W9-BZW-792

Living Liturgy™

Using this book for small group sharing

Groups using *Living Liturgy*™ for prayer and faith-sharing
might begin with the following general format and then adjust
it to fit different needs.

OPENING PRAYER
- Begin with a hymn
- Pray the collect for the Sunday or solemnity

GOD'S WORD
- Read aloud the gospel
- Observe a brief period of silence

INDIVIDUAL STUDY, REFLECTION, PRAYER
- Read and consider "Reflecting on the Gospel" or "Living
  the Paschal Mystery"
- Spend some time in reflection and prayer

FAITH-SHARING
- Use the "Assembly & Faith-sharing Groups" spirituality
  statements (and the specific liturgical ministry statements
  if they apply)
- Consider what ways the gospel is challenging you to *live*
  the liturgy you will celebrate on Sunday

CONCLUDING PRAYER
- Pray the "Model Universal Prayer (Prayer of the Faithful)"
- Pray the Our Father at the end of the intercessions
- Conclude with a hymn

Give Us ThisDay®
DAILY PRAYER FOR TODAY'S CATHOLIC

Living Liturgy™

Using this book for personal prayer

The best preparation for Sunday celebration of Eucharist is prayer. Here are two suggested approaches for an individual to use this book for personal prayer.

Daily Prayer

MONDAY
- Read the gospel prayerfully

TUESDAY
- Read the gospel again
- Reflect on the statements from "Assembly and Faith-sharing Groups" and let your reflection lead you to prayer

WEDNESDAY
- Read again the gospel
- Read "Reflecting on the Gospel" and let it lead you to prayer

THURSDAY
- Read and study "Living the Paschal Mystery"
- Pray the "Model Universal Prayer (Prayer of the Faithful)"

FRIDAY
- Pray the responsorial psalm
- Read "Connecting the Responsorial Psalm to the readings"

SATURDAY
- Read the gospel and first reading
- Read and study "Focusing the Gospel"
- Reflect on how you have been able to live this gospel during the week

SUNDAY
- Enter fully into the celebration of Eucharist
- Enjoy a day of rest

Prayer as Time and Opportunity Permit

A daily routine of study and prayer is not always possible. As time and opportunity permit:
- Read the gospel prayerfully
- Reflect on "Living the Paschal Mystery"
- Pray the "Model Universal Prayer (Prayer of the Faithful)"

Give Us
ThisDay®

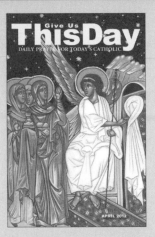

Daily Prayer for Today's Catholic

Give Us This Day ™ establishes prayer as a part of your parishioners' lives, enhancing their existing practices and deepening their encounter with God:

- ▶ Prayers and readings for daily Mass
- ▶ Daily prayer, Morning and Evening
- ▶ A reflection on the Scriptures for each day
- ▶ Profiles of Christian living from the cloud of witnesses

Parish Partnership / Group Subscriptions
1-year (12 issues)

5-19	copies	$29.95	200-499 copies	$17.95
20-49	copies	$24.95	500+copies	$15.95
50-199	copies	$19.95	(All prices include shipping to a single address).	

Standard Print Edition

2 years	(24 issues)	$79.95	$74.95
1 year	(12 issues)	$44.95	$39.95

Large Print Edition

2 years	(24 issues)	$190.80	$94.95
1 year	(12 issues)	$95.40	$49.95

Print subscribers also receive FREE access to the *Give Us This Day* ™ Digital Edition!

Digital Edition

2 years	(24 issues)	$37.95
1 year	(12 issues)	$19.95

Digital edition delivered via web browser (with pdf download option) on your computer or mobile device.

FREE SAMPLE COPIES FOR YOUR PARISH

Visit us at **www.giveusthisday.org**

Or call **1-800-858-5450**

Living Liturgy™

Living Liturgy™

Spirituality, Celebration, and Catechesis for Sundays and Solemnities

Year C • 2013

Joyce Ann Zimmerman, C.PP.S.
Kathleen Harmon, S.N.D. de N.
Christopher W. Conlon, S.M.

LITURGICAL PRESS
Collegeville, Minnesota

www.litpress.org

Design by Ann Blattner. Art by Julie Lonneman.

Excerpts from the *Lectionary for Mass for use in the Dioceses of the United States* Copyright © 2001, 1998, 1997 and 1970 Confraternity of Christian Doctrine, Inc., Washington, D.C. Used with permission. All rights reserved. No portion of this text may be reproduced without permission in writing from the copyright holder.

The English translation of some Psalm Responses, Alleluia Verses, and Gospel Verses from *Lectionary for Mass* © 1969, 1981, 1997, International Commission on English in the Liturgy Corporation (ICEL); excerpts from the English translation of *Book of Blessings* © 1988, ICEL; excerpts from the English translation of *The Roman Missal* © 2010, ICEL. All rights reserved.

The poetic English translations of the sequences of the Roman Missal are taken from the *Roman Missal* approved by the National Conference of Catholic Bishops of the United States © 1964 by the National Catholic Welfare Conference, Inc. All rights reserved.

© 2012 by Order of Saint Benedict, Collegeville, Minnesota. All rights reserved. No part of this book may be reproduced in any form, by print, microfilm, microfiche, mechanical recording, photocopying, translation, or by any other means, known or yet unknown, for any purpose except brief quotations in reviews, without the previous written permission of Liturgical Press, Saint John's Abbey, P.O. Box 7500, Collegeville, Minnesota 56321-7500. Printed in the United States of America.

ISSN 1547-089X

ISBN 978-0-8146-3389-2

CONTENTS

CONTRIBUTORS

Joyce Ann Zimmerman, C.PP.S., is the director of the Institute for Liturgical Ministry in Dayton, Ohio, and is an adjunct professor of liturgy, liturgical consultant, and frequent facilitator of workshops. She is consultant to the Committee on Divine Worship and has published numerous scholarly and pastoral liturgical works. She holds civil and pontifical doctorates of theology.

Kathleen Harmon, S.N.D. de N., is the music director for programs of the Institute for Liturgical Ministry in Dayton, Ohio, and is the author of numerous publications. An educator and musician, she facilitates liturgical music workshops and cantor formation programs. She holds a graduate degree in music and a doctorate in liturgy.

Christopher W. Conlon, S.M., is a Marianist priest who works with faculty and staff and has taught Scripture at the University of Dayton. He has been an educator for over a half century and is a highly respected homilist, a workshop presenter, and a spiritual director. He holds a graduate degree in religious education and the licentiate in theology.

USING THIS RESOURCE

As with all electronics, GPS devices continually upgrade with newer and more helpful features. When they were first out, we were happy with the basic model that got us from point A to point B. Now these GPS devices can tell us speed limits, provide us with lane assistance, inform us of traffic problems, help us with detours, and who knows what else is coming? Of course, each new model with more features is more costly. But many of us are more than willing to spend the extra money. Nonetheless, the price we pay for the latest GPS model is not the only cost entailed when we travel. So it is with our spiritual journey. Using a worship preparation aid such as *Living Liturgy*™ can facilitate our journey through the liturgical year, but this energy spent getting ready to celebrate liturgy well is not the only cost. To pray liturgy well takes time, effort, commitment. In our busy world, these are expensive commodities. But who would consider skimping on such an important journey as our journey toward God?

EASY JOURNEYS STILL HAVE COST

Despite all the changes we experience in our daily journeying, *Living Liturgy*™ still continues its original purpose: to help us prepare well for liturgy and live a liturgical spirituality (that is, a way of living that is rooted in liturgy) which opens our vision to our baptismal identity as the Body of Christ and shapes our living according to the rhythm of paschal mystery dying and rising. The paschal mystery is the central focus of liturgy, of the gospels, and of every volume of *Living Liturgy*™.

PASCHAL MYSTERY STILL CENTRAL FOCUS

A threefold dynamic of daily living, prayer, and study continues to determine the basic structure of *Living Liturgy*™, captured in the layout under the headings "Spirituality," "Celebration," and "Catechesis." This threefold dynamic is lived by the three authors; this is why each year the new volume is fresh with new material. The features don't always change (and there are no new features for this year), but the content does.

SPIRITUALITY, CELEBRATION, AND CATECHESIS

A word about the music suggestions on the Catechesis page: at the time of writing this volume of *Living Liturgy*™, many hymnbooks and music resources being revised by the major Catholic publishers to accord with The *Roman Missal, Third Edition* were not yet available. Consequently, no references to sources are given here other than citations of hymn collections not generally classified as resources meant to be used by the people in the pews. We do continue to suggest hymns for most of the Sundays and solemnities, and liturgical musicians will know whether these suggestions are part of the community's repertoire and where to find them. Our intention here is not to provide a complete list of music suggestions for each Sunday or solemnity (these are readily available in other publications), but to make a few suggestions with accompanying catechesis; thus, we hope this is a learning process.

A NOTE ABOUT MUSIC SUGGESTIONS

During Ordinary Time of the 2013 liturgical year, we read from Luke's gospel with its special focus on Jesus' resolute journey to Jerusalem and the cross and resurrection. Our faithful weekly preparation for the Sunday proclamation of the word is our way to walk with Jesus as faithful disciples, bearing our own crosses each day and opening ourselves to the new Life God always offers those who are resolute. Yes, our journey may have a cost—sometimes a very high cost, indeed—but the cost we might bear pales in relation to the graces we receive as we journey. God is always with us, accompanying us, guiding us, helping us to make our journey toward fullness of Life as fruitful as possible.

JESUS DESIRES THAT WE JOURNEY WITH HIM TO JERUSALEM

INTRODUCTION to the Gospel of Luke

Luke, who lived in Antioch, wrote his gospel for a Gentile community somewhere between 80 and 85 A.D. The people for whom he wrote never saw Jesus and probably never even knew anyone who did. Consequently, a problem facing the community was how to maintain faithful continuity with the teaching and spirit of Jesus. Luke's response to this problem was the post-resurrection story on the road to Emmaus, where the two disciples realized that they had experienced the presence of Jesus after they heard him explain what the Scriptures said and recognized him in the breaking of the bread. Jesus' presence certainly was not limited to when he was historically present, but extends beyond time and space to his being present in word and sacrament today and every day.

The gospel begins with the historical Jesus in Galilee, but this is not the focus of Luke's gospel. Jesus sets about preaching in Galilee, but then he "sets his face" toward Jerusalem, where he will meet suffering and death. This gospel, then, is structured around this resolute journey to Jerusalem and accomplishing the mission of salvation for which Jesus came. The Acts of the Apostles (considered to be the second part of Luke's gospel) picks up in Jerusalem after Jesus' death and tells of his ascension to heaven and the coming of the Spirit upon the disciples. Filled with this Spirit of the risen Jesus, the disciples go out to preach and live the Good News. Whereas Jesus began his preaching in Galilee and was crucified in Jerusalem, the disciples—filled with the Spirit of the risen Christ—began their preaching and healing in Jerusalem and went forth from there to the four corners of the world to preach the Good News. Moreover, the preaching of the Good News does not die with the martyrdom of great apostles like Peter and Paul (highlighted in the Acts), but is taken up all over the known world. Now, in our own day, we are also called to continue the preaching of the Good News by the way we live as followers of Jesus, filled with this same Spirit.

Jesus born in a stable and placed in a manger, the shepherds who visited him, the elderly Simeon and Anna who recognized him in the Temple, the Good Samaritan, the Prodigal Son, the Widow of Naim: the narratives around these people are among the best known and loved stories in the whole New Testament, and they are stories unique to the Gospel of Luke. Such people as the poor, outcasts, and sinners who figure so prominently in Luke lead us to refer to the third gospel as the "gospel of mercy." A few more examples illustrate this further.

Whereas in Matthew's gospel Jesus calls us to "be perfect, just as your heavenly Father is perfect" (Matt 5:48), Luke replaces "perfect" with "merciful" (Luke 6:36). Luke 15 contains three familiar parables of mercy (the lost sheep, lost coin, and prodigal son; the last two are unique to Luke) that compare God to those who go out of their way to help the lost. We are called to be compassionate like the rich merchant who forgave a servant who owed him much (but a servant who, in turn, refused to forgive the much smaller debts that fellow servants owed him).

Likewise this gospel is also called the "gospel of prayer" (Jesus often goes off by himself to pray) and the "gospel of women" (because of the prominent role of women in this gospel, for example, the angel appears to Mary). It is precisely these people who play such significant roles that highlight Luke's message: salvation is for all, God cares for the poor, God's care and mercy is wonderfully shown through the life and ministry of Jesus. We, disciples today who carry forth Jesus' saving mission, are likewise to show God's care and mercy through our own lives of prayer and care for others. Luke's gospel, in its gentleness and imagery, is nevertheless a gospel of challenge. We are to live as Jesus did. We are to journey as Jesus did: toward Jerusalem and the cross. Toward new, risen life.

ABBREVIATIONS

LITURGICAL RESOURCES

BofB   *Book of Blessings*. International Commission on English in the Liturgy. Collegeville: Liturgical Press, 1989.

BLS   *Built of Living Stones: Art, Architecture, and Worship.* Guidelines of the National Conference of Catholic Bishops, 2000.

CCC   *Catechism of the Catholic Church.* USCCB, 2004.

GIRM   General Instruction of the Roman Missal, 2010.

ILM   Introduction to the Lectionary for Mass, 1981.

SC   *Sacrosanctum Concilium*. The Constitution on the Sacred Liturgy. Vatican II, 1963.

ST   *Sing to the Lord: Music in Divine Worship,* 2007.

UNYC   Universal Norms on the Liturgical Year and the General Roman Calendar, 1969.

MUSICAL RESOURCES

GIA   GIA Publications, Inc.

OCP   Oregon Catholic Press

WLP   World Library Publications

NOTE: At the time of writing this volume of *Living Liturgy*™ many hymnbooks and music resources being revised by the major Catholic publishers to accord with The *Roman Missal, Third Edition* were not yet available. Consequently, no references to sources are given here other than citations of hymn collections not generally classified as resources meant to be used by the people in the pews.

Advent

✠ SPIRITUALITY

GOSPEL ACCLAMATION
Ps 85:8

℟. Alleluia, alleluia.
Show us Lord, your love;
and grant us your salvation.
℟. Alleluia, alleluia.

Gospel

Luke 21:25-28, 34-36; L3C

**Jesus said to his disciples:
"There will be signs in the sun, the
moon, and the stars,
and on earth nations will be in
dismay,
perplexed by the roaring of the sea
and the waves.
People will die of fright
in anticipation of what is coming
upon the world,
for the powers of the heavens will
be shaken.
And then they will see the Son of Man
coming in a cloud with power and
great glory.
But when these signs begin to happen,
stand erect and raise your heads
because your redemption is at hand.**

**"Beware that your hearts do not
become drowsy
from carousing and drunkenness
and the anxieties of daily life,
and that day catch you by surprise
like a trap.
For that day will assault everyone
who lives on the face of the earth.
Be vigilant at all times
and pray that you have the strength
to escape the tribulations that are
imminent
and to stand before the Son of Man."**

Reflecting on the Gospel

Waiting can be a process that strikes us as quite relative. If we are waiting for a dentist appointment to undergo a root canal, the wait can pass all too quickly. If we are waiting for a desperately needed check to come in the mail, the wait can seem interminable. These are concrete situations where we can "measure" our waiting. They are experiences we actually might have in our daily living. The gospel, however, admonishes us to be vigilant for a future event—the Second Coming of "the Son of Man"—of which none of us has any experience. How do we wait in anticipation of something so utterly beyond our experience?

The answer to this question comes when we take a deeper look at the gospel. Yes, Jesus is surely talking about his coming when the world as we know it will end. But this gospel is not really about the end of the world; it is about the completion of the kingdom. The Second Coming is not a deadline; it is an invitation and incentive to live in a certain way in the present time. The gospel calls us to be vigilant not about a future event but about a present way of living shaped by the Jesus before whom we stand.

The signs of the end of the world are not disastrous cosmic events which we anticipate with dread, but the fullness of our own Gospel living. The signs we ordinarily think will accompany the end of the world—cosmos in disarray and nations in dismay—are really signs of how far we still have to go to implant Gospel values in our lives and world. Our care and love for others, our fruitful response to the challenge of Gospel living, are the definitive signs of Christ's presence among us. These are the signs of God's kingdom coming to completion.

Rather than think of the end of the world as a disastrous, punishing time, this gospel really challenges us to think of the end of the world as a celebration of Gospel living. If we followers of Christ are vigilant and have lives "blameless in holiness" (second reading), we can live without fear for we are united with Christ. Good Gospel living results in joyful anticipation of our redemption. Our destiny is to share in the Son of Man's "great glory." On the way, we are privileged to cooperate in Christ's mission to establish the reign of God.

Living the Paschal Mystery

What are the signs of our times and how ought we to read them? In order for the kingdom to come fully, we must address more forcefully those things which impede the kingdom (genocide, domination of one nation over another, poverty, violence and abuse of all kinds). And we begin this process of addressing the world's ills by addressing what is immediately at hand in our own lives.

The way we ought to live *now* is shaped by this particular time of the liturgical year, Advent, with its motif of joyful anticipation. During Advent we Christians wait for more than a *day* (Christmas); we await a *Person*—Jesus Christ who now reigns in glory. This Jesus is among us now, inviting us to live as he did—with care for others, with unselfish response to others' needs, with the kind of self-giving that draws people into a venue of joy and peace. When we live the Gospel well, the future is now. Our waiting is pregnant with life. That's nice waiting.

Focusing the Gospel

Key words and phrases: what is coming upon the world, great glory, Be vigilant, stand before the Son of Man

To the point: This gospel is not really about the end of the world; it is about the completion of the kingdom. The Second Coming is not a deadline; it is an invitation and incentive to live in a certain way in the present time. The gospel calls us to be vigilant not about a future event but about a present way of living shaped by the Jesus before whom we stand. Our destiny is to share in the Son of Man's "great glory."

Connecting the Gospel

to the second reading: The second reading spells out quite clearly what our daily vigilance looks like. We are to abound in love, be blameless in holiness, conduct ourselves to be pleasing to God, receive instructions given "through the Lord Jesus."

to experience: Given our present experience of wars, poverty, natural disasters, some people conclude that the end of the world is at hand and are fearful. Rather than inviting fear of an imminent end, these same things call us to become more vigilant about the way we live and witness to the Gospel.

Connecting the Responsorial Psalm

to the readings: The Hebrew word for "way" or "path"(*derek*) has many connotations: road, travel, voyage, life-direction. The word means not only a path one is walking, but also a habitual manner of acting. In these verses from Psalm 25 we ask God to point us in the right direction. Even more, we ask for the grace to live and act as God does. We ask that God's way become our way. We know this will mean doing what is "right and just" (first reading). It will mean conducting ourselves as Christ has instructed us (second reading). It will mean remaining steadfast in this way when times are rough, when even the "anxieties of daily life" (gospel) tempt us to abandon fidelity to this way. We pray in this psalm, then, for the grace of fidelity, knowing that our fidelity rests in the God who is first faithful to us.

to psalmist preparation: In this psalm the "way" you beg to come to know is not a set of rules, but a Person: God who is good and upright, kind and constant, faithful and forgiving. How might you "lift [your] soul" to God during this week so that you might sing this psalm on Sunday with more power and conviction?

ASSEMBLY & FAITH-SHARING GROUPS
- When I observe wars, poverty, natural disasters, I become more . . .
- Advent calls me to grow in Gospel living by . . .
- I experience sharing already in Christ's "great glory" in that . . .

PRESIDERS
My manner of living encourages those whom I serve to be more vigilant about Gospel living when I . . .

DEACONS
My service is an expression of vigilance for the coming of the kingdom when I . . .

HOSPITALITY MINISTERS
Advent challenges me to change the way I greet others at church and in my daily life by . . .

MUSIC MINISTERS
In my music ministry I must be vigilant about . . . This vigilance furthers the coming of the kingdom in that . . .

ALTAR MINISTERS
My vigilance when I serve at the altar reflects my growing in living the Gospel when I . . .

LECTORS
My preparations with the word keep me vigilant for Christ's coming in that . . . My proclamation communicates this by . . .

EXTRAORDINARY MINISTERS OF HOLY COMMUNION
In the faces of those who come to receive Holy Communion, I see "great glory" and this invites me to . . .

Model Penitential Act

Presider: As we begin this season of Advent, Christ is present with us now even as we await his final coming in glory. Let us prepare ourselves to celebrate this mystery of his presence . . . [pause]

   Lord Jesus, you will come in great glory: Lord . . .

   Christ Jesus, your coming is our redemption: Christ . . .

   Lord Jesus, you strengthen us to live your Gospel as we await the full coming of your kingdom: Lord . . .

Homily Points

• All around us we see people collecting food for the poor, giving time to Habitat for Humanity, volunteering in homeless shelters and safe havens for those abused. Many people are already helping the kingdom to come fully. In face of disastrous things in the world, these people do not "die of fright" and give up, but they "stand erect" and address causes and outcomes.

• Although the gospel does not explicitly talk about the kingdom, it does so indirectly. What "is coming upon the world" is not simply calamity, but the reign of God. Christ's coming now and at the end of time is the presence of the kingdom. Our standing erect before God by doing God's will is bringing about the kingdom. The kingdom is not a place but a faithful relationship to God and each other mediated by the Spirit of Jesus Christ.

• The "anxieties of daily life" can sometimes overwhelm us. We can so easily lose sight of the fact that the simple daily choices to do good—lending a helping hand to a family member, being patient with someone struggling, checking one's anger or frustration—are practical ways we are cooperating with Christ in bringing about the kingdom. These are ways we remain vigilant, ways we "stand erect" before Christ, ways we already share in Christ's "great glory."

Model Universal Prayer (Prayer of the Faithful)

Presider: We make known our needs to God, so that we can be vigilant and respond to Christ coming among us.

Response:

Lord, hear our prayer.

Cantor:

we pray to the Lord,

That the church may be vigilant at all times and assist others to stand confidently before Christ . . . [pause]

That the people of the world may always conduct themselves so as to please God . . . [pause]

That those who experience anxiety over the things of daily life may find comfort in the God who is always faithful . . . [pause]

That we here gathered may see in the signs of the times the call to live the Gospel more fully . . . [pause]

Presider: All-powerful God, your Son will come with great glory and power to gather us into your loving embrace: hear these our prayers that we may be ready for his coming. We ask this through that same Christ our Lord. **Amen.**

COLLECT

Let us pray

Pause for silent prayer

Grant your faithful, we pray, almighty God,
the resolve to run forth to meet your Christ
with righteous deeds at his coming,
so that, gathered at his right hand,
they may be worthy to possess the heavenly Kingdom.
Through our Lord Jesus Christ, your Son,
who lives and reigns with you in the unity of the Holy Spirit,
one God, for ever and ever.
Amen.

FIRST READING

Jer 33:14-16

The days are coming, says the LORD,
   when I will fulfill the promise
   I made to the house of Israel and Judah.
In those days, in that time,
   I will raise up for David a just shoot;
   he shall do what is right and just in the land.
In those days Judah shall be safe
   and Jerusalem shall dwell secure;
   this is what they shall call her:
   "The LORD our justice."

RESPONSORIAL PSALM
Ps 25:4-5, 8-9, 10, 14

R︎. (1b) To you, O Lord, I lift my soul.

Your ways, O LORD, make known to me;
    teach me your paths,
guide me in your truth and teach me,
    for you are God my savior,
    and for you I wait all the day.

R︎. To you, O Lord, I lift my soul.

Good and upright is the LORD;
    thus he shows sinners the way.
He guides the humble to justice,
    and teaches the humble his way.

R︎. To you, O Lord, I lift my soul.

All the paths of the LORD are kindness and
      constancy
    toward those who keep his covenant
      and his decrees.
The friendship of the LORD is with those
      who fear him,
    and his covenant, for their instruction.

R︎. To you, O Lord, I lift my soul.

SECOND READING
1 Thess 3:12–4:2

Brothers and sisters:
May the Lord make you increase and
      abound in love
    for one another and for all,
    just as we have for you,
    so as to strengthen your hearts,
    to be blameless in holiness before our
      God and Father
    at the coming of our Lord Jesus with all
      his holy ones. Amen.

Finally, brothers and sisters,
    we earnestly ask and exhort you in the
      Lord Jesus that,
    as you received from us
    how you should conduct yourselves to
      please God
    —and as you are conducting
      yourselves—
you do so even more.
For you know what instructions we gave
    you through the Lord Jesus.

About Liturgy

Advent waiting: Most Catholics understand Advent as a time of waiting and anticipation. However, we await not just the celebration of Christmas, that festival commemorating Christ's coming into the world incarnated in the flesh of an infant, but also the celebration of Christ's Second Coming at the end of the world. We begin Advent with looking forward to Christ's Second Coming.

Accompanying Christ's Second Coming will be the general judgment and resurrection. As we await the Second Coming, we know that we will face this cosmic event either with calmness and joyful anticipation begotten by lives lived in fidelity to the Gospel, or we will face this cosmic event with dread because we know we have been unfaithful to our relationship with God. Thus Advent calls us to renewed Gospel living—lives patterned after Christ—so that we will be ready for the end times.

Each liturgy we celebrate helps strengthen our relationship with God and each other. In a real way, then, each liturgy prepares us for Christ's Second Coming, brings us to cooperate in Christ's mission to establish God's reign in our world, and helps us overcome any fear of the judgment which will accompany Christ's coming. This is one sense of how we call all liturgy "eschatological," that is, having to do with the end times.

About Liturgical Music

Appropriate music for Advent: GIRM no. 313 guides the type of music to be sung during the season of Advent: "In Advent the use of the organ and other musical instruments should be marked by a moderation suited to the character of this time of year, without expressing in anticipation the full joy of the Nativity of the Lord." In other words, a certain restraint should mark the music during this season. This restraint does not have the penitential character of Lent, but is a kind of "fasting" before the "feasting" that accords with the character of Advent as a season of waiting. Indeed, we wait in hope and sing songs expressing joy and expectation (many of the Advent readings do this very thing), yet the music overall should be characterized by a sense of holding back until the time for full celebration arrives.

Advent service music: One of the functions of service music is to mark the liturgical season or feast. The parish needs to have a set reserved for use only during Advent, a setting which draws people into joyful expectation without spilling over into the total exuberance of Christmas and expresses quiet waiting without the penitential somberness of Lent. Since Advent and Christmas together form a unified festal season, it would be good to use a setting which can be sung simply during Advent and then embellished with choral and instrumental parts between Christmas and Epiphany.

✢ SPIRITUALITY

GOSPEL ACCLAMATION
cf. Luke 1:28

℟. Alleluia, alleluia.
Hail, Mary, full of grace, the Lord is with you;
blessed are you among women.
℟. Alleluia, alleluia.

Gospel   Luke 1:26-38; L689

The angel Gabriel was sent from God
  to a town of Galilee called Nazareth,
  to a virgin betrothed to a man named
      Joseph,
  of the house of David,
  and the virgin's name was Mary.
And coming to her, he said,
  "Hail, full of grace! The Lord is with
      you."
But she was greatly troubled at what was
      said
  and pondered what sort of greeting this
      might be.
Then the angel said to her,
  "Do not be afraid, Mary,
  for you have found favor with God.
Behold, you will conceive in your womb and
      bear a son,
  and you shall name him Jesus.
He will be great and will be called Son of
      the Most High,
  and the Lord God will give him the throne
      of David his father,
  and he will rule over the house of Jacob
      forever,
  and of his Kingdom there will be no end."

Continued in Appendix A, p. 263.

See Appendix A, p. 263, for the other readings.

Reflecting on the Gospel

Only two human beings have not shared in human sinfulness—Jesus and his mother Mary. This festival in honor of Mary celebrates her innocence from the very moment of her conception in her mother's womb. She is the new Eve and, through her, God reverses the shame brought forth by the first mother of the living. Mary's innocence gained her a singular intimacy with God, for it was she who conceived by the Holy Spirit (gospel) and carried within her womb for nine months the very Son of God. Her body—conceived in innocence and kept free from the stain of sin throughout her life—was a fitting temple to nurture the human life of the divine Son. Yet, the gospel suggests to us that Mary's innocence did not protect her from normal human responses in face of great mystery. We can only strive for Mary's purity and innocence. But we can readily identify with her human response to Gabriel.

The Holy Spirit overshadowed Mary and she gave birth to the "Son of the Most High." This was brought about in the aftermath of Mary's pondering, questioning, and, finally, saying yes. Mary's dialogue with Gabriel does not reveal obstinacy or belligerence or unwillingness. The dialogue simply reveals that Mary did not take all this for granted. It reveals that Mary truly did have a choice. It reveals that Mary, while not knowing fully what her yes would entail, was aware that she was encountering something totally out of the ordinary, she was encountering previously unrevealed mystery.

We, too, are overshadowed by the Holy Spirit which enables us to be holy and unblemished, adopted, beloved, chosen (see second reading). Like Mary, we ponder, question, and, finally, say yes by how we live. Like Mary, our dialogues with God, self, others that bring us to say yes are not weakness or hesitation. Rather, our own pondering and questioning lead to an informed choice and a deeper commitment.

Like Mary, we must respond to God's offer of grace with our "Behold, I am the handmaid [servant] of the Lord." Then, like Mary, we, too, bear the Son of God within us. She is the model for God-bearing. She is our Mother and helps us attain for ourselves the fruits of her great privilege—Emmanuel, God is with us!

Living the Paschal Mystery

This is a feast of grace. The sin of Adam and Eve is met by God's promise that the ancient enemy will be crushed. Mary is chosen to be "holy and without blemish" (second reading) and is, indeed, "full of grace" (gospel). The grace which preserved Mary free from all sin is the same grace by which "we were also chosen" and are "blessed . . . with every spiritual blessing" (second reading).

Thus, God chose us, too! This is the Good News! Our baptism is our "conception" into new, divine life. Mary is the model for a lifelong yes to fidelity to God's will which brings us life. Rather than a distant model, Mary is one who is close to us because she was close to her divine Son. Mary is a model for us of grace-filled living; all we need to do is say yes!

But our yes is much more than a word. Our yes is borne out in the good deeds and care we show others. We are Christ-bearers when we bring his presence that heals and saves, that cares and loves, that brings hope and fulfills promises.

Focusing the Gospel

Key words and phrases: pondered, Son of the Most High, How can this be, Holy Spirit will come upon you, May it be done to me

To the point: The Holy Spirit overshadowed Mary and she gave birth to the "Son of the Most High." This was brought about in the aftermath of Mary's pondering, questioning, and, finally, saying yes. We, too, are overshadowed by the Holy Spirit which enables us to be holy and unblemished, adopted, beloved, chosen (see second reading). Like Mary, we ponder, question, and, finally, say yes by how we live.

Model Penitential Act

Presider: God kept Mary free from sin from the very moment of her conception. As we begin our celebration, let us ask God to free us from our sinfulness . . . [pause]

Lord Jesus, you are the son of Mary: Lord . . .

Christ Jesus, you are the Son of the Most High: Christ . . .

Lord Jesus, your kingdom will have no end: Lord . . .

Model Universal Prayer (Prayer of the Faithful)

Presider: Let us make known our needs to the God for whom nothing is impossible.

Response:

Cantor:

That members of the church hear what God desires of them and say yes . . . [pause]

That all peoples of the world ponder God's ways and say yes to God's will . . . [pause]

That all those in need remember that nothing will be impossible with God . . . [pause]

That we here gathered may be preserved from sin and grow in holiness . . . [pause]

Presider: O God, you preserved Mary from all sin: hear our prayers that we, with Mary, might one day enjoy everlasting life with you. We pray through Christ our Lord. **Amen**.

COLLECT

Let us pray

Pause for silent prayer

O God, who by the Immaculate Conception
    of the Blessed Virgin
prepared a worthy dwelling for your Son,
grant, we pray,
that, as you preserved her from every stain
by virtue of the Death of your Son, which
    you foresaw,
so, through her intercession,
we, too, may be cleansed and admitted to
    your presence.
Through our Lord Jesus Christ, your Son,
who lives and reigns with you in the unity
    of the Holy Spirit,
one God, for ever and ever.
Amen.

FOR REFLECTION

• I find myself pondering and questioning the ways of God when . . .

• I experience the presence of the Holy Spirit upon me when . . .

• Where I am resistant to saying "May it be done unto me according to your word" is . . . What helps me say yes is . . .

Homily Points

• How do we experience what God asks of us? Unlike Mary at the Annunciation, an angel will not appear to us. We hear God by pondering Scripture, by listening to others, by reflecting on the events in our lives (including the mistakes we make), by growing in consciousness and conscience.

• What frees us to say yes to whatever God asks of us? Certainly not total clarity about the request, nor complete easiness with the manner of its coming to us. Only trust in the God for whom nothing is impossible. Despite being troubled at the angel's greeting, despite needing to question the angel's message, Mary said yes to God—and the Word was made flesh. So must we say yes—and new life is given.

SPIRITUALITY

GOSPEL ACCLAMATION
Luke 3:4, 6

R̷. Alleluia, alleluia.
Prepare the way of the Lord, make
straight his paths:
all flesh shall see the salvation of God.
R̷. Alleluia, alleluia.

Gospel

Luke 3:1-6; L6C

**In the fifteenth year of the reign
of Tiberius Caesar,
when Pontius Pilate was
governor of Judea,
and Herod was tetrarch of
Galilee,
and his brother Philip tetrarch
of the region of Ituraea
and Trachonitis,
and Lysanias was tetrarch of Abilene,
during the high priesthood of Annas
and Caiaphas,
the word of God came to John the
son of Zechariah in the desert.
John went throughout the whole region
of the Jordan,
proclaiming a baptism of repentance
for the forgiveness of sins,
as it is written in the book of the
words of the prophet Isaiah:**
*A voice of one crying out in the
desert:*
*"Prepare the way of the Lord,
make straight his paths.
Every valley shall be filled
and every mountain and hill
shall be made low.
The winding roads shall be made
straight,
and the rough ways made smooth,
and all flesh shall see the salvation
of God."*

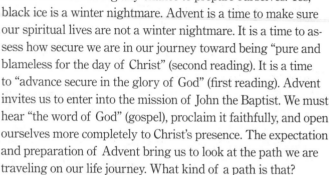

Reflecting on the Gospel

Black ice is a winter nightmare for anyone living in cold regions. It's nearly invisible. The pavement can look clear, but one false step and the feet fly out from under us and down we go. When we suspect or are warned about black ice, we tend to walk tentatively, gingerly. We are not secure walking on black ice, and we move very carefully. If we are driving, black ice can cause us to totally lose control without having any chance to prepare ourselves. Yes, black ice is a winter nightmare. Advent is a time to make sure our spiritual lives are not a winter nightmare. It is a time to assess how secure we are in our journey toward being "pure and blameless for the day of Christ" (second reading). It is a time to "advance secure in the glory of God" (first reading). Advent invites us to enter into the mission of John the Baptist. We must hear "the word of God" (gospel), proclaim it faithfully, and open ourselves more completely to Christ's presence. The expectation and preparation of Advent bring us to look at the path we are traveling on our life journey. What kind of a path is that?

John proclaims that we must "[p]repare the way of the Lord" by repenting. Isaiah and John both describe repentance as a leveling and a straightening out of the uneven and crooked shape of our lives. When the paths of our lives are not straight and smooth, we can at best move only tentatively, as we do on black ice. We cannot be free to enter wholeheartedly into our journey toward God. If our eyes are too closely focused on the rocks and crags of our lives, we cannot see the presence of God beckoning us toward smoother going. Isaiah's image of a straight and smooth way is a metaphoric, descriptive definition of repentance. It is Isaiah's (and Advent's) way to call us to faithful living in right relationship with God.

Isaiah and John call us to ask whether our path is taking us closer to God as well as opening up for others the way to God. Smooth paths—those unmarred by false knowledge, misguided perceptions, forgotten values (cf. second reading)—are those which help us focus on God and root out anything that keeps us from God. Smooth paths are those that increase our love for God and others, prompting us to bring others along the same smooth and straight path on which we are journeying toward final fulfillment with God. Then "all flesh shall see the salvation of God."

Living the Paschal Mystery

The Liturgy of the Word challenges us to take the real events of our everyday lives—all the suffering and pain, all the anxiety and hopelessness, all the joy and peace—and see them as means to recognize the presence of Christ to us. These events are deeds enacted in love increased, knowledge shared, discernment embraced, righteousness integrated into the very fabric of our being (see second reading). In this way we make our Advent something more than the preparation for a single-day feast of a birth.

This is what Advent is all about—recognizing the presence of Christ in our lives as salvation already come because God's Word has already been spoken to us. Christian living challenges us to stop our busyness long enough to hear that Word, to be overshadowed by the Word, to allow the Word to make straight our paths.

Focusing the Gospel

Key words and phrases: repentance, prepare the way of the Lord, make straight, shall be filled, made low, made straight, made smooth, all flesh shall see the salvation of God

To the point: John proclaims that we must "[p]repare the way of the Lord" by repenting. Isaiah and John both describe repentance as a leveling and a straightening out of the uneven and crooked shape of our lives. They call us to ask whether our path is taking us closer to God as well as opening up for others the way to God. Then "all flesh shall see the salvation of God."

Connecting the Gospel

to the first reading: Isaiah gives us a vision of the eschatological end times when the full flowering of repentance is made visible.

to experience: GPS devices have taken the meandering out of our road trips and guaranteed smooth travel toward our destination. Repentance is the "GPS" of our Gospel journey toward final glory.

Connecting the Responsorial Psalm

to the readings: When God delivered Israel from their captivity in Babylon, they responded by creating Psalm 126. Over time they came to use this psalm as a song of confidence any time they were in danger of destruction. The text moves from memorial of past deliverance (strophes 1 and 2) to petition for new deliverance (strophes 3 and 4). Israel's confidence was based on real historical event, not dreamed imaginings. Of this they were certain: the God who *had* saved them *would* save them again.

Advent is the season when we look as did the Israelites toward the redemption coming on our behalf from the hand of God (first reading). Truly "the one who began a good work in [us] will . . . complete it" (second reading). Luke tells us this redemption will take place in real history ("In the fifteenth year of . . . when . . .") and that it will demand choices and changes (gospel). This Advent may we recognize what God is doing. May we make the choices and changes redemption requires. May we make Psalm 126 our story and our song.

to psalmist preparation: In this responsorial psalm you call the community to dream about the future by remembering what God has done in the past. You remind them that the God who *has* saved *will* save again. What past experiences help you maintain this hope? When has God transformed your "weeping" into "rejoicing"?

ASSEMBLY & FAITH-SHARING GROUPS

- The call to "prepare the way of the Lord" means I must . . .
- My daily living opens up for others the way to the Lord when I . . .
- Repentance means to me . . .

PRESIDERS

While I minister I "prepare the way of the Lord" and "see the salvation of God" in that . . .

DEACONS

My ministry opens up the way to the Lord for those in need when I . . .

HOSPITALITY MINISTERS

Ways that my hospitality aids others to experience "see[ing] the salvation of God" are . . .

MUSIC MINISTERS

The music I lead helps the assembly "prepare the way of the Lord" when . . .

ALTAR MINISTERS

Serving others is a way of preparing for the Lord in that . . .

LECTORS

The manner of my proclamation opens up for others the way to God whenever I . . .

EXTRAORDINARY MINISTERS OF HOLY COMMUNION

Like the Eucharist, I am food for others as they struggle to prepare the way of the Lord in that . . .

Model Penitential Act

Presider: John the Baptist calls us to "[p]repare the way of the Lord." As we prepare to celebrate this liturgy, let us consider how we have not stayed on a straight path to the Lord in our daily living . . . [pause]

Lord Jesus, you are the Word which John announced: Lord . . .

Christ Jesus, you are the salvation of God: Christ . . .

Lord Jesus, you lead us along a straight path to everlasting life: Lord . . .

Homily Points

• We use the word "straight" in many ways: set the record straight, get this straight, look me straight in the eye. All these phrases essentially mean the same thing: be direct, correct, truthful, upright, emphatic. At stake is right relationship. John is direct and emphatic in calling us to right relationship with God and one another.

• For John, preparing the way of the Lord is clear and simple: we must straighten out our lives. The way to do this is by repenting. Repentance comes from a single-minded focus on how the Word dwells among us and forms us. God leads us along right ways.

• Are our relationships marred by the unevenness of being moody, the crookedness of dishonesty, the uppityness of being haughty, the lowness of self-deprecation, the roughness of vulgarity? John's call to repentance challenges us to examine our behaviors and our relationships with God, self, and others. Only through repentance—genuine building of right relationships—will we "see the salvation of God."

Model Universal Prayer (Prayer of the Faithful)

Presider: Let us place our needs before God that we may truly prepare the way of the Lord.

Response:

Cantor:

That all members of the church may grow in right relationship with God and each other . . . [pause]

That all peoples of the world may see the salvation of God . . . [pause]

That those who have lost their way may find guidance in God's word . . . [pause]

That each of us here gathered may live Advent in such a way that our repentance leads to new life . . . [pause]

Presider: O God, you sent your Son to bring salvation: hear these our prayers that one day we might live with you forever. We pray through Christ our Lord. **Amen.**

COLLECT

Let us pray

Pause for silent prayer

Almighty and merciful God,
may no earthly undertaking hinder those
who set out in haste to meet your Son,
but may our learning of heavenly wisdom
gain us admittance to his company.
Who lives and reigns with you in the unity
    of the Holy Spirit,
one God, for ever and ever.
Amen.

FIRST READING

Bar 5:1-9

Jerusalem, take off your robe of mourning
    and misery;
      put on the splendor of glory from God
      forever:
wrapped in the cloak of justice from God,
      bear on your head the mitre
      that displays the glory of the eternal
      name.
For God will show all the earth your
    splendor:
      you will be named by God forever
      the peace of justice, the glory of God's
      worship.

Up, Jerusalem! stand upon the heights;
    look to the east and see your children
gathered from the east and the west
    at the word of the Holy One,
      rejoicing that they are remembered by
      God.
Led away on foot by their enemies they
    left you:
      but God will bring them back to you
      borne aloft in glory as on royal thrones.
For God has commanded
    that every lofty mountain be made low,
and that the age-old depths and gorges
    be filled to level ground,
      that Israel may advance secure in the
      glory of God.
The forests and every fragrant kind of
    tree
      have overshadowed Israel at God's
      command;
for God is leading Israel in joy
    by the light of his glory,
      with his mercy and justice for company.

RESPONSORIAL PSALM

Ps 126:1-2, 2-3, 4-5, 6

R⁘. (3) The Lord has done great things for us; we are filled with joy.

When the LORD brought back the captives
of Zion,
    we were like men dreaming.
Then our mouth was filled with laughter,
    and our tongue with rejoicing.

R⁘. The Lord has done great things for us;
we are filled with joy.

Then they said among the nations,
    "The LORD has done great things for
        them."
The LORD has done great things for us;
    we are glad indeed.

R⁘. The Lord has done great things for us;
we are filled with joy.

Restore our fortunes, O LORD,
    like the torrents in the southern desert.
Those who sow in tears
    shall reap rejoicing.

R⁘. The Lord has done great things for us;
we are filled with joy.

Although they go forth weeping,
    carrying the seed to be sown,
they shall come back rejoicing,
    carrying their sheaves.

R⁘. The Lord has done great things for us;
we are filled with joy.

SECOND READING

Phil 1:4-6, 8-11

Brothers and sisters:
I pray always with joy in my every prayer
        for all of you,
    because of your partnership for the
        gospel
    from the first day until now.
I am confident of this,
    that the one who began a good work
        in you
    will continue to complete it
    until the day of Christ Jesus.
God is my witness,
    how I long for all of you with the
        affection of Christ Jesus.
And this is my prayer:
    that your love may increase ever more
        and more
    in knowledge and every kind of
        perception,
    to discern what is of value,
    so that you may be pure and blameless
        for the day of Christ,
    filled with the fruit of righteousness
    that comes through Jesus Christ
    for the glory and praise of God.

About Liturgy

Advent and Morning Prayer: Two cautions may be in order as we celebrate this Second Sunday of Advent. (1) We might move too quickly to thinking about Christmas; the readings for this Sunday still orient us toward Christ's Second Coming. (2) In spite of the opening lines of this Sunday's gospel, we want to be careful about "historicizing" these feasts. We are celebrating a mystery which both opens up God's saving event and eludes us.

Advent is the time par excellence for preparation for Christ's comings. But it is not the only time when the church opens and prepares us for Christ's comings. Each morning, if we join ourselves to the whole church in praying Morning Prayer from the Liturgy of the Hours, we are preparing for the way of the Lord. Part of the intent of the church's Morning Prayer is to open the mystery of Christ as it comes to us during the day. Liturgy is not something which merely happens in church or during formal times of prayer. Liturgy is an immersion in Christ's paschal mystery and unfolds in each and every event of our lives. We need to simply look for Christ all around us. Looking is a kind of preparing!

Morning Prayer, too, always includes Scripture and so this prayer affords us an opportunity at the beginning of our day to open ourselves to God's word. Thus fortified, we are more equipped, then, to recognize in the many deeds of the day our own faithful living of this word. Morning Prayer can help make smooth and straight the path of our day.

About Liturgical Music

Music suggestions: As with the First Sunday of Advent, the songs we sing this day need to focus on the final coming of Christ and the completion of redemption at the end of time. An excellent entrance hymn that interrelates Christ's final coming with John the Baptist's call to repentance is Genevieve Glen's "Arise, Stand on the Height" (in *Voices from the Valley*, OCP). Two very fine hymns that speak of all three comings of Christ (at the Incarnation, in the sacraments, and at the Second Coming) are Herman G. Stuempfle's "O Christ at Your Appearing" (in *Awake our Hearts to Praise!*, GIA) and Carl Daw's "For the Coming of the Savior." A hymn that relates particularly well to the first reading and the psalm is Genevieve Glen's "When Christ in Majesty Returns" (in *The Listening Heart,* OCP). Delores Dufner's "Wait When the Seed Is Planted" (in *The Glimmer of Glory in Song,* GIA) would be a good choice for preparation of the gifts or Communion on any Sunday. Good verse-refrain choices for Communion include Frances Patrick O'Brien's "Maranatha, Come"; Paul Page's "Lord, Come" (in *Mantras for the Season,* WLP); and Kathy Powell's "Maranatha, Lord Messiah."

DECEMBER 9, 2012
SECOND SUNDAY OF ADVENT

SPIRITUALITY

GOSPEL ACCLAMATION
Isa 61:1 (cited in Luke 4:18)

R̶. Alleluia, alleluia.
The Spirit of the Lord is upon me,
because he has anointed me
to bring glad tidings to the poor.
R̶. Alleluia, alleluia.

Gospel

Luke 3:10-18; L9C

The crowds asked John the Baptist,
  "What should we do?"
He said to them in reply,
  "Whoever has two cloaks
  should share with the person who
    has none.
And whoever has food should do
    likewise."
Even tax collectors came to be baptized
    and they said to him,
  "Teacher, what should we do?"
He answered them,
  "Stop collecting more than what is
    prescribed."
Soldiers also asked him,
  "And what is it that we should do?"
He told them,
  "Do not practice extortion,
  do not falsely accuse anyone,
  and be satisfied with your wages."

Now the people were filled with
    expectation,
  and all were asking in their hearts
  whether John might be the Christ.
John answered them all, saying,
  "I am baptizing you with water,
  but one mightier than I is coming.
I am not worthy to loosen the thongs of
    his sandals.
He will baptize you with the Holy Spirit
    and fire.
His winnowing fan is in his hand to
    clear his threshing floor
  and to gather the wheat into his barn,
  but the chaff he will burn with
    unquenchable fire."
Exhorting them in many other ways,
  he preached good news to the people.

Reflecting on the Gospel
"What should we do?" This can be a loaded question! Sometimes it is simply a matter of mulling over two attractive choices for a night out at the movies. Sometimes the question is prompted by a perplexing situation to resolve, for example, the gift tags on the Advent Giving Tree for families in need haven't all been taken. Sometimes, like in this Sunday's gospel, the question comes when we are faced with changing our behaviors. How we answer the question has life-giving consequences.

John's clear and unequivocal answers to "What should we do?" gave direction to people's lives. He challenged the crowds, tax collectors, and soldiers to change their behavior, to make other people their focus and care. John's good news, however, went beyond merely telling the people how to behave toward each other, but also instilled expectation in them. His answers indicated that something new is happening. His good news pointed to the One who is all Good News, "a mighty savior" who is in our midst (first reading), who is near (see second reading). The Good News is not a message but a person—Jesus.

"What should we do?" The gospel gives a simple challenge: make Jesus the center of our lives. Make how he responded to people the way we respond to people. Make his fire well up in our hearts so that our baptism with the Holy Spirit conforms us more perfectly to him. Make our answer to the question one that leads us to preach to others the same Good News Jesus preached to us. And we must preach the same way he did: not simply with words, but with deeds.

Traditionally, this is "Gaudete," "rejoice," Sunday, named after the Introit antiphon in the *Roman Missal*. The second reading also refers to rejoicing and suggests to us that the cause of our joy is Christ and Christ alone ("The Lord is near"). When we say "The Lord is near," we mean not that Christmas is almost here, but that Christ is always being enfleshed in our midst. "What should we do?" to celebrate this Presence already and always so near to us? John tells us, and so does Jesus. All we need to do is answer the question by the quality of how we live.

Living the Paschal Mystery
The gospel imagery of chaff and wheat captures well the dying and rising of the paschal mystery. Those who refuse to die to themselves and be transformed into those over whom God rejoices (see first reading) will "burn with unquenchable fire." "What should we do" to avoid this judgment? The gospel is clear: live as green wheat rising to new life. The second reading is specific: "Your kindness should be known to all." Only by dying to self now do we avoid the everlasting judgment to "burn with unquenchable fire." Only by dying to self now can we claim to be conformed to Jesus, can we claim to have answered with integrity the question, "What should we do?"

Here is the key to Gospel living: when we live as wheat risen to new life in Christ, when we make our kindness known to all, we preach the Good News by our very lives. We announce with John that the Lord is near and that we have discovered anew what we should do. Yes, indeed, something new is happening here. What is new is a fresh attentiveness to Jesus' abiding presence within and among us.

Focusing the Gospel

Key words and phrases: What should we do?, filled with expectation, one . . . is coming, good news

To the point: John's clear and unequivocal answers to "What should we do?" gave direction to people's lives. John's good news, however, went beyond merely telling the people how to behave toward each other, but also instilled expectation in them. His good news pointed to the One who is all Good News, "a mighty savior" who is in our midst (first reading), who is near (see second reading). The Good News is not a message but a person—Jesus.

Connecting the Gospel

to the first and second readings: The first and second readings both speak of rejoicing and suggest to us that the cause of our joy is Christ ("in your midst, a mighty savior"; "The Lord is near"). Christ is always being enfleshed in our midst.

to experience: All of us have experienced the sheer goodness of another person, the utter joy of an event, the complete surprise of intimacy. With reflection we conclude that we have indeed experienced the nearness of Christ in the flesh among us.

Connecting the Responsorial Psalm

to the readings: Instead of singing verses from a psalm this Sunday, we sing a text from Isaiah, who tells us the Holy One we await is already in our midst. Three times the crowd around John the Baptist asks, "What should we do?" to prepare for the presence of God. The words from Isaiah answer: cry out with joy, sing praise, give thanks, shout with exultation, make God's deeds known. We are to do so not only by singing, however, but also by putting into practice the Good News the Holy One has come into our midst to proclaim. We are to care for the needy and to act with justice (gospel). We are to show kindness to all (second reading). We are to invite all nations into our song of salvation (psalm). Then all peoples will hear the Lord singing over them with joy (first reading). What a chorus that will be!

to psalmist preparation: In singing these verses you are the prophet Isaiah announcing God's saving presence in the midst of the people. How does your manner of living announce this presence of the Holy One? How in your singing will the people hear God singing joyfully over them?

ASSEMBLY & FAITH-SHARING GROUPS

- When the question, "What should we do?" arises in me, I turn to . . .
- What instills expectation in me is . . . What I expect is . . .
- The Good News for me is . . .

PRESIDERS

Like John, my preaching is explicit, challenging, and "good news" in that . . .

DEACONS

I help those I serve experience the nearness of the Lord (see second reading) whenever I . . .

HOSPITALITY MINISTERS

My ministry helps others experience the nearness of the Lord during the liturgy when I . . .

MUSIC MINISTERS

If I were to ask John the Baptist "What should I do?" as a music minister, he would answer . . .

ALTAR MINISTERS

The manner of my serving at the altar announces that I have experienced the nearness of the Lord when . . .

LECTORS

My proclamation helps others encounter Jesus as the Good News when I . . .

EXTRAORDINARY MINISTERS OF HOLY COMMUNION

I see Jesus, the Good News, in those who come to me for Holy Communion whenever I . . .

Model Penitential Act

Presider: We gather to hear the good news of Christ's coming. Let us quiet our hearts that we may encounter this Good News . . . [pause]

    Lord Jesus, you are the Christ, the Good News who comes to us: Lord . . .

    Christ Jesus, you are the fulfillment of all expectation: Christ . . .

    Lord Jesus, you are God's peace among us: Lord . . .

Homily Points

• We naturally tend to gravitate toward relationships with persons who share our values, desires, and expectations. However, at the same time, we also gravitate toward persons whose experiences, wisdom, and knowledge can challenge us and lead us beyond where we are.

• Our desires and expectations to know what we should do and who we should be lead us to seek Jesus. John pointed his listeners to Jesus as the One who would fulfill their expectations. Each day brings us persons who point us to that same presence of Jesus. Then as now, Jesus is the Good News who shows us what we should do and how we should be.

• Our hearts long to know not only a good direction for our lives, but also to know someone who might show us the way. At some time or other we have all chosen a mentor, spiritual director, counselor, teacher, idol, coach—someone whom we trust, respect, and who can engender in us the willingness to give ourselves over to their judgment. Such persons incarnate Jesus who, indeed, acts through them.

Model Universal Prayer (Prayer of the Faithful)

Presider: John the Baptist announced to his listeners that One who is mightier than he is coming. With confidence we lift our needs to this mighty Savior.

Response:

Cantor:

That all members of the church lead lives that inspire others to encounter Christ . . . [pause]

That the people of the world encounter the Savior of the world . . . [pause]

That those who desire a closer relationship with God encounter the Christ who is near . . . [pause]

That we here gathered may hear the Good News and rejoice in Christ's nearness . . . [pause]

Presider: O saving God, you hear those who cry to you: answer our prayers and help us to ready ourselves for the coming of your Son, Jesus Christ our Lord. **Amen.**

COLLECT

Let us pray

Pause for silent prayer

O God, who see how your people
faithfully await the feast of the Lord's
    Nativity,
enable us, we pray,
to attain the joys of so great a salvation
and to celebrate them always
with solemn worship and glad rejoicing.
Through our Lord Jesus Christ, your Son,
who lives and reigns with you in the unity
    of the Holy Spirit,
one God, for ever and ever.
Amen.

FIRST READING

Zeph 3:14-18a

Shout for joy, O daughter Zion!
    Sing joyfully, O Israel!
Be glad and exult with all your heart,
    O daughter Jerusalem!
The LORD has removed the judgment
    against you,
    he has turned away your enemies;
the King of Israel, the LORD, is in your
    midst,
    you have no further misfortune to fear.
On that day, it shall be said to Jerusalem:
    Fear not, O Zion, be not discouraged!
The LORD, your God, is in your midst,
    a mighty savior;
he will rejoice over you with gladness,
    and renew you in his love,
he will sing joyfully because of you,
    as one sings at festivals.

RESPONSORIAL PSALM
Isa 12:2-3, 4, 5-6

R̸. (6) Cry out with joy and gladness: for among you is the great and Holy One of Israel.

God indeed is my savior;
    I am confident and unafraid.
My strength and my courage is the LORD,
    and he has been my savior.
With joy you will draw water
    at the fountain of salvation.

R̸. Cry out with joy and gladness: for among you is the great and Holy One of Israel.

Give thanks to the LORD, acclaim his name;
    among the nations make known his
        deeds,
    proclaim how exalted is his name.

R̸. Cry out with joy and gladness: for among you is the great and Holy One of Israel.

Sing praise to the LORD for his glorious
        achievement;
    let this be known throughout all the
        earth.
Shout with exultation, O city of Zion,
    for great in your midst
    is the Holy One of Israel!

R̸. Cry out with joy and gladness: for among you is the great and Holy One of Israel.

SECOND READING
Phil 4:4-7

Brothers and sisters:
Rejoice in the Lord always.
I shall say it again: rejoice!
Your kindness should be known to all.
The Lord is near.
Have no anxiety at all, but in everything,
    by prayer and petition, with
        thanksgiving,
    make your requests known to God.
Then the peace of God that surpasses all
        understanding
    will guard your hearts and minds in
        Christ Jesus.

About Liturgy

Advent's uniqueness: Sometimes we treat Advent like a "mini" Lent. Both seasons are preparation for great feasts. Both seasons call us to penance and repentance. But Advent is very different from Lent.

This is the last full week of Advent. Next Sunday, the Fourth Sunday of Advent, will leave us with only two more days of Advent. This deftly underscores that Advent is a season of four Sundays rather than one of four weeks.

Monday, December 17 begins the time for Advent weekday propers, including the great "O" antiphons. The liturgies for these final weekdays before Christmas specifically focus our attention on the coming feast. Prior to December 17, the weekdays of Advent have a one-week series of propers which are repeated. Now, with only one week to go, there are propers for every day. We are nearing the feast. We are nearing our celebration of God incarnate. We are preparing ourselves with special hymns and prayers so that we can celebrate with full hearts and voices.

The "O" antiphons, dating from about the seventh century, are magnificent poetic compositions extolling name-imagery for the Savior combined with a petition; they are used as gospel acclamations and as antiphons for the *Magnificat* sung during Evening Prayer from December 17 to 23 (see the weekday Lectionary, L201). The name-imagery extols Christ as Wisdom, Leader, Root of Jesse, Key of David, Emmanuel, King (on both December 22 and 23), and Radiant Dawn.

About Liturgical Music

Music suggestions: This Sunday the focus of Advent turns from looking toward the final coming of Christ at the end of time to remembering his coming at the Incarnation two thousand years ago. Hymns expressing this focus include "O Come, O Come, Emmanuel"; "On Jordan's Bank"; "Savior of the Nations, Come"; "O Come, Divine Messiah"; "Come, O Long Expected Jesus"; "People, Look East"; "Creator of the Stars of Night" (also titled "O Lord Who Made the Stars of Night"); "Awake! Awake, and Greet the New Morn"; "Emmanuel"; "See How the Virgin Waits"; and "Each Winter as You Grow Older."

SPIRITUALITY

GOSPEL ACCLAMATION
Luke 1:38

℟. Alleluia, alleluia.
Behold, I am the handmaid of the Lord.
May it be done to me according to your word.
℟. Alleluia, alleluia.

Gospel

Luke 1:39-45; L12C

**Mary set out
and traveled to the hill country in
haste
to a town of Judah,
where she entered the house of
Zechariah
and greeted Elizabeth.
When Elizabeth heard Mary's greeting,
the infant leaped in her womb,
and Elizabeth, filled with the Holy
Spirit,
cried out in a loud voice and said,
"Blessed are you among women,
and blessed is the fruit of your
womb.
And how does this happen to me,
that the mother of my Lord should
come to me?
For at the moment the sound of your
greeting reached my ears,
the infant in my womb leaped for joy.
Blessed are you who believed
that what was spoken to you by the
Lord
would be fulfilled."**

Reflecting on the Gospel

When two people are unsure of themselves, encounters can surely be most awkward! Suppose a wife and husband have had a disagreement before they go off to work; coming home in the evening might be awkward until someone takes the initiative to smooth things out. Or perhaps an important birthday or anniversary of a friend has been forgotten and one encounters the friend unexpectedly in the grocery store; the exchange might be awkward until the social breach has been admitted and repaired. This Sunday's gospel features an encounter between two pregnant women. All the ingredients are there for an awkward encounter: both pregnancies occur under most unusual circumstances. Yet, instead of awkwardness there is immediate recognition and blessing.

Two days before Christmas, this Sunday is priming us to encounter the Word made flesh. The gospel alerts us to recognize the mystery of Christ's presence through encounter, and highlights the fitting response we make to these encounters. Mary does a natural thing when one has good news to share—she makes a visit to a relative, especially this relative because Elizabeth is pregnant, too. Both pregnancies are wrapped in mystery. Both pregnancies burst with something new.

Mary went in haste to Elizabeth's house, entered, and greeted her. Elizabeth recognized and responded to the mystery taking place. She expressed astonishment, wonder, amazement: "how does this happen to me, that the mother of my Lord should come to me?" There is encounter. There is blessing. There is praise. One woman carries the infant who is born to be precursor. The other carries the infant who is born to be Savior.

It is too easy to dismiss this encounter. We might be astonished at the singularity of these two women; we might wonder at their holiness and obedience; we might be amazed at their openness to God's grace. An even greater astonishment, wonder, amazement, however, is also at work: the Lord himself comes to *us*. How do *we* respond? Mary responded by believing and saying yes to God's will. Elizabeth responded by opening herself to be a participant in the mystery of salvation and uttering praise and blessing when she encountered her Lord. Our response to the mystery of the Word made flesh must be similar to theirs: believing, saying yes, praising, blessing. This response primes us to celebrate the mystery of Christmas in all its fullness.

Living the Paschal Mystery

What is Christmas about? Encounter! More than gifts which bring temporary joy, Christmas is about self-giving which makes possible everlasting joy. What has Advent really been about? We have been getting ready for our own bodies to be "consecrated" (second reading), like Christ's. Like Mary, we must believe so that what God speaks might be fulfilled in us.

By giving do we receive and convey the blessedness we have received in Christ. During these holidays, with family and friends gathering, there will be many opportunities for encounters and self-giving. Perhaps it is a matter of taking a few minutes to be present individually to the elderly. Perhaps it means playing awhile with the little ones. Perhaps it means simply helping to clean up and do dishes. However the opportunity for self-giving presents itself, it always is an opportunity for blessing.

Focusing the Gospel

Key words and phrases: how does this happen to me, the mother of my Lord should come to me

To the point: Mary went in haste to Elizabeth's house, entered, and greeted her. Elizabeth recognized and responded to the mystery taking place. She expressed astonishment, wonder, amazement: "how does this happen to me, that the mother of my Lord should come to me?" An even greater astonishment, wonder, amazement: the Lord himself comes to *us*. How do *we* respond?

Connecting the Gospel

to the first reading: How astounding and unexpected that the majestic ruler of Israel should come from so small and insignificant a place as Bethlehem. Even more astounding is that the Son of God should come to share our humanity.

to experience: We are overjoyed at a visit from a beloved relative or friend whom we have not seen for some time. We are being invited this Sunday to recognize and rejoice over the abiding presence of Jesus, who is beloved relative (brothers and sisters in Christ) and friend.

Connecting the Responsorial Psalm

to the readings: Psalm 80 was a lament prayed by the Israelite community during times of national destruction. The community begged God to "look down from heaven," see their suffering, and "come to save" them. The "man of your right hand" they prayed for in verse 18 was the king who represented them all. The people asked to be turned back toward God so that they would no longer "withdraw" from divine love and presence.

This Sunday we, too, ask God to "let us see your face" that we may be saved. And where does God direct our vision? First to the face of the Son made flesh in the womb of Mary (gospel). Then to the face of the adult Christ carrying out God's will (second reading). Then to the faces of one another who, "consecrated" through Christ's offering, continue to shine the face of salvation upon the world. In the human flesh of Christ and one another God has indeed shown us the divine face—all we need to do is look and be saved.

to psalmist preparation: As you prepare to sing this psalm, spend some time reflecting on where and when you see the face of God and where and when you struggle to see that face. In what direction do you need to "turn" that you might better see?

ASSEMBLY & FAITH-SHARING GROUPS
- Like Elizabeth, I have been astounded to find the Lord's presence when . . . in . . . through . . .
- My response to the Lord's presence tends to be . . .
- Like Mary, I bring the Lord's presence to others when I . . .

PRESIDERS
Like Mary, I best bring Christ to others when I . . . Like Elizabeth, I respond to the Christ in others by . . .

DEACONS
I bring the presence of Christ to those in need in these ways . . .

HOSPITALITY MINISTERS
I recognize the presence of the Lord in those I greet whenever I . . . and I respond by . . .

MUSIC MINISTERS
In my music making I am the presence of Christ to the assembly when I . . .

ALTAR MINISTERS
My service at the altar leads others to experience the Lord among us when I . . .

LECTORS
When I have grown in my ability to recognize Christ in others, my proclamation sounds like . . .

EXTRAORDINARY MINISTERS OF HOLY COMMUNION
Beyond bringing Holy Communion to the sick and homebound, I myself am a presence of Christ for others when I . . .

Model Penitential Act

Presider: Elizabeth recognized the infant in Mary's womb as her Lord. Let us reflect on how we recognize the Lord and prepare for his coming . . . [pause]

Lord Jesus, your coming brings us joy: Lord . . .

Christ Jesus, your coming brings us blessing: Christ . . .

Lord Jesus, your coming brings us life: Lord . . .

Homily Points

• What joy a child exhibits when receiving the loving attention of an adult! What joy all of us feel whenever we are acknowledged as loved, valued, and good! Yet in our society our tendency is to speak and hear less-than-positive words about each other. In our hunger to hear good words, God comes to us speaking the good Word.

• Gabriel reveals to Mary the good news about Elizabeth's pregnancy. Mary sets out immediately to go to Elizabeth—and what an exchange of good news! To both women, God had come. Both women responded with joyful recognition of God's presence.

• Mary "set out . . . in haste" to go to Elizabeth. God also comes to us "in haste." For us time-trapped, impatient humans, however, God's coming might seem immeasurably slow. God simply doesn't always come in ways we expect, and so we often miss divine Presence. Yet God does faithfully come in every moment, every event, every encounter with another. How do we respond?

Model Universal Prayer (Prayer of the Faithful)

Presider: We are confident to make known our needs to a God who is always present and attentive to us.

Response:

Lord, hear our prayer.

Cantor:

we pray to the Lord,

That all members of the church might faithfully proclaim the saving presence of the Word made flesh . . . [pause]

That all people of the world might share more fully in Christ's joy and peace . . . [pause]

That those who are poor, hungry, and without shelter may be helped by the generosity of those who bear Christ's presence . . . [pause]

That we here present may recognize more fully Christ's presence among and within us . . . [pause]

Presider: O God, you sent your Son into the world that we might have life: bless us now with joy and expectation and grant what we ask through Christ our Lord. **Amen.**

COLLECT

Let us pray

Pause for silent prayer

Pour forth, we beseech you, O Lord,
your grace into our hearts,
that we, to whom the Incarnation of Christ
    your Son
was made known by the message of an
    Angel,
may by his Passion and Cross
be brought to the glory of his
    Resurrection.
Who lives and reigns with you in the unity
    of the Holy Spirit,
one God, for ever and ever.
Amen.

FIRST READING

Mic 5:1-4a

Thus says the LORD:
You, Bethlehem-Ephrathah
    too small to be among the clans of
        Judah,
from you shall come forth for me
    one who is to be ruler in Israel;
whose origin is from of old,
    from ancient times.
Therefore the Lord will give them up, until
    the time
    when she who is to give birth has borne,
and the rest of his kindred shall return
    to the children of Israel.
He shall stand firm and shepherd his flock
    by the strength of the LORD,
    in the majestic name of the LORD, his
        God;
and they shall remain, for now his
    greatness
    shall reach to the ends of the earth;
he shall be peace.

RESPONSORIAL PSALM
Ps 80:2-3, 15-16, 18-19

R⁄. (4) Lord, make us turn to you; let us see your face and we shall be saved.

O shepherd of Israel, hearken,
    from your throne upon the cherubim,
        shine forth.
Rouse your power,
    and come to save us.

R⁄. Lord, make us turn to you; let us see your face and we shall be saved.

Once again, O Lord of hosts,
    look down from heaven, and see;
take care of this vine,
    and protect what your right hand has
        planted,
    the son of man whom you yourself
        made strong.

R⁄. Lord, make us turn to you; let us see your face and we shall be saved.

May your help be with the man of your
    right hand,
    with the son of man whom you yourself
        made strong.
Then we will no more withdraw from you;
    give us new life, and we will call upon
        your name.

R⁄. Lord, make us turn to you; let us see your face and we shall be saved.

SECOND READING
Heb 10:5-10

Brothers and sisters:
When Christ came into the world, he said:
    "Sacrifice and offering you did not
        desire,
    but a body you prepared for me;
    in holocausts and sin offerings you took
        no delight.
    Then I said, 'As is written of me in the
        scroll,
    behold, I come to do your will, O God.'"

First he says, "Sacrifices and offerings,
    holocausts and sin offerings,
    you neither desired nor delighted in."
These are offered according to the law.
Then he says, "Behold, I come to do your
    will."
He takes away the first to establish the
    second.
By this "will," we have been consecrated
    through the offering of the body of
        Jesus Christ once for all.

About Liturgy

Annunciation and visitation: In years A and B the Lectionary selection assigned for the gospel of the Fourth Sunday of Advent is the annunciation account. The gospel acclamation assigned to year C is also from the annunciation account. It is easy to relate this familiar gospel story to the coming Christmas celebration; after all, physiologically, conception precedes birth. However, the gospel in year C presents us with the story of the visitation. Putting aside the logic of how things happen naturally enables us to see how this story, like the story of the annunciation, leads us to the Christmas mystery. The visitation is another *annunciation*—Elizabeth recognizes and "cri[es] out in a loud voice" that her Lord is near, indeed, the fruit of Mary's womb.

Every liturgy is both an annunciation and a visitation. During each Liturgy of the Word Christ's presence is uniquely announced in the proclamation of the gospel. Even more: in the very proclamation, the person of Jesus comes to dwell within the liturgical assembly. Each Liturgy of the Eucharist is also a kind of visitation when *we ourselves* take into our very own bodies the Body and Blood of our Lord Jesus Christ and are *transformed* into being more perfect members of the Body. Each liturgy, then, is Christmas. The Word is made flesh and dwells among us!

About Liturgical Music

Music suggestions: Songs expressing the mystery of Mary's involvement in the Incarnation include "See How the Virgin Waits," "The Angel Gabriel from Heaven Came," "She Will Show Us the Promised One," and "Emmanuel." "When to Mary, the Word" (in *Hymns for the Gospels*, GIA) tells the story of Mary's visitation to Elizabeth and calls us to reach out to our neighbor as did Mary, and to see the Christ hidden within the other as did the infant John in Elizabeth's womb.

A good choice for Communion would be a setting of the *Magnificat*. Rory Cooney's "Canticle of the Turning" with its energetic refrain, "My heart shall sing of the day you bring. Let the fires of your justice burn. Wipe away all tears, for the dawn draws near, and the world is about to turn," would be particularly uplifting. Finally, even though we have two days rather than a week left to finish Advent, John A. Dalles's thought-provoking hymn "We Blew No Trumpet Blasts to Sound" (in *Swift Currents and Still Waters*, GIA) would be an excellent text to sing either as a post-Communion song or a recessional. In it we sing: "We blew no trumpet blasts. . . . We built no bonfire. . . . We spread no welc'ming canopy. . . . [instead] We hurried through another week, unheeding, and unmoved. . . . Dear God, how unprepared we were to welcome Jesus, then. We pray you, help us not to miss your priceless gift again."

Christmas Time

To whom are you like,
glad Babe, fair little One,
Whose Mother is a Virgin,
Whose Father is hidden,
Whom even the Seraphim
are not able to look upon?
Tell us whom you are like,
O Son of the Gracious!

—St. Ephraim the Syrian
Nineteen Hymns on the Nativity of Christ in the Flesh
Hymn IX

SPIRITUALITY

At the Vigil Mass

GOSPEL ACCLAMATION
R7. Alleluia, alleluia.
Tomorrow the wickedness of the earth will be
    destroyed:
the Savior of the world will reign over us.
R7. Alleluia, alleluia.

Gospel

Matt 1:1-25; L13 ABC

The book of the genealogy of
    Jesus Christ,
    the son of David, the son of
        Abraham.

Abraham became the father of
    Isaac,
    Isaac the father of Jacob,
    Jacob the father of Judah
        and his brothers.
Judah became the father of
    Perez and Zerah,
    whose mother was Tamar.
Perez became the father of
    Hezron,
    Hezron the father of Ram,
    Ram the father of Amminadab.
Amminadab became the father of
    Nahshon,
    Nahshon the father of Salmon,
    Salmon the father of Boaz,
    whose mother was Rahab.
Boaz became the father of Obed,
    whose mother was Ruth.
Obed became the father of Jesse,
    Jesse the father of David the king.

Continued in Appendix A, p. 264

or Matt 1:18-25 *in Appendix A, p. 264.*

See Appendix A, p. 265, for the other readings.

Reflecting on the Gospel and Living the Paschal Mystery

Key words and phrases: how the birth . . . came about, before they lived together, angel of the Lord appeared, he will save, God is with us, did as the angel of the Lord had commanded

To the point: This gospel begins with Joseph's experiencing inner turmoil ("unwilling to expose her," "decided to divorce her") and moves to Joseph's grasping events in which salvation is happening ("through the Holy Spirit that this child has been conceived," "he will save his people"). He did as the angel commanded: "do not be afraid," "take Mary," "name him Jesus." And so Salvation was born. Then. And now in *our* lives.

Reflection: This is how most births come about: a man and woman fall in love, marry, become pregnant, live in joyful anticipation for months, pack suitcases early, anxiously plan details of getting to the hospital as the time comes near, be ministered to by a myriad of medical team members, rejoice when the first cry is heard. In this Christmas gospel we, too, hear about how a birth came about.

Mary is betrothed to Joseph. So far so good. But then the gospel relates a truly extraordinary circumstance: Mary has conceived by the Holy Spirit. Clearly this will be no ordinary child. Then another extraordinary circumstance occurs. Naturally, Joseph is experiencing inner turmoil: shall he divorce his betrothed? His answer comes in a dream: he is not to be afraid to take Mary as his wife into his home. Further, he is to "name him Jesus," for "he will save his people from their sins." The inner turmoil gives way to obedience. And so Salvation was born.

This gospel centers on the *who* of Mary and Joseph. They were ordinary people doing ordinary things. Then God visited them both and their lives were changed forever. No longer would they simply be a married couple. No longer would they simply be husband and wife. No longer would they simply be housewife and carpenter. No longer would they simply be parents. Now they are the first witnesses of the *who* of salvation. Their child is "Emmanuel . . . God is with us." God was with Mary and Joseph. God is with us now. Salvation was born through Mary and Joseph. Salvation lives within us, now. Salvation is not a "what" but a *Who*: "God is with us."

As these extraordinary circumstances changed Mary and Joseph's lives, so do they change our lives. Since this is the birth of Salvation, then this day calls us to live lives that proclaim "God is with us." This blessed season is an opportunity to reach out to the less fortunate. We are invited by this festival to put these wonderful charitable acts into the larger picture of the Incarnation's reminder of the closeness of all humanity in Christ. In reaching out to others we ourselves are making present a kind of "incarnation"—we are enfleshing the intimacy we share with our God through care and mercy and compassion for others. We, too, then, are giving birth to salvation through these loving acts.

Incarnation is about much more than the birth of a Baby. What we celebrate at Christmas is the incarnation of God among us which transforms us into God's very presence for others. In this we are all most blessed. In this we proclaim our own share in Salvation. In this we proclaim that Salvation has been born in our own lives. In this gospel we hear not simply that a birth came about long ago, but still today. In us.

SPIRITUALITY

At the Mass during the Night

GOSPEL ACCLAMATION
Luke 2:10-11

R̸. Alleluia, alleluia.
I proclaim to you good news of great joy:
today a Savior is born for us,
Christ the Lord.
R̸. Alleluia, alleluia.

Gospel

Luke 2:1-14; L14ABC

In those days a decree went out from
    Caesar Augustus
  that the whole world should be enrolled.
This was the first enrollment,
  when Quirinius was governor of Syria.
So all went to be enrolled, each to his
    own town.
And Joseph too went up from Galilee
    from the town of Nazareth
  to Judea, to the city of David that is
    called Bethlehem,
  because he was of the house and
    family of David,
  to be enrolled with Mary, his
    betrothed, who was with child.
While they were there,
  the time came for her to have her child,
  and she gave birth to her firstborn son.
She wrapped him in swaddling clothes
    and laid him in a manger,
  because there was no room for them
    in the inn.

Continued in Appendix A, p. 265.

See Appendix A, p. 266, for the other readings.

Reflecting on the Gospel and Living the Paschal Mystery

Key words and phrases from the gospel: from the town of Nazareth, to the city of David, glory . . . shone around them, a savior has been born for you, Glory to God in the highest

To the point: The journey from Nazareth to Bethlehem points to a cosmic movement from a "people who walked in darkness" to a people who have "seen a great light" (first reading). The shepherds are among the first of this people of light: "the glory of the Lord shone around them." Revealed to them is "good news of great joy": "a savior has been born." Now we are the shepherds surrounded by God's glory, whose very lives must sing "Glory to God in the highest."

Reflection: Christmas is one of the busiest travel times of the year. Airports move millions of travelers. Highways move countless millions more. Buses and trains are crowded. It seems like everyone is on the move to get home, to get to family or friends, to join somewhere in a celebration larger than themselves. Long ago people were also on the move. Mary and Joseph traveled from Nazareth to "the city of David," to Bethlehem. They were going "home," too. Mary and Joseph were returning to the city of their lineage. Their Child is no ordinary child. Their Child is a King—not an earthly king like David, but a King-Savior.

Luke passes rather quickly over the fact that "there was no room for them in the inn" and that Jesus was "laid . . . in a manger." This King-Savior was hardly born in luxury and comfort. Our Christmas crèche statues paint the shepherds in nice clothes and beautiful colors, but in reality they were a scruffy bunch assigned to the night watch because they were the "outcasts." So who were the first witnesses of this King-Savior? These shepherds, these folks who have no "home" but now find a home in singing out "Glory to God in the highest."

The Savior of the world was born during the night of the year when darkness is the longest. Jesus comes for the people in dark places. The real, lasting, and deep joy of Christmas is that the Light shines wherever this King-Savior is acknowledged and adored. Now we are the shepherds surrounded by God's glory, whose very lives must sing "Glory to God in the highest." Now we are to find our home in this King-Savior.

In a manger, in a town far away, among shepherds, and in the dark of night, Jesus was born. Our salvation dawned in the messiness, poverty, and weakness of ordinary human life. This hardly seems like a very auspicious beginning to the dawn of salvation! Yet, we have hope not because we are perfect or because our world is perfect, but because Jesus was born into the house and family of our humanity. His birth gives us a new home and calls us to come home. His birth dispels darkness and raises us up to new heights within the Light of life. This is the cosmic movement for us that this birth brought about: we dispel darkness and bring light by how we live. We come home.

Our daily lives must reflect this mystery: we ourselves must enter into the dark reaches of people and places and bring light and hope and peace. God's glory is proclaimed not simply by words but by our own mighty deeds of salvation. We only need to reach out and be the presence for others of this firstborn Son. We must be home to others who seek this King-Savior. We must lead others to sing the same "Glory to God in the highest" that helped the shepherds of long ago know they had come home. We must know our home is in this King-Savior.

SPIRITUALITY

At the Mass at Dawn

GOSPEL ACCLAMATION
Luke 2:14

R̸. Alleluia, alleluia.
Glory to God in the highest,
and on earth peace to those
on whom his favor rests.
R̸. Alleluia, alleluia.

Gospel

Luke 2:15-20; L15ABC

When the angels went away
    from them to heaven,
    the shepherds said to one
    another,
"Let us go, then, to
    Bethlehem
to see this thing that has
    taken place,
which the Lord has made
    known to us."
So they went in haste and found Mary
    and Joseph,
and the infant lying in the manger.
When they saw this,
    they made known the message
    that had been told them about this
    child.
All who heard it were amazed
    by what had been told them by the
    shepherds.
And Mary kept all these things,
    reflecting on them in her heart.
Then the shepherds returned,
    glorifying and praising God
    for all they had heard and seen,
    just as it had been told to them.

See Appendix A, p. 266, for the other readings.

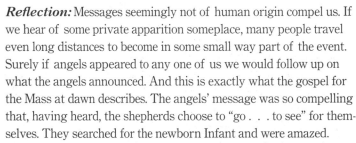

Reflecting on the Gospel and Living the Paschal Mystery

Key words and phrases from the gospel: shepherds, this . . . the Lord has made known, they made known the message, amazed

To the point: What about the message was so compelling that the people were amazed at hearing it even from the likes of shepherds? A newborn baby? Not really. An event taking place in a stable? Hardly. Appearance of angels? Not even this. The startling message made known is a revelation of a new inbreaking of divine-human presence: "[Y]our savior comes" (first reading). This same startling message is made known to us today. How amazed are we?

Reflection: Messages seemingly not of human origin compel us. If we hear of some private apparition someplace, many people travel even long distances to become in some small way part of the event. Surely if angels appeared to any one of us we would follow up on what the angels announced. And this is exactly what the gospel for the Mass at dawn describes. The angels' message was so compelling that, having heard, the shepherds choose to "go . . . to see" for themselves. They searched for the newborn Infant and were amazed.

What they found—Mary, Joseph, "the infant lying in the manger"—compelled them even more. When they left that manger scene they themselves became like messenger-angels for "they made known the message." Then something even more compelling happens. The message they announced—that "our savior comes" (first reading) compelled all who heard the shepherds to be amazed. The gospel does not indicate so, but it's not a stretch of the imagination to suppose that all who heard the shepherds could hardly keep this message to themselves. They, too, became messenger-angels who heralded this newborn Savior. No doubt the message, too, caused amazement in their own hearers.

And so it goes, on down through the centuries. People have been compelled to make known the same message of salvation. All through the centuries people have been amazed enough at this message to be compelled themselves to announce the message. Now this same amazing message—a revelation of a new in-breaking of divine-human presence bringing salvation—is made known to us. We hear the gospel proclaimed. How amazed are we? How compelled are we to announce to others who this newborn Infant is?

Like the shepherds, we, too, must make "known the message" and we do this by the very way we live each day, always remembering that any good we do is possible because of God's dwelling *with* us and *within* us. Our own priceless gift to each other during this season of giving (and all year long) is to bring Christ's presence to others. We are to help people be amazed by God's many gifts to us, but especially the Gift of the divine Son, our Savior, and then be compelled to give this Gift to others. This Gift may be as simple as helping to pick up the wrapping paper and clean up after a family party. It may be as demanding as choosing to do with less food and drink this festive season so that others with so much less might have a bit more.

So, some final questions: Do we amaze other people by the way we live? Do we amaze other people by the way we live the gift of salvation given to us by Jesus Christ? Are we ourselves amazed enough by these events to glorify and praise God? How great is our amazement at this amazing mystery we celebrate?

SPIRITUALITY

At the Mass during the Day

GOSPEL ACCLAMATION
R℟. Alleluia, alleluia.
A holy day has dawned upon us.
Come, you nations, and adore the Lord.
For today a great light has come upon the earth.
R℟. Alleluia, alleluia.

Gospel

John 1:1-18; L16ABC

In the beginning was the
    Word,
  and the Word was with
    God,
  and the Word was God.
He was in the beginning
    with God.
All things came to be
    through him,
  and without him nothing
    came to be.
What came to be through him was life,
  and this life was the light of the
    human race;
the light shines in the darkness,
  and the darkness has not
    overcome it.
A man named John was sent from God.
He came for testimony, to testify to the
    light,
  so that all might believe through him.
He was not the light,
  but came to testify to the light.

Continued in Appendix A, p. 267

or John 1:1-5, 9-14 *in Appendix A, p. 267.*

See Appendix A, pp. 267–268, for the other readings.

Reflecting on the Gospel and Living the Paschal Mystery

Key words and phrases from the gospel: In the beginning was the Word, the Word became flesh, From his fullness we have all received

To the point: Who is Jesus? Word, God, light, became flesh, only Son. And "[f]rom his fullness we have all received." So who are we? For believers, we are "children of God," "born . . . of God," "grace in place of grace." In us this Word continues to be enfleshed and dwells within and among us. We are the "feet" of those "announcing salvation" (first reading).

Reflection: What parent, gazing upon the innocence and beauty of a newborn infant, doesn't muse over what the child will be? Does a father imagine the child choosing his profession? Does a mother imagine the child walking down the aisle on the wedding day radiant with happiness? We celebrate at Christmas the greatest birth that ever occurred. From the beginning this "Word was with God," the only Son. From the beginning what this Child will be was known: divine Word becoming the incarnate Light of the world.

This gospel states in startling clarity the deepest meaning of the Christmas stories: "And the Word became flesh and made his dwelling among us." Christmas is about more than the Son taking on human flesh. It is about Jesus dwelling with us, throwing his lot in with us, showing us how to live all that we can become. Because Jesus participates fully in our humanity, we participate in his divinity: "[f]rom his fullness we have all received." Surely the first and foremost fullness we receive because of the Incarnation is to have that divine life dwell *within* us and thereby raise humanity up to a unique share in divinity. God's desire for us from the very beginning of creation has been that we enjoy a most intimate relationship with God. Moreover, the relationship we enjoy is exactly that of the Son: we are "children of God," born through baptism "of God."

The old dispensation of grace—the covenantal relationship with God expressed through fidelity to the law "given through Moses"—gives way to a new dispensation of grace. Jesus brings the truth of new life, a whole new relationship with God. The fullness from which we receive is nothing less than divine Life itself. This fullness is unprecedented in the gradual revealing of God's offer of salvation. When "the Word became flesh" not only did the Son of God take on the identity of being human, but this self-giving act made possible our participation in divine life so that we ourselves are an incarnation of divine presence.

In Christ God has spoken to us and "sustains . . . [us] by his mighty word" (second reading). God's Word, now the divine Son, came to dwell among us and live as an example of how we should live. Rather than mere *receivers* of the "fullness we have all received," by Christ's taking on flesh, he identified with us to the extent that we, too, participate in salvation, in restoring all things to God as it was in the beginning. The mighty act of God's Son taking on flesh and "dwelling among us" does not diminish the good enfleshed in every small and seemingly insignificant act we do for the sake of others. After the Incarnation no good, no truth is insignificant. In a very real way our acts of kindness and mercy toward others are incarnations of the "fullness we have all received." In this way we ourselves become a light for the nations and our good acts testify to the truth. With such an intimate relationship with God and with Christ as our Light, we cannot help but sing out God's glory and praise.

Model Penitential Act

Presider: Today we lift our hearts with joy to praise our God who sends his Son to dwell among us. Let us prepare ourselves to hear the word of salvation and receive the gift of life God offers us . . . [pause]

Lord Jesus, you are the Word made flesh: Lord . . .

Christ Jesus, you are the Light dispelling darkness: Christ . . .

Lord Jesus, you are the Savior of the world: Lord . . .

Model Universal Prayer (Prayer of the Faithful)

Presider: Our Savior dwells among us. With confidence we make our prayers known to God.

Response:

Lord, hear our prayer.

Cantor:

we pray to the Lord,

That the church may grow in the joy of Christ's abiding presence among us . . . [pause]

That all peoples may share in the salvation and peace that Christ brings . . . [pause]

That the poor and disadvantaged experience joy in the nearness of God . . . [pause]

That we here gathered may give God glory by faithfully heralding the Good News of salvation . . . [pause]

Presider: O wondrous God, you give us joy in this celebration of the birth of your Son: hear these our prayers that we may sing with the angels your glory and praise always. We pray through that same Son, Jesus Christ our Lord. **Amen**.

COLLECT

(from At the Mass during the Night)

Let us pray

Pause for silent prayer

O God, who have made this most sacred night radiant with the splendor of the true light, grant, we pray, that we, who have known
the mysteries of his light on earth,
may also delight in his gladness in heaven.
Who lives and reigns with you in the unity
of the Holy Spirit,
one God, for ever and ever.
Amen.

FOR REFLECTION

• Ways I have assisted others to recognize and experience Christ in the midst of their darkness, messiness, poverty, and weakness are . . .

• When I reflect on the Christmas mystery, I come to greater recognition of my identity as . . .

• Like the angels and shepherds that first Christmas night, I glorify and praise God by . . .

Homily Points

• Everybody knows that Christmas is a time of gift-giving. Even those who have little manage to find a way to give at least a small gift. The meaningfulness of a gift is not dependent upon the amount spent but on the heart given. The greatest gift ever given is the greatest heart ever given: God sent the only Son to dwell among us.

• Jesus came among us as God's gift of salvation to us. Jesus himself is gift and salvation. As gift and salvation, Jesus is the incarnation of God's loving presence among us. The invitation of the Christmas mystery is for each of us to discover that our own deepest identity is to be an incarnated presence of the One whose birth we celebrate, and to share his gift of love with each other. This gift costs us no money. It does cost us our own life: a heart turned to God.

✠ SPIRITUALITY

GOSPEL ACCLAMATION
Col 3:15a, 16a

R̸. Alleluia, alleluia.
Let the peace of Christ control your hearts;
let the word of Christ dwell in you richly.
R̸. Alleluia, alleluia.

Gospel Luke 2:41-52; L17C

Each year Jesus' parents went to
  Jerusalem for the feast of Passover,
 and when he was twelve years old,
 they went up according to festival
     custom.
After they had completed its days, as
    they were returning,
 the boy Jesus remained behind in
     Jerusalem,
 but his parents did not know it.
Thinking that he was in the caravan,
 they journeyed for a day
 and looked for him among their
     relatives and acquaintances,
 but not finding him,
 they returned to Jerusalem to look for
    him.
After three days they found him in the
    temple,
 sitting in the midst of the teachers,
 listening to them and asking them
     questions,
 and all who heard him were astounded
 at his understanding and his answers.

Continued in Appendix A, p. 268.

Reflecting on the Gospel

Losing something can be quite disconcerting! If it's something relatively unimportant (like dropping a penny), we might take a casual look around and then not put forth any more time or energy. If it's something so important as losing a child, parents never give up. In the case of searching for something significant, there is usually a pattern. Searching a wood for a child begins with sectioning off the area and assigning units who search in meticulous ways. In

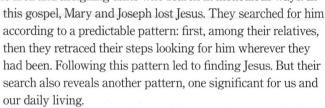

this gospel, Mary and Joseph lost Jesus. They searched for him according to a predictable pattern: first, among their relatives, then they retraced their steps looking for him wherever they had been. Following this pattern led to finding Jesus. But their search also reveals another pattern, one significant for us and our daily living.

Mary and Joseph looked for Jesus. In reality, this describes our own Christian living. We look for Jesus when we, like him, seek to be in God's presence; when we, like him, choose to be obedient; when we, like him, grow in wisdom. Along the way we discover that Jesus enlarges where we look for him, how we find him, and what new understanding comes to us through our encounters with him. This is the pattern of faithful Christian living that brings us to fullness of life.

The second reading suggests actions that parallel the pattern of gospel looking. Jesus chose to be in God's presence; this might be a metaphor for St. John's admonition to "believe in the Name of . . . Jesus Christ." Believing here is not an intellectual pursuit (as in believing in doctrines) but an active pursuing of being with God. Saint John also says we are to "keep [God's] commandments"; like Jesus, we are to submit ourselves to obedience. Finally, we are told in the second reading to "love one another" and this is how we grow in "wisdom . . . and favor . . . before God."

Looking for Jesus is probably not a conscious element of our daily living, at least not in the sense that Mary and Joseph looked for him as told in the gospel. Yet, every time we seek to be in God's presence, choose to be obedient to what God wants of us, go out of our way to love one another, we are seeking Jesus. And we will always find him.

Living the Paschal Mystery

Every good family strives for continued growth in fidelity to God and each other. Each time we let go of one attitude, habit, annoying behavior (that is, each time we choose to love one another) we grow into a newer and deeper relationship with those around us. The family is stronger and so are we for it.

A holy family is one in which relationships place God at the center. Parenting is a great entry into the paschal mystery! Good parents spend their children's growing-up years emptying themselves of their own desires for the sake of the well-being of their children, endlessly and willingly sacrificing for them. Then, when the children are adults, parents must be willing to "cut the apron strings" and let go so the children can be about their own business. Like Mary and Joseph, good parents always nurture and take care of their children but, then, they willingly give back what they have received. Such is what holy family living is really all about: seeking, obeying, loving.

Focusing the Gospel

Key words and phrases: looked for him, look for him, looking for you, Why were you looking for me, in my Father's house, obedient to them, advanced in wisdom

To the point: Mary and Joseph looked for Jesus. In reality, this describes our own Christian living. We look for Jesus when we, like him, seek to be in God's presence; when we, like him, choose to be obedient; when we, like him, grow in wisdom. Along the way we discover that Jesus enlarges where we look for him, how we find him, and what new understanding comes to us through our encounters with him. This is the pattern of faithful Christian living that brings us to fullness of life.

Connecting the Gospel

to the second reading: The second reading parallels what the gospel suggests about looking for Jesus. We look for Jesus by believing in him, loving one another, and keeping the commandments.

to experience: Our experience of divine presence, obedience, and growing in wisdom unfolds first and foremost in our family life. The joys, challenges, and pains of family life are all opportunities to look for and find Jesus.

Connecting the Responsorial Psalm

to the readings: For the Israelites God's dwelling place was the Temple in Jerusalem. There they journeyed three times a year to keep festival. These annual pilgrimages were joyous occasions, expressing the community's sense of identity as God's chosen people and their longing to be with God forever. Psalm 84 communicates this joy and this hope.

Knowing they were part of God's chosen people, Hannah could give her son to God (first reading) and Jesus could recognize where his true home was (gospel). On this feast of the Holy Family we celebrate who we are—"the children of God"—and where our true home is—"in him" (second reading). Like Hannah, Jesus, Mary, and Joseph, we give ourselves in obedience and trust to the God who has made us God's own. We sing Psalm 84 to celebrate *our* blessedness as God's chosen ones and to express our desire to dwell more fully in God's presence.

to psalmist preparation: In this responsorial psalm you call the assembly to become conscious of who they are—a holy family who dwell in the house of the Lord. What would strengthen your own sense of yourself as a member of God's family? How might you live this week so that this identity be more evident to others?

**ASSEMBLY &
FAITH-SHARING GROUPS**
- My family (birth family, friendship family, work family) helps me look for Jesus by . . . I help them look for Jesus by . . .
- Like Mary and Joseph, I have come to a deeper understanding of who Jesus is when . . .
- What best describes my own Christian living is . . .

PRESIDERS
I look for Jesus in . . . This affects my ministry in that . . . This shapes my preaching because . . .

DEACONS
I look for Jesus in the faces of the poor and needy and find . . .

HOSPITALITY MINISTERS
Those who gather for liturgy come looking for Jesus. My hospitality helps them find him when I . . .

MUSIC MINISTERS
Looking for Jesus in my music ministry has led me to grow in wisdom in these ways . . .

ALTAR MINISTERS
My manner of serving at the altar helps the assembly members find the One for whom they are looking when I . . .

LECTORS
How God's word is advancing me "in wisdom and . . . favor before God and [humanity]" is . . .

**EXTRAORDINARY MINISTERS
OF HOLY COMMUNION**
Communicants come forward looking for Jesus. They find him . . .

Model Penitential Act

Presider: We come together as God's family in our Father's house. Let us open our hearts to the gift of God's grace and mercy . . . [pause]

Lord Jesus, you are the son of Mary and Joseph who grew in wisdom and age and favor: Lord . . .

Christ Jesus, you are the divine Son who shows us the way to the Father's house: Christ . . .

Lord Jesus, you are the obedient Son who leads us to the fullness of life: Lord . . .

Homily Points

• Internet searches have made finding information and products so easy. However, there is no "heavenly Internet" that makes finding Jesus and what he asks of us easy. It takes work to look fruitfully for Jesus. And even more work to know what he wants of us. Yet it is this pattern of searching and discerning that helps us encounter Jesus, be obedient to what he wants of us, and grow in wisdom.

• Mary and Joseph searched diligently for Jesus: first, for a whole day among their caravan, then anxiously retracing their steps back to Jerusalem looking for him. When they found him, Jesus challenged their understanding of who he is and what he is to be about. Like Mary and Joseph, we search for Jesus. When we find him, we come to new understanding of who he is and who we are to be in relation to him.

• We have no "heavenly Internet" to help us with our search, but we do have even more sure help. For example, when we have an important decision to make, we find Jesus and come to new understanding by going to other people who have made similar decisions and share their wisdom with us. We also can find Jesus through prayer and through reflection on our own past experiences of the events and complexities of life. Searching for Jesus in these and other ways, we grow in wisdom and come to fuller life.

Model Universal Prayer (Prayer of the Faithful)

Presider: As members of the family of God, we have confidence that God hears and answers our prayers. And so we pray.

Response:

Lord, hear our prayer.

Cantor:

we pray to the Lord,

That all members of the church diligently search for Jesus and discern his desire for them . . . [pause]

That all parents may help their children grow in wisdom and love of God . . . [pause]

That those who live in isolation, confusion, or anxiety be eased by an encounter with Jesus mediated by the care of others . . . [pause]

That as Mary and Joseph sought and found Jesus, all of us here gathered may seek and find Jesus in one another . . . [pause]

Presider: God our Father, you call us your children: hear these our prayers that we may grow in your love and attain life everlasting with you. We pray through Christ our Lord. **Amen.**

COLLECT

Let us pray

Pause for silent prayer

O God, who were pleased to give us
the shining example of the Holy Family,
graciously grant that we may imitate them
in practicing the virtues of family life and
    in the bonds of charity,
and so, in the joy of your house,
delight one day in eternal rewards.
Through our Lord Jesus Christ, your Son,
who lives and reigns with you in the unity
    of the Holy Spirit,
one God, for ever and ever. **Amen**.

FIRST READING

1 Sam 1:20-22, 24-28

In those days Hannah conceived, and at
    the end of her term bore a son
      whom she called Samuel, since she had
      asked the LORD for him.
The next time her husband Elkanah was
    going up
    with the rest of his household
to offer the customary sacrifice to the
    LORD and to fulfill his vows,
    Hannah did not go, explaining to her
    husband,
    "Once the child is weaned,
I will take him to appear before the LORD
and to remain there forever;
I will offer him as a perpetual nazirite."

Once Samuel was weaned, Hannah
    brought him up with her,
    along with a three-year-old bull,
    an ephah of flour, and a skin of wine,
    and presented him at the temple of the
    LORD in Shiloh.
After the boy's father had sacrificed the
    young bull,
    Hannah, his mother, approached Eli and
    said:
    "Pardon, my lord!
As you live, my lord,
    I am the woman who stood near you
    here, praying to the LORD.
I prayed for this child, and the LORD
    granted my request.
Now I, in turn, give him to the LORD;
    as long as he lives, he shall be dedicated
    to the LORD."
Hannah left Samuel there.

RESPONSORIAL PSALM

Ps 84:2-3, 5-6, 9-10

℟. (cf. 5a) Blessed are they who dwell in
your house, O Lord.

How lovely is your dwelling place, O Lᴏʀᴅ
  of hosts!
  My soul yearns and pines for the courts
  of the Lᴏʀᴅ.
My heart and my flesh cry out for the
  living God.

R℣. Blessed are they who dwell in your
house, O Lord.

Happy they who dwell in your house!
  Continually they praise you.
Happy the men whose strength you are!
  Their hearts are set upon the
  pilgrimage.

R℣. Blessed are they who dwell in your
house, O Lord.

O Lᴏʀᴅ of hosts, hear our prayer;
  hearken, O God of Jacob!
O God, behold our shield,
  and look upon the face of your
  anointed.

R℣. Blessed are they who dwell in your
house, O Lord.

SECOND READING
1 John 3:1-2, 21-24

Beloved:
See what love the Father has bestowed
    on us
  that we may be called the children of
    God.
And so we are.
The reason the world does not know us
    is that it did not know him.
Beloved, we are God's children now;
  what we shall be has not yet been
    revealed.
We do know that when it is revealed we
    shall be like him,
  for we shall see him as he is.

Beloved, if our hearts do not condemn us,
  we have confidence in God and receive
    from him whatever we ask,
  because we keep his commandments
    and do what pleases him.
And his commandment is this:
  we should believe in the name of his
    Son, Jesus Christ,
  and love one another just as he
    commanded us.
Those who keep his commandments
  remain in him, and he in them,
  and the way we know that he remains
    in us
  is from the Spirit he gave us.

*See Appendix A, pp. 268–269, for
optional readings.*

About Liturgy

Children and liturgy: A great deal of the parish catechesis and liturgical energy is directed to the children, as well it should be. We have an important liturgical document (Directory for Masses with Children) as well as a Lectionary for Children to help us draw the younger members of our liturgical communities into the Christian family. These two resources and many others available through various Catholic publishers can help us do well the sometimes daunting task of teaching the children about the deepest meaning of liturgy and helping them be in their "Father's house" fruitfully, leading them to growth. There are some important principles to keep in mind as we help children celebrate liturgy.

1. The children's Lectionary is not a "watered down" set of readings. The readings are simplified, surely, but the selections remain faithful to Scripture. We always proclaim Scripture at liturgy, never a paraphrase, even with children.

2. It is better not to have the children do something simply to keep them occupied (and, hopefully, quiet). For example, rather than teach gestures which might be peripheral to the liturgical action (such as gesturing during a song), we need to teach and explain well the many postures and gestures which are part of liturgy.

3. We need to teach the children how to pray. This is best supported by family prayer at home, especially family prayer which coincides and is respectful of the liturgical seasons and festivals.

4. Whatever we teach the children, it ought not be in opposition to what takes place at an "adult" liturgy. We are always to help the children grow into full, conscious, and active participation in any parish celebration.

5. If children are to know what to do at Mass (and how to behave), they must be taught that and practice it with "quiet times" at home during which they are helped to pray.

About Liturgical Music

Music suggestions: The feast of the Holy Family confronts us with the disappearance of the twelve-year-old Jesus in Jerusalem and Mary and Joseph's struggle with who he is and what his life must be about. Christmas songs which speak about the revelation of who this Child will become would be most appropriate on this day. One good choice, for example, would be "Once in Royal David's City." A good choice for the preparation of the gifts would be "Within the Father's House" (in *Hymns for the Gospels*, GIA), which retells the story of the gospel and asks God to reveal Jesus' hidden identity to us in "full epiphany." "Come, Sing a Home and Family," appropriate either for the entrance procession or the preparation of the gifts, suggests concrete ways Mary and Joseph would have influenced who the adult person Jesus was to become.

Delores Dufner's "What Feast of Love" (in *Sing a New Church*, OCP) exemplifies a way of introducing an excellent eucharistic text for the Christmas season via use of a traditional text and tune. Using "What Child Is This," Dufner moves from the gift of Jesus in his birth at Bethlehem to his ongoing gift of self in the Eucharist. Because of our familiarity with the original, we will sing this new hymn with ease. Singing it will also enable us to reflect on the traditional text with deepened insight. Dufner suggests that cantor(s) or choir only sing the first four lines of each verse and the assembly respond with the refrain ("This, this is Christ the King . . ."). Unlike the traditional refrain, Dufner's refrain changes wording with each repetition, so people will need copies in hand in order to sing their part.

DECEMBER 30, 2012
THE HOLY FAMILY OF JESUS, MARY, AND JOSEPH

✠ SPIRITUALITY

GOSPEL ACCLAMATION

℟. Alleluia, alleluia.
In the past God spoke to our ancestors through
    the prophets;
in these last days, he has spoken to us through
    the Son.
℟. Alleluia, alleluia.

Gospel

Luke 2:16-21; L18ABC

**The shepherds went in haste to
    Bethlehem and found Mary and
    Joseph,
    and the infant lying in the manger.
When they saw this,
    they made known the message
    that had been told them about this
        child.
All who heard it were amazed
    by what had been told them by the
        shepherds.
And Mary kept all these things,
    reflecting on them in her heart.
Then the shepherds returned,
    glorifying and praising God
    for all they had heard and seen,
    just as it had been told to them.**

**When eight days were completed for
        his circumcision,
    he was named Jesus, the name given
        him by the angel
    before he was conceived in the womb.**

See Appendix A, p. 269, for the other readings.

Reflecting on the Gospel

Youngsters are notorious for dilly-dallying around, especially when they don't want to do something. Chores and homework get put off until the last minute, often only after much harping from parents. A fifteen minute bedtime routine all too frequently stretches into an hour or more. Yet if a friend calls and wants them to go out, they can change clothes and be on their way in an instant. All of us tend to make haste when we are pursuing something we enjoy, something that is interesting and exciting, something that is extraordinary. This solemnity's gospel begins with the shepherds making haste after the angels announced to them that a Savior was born in Bethlehem. No dilly-dallying around to secure the sheep or change into clean clothes or even check on the truth of what had been told them. The angels' announcement was so startling, interesting, exciting, extraordinary that they made haste.

Having heard the angels' announcement of the birth of the Savior, the shepherds "went in haste" to find him. But it doesn't seem like the shepherds dilly-dallied around once they found "the infant lying in the manger" either. This encounter propelled them into further quick action. Having found him, they returned to their sheep, their everyday life, but they were no longer the same shepherds. Their encounter with the newborn Infant had changed them: they became messengers of the Good News of Jesus' birth and could not stop "glorifying and praising God for all they had heard and seen." While the search for Jesus is important—we must find him—our response to finding him is even more important. This is the pattern for response to the Christmas mystery: come to Jesus, find him, and be changed. This was Mary's response; it is to be ours.

It is quite fitting that one of our Christmas season festivals focuses on Mary's motherhood. For who ever conceived by the Holy Spirit? Who ever gave birth to God's very Son? Jesus' birth is like no other birth! The greatest blessing for Mary and for us is that Jesus is born for us and *within* us. Mary is not the only "Christ-bearer." We are to be Christ-bearers in our daily living as well. We encounter Christ, are changed by him, and then are charged to announce this Good News of salvation to all we meet. Like the shepherds, we must make haste to instill this pattern into our daily Christian living.

Living the Paschal Mystery

"Don't get in my face!" It's an expression we all understand readily: "leave me alone; don't bug me!" On the contrary, the readings for this festival remind us that God has shown us the divine countenance, invites us into divine presence, and thus offers us salvation. Mary is the model for our response to these blessings of God in our daily lives. The shepherds show us what the blessing of God's presence means: we are to announce the Good News and constantly glorify and praise God by all we do.

This gospel prompts us to Gospel living in some surprising ways. First of all, simply taking quality time to reflect on God's mysteries and blessings is its own pattern of daily living. Gospel living also entails an abiding habit of giving God praise and glory. Worship is not limited to formal time in church, but is an attitude of opening ourselves to God's presence every moment of every day. Finally, Gospel living prompts us to listen for God's word in many different kinds of circumstances. Thus do God's many blessings become for us an invitation to a holy way of life. Let us make haste to come to Jesus, be changed, and praise him forever.

Focusing the Gospel

Key words and phrases: went in haste, found . . . the infant, made known the message, returned, glorifying and praising God

To the point: Having heard the angels' announcement of the birth of the Savior, the shepherds "went in haste" to find him. Having found him, they returned to their sheep, their everyday life, but they were no longer the same shepherds. Their encounter with the newborn Infant had changed them: they became messengers of the Good News of Jesus' birth and could not stop "glorifying and praising God for all they had heard and seen." This is the pattern for response to the Christmas mystery: come to Jesus, find him, and be changed. This was Mary's response; it is to be ours.

Model Penitential Act

Presider: Mary was blessed in becoming the mother of the divine Son. At the beginning of this New Year, we pause to reflect on God's blessings to us in Christ . . . [pause]

Lord Jesus, you were born of Mary: Lord . . .

Christ Jesus, you are the Savior of all nations: Christ . . .

Lord Jesus, you are God's blessing to us: Lord . . .

Model Universal Prayer (Prayer of the Faithful)

Presider: We have a powerful intercessor before God in our Mother Mary. And so we offer our prayers with confidence.

Response:

Cantor:

That all members of the church hasten to encounter the newborn Savior and make known the message of salvation . . . [pause]

That all peoples always and everywhere glorify and praise God for salvation . . . [pause]

That all those in any need be enriched by the generosity of those who have hastened to find the newborn Savior . . . [pause]

That we here present faithfully seek Jesus in our everyday lives, find him, and be changed . . . [pause]

Presider: Good and gracious God, Father of us all, you shower your blessings with love upon your faithful people: hear these our prayers that we might one day live with you forever and ever. **Amen.**

COLLECT

Let us pray

Pause for silent prayer

O God, who through the fruitful virginity of
    Blessed Mary
bestowed on the human race
the grace of eternal salvation,
grant, we pray,
that we may experience the intercession of
    her,
through whom we were found worthy
to receive the author of life,
our Lord Jesus Christ, your Son.
Who lives and reigns with you in the unity
    of the Holy Spirit,
one God, for ever and ever.
Amen.

FOR REFLECTION

- What hastens me to seek Jesus is . . . This changes me when . . .
- The purpose and value of "glorifying and praising God" like the shepherds is . . .
- In this New Year, what I hope to change in my life is . . . Encounter with Jesus will make this easier because . . .

Homily Points

• New Year's resolutions are too often made simply as fodder for jokes with the assumption that they won't last. Our celebration of the Christmas mystery, however, asks of us a response that is more than a half-hearted resolution. We cannot afford to take lightly our encounter with this mystery and its power to make a real difference in how we live.

• After their marvelous encounter with the newborn Savior lying in a manger, the shepherds returned to the ordinariness of their lives. Yet they were not the same. These scruffy shepherds had become messengers of the in-breaking of God's salvation. When we come to the end of this year's celebration of the Christmas mystery, we will return to the ordinariness of our lives. How will we have been changed? What message will we proclaim to others during the rest of the year?

SPIRITUALITY

GOSPEL ACCLAMATION
Matt 2:2

R⁊. Alleluia, alleluia.
We saw his star at its rising
and have come to do him homage.
R⁊. Alleluia, alleluia.

Gospel Matt 2:1-12; L20ABC

When Jesus was born in
    Bethlehem of Judea,
in the days of King Herod,
behold, magi from the east
    arrived in Jerusalem,
    saying,
"Where is the newborn king
    of the Jews?
We saw his star at its rising
    and have come to do him
    homage."
When King Herod heard this,
    he was greatly troubled,
    and all Jerusalem with him.
Assembling all the chief priests and the
    scribes of the people,
    he inquired of them where the Christ was
    to be born.
They said to him, "In Bethlehem of Judea,
    for thus it has been written through the
        prophet:
And you, Bethlehem, land of Judah,
    are by no means least among the
        rulers of Judah;
since from you shall come a ruler,
    who is to shepherd my people Israel."
Then Herod called the magi secretly
    and ascertained from them the time of
        the star's appearance.
He sent them to Bethlehem and said,
"Go and search diligently for the child.
When you have found him, bring me word,
    that I too may go and do him homage."
After their audience with the king they set
    out.

Continued in Appendix A, p. 269.

Reflecting on the Gospel

Many of us have had the experience of restlessness, but we can't quite put a finger on why. Perhaps we toss and turn at night although nothing particular is worrying us. Maybe we have a hard time sitting still and concentrating. Or we find ourselves talking incessantly, even when no one is there to listen. As we get to the bottom of our restlessness, we might discover that the real issue is a sense that something is about to happen. Or we have a deep longing, but are not sure for what. Or we have a sense of emptiness, but don't know why. At these times we must begin to ask ourselves critical questions: What is the meaning of my life? Am I satisfied? Am I on the right track? In this Sunday's gospel "magi from the east" are on a search-journey that leads to a critical question.

Arriving in Jerusalem, the magi ask, "Where is the newborn king of the Jews?" This is the burning question that prompted them to follow a distant star to a distant place. What planted this burning question in their hearts surely was some wisdom that their lives were not complete; no doubt they experienced a restlessness that prompted them to follow the light of a star. Their journey to find the Infant was long and convoluted, yet guided by heavenly light.

Of course, the light of the guiding star is not just any light. For Isaiah, the "light [which] has come" to Jerusalem is God's glory. For us the light is Christ himself. In Christ God's light and glory have taken flesh. Moreover, this light is not something possessed by a single people or nation, but it shines so that "all might gather and come to" (first reading) Christ. The Light of Christ shines beyond the boundaries of Israel, extending the gift of salvation to Gentiles. Ironically, it is not the king nor the chief priests and scribes, but magi-foreigners who model a driving desire to find the Christ.

We, too, will find Christ if we search. We, too, will be led by God's light. We, too, will be satisfied with Fullness of life. What leads us and prompts us to seek the divine is more than simple light; it is always God's power acting in Christ to lead us to encounter the divine. The Light brings us to God and elicits from us the homage we instinctually know we must render God.

The magi's epiphany journey is the pattern of our Christian living: we follow God's promptings, seek God diligently, overcome many obstacles, and finally, finding God, we offer homage and give over the treasure of our heart. Rather than gifts of things, we offer God the greatest gift we can—our very selves.

Living the Paschal Mystery

God leads us just as surely as the star led the magi to Bethlehem. We are not in control but must trust in God's loving presence and sure guidance. There will be setbacks and challenges before we attain that for which we seek: our everyday lives are filled with obstacles and restlessness which can get us off track. We must "search diligently": God and God's will can be found in many circumstances of our family life, work, and leisure times. Sometimes we must change course and take "another way": conversion is an ongoing milestone in Christian living.

This feast day of the Lord's epiphany reminds us that the Light of Christ is a diffuse one; it permeates all the world, and diffuses salvation everywhere. Our response: give of the treasure of our hearts.

Focusing the Gospel

Key words and phrases: Where is the newborn king of the Jews, saw his star, search diligently, saw the child

To the point: Arriving in Jerusalem, the magi ask a critical question: "Where is the newborn king of the Jews?" This is the burning question that prompted them to follow a distant star to a distant place. What planted this burning question in their hearts surely was some wisdom that their lives were not complete. Their journey to find the Infant was long and convoluted, yet guided by heavenly light. We, too, will find Christ if we search. We, too, will be led by God's light. We, too, will be satisfied with Fullness of life.

Connecting the Gospel

to the first reading: For Isaiah the "light [which] has come" to Jerusalem is God's glory. The story of the magi in the gospel reveals that the light is Christ himself, manifested to all nations.

to experience: We tend to rely on logic when setting a direction for our lives, for example, when choosing a spouse, a profession, a neighborhood, or a school. From the magi we learn that life-directing choices must also be guided by unexpected in-breakings of wisdom that come from sudden light, the counsel of others, inspiration, insight, dreams.

Connecting the Responsorial Psalm

to the readings: Historically, the purpose of Psalm 72 was to intercede for the king of Israel who represented God. The people asked God to endow the king with divine judgment so that justice might reign, the poor and afflicted might be rescued, and peace might blossom for all time. Then light would shine from Jerusalem and all peoples would recognize and pay homage to the true King, the Lord God (first reading).

The Lectionary uses these verses from Psalm 72 to identify Christ as the fulfillment of Israel's prayer: this newborn Babe is the King par excellence, God's justice and mercy in the flesh, come to rescue the poor and bring peace to all nations. Those who "see" recognize who he is (gospel). But the gospel also casts a paschal mystery shadow. We know the conclusion of this story: some, even those deputed to represent God, will seek to destroy Christ rather than pay him homage. While the revelation made known in the coming of Christ is complete and universal (second reading), leading all people to see and acknowledge him awaits our choice and needs our prayer. And so we sing this psalm with jubilation for what has already been given in Christ and longing for what is yet to be recognized and received.

to psalmist preparation: When you sing this responsorial psalm, you reveal who Christ is: the justice, peace, and mercy of God in full flesh. You also participate in the church's prayer that all peoples recognize who Christ is and come to adore him. What might you do this week to be the justice of God in human flesh for someone? Who needs you to be the mercy of God made flesh?

ASSEMBLY & FAITH-SHARING GROUPS
- Like the magi I feel a driving desire to find Christ when . . .
- I know my life is incomplete when . . . Wisdom to find completeness comes to me through . . .
- Christ satisfies me with fullness when . . .

PRESIDERS
I am best a guiding light for others when I . . . Others guide me in these ways . . .

DEACONS
I can turn the burning need inside others into a burning quest for Christ when I . . .

HOSPITALITY MINISTERS
My manner of greeting those gathering for liturgy helps them to find Christ when I . . .

MUSIC MINISTERS
The "star" I follow in my music ministry is . . . When I find myself following the wrong star, what helps me redirect my sight to Christ is . . .

ALTAR MINISTERS
My diligence in serving at the altar manifests a quest for Christ when I . . .

LECTORS
My proclamation is an epiphany of Christ to the assembly whenever I . . .

EXTRAORDINARY MINISTERS OF HOLY COMMUNION
When I view those coming for Holy Communion as magi in search of Christ, my ministry becomes . . .

35

Model Penitential Act

Presider: The magi were guided by the light of God's star to the newborn King. Let us open ourselves to God's light guiding us to encounter God's mercy and love during this liturgy . . . [pause]

Lord Jesus, you are Light for all nations: Lord . . .

Christ Jesus, you are the revelation of God's love: Christ . . .

Lord Jesus, you are the Savior of the world: Lord . . .

Homily Points

• To what ends do we go when we really want something? We might refinance our home to help pay college tuition. We might stick to a rigorous diet and exercise program to reach an ideal weight. The magi traveled a great distance down an unmarked road to find the newborn King. How far do we go to find him?

• The magi had the wisdom to follow the star, to seek help in their quest, and to protect the newborn King by taking a different route home. They went home minus their treasures of gold, frankincense, and myrrh, but having gained the treasure of encountering the Savior of the world. They went to great ends to find Jesus; in return they received a fullness beyond imagining.

• What wisdom guides our own diligent search for Jesus? Who and what are the stars that lead the way to him? How far will we go to find him? There are no easy or quick answers to these questions. Nevertheless, our faithful Christian journeying answers them, for along the way it is God who leads, God who fills.

Model Universal Prayer (Prayer of the Faithful)

Presider: Just as surely as God's star led the magi to find the infant, so will God guide us to fullness of life. Let us pray for this guidance.

Response:

Cantor:

That the church may be the light guiding all people to salvation . . . [pause]

That all people of the world may be enlightened by God's guiding presence . . . [pause]

That those who search may find God patiently and lovingly waiting for them . . . [pause]

That all of us here gathered may search diligently for Christ in our lives and receive the fullness of life he brings . . . [pause]

Presider: O God, your light guides us to fullness of life: hear these prayers we offer you and bring us to life everlasting. We pray through Christ our Lord. **Amen**.

COLLECT

Let us pray

Pause for silent prayer

O God, who on this day
revealed your Only Begotten Son to the
    nations
by the guidance of a star,
grant in your mercy
that we, who know you already by faith,
may be brought to behold the beauty of
    your sublime glory.
Through our Lord Jesus Christ, your Son,
who lives and reigns with you in the unity
    of the Holy Spirit,
one God, for ever and ever.
Amen.

FIRST READING

Isa 60:1-6

Rise up in splendor, Jerusalem! Your light
    has come,
    the glory of the Lord shines upon you.
See, darkness covers the earth,
    and thick clouds cover the peoples;
but upon you the LORD shines,
    and over you appears his glory.
Nations shall walk by your light,
    and kings by your shining radiance.
Raise your eyes and look about;
    they all gather and come to you:
your sons come from afar,
    and your daughters in the arms of their
        nurses.

Then you shall be radiant at what you see,
    your heart shall throb and overflow,
for the riches of the sea shall be emptied
        out before you,
    the wealth of nations shall be brought
        to you.
Caravans of camels shall fill you,
    dromedaries from Midian and Ephah;
all from Sheba shall come
    bearing gold and frankincense,
    and proclaiming the praises of the LORD.

RESPONSORIAL PSALM
Ps 72:1-2, 7-8, 10-11, 12-13

R⍭. (cf. 11) Lord, every nation on earth will adore you.

O God, with your judgment endow the
 king,
 and with your justice, the king's son;
he shall govern your people with justice
 and your afflicted ones with judgment.

R⍭. Lord, every nation on earth will adore you.

Justice shall flower in his days,
 and profound peace, till the moon be no
 more.
May he rule from sea to sea,
 and from the River to the ends of the
 earth.

R⍭. Lord, every nation on earth will adore you.

The kings of Tarshish and the Isles shall
 offer gifts;
 the kings of Arabia and Seba shall
 bring tribute.
All kings shall pay him homage,
 all nations shall serve him.

R⍭. Lord, every nation on earth will adore you.

For he shall rescue the poor when he cries
 out,
 and the afflicted when he has no one to
 help him.
He shall have pity for the lowly and the
 poor;
 the lives of the poor he shall save.

R⍭. Lord, every nation on earth will adore you.

SECOND READING
Eph 3:2-3a, 5-6

Brothers and sisters:
You have heard of the stewardship of
 God's grace
 that was given to me for your benefit,
 namely, that the mystery was made
 known to me by revelation.
It was not made known to people in other
 generations
 as it has now been revealed
to his holy apostles and prophets by the
 Spirit:
that the Gentiles are coheirs, members
 of the same body,
 and copartners in the promise in Christ
 Jesus through the gospel.

About Liturgy

Connecting the two great festal seasons: There are hints in this Sunday's gospel which help us connect the two great festal seasons (Advent-Christmas-Epiphany and Lent-Triduum-Easter) as two sides of salvation. (1) The magi saw the "star at its rising"; that is, in the East. This is the direction from which Israel expected the Messiah to come and the direction from which the early church expected Christ to come at the parousia. (2) King Herod has an exchange with the Jewish leaders, as happened at the trial of Jesus. (3) Jesus manifested himself to Gentiles as an infant, as it was a Gentile (the centurion) who recognized Jesus on the cross as the Son of God. (4) There is fear and a power struggle among the leadership at Jesus' birth as there was at his trial, suffering, and death.

These connections help us realize that the liturgical year is a seamless celebration of the whole mystery of Christ. The year unfolds event by event and invites us to enter into Jesus' paschal journey. But this is not a historical journey; it is a liturgical journey calling us to pattern our lives more closely on that of Jesus. All the various events actually collapse into the one mystery of salvation.

About Liturgical Music

Music suggestions: "Hail to the Lord's Anointed" identifies Christ as "David's greater Son" come to fulfill God's saving plan for all the earth. Its text is based on Psalm 72 (the responsorial psalm for this day). Its majestic tune would work well for the entrance procession. Another hymn suitable for the entrance procession would be "What Star Is This." The song has been widely used since the early eighteenth century as a hymn for vespers on Epiphany. Its delightful dance-like quality expresses well the festive mood of this day. "How Brightly Shines the Morning Star" speaks of Christ as the Morning Star and calls all earth and heaven to give praise. The tune's broad pace makes this hymn suitable for the preparation of the gifts.

Ruth Duck's "O Radiant Christ, Incarnate Word" (in *Dancing in the Universe*, GIA) captures both the confidence we feel in the revelation brought by Christ and the struggle we experience with choosing to let that revelation guide human affairs: "Our bartered, busy lives burn dim, too tired to care, too numb to feel. . . . Come, shine upon our shadowed world. . . . illumine all we say and do. . . . lead the peoples to your peace, as stars once lead the way to you." The text is set to a specifically commissioned tune (David Cherwien's RADIANT LIGHT) whose shifts between C major and C minor aptly express the light-darkness-light shifts in the text itself. As this tune will be unknown to most assemblies, the choir only could sing the hymn during the preparation of the gifts, or, as Duck suggests, the hymn could be sung by everyone using a familiar tune such as WAREHAM.

SPIRITUALITY

GOSPEL ACCLAMATION
cf. Luke 3:16

℟. Alleluia, alleluia.
John said: One mightier than I is coming;
he will baptize you with the Holy Spirit and with
    fire.
℟. Alleluia, alleluia.

Gospel

Luke 3:15-16, 21-22; L21C

**The people were filled with
    expectation,
    and all were asking in their hearts
    whether John might be the Christ.
John answered them all, saying,
    "I am baptizing you with water,
    but one mightier than I is coming.
I am not worthy to loosen the thongs of
    his sandals.
He will baptize you with the Holy Spirit
    and fire."**

**After all the people had been baptized
    and Jesus also had been baptized and
        was praying,
    heaven was opened and the Holy
        Spirit descended upon him
    in bodily form like a dove.
And a voice came from heaven,
    "You are my beloved Son;
    with you I am well pleased."**

Reflecting on the Gospel

Five-year-old Robbie was dressed to the hilt. He had on a brand new suit, white shirt and tie. He strutted a bit as he came into church and sat with his family in the first row. Today was a big day for him. He was being baptized. Clearly he had been well prepared; there was no fear as he was signed, anointed with the oil of catechumens, then lifted by his father into the fount to be washed in the "bath of rebirth" (second reading). As his parents were drying him off, Father whispered (and because of the lapel mic everyone in the assembly heard), "Good boy." The assembly members smiled, some chuckled out loud. This fatherly comment was meant to convey to Robbie that he had behaved well. But underneath the comment, there is another truth. Baptism changes us. Robbie is now "good"—filled with the Holy Spirit, with God's life.

With John's baptism, the onus was on the people to repent. With Jesus' baptism, the onus is on the people to receive the gift that God offers. This gift is nothing less than the Holy Spirit, the very life of God, who empowers us to be God's children, God's beloved. When we embrace this gift, we, like Jesus, are those in whom God is well pleased.

Because of the power of John's baptism, the expectation of the people in the gospel is that they have found the Christ in John. John points the people, however, to Jesus, who will bring an even more powerful baptism. This is the baptism Robbie and each of us has received. This is the baptism that showers on us unexpected gifts. The Holy Spirit descended on Jesus, so does the Holy Spirit descend upon us; Jesus is the beloved Son, so are we beloved children; God was well pleased with Jesus, so is God well pleased with us. To what does such a baptism call us? What do we expect? What does God expect?

These are not questions with simple answers. Yes, in one sense, we can answer the questions with Paul's admonition in the second reading to reject anything that turns us from God and embrace whatever strengthens our relationship with God and each other. But all of us who share in the wisdom of Christian living through the years know that it takes a whole lifetime to repent, to turn toward God, to internalize the appropriate response to the great gifts God freely and lovingly gives us. Baptismal living takes a lifetime of fidelity. It takes a lifetime of learning. It takes a lifetime of discerning expectations—our own and God's—and doing whatever we need to fulfill those expectations. It takes a lifetime of opening ourselves to the Holy Spirit, hearing God's voice calling us beloved, living in such a way that God continues to be well pleased.

Living the Paschal Mystery

As in Jesus, baptism must be made flesh in us. Father's "good boy" is, therefore, also an admonition to Robbie and to all of us: reborn in Christ, he and we are to lead good lives; we are to "reject godless ways" and live rightly (second reading). Robbie had a big day one Sunday. He will spend his whole life growing into the realization that baptism doesn't happen on one day, but calls us to a way of living. Each time we say yes to doing good, we are living our baptism. Each time we recognize the giftedness of others, we are living our baptism. Each time we avoid doing something harmful, we are living our baptism. But most of all, we live our baptism when we relish the gift of God's life within us.

Focusing the Gospel

Key words and phrases: filled with expectation, he will baptize you, Holy Spirit, beloved Son, well pleased

To the point: Because of the power of John's baptism, the people's expectation is that they have found the Christ in John. John points the people, however, to Jesus, who will bring an even more powerful baptism. The Holy Spirit descended on Jesus, so does the Holy Spirit descend upon us; Jesus is the beloved Son, so are we beloved children; God was well pleased with Jesus, so is God well pleased with us. To what does such a baptism call us? What do we expect? What does God expect?

Connecting the Gospel

to the second reading: The second reading spells out what baptismal living looks like: "reject godless ways and worldly desires and to live temperately, justly, and devoutly." This is the rebirth to which God calls us.

to experience: Over time and experience we grow to maturity as human beings, appreciating more and more fully both our roots and our potential. So, too, with baptism. We grow over time into understanding its meaning and its power.

Connecting the Responsorial Psalm

to the readings: The verses from Psalm 104 used for this responsorial psalm recite the many ways God's glory is revealed: God generates the heavens, rules water and wind, creates all that roams earth and swims seas, gives all creatures their food in due season, and, above all, continuously sends the Spirit, the breath of life and renewal.

The first and second readings proclaim that in Christ the fullness of God's glory has appeared. His identity is confirmed at his baptism: "You are my beloved Son" who will "baptize . . . with the Holy Spirit and fire" (gospel). The power of God has become fully manifest in Christ who cleanses us from sin and recreates us as a people "eager to do . . . good" (second reading). What better response can we make than "O bless the Lord, my soul"? May this response acknowledge our baptismal identity and our willingness to enter with Christ into the Ordinary Time journey of our discipleship.

to psalmist preparation: The numerous signs of God's glory which you enumerate in these psalm verses are external revelations of the even greater glory God works within you through your baptism in Christ. What might you do this week to renew your awareness of the power and grace of baptism? What might you do to bless God for this power and grace?

**ASSEMBLY &
FAITH-SHARING GROUPS**
- My expectations for my life are . . . for my baptismal living are . . .
- What brings me to evaluate and perhaps redirect my expectations is . . .
- Knowing I am a beloved child of God, I . . . Knowing God is well pleased with me means . . .

PRESIDERS
I help the assembly members appreciate that they are God's children when I . . .

DEACONS
My service models baptismal living in these ways . . .

HOSPITALITY MINISTERS
When I realize I am welcoming God's beloved children, my greeting sounds like . . .

MUSIC MINISTERS
My music making draws others into living more fully their baptismal commitment when I . . .

ALTAR MINISTERS
In my ministry, I expect . . . the presider expects . . . God expects . . .

LECTORS
When I listen to the Holy Spirit in preparing for my ministry, my proclamation has this effect . . .

**EXTRAORDINARY MINISTERS
OF HOLY COMMUNION**
I relate my ministry to my baptismal living in these ways . . .

✚ CELEBRATION

Model Penitential Act

Presider: John points to Jesus as One greater than himself who baptizes with the Holy Spirit. Let us open our hearts to this Spirit who dwells within us, that we may be pleasing to God in our celebration . . . [pause]

Lord Jesus, you are God's beloved Son: Lord . . .

Christ Jesus, you are the One in whom God is well pleased: Christ . . .

Lord Jesus, you baptize us in the Holy Spirit: Lord . . .

Homily Points

• Growing in their personal identity, adolescents are often difficult to deal with because they so mightily struggle to discover who they are apart from their parents and others who guide them. Growing in baptismal identity has the opposite dynamic: we choose to depend more and more upon the Holy Spirit to guide us and work mightily never to depart from that divine presence.

• The Holy Spirit is the spirit of Jesus himself. To open ourselves to guidance by the Holy Spirit means that we look to Jesus: how he lived, how he prayed, how he made decisions, how he related to others, how he loved.

• Growing into baptismal living means that our lives are not guided by our own preferences but by a deeper integration of Gospel values. These values are discerned through our relationships with others, through the wealth of experience we gain from daily decisions and actions, through our reflection on Scripture and faithful participation in liturgy. What motivates us to this kind of baptismal living is growing awareness that God embraces us as beloved children.

Model Universal Prayer (Prayer of the Faithful)

Presider: The God who bestows the Spirit upon us and calls us beloved children will grant us all we need to grow to fullness of life. And so we pray for our needs with confidence.

Response:

Lord, hear our prayer.

Cantor:

we pray to the Lord,

That the leadership of the church may be guided by the Holy Spirit and lead all the baptized to full maturity in Christ . . . [pause]

That all people of the world may come to know themselves as God's beloved children . . . [pause]

That the sick and the suffering may be comforted by the care of the community of God's beloved . . . [pause]

That all of us here gathered may live Gospel values in such a way as to bring God's love to others . . . [pause]

Presider: Loving God, you send the Spirit of your divine Son upon us: hear these our prayers that we may be faithful to our baptism and one day share the fullness of life with you forever. We pray through Christ our Lord. **Amen.**

COLLECT

Let us pray
[that we will be faithful to our baptism]

Pause for silent prayer

Almighty ever-living God,
who, when Christ had been baptized in the
    River Jordan
and as the Holy Spirit descended upon
    him,
solemnly declared him your beloved Son,
grant that your children by adoption,
reborn of water and the Holy Spirit,
may always be well pleasing to you.
Through our Lord Jesus Christ, your Son,
who lives and reigns with you in the unity
    of the Holy Spirit,
one God, for ever and ever. **Amen.**

FIRST READING
Isa 40:1-5, 9-11

Comfort, give comfort to my people,
    says your God.
Speak tenderly to Jerusalem, and proclaim
    to her
    that her service is at an end,
    her guilt is expiated;
indeed, she has received from the hand of
    the LORD
    double for all her sins.

A voice cries out:
In the desert prepare the way of the LORD!
    Make straight in the wasteland a
        highway for our God!
Every valley shall be filled in,
    every mountain and hill shall be made
        low;
the rugged land shall be made a plain,
    the rough country, a broad valley.
Then the glory of the LORD shall be
    revealed,
    and all people shall see it together;
    for the mouth of the LORD has spoken.

Go up onto a high mountain,
    Zion, herald of glad tidings;
cry out at the top of your voice,
    Jerusalem, herald of good news!
Fear not to cry out
    and say to the cities of Judah:
    Here is your God!
Here comes with power
    the Lord GOD,
    who rules by a strong arm;
here is his reward with him,
    his recompense before him.
Like a shepherd he feeds his flock;
    in his arms he gathers the lambs,
carrying them in his bosom,
    and leading the ewes with care.

RESPONSORIAL PSALM
Ps 104:1b-2, 3-4, 24-25, 27-28, 29-30

R. (1) O bless the Lord, my soul.

O Lord, my God, you are great indeed!
  You are clothed with majesty and glory,
robed in light as with a cloak.
  You have spread out the heavens like a
    tent-cloth.

R. O bless the Lord, my soul.

You have constructed your palace upon the
    waters.
  You make the clouds your chariot;
you travel on the wings of the wind.
  You make the winds your messengers,
and flaming fire your ministers.

R. O bless the Lord, my soul.

How manifold are your works, O Lord!
  In wisdom you have wrought them all—
the earth is full of your creatures;
  the sea also, great and wide,
in which are schools without number
  of living things both small and great.

R. O bless the Lord, my soul.

They look to you to give them food in due
    time.
  When you give it to them, they gather it;
when you open your hand, they are filled
    with good things.

R. O bless the Lord, my soul.

If you take away their breath, they perish
    and return to the dust.
  When you send forth your spirit, they
    are created,
and you renew the face of the earth.

R. O bless the Lord, my soul.

SECOND READING
Titus 2:11-14; 3:4-7

Beloved:
The grace of God has appeared, saving all
  and training us to reject godless ways
      and worldly desires
  and to live temperately, justly, and
      devoutly in this age,
  as we await the blessed hope,
  the appearance of the glory of our great
      God
  and savior Jesus Christ,
  who gave himself for us to deliver us
      from all lawlessness
  and to cleanse for himself a people as
      his own,
  eager to do what is good.

Continued in Appendix A, p. 270.

About Liturgy

Symbols of baptism: The symbols of the baptismal rite put into focus the primary gift of baptism—the indwelling of the Holy Spirit, a share in divine life:

Water—plunged into the baptismal waters, we are plunged into Christ's death; rising, we share in his risen life. Water brings both death (to our old selves) and life (new life of rebirth in God).

Chrism—anointed with Chrism, we share in the threefold office of Christ—priest, prophet, king. Our being anointed with Chrism is a consecration of ourselves to conform our life to Christ's.

White garment—clothed in a white garment, we are reminded of our new, risen life in Christ. We have been given a new identity as beloved daughters and sons of God. We are to live unstained until we come to enjoy eternal life with God.

Lighted candle—enlightened by Christ, we are also to be the light of Christ dispelling sin and darkness in the world. We ourselves are to be living examples that in Christ the light of salvation has come into the world.

Although all of these symbols also imply the demands of discipleship (*water*—dying to self; *Chrism*—conforming ourselves to Christ; *white garment*—living lives worthy of who we are; *lighted candle*—overcoming the darkness of evil), they primarily help us understand who we become in baptism—members of the Body of Christ sharing in divine identity. Greater awareness and appreciation of our identity eases the way for us to be more faithful in our discipleship.

About Liturgical Music

Service music for Ordinary Time: The celebration of the Baptism of the Lord is the hinge Sunday, marking the change-over from the Christmas season to Ordinary Time. Because the feast stands as a turning point and faces both directions, it would be appropriate either to sing the service music used during Christmas season one last time or to begin using the Ordinary Time setting.

Hymn suggestions: "Jesus Christ, by Faith Revealed" would be an excellent entrance song for this celebration of the baptism of the Lord. "Baptized by Living Waters" would serve well during the preparation of the gifts as a reminder of our participation in the mystery and mission of baptism. A hymn well suited to the return next Sunday to Ordinary Time would be Herman Stuempfle's "The Hills Are Still, the Darkness Deep" (in *The Word Goes Forth*, GIA). Stuempfle brings us down from the glories of Christmas and plants us firmly in the reality of ordinary life. The song of angels no longer fills the sky, but instead a "hungry cry"; shepherds once roused by glorious light have returned to "cold and lonely vigil"; the kings have departed leaving Mary to tend a child in the night. The final verse captures the challenge of Ordinary Time: "O God, when glory fades away And duties fill the night, the day: By grace unseen but present still, Give strength to heart and hand and will." This would make an excellent text for the assembly to sing after Communion as an act of quiet renewal of their baptism and its meaning for daily life.

Ordinary Time I

SPIRITUALITY

GOSPEL ACCLAMATION
See 2 Thess 2:14

R̸. Alleluia, alleluia.
God has called us through the Gospel
to possess the glory of our Lord Jesus Christ.
R̸. Alleluia, alleluia.

Gospel   John 2:1-11; L66C

There was a wedding at Cana in
    Galilee,
    and the mother of Jesus was
        there.
Jesus and his disciples were also
    invited to the wedding.
When the wine ran short,
    the mother of Jesus said to him,
    "They have no wine."
And Jesus said to her,
    "Woman, how does your concern affect
        me?
My hour has not yet come."
His mother said to the servers,
    "Do whatever he tells you."
Now there were six stone water jars there
    for Jewish ceremonial washings,
    each holding twenty to thirty gallons.
Jesus told them,
    "Fill the jars with water."
So they filled them to the brim.
Then he told them,
    "Draw some out now and take it to the
        headwaiter."
So they took it.
And when the headwaiter tasted the
    water that had become wine,
    without knowing where it came from
    —although the servers who had drawn
        the water knew—,
    the headwaiter called the bridegroom
        and said to him,
    "Everyone serves good wine first,
    and then when people have drunk
        freely, an inferior one;
    but you have kept the good wine until
        now."
Jesus did this as the beginning of his
    signs at Cana in Galilee
    and so revealed his glory,
    and his disciples began to believe in him.

Reflecting on the Gospel

The critical line in the gospel comes in the very last sentence: "Jesus did this as the beginning of his signs at Cana in Galilee and so revealed his glory, and his disciples began to believe in him." Thus does John's Gospel mark the beginning of Jesus' public ministry. But as beginning, it also contains a preview of the end and purpose of his ministry. The abundance and worth of the water made into wine announce the age of the Messiah when messianic abundance will be evident. This abundance reveals the glory of God, leads us to believe in Jesus, and invites us to become his intimate friends.

Jesus' epiphany—the revelation of his glory—did not end with the sign he performed but with the belief to which his followers came. Not only does Jesus change water into wine, but he transforms his disciples from being mere companions to becoming those who believe in him. They move from fellowship to the intimacy of belief and their lives will never be the same. He changed them. He will change us. And our lives will never be the same.

The intimacy of belief is not passive. This is Jesus' true glory and his whole ministry: not only turning water into wine but spending himself for the good of others. His total attentiveness and response to others is the model for our own active believing, the way to sustain intimacy with him, and is the promise of our own glory. This kind of active believing changes us into those who do as Jesus did. We spend ourselves for others.

It's telling that at the very beginning of his public ministry, Jesus manifests his glory in terms of a sign that brings his disciples to the intimacy of belief. Here is the Good News: spending oneself for the sake of another is how we actively believe, how we achieve salvation, how we march steadily toward messianic abundance, how we share in Jesus' glory. By thus spending ourselves do we achieve the fullness of abundance Jesus promises in the age to come. No, our lives will never be the same.

Living the Paschal Mystery

The messianic age announced in the gospel is given a different concrete description in the first reading from Isaiah. There God is the Spouse and rejoices in us who are God's beloved. Like the disciples in the gospel, we are to "believe in him."

This lays out for us a lifelong task of accepting all the signs of Jesus' presence and messianic abundance among us. It means that we are to make a lifelong covenant with God. Traditionally, this is how we understand our baptism. It is our initial celebration of a relationship with God that is intimate, loving, lasting. Our fidelity during this life assures us that death is not a separation but an entrance into eternal life where the wine never runs out, the rejoicing never ceases, and the depths of love are never exhausted.

During Ordinary Time we journey with Jesus through a gospel (this year, Luke's Gospel) toward our fulfillment at the messianic banquet. Let us taste the wine, and know that the good only gets better!

Focusing the Gospel

Key words and phrases: disciples were also invited, water that had become wine, beginning of his signs, revealed his glory, disciples began to believe in him

To the point: Jesus' epiphany—the revelation of his glory—did not end with the sign he performed but with the belief to which his followers came. Not only does Jesus change water into wine, but he transforms his disciples from being mere companions to becoming those who believe in him. They move from fellowship to the intimacy of belief and their lives will never be the same. He changed them. He will change us. And our lives will never be the same.

Connecting the Gospel

to the first reading: Isaiah provides us with language to describe believing: "I will not be silent . . . I will not be quiet." He gives us as well language to describe the intimacy of belief: "My delight," "Espoused," "the LORD delights in you," "your Builder shall marry you," "God rejoice in you."

to experience: Some changes are self-initiated, for example, we stop smoking, resolve to exercise daily, watch less TV. Other changes are generated by an outside catalyst, such as a natural disaster or the loss of a job because of a bankrupt company. When we open ourselves to God's actions within us, the most life-changing transformations occur.

Connecting the Responsorial Psalm

to the readings: What marvelous deeds are we proclaiming in this Sunday's responsorial psalm? We attest to God's saving actions in transforming Jerusalem from "forsaken" and "desolate" to "delight" and "espoused" (first reading). We attest to Christ's action in transforming simple water into lush wine and to the revelation this miracle made about his identity and mission (gospel). And we attest to the change that was wrought in the hearts and minds of the disciples at Cana who let themselves be transformed by this sign from mere onlookers to true believers in the person of Jesus. In singing this psalm we announce that we, too, have seen the signs and have come to believe in the One sent for the world's salvation. We proclaim our belief in him and invite all nations to join us in praise and worship.

to psalmist preparation: You can only sing about the saving acts of God if you recognize them. Sometimes these saving acts come in extraordinary ways, but most often they come in the quiet events of ordinary, everyday living. The trick is to see them so that you can believe. Be on the lookout this week for how Christ will turn the ordinary water of your life into the wine of salvation.

ASSEMBLY & FAITH-SHARING GROUPS

- To me believing means . . . My believing in Jesus is deepened when I . . .
- Jesus has transformed me from . . . to . . .
- I experience intimacy with Jesus when . . .

PRESIDERS

My ministry leads others to greater intimacy with Jesus when I . . .

DEACONS

My ministry manifests Jesus' glory to others when I . . .

HOSPITALITY MINISTERS

My hospitality is an expression of my intimate believing when I greet others with . . .

MUSIC MINISTERS

Through my participation in music ministry, Jesus transforms me by . . .

ALTAR MINISTERS

Serving others has taught me that God's glory is like . . .

LECTORS

When it comes to God's word I cannot be "silent" or "quiet" (first reading) because . . .

EXTRAORDINARY MINISTERS OF HOLY COMMUNION

Distributing the Body (or Blood) of Christ is transforming for me when I . . .

Model Penitential Act

Presider: Today's gospel tells the story of the wedding feast at Cana where Jesus reveals his glory. As we stand before the glory of God, let us prepare ourselves to celebrate this liturgy . . . [pause]

Lord Jesus, you are the Glory of God in our midst: Lord . . .

Christ Jesus, you are our Delight: Christ . . .

Lord Jesus, you are the One who calls us to believe: Lord . . .

Homily Points

• What brings us to embrace change? A closed bridge might bring us to find a new route to work. Sickness might bring us to lead a healthier lifestyle. Falling in love might bring us to an unprecedented self-giving. What brings us to embrace belief?

• The disciples of Jesus saw him change water into wine. This sign, worked at the beginning of Jesus' public ministry, "revealed his glory" and changed the disciples' relationship with him—they "began to believe in him." The sign was the catalyst of their belief bringing them to new intimacy with Jesus.

• We don't see Jesus changing more than a hundred gallons of water into wine! But we do see signs of Jesus' power and presence in our lives when we observe someone entrusting self to another, when forgiveness is offered and accepted, when a friend confronts someone about hurtful behavior. The more we see in others the signs of Jesus' power and presence, the more we, like the disciples, are drawn to grow in belief and intimacy with him.

Model Universal Prayer (Prayer of the Faithful)

Presider: God loves us and desires intimacy with us through Jesus. We have trust in this God to give us what we need. And so we pray.

Response:

Lord,——— hear our prayer.

Cantor:

we pray to the Lord,

May all members of the church grow in their belief in and love of Jesus . . . [pause]

May all peoples of the world come to believe in the salvation offered by a loving God . . . [pause]

May those who are hungry or homeless have their lives transformed by the generosity of those who believe in Jesus . . . [pause]

May we here gathered grow in our intimacy with Jesus through our love for each other . . . [pause]

Presider: O God of love, you fulfill the needs of those who come to you: hear these our prayers that we might one day enjoy life eternal with you. We pray through Christ our Lord. **Amen.**

COLLECT
Let us pray

Pause for silent prayer

Almighty ever-living God,
who govern all things,
both in heaven and on earth,
mercifully hear the pleading of your
    people
and bestow your peace on our times.
Through our Lord Jesus Christ, your Son,
who lives and reigns with you in the unity
    of the Holy Spirit,
one God, for ever and ever.
Amen.

FIRST READING
Isa 62:1-5

For Zion's sake I will not be silent,
    for Jerusalem's sake I will not be quiet,
until her vindication shines forth like the
    dawn
    and her victory like a burning torch.

Nations shall behold your vindication,
    and all the kings your glory;
you shall be called by a new name
    pronounced by the mouth of the Lord.
You shall be a glorious crown in the hand
    of the Lord,
    a royal diadem held by your God.
No more shall people call you "Forsaken,"
    or your land "Desolate,"
but you shall be called "My Delight,"
    and your land "Espoused."
For the Lord delights in you
    and makes your land his spouse.
As a young man marries a virgin,
    your Builder shall marry you;
and as a bridegroom rejoices in his bride
    so shall your God rejoice in you.

RESPONSORIAL PSALM

Ps 96:1-2, 2-3, 7-8, 9-10

R̯. (3) Proclaim his marvelous deeds to all the nations.

Sing to the LORD a new song;
    sing to the LORD, all you lands.
Sing to the LORD; bless his name.

R̯. Proclaim his marvelous deeds to all the nations.

Announce his salvation, day after day.
Tell his glory among the nations;
    among all peoples, his wondrous deeds.

R̯. Proclaim his marvelous deeds to all the nations.

Give to the LORD, you families of nations,
    give to the LORD glory and praise;
    give to the LORD the glory due his name!

R̯. Proclaim his marvelous deeds to all the nations.

Worship the LORD in holy attire.
    Tremble before him, all the earth;
say among the nations: The LORD is king.
    He governs the peoples with equity.

R̯. Proclaim his marvelous deeds to all the nations.

SECOND READING

1 Cor 12:4-11

Brothers and sisters:
There are different kinds of spiritual gifts
    but the same Spirit;
    there are different forms of service but
        the same Lord;
    there are different workings but the
        same God
    who produces all of them in everyone.
To each individual the manifestation of
    the Spirit
    is given for some benefit.
To one is given through the Spirit the
    expression of wisdom;
    to another, the expression of knowledge
        according to the same Spirit;
    to another, faith by the same Spirit;
    to another, gifts of healing by the one
        Spirit;
    to another, mighty deeds;
    to another, prophecy;
    to another, discernment of spirits;
    to another, varieties of tongues;
    to another, interpretation of tongues.
But one and the same Spirit produces all
    of these,
    distributing them individually to each
        person as he wishes.

About Liturgy

Ordinary Time: After weeks of preparing for and celebrating the mystery of the Incarnation, it seems as though the church knows and expresses in the rhythm of her liturgical year that we are ready to get on with our journey toward salvation. We are ready to let go of the exuberance of festivity and begin to follow through with the demands of the gospel and the mystery of salvation: living as Jesus did. Ordinary Time leads us through a gospel journey with Jesus (during this Year C we read from Luke's Gospel), through his public ministry to his death and resurrection. This liturgical journey symbolizes our life journey as Christians.

This gospel of the wedding feast at Cana is associated with the celebration of Epiphany in the Eastern Church and has strong baptismal overtones. Even at this placement in the Western Lectionary (separate from Epiphany and the Baptism of the Lord), the feast can still speak to us about our baptism. In the gospel selection for this Sunday Jesus inaugurates his public ministry. Baptism is our own "inauguration" of our public ministry and an ongoing expression of our belief in and commitment to Jesus. It is our public avowal to make Jesus the very center of our lives. It is the formal covenant we make with God to live as Jesus did. Baptism leads us into the task of Ordinary Time: to walk with Jesus through death to resurrection.

About Liturgical Music

Service music for Ordinary Time: The purpose of liturgical music is not to entertain us but to help us surrender to the transforming action of the liturgy. During Ordinary Time the liturgy pulls us into the paschal mystery journey of ongoing Christian living. The liturgical music we sing during this period is meant to help us deepen our understanding of and participation in that journey. For this we need music which is ritually consistent rather than constantly changing. We need, for example, to sing the same service music—from the gospel acclamation to the Lamb of God—throughout these weeks between the end of the Christmas season and the beginning of Lent. Only then will we find ourselves singing this music with greater understanding and deeper intentionality.

✚ SPIRITUALITY

GOSPEL ACCLAMATION
See Luke 4:18

R̶. Alleluia, alleluia.
The Lord sent me to bring glad tidings to the
     poor,
and to proclaim liberty to captives.
R̶. Alleluia, alleluia.

Gospel   Luke 1:1-4; 4:14-21; L69C

Since many have undertaken to
     compile a narrative of the
     events
   that have been fulfilled among
     us,
   just as those who were
     eyewitnesses from the
     beginning
and ministers of the word have
     handed them down to us,
I too have decided,
after investigating everything
     accurately anew,
to write it down in an orderly
     sequence for you,
most excellent Theophilus,
so that you may realize the certainty
     of the teachings
you have received.

Jesus returned to Galilee in the power
     of the Spirit,
   and news of him spread throughout
     the whole region.
He taught in their synagogues and was
     praised by all.

He came to Nazareth, where he had
     grown up,
   and went according to his custom
into the synagogue on the sabbath day.
He stood up to read and was handed a
     scroll of the prophet Isaiah.
He unrolled the scroll and found the
     passage where it was written:
   The Spirit of the Lord is upon me,
     because he has anointed me
     to bring glad tidings to the poor.

Continued in Appendix A, p. 270.

Reflecting on the Gospel

Words are powerful. They can bring comfort and joy. They can heal and nourish spiritually and emotionally. Encouraging words can bring success to those faltering in a task. Words of praise lift the self-esteem of not just children but adults as well. Words of beauty couched in poetry or sublime prose immortalize our deepest sense of worth and reality, heroes, or heroic actions. Words can provide moral guidance as well as a challenge to mend our ways. Words can bring laughter and joy, lightness and humor, meaning and understanding. Yes, words are powerful. So it is not at all surprising that Luke, beginning his written account of Jesus, took the time to investigate "everything accurately anew." Luke needed to get it right. These words he writes are words that have divine origin. The Good News ("glad tidings") is that God's desire is being fulfilled *now* in Jesus. The Word of God is given for the life of the community. And this life is Jesus.

Luke portrays Jesus as One who had a clear understanding of who he was and his mission. Who he was: the One "in the power of the Spirit." His mission: "to bring glad tidings" to the poor, captives, blind, oppressed. Luke also had a clear understanding of who he was and his mission: he investigated "everything accurately anew" in order to proclaim the Good News. From the very beginning, what Jesus came to fulfill has been observed, treasured, handed down.

But the Good News cannot be proclaimed only by Jesus. Those who come after Jesus are "to bring glad tidings" in many ways to many people. Luke wrote a gospel, and in this fulfilled who he was and his mission. Now we ourselves are to be the bearers of the Good News so that others may "realize the certainty" of the story we have received. We are certain about our story and how we live when Jesus is the model from whom we draw our words and make the decisions which shape our life. We are certain when we speak "in the power of the Spirit." It is not our words we speak, but God's words of eternal life. The gospel each of us writes is written by the way we live. And when this living is in accordance with the Gospel, then we fulfill who we are and our mission, too.

So much is at stake in words! May our words speak—our deeds live—eloquently the Spirit who dwells within us!

Living the Paschal Mystery

We are all familiar with the power of words to shape our identity and way of living. Society offers conflicting messages which often pull us in many directions. In the midst of all these competing words, God's word is the true source of our identity as Christian people.

As the Lukan community received Jesus' teachings, so have we. Our ministry? Transpose Jesus' teachings from words on a page to a way of living. Who are the poor, the captives, the sightless in our midst? Who needs the glad tidings of God's mercy and presence preached to them? How is our word Jesus' word that "is fulfilled in [our] hearing"? Do our lives bear out our own certainty about the "teachings [we] have received"? Christian living is none other than taking God's word and making it concrete by the very way we live. Our daily living is the Word made flesh among us. Such powerful words!

Focusing the Gospel

Key words and phrases: have been fulfilled, investigating everything accurately anew, realize the certainty, power of the Spirit, bring glad tidings, fulfilled in your hearing

To the point: Luke portrays Jesus as One who had a clear understanding of who he was and his mission. Who he was: the One "in the power of the Spirit." His mission: "to bring glad tidings" to the poor, captives, blind, oppressed. Luke also had a clear understanding of who he was and his mission: he investigated "everything accurately anew" in order to proclaim the Good News. From the very beginning, what Jesus came to fulfill has been observed, treasured, handed down. Now we ourselves are to be the bearers of the Good News so that others may "realize the certainty" of the story we have received.

Connecting the Gospel

to the first reading: Nehemiah provides details that assure the people the words proclaimed by Ezra were, indeed, the words of God. As Jesus proclaimed glad tidings "in the power of the Spirit," so must our proclamation of the Good News come from the Spirit who dwells within us. The details of our daily living must assure others that the words we proclaim are, indeed, from God.

to experience: We are all familiar with the power of words to shape our identity and way of life. Society offers conflicting messages that often pull us in many directions. In the midst of all these competing words, God's word is the true source of our identity as Christian people.

Connecting the Responsorial Psalm

to the readings: In the refrain to the responsorial psalm we sing that the word of God is "Spirit and life." In the verses we call God's Law perfect, trustworthy, right, and clear. Hearing God's Law read to them by Ezra, the people weep (first reading). Hearing God's word proclaimed to them by Jesus, the people "look intently at him" for its interpretation (gospel). His interpretation stuns them: this word, "fulfilled in your hearing," is his very person.

Jesus' interpretation takes our understanding of the psalm to a new level. The word of God given in the law and the prophets expresses God's will for human salvation. Jesus reveals that this will is himself, the Word-will of God in flesh and bone, bringing Good News to the poor, restoring sight to the blind, and granting freedom to the oppressed. The Word which is trustworthy and clear, which rejoices the heart and enlightens the eye is the very person of Christ. Such a Word is truly salvation for the world. This is the Word about which we sing, the Law upon which we base our lives.

to psalmist preparation: The Word of God about which you sing in this responsorial psalm is fulfilled in the person of Christ. As you pray the psalm in preparation this week, substitute the name of Christ for the words "law," "decree," "precept," etc. How does this deepen your understanding of the psalm? Your personal relationship with Christ? How might this affect your singing of the psalm for the assembly?

**ASSEMBLY &
FAITH-SHARING GROUPS**
• My manner of living compiles a narrative of Jesus' life and mission in that . . .
• The Isaian prophecy read by Jesus is being fulfilled through me whenever I . . .
• What I observe, treasure, and hand down is . . .

PRESIDERS
I find and nurture my identity and mission through God's word by . . .

DEACONS
I embody Jesus' "glad tidings" for the disadvantaged by . . .

HOSPITALITY MINISTERS
Ways I open the assembly to hear the Good News are . . .

MUSIC MINISTERS
My music ministry embodies observing, treasuring, and handing down the Good News in that . . .

ALTAR MINISTERS
My serving at the altar is a fulfillment of the Good News when I . . .

LECTORS
My daily living is a genuine interpretation of God's word for others whenever I . . .

**EXTRAORDINARY MINISTERS
OF HOLY COMMUNION**
The manner of my distributing Holy Communion arouses in others the certainty of the Good News in that . . .

Model Penitential Act

Presider: Jesus inaugurates his public ministry in the power of the Spirit. Let us prepare ourselves to celebrate this liturgy well as we hear his Good News and share in his Meal . . . [pause]

Lord Jesus, you are the fulfillment of the Good News: Lord . . .

Christ Jesus, you are the Christ, the anointed One: Christ . . .

Lord Jesus, you are glad tidings for the poor: Lord . . .

Homily Points

• When families gather for special threshold occasions—weddings, funerals, anniversaries, significant birthdays, graduations, First Communions—conversation inevitably includes the sharing of family lore. This is how younger members internalize who they are and how they belong to this family. It is no different for the community who follows Christ and hands on the Good News.

• Luke undertook a conscientious telling of the story of Jesus. His and other accounts have nurtured the faith of generations of Christians and brought them to take up Jesus' mission to proclaim the glad tidings of what is "acceptable to the Lord."

• For our part we are to "bring glad tidings" to our families, neighborhoods, cities and in this fulfill who we are and our mission as faithful followers of Christ. We do this in word but, even more importantly, in deed. Our challenge is to proclaim the story in a manner that is relevant for today's world in words and deeds that remain true to the original Good News.

Model Universal Prayer (Prayer of the Faithful)

Presider: Let us pray that we can hear and proclaim faithfully the Good News given us in Christ.

Response:

Lord,—— hear our prayer.

Cantor:

we pray to the Lord,

That each member of the church faithfully observe, treasure, and hand down the Good News of Jesus . . . [pause]

That leaders of the world work tirelessly to establish justice for the poor and oppressed . . . [pause]

That those who are downtrodden or depressed hear the glad tidings of God's love . . . [pause]

That each of us here faithfully proclaim the certainty of the Good News . . . [pause]

Presider: O loving God, the Word made flesh proclaimed the glad tidings of salvation: hear these our prayers that your desire for our salvation may be fulfilled. We ask this through that same Christ our Lord. **Amen**.

COLLECT

Let us pray

Pause for silent prayer

Almighty ever-living God,
direct our actions according to your good
    pleasure,
that in the name of your beloved Son
we may abound in good works.
Through our Lord Jesus Christ, your Son,
who lives and reigns with you in the unity
    of the Holy Spirit,
one God, for ever and ever.
Amen.

FIRST READING

Neh 8:2-4a, 5-6, 8-10

Ezra the priest brought the law before the
    assembly,
    which consisted of men, women,
    and those children old enough to
        understand.
Standing at one end of the open place that
    was before the Water Gate,
    he read out of the book from daybreak
        till midday,
    in the presence of the men, the women,
    and those children old enough to
        understand;
    and all the people listened attentively to
        the book of the law.
Ezra the scribe stood on a wooden
    platform
    that had been made for the occasion.
He opened the scroll
    so that all the people might see it
    —for he was standing higher up than
        any of the people—;
    and, as he opened it, all the people rose.
Ezra blessed the LORD, the great God,
    and all the people, their hands raised
        high, answered,
    "Amen, amen!"
Then they bowed down and prostrated
    themselves before the LORD,
    their faces to the ground.
Ezra read plainly from the book of the law
    of God,
    interpreting it so that all could
        understand what was read.
Then Nehemiah, that is, His Excellency,
    and Ezra the priest-scribe
    and the Levites who were instructing
        the people
    said to all the people:
    "Today is holy to the LORD your God.
Do not be sad, and do not weep"—
    for all the people were weeping as they
        heard the words of the law.

He said further: "Go, eat rich foods and
   drink sweet drinks,
   and allot portions to those who had
      nothing prepared;
   for today is holy to our LORD.
Do not be saddened this day,
   for rejoicing in the LORD must be your
      strength!"

RESPONSORIAL PSALM
Ps 19:8, 9, 10, 15

R̸. (cf. John 6:63c) Your words, Lord, are
Spirit and life.

The law of the LORD is perfect,
   refreshing the soul;
the decree of the LORD is trustworthy,
   giving wisdom to the simple.

R̸. Your words, Lord, are Spirit and life.

The precepts of the LORD are right,
   rejoicing the heart;
the command of the LORD is clear,
   enlightening the eye.

R̸. Your words, Lord, are Spirit and life.

The fear of the LORD is pure,
   enduring forever;
the ordinances of the LORD are true,
   all of them just.

R̸. Your words, Lord, are Spirit and life.

Let the words of my mouth and the
      thought of my heart
   find favor before you,
O LORD, my rock and my redeemer.

R̸. Your words, Lord, are Spirit and life.

SECOND READING
1 Cor 12:12-14, 27

Brothers and sisters:
As a body is one though it has many parts,
   and all the parts of the body, though
      many, are one body,
   so also Christ.
For in one Spirit we were all baptized into
      one body,
   whether Jews or Greeks, slaves or free
      persons,
   and we were all given to drink of one
      Spirit.
Now the body is not a single part, but
   many.
You are Christ's body, and individually
   parts of it.

or 1 Cor 12:12-30

See Appendix A, p. 271.

About Liturgy

Importance of the Liturgy of the Word: One of the most significant liturgical reforms since Vatican II has been to restore a Liturgy of the Word to every celebration of a sacrament (see SC no. 24). This underscores the relationship of word to sacrament, of word to action. It also says that the context for God's work of salvation in and among the people is always the efficacious word of God proclaimed. The Liturgy of the Word, then, at Sunday Mass is hardly a preamble so that the assembly can get to the "good part," Holy Communion. The word is the context and Holy Communion is the response for our great thanksgiving for all God has said and done for us. Further, Christ is present in the word proclaimed (see SC no. 7). In the Liturgy of the Word, then, we celebrate a presence of Christ just as we do in the Liturgy of the Eucharist.

Just as this Sunday's gospel passage quoting the prophet Isaiah is challenging to us—we, too, are sent to "proclaim liberty to captives and recovery of sight to the blind, and let the oppressed go free"—so is this true for every proclamation of the word. There is always the challenge to hear God in a new way, to discern afresh how we are to respond in our daily living, and to examine the fruitfulness of our responses. For us, God's word must become as "rich foods and . . . sweet drinks"; thus we already share in an abundance of ways in the Lord's table.

About Liturgical Music

The gospel acclamation: Both the first reading and the gospel this Sunday relate occasions when the word of God is proclaimed in the midst of the community. This offers a good opportunity to examine the meaning and importance of the gospel acclamation. While we remain seated during the proclamation of the first and second readings, we stand for the proclamation of the gospel and we greet this proclamation by singing the acclamation. Singing this acclamation announces our belief that the person of Christ becomes present in our midst in the proclamation of the gospel (GIRM, no. 62). The accompanying verse sung by cantor or choir is usually taken from the gospel text and acts as an invitation that we open our hearts to truly hear what will be proclaimed and let ourselves be transformed by it (like a "liturgical hors d'oeuvre" offered to whet our appetites for the meat to come). The most suitable gesture during the singing of the acclamation would be to turn our bodies toward the *Book of the Gospels* as it is carried to the ambo.

SPIRITUALITY

GOSPEL ACCLAMATION
Matt 4:18

GOSPEL ACCLAMATION
Matt 4:18

R̸. Alleluia, alleluia.
The Lord sent me to bring glad tidings to the
   poor,
to proclaim liberty to captives.
R̸. Alleluia, alleluia.

Gospel   Luke 4:21-30; L72C

Jesus began speaking in the
   synagogue, saying:
   "Today this Scripture passage is
      fulfilled in your hearing."
And all spoke highly of him
   and were amazed at the
      gracious words that came
      from his mouth.
They also asked, "Isn't this the son of
   Joseph?"
He said to them, "Surely you will quote me
   this proverb,
   'Physician, cure yourself,' and say,
   'Do here in your native place
   the things that we heard were done in
      Capernaum.'"
And he said, "Amen, I say to you,
   no prophet is accepted in his own native
      place.
Indeed, I tell you,
   there were many widows in Israel in the
      days of Elijah
   when the sky was closed for three and a
      half years
   and a severe famine spread over the
      entire land.
It was to none of these that Elijah was sent,
   but only to a widow in Zarephath in the
      land of Sidon.
Again, there were many lepers in Israel
   during the time of Elisha the prophet;
   yet not one of them was cleansed, but
      only Naaman the Syrian."
When the people in the synagogue heard this,
   they were all filled with fury.
They rose up, drove him out of the town,
   and led him to the brow of the hill
   on which their town had been built,
   to hurl him down headlong.
But Jesus passed through the midst of them
   and went away.

Reflecting on the Gospel

We are hearing words from Jesus at the very beginning of his public ministry as reported by Luke. The first line of this Sunday's gospel is the last line from last Sunday's gospel: "Today this Scripture passage is fulfilled in your hearing." Jesus speaks "gracious words" to the people of Nazareth about bringing glad tidings of freedom for captives and the oppressed, sight for the blind (see last Sunday's gospel). These words, however, are not only applied to Jesus and his ministry, but to the people as well. Hearing these words challenges the people themselves to do what they hear (thus are the words "fulfilled in your hearing"), and for this they reject Jesus and want to destroy him. Yet God, whose word Jesus speaks, delivers him ("passed through the midst of them"). Eventually enemies do destroy Jesus on the cross. But do they? In the end God's gracious words of deliverance prevail. The ultimate word is Jesus; the ultimate deliverance is risen life, which is ours when we hear and heed the gracious divine words spoken to us.

In the prophetic tradition Jeremiah is the classic example of the rejected prophet. Prophets are rejected because their message is rejected. Jeremiah contrasts the tenderness and protection of God toward those who faithfully hear God's word with the inevitable resistance that God's word wells up in those who cannot or will not hear its message of challenge and salvation. God's word inevitably stirs up conflict. Just as inevitably, it is a word of deliverance.

Jesus understood his own prophetic role as one which would lead to rejection and, ultimately, death. When he spoke "gracious words" his message "amazed" his hearers and his message was accepted. But when he spoke challenging words, his hearers were "filled with fury." Ultimately, God's words not only lead to a new understanding of God and God's ways of bringing salvation to all (even the Gentiles), but they also lead to a new understanding of ourselves and our own call to hear Jesus' words and live them. When God's words satisfy us, we are faced with the goodness in ourselves and how we are already responding to God. When God's words make demands on us, we are faced with new ways we must die to ourselves in order to become better disciples.

Living the Paschal Mystery

All of us struggle to hear and respond to God's word in our lives. This Sunday we are confronted with the reality that we are not always going to like what we hear in God's word. God's word always takes us beyond where we are (or where we want to go). It is the very word which questions our status quo and asks us to give up our own wills and embrace God's will. It is the very word which nudges us to surrender ourselves and our own small world to encompass the larger vision of a world in which God assures that all are met with love and dignity.

Announcing the message of the gospel is one way we express our faithfulness in hearing God's word. And, as those baptized into Christ's death and resurrection, being faithful to God's word always means dying to self for the sake of others. Like Jesus, we ought not fear the fury of others. When we witness to a way of living that challenges others and their assumptions, we may well cause fury. But as Jesus' enemies did not, in the end, destroy him, neither will those whom we anger by the goodness of our lives destroy us. God delivers.

Focusing the Gospel

Key words and phrases: fulfilled in your hearing, gracious words, filled with fury, hurl him down, passed through the midst of them

To the point: Jesus speaks "gracious words" to the people of Nazareth about bringing glad tidings of freedom for captives and the oppressed, sight for the blind (see last Sunday's gospel). Hearing these words challenges the people to do what they hear ("fulfilled in your hearing"), and for this they reject Jesus and want to destroy him. Yet God, whose word Jesus speaks, delivers him ("passed through the midst of them"). Eventually enemies do destroy Jesus on the cross. But do they?

Connecting the Gospel

to the first reading: In the prophetic tradition Jeremiah is the classic example of the rejected prophet. How tender are the words of God to Jeremiah, that no matter how people attempt to crush him, God will strengthen, protect, and deliver the prophet.

to experience: Often in our desire to be accepted, we adjust what we say to what our audience will accept. Announcing the message of the gospel is not undertaken for the sake of being accepted, but in order to be faithful to God's word.

Connecting the Responsorial Psalm

to the readings: Like Jesus (gospel) and Jeremiah (first reading), we are sent to proclaim salvation to the world. Like Jesus and Jeremiah we will meet opposition, persecution, even death as we fulfill this mission. But the responsorial psalm promises we shall be protected even as we are persecuted, for the one who has loved us since before our birth will be our salvation. The psalm invites us to fulfill our mission fully conscious of the suffering it will bring, but equally conscious of the salvation which has been promised beyond that suffering. This is not a psalm which we sing naively, but with hope-filled realism. And Jesus sings with us.

to psalmist preparation: The confidence of this psalm is perfect counterbalance to the reality of persecution spoken of in both the first reading and the gospel. If you choose to be faithful to the mission you share with Christ, you will know rejection. But you will also know the intimate presence of the God who guides and protects you. Are you willing to take the risk?

**ASSEMBLY &
FAITH-SHARING GROUPS**
- The prophetic words of Jesus which amaze me are . . . Those which I embrace wholeheartedly are . . .
- The prophetic words of Jesus which are upsetting and which I am resisting are . . .
- What sustains me to live Jesus' words even in the face of opposition and anger from others is . . .

PRESIDERS
Times when I have preached "less than" the gospel are . . . because . . .

DEACONS
Where Jesus' prophetic word is challenging how I minister is . . .

HOSPITALITY MINISTERS
Ways I might assist the assembly to ready themselves for a challenging word from God are . . .

MUSIC MINISTERS
As a music minister, I am comforted by God's word when . . . God's word challenges me as a music minister when . . .

ALTAR MINISTERS
I serve the prophetic word by . . .

LECTORS
When the word of God I am preparing to proclaim demands more of me than I am willing to live, I . . .

**EXTRAORDINARY MINISTERS
OF HOLY COMMUNION**
Distributing and receiving Holy Communion is a prophetic challenge in that . . .

Model Penitential Act

Presider: In today's gospel Jesus is a prophet not accepted in his hometown. As we prepare to celebrate this liturgy, we ask God to open our ears so that we may receive Jesus and his word wholeheartedly . . . [pause]

 Lord Jesus, you are the Prophet who proclaims Good News: Lord . . .

 Christ Jesus, you are the gracious Word of salvation: Christ . . .

 Lord Jesus, you strengthen us to live your word: Lord . . .

Homily Points

• When do words motivate us to act? Sometimes when the speaker is a beloved figure whom we trust. At other times when the words align with our own dreams and expectations. Or when the words are new and promising. When do the words of Jesus motivate us to act?

• The people's response to Jesus' initial words in the synagogue (last Sunday's gospel) was positive—these were "gracious words." Their reaction to his subsequent words about "a widow of Zarephath" and "Naaman the Syrian" (in this Sunday's gospel), however, was rage and vengeance. What triggered this change?

• Jesus' prophetic words are not just nice sayings. They are challenges to change how we think, how we relate, how we live. As human beings, we resist such challenges that get to the core of who and how we are. What motivates us to hear Jesus' prophetic words and internalize them is that he is the beloved One whom we can trust, who fulfills our truest dreams, who promises newness of life. What do we hear Jesus saying to us today? What is our response?

Model Universal Prayer (Prayer of the Faithful)

Presider: Let us pray that we hear Jesus' words and act on them faithfully.

Response:

Lord, hear our prayer.

Cantor:

we pray to the Lord,

That all members of the church may faithfully hear God's word, speak God's word, live God's word . . . [pause]

That all world leaders be guided by God's word to act with truth and justice . . . [pause]

That those who are sick and suffering be lifted up by those who hear God's word and act on it . . . [pause]

That we here gathered may find in the gracious words of Jesus the courage to live the prophetic words of Jesus . . . [pause]

Presider: Almighty God, your word brings life: hear these our prayers and lead us to everlasting life. We ask this through Christ our Lord. **Amen**.

COLLECT

Let us pray

Pause for silent prayer

Grant us, Lord our God,
that we may honor you with all our mind,
and love everyone in truth of heart.
Through our Lord Jesus Christ, your Son,
who lives and reigns with you in the unity
 of the Holy Spirit,
one God, for ever and ever.
Amen.

FIRST READING

Jer 1:4-5, 17-19

The word of the LORD came to me, saying:
 Before I formed you in the womb I knew
  you,
 before you were born I dedicated you,
 a prophet to the nations I appointed you.

But do you gird your loins;
 stand up and tell them
 all that I command you.
Be not crushed on their account,
 as though I would leave you crushed
  before them;
for it is I this day
 who have made you a fortified city,
a pillar of iron, a wall of brass,
 against the whole land:
against Judah's kings and princes,
 against its priests and people.
They will fight against you but not
  prevail over you,
 for I am with you to deliver you, says
  the LORD.

RESPONSORIAL PSALM

Ps 71:1-2, 3-4, 5-6, 15, 17

R. (cf. 15ab) I will sing of your salvation.

In you, O LORD, I take refuge;
 let me never be put to shame.
In your justice rescue me, and deliver me;
 incline your ear to me, and save me.

R. I will sing of your salvation.

Be my rock of refuge,
 a stronghold to give me safety,
 for you are my rock and my fortress.
O my God, rescue me from the hand of the
  wicked.

R. I will sing of your salvation.

For you are my hope, O Lord;
   my trust, O God, from my youth.
On you I depend from birth;
   from my mother's womb you are my
      strength.

R̸. I will sing of your salvation.

My mouth shall declare your justice,
   day by day your salvation.
O God, you have taught me from my
   youth,
   and till the present I proclaim your
      wondrous deeds.

R̸. I will sing of your salvation.

SECOND READING
1 Cor 13:4-13

Brothers and sisters:
Love is patient, love is kind.
It is not jealous, it is not pompous,
   it is not inflated, it is not rude,
   it does not seek its own interests,
   it is not quick-tempered, it does not
      brood over injury,
   it does not rejoice over wrongdoing but
      rejoices with the truth.
It bears all things, believes all things,
   hopes all things, endures all things.

Love never fails.
If there are prophecies, they will be
      brought to nothing;
   if tongues, they will cease;
   if knowledge, it will be brought to
      nothing.
For we know partially and we prophesy
      partially,
   but when the perfect comes, the partial
      will pass away.
When I was a child, I used to talk as a
      child,
   think as a child, reason as a child;
   when I became a man, I put aside
      childish things.
At present we see indistinctly, as in a
      mirror,
   but then face to face.
At present I know partially;
   then I shall know fully, as I am fully
      known.
So faith, hope, love remain, these three;
   but the greatest of these is love.

or 1 Cor 12:31–13:13

See Appendix A, p. 271.

About Liturgy

Liturgy and words: There is always a danger that we speak so many words at liturgies, they fall on unhearing ears. There must be a right balance between the words, gestures, and symbols of the liturgy. For this reason, great care must be taken that we don't add many extra words, even in those places where they are permitted. For example, introductions are best kept short and simple. Further, although brief descriptions of the readings are permitted to be given before the proclamation in order to help people listen better (see GIRM no. 31), this practice runs a high risk of constraining God's word. Finally, God's word spoken in liturgy is proclamation, not didactic teaching; it is encounter rather than explanation.

Another problematic area concerns announcements. Although announcements are permitted "should they be necessary" (GIRM no. 90), too many parishes still read most of the upcoming week's events already listed on the parish bulletin. Examples of "necessary" announcements would include mentioning approaching funerals which were scheduled after the bulletin was printed (but not other pertinent information such as visitation times; that can be handled on a parish bulletin board), or anything else for the coming week which didn't get printed in the bulletin.

The placement of announcements is also critical. Structurally, the announcements belong to the concluding rites. They are made after the Communion prayer but before the presider's greeting and blessing. The place for the announcements is not the ambo but some other place, for example, the cantor stand.

About Liturgical Music

Music suggestions: A number of songs express the struggle with God's word and opposition to Jesus exemplified in this Sunday's gospel. "Good News" is based on the gospel and speaks of Jesus as the fulfillment of Isaiah's prophecy of good news for the needy, of the opposition Jesus met, and of his refusal to flee his mission no matter what the cost. Its dancing and joyful Ethiopian melody would work well at the preparation of the gifts or as a hymn of praise after Communion. "Christus Paradox" captures our mixed reactions to Jesus, the "peace-maker and sword-bringer" whom we "both scorn and crave," and would work well during the preparation of the gifts.

Songs expressing willingness to accept Jesus and his word include "Praise to You, O Christ, Our Savior," a hymn of praise to Christ the Word who calls, leads, and teaches us. It would work well as an entrance hymn, and can be sung either responsorially between cantor/choir and assembly, or in direct fashion by everyone. Another appropriate text can be found in "God Has Spoken by His Prophets" which progresses from "God has spoken by his prophets . . ." to "God has spoken by Christ Jesus . . ." to "God is speaking by his Spirit . . ." This strong text and tune would suit the entrance procession.

✠ SPIRITUALITY

GOSPEL ACCLAMATION
Matt 4:19

R⁊. Alleluia, alleluia.
Come after me
and I will make you fishers of men.
R⁊. Alleluia, alleluia.

Gospel   Luke 5:1-11; L75C

While the crowd was pressing in on
    Jesus and listening to the word of
    God,
  he was standing by the Lake of
    Gennesaret.
He saw two boats there alongside the
    lake;
  the fishermen had disembarked
    and were washing their nets.
Getting into one of the boats, the one
    belonging to Simon,
  he asked him to put out a short
    distance from the shore.
Then he sat down and taught the
    crowds from the boat.
After he had finished speaking, he said
    to Simon,
  "Put out into deep water and lower
    your nets for a catch."
Simon said in reply,
  "Master, we have worked hard all
    night and have caught nothing,
  but at your command I will lower the
    nets."
When they had done this, they caught a
    great number of fish
  and their nets were tearing.
They signaled to their partners in the
    other boat
  to come to help them.
They came and filled both boats
  so that the boats were in danger of
    sinking.

Continued in Appendix A, p. 272.

Reflecting on the Gospel

Having someone take command of us can bring opposite effects from us. If, for example, we are planting our flower beds and a neighbor comes along and tells us where to plant what, we might get testy. Contrary, if we are in a perilous situation, for example, a fire has broken out, to have an off-duty firefighter handy who takes over, gives orders, and quickly gets people to safety is a good thing. No one objects, and when orders are given no one thinks about disobeying. In this gospel story Peter and the other fishermen are docked and cleaning up after a night of unsuccessful fishing. One might surmise that they were a bit testy. Jesus gets into Simon's boat and asks him to move away from the shore a bit where he sits down and teaches. Then Jesus commands him to put out into the deep. Peter must have had some sense of who Jesus was, because he responds affirmatively to his command. His inkling led to what Simon could never have imagined.

Simon Peter begins a more sure relationship with Jesus by allowing him to take command of his boat. He moves to allowing Jesus to take command of his heart, openly confessing the truth about himself ("I am a sinful man"). Finally, he allows Jesus to take command of his whole life ("left everything and followed him"). Like Peter, we are to allow Jesus to take command of us—our possessions, our hearts, our lives. We are to see that what is at stake in Jesus' commands to us is life-threatening and life-giving. Life-threatening because choosing to follow Jesus costs us our all—we "leave everything." At the same time, we receive all—more than even an abundant "catch of fish," we receive Life.

Both the first reading and gospel make clear that while God is present to us and calls us, our freedom is respected—God truly does give us a choice about answering the call. In the first reading God asks, "Whom shall I send?" In the gospel Jesus merely announces, "from now on you will be catching men." In both cases Isaiah and Peter were free to respond or not. Such is divine graciousness—God calls, but in the divine encounter gives us the strength and grace to respond. How can we not answer, "Send me!"

Living the Paschal Mystery

If we pay attention to details in this gospel beyond the immediate call and response events, we might be caught by surprise. Too often we feel the burden of discipleship is solely on our own shoulders. The gospel depicts Jesus initiating the call—he comes to Peter at his boat; he invites Peter to follow. Our discipleship rests upon Jesus long before we begin to follow. The surprise of the gospel is that we are never alone when we hear and follow God's call; divine Presence always abides within us, enables us to hear the commands and call of God, and to answer the call and remain faithful to it.

God meets people where they are. Sinfulness isn't a stumbling block to following God's call. We simply go deeper, beyond our sinfulness to hear God call each of us (because of our baptism) to discipleship. In spite of our objections, God gently and persistently says to each of us, "You're still the one I want." Like Isaiah and Peter, we are invited to be overwhelmed by God's graciousness and self-revelation and answer, "Send me!" God's is a gentle command. Our response must be strong.

Focusing the Gospel

Key words and phrases: Getting into one of the boats, at your command, I am a sinful man, left everything and followed him

To the point: In this gospel story Peter begins by allowing Jesus to take command of his boat. He moves to allowing Jesus to take command of his heart, openly confessing the truth about himself ("I am a sinful man"). Finally, he allows Jesus to take command of his whole life ("left everything and followed him"). Like Peter, we are to allow Jesus to take command of us—our possessions, our hearts, our lives.

Connecting the Gospel

to the first reading: Both Isaiah and Peter declare themselves to be sinful people. But the call of God comes to sinful people and in diverse places (Temple, boats). The call depends not on the individual or the place, but on the graciousness of God.

to experience: Too often we feel the burden of discipleship rests solely on our own shoulders. The gospel depicts Jesus initiating the call—he comes to Peter at his boat; he invites Peter to follow. Our discipleship rests upon Jesus long before we begin to follow.

Connecting the Responsorial Psalm

to the readings: Encounter with the Holy One, be it the Lord of hosts in heaven (first reading) or Jesus in an ordinary life situation (gospel), is a wake-up call. Individuals are shaken out of their complacency and change the direction of their lives. Both Isaiah and Peter acknowledge their own unholiness, and then find themselves sent on mission. The responsorial psalm reveals more beneath the surface, however. God heard the "words of my mouth" uttered by each individual. God perceived the weakness each felt and replaced it with strength. Supported by such divine initiative, these two readily accept their mission, for they are confident that God "will complete what he has" begun in them.

The Holy One comes to us, too, sometimes in extraordinary ways, most times in the ordinary circumstances of our daily lives. Each time the Holy One shows us ourselves as we really are, strengthens us, then sends us to continue our baptismal mission. Like Isaiah and Peter we can give a ready "Send me!" for we know, as does the psalmist, who has begun and who will complete this work in us.

to psalmist preparation: Your role as cantor requires humility and vulnerability. This Sunday's psalm reminds you that God will accomplish in you what needs to be done. You have only to sing God's praises, and let God's Spirit do the work.

**ASSEMBLY &
FAITH-SHARING GROUPS**
- I hear God calling me to . . . Some of my excuses for not accepting God's call are . . .
- I allow Jesus to take command of my possessions when I . . . of my heart when I . . . of my life when I . . .
- I feel the challenge of discipleship when . . . I feel the joys of discipleship when . . .

PRESIDERS
The progression of my allowing Jesus to take command of my possessions, my heart, my life is . . . This has made a difference in my ministry in that . . .

DEACONS
My manner of serving others encourages them to hear and heed God's call in their life when . . .

HOSPITALITY MINISTERS
My manner of greeting others as they gather for liturgy helps them allow God to take greater command of their lives when I . . .

MUSIC MINISTERS
I am most aware of God's having called me to the ministry of music when . . . When I am aware of my inadequacies, I feel God strengthening me by . . .

ALTAR MINISTERS
In order for me to serve well at the altar, I must leave behind . . .

LECTORS
Being a faithful follower of Jesus impacts the way I proclaim Scripture in that . . .

**EXTRAORDINARY MINISTERS
OF HOLY COMMUNION**
The privilege of distributing Holy Communion calls me to . . . in my daily living.

Model Penitential Act

Presider: Simon Peter, James, and John left everything to follow Jesus. Let us reflect on our response to Jesus' call and our willingness to be his disciples . . . [pause]

Lord Jesus, you are the Master who calls us to follow you: Lord . . .

Christ Jesus, you are the Teacher who brings words of life: Christ . . .

Lord Jesus, you are the One who strengthens and sustains those who follow you: Lord . . .

Homily Points

• Serious commitment often begins with an inkling which takes time to grow into a wholehearted response. For example, we might admire the dedication of St. Vincent de Paul Society volunteers, come to help at a bundle Sunday collection, and then commit ourselves to be involved regularly. Similarly, discipleship begins with an inkling about who Jesus is and what he asks of us, and gradually grows over our lifetime.

• Some inkling about who Jesus was ("Master") and what he was about must have prompted Peter to be open to what Jesus would ask of him. Then his encounter with the abundance Jesus offered (great "catch of fish") elicited the total commitment to leave "everything and [follow] him." Jesus provided the "boost" Peter needed to make his leap to full discipleship. Jesus calls followers to a discipleship that is demanding, but always gives them what they need to say yes and continue growing in fidelity.

• What inklings have we been given about who Jesus is and what he asks of us? What signs of abundance—"boosts"—does Jesus give us that prompt us to leave "everything and [follow] him"? How do our responses indicate that we are allowing Jesus to take command of us—our possessions, our hearts, our lives? As with all commitments, our answers will become clear only gradually through the choices we make in daily living as we grow into a lifetime of faithful discipleship.

Model Universal Prayer (Prayer of the Faithful)

Presider: To be faithful disciples, we need God's strength and help. And so we make our needs known.

Response:

Lord,—— hear our prayer.

Cantor:

we pray to the Lord,

That all members of the church may allow Jesus to take command of their possessions, their hearts, their lives . . . [pause]

That all people of the world may hear God's call to salvation . . . [pause]

That those struggling with fidelity in their lives may be strengthened and encouraged . . . [pause]

That all of us here may encounter Jesus and heed his call in our everyday lives . . . [pause]

Presider: Good and gracious God, your Son Jesus calls us to be his followers: strengthen us and help us to be faithful. We ask this through that same Son, Jesus Christ our Lord. **Amen**.

COLLECT

Let us pray

Pause for silent prayer

Keep your family safe, O Lord, with
    unfailing care,
that, relying solely on the hope of
    heavenly grace,
they may be defended always by your
    protection.
Through our Lord Jesus Christ, your Son,
who lives and reigns with you in the unity
    of the Holy Spirit,
one God, for ever and ever.
Amen.

FIRST READING

Isa 6:1-2a, 3-8

In the year King Uzziah died,
    I saw the Lord seated on a high and
        lofty throne,
    with the train of his garment filling the
        temple.
Seraphim were stationed above.

They cried one to the other,
    "Holy, holy, holy is the LORD of hosts!
All the earth is filled with his glory!"
At the sound of that cry, the frame of the
        door shook
    and the house was filled with smoke.

Then I said, "Woe is me, I am doomed!
For I am a man of unclean lips,
    living among a people of unclean lips;
    yet my eyes have seen the King,
        the LORD of hosts!"
Then one of the seraphim flew to me,
    holding an ember that he had taken
        with tongs from the altar.

He touched my mouth with it, and said,
    "See, now that this has touched your
        lips,
    your wickedness is removed, your sin
        purged."

Then I heard the voice of the Lord saying,
    "Whom shall I send? Who will go for
        us?"
"Here I am," I said; "send me!"

RESPONSORIAL PSALM

Ps 138:1-2, 2-3, 4-5, 7-8

℟. (1c) In the sight of the angels I will sing
your praises, Lord.

I will give thanks to you, O Lord, with all
    my heart,
    for you have heard the words of my
        mouth;
    in the presence of the angels I will sing
        your praise;
I will worship at your holy temple
    and give thanks to your name.

R⁊. In the sight of the angels I will sing
your praises, Lord.

Because of your kindness and your truth;
    for you have made great above all things
        your name and your promise.
When I called, you answered me;
    you built up strength within me.

R⁊. In the sight of the angels I will sing
your praises, Lord.

All the kings of the earth shall give
        thanks to you, O Lord,
    when they hear the words of your mouth;
and they shall sing of the ways of the Lord:
    "Great is the glory of the Lord."

R⁊. In the sight of the angels I will sing
your praises, Lord.

Your right hand saves me.
    The Lord will complete what he has
        done for me;
your kindness, O Lord, endures forever;
    forsake not the work of your hands.

R⁊. In the sight of the angels I will sing
your praises, Lord.

SECOND READING
1 Cor 15:3-8, 11

Brothers and sisters,
    I handed on to you as of first
        importance what I also received:
    that Christ died for our sins
        in accordance with the Scriptures;
    that he was buried;
    that he was raised on the third day
        in accordance with the Scriptures;
    that he appeared to Cephas, then to the
        Twelve.
After that, he appeared to more
        than five hundred brothers at once,
    most of whom are still living,
    though some have fallen asleep.
After that he appeared to James,
    then to all the apostles.
Last of all, as to one born abnormally,
    he appeared to me.
Therefore, whether it be I or they,
    so we preach and so you believed.

or 1 Cor 15:1-11

See Appendix A, p. 272.

About Liturgy
Parish call and response: The average Catholic parish in North America has fewer than 10 percent of its registered members involved in various parish activities. This raises an important question: Do we understand that part of the response to our baptismal call is to help build up the Body of Christ? We cannot simply *belong* to a parish; we must be *involved* in its life and ministry. In a general way, Christian discipleship means spreading the Good News of Jesus Christ to all those one meets, living an upright life, doing as Jesus would do. More specifically, each baptized person, as a member of a parish, is called to be involved actively in the affairs of the parish, thus building up the Body of Christ.

Generally, the activity involving the largest number of parishioners is some form of liturgical ministry. In order to keep these ministries from mere "doing" and clearly understanding the liturgical ministries as our response to God's presence and call, we must include a spiritual component in our preparation for the ministry (which is much more than simply practicing "how to"). That is, we must ensure that our liturgical ministers understand that ours is a ministry, not a "job," and that we are called to live the deep meaning of the ministry. For example, lectors must live the word of God throughout the week before they proclaim the word. Hospitality ministers must practice hospitality in their own homes and inclusivity at church in welcoming others into the community. Extraordinary ministers of Holy Communion must treat all those they meet each day as members of the Body of Christ. By growing in this spiritual dimension of the liturgical ministry, we grow in our awareness of God's abiding presence as well as in our awareness that our call to serve reaches way beyond the hour or so that we spend weekly in church.

About Liturgical Music
Music suggestions: Songs about the call to discipleship would be suitable this Sunday, as would songs which speak of how encounter with Christ transforms us and changes our lives. The bilingual "Pescador de Hombres" flows directly from the gospel story and would be a good choice for Communion. Christopher Walker's "Out of Darkness" would work well for the entrance, the preparation of the gifts, or Communion. In Michael Ward's "Here I Am, Lord" we can hear the sinful Peter saying to Jesus, "What joy it is to stand amid your glory. Let me always stay in your presence, O God" (v. 2). This verse-refrain song would be suitable for Communion. In "Lead Me, Guide Me" we speak to Jesus about our weakness and our need for his strength and power, praying to be led by him all along the way of discipleship. This hymn could be sung for Communion or as a recessional.

Also appropriate this Sunday would be songs proclaiming God as holy, such as "Holy, Holy, Holy," a good choice for the entrance procession, and "Holy God We Praise Thy Name," a fitting choice for the recessional.

Lent

ASH WEDNESDAY

SPIRITUALITY

GOSPEL ACCLAMATION
See Ps 95:8

If today you hear his voice,
harden not your hearts.

Gospel   Matt 6:1-6, 16-18; L219

Jesus said to his disciples:
"Take care not to perform righteous
     deeds
in order that people may see them;
otherwise, you will have no recompense
     from your heavenly Father.
When you give alms,
do not blow a trumpet before you,
as the hypocrites do in the synagogues
     and in the streets
to win the praise of others.
Amen, I say to you,
they have received their reward.
But when you give alms,
do not let your left hand know what
     your right is doing,
so that your almsgiving may be secret.
And your Father who sees in secret will
     repay you.

"When you pray,
do not be like the hypocrites,
who love to stand and pray in the
     synagogues and on street corners
so that others may see them.
Amen, I say to you,
they have received their reward.
But when you pray, go to your inner room,
close the door, and pray to your Father in
     secret.
And your Father who sees in secret will
     repay you.

"When you fast,
do not look gloomy like the hypocrites.
They neglect their appearance,
so that they may appear to others to be
     fasting.
Amen, I say to you, they have received their
     reward.
But when you fast,
anoint your head and wash your face,
so that you may not appear to be fasting,
except to your Father who is hidden.
And your Father who sees what is hidden
     will repay you."

See Appendix A, p. 273, for other readings.

62

Reflecting on the Gospel

Ashes remind us of fire, which reminds us of destruction. Burning logs in a fireplace leave a heap of ashes to clean up. A burnt-to-the-ground house leaves a big heap of ashes to clean up. At the beginning of Lent the palms from the previous year's holy week are burned and leave ashes. These ashes, too, mean cleaning up. But not just the place where they were burned; the cleaning up they move us to embrace is a soul-searching cleaning of self that leads to Easter new Life. Lenten penance is our act of cleaning up. It is a kind of spring housecleaning during which we rid ourselves of anything that gets in the way of opening ourselves anew to God and each other.

Lenten penance is not about self-denial for its own sake, but is directed toward renewing our relationship with others, God, and self through acts of charity, prayer, and fasting. Lenten penance is not undertaken for our own sake (to receive rewards), but for the sake of returning to God with our whole heart (see first reading). These two gospel teachings about penance make clear that renewed relationships can only be realized through the self-denial that turns us away from ourselves. We deny self so that we may better give self. A whole heart is a giving heart.

The task of renewing relationships necessitates a forgetfulness of self that compels self-giving. In the gospel Jesus points beyond *behaviors* to a *conversion* of heart, as was also commanded by Joel in the first reading: "return to me with your whole heart." This kind of conversion demands of us a unique self-giving—a forgetting about ourselves which places God at the very center of our lives. Behaviors are important, to be sure; changed behaviors and habits are also a goal of Lent and often witness to a conversion of heart. But changed behaviors are worthless if they don't lead to and express something deeper: that conversion of heart which brings us closer to God and each other. A whole heart is a giving heart.

If we understand clearly that we share a solidarity of identity (as God's chosen people, as the Body of Christ), then all we do affects all our relationships—to God, others, self. Sometimes it is the challenge of rubbing shoulders with others which brings about conversion. At other times it is the solace of being alone and wrestling with our own demons which brings conversion. Lent is an opportunity to change behaviors and come to conversion. In either case, we surrender ourselves to God and seek mercy and forgiveness.

The only way we come to conversion, come to surrendering ourselves to God is through self-giving. Beyond just doing good for others, self-giving is the practice of turning our hearts outward beyond ourselves. Self-giving turns our hearts to others. Self-giving turns our hearts to God. Yes, a whole heart is a giving heart.

Living the Paschal Mystery

The size or difficulty or quantity of our penance during Lent isn't the measure of a successful Lent; conversion of heart is. Greater practice of self-giving is. During Lent we practice dying to self in new ways which bring us to a true celebration of Easter life. It's better to accomplish something small which makes a difference in our relationships with God and others than to tackle something large which may bring failure. Our penance does not have to be big, but it must be serious enough to make a difference in our relationships with God, self, and others. Whatever the penance we choose, it must be self-giving and lead to conversion. The choice is ours.

Focusing the Gospel

Key words and phrases: give alms, pray, fast, received their reward

To the point: Lenten penance is not about self-denial for its own sake, but is directed toward renewing our relationship with others, God, and self through acts of charity, prayer, and fasting. Lenten penance is not undertaken for our own sake (to receive rewards), but for the sake of returning to God with our whole heart (see first reading). These two gospel teachings about penance make clear that renewed relationships can only be realized through the self-denial that turns us away from ourselves. We deny self so that we may better give self. A whole heart is a giving heart.

Model Universal Prayer (Prayer of the Faithful)

Presider: Let us pray that the God who calls us to penance and the renewal of life will hear our prayers.

Response:

Lord,   hear   our   prayer.

Cantor:

we   pray   to   the   Lord,

That all the members of the church take to heart the Lenten work of penance and renewal of life . . . [pause]

That peoples and nations at war open their hearts to reconciliation and peace . . . [pause]

That those alienated from God, family, or friends turn their hearts toward forgiveness and unity . . . [pause]

That all of us here gathered deny self so that we may better give self for the good of others . . . [pause]

Presider: God of new life, you hear the prayers of those who turn to you: keep us faithful during this Lent so that at Easter we may fully rejoice in the renewal of life. We ask this through Christ our Lord. **Amen.**

COLLECT

Let us pray

Pause for silent prayer

Grant, O Lord, that we may begin with holy fasting
this campaign of Christian service,
so that, as we take up battle against spiritual evils,
we may be armed with weapons of self-restraint.
Through our Lord Jesus Christ, your Son,
who lives and reigns with you in the unity of the Holy Spirit,
one God, for ever and ever.
Amen.

FOR REFLECTION

- My Lenten practices go beyond mere self-denial to renewing my relationships with God, self, and others by . . .
- I can better give myself to . . .
- I experience having a whole heart when . . . having a giving heart when . . .

Homily Points

- The stronger our desire to achieve a goal, the more rigorously do we embrace and maintain a regimen of self-denial necessary to achieve the goal. The goal entices and drives us. The goal of Lent is renewal of life—Easter. How much does this goal entice and drive us?

- In order to have a fruitful Lent, we must keep clearly in mind that renewal of life—opening our hearts more perfectly toward God and others, reconciling our divisions, embracing God's mercy and forgiveness—is the goal of Lent. Tallying up acts of self-denial for their own sake will not get us to the goal. Treating Lent like any other time of the year will not get us to the goal. Lent is a special time of the church year when we deny self so that we may better give self. A whole heart is a giving heart. This is renewal of life. How much does this entice and drive us?

✝ SPIRITUALITY

GOSPEL ACCLAMATION
Matt 4:4b

One does not live on bread alone,
but on every word that comes forth from the
    mouth of God.

Gospel   Luke 4:1-13; L24C

Filled with the Holy Spirit, Jesus
    returned from the Jordan
and was led by the Spirit into the
    desert for forty days,
to be tempted by the devil.
He ate nothing during those days,
    and when they were over he was
    hungry.
The devil said to him,
    "If you are the Son of God,
    command this stone to become bread."
Jesus answered him,
    "It is written, *One does not live on bread
    alone.*"
Then he took him up and showed him
    all the kingdoms of the world in a single
    instant.
The devil said to him,
    "I shall give to you all this power and glory;
    for it has been handed over to me,
    and I may give it to whomever I wish.
All this will be yours, if you worship me."
Jesus said to him in reply,
    "It is written:
    *You shall worship the Lord, your God,
    and him alone shall you serve.*"
Then he led him to Jerusalem,
    made him stand on the parapet of the
        temple, and said to him,
    "If you are the Son of God,
    throw yourself down from here, for it is
        written:
    *He will command his angels
        concerning you, to guard you,*
and:
    *With their hands they will support you,
    lest you dash your foot against a stone.*"
Jesus said to him in reply,
    "It also says,
    *You shall not put the Lord, your God, to
    the test.*"
When the devil had finished every
    temptation,
    he departed from him for a time.

Reflecting on the Gospel

Jesus' identity as the Son of God was revealed at his baptism—he is the beloved Son (see Luke 3:22). Following this, Jesus was led into the desert "by the Spirit" and there confronted evil. To violate basic human laws—turn stones into bread, worship the devil as a good, deny death—would have been consistent with the revelation that Jesus is the divine One, but would have called into question both his identity with us humans and the credibility of the public ministry upon which he was about to embark. By resisting the temptations Jesus models for us how we are to respond to the inevitable temptations we face as human beings. In the desert he was faced with the balance between human need and divine goodness. He was mightily tempted, yet remained strong and never succumbed to the wiles of the devil. By choosing good, he models for us the choices we are to make.

Twice the devil entices Jesus to give into temptation by saying, "If you are the Son of God . . ." True, Jesus is divine, but he is also fully human. Jesus resists the devil's temptation to put aside his humanity and act like God, thus remaining true to himself and to why he came. But Jesus' resisting the temptations has implications for us, too. By fully embracing his humanity Jesus lifts us up to be who we are in our relationship with God. Only from this relationship do we have the inner strength and conviction to make right choices in face of the temptations that are an inevitable part of being human.

Jesus resisted the temptation to act divine, and in this remained true to his identity also as being fully human. When we resist temptation, we remain true to our identity—an identity as both humans who are tempted and persons who share in God's very divine life (through baptism). Choosing goodness is choosing who we are and who God intends us to be. We, too, are the beloved children.

Living the Paschal Mystery

Whatever Lenten practices we undertake, it is important to remember their purpose. Lenten practices are not about losing weight or finally stopping smoking, but they are about deepening our baptismal identity as children of God and members of the Body of Christ. "If you are [children] of God" . . . this is the identity conferred upon us at baptism. This is the identity out of which we enter into our own Lenten desert. This is the identity out of which we face our own worst temptations. By remaining faithful to who we are—God's children, members of the Body of Christ—we can resist temptations and grow in our relationships with God, self, and others.

Traditionally, Christian penance has always included three prongs: fasting, prayer, and almsgiving (charity). This suggests to us that penance isn't only a matter of "giving up" something, nor is it a single act—even if performed faithfully over a long period like forty days. Christian penance has as its purpose genuine conversion of life, so that at the end of Lent when we renew our baptismal promises we are able to do so with full throat, well aware of our own wonderful identity as sons and daughters of God. The new life we celebrate at Easter cannot happen without our dying to ourselves, without our going to Jerusalem with Jesus and willingly embracing whatever death is in store for us. For that is the road to new life. That is the road we travel during Lent.

Focusing the Gospel

Key words and phrases: tempted by the devil, If you are the Son of God, Jesus answered him, Jesus said to him, Jesus said to him

To the point: Twice the devil entices Jesus to give into temptation by saying, "If you are the Son of God . . ." True, Jesus is divine, but he is also fully human. Jesus resists the devil's temptation to put aside his humanity and act like God, thus remaining true to himself and to why he came. But Jesus' resisting the temptations has implications for us, too. By fully embracing his humanity Jesus lifts us up to be who we are in our relationship with God. Only from this relationship do we have the inner strength and conviction to make right choices in face of the temptations that are an inevitable part of being human.

Connecting the Gospel

to the second reading: In the gospel the devil sets himself up as Lord when he tempts Jesus to worship him. Paul reminds us in the second reading that the One whom we are to profess as Lord is Jesus, and when we proclaim him as Lord we are saved.

to experience: All temptation presents us with a choice in the face of a perceived good. We are able to see through the ruse of the perceived good to the inherent selfishness of all temptation when we spend our lives deepening our sense of who we are in relation to God.

Connecting the Responsorial Psalm

to the readings: As the psalm refrain indicates, Jesus is in "trouble." Hungry after forty days of fasting, he is accosted by Satan with every possible temptation. Yet he steadfastly "clings" to God (psalm). He chooses to "bow down" (first reading) only before God; he chooses to live not by bread, but by the word of God; he refuses to test God, but chooses to trust instead on a guarantee already given (psalm). Jesus' mission will lead to his death, but he knows God will "deliver him and glorify him" because this is what God has promised to do. Jesus remains true to who he is because he knows he can count on God remaining true to who God is. As we enter this new season of Lent, our own forty-day testing period, we sing this psalm with Jesus, we stand with Jesus on God's promise.

to psalmist preparation: The gospel reading suggests a specific shape to the "trouble" about which you sing in the responsorial psalm: the temptation at the beginning of Lent to abandon fidelity to God when the task is too hard, the time too long, and more alluring prospects offer themselves. In this psalm Christ shares with you his certainty of God's presence and protection in the face of such "trouble." How might you share his certainty with the assembly when you sing this psalm?

**ASSEMBLY &
FAITH-SHARING GROUPS**

- When I remember that Jesus is both fully divine and fully human, his temptations in the desert seem like . . .
- I find myself struggling most with temptations about . . . They tell me this about myself . . .
- I find myself drawing on my relationship with God when . . .

PRESIDERS
In my preaching I help people come closer to God when I . . . I help them discover more clearly who they are when I . . .

DEACONS
I assist those in need to remain faithful to their true dignity as human beings by . . .

HOSPITALITY MINISTERS
My manner of greeting those gathering for liturgy helps them deepen their relationship to God when I . . .

MUSIC MINISTERS
My music ministry helps me to be true to who I am when . . . It helps the assembly to grow in their relationship with God when . . .

ALTAR MINISTERS
Serving at liturgy reminds me of my true identity because . . .

LECTORS
When I prepare well to proclaim the Scriptures, I learn this about myself . . .

**EXTRAORDINARY MINISTERS
OF HOLY COMMUNION**
Some ways I serve and strengthen those enduring temptations are . . .

Model Penitential Act

Presider: As we come together on this First Sunday of Lent, let us ask for forgiveness for the times we have given in to temptation . . . [pause]

 Confiteor: I confess . . .

Homily Points

• Lent is about growing in our relationship with God, which informs choices affecting how we understand ourselves and how we relate to others. Special helps are given to us: the rich Lenten Scriptures, the penitential practices we embrace, the extra prayer and devotional opportunities. Lent is a rich time to grow in who we are and strengthen the clarity about which we face temptations and make choices.

• Just before embarking on his public ministry, Jesus spent forty days in the desert fasting and praying—Jesus focuses fully on God. With the temptations the devil focuses fully on Jesus. In their confrontation the cosmic powers of good and evil face one another, and in clear and committed choice Jesus reveals who the victor is. At this moment and in the ultimate future.

• Our forty days in the Lenten desert must include the prayer and fasting that marked Jesus' time in the desert and will help us focus our lives more perfectly on God. We, too, will face our own demons. We, too, will have the opportunity to make clear and committed choices that reveal who we are and our relationship with God. We are encouraged and strengthened to make right choices because of the victory over evil already won by Jesus. This is the victory we celebrate at Easter. This is the new life toward which we journey during Lent.

Model Universal Prayer (Prayer of the Faithful)

Presider: God sustains us when facing temptations. Let us ask for God's help and strength.

Response:

Lord, hear our prayer.

Cantor:

we pray to the Lord,

That all members of the church enter this season of prayer and fasting with confidence in their ultimate victory over evil . . . [pause]

That all people of the world may recognize and overcome every form of evil . . . [pause]

That those who are hungry and in need be delivered through the generous charity of others . . . [pause]

That our identity as sons and daughters of God may be strengthened through our Lenten penance . . . [pause]

Presider: Ever-faithful God, you hear the prayers of those who turn to you in faith and trust: hear our prayers that our Lenten journey may bring us closer to you and each other. We ask this through Christ our Lord. **Amen.**

Let us pray

Pause for silent prayer

Grant, almighty God,
through the yearly observances of holy
 Lent,
that we may grow in understanding
of the riches hidden in Christ
and by worthy conduct pursue their
 effects.
Through our Lord Jesus Christ, your Son,
who lives and reigns with you in the unity
 of the Holy Spirit,
one God, for ever and ever.
Amen.

FIRST READING
Deut 26:4-10

Moses spoke to the people, saying:
 "The priest shall receive the basket from
  you
 and shall set it in front of the altar of
  the LORD, your God.
Then you shall declare before the LORD,
 your God,
'My father was a wandering Aramean
 who went down to Egypt with a small
  household
 and lived there as an alien.
But there he became a nation
 great, strong, and numerous.
When the Egyptians maltreated and
  oppressed us,
 imposing hard labor upon us,
 we cried to the LORD, the God of our
  fathers,
 and he heard our cry
 and saw our affliction, our toil, and our
  oppression.
He brought us out of Egypt
 with his strong hand and outstretched
  arm,
 with terrifying power, with signs and
  wonders;
 and bringing us into this country,
 he gave us this land flowing with milk
  and honey.
Therefore, I have now brought you the
 firstfruits
 of the products of the soil
 which you, O LORD, have given me.'
And having set them before the LORD, your
 God,
 you shall bow down in his presence."

RESPONSORIAL PSALM

Ps 91:1-2, 10-11, 12-13, 14-15

R̸. (cf. 15b) Be with me, Lord, when I am in trouble.

You who dwell in the shelter of the Most High,
    who abide in the shadow of the Almighty,
say to the Lord, "My refuge and fortress,
    my God in whom I trust."

R̸. Be with me, Lord, when I am in trouble.

No evil shall befall you,
    nor shall affliction come near your tent,
for to his angels he has given command about you,
    that they guard you in all your ways.

R̸. Be with me, Lord, when I am in trouble.

Upon their hands they shall bear you up,
    lest you dash your foot against a stone.
You shall tread upon the asp and the viper;
    you shall trample down the lion and the dragon.

R̸. Be with me, Lord, when I am in trouble.

Because he clings to me, I will deliver him;
    I will set him on high because he acknowledges my name.
He shall call upon me, and I will answer him;
    I will be with him in distress;
I will deliver him and glorify him.

R̸. Be with me, Lord, when I am in trouble.

SECOND READING

Rom 10:8-13

See Appendix A, p. 273.

About Liturgy

Lent, forty days, and fasting: "Forty" is a number which comes up often in Scripture (see, for example, Gen 7:4; Exod 16:35; 24:18; Num 14:33; Judg 3:11; 1 Kgs 2:11; Jon 3:4; Acts 1:3) and it means "for a sufficient time." When Lent began to be a more extended period of time, it first lasted forty days. But since Sundays have always been excluded as fast days (because that is the day of the Lord, the day of resurrection, the day when we celebrate the Bridegroom's presence), that meant Lent consisted of fewer than forty fast days. During a time when the church emphasized the sinfulness and unworthiness of the baptized rather than their blessedness, Lent was extended back to the Wednesday before the First Sunday of Lent in order to have forty fast days (hence, the origin of Ash Wednesday, in place by the eighth–ninth centuries). The reform of the liturgical year in the wake of Vatican II kept intact the period of Lent with forty fast days. This being said, we cannot understand Lent properly only in terms of fasting. Lent is, essentially, a period of conversion which culminates in the renewal of baptismal promises at the Easter Vigil or Easter Sunday Mass.

The Confiteor: In the model penitential act we recommend using the *Confiteor* during Lent. In this prayer we publicly profess that we have "greatly sinned." The point isn't that we are great sinners, but that anything at all that weakens our relationship with God, self, or others is grievous. As we embrace a life of conversion, turning ever more perfectly to God as the center of our being, sin (small or great) becomes even more abhorrent to us. As we pray the *Confiteor* during Lent, may it remind us that God calls us to lives of holiness.

About Liturgical Music

Service music for Lent: As directed in GIRM no. 313, the penitential character of Lent calls for quieter, more "spare" service music. Lent is a good season to sing the unaccompanied chant setting of the Mass, in either Latin or English.

Music suggestions: "Jesus, Tempted in the Desert" is an excellent hymn for both this Sunday's gospel and the beginning of Lent. Barely moving outside the tonic triad, the melody conveys a sense of being in place, of being grounded in faith. At the same time its triplet figures and dotted rhythms propel us into the challenges of Lent. The text reassures that as faithful disciples we do not face temptation alone: "When we face temptation's power, Lonely, struggling, filled with dread, Christ, who knew the tempter's hour, Come and be our living bread" (v. 4). The hymn would work well during the preparation of the gifts after the gospel has been proclaimed.

A second excellent hymn for this Sunday is Sylvia Dunstan's "From the River to the Desert" (in *Hymns for the Gospels*, © 2001 GIA). The text provides a poetic narration of the story of Christ's temptation in the desert. Following the pattern of the gospel story, verses 2 to 4 unfold as a dialogue between Satan and Jesus. Verse 5 is a prayer begging Jesus who "knows our weakness" to plead for us for whom "your grace is all we need." The lengthy text needs to be sung in its entirety. If there is sufficient time, it could be sung during the preparation of the gifts. Otherwise the choir could sing it as a prelude. An effective way for them to sing it would be to have a soloist sing verse 1 to set the scene, antiphonal sections sing verses 2 to 4 to highlight the dialogue between Satan and Christ, and everyone sing the final verse as a communal prayer.

✝ SPIRITUALITY

GOSPEL ACCLAMATION

cf. Matt 17:5
From the shining cloud the Father's voice is
   heard:
This is my beloved Son, hear him.

Gospel   Luke 9:28b-36; L27C

Jesus took Peter, John, and James
   and went up the mountain to pray.
While he was praying his face
   changed in appearance
   and his clothing became dazzling
      white.
And behold, two men were
   conversing with him, Moses and
   Elijah,
who appeared in glory and spoke
   of his exodus
that he was going to accomplish in
   Jerusalem.
Peter and his companions had been
   overcome by sleep,
but becoming fully awake,
   they saw his glory and the two men
      standing with him.
As they were about to part from him,
   Peter said to Jesus,
"Master, it is good that we are here;
   let us make three tents,
one for you, one for Moses, and one
   for Elijah."
But he did not know what he was
   saying.
While he was still speaking,
   a cloud came and cast a shadow over
      them,
   and they became frightened when
      they entered the cloud.
Then from the cloud came a voice that
   said,
"This is my chosen Son; listen to
   him."
After the voice had spoken, Jesus was
   found alone.
They fell silent and did not at that time
   tell anyone what they had seen.

Reflecting on the Gospel

This gospel about the transfiguration is a familiar one. The temptation is to
all too quickly limit its meaning and power. There is more to this event than
a glimpse of future glory. It tells us of what we can expect along the journey
toward glory.

"Jesus . . . went up the mountain to pray." Like us, Jesus sought communion
with his God and Father. He most likely didn't go up the mountain expecting to
be transfigured, but his prayerful union with his Father manifested his identity
as One who shares in the Father's glory. During prayer Jesus' "face changed."

This phrase is biblical language indicating that Jesus himself
changed. When the transfiguration takes place Jesus is already
on the journey to Jerusalem. To come to the glory promised
by the transfiguration, however, Jesus could not remain on
the mountain, but had to continue his journey to Jerusalem
and the Cross.

Luke explicitly relates the glory of the transfiguration to
the glory of the new life that Jesus shares after his resurrection. At the same time, Luke is the only synoptic evangelist
who gives us a hint about the conversation among Jesus,
Moses, and Elijah—they talked about Jesus' "exodus," that
is, his "passover" which would be "accomplish[ed] in Jerusalem." This glory has a cost. And it is no small cost. It is
one's very life.

On the mountain of transfiguration the disciples wit-
nessed the glory of Jesus' identity as the "chosen Son." We, too, are destined for
glory when Christ will "change our lowly body to conform with his glorified
body" (second reading). During prayer we, too, encounter God in such a way
that we are invited to change. We, too, are emboldened to follow our life journey and embrace the Cross. And we, too, will be glorified. Now and forever.

Living the Paschal Mystery

At the beginning of Lent, the goal is laid out for us. Jesus went up the mountain to pray and was transformed. Lent is not only a desert (as in last Sunday)
but is also the "mountain" we go up to pray in order to be transformed. Jesus
talks about his exodus, his passing through suffering and death to the glory of
risen life. Our salvation is to follow Jesus into his passion and death so that we,
too, might attain the glory of new life.

Our following Jesus is spelled out in the ordinary "dyings" of our everyday
living: reaching out to visit a lonely elderly person, listening to a troubled
adolescent, biting our tongue instead of saying sharp words, still having patience when we've been pushed too far or simply run out of energy. The utterly
amazing thing about our embracing these little, everyday "dyings" is that we
ourselves experience a kind of transfiguration. As we learn to say yes to God
and others, we grow deeper into our own identity as the chosen ones of God.
We become more perfect members of Christ's Body when we act like Jesus
did—when we reach out to others who are in need, when we bring a comforting touch, when we forgive. All these are ways we are faithful on our journey
to Jerusalem. Our whole life, then, is a transfiguration, a passing over from our
old sinful ways to the ways of light and grace offered by God.

Focusing the Gospel

Key words and phrases: his face changed, going to accomplish in Jerusalem, saw his glory, good that we are here

To the point: During prayer Jesus' "face changed." This phrase is biblical language indicating that Jesus himself changed. The transfiguration is a fleeting glimpse of the glory of his risen life. To come to this glory, however, Jesus could not remain on the mountain, but had to continue his journey to Jerusalem and the Cross. During prayer we, too, encounter God in such a way that we are invited to change. We, too, are emboldened to follow our life journey and embrace the Cross. And we, too, will be glorified. Now and forever.

Connecting the Gospel

to the second reading: On the mountain of transfiguration the disciples witnessed the glory of Jesus' identity as the "chosen Son." We, too, are destined for glory when Christ will "change our lowly body to conform with his glorified body" (second reading).

to experience: We often have glimpses of glory: in a remarkable sunset, in the shining face of a delighted child, in the radiant joy of new parents. Like the transfiguration, these glimpses of glory encourage and strengthen us to continue the journey of life toward eternal glory.

Connecting the Responsorial Psalm

to the readings: Psalm 27 proclaims that those who seek the Lord will see the Lord. Such confidence enables the faithful to wait for salvation with courage and stoutheartedness. Nonetheless, as the middle verses of the psalm reveal, such confidence does not exempt one from anxiety. Just so must the righteous and obedient Abraham sit through a "terrifying darkness" before hearing God's word of promise (first reading). Just so are Peter, James, and John overcome by darkness and fear after seeing Christ glorified (gospel). Jesus' identity as God's Son has been revealed to them and they can only remain silent about what they have seen.

As we journey through Lent—and through all of Christian life—we, too, have moments of revelation and periods of darkness. There are moments when we see the transfigured Christ and know his glory to be our future (second reading). And there are long periods when, as if asleep (gospel) or in a trance (first reading), we can neither see nor speak but only wait in hope. These verses from Psalm 27 capture both sides of our experience and frame them with faith.

to psalmist preparation: As you prepare to sing these verses from Psalm 27, spend some time reading and praying the entire psalm. The psalm is shot through with images of danger and death, all the while maintaining its confidence in God's promise of salvation. As a baptized person the danger you face is the struggle with evil and the death to self this entails (see last Sunday's gospel). How are you being called this Lent to die to yourself? What keeps you confident of God's promise of ultimate transformation?

**ASSEMBLY &
FAITH-SHARING GROUPS**

- Where I have witnessed the glory of Jesus is . . .
- What it means to me that I am destined to share in Jesus' glory is . . .
- My Lenten practices are bringing about this change in me . . . These changes direct me toward glory in that . . .

PRESIDERS
I keep the Lenten work of transformation before the assembly by . . .

DEACONS
The glory of Jesus revealed in serving others is . . .

HOSPITALITY MINISTERS
My ministry points to the glory of Christ and his body when I . . .

MUSIC MINISTERS
The glory of my music making invites the assembly to open themselves to change and participate more fully in Jesus' glory when I . . .

ALTAR MINISTERS
My serving at liturgy manifests the glory of God to the assembly in that . . .

LECTORS
I proclaim to the assembly that our "citizenship is in heaven" (second reading) by . . .

**EXTRAORDINARY MINISTERS
OF HOLY COMMUNION**
My ministry becomes a moment of glory for others when I . . .

Model Penitential Act

Presider: Peter, John, and James went up the mountain with Jesus and saw his glory. Let us repent of our sins which mar God's glory in us . . . [pause]

   Confiteor: I confess . . .

Homily Points

• We human beings tend not to like change. We are creatures of habit and status quo. So what spurs us on to embrace change? Encounter with another who has accepted change and become more successful. Growing impatient with not getting ahead. Being presented with a creative and exciting new opportunity. Even with these catalysts of change the road is still often rocky, but keeping the goal in mind is enough to spur us on. The Transfiguration shows us the goal; it also shows us the rocky road.

• The Transfiguration is a foreshadowing not only of Jesus' risen glory, but also of what Jesus will embrace on the journey. Jesus' prayer encounter with his Father reinforces his self-understanding as the "chosen Son" and why he was sent. Moreover, the road he walked is the road we must walk. Our own prayer encounters with the Father reinforce our self-understanding and keep us faithful on our life journey toward glory.

• It is well established that the journey of life follows a rocky road. We live through the death of loved ones, loss of a job or home, disappointments and failures, pain and illness. Followers of Christ are not exempt from such a rocky road. But they do have a clear goal that encourages and strengthens them: Christ's risen presence (often through the support and help of others) and an experience of glory (now and forever).

Model Universal Prayer (Prayer of the Faithful)

Presider: We make our prayers known to God whose Son came that we might share in his risen glory.

Response:

Lord, hear our prayer.

Cantor:

we pray to the Lord,

That all members of the church may embrace the challenges of the cross and experience risen glory . . . [pause]

That all peoples of the world seek the glory of salvation . . . [pause]

That those bowed down by the burdens of life might be lifted to glory through the care of others . . . [pause]

That all of us use these Lenten days as a time of deepened prayer and personal transformation . . . [pause]

Presider: Gracious God, you hear the prayers of those who turn to you: may we be transformed by your grace and enjoy everlasting glory with you. We ask this through Christ your transfigured Son. **Amen.**

COLLECT

Let us pray

Pause for silent prayer

O God, who have commanded us
to listen to your beloved Son,
be pleased, we pray,
to nourish us inwardly by your word,
that, with spiritual sight made pure,
we may rejoice to behold your glory.
Through our Lord Jesus Christ, your Son,
who lives and reigns with you in the unity
   of the Holy Spirit,
one God, for ever and ever.
Amen.

FIRST READING

Gen 15:5-12, 17-18

The Lord God took Abram outside and
   said,
   "Look up at the sky and count the stars,
      if you can.
Just so," he added, "shall your descendants
      be."
Abram put his faith in the LORD,
   who credited it to him as an act of
      righteousness.

He then said to him,
   "I am the LORD who brought you from Ur
      of the Chaldeans
   to give you this land as a possession."
"O Lord GOD," he asked,
   "how am I to know that I shall possess
      it?"
He answered him,
   "Bring me a three-year-old heifer, a
      three-year-old she-goat,
   a three-year-old ram, a turtledove, and a
      young pigeon."
Abram brought him all these, split them
   in two,
   and placed each half opposite the other;
   but the birds he did not cut up.
Birds of prey swooped down on the
   carcasses,
   but Abram stayed with them.
As the sun was about to set, a trance fell
   upon Abram,
   and a deep, terrifying darkness
      enveloped him.

When the sun had set and it was dark,
   there appeared a smoking fire pot and a
      flaming torch,
   which passed between those pieces.
It was on that occasion that the LORD made
   a covenant with Abram,
   saying: "To your descendants I give this
      land,
   from the Wadi of Egypt to the Great
      River, the Euphrates."

RESPONSORIAL PSALM

Ps 27:1, 7-8, 8-9, 13-14

R̸. (1a) The Lord is my light and my salvation.

The LORD is my light and my salvation;
   whom should I fear?
The LORD is my life's refuge;
   of whom should I be afraid?

R̸. The Lord is my light and my salvation.

Hear, O LORD, the sound of my call;
   have pity on me, and answer me.
Of you my heart speaks; you my glance
     seeks.

R̸. The Lord is my light and my salvation.

Your presence, O LORD, I seek.
   Hide not your face from me;
do not in anger repel your servant.
   You are my helper: cast me not off.

R̸. The Lord is my light and my salvation.

I believe that I shall see the bounty of the
     LORD
   in the land of the living.
Wait for the LORD with courage;
   be stouthearted, and wait for the LORD.

R̸. The Lord is my light and my salvation.

SECOND READING

Phil 3:17–4:1

Join with others in being imitators of me,
   brothers and sisters,
   and observe those who thus conduct
     themselves
   according to the model you have in us.
For many, as I have often told you
   and now tell you even in tears,
   conduct themselves as enemies of the
     cross of Christ.
Their end is destruction.
Their God is their stomach;
   their glory is in their "shame."
Their minds are occupied with earthly
     things.
But our citizenship is in heaven,
   and from it we also await a savior, the
     Lord Jesus Christ.
He will change our lowly body
   to conform with his glorified body
   by the power that enables him also
   to bring all things into subjection to
     himself.

Therefore, my brothers and sisters,
   whom I love and long for, my joy and
     crown,
   in this way stand firm in the Lord.

or Phil 3:20–4:1, see Appendix A, p. 273.

About Liturgy

Lent, first reading, and gospel: For most of the liturgical year the Roman Catholic Lectionary's first reading for Sundays relates well to the gospel. The first reading may relate to the gospel thematically (sometimes with a parallel incident from the Old Testament) or it may include a promise/fulfillment relationship. However, during Lent the first reading and gospel are not harmonized, but the first reading runs its own course with its own purpose.

Always during Lent the first reading gives us a glimpse of major salvation events. For example, in this year C, the Old Testament reading from Deuteronomy for the First Sunday of Lent relates Israel's passover from slavery to freedom and reminds them of God's mighty deeds in making them God's own chosen people, eliciting from them a profession of faith. On the Second Sunday of Lent we hear about God's covenant with Abraham; Third Sunday, Moses' encounter with God in the burning bush; Fourth Sunday, Israel celebrates the Passover in the promised land; Fifth Sunday, prophecy about God doing something new for the people; and Palm Sunday, the opening verses of the Third Song of the Suffering Servant.

None of these readings are repeated on Holy Saturday at the Vigil, although there, too, the Old Testament readings recount for us salvation history. It is as though these first readings during Lent prepare us for the Easter Vigil—we've been hearing our salvation history unfolding throughout Lent.

About Liturgical Music

Music suggestions: There exists a number of hymns specific to the transfiguration event proclaimed every year on the Second Sunday of Lent: "'Tis Good, Lord, to Be Here"; "Christ upon the Mountain Peak"; "Jesus, Take Us to the Mountain"; "Transform Us"; "From Ashes to the Living Font." Particularly appropriate this year when the gospel speaks about the "exodus" Jesus must "accomplish in Jerusalem" would be a song explicitly relating Christ's transfiguration to his passion and death.

Another good choice for the entrance procession would be "O Sun of Justice." The text speaks of the light of Christ dispelling darkness and bringing new life. The traditional tune (JESU DULCIS MEMORIA) can be effectively accompanied with simple tone chimes or bells playing open chords or chord clusters at the places of rhythmic pulse. Also fitting for the entrance or the preparation of the gifts would be "Eternal Lord of Love," which speaks of the journey of Lent and the glory awaiting us at its end.

THIRD SUNDAY OF LENT

✝ SPIRITUALITY

GOSPEL ACCLAMATION
Matt 4:17

Repent, says the Lord;
the kingdom of heaven is at hand.

Gospel   Luke 13:1-9; L30C

Some people told Jesus about the
    Galileans
  whose blood Pilate had mingled with
      the blood of their sacrifices.
Jesus said to them in reply,
  "Do you think that because these
      Galileans suffered in this way
  they were greater sinners than all
      other Galileans?
By no means!
But I tell you, if you do not repent,
  you will all perish as they did!
Or those eighteen people who were
    killed
  when the tower at Siloam fell on
      them—
  do you think they were more guilty
  than everyone else who lived in
      Jerusalem?
By no means!
But I tell you, if you do not repent,
  you will all perish as they did!"

And he told them this parable:
  "There once was a person who had
      a fig tree planted in his orchard,
  and when he came in search of fruit
      on it but found none,
  he said to the gardener,
  'For three years now I have come in
      search of fruit on this fig tree
  but have found none.
So cut it down.
Why should it exhaust the soil?'
He said to him in reply,
  'Sir, leave it for this year also,
  and I shall cultivate the ground
      around it and fertilize it;
  it may bear fruit in the future.
If not you can cut it down.'"

*See Appendix A, pp. 274–276, for optional
readings.*

72

Reflecting on the Gospel

We tend to take special care of a possession we prize deeply. Perhaps we have a special place for it so it can't get lost or broken. Or we clean it regularly or make sure it is in great working order. On the other hand, we tend to use casually, and even discard, things for which we have no great emotional attachment. The parable in this Sunday's gospel presents us with two characters: one cares only casually for a fruit tree he judges to be of little value; the other cares deeply for the tree because of the potential he sees in it.

The owner of the fig tree only cares about whether the tree bears fruit—he has no regard for the tree and its life. The gardener, on the other hand, cares about the fig tree, sees the life still there, and wants to give it every chance ("I shall cultivate . . . and fertilize it") to produce. He understands that as long as there's life, there's potential to bear fruit. He understands that it's not only the fruit that is worthwhile, but the very life of the tree itself. As long as there's life, something more can come.

Repentance is ultimately about life and about choosing life. Sin is selfishness, weakened or broken relationships, disregard for the value of life and what good can come from life. What wastes away life within us and prevents us from bearing fruit is sin. Repentance, then, means choosing to nurture new life and all the fullness it can bring.

While the stakes are high (repent or perish, bear fruit or be cut down), the parable offers this hope: that in our work of repentance God shows us patience ("leave it for this year"), assists us ("I shall cultivate . . . and fertilize"), and shows great compassion. Repentance is an *attitude* of relationship—we receive God's compassion which strengthens us to change our behaviors and conform more perfectly to Christ. Repentance is as much a part of Christian living as is loving and caring for others. In fact, without repentance we cannot bear the fruit of right relationships with God, self, and others. Much is at stake in our choice to repent or perish, in choosing life!

Living the Paschal Mystery

The challenge of Lent is urgent: "repent or perish; bear fruit or be cut down." But what does this urgency mean for most of us who are scarcely huge sinners! Although murder and adultery and apostasy (giving up the faith) and other public, scandalous, heinous sins are as much a part of our church now as they were when the early church practiced public penitence, the vast majority of us are just common sinful folk. Sometimes it's not so obvious to us of what we must repent. We are sort of stuck—like the fig tree; it was still alive, just wasn't doing much.

The challenge of Lent is to allow Jesus to "cultivate" and "fertilize" us so that we know of what we are to repent and can begin bearing even more fruit. Heeding the message of the gospels is one way we prune ourselves of sins. The gospels are the measure against which we can examine our daily living. Another way is to pay attention to the people around us. They can reflect back to us behaviors we need to change as well as draw us out of ourselves to act in charity and graciousness. Christian living—and repenting—isn't something undertaken in isolation. It always involves other people. They are the "examples" who teach us what needs to change in us so that we can bear fruit—even a bumper crop!

Focusing the Gospel

Key words and phrases: sinners, repent, cut it down, I shall cultivate . . . and fertilize it, may bear fruit

To the point: The owner of the fig tree only cares about whether the tree bears fruit—he has no regard for the tree and its life. The gardener, on the other hand, cares about the fig tree, sees the life still there, and wants to give it every chance ("I shall cultivate . . . and fertilize it") to produce. He understands that as long as there's life, there's potential to bear fruit. What wastes away life within us and prevents us from bearing fruit is sin. Repentance, then, means choosing to nurture new life and all the fullness it can bring.

Connecting the Gospel

to the second reading: Paul, like Jesus, offers examples from Israel's history as a "warning to us" (second reading) not to stray from God's guidance. God offered every means for coming to new life to the people of Israel; so, too, Jesus offers us every means for coming to new and fruitful life ("I shall cultivate the ground . . . and fertilize it").

to experience: Growing up takes hard work. Getting ahead in life takes hard work. Deepening our relationship with God and others takes hard work. It is no surprise, then, that repenting takes hard work. The discipline of Lent includes this kind of hard-work repentance which leads to the new life Easter promises.

Connecting the Responsorial Psalm

to the readings: This Sunday's gospel and second reading demand that we repent and do so immediately. The demand is unequivocal: if we do not repent we shall perish. Yet Jesus, in his parable of the fig tree, seems to soften his own demand. God, he says, will always give us one more chance. The psalm reveals why. With numerous images the psalm tells us how merciful God is, how compassionate, forgiving, and kind. God is not vindictive, but "slow to anger" and quick to "pardon . . . iniquities." The demand that we repent remains, but the way there is to reach out and accept this mercy offered without stint. This is the task of Lent: that we let our hearts be cultivated by a divine mercy that transforms whatever is barren into new life.

to psalmist preparation: As during previous weeks, you need to prepare yourself to sing the responsorial psalm by praying the whole of the psalm from which its verses have been taken. Jesus' insistence on repentance (gospel) cannot be understood outside of God's continuing compassion for human weakness (psalm). Do you see the mercy behind God's call to repentance? What do you need to do so that you can effectively tell the assembly about it?

**ASSEMBLY &
FAITH-SHARING GROUPS**

- Like the owner of the fig tree, I show little regard for how my actions waste away life when . . .
- Jesus' call to repent and choose new life means to me . . .
- Jesus is patiently "cultivating" and "fertilizing" my life by . . .

PRESIDERS
My ministry demonstrates the patience of God when I . . . In this I foster new life in the people I serve in that . . .

DEACONS
My service of others best draws out the potential for new life in those who are sick or suffering when I . . .

HOSPITALITY MINISTERS
My care and concern for others assists them in bearing the good fruit of discipleship by . . .

MUSIC MINISTERS
God uses my participation in music ministry to cultivate a conversion to fuller life in Christ by . . .

ALTAR MINISTERS
I serve the assembly in their work of repentance and choosing life by . . .

LECTORS
My own work of repentance bears fruit in my Sunday proclamation in that . . .

**EXTRAORDINARY MINISTERS
OF HOLY COMMUNION**
As a member of the Body of Christ I "cultivate" and "fertilize" the discipleship of others by . . .

Model Penitential Act

Presider: During Lent we are called to repent and bear the good fruit of new life. Let us reflect on how we have failed to use opportunities this week to repent and bear fruit . . . [pause]

  Confiteor: I confess . . .

Homily Points

• We all have a "bottom line." Children can push parents just so far, and then when their patience is exhausted, the children pay. Employers can raise production quotas to the point where employees strike. "Bottom line" is the limit of what is acceptable for us. Since our God is a God of life, there is no "bottom line" that exhausts God's patience. There is always time for our repentance and choosing new life.

• As long as there is life, there is potential to bear fruit. This gospel contrasts the reality of sin and the alienation it brings with the utter patience of God who always calls us to new life. With God we always have another chance. This "another chance" is what we call repentance—choosing new life and bearing good fruit.

• Lent is the church's gift to us—an opportunity to reflect deeply on how we live and relate. During Lent we discern how we have wasted away opportunities for new life. During Lent we discern for what we need to repent. During Lent we make a conscious choice for new life. During Lent we renew our commitment to bear good fruit. During Lent we raise our "bottom line" behavior from unfruitful self-absorption to bearing the good fruit of faithful discipleship.

Model Universal Prayer (Prayer of the Faithful)

Presider: God is patient and understanding of our needs and so we are encouraged to pray.

Response:

Lord, hear our prayer.

Cantor:

we pray to the Lord,

That all people of God choose the new life repentance promises . . . [pause]

That all people of the world cultivate justice and peace . . . [pause]

That those for whom life is wasting away may turn with confidence to the God of patience and care . . . [pause]

That all of us here present remain faithful to God's ways and bear much fruit for the good of others . . . [pause]

Presider: Patient and merciful God, you hear the prayers of your people who cry out to you: help us to bear much fruit and lead us to life everlasting. Grant this through Christ our Lord. **Amen**.

COLLECT

Let us pray

Pause for silent prayer

O God, author of every mercy and of all
  goodness,
who in fasting, prayer and almsgiving
have shown us a remedy for sin,
look graciously on this confession of our
  lowliness,
that we, who are bowed down by our
  conscience,
may always be lifted up by your mercy.
Through our Lord Jesus Christ, your Son,
who lives and reigns with you in the unity
  of the Holy Spirit,
one God, for ever and ever.
Amen.

FIRST READING
Exod 3:1-8a, 13-15

Moses was tending the flock of his father-
  in-law Jethro,
  the priest of Midian.
Leading the flock across the desert, he
  came to Horeb,
  the mountain of God.
There an angel of the LORD appeared to
  Moses in fire
  flaming out of a bush.
As he looked on, he was surprised to see
  that the bush,
  though on fire, was not consumed.
So Moses decided,
  "I must go over to look at this
    remarkable sight,
  and see why the bush is not burned."
When the LORD saw him coming over to
  look at it more closely,
  God called out to him from the bush,
    "Moses! Moses!"
He answered, "Here I am."
God said, "Come no nearer!
Remove the sandals from your feet,
  for the place where you stand is holy
    ground.
I am the God of your fathers," he
  continued,
  "the God of Abraham, the God of Isaac,
    the God of Jacob."
Moses hid his face, for he was afraid to
  look at God.
But the LORD said,
  "I have witnessed the affliction of my
    people in Egypt
  and have heard their cry of complaint
    against their slave drivers,
  so I know well what they are suffering.
Therefore I have come down to rescue
  them
  from the hands of the Egyptians

and lead them out of that land into a
        good and spacious land,
    a land flowing with milk and honey."

Moses said to God, "But when I go to the
        Israelites
    and say to them, 'The God of your
        fathers has sent me to you,'
    if they ask me, 'What is his name?'
        what am I to tell them?"
God replied, "I am who am."
Then he added, "This is what you shall tell
        the Israelites:
    I AM sent me to you."

God spoke further to Moses, "Thus shall
        you say to the Israelites:
    The LORD, the God of your fathers,
    the God of Abraham, the God of Isaac,
        the God of Jacob,
    has sent me to you.

"This is my name forever;
    thus am I to be remembered through all
        generations."

RESPONSORIAL PSALM
Ps 103:1-2, 3-4, 6-7, 8, 11

R̆. (8a) The Lord is kind and merciful.

Bless the LORD, O my soul;
    and all my being, bless his holy name.
Bless the LORD, O my soul,
    and forget not all his benefits.

R̆. The Lord is kind and merciful.

He pardons all your iniquities,
    heals all your ills.
He redeems your life from destruction,
    crowns you with kindness and
        compassion.

R̆. The Lord is kind and merciful.

The LORD secures justice
    and the rights of all the oppressed.
He has made known his ways to Moses,
    and his deeds to the children of Israel.

R̆. The Lord is kind and merciful.

Merciful and gracious is the LORD,
    slow to anger and abounding in
        kindness.
For as the heavens are high above the
        earth,
    so surpassing is his kindness toward
        those who fear him.

R̆. The Lord is kind and merciful.

SECOND READING
1 Cor 10:1-6, 10-12

*See Appendix A, pp. 274–276, for optional
readings.*

About Liturgy

Lenten Sundays connect: In our personal and parish preparations for this and
the next two Sundays, it is good to keep in mind that these Sundays are linked during
all three years. During Year A (and at Masses when the Scrutinies are celebrated) a
baptismal motif runs through the gospels; during Year B, the third to fifth Sundays of
Lent have as a motif the dying and rising mystery of Christ; and during this Year C,
the motif for these three Sundays is repentance. Moreover, not only are the three Sundays during each year linked, but the years are linked together as well. The baptismal
motif (Year A) reminds us that it is through our baptism that we are plunged into the
mystery of Christ (Year B), and we remain faithful to that mystery through continuing
repentance (Year C).

Further, the first two Sundays (temptations and transfiguration) as well as Palm
Sunday (hosannah! gospel at the procession with palms and Passion gospel during
the Liturgy of the Word) also frame Lent with the paschal mystery rhythm of dying
and rising. The more effort we make to connect the Sundays, the more able are we to
experience the liturgical year as an unfolding of the paschal mystery, as an invitation
to enter more deeply into our Christian identity as disciples, and as an encounter with
God who offers us salvation.

About Liturgical Music

Music suggestions: This Sunday invites us to sing songs with a motif of repentance. Examples include Francis Patrick O'Brien's "The Cross of Christ," suitable for
the entrance procession or the preparation of the gifts; "Our Father, We have Wandered," also fitting for the entrance procession or the preparation of the gifts; "Come
You Sinners, Poor and Needy," appropriate for the preparation of the gifts; and "Draw
Near, O Lord/*Attende Domine*" and "Spare Us, Lord/*Parce Domine*," both suitable for
the Communion procession.

Reginald Heber's "Bread of the World" is a particularly appropriate text for Communion: "Bread of the world, in mercy broken, Wine of the soul in mercy shed, By
whom the words of life were spoken, And in whose death our sins are dead. Look on
the heart by sorrow broken, Look on the tears by sinners shed; And be your feast to
us the token That by your grace our souls are fed." Paul Tate has set the text to an appealing pentatonic melody and added verses which can be sung either by cantor/choir
or the whole assembly. His SAB choral harmonization is simple yet rich, and satisfying
to sing (WLP, 008844).

✠ SPIRITUALITY

GOSPEL ACCLAMATION
Luke 15:18

I will get up and go to my Father and shall say
to him:
Father, I have sinned against heaven and against
you.

Gospel   Luke 15:1-3, 11-32; L33C

Tax collectors and sinners were all
    drawing near to listen to Jesus,
  but the Pharisees and scribes began
    to complain, saying,
  "This man welcomes sinners and eats
    with them."
So to them Jesus addressed this
    parable:
"A man had two sons, and the younger
    son said to his father,
  'Father give me the share of your
    estate that should come to me.'
So the father divided the property
    between them.
After a few days, the younger son collected
    all his belongings
  and set off to a distant country
  where he squandered his inheritance on
    a life of dissipation.
When he had freely spent everything,
  a severe famine struck that country,
  and he found himself in dire need.
So he hired himself out to one of the local
    citizens
  who sent him to his farm to tend the
    swine.
And he longed to eat his fill of the pods on
    which the swine fed,
  but nobody gave him any.
Coming to his senses he thought,
  'How many of my father's hired workers
  have more than enough food to eat,
  but here am I, dying from hunger.
I shall get up and go to my father and I
    shall say to him,
  "Father, I have sinned against heaven
    and against you.

Continued in Appendix A, p. 276.

*See Appendix A, pp. 277–278, for optional
readings.*

Reflecting on the Gospel

Desperation can push us to do things we wouldn't ordinarily choose. Lack of money for food can push an out-of-work parent to take any job, even one below their qualification level and at minimum wage. A coach donated one of his kidneys to a ball player. He commented that this act was not about desperately gaining back his star player and winning ball games, but it was about giving this young man his life back. Desperation is often a matter of life and death. Faced with this choice, we choose life.

This gospel parable is a familiar one and is often referred to as the parable of the prodigal son. How in the world is the son prodigal—lavish, extravagant—when he acted so selfishly? On the one hand, the younger son is prodigal when he prodigiously squanders his inheritance. On the other hand, the real prodigality of the son lay in that he loved his life enough to swallow his pride, return home, and throw himself on the mercy of his father. While this son's situation was desperate enough—he was "dying from hunger"—he also knew his father well enough to know with confidence that he would not be turned away. He would not let him die. The younger son chooses life, even if it might be different.

The father, too, is prodigal: he welcomes him as son (not as a hired worker), clothes him in the finest array, and throws a lavish feast. The surprise of the parable is that the father expresses his forgiveness by restoring the younger son to their former relationship. He restored the wayward fellow back to his identity as son. He gave him new life. This is the most prodigal act possible: to give new life. The father chose life for both himself and his son when he restored the broken relationship.

Both the younger son and the father give us an example of how reconciliation must work. The younger son had to admit his wrongdoing, admit the punishment he deserves, and seek his father's forgiveness. The father forgives, imparts identity and life, and celebrates the restored relationship. Reconciliation always makes demands on both of the parties involved. Both must reach out to the other. Both must be willing to choose life.

Living the Paschal Mystery

Our Lenten penance calls us to go beyond where we are and come to the compassion and generosity of the father. Every day in countless ways we are faced with a choice to repent and make stronger our relationships with others. Ultimately, our Lenten (and life) journey is one of reconciliation which brings healing and restored relationship. Reconciliation implies a letting go of whatever binds us or hinders us or turns us in on ourselves and a "passing over" to receiving the compassion and mercy which can only be celebrated as new life.

Lent tends to pass all too quickly. We cannot let it go by and be satisfied only with "giving up" something. Lent also offers us a positive opportunity to reflect on our many relationships, especially with those closest to us (family, parish community, colleagues at work). Repentance challenges us to look deeply into our own selves and root out whatever self-centeredness keeps us from receiving God's mercy and compassion and from offering forgiveness to (or seeking it from) others. Repentance invites us to choose life. Reconciliation compels us to give life to others.

Focusing the Gospel

Key words and phrases: squandered his inheritance, dying from hunger, treat me as . . . hired workers, father . . . filled with compassion, come to life again

To the point: This parable is a familiar one and is often referred to as the parable of the prodigal son. On the one hand, the younger son is prodigal when he prodigiously squanders his inheritance. On the other hand, the real prodigality of the son lay in that he loved his life enough to swallow his pride, return home, and throw himself on the mercy of his father. The father, too, is prodigal: he welcomes him as son (not hired worker), clothes him in the finest array, and throws a lavish feast. He gave him new life. This is the most prodigal act possible: to give new life.

Connecting the Gospel

to the second reading: Paul reinforces what the gospel parable points to: sureness in the Father's prodigiousness—"new things have come." As the younger son is reconciled with his father, we are all reconciled to God "through Christ."

to experience: Good parents spare nothing for the sake of their children. Sometimes they are prodigious even beyond their means. How much more so is our loving Father prodigious with us!

Connecting the Responsorial Psalm

to the readings: The verses of this responsorial psalm move back and forth between first-person declaration ("I will bless . . ."; "I sought the LORD . . .") and direct address ("Glorify the LORD . . ."; "Look to him . . ."). This grammatical structure implicates us directly in the psalm and the readings. We are the ones who have tasted the goodness of the Lord and now call upon the lowly to cry for help and be saved. We are the Israelites once enslaved in Egypt who having survived the terrible desert journey now feast in the land of God's deliverance (first reading). We are the prodigal son once distant and dissipated who having crossed the terrain of regret and repentance now feast at our father's table (gospel). We are the ones who, having become a new creation in Christ (second reading), are now ambassadors of the message: repent, come home, the feast is ready and—oh, so good—it is God.

to psalmist preparation: In this psalm you call those who have abandoned God or sinned in any way to repent, come home, and feast on God's mercy. What personal experience of God's goodness and mercy can inspire your singing of this psalm? What radiance (see last strophe) will shine on your face?

ASSEMBLY & FAITH-SHARING GROUPS

- I am most prodigious with others when . . . Others are most prodigious with me when . . .
- The lavishness of God that I have experienced in my life is . . .
- I love life so much that I . . . I have received new life from . . .

PRESIDERS

My most prodigious act as one who presides and preaches is . . .

DEACONS

My acts of kindness when I serve others bring new life in that . . .

HOSPITALITY MINISTERS

I am extravagant in hospitality when I . . .

MUSIC MINISTERS

My music making calls me back "home" to right relationship with God and others in that . . .

ALTAR MINISTERS

My serving witnesses to God's extravagance toward us when I . . .

LECTORS

When I reflect on God's extravagance toward me, my proclamation sounds like . . .

EXTRAORDINARY MINISTERS OF HOLY COMMUNION

Others "taste and see" (psalm) in me God's extravagance whenever I . . .

✠ CELEBRATION

Model Penitential Act

Presider: God invites us to the extravagance of this eucharistic feast. To celebrate worthily, let us come home to God and ask for mercy . . . [pause]

    Confiteor: I confess . . .

Homily Points

• Our love for life most strongly motivates us when life itself is threatened. Destitute parents give what little food they have first to the children rather than themselves. Doctors and nurses work tirelessly to help heal a person diagnosed with a life-threatening disease. Even a perfect stranger donates a kidney to a person in renal failure. The most prodigal act we can do is give another life.

• Pushed by desperation, the younger son in the gospel returns home confident that his father won't let him die. The son is seeking only to live. The prodigality of the father is about even more than this. The father is concerned about both his son's identity and his life. The father not only guarantees his son's life, but gives new life when he restores him as his son.

• Lent, too, is about identity and new life. It is a desert time when we come to thirst more deeply for the life only made possible by growing in our relationship with Christ. By returning home to Christ (by being reconciled with God and each other), we become "a new creation" in him (second reading). Lent helps us seek new life; reconciliation guarantees new life. God's most prodigal act is to give us this new life.

Model Universal Prayer (Prayer of the Faithful)

Presider: God greatly desires to share with us new life. Let us confidently place our needs before this generous God.

Response:

Cantor:

For all members of the church to seek new life for themselves and to give new life to others . . . [pause]

For all those alienated from families and for countries alienated from each other to be reconciled . . . [pause]

For those whose lives are threatened by illness, poverty, or violence to come to peace . . . [pause]

For those of us here gathered to be reconciled with those whom we have hurt and come to new life during Lent . . . [pause]

Presider: Gracious and merciful God, you sent your Son Jesus to reconcile us to you and each other: hear these our prayers that we might come joyfully to your eternal Feast. We ask this through Christ our Lord. **Amen.**

COLLECT

Let us pray

Pause for silent prayer

O God, who through your Word
reconcile the human race to yourself in a
    wonderful way,
grant, we pray,
that with prompt devotion and eager faith
the Christian people may hasten
toward the solemn celebrations to come.
Through our Lord Jesus Christ, your Son,
who lives and reigns with you in the unity
    of the Holy Spirit,
one God, for ever and ever.
Amen.

FIRST READING
Josh 5:9a, 10-12

The LORD said to Joshua,
    "Today I have removed the reproach of
        Egypt from you."

While the Israelites were encamped at Gilgal
    on the plains of Jericho,
    they celebrated the Passover
    on the evening of the fourteenth of the
        month.
On the day after the Passover,
    they ate of the produce of the land
    in the form of unleavened cakes and
        parched grain.
On that same day after the Passover,
    on which they ate of the produce of the
        land, the manna ceased.
No longer was there manna for the
    Israelites,
    who that year ate of the yield of the
        land of Canaan.

RESPONSORIAL PSALM

Ps 34:2-3, 4-5, 6-7

R̺. (9a) Taste and see the goodness of the Lord.

I will bless the LORD at all times;
  his praise shall be ever in my mouth.
Let my soul glory in the LORD;
  the lowly will hear me and be glad.

R̺. Taste and see the goodness of the Lord.

Glorify the LORD with me,
  let us together extol his name.
I sought the LORD, and he answered me
  and delivered me from all my fears.

R̺. Taste and see the goodness of the Lord.

Look to him that you may be radiant with
    joy,
  and your faces may not blush with
    shame.
When the poor one called out, the LORD
    heard,
  and from all his distress he saved him.

R̺. Taste and see the goodness of the Lord.

SECOND READING

2 Cor 5:17-21

Brothers and sisters:
Whoever is in Christ is a new creation:
  the old things have passed away;
  behold, new things have come.
And all this is from God,
  who has reconciled us to himself
    through Christ
  and given us the ministry of
    reconciliation,
  namely, God was reconciling the world
    to himself in Christ,
  not counting their trespasses against
    them
  and entrusting to us the message of
    reconciliation.
So we are ambassadors for Christ,
  as if God were appealing through us.
We implore you on behalf of Christ,
  be reconciled to God.
For our sake he made him to be sin who
    did not know sin,
  so that we might become the
    righteousness of God in him.

See Appendix A, pp. 277–278, for optional readings.

About Liturgy

Eucharist and reconciliation: Eucharist is considered the sacrament of reconciliation par excellence. This is so for two reasons. First, Eucharist is a sacrament of reconciliation because Eucharist celebrates and strengthens our unity in the Body of Christ. At Eucharist we are nourished at both the table of the Word and the table of the Sacrament. The word helps us shape our lives after Christ's, challenging us to lead lives characterized by compassion and forgiveness. At the table we share in the same Body and Blood of Christ, enabling us to grow together in our common identity. Second, Eucharist is a sacrament of reconciliation because in Eucharist we come to the feast—God's messianic feast whereby we already share in the fullness of life (and relationships) which is to come. There is a price to pay for this reconciliation: both becoming one in Christ and sharing in the feast entails a letting go of whatever behaviors are stumbling blocks to unity and feasting.

The Sacrament of Penance, the church's specific ritual of reconciliation, is not unrelated to Eucharist's reconciliation. In this sacrament we acknowledge to another our sinfulness and seek the forgiveness and reconciliation of Christ through the church. Having healed broken or weakened relationships (with God, self, others), we come to the eucharistic feast to celebrate our restored relationships.

About Liturgical Music

Music suggestions: As last Sunday, the readings this week celebrate the mercy of God which supports human repentance. A particularly appropriate hymn for this Sunday is "Our Father, We Have Wandered." Based on the parable of the prodigal son, this hymn is set to the PASSION CHORALE tune so strongly associated with the season of Lent. The hymn could be used for either the entrance procession or the preparation of the gifts. Another excellent choice for either the entrance or the preparation of the gifts is "Eternal Lord of Love." The image in the first verse of God's watching and leading the church on its "pilgrim way of Lent" identifies the church with the Israelites on their journey to the promised land, but it is also reminiscent of the journey home of the prodigal son, with the father compassionately watching for his return. To all—the Israelites in the desert, the church on her Lenten journey, the prodigal son returning home—the conclusion of the verse beautifully applies: "Moved by your love and toward your presence bent: Far off yet here, the goal of all desire." Herman Stuempfle's "Far From Home We Run Rebellious" (in *Hymns for the Gospels*, GIA) retells the gospel story of our return home after having abandoned God's love for false treasures and empty, self-centered dreams. This hymn would be very effective during the preparation of the gifts.

✠ SPIRITUALITY

GOSPEL ACCLAMATION
Joel 2:12-13

Even now, says the Lord,
return to me with your whole heart;
for I am gracious and merciful.

Gospel   John 8:1-11; L36C

Jesus went to the Mount of Olives.
But early in the morning he arrived
    again in the temple area,
    and all the people started coming
        to him,
    and he sat down and taught
        them.
Then the scribes and the Pharisees
        brought a woman
    who had been caught in adultery
    and made her stand in the middle.
They said to him,
    "Teacher, this woman was caught
    in the very act of committing adultery.
Now in the law, Moses commanded us to
        stone such women.
So what do you say?"
They said this to test him,
    so that they could have some charge to
        bring against him.
Jesus bent down and began to write on
        the ground with his finger.
But when they continued asking him,
    he straightened up and said to them,
    "Let the one among you who is without
        sin
    be the first to throw a stone at her."
Again he bent down and wrote on the
        ground.
And in response, they went away one by
        one,
    beginning with the elders.
So he was left alone with the woman
        before him.
Then Jesus straightened up and said to her,
    "Woman, where are they?
Has no one condemned you?"
She replied, "No one, sir."
Then Jesus said, "Neither do I condemn
        you.
Go, and from now on do not sin any more."

*See Appendix A, pp. 279–281, for optional
readings.*

Reflecting on the Gospel

Some people like to be center stage. They are natural-born entertainers who feed off of and thrive on audience responses. Other people avoid this kind of attention focused on themselves. We might surmise that the adulterous woman in this gospel story was hardly happy about being center stage! She was facing death by stoning—not a very inviting prospect! Her life hung in the balance.

How would Jesus respond to the challenge of the scribes and Pharisees? Hardly the way anyone anticipated!

The scribes and Pharisees brought an adulterous woman to Jesus and "made her stand in the middle." In their self-righteousness they wished to make an example of her as a grave sinner deserving of death. Ironically, Jesus makes an example of them as sinners: they turned away from him and "went away one by one." Once they were faced with their own sinfulness and the futility of their "test," they chose not to remain with the One who would grant them forgiveness and mercy, reconciliation and new life. The woman, however, remained with Jesus. And for this choice she received forgiveness, mercy, new life.

Encountering Jesus always exposes the truth—both the woman *and* the crowd learn the truth about their own sinfulness. They and we are not all that different: we are all sinners who need to encounter Jesus, ask the truth about ourselves, and receive Jesus' mercy. Encounter with Jesus is the occasion for changing both the condemners and the condemned. Our own work during Lent is like that of the adulterous woman: truthfully face our sinfulness and faithfully remain with Jesus. Though we sin, Jesus only wishes new life for us.

The center of this gospel, then, is not really the woman or her sin of adultery, but Jesus himself. He is the One who draws people to himself, teaches, challenges others about the truth of their lives, forgives, commands not to sin again. This is the same Jesus we encounter during Lent. This is the same Jesus who offers us forgiveness and new life. We are not so different from the scribes and Pharisees and the adulterous woman in this gospel. We are all sinners who need to encounter Jesus, face the truth about ourselves, and receive Jesus' mercy. We are all sinners who seek new life.

Living the Paschal Mystery

Jesus never denied others' shortcomings or sinfulness, as is clear when he commands the adulterous woman to "not sin any more." But neither did he deny their goodness. Jesus did not imprison people by their past actions, but called them to the truth of who they were and the goodness within them. He freed people from the "death" of their own sinful actions and offered to those who would remain with him new life.

Repentance, turning from our sinfulness, includes both a dying and a rising. Changing our ways is the dying; a new relationship with Christ is the rising. The deepest truth about ourselves lies not so much in recognizing our sinfulness (as important as that is!) as it lies in deepening our relationship with Christ. Encountering Christ and desiring to be more like him is what calls forth from us a repentant attitude. The closer we become to Christ, the more able are we to recognize our own sinfulness (that which weakens our relationship with him) and repent of our ways. Then we hear Christ say to us, "Neither do I condemn you." Then we may be assured of receiving new life.

Focusing the Gospel

Key words and phrases: woman . . . caught in adultery, stand in the middle, one . . . without sin, went away one by one, woman before him, do not sin any more

To the point: The scribes and Pharisees brought an adulterous woman to Jesus and "made her stand in the middle." In their self-righteousness they wished to make an example of her as a grave sinner deserving of death. Ironically, Jesus makes an example of them as sinners: they turned away from him and "went away one by one." The woman, however, remained with Jesus. Our own work during Lent is like that of the adulterous woman: truthfully face our sinfulness and faithfully remain with Jesus. Though we sin, Jesus only wishes new life for us.

Connecting the Gospel

to the second reading: Paul admonishes us not to be prisoners of our sinfulness but to strain forward to the new life that lies ahead. This new life is the "supreme good of knowing Christ Jesus" and remaining with him ("be found in him").

to experience: When we focus exclusively on our own sinfulness we can easily lose sight of our goodness and God's mercy. Jesus responds even to profound sin with even more profound mercy.

Connecting the Responsorial Psalm

to the readings: The first reading from Isaiah recounts God's mighty acts in restoring Israel as a nation after the Babylonian captivity. As Isaiah asserts, this restoration will make the Exodus look as if it were nothing ("Remember not the events of the past . . . I am doing something new!"). The gospel reading recounts God's acting again to do something new in Jesus. Salvation becomes personalized in the adulterous woman whom Jesus does not condemn but grants new life, both physically and spiritually. God constantly revolutionizes our expectations by saving us in newer, deeper ways. Psalm 126 is our "pinch me" response: we are not dreaming; this salvation is really happening. The readings remind us, however, that the challenge is not just to see but to believe. We must let this new righteousness take possession of us (second reading). We must change our ways and let go of our judgments (gospel). Only then can we "forget [ ] what lies behind" and look toward the future (second reading). Only then can we realize the past about which we sing is just the beginning.

to psalmist preparation: As you sing this psalm, you do not just retell past events; you establish hope for the future. The great things God has already done are nothing compared to what God is yet to do for us in Christ. In what way this week might you let Christ take possession of you (second reading) so that you can sing of this hope with conviction?

ASSEMBLY & FAITH-SHARING GROUPS

- Like the gospel scribes and Pharisees, I tend to be self-righteous when . . .
- Those I tend to make an example of are . . . The good I came to see in them is . . .
- I remain with Jesus when . . . The new life I receive from him is . . .

PRESIDERS

The truth about myself that Jesus is exposing is . . . Addressing this honestly impacts my ministry in that . . .

DEACONS

My service to others brings them to remain more faithfully with Jesus when I . . .

HOSPITALITY MINISTERS

My hospitality prepares others to encounter and remain with Jesus when I . . .

MUSIC MINISTERS

One way my participation in music ministry has led me to deeper encounter with Jesus is . . . One way it has helped me become more honest about myself is . . .

ALTAR MINISTERS

The way I minister puts me "in the middle" and in this I witness to . . .

LECTORS

My manner of proclaiming Scripture invites the assembly to be truthful about themselves and remain with Jesus when I . . .

EXTRAORDINARY MINISTERS OF HOLY COMMUNION

My manner of distributing Holy Communion encourages others to remain with Jesus beyond the celebration when I . . .

Model Penitential Act

Presider: Jesus does not condemn the adulterous woman we will hear about in today's gospel, but he does command her to go and sin no more. As we prepare for this liturgy, let us be truthful about our own sinfulness and ask for Jesus' forgiveness and mercy . . . [pause]

    Confiteor: I confess . . .

Homily Points

• It seems to be a common human tendency to stand someone "in the middle," in other words, we tend to be quick to condemn the actions of others. Often we focus so much on others that we fail to see our own shortcomings. In this we miss opportunities to grow in our relationship with God and others. Consequently, we choose death for ourselves rather than life.

• Jesus did not tell the scribes and Pharisees to leave; they chose not to remain with him. They could not let go of death, could not let go of their ill will toward him. How sad! They left Jesus! Jesus does not desire to condemn us to death, but to bring us to new life. The adulterous woman chose not to leave. Jesus does not condemn her for her sinfulness but calls her to continue her journey of remaining with him and choosing life.

• Jesus helped the characters in the gospel to recognize their own sinfulness. He does the same with us today, often with the help of others. The unacceptable behavior of others might speak to us of our own sinfulness. The truthfulness of what someone says to us in anger might finally hit home about how we must change. Painful as these admissions may well be, they are exactly what can bring us to choose life. We are strengthened in our choice by remaining with Jesus.

Model Universal Prayer (Prayer of the Faithful)

Presider: God wants for us life, not death, forgiveness and mercy, not condemnation. This graciousness encourages us to make our needs known to such a caring God.

Response:

Lord, hear our prayer.

Cantor:

we pray to the Lord,

That all members of the church may witness to others what it means to remain with Jesus who is merciful, compassionate, and truthful . . . [pause]

That all leaders of nations be slow to condemn and quick to show compassion . . . [pause]

That those who stand condemned receive justice, mercy, and compassion . . . [pause]

That each of us gathered here may choose to grow in new life by acknowledging our sinfulness and need for God's mercy . . . [pause]

Presider: God of mercy and compassion, you sent your Son to call us to new life: hear our prayers that we might one day have eternal life. We ask this through Christ our Lord. **Amen**.

COLLECT

Let us pray

Pause for silent prayer

By your help, we beseech you, Lord our
    God,
may we walk eagerly in that same charity
with which, out of love for the world,
your Son handed himself over to death.
Through our Lord Jesus Christ, your Son,
who lives and reigns with you in the unity
    of the Holy Spirit,
one God, for ever and ever.
Amen.

FIRST READING

Isa 43:16-21

Thus says the LORD,
    who opens a way in the sea
    and a path in the mighty waters,
who leads out chariots and horsemen,
    a powerful army,
till they lie prostrate together, never to rise,
    snuffed out and quenched like a wick.
Remember not the events of the past,
    the things of long ago consider not;
see, I am doing something new!
    Now it springs forth, do you not
        perceive it?
In the desert I make a way,
    in the wasteland, rivers.
Wild beasts honor me,
    jackals and ostriches,
for I put water in the desert
    and rivers in the wasteland
    for my chosen people to drink,
the people whom I formed for myself,
    that they might announce my praise.

RESPONSORIAL PSALM

Ps 126:1-2, 2-3, 4-5, 6

℟. (3) The Lord has done great things for us; we are filled with joy.

When the LORD brought back the captives
    of Zion,
    we were like men dreaming.
Then our mouth was filled with laughter,
    and our tongue with rejoicing.

℟. The Lord has done great things for us; we are filled with joy.

Then they said among the nations,
    "The LORD has done great things for
        them."
The LORD has done great things for us;
    we are glad indeed.

℟. The Lord has done great things for us; we are filled with joy.

Restore our fortunes, O Lord,
   like the torrents in the southern desert.
Those that sow in tears
   shall reap rejoicing.

R̸. The Lord has done great things for us;
we are filled with joy.

Although they go forth weeping,
   carrying the seed to be sown,
they shall come back rejoicing,
   carrying their sheaves.

R̸. The Lord has done great things for us;
we are filled with joy.

SECOND READING
Phil 3:8-14

Brothers and sisters:
I consider everything as a loss
   because of the supreme good of
      knowing Christ Jesus my Lord.
For his sake I have accepted the loss of all
      things
   and I consider them so much rubbish,
   that I may gain Christ and be found in
      him,
   not having any righteousness of my
      own based on the law
   but that which comes through faith in
      Christ,
   the righteousness from God,
   depending on faith to know him and the
      power of his resurrection
   and the sharing of his sufferings by being
      conformed to his death,
   if somehow I may attain the
      resurrection from the dead.

It is not that I have already taken hold of it
   or have already attained perfect maturity,
   but I continue my pursuit in hope that I
      may possess it,
   since I have indeed been taken
      possession of by Christ Jesus.
Brothers and sisters, I for my part
   do not consider myself to have taken
      possession.
Just one thing: forgetting what lies behind
   but straining forward to what lies
      ahead,
   I continue my pursuit toward the goal,
   the prize of God's upward calling, in
      Christ Jesus.

*See Appendix A, pp. 279–281, for optional
readings.*

About Liturgy
Lent and personal relationship with Christ: Sometimes we can get so caught up during Lent with doing "penance" that we forget that Lent is ultimately about encountering Jesus and coming to a deeper union with him. Our Lenten penance is never an end in itself, but is always a means to a deeper relationship with Christ. Our Lenten penance is always directed to strengthening our resolve to remain with Jesus, never to turn away from him. As we discipline ourselves, we gradually learn new priorities and what's most important in our lives and are then better able to keep Christ at the center of our lives.

We are a full four weeks into our Lenten journey. Now is a good time to assess how well our Lenten penance has helped us overcome sin and come closer to Jesus. At liturgy during Lent we particularly focus the act of penitence at the beginning of Mass on begging God's mercy for our sinfulness. We might evaluate whether this act is simply a ritual element that we "go through" or whether it is truly a time for seeking God's mercy and forgiveness.

About Liturgical Music
Music suggestions: Any Lenten hymns acknowledging our need for God's mercy and forgiveness are appropriate on this Sunday, but those which also call us to give up condemning one another are particularly suitable. "The Master Came to Bring Good News," set to the forceful tune ICH GLAUB AN GOTT, would be a good entrance song, as would "Help Us Accept Each Other," set to the metrically strong tune EL-LACOMBE. "Help Us Forgive, Forgiving Lord" (in *Hymns for the Gospel*, GIA), set to a gentler tune, would work well during the preparation of the gifts. "Forgive Our Sins [As We Forgive]" acknowledges our need for God's grace to put into practice these challenging words from the Our Father. Its style and tempo make it suitable for the preparation of the gifts. "As We Forgive" draws even more of its text from the Our Father, adding at verse 3: "Our Father in heaven, heal our jealous hearts. May we not judge, lest we be judged; help us to practice mercy." This refrain-verse song can be led by cantor or choir and would be suitable during the preparation of the gifts.

SPIRITUALITY

GOSPEL ACCLAMATION
Ps 84:5

Blessed are those who dwell in your house, O Lord;
they never cease to praise you.

Gospel   Luke 2:41-51a; L543

Each year Jesus' parents went to
Jerusalem for the feast of
Passover,
and when he was twelve years
old,
they went up according to
festival custom.
After they had completed its days,
as they were returning,
the boy Jesus remained behind
in Jerusalem,
but his parents did not know it.
Thinking that he was in the caravan,
they journeyed for a day
and looked for him among their relatives
and acquaintances,
but not finding him,
they returned to Jerusalem to look for
him.
After three days they found him in the
temple,
sitting in the midst of the teachers,
listening to them and asking them
questions,
and all who heard him were astounded
at his understanding and his answers.
When his parents saw him,
they were astonished,
and his mother said to him,
"Son, why have you done this to us?
Your father and I have been looking for you
with great anxiety."
And he said to them,
"Why were you looking for me?
Did you not know that I must be in my
Father's house?"
But they did not understand what he said to
them.
He went down with them and came to
Nazareth,
and was obedient to them.

or Matt 1:16, 18-21, 24a in Appendix A, p. 282.

See Appendix A, p. 282, for the other readings.

Reflecting on the Gospel

How often do parents exclaim with respect to their children, "They grow up so fast!" This gospel helps us see Joseph and Mary as two very normal parents coping with a very unusual Son. The occasion is Passover; but personal "passovers" are revealed, two of them in fact—one for Jesus and one for Joseph and Mary. Jesus announces that he "must be in [his] Father's house" and indicates that he is "passing over" in his life journey from his hidden childhood toward assuming his public ministry of announcing that God's reign is at hand. Joseph and Mary continue the normal care and concern of parents, but they also are challenged to "pass over" into secondary roles as Jesus will soon take up his adult ministry. No doubt Joseph and Mary were thinking on the journey back to Nazareth after they found Jesus, "He is growing up so fast!"

At the very center of this gospel is a diligent search by Joseph and Mary for Jesus. However, the Jesus for whom they search (the "boy Jesus") is not the Jesus whom they find (the One in his "Father's house"). Joseph models for us not only that we must spend our lives diligently searching for Jesus, but also that we cannot be narrow in who is the One we expect to find. Each of us must let go of our narrow perception of who Jesus is to be for us and where we might find him.

We celebrate this solemnity in honor of St. Joseph because he was so willing to let Jesus be who he was born to be. In this gospel Joseph models three particular virtues. First, he is obedient to the requirements of Jewish Law ("Each year . . . went to Jerusalem for . . . Passover"). Thus Joseph reminds us that our "passing over" into greater maturity in Christ through our own decisions to live as he taught is in continuity with a whole tradition of holy people who placed their lives at God's disposition. Second, Joseph takes responsibility for his son's whereabouts and welfare ("your father and I have been looking for you with great anxiety"). Joseph challenges us to take responsibility for how we are disciples of Jesus, how we have assumed our own role in the tradition of saving events. Third, Joseph humbly accepts the secondary role assigned to him when Jesus acknowledges God as his Father. We, too, find our deepest identity and ministry not in a holy city or feast or sacred space, but in a person: Jesus Christ. Our whole lives must be lived by keeping our focus on Jesus whom we serve. And sometimes be surprised by the Jesus we find.

Living the Paschal Mystery

This festival and the virtues Joseph models for us provide an opportunity for us to reflect on our own "passing over" into more perfectly continuing Jesus' saving ministry. So little is known about Joseph; he achieved sainthood not by big, ostentatious saving actions but by simply, obediently following the role in salvation history God asked of him. We, too, are called to simply, obediently follow the saving role God asks of us and we do so most faithfully when we discern the pattern of Jesus' own dying and rising in our lives and continually grow in our ability to give of ourselves for the sake of others.

Like Joseph, we must continually search for Jesus in our daily lives, but not be surprised by the Jesus we might find. We find him not only in invitations to do acts of kindness and compassion, but also when we see his countenance on the face of others. Our role in bringing about salvation is to remain faithful to the presence of Jesus, however he shows himself.

Focusing the Gospel
Key words and phrases: went to Jerusalem, boy Jesus, looked for him, they were astonished, I must be in my Father's house

To the point: At the very center of this gospel is a diligent search by Joseph and Mary for Jesus. However, the Jesus for whom they search (the "boy Jesus") is not the Jesus whom they find (the One in his "Father's house"). Joseph models for us not only that we must spend our lives diligently searching for Jesus, but also that we cannot be narrow in who is the One we expect to find.

Model Penitential Act
Presider: Saint Joseph is the patron of the universal church and model of how we make Jesus the center of our lives. As we prepare for this liturgy celebrating the faithfulness of Joseph, let us open ourselves to how God makes us more faithful . . . [pause]

Lord Jesus, you are the son of David: Lord . . .

Christ Jesus, you dwell in your Father's house: Christ . . .

Lord Jesus, you are the obedient Son of your Father: Lord . . .

Model Universal Prayer (Prayer of the Faithful)
Presider: With St. Joseph as our protector and intercessor, we are encouraged to make our needs known to God.

Response:

Lord, hear our prayer.

Cantor:

we pray to the Lord,

That all members of the church never cease from searching diligently for Jesus and keeping him at the center of their lives . . . [pause]

That all leaders of the world may protect and care for their people with justice and diligence . . . [pause]

That those suffering from the anxiety of lost loved ones may be comforted . . . [pause]

That each of us here present may be open to the many ways Jesus is present to us . . . [pause]

Presider: Loving God, you provided a loving family for your Son: show us the same love and grant our prayers through Christ our Lord. **Amen**.

COLLECT
Let us pray

Pause for silent prayer

Grant, we pray, almighty God,
that by Saint Joseph's intercession
your Church may constantly watch over
the unfolding of the mysteries of human
    salvation,
whose beginnings you entrusted to his
    faithful care.
Through our Lord Jesus Christ, your Son,
who lives and reigns with you in the unity
    of the Holy Spirit,
one God, for ever and ever. **Amen.**

FOR REFLECTION
• I diligently look for Jesus when . . . The Jesus I find is . . .

• What I have learned about Jesus after finding him in some surprising places is . . .

• Saint Joseph teaches me that my life journey is . . .

Homily Points
• When Joseph and Mary discovered Jesus was missing from their company, they knew where to search: back to Jerusalem and to the Temple. They also thought they knew for whom they were looking: their twelve-year-old boy. Our challenge in searching for Jesus is to discover where is Jerusalem, where is the Temple? Where do we find Jesus? Also, we are challenged to be open to the Jesus we find.

• Sometimes we miss finding Jesus because we are looking for the wrong Jesus in the wrong places. With diligent search, we can find Jesus in surprising places: in the routine of faithful daily living; in the quiet of a moment spent in peace with a loved one; in the hustle and bustle of the supermarket. With diligent search, the Jesus we might find is in the face of an exhausted parent, in the scruffiness of the homeless person, in the innocence of a child. Wherever and however we find Jesus, we must allow ourselves to be astonished at who he is.

✠ SPIRITUALITY

GOSPEL ACCLAMATION
Phil 2:8-9

Christ became obedient to the point of death,
even death on a cross.
Because of this, God greatly exalted him
and bestowed on him the name which is above
    every name.

Gospel at the procession with
palms
Luke 19:28-40; L37C

**Jesus proceeded on his
    journey up to Jerusalem.
As he drew near to
    Bethphage and Bethany
at the place called the
    Mount of Olives,
he sent two of his disciples.
He said, "Go into the village
    opposite you,
and as you enter it you will find a colt
    tethered
on which no one has ever sat.
Untie it and bring it here.
And if anyone should ask you,
    'Why are you untying it?'
you will answer,
    'The Master has need of it.'"
So those who had been sent went off
    and found everything just as he had
        told them.
And as they were untying the colt, its
    owners said to them,
    "Why are you untying this colt?"
They answered,
    "The Master has need of it."
So they brought it to Jesus,
    threw their cloaks over the colt,
    and helped Jesus to mount.
As he rode along,
    the people were spreading their cloaks
        on the road;
    and now as he was approaching the
        slope of the Mount of Olives,
    the whole multitude of his disciples
    began to praise God aloud with joy
    for all the mighty deeds they had seen.**

Continued in Appendix A, p. 283.

Gospel at Mass   Luke 22:14–23:56; L38ABC
or Luke 23:1-49 *in Appendix A, pp. 283–286.*

Reflecting on the Gospel

Most of us probably don't think very often about whether we love our life or not. We tend to take it for granted. Yet, we do all kinds of things that indicate we really do love our life: we take care of our health, do activities that we enjoy and refresh us, share our joys and sorrow with others. Loving life keeps us energized. Loving life keeps us moving forward. Loving life keeps us engaged.

Luke's Passion account highlights how much Jesus loved life. His struggle to say yes to his Father's will ("take this cup away from me") was so intense that he sweat blood. He also intensely loved others and their lives: he healed the man with the severed ear, comforted the women of Jerusalem, forgave his executioners, promised Paradise to the repentant thief. For the sake of others' life he was willing to give over his own life ("not my will but yours be done"). Already in his suffering and death Jesus is showing us that the very dying includes life-giving to others.

The first reading illustrates this point most profoundly, for Isaiah's prophecy finds its fulfillment in Jesus: it not only describes his suffering but also his concern for others, "speak[ing] to the weary a word" of comfort. Jesus' concern for others in the midst of suffering speaks not only of his own startling self-giving, but also of the startling *value of the needy person*. Even when suffering, Jesus loves the other so much! Jesus loves the life of the other as much as he loves his own life. Such is the care modeled by our Savior. Such is the life of his disciples. Jesus' struggle and self-giving is to be ours. While intensely loving the Life given us, we also are to give it over for others.

Living the Paschal Mystery

In spite of the fact that we have two distinct gospels with two distinct "feelings" at Mass this Sunday (quite unusual in itself), the purpose of the first gospel and procession is to ready us in a most profound way to hear the proclamation of the passion and to celebrate well the Triduum. Our procession with the palms is a way to engage our whole selves—including the actual bodily movement from one place to another—in symbolizing our own paschal journey with Christ. This procession with palms brings us, literally, to the doorstep of the passion and in this way it prepares and readies us for the proclamation of the passion. Giving ourselves over wholeheartedly during the procession with the palms prepares us to do what hearing this passion account reminds us: that our lives are about giving life to others.

This suggests two ways to live Holy Week. First, to see all our actions this week as a continuation of the procession with palms, joining ourselves with Jesus on his journey to the cross, on the journey to receiving new life. Rather than a somber, morbid week, we live in anticipation of embracing the cross so that we might experience new life on Easter.

Second, knowing full well that the journey this week (and of our whole Christian life) leads to the cross, to commit ourselves to be especially aware of those around us in need, as Jesus was always compassionate toward those in need—evening in his darkest hour. No matter how busy we might be while preparing for a holiday weekend, we want to redouble our efforts to be mindful of the countless ways each day we are called to die to self for the sake of others.

Focusing the Gospel

Key words and phrases: take this cup from me, drops of blood, not my will but yours be done, healed him, do not weep for me, forgive them, you will be with me in Paradise

To the point: Luke's Passion account highlights how much Jesus loved life. His struggle to say yes to his Father's will ("take this cup away from me") was so intense that he sweat blood. He also intensely loved others and their lives: he healed the man with the severed ear, comforted the women of Jerusalem, forgave his executioners, promised Paradise to the repentant thief. For the sake of others' life he was willing to give over his own life ("not my will but yours be done"). Jesus' struggle and self-giving is to be ours. While intensely loving the Life given us, we also are to give it over for others.

Connecting the Gospel

to the first reading: Isaiah's prophecy finds its fulfillment in Jesus: it not only describes his suffering but also his concern for others, "speak[ing] to the weary a word" of comfort.

to experience: When we hear the proclamation of the Passion, we are most mindful of all the suffering Jesus endured. Luke reminds us that the passion also proclaims Jesus' ultimate self-giving ministry for others.

Connecting the Responsorial Psalm

to the readings: The whole of Psalm 22 is a masterpiece of poetry and theology. The psalmist struggles with an increasing sense of being abandoned (from "My God, my God, why have you abandoned me?" to "All who see me scoff at me," to violent imagery of destruction and death) while also experiencing deepening intimacy with God (the One who is far away and does not answer is also the One who has been present "from my mother's womb"). The psalmist begs to be saved from suffering and violence, then offers God lengthy praise. Most lament psalms end with one or two short verses of praise but here the praise continues for nearly one-third of the text. Furthermore, the psalmist invites an ever-widening circle to join in the praise: first the psalmist's immediate family, then all of Israel, then all nations, then generations yet unborn, and finally, even the dead.

Psalm 22 helps us understand the passion, both Christ's and ours. God is not distant from the suffering, but very near. And the depth of the suffering can be the wellspring of the most profound praise. May our singing of these verses from Psalm 22 give us the courage we need to enter Holy Week aware of both the sorrow and the praise to which it will lead.

to psalmist preparation: To help yourself sing this psalm well, take some time to pray the full text of Psalm 22. You sing not only about Christ's suffering, but about his transformation into risen life through his suffering and death. You sing about your own transformation as well, for through baptism you have been incorporated into Jesus' death and resurrection. How willing are you to undergo this transformation? How willing are you to invite the assembly to do so?

**ASSEMBLY &
FAITH-SHARING GROUPS**

- I love my life so much that I . . . What helps me be other-centered is . . .
- I struggle to say yes to God when . . . I struggle to say yes to others when . . .
- When I reach out to others, I experience . . .

PRESIDERS
Where I am challenged to be compassionate in the busyness of my ministry is . . .

DEACONS
My service not only comforts but also assists others to grow in their own compassion in that . . .

HOSPITALITY MINISTERS
My hospitality includes a spirit of compassion toward others in that . . .

MUSIC MINISTERS
In the midst of the intense music demands during Holy Week, one way I can focus not on myself but on the needs of others is . . .

ALTAR MINISTERS
My serving is an expression of my own intense love for life when . . .

LECTORS
My proclamation is a word of comfort and encouragement for the life-weary when I . . .

**EXTRAORDINARY MINISTERS
OF HOLY COMMUNION**
My manner of offering the Body (Blood) of Christ to others helps intensify their love of life when . . .

Model Penitential Act *(only at Masses with the simple entrance)*

Presider: In the Garden of Gethsemane Jesus struggles to say yes to his Father's will. To prepare ourselves to enter into these sacred mysteries, let us examine when we have not been faithful to God . . . [pause]

    Confiteor: I confess . . .

Homily Points

• Most of us don't think often about intensely loving our own life. Yet we make choices every day that show we really do love life. For example, we opt to eat healthy food, to do daily exercise, to get seven or eight hours of good sleep. These choices lead to a more healthy and energetic self, and also give us the sense of well-being essential for looking beyond ourselves and our own needs to others.

• Reaching out to help others was so much a part of the very fabric of who Jesus was and his love for his own life that even during his great suffering and darkest hour he still instinctively reached out to others. Love of his own life enabled Jesus to love the life of others.

• Intense love engenders action. During his passion, Jesus still healed, comforted, forgave, instilled hope in others. During his passion, in spite of his own ebbing life, he gave life to others. We also must live and love so intensely.

Model Universal Prayer (Prayer of the Faithful)

Presider: As Jesus was concerned for others, we now bring our concerns for others to God.

Response:

Lord, hear our prayer.

Cantor:

we pray to the Lord,

That all members of the church may manifest Christ's compassion by lives of generous self-giving . . . [pause]

That all people may extend to one another the intense love God has shown the whole world . . . [pause]

That those who are sick, suffering, or dying may find comfort in Christ's compassionate embrace . . . [pause]

That all of us here may walk with Jesus through death to new life during this holiest of weeks . . . [pause]

Presider: Loving God, you sent your Son to be one with us: hear these our prayers that we might unite ourselves with the passion of Jesus Christ and so rise with him to new life. We pray through that same Jesus Christ our Lord. **Amen**.

COLLECT

Let us pray

Pause for silent prayer

Almighty ever-living God,
who as an example of humility for the
    human race to follow
caused our Savior to take flesh and submit
    to the Cross,
graciously grant that we may heed his
    lesson of patient suffering
and so merit a share in his Resurrection.
Who lives and reigns with you in the unity
    of the Holy Spirit,
one God, for ever and ever.
Amen.

FIRST READING

Isa 50:4-7

The Lord God has given me
    a well-trained tongue,
that I might know how to speak to the
    weary
    a word that will rouse them.
Morning after morning
    he opens my ear that I may hear;
and I have not rebelled,
    have not turned back.
I gave my back to those who beat me,
    my cheeks to those who plucked my
        beard;
my face I did not shield
    from buffets and spitting.

The Lord God is my help,
    therefore I am not disgraced;
I have set my face like flint,
    knowing that I shall not be put to
        shame.

RESPONSORIAL PSALM

Ps 22:8-9, 17-18, 19-20, 23-24

℟. (2a) My God, my God, why have you
abandoned me?

All who see me scoff at me;
    they mock me with parted lips, they
        wag their heads:
"He relied on the Lord; let him deliver him,
    let him rescue him, if he loves him."

℟. My God, my God, why have you
abandoned me?

Indeed, many dogs surround me,
    a pack of evildoers closes in upon me;
they have pierced my hands and my feet;
    I can count all my bones.

R℣. My God, my God, why have you
abandoned me?

They divide my garments among them,
    and for my vesture they cast lots.
But you, O LORD, be not far from me;
    O my help, hasten to aid me.

R℣. My God, my God, why have you
abandoned me?

I will proclaim your name to my brethren;
    in the midst of the assembly I will
        praise you:
"You who fear the LORD, praise him;
    all you descendants of Jacob, give glory
        to him;
    revere him, all you descendants of
        Israel!"

R℣. My God, my God, why have you
abandoned me?

SECOND READING
Phil 2:6-11

Christ Jesus, though he was in the form
        of God,
    did not regard equality with God
    something to be grasped.
Rather, he emptied himself,
    taking the form of a slave,
    coming in human likeness;
    and found human in appearance,
    he humbled himself,
    becoming obedient to the point of
        death,
    even death on a cross.
Because of this, God greatly exalted him
    and bestowed on him the name
    which is above every name,
    that at the name of Jesus
    every knee should bend,
    of those in heaven and on earth and
        under the earth,
    and every tongue confess that
    Jesus Christ is Lord,
    to the glory of God the Father.

CATECHESIS

About Liturgy

Palm Sunday entrances: The liturgy provides three forms of entrance. The *procession* includes the ministers and assembly processing together from a building or place at a distance from or separate from the worship space. The procession may take place only once, at the principal Mass. The *solemn entrance* includes the ministers and assembly who process into the worship space either from in front of the church doors or from just inside the building. This may take place at any Mass. Therefore, the difference between the procession and solemn entrance is a matter of starting point—a place separate and at some distance from the worship space or near the entrance. Both of these forms replace the penitential act. The *simple entrance* (including only the priest and ministers) would not be the usual form for a parish liturgy. If this is used (for example, in a retirement center community or other smaller group setting), then the penitential act is used. With both the procession and solemn entrance, the intention is to underscore the expansiveness of liturgical gesture and movement and the involvement of the whole self in celebrating the paschal mystery.

Name for Palm Sunday: The name assigned to this Sunday in *The Roman Missal*—Palm Sunday of the Passion of the Lord—already indicates something of a contrast between triumph and dying, between the gospel proclaimed before the procession with palms begins and the proclamation of the Passion gospel during the Liturgy of the Word. In the popular mind, the core of this Sunday's liturgy is the blessing of palms and taking them home. In fact, the core of this liturgy is the proclamation of the Passion.

About Liturgical Music

Music and the procession: Because the procession or the solemn entrance which opens this Sunday's liturgy is meant to symbolize the assembly's willingness to enter into the mystery of the cross and resurrection, it needs to be done with as many assembly members as possible participating. Singing whatever music is involved always takes logistical planning, especially when the procession begins in a place other than the church. One way to support the singing is to have the choir flank the procession on either side. Another way is to divide the choir into small groups interspersed throughout the procession. A third option is to have the assembly sing a well-known Christ the King hymn while standing in place, then process in silence to the door of the church (or in the case of the solemn entrance, into the body of the church). With this option it is important to encourage the assembly to process slowly and reflectively, letting each step truly be a choice to move closer to the cross. Processing in silence may take some catechizing of the assembly, but doing it can move participants from historical reenactment of Jesus' entry into Jerusalem to actual enactment of their here-and-now choice to walk with Jesus to the cross.

The Sacred Paschal Triduum

How blessed and amazing
are God's gifts, dear friends!
Life with immortality,
splendor with righteousness,
truth with confidence,
faith with assurance,
self-control with holiness!

—1 Clement 35:1-2

Reflecting on the Triduum

Choose life: The late first century letter from the Church in Rome to the Church in Corinth (commonly ascribed to the third pope, Clement) extols life as a "blessed and amazing" gift from God. It also makes a bold claim that our gift of life includes immortality. Now, we all know that death entered the world when Adam and Eve disobeyed God. Rather than life, they chose death. Jesus is an even more "blessed and amazing" gift from God, for through him death has been overcome. Through his obedience he chose life—not only for himself, but made it possible for all of us who are his faithful followers to share in that same life: risen life, immortality. Through Christ we are invited to live forever.

Jesus chose life through his self-giving. His life was for the sake of others. The paradox is that self-giving doesn't lead to emptiness or nothingness, but to fullness of life. Through surrendering ourselves for the good of others we give ourselves over to the divine Mystery which beckons us to become fully who we are; we choose to be what God wants of us and what Christ modeled for us—dying to self which leads to the exaltation of new life. The invitation not only during these three sacred days of the paschal Triduum but through all our Christian journey is to choose life.

We spend our lives stretched between the two greatest events of our lives—birth and death. In a real sense we are born to die and spend our whole lives dying. However, more is happening in this dying process than the gradual diminishment of life. The movement from birth to death captures the very rhythm which defines us in relation to God. Dying and rising are but two poles of the same mystery of coming into our own humanity in such a way that we grow to realize that our truest selves are found in surrendering into divinity.

These Triduum days call us to empty ourselves and become more like Jesus in his self-giving. Only by self-giving do we realize the full potential of who we can become; only by self-giving can we grow into the divine life which is offered to us. Just as Christ was raised up, so does God raise us up. This is the mystery we celebrate these days: obedience brings victory and death brings exaltation. Choose life!

Living the Paschal Mystery

In everyday terms, self-giving demands of us that we let go of all that distracts us from fully embracing our humanity. Only by reaching out to others can we realize our own full potential. Locked in ourselves, we die. Opening ourselves to others, we live.

In an age of abundant goods, perhaps self-giving means that we buy less so others can have their basic needs fulfilled. At a time of ravishing our good earth, perhaps it means that we pay more attention to how we use our natural resources so that others can share in these life-giving and sustaining gifts of God. In societies which depreciate the value of lasting human relationships, perhaps self-giving means that we let go of our own expectations of others so that they can be who they were created to be. An attitude of self-giving helps us look afresh at all our relationships—to God, self, others—and reevaluate what is truly important to us. Self-giving calls us to set right priorities—that entering into Jesus' dying and rising is why we were created in God's image, why we were given this precious gift that is life. Here is the paradox of this mystery we celebrate: by giving we receive, by dying we live, by reaching out to others we ourselves come to the fullness of joy, peace, life that God intends for us. Choose life!

TRIDUUM

"Triduum" comes from two Latin words (*tres* and *dies*) which mean "a space of three days." But since we have four days with special names—Holy Thursday, Good Friday, Holy Saturday, and Easter Sunday—the "three" may be confusing to some.

The confusion is cleared up when we understand how the days are reckoned. On all high festival days the church counts a day in the same way as Jews count days and festivals; that is, from sundown to sundown. Thus, the Triduum consists of *three* twenty-four-hour periods that stretch over four calendar days.

Therefore, the Easter Triduum begins at sundown on Holy Thursday with the Mass of the Lord's Supper and concludes with Easter evening prayer at sundown on Easter Sunday; its high point is the celebration of the Easter Vigil (UNYC no. 19).

SOLEMN PASCHAL FAST

According to the above calculation, Lent ends at sundown on Holy Thursday; thus, Holy Thursday itself is the last day of Lent. This doesn't mean that our fasting concludes on Holy Thursday, however; the church has traditionally kept a solemn forty-hour fast from the beginning of the Triduum until the fast is broken at Communion during the Easter Vigil.

SPIRITUALITY

I give you a new commandment, says the Lord:
love one another as I have loved you.

Gospel   John 13:1-15; L39ABC

Before the feast of Passover, Jesus knew
    that his hour had come
  to pass from this world to the Father.
He loved his own in the world and he loved
    them to the end.
The devil had already induced Judas, son of
    Simon the Iscariot, to hand him over.
So, during supper,
  fully aware that the Father had put
    everything into his power
  and that he had come from God and was
    returning to God,
  he rose from supper and took off his
    outer garments.
He took a towel and tied it around his waist.
Then he poured water into a basin
  and began to wash the disciples' feet
  and dry them with the towel around his
    waist.
He came to Simon Peter, who said to him,
  "Master, are you going to wash my feet?"
Jesus answered and said to him,
  "What I am doing, you do not understand
    now,
  but you will understand later."
Peter said to him, "You will never wash my
    feet."
Jesus answered him,
  "Unless I wash you, you will have no
    inheritance with me."

Continued in Appendix A, p. 287.
See Appendix A, p. 287, for the other readings.

Reflecting on the Gospel and Living the Paschal Mystery

Key words and phrases from the gospel: loved his own in the world, Unless I wash you . . . no inheritance with me, model to follow, you should also do

To the point: Peter desires to maintain the Master-disciple relationship: "Master, are you going to wash my feet?" Because Jesus "loved his own in the world," he knew the more desirable relationship to preserve is that of serving others in such a way that they grow into the fullness of life. The model Jesus gives us is more even than serving others—it is choosing life. It is seeking the inheritance only Jesus can give.

Reflection: Sometimes it's hard to love another. Little Noah can love his grandparents and aunts and uncles and cousins. That's easy. But when it gets down to loving his little sister, being patient with her, sharing his toys with her, he's not so sure. His little sister makes demands on him. He's the big brother; she should look up to him, but leave him alone. What Noah needs to learn—and he will as he grows and matures—is that loving another means self-giving. Putting ourselves first always breeds resentment, strained relations, being distanced from another. Lack of self-giving diminishes self. On the other hand, the most profound self-giving lifts up both the other and self to new dignity, new life. On this night before he died, Jesus embarks on the most profound acts of self-giving fathomable. And he offers us the most unfathomable life: his own eternal life. Jesus offers others the fullness of life. We are invited to respond by choosing this life Jesus offers.

First, he gave us Food for our disciple journey. But this Food isn't the making of human industry; it is the very bread of his Body and the wine of his Blood. In giving us the Eucharist Jesus gave us Life—he gave his very Body and Blood as a new covenant for our salvation, a new relationship with God based on our receiving the very Life of God. Giving oneself for the sake of another is taken to unprecedented heights; we commune with the Divine by eating and drinking the very Body and Blood of the divine Son. Eucharist is about giving Life and choosing Life.

Second, Jesus (teacher and master) did what only a slave would do. In this act of foot-washing, Jesus showed us a most profound example of self-giving. He did not cling to power, wealth, or divine attributes. He did not cling to the leadership status of being teacher and master. He let go of all this to enter into a whole new relationship with his disciples—he became one with them in their weak, impoverished humanity. This self-giving act profoundly exemplifies for us the extent to which Jesus became one like us. It exemplifies how much Jesus loved life. It exemplifies for us how much Jesus wanted to give us life. It exemplifies for us what Eucharist truly is: self-giving, new relationships, new Life.

This night Jesus showed the depths of his love for humanity: he gave us heavenly Food that promises new and eternal life. This night invites us: "as I have done for you, you should also do." We become truly alive and life-giving by partaking in the heavenly Food which transforms us more perfectly into being members of the Body of Christ. We become truly alive and life-giving by becoming the slave to all by our own self-giving for the sake of others. We become truly alive and life-giving when we choose life by responding to others with dignity, reaching out to those in need, being for others the very presence of our loving God.

Model Penitential Act

Presider: On this night we remember Jesus' great love for us and his desire that we share this love with each other. Let us prepare to celebrate this great mystery by opening ourselves even more to God's love . . . [pause]

Lord Jesus, you love your own in the world: Lord . . .

Christ Jesus, you model for us a life of loving service: Christ . . .

Lord Jesus, you invite us to a share in your eternal inheritance: Lord . . .

Homily Points

- The discussion between Peter and Jesus is not principally about how much or what of Peter's body should be washed, but about choosing life. Choosing life entails getting rid of whatever "dirt" we have accrued that keeps us from faithfully following Jesus. Its fuller meaning, however, demands loving and serving others as Jesus did. His inheritance—eternal Life—is the real choice we make. Holy Thursday is about choosing life: loving and serving others, receiving the Gift of Eucharist Jesus has given us.

- The goal of those who follow Jesus is really not serving others nor even loving, but choosing life. Serving and loving others are the *only* means for achieving the more long-range goal of receiving eternal inheritance.

- We all have "dirty feet" at times! Harmful attitudes, prejudices, unwarranted fears, compulsions, excessive ego-centeredness are all behaviors that lead us away from Jesus. Loving service is the cleansing that expresses our choice for life and promises us a share in Jesus' inheritance. Eucharist strengthens us for this loving service.

Model Universal Prayer (Prayer of the Faithful)

Presider: Let us pray that this Eucharist might strengthen us to walk in the loving service of Jesus.

Response:

Lord,   hear   our prayer.

Cantor:

we pray to the Lord,

That all members of the church choose a life of lovingly serving others as Jesus did . . . [pause]

That all people of the world receive the eternal inheritance promised to those who lovingly serve others . . . [pause]

That those who serve the poor and needy be strengthened in their faithfulness in following Jesus . . . [pause]

That each of us here gathered be drawn closer to Jesus by receiving the Eucharist and sharing the Life we have received . . . [pause]

Presider: Gracious God, you strengthen us by the Gift of Eucharist: help us to love and serve others more faithfully and one day receive eternal inheritance with all the saints. We ask this through Christ our Lord. **Amen.**

COLLECT

Let us pray

Pause for silent prayer

O God, who have called us to participate
in this most sacred Supper,
in which your Only Begotten Son,
when about to hand himself over to death,
entrusted to the Church a sacrifice new for
    all eternity,
the banquet of his love,
grant, we pray,
that we may draw from so great a mystery,
the fullness of charity and of life.
Through our Lord Jesus Christ, your Son,
who lives and reigns with you in the unity
    of the Holy Spirit,
one God, for ever and ever.
Amen.

FOR REFLECTION

- What helps me choose to serve others more lovingly is . . .
- Eucharist gives me life and helps me love more deeply because . . .
- I have chosen life when . . . This choice has helped me experience the inheritance only Jesus can give when . . .

SPIRITUALITY

GOSPEL ACCLAMATION
Phil 2:8-9

Christ became obedient to the point of death,
even death on a cross.
Because of this, God greatly exalted him
and bestowed on him the name which is above
every other name.

Gospel John 18:1–19:42; L40ABC

Jesus went out with his disciples across
the Kidron valley
to where there was a garden,
into which he and his disciples entered.
Judas his betrayer also knew the place,
because Jesus had often met there with
his disciples.
So Judas got a band of soldiers and
guards
from the chief priests and the
Pharisees
and went there with lanterns, torches,
and weapons.
Jesus, knowing everything that was going
to happen to him,
went out and said to them, "Whom are
you looking for?"
They answered him, "Jesus the Nazorean."
He said to them, "I AM."
Judas his betrayer was also with them.
When he said to them, "I AM,"
they turned away and fell to the ground.
So he again asked them,
"Whom are you looking for?"
They said, "Jesus the Nazorean."
Jesus answered,
"I told you that I AM.
So if you are looking for me, let these men
go."
This was to fulfill what he had said,
"I have not lost any of those you gave me."
Then Simon Peter, who had a sword, drew
it,
struck the high priest's slave, and cut off
his right ear.
The slave's name was Malchus.
Jesus said to Peter,
"Put your sword into its scabbard.
Shall I not drink the cup that the Father
gave me?"

Continued in Appendix A, pp. 288–289.
See Appendix A, p. 290, for the other readings.

Reflecting on the Gospel and Living the Paschal Mystery
Key words and phrases from the gospel: I AM, I have not lost any, my kingdom is not here, blood and water flowed out

To the point: No one had power over Jesus: not the Jewish leaders, not even Pilate. He was the Son of God whose "kingdom is not here." He is the divine I AM, one with God who gives life from the very beginning of creation. Humans could take away Jesus' human life ("he was . . . dead"), but could not take away what he came to accomplish: "I have not lost any of those you gave me." Nor could they take away the gift of life and inheritance he assured to those who faithfully follow him. The blood and water that flowed from his pierced side is the new covenant that calls us to choose his life.

Reflection: During the religion class before the Triduum, knowing that the singing of the passion in their parish would be very long for the children, the teacher gave them a concrete challenge. So she explained to them that because the gospel on Good Friday is very special they were to listen carefully and count how many times they heard the word "king." After Easter the children were all excited to tell their teacher how many times. Most didn't get it quite right, but some hit the nail on the head: twelve times. This was the springboard for her to catechize the little ones about Jesus as the King who died for us, but Jesus' kingdom is not like England is a kingdom. His kingdom is wherever we do whatever God asks of us. In turn our King gives us a special gift of life in which we all share now.

By his own humble obedience (see the gospel acclamation), Jesus drank the cup of suffering and passed over from death to life. His Passover opened the gates for us to pass over from mortal humanity to immortality: a share in divine life. Jesus' embrace of death is the ultimate act of throwing his lot in with us humans—he embraced *mortality*, one trait which distinguishes us clearly from God. At the same time that he embraced death he conquered death. John's passion account does not focus on Jesus' suffering, but on his will to bring life. Good Friday is not so much a somber recollection of suffering and death by one Man, as it is the sober remembering that this loving servant of all surrendered himself to death so that all might have life. This divine Son passes over from death to risen life, yet never forsakes us, always beckons us to embrace death and in that embrace choose life.

Each time we sign ourselves with the cross or look upon a cross we've hung upon a wall in our home, we surrender ourselves to the Mystery which enables us to pass over from death to new life. To live this Mystery to the fullest we must obediently become the servant of all as Jesus did. This is really more than a matter of saying yes to the obvious ways to die to self which come our way each day—getting to work on time so the family has the sustenance they need; spending a few minutes of our coffee break to listen to someone who needs to share a difficulty; being patient with the children when they need our attention. To live this Mystery well means that we surrender ourselves to do as Jesus did—die to self for the sake of others. We actually *look for* ways to embrace death, to be self-giving, to die to self. This is how we live. This is how we choose life.

Homily Points

• When we hear the voice on a GPS device say, "Recalculating," we feel both alarm and confident hope. Alarm, because it means we missed a turn which puts us in unfamiliar territory. Confident hope, because experience has taught us that the new directions will get us back on track to our destination. Hearing and following Jesus' voice brings to us confident hope that we will reach our final destination of life. This is what we celebrate on Good Friday.

• Facing death, Jesus is still caught up in giving life. Through his death his kingdom was established, new life was given, and eternal inheritance gained (first reading: "he shall see his descendants in a long life"; second reading: "he became the source of eternal salvation"). His death, rather than an end, was a beginning—a new covenant for those who hear his voice and choose his life. This is what we celebrate on Good Friday.

Suggestions for Music

Singing the solemn intercessions: Just as the Easter Vigil is the mother of all vigils, so the Good Friday solemn intercessions are the mother and model of all general intercessions. Because of their solemnity they are meant to be sung, using the simple chant given in *The Roman Missal*, and to include short periods of silent prayer after each statement of intention. If it is not possible that these intercessions be sung, they should be spoken with solemnity, with time allowed for the appropriate silent pauses.

Music during the adoration of the cross: As the title —"Adoration of the Holy Cross"— of this part of the Good Friday liturgy indicates, what we honor in this procession is not the One crucified but the *cross* which embodies the mystery of his—and our—redemptive triumph over sin and death. Because we are not *historicizing* nor *reenacting* a past event, but *ritualizing* the meaning of this event for our lives here and now, this procession is not one of sorrow or expiation but of gratitude, of triumph, and of quiet and confident acceptance (the very sentiments expressed in the responsorial psalm).

The music during this procession needs, then, to sing about the mystery and triumph of the cross rather than about the details of Jesus' suffering and death. Examples of appropriate music include "We Acclaim the Cross of Jesus"; "O Cross of Christ, Immortal Tree"; "Behold, Before Our Wond'ring Eyes"; and Francis Patrick O'Brien's "Tree of Life and Glory" (GIA G-5452). Steve Janco's choral setting of the entrance antiphon for Holy Thursday ("Glory In the Cross," GIA-4213), Gerard Chiusano's setting ("We Should Glory in the Cross," OCP 10884), or Ricky Manalo's setting ("We Should Glory in the Cross," OCP 11355CC) would be an excellent piece to sing with choir leading. If already sung as part of the Holy Thursday liturgy, repeating it would express the unity of these celebrations.

COLLECT

Let us pray

Pause for silent prayer

Remember your mercies, O Lord,
and with your eternal protection sanctify
　　your servants,
for whom Christ your Son,
by the shedding of his Blood,
established the Paschal Mystery.
Who lives and reigns for ever and ever.
Amen.

FOR REFLECTION

• I feel lost and alienated from Jesus when . . . What brings me to new life is . . .

• What helps me be faithful to my baptismal covenant is . . .

• What I appreciate about Jesus' gift of life to me is . . . I express this in my life in these ways . . .

✝ SPIRITUALITY

Gospel Luke 24:1-12; L41ABC

At daybreak on the first day of the week
  the women who had come from
    Galilee with Jesus
  took the spices they had prepared
  and went to the tomb.
They found the stone rolled
    away from the tomb;
  but when they entered,
  they did not find the body of
    the Lord Jesus.
While they were puzzling over
    this, behold,
  two men in dazzling garments
    appeared to them.
They were terrified and bowed
    their faces to the ground.
They said to them,
  "Why do you seek the living
    one among the dead?
He is not here, but he has been
    raised.
Remember what he said to you while
    he was still in Galilee,
  that the Son of Man must be handed
      over to sinners
  and be crucified, and rise on the
    third day."
And they remembered his words.
Then they returned from the tomb
  and announced all these things to the
    eleven
  and to all the others.
The women were Mary Magdalene,
    Joanna, and Mary the mother of
    James;
  the others who accompanied them
    also told this to the apostles,
  but their story seemed like nonsense
  and they did not believe them.
But Peter got up and ran to the tomb,
  bent down, and saw the burial cloths
    alone;
  then he went home amazed at what
    had happened.

Readings continued in Appendix A, pp. 291–296.

Reflecting on the Gospel and Living the Paschal Mystery
Key words and phrases from the gospel: did not find the body, he has been raised, rise on the third day, burial cloths alone, went home amazed

To the point: The disciples "did not believe" the women's announcement about what they had found. Peter, not relying on the women's testimony, went to the tomb to see for himself and was amazed. What amazed Peter? The empty tomb? The burial cloths lying there without a body? Or, perhaps, the hope against hope that Jesus' promise that he would "rise on the third day" was realized. Peter's amazement points to a soon-to-be-fulfilled expectation that he would encounter an alive Jesus. Our own Easter amazement must also bring us to an expectation of new Life through an encounter with the risen Lord. The women "went to the tomb" to seek the dead but found the Living. So must we.

Reflection: This is the night when we sing out with full voice our Easter alleluias. Yes, this is the night when we come to the deepest conviction about who we are: those united with their risen Lord, ringing out our *Gloria*, so mindful that on this night we celebrate death's giving way to life.

As we listen to an Easter gospel proclamation for the first time this year, we might remember Jesus' words, too, and be "amazed at what had happened" (gospel). We have heard over and over that dying is the way to life. Now, on this night, we remember how true this is. Yes, we are reminded about the utter truth of Jesus' words: he will die and in three days rise. We are eager to celebrate our own risen life in Christ. We are awed as we celebrate during this night the consummate identity of who Jesus is: the man who died and was raised up three days later. We are delighted as we celebrate our own identity: the baptized ones who have been plunged into Christ's death so that we might share in his risen life. This night, like no other, bids us to choose life.

We sing our alleluias during this night with joy in our hearts because Christ is risen from the dead. But no small part of our alleluias comes from the joy we receive by sharing in Christ's life. As members of his Body, we share in his identity, his life. This is a night when we come face to face with who Christ is and a challenge to become more perfectly that risen life for others. This is a night when we learn through darkness giving way to light, from readings of promise giving way to a proclamation of victory, that new life is ours who choose it.

As the women in the gospel were terrified and questioned and remembered and announced, we find ourselves struggling with the same sentiments. Even as we celebrate Easter the immensity of the mystery is not easy to grasp. We, too, struggle with "seek[ing] the living one among the dead." Perhaps part of our struggle comes because risen life—immortality—is outside of our ordinary human experience. Yet the risen One has promised: for those who love, new life is theirs.

As we sing alleluia during this night and throughout our Easter celebration, we remember that our alleluia can be true only if we conform our life to Christ's. To do so means that even in this season of celebrating risen life, we also remember that our share in this life only comes by self-giving. We find life in dying to self. We share life in loving others. We come to the fullness of life when we do as Jesus did. The Easter invitation is to choose life. Alleluia!

Homily Points

• What amazes us? A beautiful sunset. An act of superhuman strength that saves someone's life. An insight that leads to a breakthrough for new understanding. Can any of us be prepared for what amazed Peter on that first Easter? What led these disciples from unbelief to belief was an actual encounter with risen Life.

• Our Easter celebration calls us to seek to strengthen our belief that new Life comes from an empty tomb. Our Easter celebration calls us to seek encounters with the risen Lord and believing that we in turn can be that presence of new Life for others. Our Easter amazement does not center so much on whether or not we believe in Jesus' resurrection—we do! Our amazement is over the fact that we can encounter the risen Lord ourselves, that Jesus' new life is our own Life, and that he works through us to bring his risen Life to others.

Model Universal Prayer (Prayer of the Faithful)

Presider: On this night when we celebrate the risen life of our Savior, Jesus Christ, we pray for our church and world that all might share in the gift of new life.

Response:

Lord, hear our prayer.

Cantor:

we pray to the Lord,

That the church might always light the way to new life for all who come seeking the risen Christ . . . [pause]

That all peoples of the world strive ever more diligently to live worthy of the salvation offered by God . . . [pause]

That all those whose lives are darkened by poverty, sickness, anxiety, or uncertainty might find peace in the new life offered at Easter . . . [pause]

That all of us here celebrate our Easter joy by faithfully living as those filled with the life of Christ . . . [pause]

Presider: God of life, you raised your divine Son to new life: hear our prayers that we might share forever that same risen life. We pray through the risen Son, Jesus Christ our Lord. **Amen.**

COLLECT
Let us pray

Pause for silent prayer

O God, who make this most sacred night
    radiant
with the glory of the Lord's Resurrection,
stir up in your Church a spirit of adoption,
so that, renewed in body and mind,
we may render you undivided service.
Through our Lord Jesus Christ, your Son,
who lives and reigns with you in the unity
    of the Holy Spirit,
one God, for ever and ever.
Amen.

FOR REFLECTION

• I am amazed at Jesus' presence and offer of new life when . . .

• My expectations about life are . . . Jesus' risen life leads me to expect . . .

• How I have experienced risen life in me is . . . What it means to me to be the living presence of the risen Christ in the world is . . .

SPIRITUALITY

GOSPEL ACCLAMATION
cf. 1 Cor 5:7b-8a

℞. Alleluia, alleluia.
Christ, our paschal lamb, has been sacrificed;
let us then feast with joy in the Lord.
℞. Alleluia, alleluia.

Gospel

John 20:1-9; L42ABC

On the first day of the week,
  Mary of Magdala came to the
    tomb early in the morning,
  while it was still dark,
  and saw the stone removed from
    the tomb.
So she ran and went to Simon Peter
  and to the other disciple whom
    Jesus loved, and told them,
  "They have taken the Lord from
    the tomb,
  and we don't know where they put him."
So Peter and the other disciple went out
  and came to the tomb.
They both ran, but the other disciple ran
    faster than Peter
  and arrived at the tomb first;
  he bent down and saw the burial cloths
    there, but did not go in.
When Simon Peter arrived after him,
  he went into the tomb and saw the
    burial cloths there,
  and the cloth that had covered his head,
  not with the burial cloths but rolled up
    in a separate place.
Then the other disciple also went in,
  the one who had arrived at the tomb
    first,
  and he saw and believed.
For they did not yet understand the
    Scripture
  that he had to rise from the dead.

or

Luke 24:1-12; L41C *in Appendix A, p. 297*

or, at an afternoon or evening Mass

Luke 24:13-35; L46 *in Appendix A, p. 297.*

See Appendix A, p. 298, for the other readings.

Reflecting on the Gospel and Living the Paschal Mystery

Key words and phrases from the gospel: came to the tomb, early in the morning, stone removed from the tomb, taken the Lord from the tomb, came to the tomb, arrived at the tomb, went into the tomb, arrived at the tomb, had to rise from the dead

To the point: Mary arose "early in the morning" to go to Jesus' tomb. This image of a new day speaks to us of a new beginning, new opportunities, new encounters. Early morning speaks to us of the freshness of new life. By contrast, this gospel uses the word "tomb" seven times, speaking to us about the seeming finality of Jesus' death. By even greater contrast, the gospel ends with the Scripture certitude that Jesus "*had* to rise from the dead" (emphasis added). Death is overcome. Death has no victory. God is the Lord of life. Easter celebrates a new beginning, our certitude of new life. May we choose that Life.

Reflection: The whimsical saying has it that the only thing of which we are certain is dying and paying taxes. Not true! This Easter morning gospel tells us of a far more reliable and important certitude: Jesus "*had* to rise from the dead" (emphasis added). Herein is the paradox of the resurrection: we believe but do not understand. We believe because we encounter the risen Lord in our good works and in the holiness of each other, because we experience the nearness of our loved ones who have died, because we see the recurring newness of life all around us. This gospel shows the extent to which Jesus' resurrection calls all of us to examine the deepest truth about ourselves, our most intensified act of self-giving: Jesus' resurrection calls us to surrender misunderstanding to belief, to give ourselves over to the life Jesus offers us. In Christ we are all members of his Body, we all share in his risen life. After the resurrection the one thing that matters is that we surrender our all (even as Christ surrendered his all) to the Father and Christ, who clothe us with an identity beyond our just deserts.

The resurrection is a mystery which we can never understand but only believe. This mystery takes us beyond all which is familiar to us—the certitude of our everyday living—to a realm where God's glory and majesty and power lift us up to a share in the new dignity of risen life. Easter is a celebration of Jesus' taking his rightful place in the divine kingdom of his Father where the truth of his divine being is known. Easter is also a celebration whereby we ourselves acknowledge who Christ really is—the One who shared in our humanity even to the point of accepting death, but who conquered death to raise us up to a share in his life. The tomb has no finality, really. The final word is risen life. In Jesus Christ death is overcome. In Jesus Christ each of us is invited to share in immortality—the gift of risen life.

This new life and dignity isn't something which can be measured or calculated or grasped. It is a freely given gift by the Divine One who has loved us from the beginning of creation, who breathed life into us, and who continues to beckon us to grow into the fullness of life. In the morning we see the freshness of the dew fall, the glory of a risen sun, the clean smell of fresh beginnings, the sweet sounds of people waking to new beginnings, new certitude, new life. Easter beckons us to choose this life, this being with the risen One, this Alleluia that rings out our certitude in the God of love who gives us life.

Model Penitential Act

Presider: Today is the day for which we've been preparing during Lent; today is the day we celebrate Jesus' risen life. Let us pause to acknowledge God's gracious mercy to us and open ourselves to God's offer of new life . . . [pause]

Lord Jesus, you were raised from the dead: Lord . . .

Christ Jesus, you conquered sin and death: Christ . . .

Lord Jesus, you share your new life with us at this banquet: Lord . . .

Homily Points

• New schools promise new friends; new work promises new skills being tested; a new book opens up new vistas; a new movie brings new enjoyment; a new car brings new ventures. New is good. But these "news" are nothing like the new that Easter promises. This new is very good.

• The Easter mystery does not unfold all at once. This Easter gospel still is only teasing us about Jesus' resurrection. We still are preoccupied with the empty tomb. We still have not actually encountered the risen Jesus. But we have—when another comes to our aid, when an unexpected opportunity for growth in grace falls in our lap, when someone gives us hope and new direction. Appropriating these and other such new things that come our way every day is how we encounter the risen Lord. Is how we choose Life. This newness of life is very good.

Model Universal Prayer (Prayer of the Faithful)

Presider: On this joyous day of celebrating risen life, we pray to the Lord of life for our needs.

Response:

Lord,   hear   our prayer.

Cantor:

we pray to the Lord,

That all members of the church might witness through word and deed to the new life God offers us in the risen Christ . . . [pause]

That all people of the world share in the joy of the new life of salvation . . . [pause]

That those whose lives are diminished by poverty and oppression might come to the fullness of life . . . [pause]

That all of us here encounter the risen Christ in the joy and goodness of others and continue to choose new life . . . [pause]

Presider: God of life, you raised up your divine Son on that first Easter: hear these our prayers that our Easter joy might be completed one day when we share in your everlasting life. We ask this through the risen Son, Jesus Christ our Lord. **Amen.**

COLLECT

Let us pray

Pause for silent prayer

O God, who on this day,
through your Only Begotten Son,
have conquered death
and unlocked for us the path to eternity,
grant, we pray, that we who keep
the solemnity of the Lord's Resurrection
may, through the renewal brought by your
   Spirit,
rise up in the light of life.
Through our Lord Jesus Christ, your Son,
who lives and reigns with you in the unity
   of the Holy Spirit,
one God, for ever and ever.
Amen.

FOR REFLECTION

• The "tombs" of my life are . . . What promises me new life is . . .

• Jesus had to rise from the dead because . . .

• I choose new beginnings when . . . new opportunities when . . . new encounters when . . . new life when . . .

Easter Time

✠ SPIRITUALITY

GOSPEL ACCLAMATION
John 20:29

R∕. Alleluia, alleluia.
You believe in me, Thomas, because you have
     seen me, says the Lord;
blessed are those who have not seen
     me, but still believe!
R∕. Alleluia, alleluia.

Gospel John 20:19-31; L45C

On the evening of that first
     day of the week,
  when the doors were
       locked, where the
       disciples were,
  for fear of the Jews,
  Jesus came and stood in their
       midst
  and said to them, "Peace be with you."
When he had said this, he showed them
     his hands and his side.
The disciples rejoiced when they saw the
     Lord.
Jesus said to them again, "Peace be with
     you.
As the Father has sent me, so I send you."
And when he had said this, he breathed on
     them and said to them,
  "Receive the Holy Spirit.
Whose sins you forgive are forgiven them,
     and whose sins you retain are retained."

Thomas, called Didymus, one of the
     Twelve,
  was not with them when Jesus came.
So the other disciples said to him, "We
     have seen the Lord."
But he said to them,
  "Unless I see the mark of the nails in
       his hands
  and put my finger into the nailmarks
  and put my hand into his side, I will not
       believe."

Now a week later his disciples were again
     inside
  and Thomas was with them.
Jesus came, although the doors were locked,
  and stood in their midst and said,
       "Peace be with you."

Continued in Appendix A, p. 298.

Reflecting on the Gospel

The disciples cowered behind locked doors, fearful that Jesus' fate would be theirs. We, too, often cower behind locked doors—locked minds, locked hearts—and are fearful of stepping into the unknown, often holding ourselves back from new experiences, new joys, new life. Easter is a time for new life. It is a time to break out of whatever locks us in and rejoice at the new life given to us. We must venture out to live in the new freedom of the resurrection. We must rejoice because we, too, can see the Lord.

What did the disciples *see* that brought them to rejoice? His wounds assured them that this was the Jesus they had seen die, the Jesus with whom they had walked the roads of Galilee, the Jesus with whom they had eaten, the Jesus who taught and encouraged them. His wounds established his identity. His tangible presence in their midst assured them that the Jesus they see now is the familiar Jesus they know; he has come back from death to new life. Yet this Jesus is also different; his presence to the disciples established his risen identity.

The disciples believed because they saw the Lord. We believe because we see the "signs and wonders" (first reading) of God's presence. We see and experience forgiveness, healing, peace, love exchanged, joy and laughter, beauty and growth, play and leisure, life lived to the fullest. Even now the risen Jesus continues to stand in the midst of the world through the "signs and wonders" worked by us who are his disciples. The risen Jesus gives his new life to us and sends us forth as his disciples. So what do others now *see* that brings them to rejoice? The risen presence of Christ in and through us.

Our Easter alleluia isn't simply a song on our lips during these weeks of Easter. It is a song in our hearts which spills out in the way we relate to others in being the risen Christ for them. Alleluia is the song of our lives which, like Jesus, brings new life to others. Alleluia is the song of our belief which calls others to utter "My Lord and my God!"

Living the Paschal Mystery

Everything Jesus did the apostles did—forgave, preached, taught, healed, added numbers to the follower-believers. Today the church brings the presence of the risen Jesus to others, and we are the church. Perhaps not in stupendous ways, but in our own simple, everyday acts we, too, do what Jesus did. Faithful disciples are Jesus' persistent presence in today's world.

We forgive when we see and treat someone who has hurt us as the risen Christ. We preach when we share with our young ones the gospels and the Christian way to live a Gospel life. We teach when we live in ways which clearly put the other ahead of ourselves, ways which speak of self-sacrificing for the good of others. We heal when we touch others physically or emotionally or psychologically, helping them realize that they are not alone but have a community to support and encourage them. It's in the moment-by-moment every-day things—even changing a diaper with a caress or being more patient with the inevitable endless bother of everyday nitty-gritty living—that we witness that we have seen the Lord.

God doesn't ask us to be heroes in our witnessing to resurrection faith and bringing Jesus' presence to others. God only asks that we be as alive to new, Easter life as was the Jesus who showed the disciples his hands and side.

Focusing the Gospel

Key words and phrases: stood in their midst, showed them his hands and his side, disciples rejoiced, I send you, We have seen the Lord

To the point: What did the disciples *see* that brought them to rejoice? His wounds assured them that this was the Jesus they had seen die. His tangible presence in their midst assured them that the Jesus they see now has come back from death to new life. The risen Jesus gives this new life to us and sends us forth as his disciples. So what do others now *see* that brings them to rejoice? The risen presence of Christ in and through us.

Connecting the Gospel

to the first reading: The risen Jesus continues to be seen through the "signs and wonders" worked by those who are his disciples.

to experience: The "signs and wonders" which reveal the presence of the risen Christ stretch far beyond miraculous healings. People see the risen Christ also in our everyday acts of kindness, sensitivity, generosity, patience, and forgiveness.

Connecting the Responsorial Psalm

to the readings: The psalmist in Psalm 118 invites an ever-widening circle to join in praising God for mercy and deliverance. This is our mission as the risen Body of Christ, to "[w]rite down what [we] have seen, and what is happening, and what will happen afterwards" (second reading). What has happened and will continue to happen is God's victory over death (second reading), disease (first reading), and sin (gospel). God takes what is flawed, useless, and inconsequential—the rejected stone (psalm), our failing lives (psalm), our diseased bodies (first reading), our doubting hearts (gospel)—and makes them the cornerstone of faith and forgiveness. This is resurrection, done "by the Lord" and "wonderful in our eyes." And it happens every day in "signs and wonders" (first reading) both great and small. For this, let us "[g]ive thanks to the Lord" (psalm refrain).

to psalmist preparation: In singing Psalm 118 you call the church to recognize and give thanks for the enduring mercy of God. You can only give a "joyful shout" because you have had personal experience of God's saving intervention, because you have been "hard pressed and falling" and known God's help. What story will you be telling when you sing?

**ASSEMBLY &
FAITH-SHARING GROUPS**
- I see the risen Christ in these persons . . . I show the risen presence of Christ to others when I . . .
- For me, new and risen life is . . .
- If I were to write an Easter gospel, signs of Christ's resurrection I would highlight are . . .

PRESIDERS
Christ's risen life shines through my ministry whenever I . . .

DEACONS
The "signs and wonders" my ministry calls me to bring about are . . .

HOSPITALITY MINISTERS
The manner of my greeting others shows the presence of the risen Christ when I . . .

MUSIC MINISTERS
The joy of my singing helps others rejoice in the presence of the risen Christ when I . . .

ALTAR MINISTERS
Others recognize the presence of the risen Christ in me when I serve in this way . . .

LECTORS
The "signs and wonders" (first reading) of Christ's resurrection which are manifested in my daily living are . . . This makes a difference in my proclamation by . . .

**EXTRAORDINARY MINISTERS
OF HOLY COMMUNION**
My ministry calls me beyond distributing the Body and Blood of Christ to living as the risen Christ in that . . .

Model Rite of Blessing and Sprinkling of Water

Presider: We are a people baptized into Christ's death and resurrection. As we ask God to bless this water, let it remind us of our baptism and of the presence of the risen Christ within us and among us . . . [pause]

> *[continue with the third choice, "during Easter time," for the blessing of water]*

Homily Points

• Some things are proven through scientific evidence (for example, the effectiveness of a new medication); others are proven through human behavior and character (for example, a person proves trustworthiness because of the way he or she acts). Still other things cannot be proved tangibly but are simply accepted on faith (for example, unexplained recovery from terminal illness). The resurrection cannot be proved, yet it is ever evident in the lives of faithful disciples.

• Before he would believe, Thomas sought tangible proof that Jesus was alive by demanding to touch his wounds. Jesus accommodated him, then went on to say, "Blessed are those who have not seen and have believed." We are the blessed who do not see Jesus as Thomas and the other disciples did, but truly come in touch with the risen Jesus through the lives of those who do believe and live accordingly.

• "What you see is what you get." When others see us, do they "get" an encounter with the risen Christ? Being a living presence of the living Jesus is expressed in everyday acts that bring new life and hope to others. For example, encouraging the discouraged, nourishing the hungry, forgiving and reconciling with those who have hurt us, confronting injustice with courage, listening to another's heartaches. In all these and countless other ways are we making tangible the risen presence of Christ. We are the living proof of the resurrection.

Model Universal Prayer (Prayer of the Faithful)

Presider: Believing in the power of the risen Christ, we confidently ask for what we need.

Response:

Lord, hear our prayer.

Cantor:

we pray to the Lord,

That all members of the church grow into the fullness of life promised to those who believe . . . [pause]

That all peoples of the world receive the salvation assured by Jesus' rising from the dead . . . [pause]

That those suffering from diminishment of life be comforted by Christ's promise of fullness of risen life . . . [pause]

That we here assembled may witness to risen life through the good works we do . . . [pause]

Presider: Ever-present God, you raised your Son to new life: hear these our prayers that we may be filled with the life of your Spirit. We ask this through your risen Son, Jesus Christ our Lord. **Amen.**

COLLECT

Let us pray

Pause for silent prayer

God of everlasting mercy,
who in the very recurrence of the paschal feast
kindle the faith of the people you have made your own,
increase, we pray, the grace you have bestowed,
that all may grasp and rightly understand
in what font they have been washed,
by whose Spirit they have been reborn,
by whose Blood they have been redeemed.
Through our Lord Jesus Christ, your Son,
who lives and reigns with you in the unity of the Holy Spirit,
one God, for ever and ever. **Amen.**

FIRST READING
Acts 5:12-16

Many signs and wonders were done among the people
    at the hands of the apostles.
They were all together in Solomon's portico.
None of the others dared to join them, but the people esteemed them.
Yet more than ever, believers in the Lord,
    great numbers of men and women, were added to them.
Thus they even carried the sick out into the streets
    and laid them on cots and mats
    so that when Peter came by,
    at least his shadow might fall on one or another of them.
A large number of people from the towns in the vicinity of Jerusalem also gathered,
    bringing the sick and those disturbed by unclean spirits,
    and they were all cured.

RESPONSORIAL PSALM
Ps 118:2-4, 13-15, 22-24

℞. (1) Give thanks to the Lord for he is good, his love is everlasting.
    or:
℞. Alleluia.

Let the house of Israel say,
    "His mercy endures forever."
Let the house of Aaron say,
    "His mercy endures forever."
Let those who fear the LORD say,
    "His mercy endures forever."

℞. Give thanks to the Lord for he is good, his love is everlasting.
    or:
℞. Alleluia.

I was hard pressed and was falling,
    but the LORD helped me.
My strength and my courage is the LORD,
    and he has been my savior.
The joyful shout of victory
    in the tents of the just:

R7. Give thanks to the Lord for he is good,
his love is everlasting.
    or:
R7. Alleluia.

The stone which the builders rejected
    has become the cornerstone.
By the LORD has this been done;
    it is wonderful in our eyes.
This is the day the LORD has made;
    let us be glad and rejoice in it.

R7. Give thanks to the Lord for he is good,
his love is everlasting.
    or:
R7. Alleluia.

SECOND READING
Rev 1:9-11a, 12-13, 17-19

I, John, your brother, who share with you
    the distress, the kingdom, and the
        endurance we have in Jesus,
    found myself on the island called
        Patmos
    because I proclaimed God's word and
        gave testimony to Jesus.
I was caught up in spirit on the Lord's day
    and heard behind me a voice as loud as
        a trumpet, which said,
    "Write on a scroll what you see."
Then I turned to see whose voice it was
    that spoke to me,
    and when I turned, I saw seven gold
        lampstands
    and in the midst of the lampstands one
        like a son of man,
    wearing an ankle-length robe, with a
        gold sash around his chest.

When I caught sight of him, I fell down at
    his feet as though dead.
He touched me with his right hand and
    said, "Do not be afraid.
I am the first and the last, the one who
    lives.
Once I was dead, but now I am alive
    forever and ever.
I hold the keys to death and the
    netherworld.
Write down, therefore, what you have
    seen,
    and what is happening, and what will
        happen afterwards."

About Liturgy

Easter octaves: Easter really has two octaves. One is the eight-day octave that this second Sunday of Easter concludes, a solemn and sustained celebration of Jesus' resurrection. The other is the fifty-day octave (seven weeks of seven days plus one; $7 \times 7 + 1 = 50$) that is sometimes called "the great octave" which concludes on Pentecost. Even the eight days of solemnities just concluded are not sufficient to plumb the depths of the Easter mystery. And so the church gives an even longer period of time to celebrate—this great octave.

Each day of the first week of Easter has the rank of solemnity. Beyond that week, however, even though the church celebrates all these fifty days as the Easter season, the weekdays no longer have the rank of solemnity. We must be careful, however, that these days don't just become like other days in the liturgical year. They are still days in the Easter season. The joyous festivity, the beautiful sacred space, the ringing alleluias must continue all the way to Pentecost.

We are given these two octaves so that we might truly embrace the Easter mystery: Christ is alive and shares that risen life with each of us. Now is our time to encounter the risen Jesus in new ways so that we can continue throughout the year to be that risen presence for the good of others.

About Liturgical Music

Music suggestions: In all three Lectionary years the gospel readings for the weeks of Easter carry the same progression. The first three weeks relate appearance stories (Christ truly has risen from the dead); the fourth Sunday presents Christ as the Good Shepherd; and the last weeks, including Pentecost, deal with our call to participate in the mission of the risen Christ.

The hymns we sing over the course of the Sundays of Easter are an effective means of reinforcing the thematic progression which unfolds in these Lectionary readings. The first three Sundays call for hymns which allow us simply to exult over Christ's resurrection (most Easter hymns fall into this category). On the fourth Sunday we need to sing songs which assure us of Christ's ongoing presence, of his tender nurturance, of his active support as we strive to live out our discipleship, hymns such as "The King of Love My Shepherd Is" and Ralph Wright's "Sing of One Who Walks Beside Us" (in *Hymnal for the Hours*, GIA). For the final Sundays we need to sing texts that call us to our mission of bringing Christ's risen life to all people, such as "We Know That Christ Is Raised"; "Christ is Alive"; "Now We Remain"; and "Go to the World."

SPIRITUALITY

GOSPEL ACCLAMATION
John 1:14ab

The Word became flesh and made his dwelling
   among us
and we saw his glory.

Gospel   Luke 1:26-38; L545

The angel Gabriel was sent from God
   to a town of Galilee called Nazareth,
   to a virgin betrothed to a man named
      Joseph,
   of the house of David,
   and the virgin's name was Mary.
And coming to her, he said,
   "Hail, full of grace! The Lord is
      with you."
But she was greatly troubled at what
      was said
   and pondered what sort of greet-
      ing this might be.
Then the angel said to her,
   "Do not be afraid, Mary,
   for you have found favor with God.
Behold, you will conceive in your
      womb and bear a son,
   and you shall name him Jesus.
He will be great and will be called Son of
      the Most High,
   and the Lord God will give him the throne
      of David his father,
   and he will rule over the house of Jacob
      forever,
   and of his Kingdom there will be no end."
But Mary said to the angel,
   "How can this be,
   since I have no relations with a man?"
And the angel said to her in reply,
   "The Holy Spirit will come upon you,
   and the power of the Most High will over-
      shadow you.
Therefore the child to be born
   will be called holy, the Son of God.
And behold, Elizabeth, your relative,
   has also conceived a son in her old age,
   and this is the sixth month for her who
      was called barren;
   for nothing will be impossible for God."
Mary said, "Behold, I am the handmaid of
      the Lord.
May it be done to me according to your word."
Then the angel departed from her.

See Appendix A, p. 299, for the other readings.

Reflecting on the Gospel

When we first meet someone and spend time getting to know each other, the tendency is to turn to what we *do*. We tend to inquire about job, education, family, recreational interests. Seldom do we inquire about who someone *is*. If we would ask, "Who are you?" we would probably get a blank stare. We tend to self-identify with what is at hand, what is visible, what is easily grasped: what we do, what interests us, what motivates us. Yet, as the relationship grows and deepens, gradually we begin to get a sense of *who* each other is: honest, trustworthy, faithful, loving, caring. Sometimes, over years of relationship, we might even begin to get a sense of the other's spiritual depth, grow in appreciation that they are holy. But, most likely, if we would share this with the other, it would be denied. "Me, holy? Oh, no!" So we can readily identify with Mary's response to the angel Gabriel's greeting her as someone who is holy. She was "greatly troubled." Wouldn't we all be?

The annunciation by the angel Gabriel to Mary that she would conceive the "Son of God" unleashed unprecedented events, much more than even the incarnation of the "Son of God." Yes, Mary is troubled, for she is addressed as no other human being before her: she is hailed as one "full of grace." Mary already fully participates in the Life of the One who "will be called holy, the Son of God" through the power of the Holy Spirit. So do we share in that same Life, by that same power by that same Spirit. This is our annunciation day, too.

This solemnity of the Annunciation of the Lord is an important festival marking much more than the beginning of Jesus' human life. It inaugurates in a "physical" way a unique relationship to God that humankind can now enjoy. The collect for this Mass asks God to grant that we "may merit to become partakers even in his divine nature." This is the other side of the mystery of the Incarnation. Jesus was conceived in the womb of the Virgin Mary by the power of the Holy Spirit. He took on the "reality of human flesh" (collect) in order to become one like us in all things except sin. By this act of self-emptying, the "holy [One], the Son of God," raises us up to share in God's Life, God's holiness. Yes, this is our annunciation day, too.

Living the Paschal Mystery

Jesus' willing obedience to his Father "consecrates" us (second reading) to a unique relationship with God, a relationship of holiness, of sharing in God's very Life. In baptism we are anointed by the Holy Spirit ("consecrated") to be members of the Body of Christ. So we receive a self-identity that involves a unique, new relationship with God.

God's gift of Life, our holiness, does have its demands. The paschal mystery always reminds us that there is no life except through death. As Mary had to die to her own expectations in saying yes to God, so must we. This means, in practical terms, that we allow our yes for the good of others to guide us into new and unexpected paths to deeper holiness. Each time we say yes we are placing our own trust in God and placing ourselves at God's disposal for bringing about salvation. We, too, might be "greatly troubled" in the face of the demands of living God's Life, a life of holiness. What enables us, like Mary, to be faithful is an intimate relationship with the divine Son who shares our "reality of human flesh." The Son knows the challenges of living God's will. And he sends the Spirit to overshadow us, too, so that we might be faithful—be holy—as was his Mother.

Focusing the Gospel

Key words and phrases: Hail, full of grace!; greatly troubled at what was said; Holy Spirit will come upon you; child . . . will be called holy

To the point: The annunciation by the angel Gabriel to Mary that she would conceive the "Son of God" unleashed unprecedented events, much more than even the incarnation of the "Son of God." Mary is troubled, for she is addressed as no other human being before her: she is hailed as one "full of grace." Mary already participates in the Life of the One who "will be called holy, the Son of God" through the power of the Holy Spirit. So do we share in that same Life, by that same power by that same Spirit. This is our annunciation day, too.

Model Penitential Act

Presider: Mary said yes to doing God's will; she said yes to being holy. As we prepare for this liturgy, let us open ourselves to the holiness God offers us . . . [pause]

> Lord Jesus, you were conceived in the womb of the Virgin Mary: Lord . . .
> Christ Jesus, you are the holy One, the Son of God: Christ . . .
> Lord Jesus, you invite us to share your Life and holiness: Lord . . .

Model Universal Prayer (Prayer of the Faithful)

Presider: God showed unbounded love for us when Jesus was conceived by the Holy Spirit, and made possible for us a share in divine Life. With this same love God hears our prayers.

Response:

Lord, hear our prayer.

Cantor:

we pray to the Lord,

That all members of the church live the holiness to which we are called . . . [pause]

That the leaders of nations be guided by the Spirit in all they do . . . [pause]

That the lonely find relationships of love and support . . . [pause]

That we here gathered faithfully imitate Mary in our response, "I come to do your will" . . . [pause]

Presider: Loving God, you hear the prayers of your holy children: may we always be faithful to doing your will so that one day we may enjoy Life with you for ever. We ask this through Christ our Lord. **Amen.**

COLLECT
Let us pray

Pause for silent prayer

O God, who willed that your Word
should take on the reality of human flesh
in the womb of the Virgin Mary,
grant, we pray,
that we, who confess our Redeemer to be
    God and man,
may merit to become partakers even in his
    divine nature.
Who lives and reigns with you in the unity
    of the Holy Spirit,
one God, for ever and ever. **Amen.**

FOR REFLECTION
- What it means to me to be overshadowed by the Holy Spirit and share in God's Life of holiness is . . .
- I am troubled about my holiness when . . .
- I am an "angel" helping others live their holiness when I . . .

Homily Points

• In these tough times, we are troubled about many things: job security, paying the bills, planning for retirement, instilling values in the children, the irresponsible use of our limited natural resources. This solemnity of the Annunciation of the Lord invites us to be troubled about something else. This festival reminds us that, like the divine Son and like Mary, we are "full of grace," we are overshadowed by the Holy Spirit, we are holy.

• We are holy because Jesus is holy. We do not earn holiness by doing good deeds, but our good deeds—our care and concern for others—is a concrete expression of our holiness, our relationship with God. We celebrate this day Jesus being made flesh in the womb of the Virgin Mary by the power of the Holy Spirit. We also celebrate this day Jesus being made flesh in our own lives by our faithful living of the divine Life that was first given us in baptism and continues to grow in us as we, like Mary, say yes to God in all we do.

✠ SPIRITUALITY

GOSPEL ACCLAMATION

℟. Alleluia, alleluia.
Christ is risen, creator of all;
he has shown pity on all people.
℟. Alleluia, alleluia.

Gospel   John 21:1-19; L48C

At that time, Jesus revealed himself
    again to his disciples at the Sea of
    Tiberias.
He revealed himself in this way.
Together were Simon Peter, Thomas
    called Didymus,
    Nathanael from Cana in Galilee,
    Zebedee's sons, and two others
    of his disciples.
Simon Peter said to them, "I am
    going fishing."
They said to him, "We also will
    come with you."
So they went out and got into the
    boat,
    but that night they caught nothing.
When it was already dawn, Jesus was
    standing on the shore;
    but the disciples did not realize that it
        was Jesus.
Jesus said to them, "Children, have you
    caught anything to eat?"
They answered him, "No."
So he said to them, "Cast the net over the
    right side of the boat
    and you will find something."
So they cast it, and were not able to pull
    it in
    because of the number of fish.
So the disciple whom Jesus loved said to
    Peter, "It is the Lord."
When Simon Peter heard that it was the
    Lord,
    he tucked in his garment, for he was
        lightly clad,
    and jumped into the sea.
The other disciples came in the boat,
    for they were not far from shore, only
        about a hundred yards,
    dragging the net with the fish.

Continued in Appendix A, pp. 299–300.

Reflecting on the Gospel

At first reading, Jesus in the longer form of this Sunday's gospel seems like the wife who is always telling her husband that he doesn't say often enough that he loves her. Three times Jesus asks Peter if he loves him. By the third time Peter is "distressed"—from the Greek we can read this as grieved or hurt, and we can well understand Peter's bruised feelings. It has been customary to interpret Jesus' thrice-given question about whether Peter loves him as a parallel to Peter's thrice denial of Jesus before his death. Peter is being faced with his own failure.

The gospel actually hints at two failures: the fishermen coming back with no fish, Peter's denial of Jesus before his death. Yet these failures became occasions for Jesus' gift of abundance: a large catch of fish, a fuller love that would "glorify God." Faithful discipleship is not measured by absence of failure, but by openness to obeying new commands from Jesus, recognition of God's abundant gifts, and willingness to grow into new life. While Jesus calls Peter (and us) to faithful love and discipleship, Jesus is also patient with us as we learn what it means to be his risen presence in the world, feeding and tending his beloved.

These three questions, "do you love me?" also hint at faithful discipleship as a constant growing into a deeper love with the risen Lord. We don't express our love once, but constantly as we grow in our perception of the risen Lord's abiding presence to us and in our own ability to witness to that presence. As the gospel indicates after Jesus' third question, we sometimes will go where we "do not want to go." Peter's loving fidelity to the risen Lord ultimately led to his death, the ultimate sign of his love for Jesus.

The risen Lord asks us the same question, "Do you love me?" Like Peter, we tend to readily respond with yes, but only gradually come to know what that yes demands of us. Love is not simply good feelings, but the tangible caring for others. The cost of loving Jesus is the cost of loving others. This great Lover of humanity and Lord of humanity is gracious in calling us to be his risen presence for others by loving them. Of such is the Easter mystery: that we love and care for others as Jesus did.

Living the Paschal Mystery

Just as Jesus' presence is persistent, so is the call. So, then, must our response to follow him be persistent. Like Peter and the early disciples, our love is to be incarnated in continuing Jesus' mission—preaching, teaching, forgiving, etc. Jesus laid down his life for us—"you had killed him by hanging him on a tree" (first reading)—and so we lay down our life for others.

Taking up Jesus' mission, however, is more than simply *doing*. We cannot forget that to *do* Jesus' mission is to bring his risen presence to others by tangible manifestations. We might not provide an abundance of fish to weary fishermen, but we can provide an abundance of nourishment, love, and care to anyone we meet.

This means that we begin to see the risen Jesus in the "everydayness" of our lives. This means that we allow ourselves to be fully nourished by Jesus (on his very Body and Blood; through his word) and gradually be transformed more and more into his risen presence for others. Like Peter, we will fail. But also like Peter, we can learn to love to the end. Easter is every day that we love ourselves and others into new life. And in our daily love, we "glorify God."

Focusing the Gospel

Key words and phrases: they caught nothing, cast your net, full of . . . large fish, do you love me, glorify God, Follow me

To the point: The gospel hints at two failures: the fishermen coming back with no fish, Peter's denial of Jesus before his death. Yet these failures became occasions for Jesus' gift of abundance: a large catch of fish, a fuller love that would "glorify God." Faithful discipleship is not measured by absence of failure, but by openness to obeying new commands from Jesus, recognition of God's abundant gifts, and willingness to grow into new life.

Connecting the Gospel

to the first reading: Strict orders from the Sanhedrin did not deter the disciples from obeying "God rather than men." Ever faithful to Jesus' command to follow him, they even rejoiced that they were able to "suffer dishonor for the sake of the name."

to experience: Sometimes we can be so discouraged by our failure to follow Jesus faithfully that we tend to give up trying. Remembering that Jesus never gives up on us can instill in us the courage to stay the course of discipleship.

Connecting the Responsorial Psalm

to the readings: From what has God rescued us (psalm refrain)? From death certainly, yet not really from death, for if we follow the Lamb who has been slain (second reading), we shall face suffering and death as surely as he did (first reading). What God rescues us from is our fear of dying for Jesus' sake, our cowardice in face of the very real costs of discipleship, and our shame for the times we have, out of fear and cowardice, abandoned discipleship and run from death (gospel). To Peter who knows he has failed in discipleship, Jesus comes with understanding and forgiveness, and says, "Follow me." Jesus shows Peter that despite all the limitations of his fears and his failures, he will nonetheless catch an abundant harvest for God's kingdom. And so for us. We are rescued from our limited courage and our tenuous fidelity by One who understands our weakness, forgives our failures, and knows our hidden strengths.

to psalmist preparation: The readings this Sunday indicate that one sign of resurrection is movement from fear of the cost of discipleship to willing embrace of its cost. Lack of confidence and commitment is a kind of death from which God's life-giving power frees you, just as it freed Peter and the apostles. In singing Psalm 30 you celebrate not a private resurrection but a very public call to mission. Can you, like Peter, rejoice in it?

**ASSEMBLY &
FAITH-SHARING GROUPS**

- The risen Jesus has manifested his love for me by . . . I manifest my love for him by . . .
- Whenever I fail to follow Jesus faithfully, he . . .
- My daily growing in love for Jesus and others "glorif[ies] God" in that . . .

PRESIDERS
The abundance the risen Christ has shared through me, despite my failures, is . . .

DEACONS
My love for the Lord motivates my love for others and my ministry to them in that . . .

HOSPITALITY MINISTERS
My greeting and concern for those who are gathering help them become more aware of God's abundant gifts to them such as . . .

MUSIC MINISTERS
One way Jesus feeds me after my labors at music ministry is . . . I find this nourishment to be . . .

ALTAR MINISTERS
The abundant gifts God has given me because of my faithful serving are . . .

LECTORS
For "the sake of [Jesus'] name" (first reading), I am willing to . . . This affects my proclamation in these ways . . .

**EXTRAORDINARY MINISTERS
OF HOLY COMMUNION**
I minister God's abundance in these ways . . .

Model Rite of Blessing and Sprinkling of Water

Presider: The risen Jesus revealed himself to his disciples and offered them an abundance of new life. We ask God to bless this water that it may be a sign of Christ's presence and gift of new life to us . . . [pause]

[*continue with the third choice, "during Easter time," for the blessing of water*]

Homily Points

• Failures in life can lead us to discouragement and paralysis of action, or they can prompt us to new growth, understanding of ourselves, and direction for our lives. Failure, then, need not be an end, but can be a beginning. Ironically, failure can bring newness of life.

• Following Jesus is never our work alone. Jesus is always present, reaching out to us, inviting us again to cast our nets in a new direction, nourishing us in abundant ways, loving us into new life. Faithful discipleship is the intersection of Jesus' presence with our obedient response.

• Faithful discipleship is not measured by never failing, but by attentiveness to Jesus' risen presence, to his encouraging voice even in the midst of failing, and to his invitation to receive the abundance of gifts he always offers. Jesus' command, "Follow me," is a call to love freely and serve faithfully. His ongoing call to "Follow me" sometimes means "start over; you'll make it this time." New life always comes. This is the promise of the resurrection.

Model Universal Prayer (Prayer of the Faithful)

Presider: The God who provided the disciples with an abundance of nourishment will surely hear our prayers. And so we lift our needs to this loving God with confidence.

Response:

Lord, hear our prayer.

Cantor:

we pray to the Lord,

That all members of the church receive God's abundant gifts and respond with faithful discipleship . . . [pause]

That all peoples of the world manifest the presence of God by their care and concern for others . . . [pause]

That those lacking in the necessities of life share in the abundance God offers . . . [pause]

That all of us here may glorify God by the faithfulness of our love for others . . . [pause]

Presider: God of abundance, you nourish your people with love and care: hear these our prayers and help us to follow your Son faithfully, who lives and reigns with you and the Holy Spirit, one God, for ever and ever. **Amen.**

COLLECT
Let us pray

Pause for silent prayer

May your people exult for ever, O God,
in renewed youthfulness of spirit,
so that, rejoicing now in the restored glory
    of our adoption,
we may look forward in confident hope
to the rejoicing of the day of resurrection.
Through our Lord Jesus Christ, your Son,
who lives and reigns with you in the unity
    of the Holy Spirit,
one God, for ever and ever.
Amen.

FIRST READING
Acts 5:27-32, 40b-41

When the captain and the court officers had
    brought the apostles in
and made them stand before the
    Sanhedrin,
the high priest questioned them,
"We gave you strict orders, did we not,
to stop teaching in that name?
Yet you have filled Jerusalem with your
    teaching
and want to bring this man's blood
    upon us."
But Peter and the apostles said in reply,
"We must obey God rather than men.
The God of our ancestors raised Jesus,
    though you had him killed by hanging
    him on a tree.
God exalted him at his right hand as
    leader and savior
to grant Israel repentance and
    forgiveness of sins.
We are witnesses of these things,
    as is the Holy Spirit whom God has given
    to those who obey him."

The Sanhedrin ordered the apostles
    to stop speaking in the name of Jesus,
    and dismissed them.
So they left the presence of the Sanhedrin,
    rejoicing that they had been found
    worthy
to suffer dishonor for the sake of the
    name.

RESPONSORIAL PSALM
Ps 30:2, 4, 5-6, 11-12, 13

R̸. (2a) I will praise you, Lord, for you have
rescued me.
    or:
R̸. Alleluia.

I will extol you, O LORD, for you drew me
   clear
   and did not let my enemies rejoice over
      me.
O LORD, you brought me up from the
   netherworld;
   you preserved me from among those
      going down into the pit.

R⁊. I will praise you, Lord, for you have
rescued me.
   or:
R⁊. Alleluia.

Sing praise to the LORD, you his faithful
   ones,
   and give thanks to his holy name.
For his anger lasts but a moment;
   a lifetime, his good will.
At nightfall, weeping enters in,
   but with the dawn, rejoicing.

R⁊. I will praise you, Lord, for you have
rescued me.
   or:
R⁊. Alleluia.

Hear, O LORD, and have pity on me;
   O LORD, be my helper.
You changed my mourning into dancing;
   O LORD, my God, forever will I give you
      thanks.

R⁊. I will praise you, Lord, for you have
rescued me.
   or:
R⁊. Alleluia.

SECOND READING
Rev 5:11-14

I, John, looked and heard the voices of
   many angels
   who surrounded the throne
   and the living creatures and the elders.
They were countless in number, and they
   cried out in a loud voice:
      "Worthy is the Lamb that was slain
         to receive power and riches,
            wisdom and strength,
            honor and glory and blessing."
Then I heard every creature in heaven and
   on earth
   and under the earth and in the sea,
   everything in the universe, cry out:
      "To the one who sits on the throne and
         to the Lamb
         be blessing and honor, glory and
            might,
            forever and ever."
The four living creatures answered,
   "Amen,"
   and the elders fell down and worshiped.

About Liturgy

Appearance accounts and hospitality ministry: The Easter Lectionary includes a number of "appearance accounts," gospel recordings of Jesus' appearances to his disciples after the resurrection. This is the third and final Sunday of Easter for which appearance accounts are the focus of the gospel selection. These accounts not only proclaim Jesus' resurrection—he is alive!—but they also remind us of the many ways Jesus is present to us. For the early disciples, he was present in encounters, seeing and believing, eating, and in calling his disciples to follow him. Today, too, Jesus is present to us in abundant ways.

The Constitution on the Sacred Liturgy explicitly mentions four liturgical ways Jesus is present (no. 7): in the presiding priest, the proclamation of the word, in the eucharistic bread and wine, in the assembly. One of the roles of the hospitality ministers and their important ministry to the assembly is to help those gathering become aware of the many presences of the risen Christ to us, but especially to help the assembly become more aware that their very coming together is already a manifestation of the presence of the risen Christ among us. The hospitality minister's greeting and welcome help those who come to Mass become the visible Body of Christ, to be the risen presence of Jesus. It is a challenge for hospitality ministers to help people understand themselves as the presence of the risen Christ for each other, and also to help the assembly understand how this is carried out in everyday, simple ways. Hospitality is so much more than a friendly hello; it is an announcement of the risen presence of Christ among us.

About Liturgical Music

Music suggestions: Bob Hurd's "Two Were Bound for Emmaus" retells the stories of both the Emmaus journey and this Sunday's gospel. Verse 4 is particularly expressive of the weariness and weakness we often feel in discipleship and the need to keep our attention turned toward the risen Jesus who will support us: "When the road makes us weary, when our labor seems but loss, when the fire of faith weakens and too high seems the cost, let the Church turn to its risen Lord, who for us bore the cross, and we'll find our hearts burning at the sound of his voice." This hymn would work well during the preparation of the gifts. A good choice for Communion would be Martin Willet's "Behold the Lamb" which integrates our sharing in the glory of the Lamb (see second reading) with our participation in eating and drinking his Body and Blood.

SPIRITUALITY

GOSPEL ACCLAMATION
John 10:14

R̸. Alleluia, alleluia.
I am the good shepherd, says the Lord;
I know my sheep, and mine know me.
R̸. Alleluia, alleluia.

Gospel

John 10:27-30; L51C

Jesus said:
"My sheep hear my voice;
I know them, and they follow me.
I give them eternal life, and they shall
never perish.
No one can take them out of my hand.
My Father, who has given them to me,
is greater than all,
and no one can take them out of the
Father's hand.
The Father and I are one."

Reflecting on the Gospel

Our being "sheep" does not mean that we blindly follow Jesus, but that we actively pursue a relationship with him by hearing his voice and heeding his words. Although following the Good Shepherd truly leads to eternal life, the way of discipleship is not easy. But Jesus is both the Good Shepherd and the Lamb who was slain. As Shepherd, Jesus is the one who cares for us and leads us. As Lamb, Jesus is the one who lays down his life in sacrifice for us. However, nothing can interfere with Jesus' care for us: we are secure in his hands. We are never alone for he is the *good* Shepherd.

Encountering Jesus as the Good Shepherd opens to us his care and love for us. The Risen One remains with us, and no one can take us "out of [his] hand" (gospel). The first task of discipleship is to open ourselves to Jesus' loving and abiding presence and to be assured that he will never abandon us, never call us to more than we can handle, never allow us to perish. Jesus' desire for us is one day to live eternally with him in the fulfillment of Easter life.

Encountering Jesus as the Lamb who was slain opens to us the cost of discipleship. Discipleship always takes us through suffering, rejection, and persecution (first reading). However, no matter what the cost of following Jesus, we are not alone nor are we abandoned to our own resources. The risen Jesus is always present within us. This is the good news of these Easter gospels.

Hearing Jesus' voice and fidelity to its call involves us in the harsh realities of the world in which we live. As the first reading reminds us, we will meet with jealousy and persecution. Not everyone we meet wants to hear a message of forgiveness and repentance, of self-sacrifice and surrender, even when there is assurance that this is the only way to new life. Yet, the tumult of the world is not a sign that God has abandoned us. Jealousy, violent abuse, persecution, expulsions, etc. have always been part of our human condition. In all of this, Jesus is at "the center," will shepherd us, lead us to "springs of life-giving water," and "wipe away every tear" (second reading). No matter what challenges we encounter in following Jesus, nothing or no one can take us out of his hand. This is, indeed, Easter Good News.

Living the Paschal Mystery

Longing for wholeness and goodness is at the very center of who we are. The ways for achieving them are up for grabs. Some people choose to focus on themselves, amassing as much money or wealth as they can since these seem to promise them security and pleasure. Some people control other people, thinking power can make them whole. Still others withdraw within themselves, trying to shut out the evil and sadness and loss of hope which surround us.

And some get it right: the only true way to wholeness and goodness is to follow Jesus along the path of self-sacrifice, willingly to be a lamb for the sake of others. We hardly need to look for opportunities to give ourselves over for the sake of others; they abound in our daily living. Easter further reminds us that when we sacrifice ourselves for others, we are never alone; the Good Shepherd is always with us, holding us tightly in his hand.

This is what Good Shepherd Sunday is all about: it's all about a God who so deeply cares for us that the only Son became the Lamb who was slain. This is why whatever we may endure in following Jesus as faithful disciples is worth the cost—because God cares for us as our Good Shepherd and "lead[s] [us] to springs of life-giving water" (second reading).

Focusing the Gospel

Key words and phrases: hear my voice, follow me, eternal life, No one can take them out of my hand

To the point: Our being "sheep" does not mean that we blindly follow Jesus, but that we actively pursue a relationship with him by hearing his voice and heeding his words. Although following the Good Shepherd truly leads to eternal life, the way of discipleship is not easy. However, nothing can interfere with Jesus' care for us: we are secure in his hands. We are never alone for he is the *good* Shepherd.

Connecting the Gospel

to the first and second readings: Jesus is both the Good Shepherd (gospel) and the Lamb who was slain (second reading). As shepherd, Jesus is the one who cares for us and leads us even when we face jealousy, abuse, and rejection (first reading). As lamb, Jesus is the one who lays down his life in sacrifice for us.

to experience: The tumult of the world is not a sign that God has abandoned us. Jealousy, violent abuse, persecution, expulsions, etc. have always been part of our human condition. In all of this, Jesus will shepherd us, lead us to "springs of life-giving water," and "wipe away every tear" (second reading).

Connecting the Responsorial Psalm

to the readings: Psalm 100 is part of a set (Pss 93; 95–100) which celebrates God's sovereignty over all things. Peoples of the ancient Near East acclaimed a god powerful because of specific acts, the greatest of which was creation. The Israelites believed their God acted not only to create the world but also to create them as a people. All forces inimical to Israel as a community—from natural disasters to human enemies—quelled before the power of God, who arranged all events in the cosmos to support Israel's coming together as a people.

In Christ God has shown the ultimate creative power by overcoming death with resurrection. Out of this act God has formed a new people beyond the boundaries of the community of Israel (first reading), a people "no one could count, from every nation, race, people, and tongue" (second reading). No hostility or persecution can prevail against this people for they are held in God's hand (gospel). In singing Psalm 100 we are recognizing who we are because of Christ's death and resurrection: a people created by God, protected by God, and shepherded by God to eternal life.

to psalmist preparation: The Israelites understood that God created them as a people and continually shepherded them. So, too, does the church recognize that she is created and shepherded by God. How have you experienced God's shepherding love for the church? How has God shepherded you as an individual disciple? In what way(s) does the church particularly need God's shepherding care today? In what way(s) do you?

**ASSEMBLY &
FAITH-SHARING GROUPS**

- I pursue a relationship with Jesus when I . . . I hear the voice of the Good Shepherd calling me to . . .

- I feel secure in Jesus' hand when . . .

- I find the way of discipleship difficult when . . . Jesus helps me by . . .

PRESIDERS
I model how to hear and follow the Shepherd's voice whenever I . . .

DEACONS
I am the hand of the Good Shepherd when I lead those in need to . . .

HOSPITALITY MINISTERS
My hospitality witnesses the care of the Good Shepherd to those gathering for liturgy when I . . .

MUSIC MINISTERS
In my music ministry right now I hear the voice of the Good Shepherd calling me to . . .

ALTAR MINISTERS
When I keep the Lamb at the center of my ministry (see second reading), my service is like . . . ; when I put myself at the center, my service is like . . .

LECTORS
Whenever I recall that the word I proclaim is the voice of the Good Shepherd to the assembly, my proclamation is like . . .

**EXTRAORDINARY MINISTERS
OF HOLY COMMUNION**
My ministry nurtures the security we have in Christ ("[N]o one can take them out of the Father's hand") by . . .

Model Rite of Blessing and Sprinkling of Water

Presider: Jesus is the Good Shepherd whose voice calls us to faithful discipleship. As we ask God to bless this water, may it remind us of our baptism and help us to hear more clearly the Good Shepherd's voice . . . [pause]

> [continue with the third choice, "during Easter time," for the blessing of water]

Homily Points

• When we say something is out of our hands, we mean we have no control over a situation, no power to influence its direction, or shape its outcome. When we wash our hands of something, we free ourselves from any connection with it. When we hand over responsibility, we entrust it to another. In all these examples, the image of "hand" represents ourselves in relation to someone or something else. In the gospel Jesus uses the image "hand" to reassure us that nothing can destroy his relationship with us.

• The gospel and this Good Shepherd Sunday promise that the risen Jesus never abandons us, never stops speaking to and guiding us, never hands us over to another power. Rather, he takes us by the hand, holds us firmly and lovingly, and leads us to fullness of life—communion with him and the Father.

• Jesus holds us in his hand; it is for us to grasp his hand in return. We do so when we listen to his voice, follow his lead as our Good Shepherd, and trust the direction he shows us for our life. We listen to his voice, for example, when we accept the guidance of the community of faithful disciples as we make decisions for our lives. We follow the Good Shepherd's lead when we give our lives over for the good of others. We trust in the direction he has shown us when we live Gospel values even when they are in opposition to what others want of us. In all of this we actively pursue a loving relationship with our Good Shepherd. We are in good hands!

Model Universal Prayer (Prayer of the Faithful)

Presider: God will never let anything or anyone take us out of Jesus' hands. This encourages us to lift our prayers to the God who loves us and cares for us.

Response:

Lord, hear our prayer.

Cantor:

we pray to the Lord,

That the church always hear the voice of the Good Shepherd and follow him faithfully to eternal life . . . [pause]

That world leaders hear the voice of the Good Shepherd and strive only for the care of their people . . . [pause]

That those who are sick or suffering feel the loving hand of the Good Shepherd upon them . . . [pause]

That all of us here gathered rejoice in our relationship to the Good Shepherd and come to love him more deeply . . . [pause]

Presider: Good and gracious God, you care for us with mercy and compassion: hear these our prayers that we might one day enjoy eternal life with you and your Son, Jesus Christ, who lives and reigns with you and the Holy Spirit, one God, for ever and ever. **Amen.**

COLLECT

Let us pray

Pause for silent prayer

Almighty ever-living God,
lead us to a share in the joys of heaven,
so that the humble flock may reach
where the brave Shepherd has gone before.
Who lives and reigns with you in the unity
    of the Holy Spirit,
one God, for ever and ever.
Amen.

FIRST READING

Acts 13:14, 43-52

Paul and Barnabas continued on from Perga
    and reached Antioch in Pisidia.
On the sabbath they entered the
    synagogue and took their seats.
Many Jews and worshipers who were
    converts to Judaism
    followed Paul and Barnabas, who spoke
        to them
    and urged them to remain faithful to the
        grace of God.

On the following sabbath almost the whole
    city gathered
    to hear the word of the Lord.
When the Jews saw the crowds, they were
    filled with jealousy
    and with violent abuse contradicted
        what Paul said.
Both Paul and Barnabas spoke out boldly
    and said,
    "It was necessary that the word of God
        be spoken to you first,
    but since you reject it
    and condemn yourselves as unworthy
        of eternal life,
    we now turn to the Gentiles.
For so the Lord has commanded us,
    I have made you a light to the Gentiles,
    that you may be an instrument of
        salvation
    to the ends of the earth."

The Gentiles were delighted when they
    heard this
    and glorified the word of the Lord.
All who were destined for eternal life came
    to believe,
    and the word of the Lord continued to
        spread
    through the whole region.

The Jews, however, incited the women of
    prominence who were worshipers
and the leading men of the city,
    stirred up a persecution against Paul
        and Barnabas,
and expelled them from their territory.
So they shook the dust from their feet in
    protest against them,
    and went to Iconium.
The disciples were filled with joy and the
    Holy Spirit.

RESPONSORIAL PSALM
Ps 100:1-2, 3, 5

℟. (3c) We are his people, the sheep of his
flock.
    or:
℟. Alleluia.

Sing joyfully to the LORD, all you lands;
    serve the LORD with gladness;
    come before him with joyful song.

℟. We are his people, the sheep of his
flock.
    or:
℟. Alleluia.

Know that the LORD is God;
    he made us, his we are;
    his people, the flock he tends.

℟. We are his people, the sheep of his
flock.
    or:
℟. Alleluia.

The LORD is good:
    his kindness endures forever,
    and his faithfulness, to all generations.

℟. We are his people, the sheep of his
flock.
    or:
℟. Alleluia.

SECOND READING
Rev 7:9, 14b-17

See Appendix A, p. 300.

About Liturgy
The Easter Lectionary and serving others: This Fourth Sunday of Easter,
Good Shepherd Sunday, is at the center of our fifty-day celebration of Easter. The appearances of the risen Lord proclaimed in the gospels of the first three Sundays open
onto this Sunday where the focus is on God's continued love and care for us. In turn,
this Sunday opens onto the next Sundays which begin to prepare the church to receive
the Holy Spirit and take up the mission of Christ—what hearing his voice and following him entails.

During this joyous time of celebrating Easter's new life, we might be fooled into
thinking that discipleship is easy since the risen Jesus is always with us. Even during
our Easter celebration, however, the Lectionary begins to move us toward the cost of
discipleship which we can take up only because we have received the Holy Spirit to
strengthen and enlighten us.

Serving others, then, is hardly something we do only during Lent (as part of our
penance) or at other specific times. Jesus has modeled for us that serving others is
what he came to teach us. Liturgical ministers model for us serving others so that we
can be dismissed from Mass to go and do likewise. Of such is Easter life: dying to self
in order to serve others.

About Liturgical Music
Music suggestions: With last Sunday's gospel Jesus already began calling the
church to ministry ("Feed my lambs"). In the coming weeks the challenge to take on
Jesus' mission will become even more intense. This week's readings couch the hardships of discipleship within the Shepherd's promise of continual care and of eternal
life. Good Shepherd songs abound (for example, "My Shepherd Will Supply My Need";
"Shepherd of Souls, Refresh and Bless"; "The King of Love My Shepherd Is"; "Shepherd Me, O God"). Most would be suitable for either the preparation of the gifts or
Communion. With so much repertoire available, however, we can overload the liturgy
with too many Good Shepherd songs. One is sufficient; two would be appropriate only
if their texts complement rather than repeat one another.

Another hymn appropriate for this Sunday is "I Know That My Redeemer Lives."
Verse 4 states, "Christ lives to silence all my fears; He lives to wipe away my tears;
Christ lives to calm my troubled heart; He lives all blessings to impart." Not all hym-
nals include this verse, in which case a cantor could interpolate it between other verses
sung by the assembly. Accordingly, the song might work best as a hymn of praise
after Communion. It would be good to vary the manner in which
the verses are sung. For example, the choir could sing the
verses with the strongest texts SATB; everyone could sing
the verses with the gentler texts a cappella.

GOSPEL ACCLAMATION
John 13:34

Ry. Alleluia, alleluia.
I give you a new commandment, says the Lord:
love one another as I have loved you.
Ry. Alleluia, alleluia.

Gospel

John 13:31-33a, 34-35; L54C

When Judas had left them, Jesus said,
  "Now is the Son of Man glorified, and
    God is glorified in him.
If God is glorified in him,
  God will also glorify him in himself,
  and God will glorify him at once.
My children, I will be with you only a
    little while longer.
I give you a new commandment: love
    one another.
As I have loved you, so you also should
    love one another.
This is how all will know that you are
    my disciples,
  if you have love for one another."

Reflecting on the Gospel

We have all seen them—those beautifully built schools with ornate facades, stained glass windows, carved massive doors rising bleakly from a neighborhood that is run down and but a shadow of what it used to be. These magnificent buildings speak to us of bygone glory days. If we have an occasion to enter, we might see a trophy case filled with reminders of past successes and prominence. The external trappings of glory remain; what makes this glory happen has gone. This Sunday's gospel speaks of glory days, too. Jesus has been raised from the dead: "Now is the Son of Man glorified, and God is glorified in him." But unlike our school above, this glory does not fade for those who hear and heed Jesus' new commandment. This glory lasts forever. This glory belongs to God. And to us who love as Jesus loved.

Jesus' new commandment is "As I have loved you, so you also should love one another." The nature of our love as disciples is specific, singular, incomparable: we are to love to the extent and in the manner Jesus loved. Our love is to be the self-sacrificing love of Jesus. It is this kind of love which brings Jesus glory. It is this kind of love which brings God glory. It is this kind of love which enables us to share in that same glory.

Yes, this love has a cost. This is a "new love" because it calls us to the same self-emptying as that of the slain Lamb. Our paschal transformation challenges us to make the norm of our love not self-love but the self-sacrificing love of Jesus. This is a demanding love because it will require that we die to self. But we do not die like the school building. Our dying to self brings new life, brings glory to God. This dying to self transforms the world! The divine love to which Jesus calls us produces dramatic results: "a new heaven and a new earth," a "new Jerusalem," indeed the making of "all things new" (second reading). This love wipes away every tear and lasts forever. Our Easter joy is not found in avoiding its costs, but in embracing its price for the sake of the new heaven and earth it promises.

Living the Paschal Mystery

We are able to love as Jesus did only because of the power and grace which come from our first being loved by God. God's dwelling is now "with the human race" (second reading). God transforms us into those who love as the divine Son loved. On our own we cannot love as Jesus did. The power of the resurrection is that Jesus' risen life now pulses within us. It is this life which gives us the ability to live Jesus' new commandment of love.

Our "paschal transformation" is our passing from keeping the old commandment to keeping the new, from loving as ourselves to loving as Jesus did, from dying to the old self-centered, sinful self to rising to a new life in Christ. What is "new" in our paschal love is that now our love is like divine love. What is "new" in our paschal living is that now our very identity is that of the risen Christ. The "new" measure of love is Jesus. He has been raised to glory and lives forever. So will we by loving in this way!

By our own self-sacrificing love, we are the presence of the risen Christ for others. Christian living is, bottom line, to love as Jesus loved, to be the risen Christ for others. By loving as Jesus did, we are transformed, and so is all the world. And this newness will last forever.

Focusing the Gospel

Key words and phrases: new commandment, Son of Man glorified, God is glorified, As I have loved you . . . love one another

To the point: Jesus' new commandment is "As I have loved you, so you also should love one another." The nature of our love as disciples is specific, singular, incomparable: we are to love to the extent and in the manner Jesus loved. Our love is to be the self-sacrificing love of Jesus. It is this kind of love which brings Jesus glory. It is this kind of love which brings God glory. It is this kind of love which enables us to share in that same glory.

Connecting the Gospel

to the second reading: When we live Jesus' new commandment of love, the results are dramatic: "a new heaven and a new earth," "new Jerusalem," indeed, "all things new" (second reading).

to experience: We are keen on underscoring obligation—we must "love one another." This is only possible because of the power and grace which come from our first being loved by God.

Connecting the Responsorial Psalm

to the readings: Paul and Barnabas are highly energetic and immensely successful in their mission to the Gentiles. All this they credit to God working in them (first reading). John relays his vision of a new heaven and new earth, God working to "make all things new" (second reading). Jesus speaks of his glorification, God's final work to complete the mission for which he was sent (gospel). In the responsorial psalm we command these works and more to give God thanks and to proclaim the power of God's might and the splendor of God's kingdom to all peoples. One work yet remains: that we who are God's people choose to love one another as Jesus has loved us (gospel). This, too, will be God's work and the one which will most definitively declare who God is and who we are because of God. May our surrender to this new and final commandment be the praise we sing, and may our praise last forever.

to psalmist preparation: Your singing of this responsorial psalm needs to invite the assembly to see themselves as a work of God, a new creation, giving praise. What might you do this week to help yourself see them in this way? To see yourself in this way? How is this way of seeing a living out of Jesus' commandment to love one another as he has loved us?

**ASSEMBLY &
FAITH-SHARING GROUPS**

- As I understand it, that which is "new" in Jesus' commandment to love is . . .
- The extent to which Jesus' love for me motivates my love for others is . . .
- I experience sharing in God's glory when . . .

PRESIDERS
I model for the people I serve Jesus' command to love as he loves us when I . . . They model this love for me when I . . .

DEACONS
My service for others models Jesus' love in that . . .

HOSPITALITY MINISTERS
My manner of greeting others indicates that I perceive the glory of God shining through them in that . . .

MUSIC MINISTERS
My participation in music ministry challenges me to love as Jesus does when . . .

ALTAR MINISTERS
When I minister to others according to the norm of Jesus' commandment, my service is like . . .

LECTORS
The way I love others is the most important way of proclaiming the risen Christ because . . .

**EXTRAORDINARY MINISTERS
OF HOLY COMMUNION**
My ministry nourishes and strengthens others to embrace the self-sacrificing love of Jesus in their daily living when I . . .

Model Rite of Blessing and Sprinkling of Water

Presider: Jesus gives us a new commandment to love others as he loves us. We now ask God to bless this water as a reminder of our baptism which bathes us in the self-sacrificing love of Jesus . . . [pause]

> *[continue with the third choice, "during Easter time," for the blessing of water]*

Homily Points

• We experience many kinds of self-sacrificing love. There is honest-love, where someone finds a briefcase of money and turns it in to the authorities rather than keeping it. There is caring-love, where a stranger helps someone who trips and falls. There is tough-love, where parents hold the line in face of a youth's destructive behavior. There is also compassion-love, forgiving-love, healing-love, tender-love, peace-love, just-love. So much love! So much glory!

• What Jesus commanded in his time was well beyond the expected behavior of even good people. His *new* commandment is that we live by Jesus-love. Jesus-love demands a total giving of self. Jesus-love is the only love that brings God glory.

• What raises our love quotient? To love as Jesus loves us means we must put self and self-interest aside: we must open our eyes to see the needs of others, empathize with the plight of others, act to correct injustices, defend another who is wronged, reach out to the disabled. So many opportunities to love! So much love! So much glory!

Model Universal Prayer (Prayer of the Faithful)

Presider: The God who first loves us will hear our prayers and grant our needs. And so we pray.

Response:

Lord, hear our prayer.

Cantor:

we pray to the Lord,

That all members of the church be recognized as disciples of Jesus by their self-sacrificing love . . . [pause]

That all world leaders promote justice and peace through self-sacrificing love . . . [pause]

That the homeless and lonely find a haven of love . . . [pause]

That we here gathered grow in our love for one another and by our love give God greater glory . . . [pause]

Presider: Generous God, you revealed your love for us in Christ your risen Son: hear these our prayers that we might love one another as you have loved us. We ask this through Christ our Lord. **Amen.**

COLLECT

Let us pray

Pause for silent prayer

Almighty ever-living God,
constantly accomplish the Paschal
    Mystery within us,
that those you were pleased to make new
    in Holy Baptism
may, under your protective care, bear
    much fruit
and come to the joys of life eternal.
Through our Lord Jesus Christ, your Son,
who lives and reigns with you in the unity
    of the Holy Spirit,
one God, for ever and ever. **Amen.**

FIRST READING
Acts 14:21-27

After Paul and Barnabas had proclaimed
    the good news to that city
and made a considerable number of
    disciples,
they returned to Lystra and to Iconium
    and to Antioch.
They strengthened the spirits of the
    disciples
and exhorted them to persevere in the
    faith, saying,
"It is necessary for us to undergo many
    hardships
to enter the kingdom of God."
They appointed elders for them in each
    church and,
with prayer and fasting, commended
    them to the Lord
in whom they had put their faith.
Then they traveled through Pisidia and
    reached Pamphylia.
After proclaiming the word at Perga they
    went down to Attalia.
From there they sailed to Antioch,
    where they had been commended to the
        grace of God
for the work they had now
    accomplished.
And when they arrived, they called the
    church together
and reported what God had done with
    them
and how he had opened the door of
    faith to the Gentiles.

RESPONSORIAL PSALM
Ps 145:8-9, 10-11, 12-13

R℣. (cf. 1) I will praise your name forever,
my king and my God.
    or:
R℣. Alleluia.

The Lord is gracious and merciful,
  slow to anger and of great kindness.
The Lord is good to all
  and compassionate toward all his
    works.

R℣. I will praise your name forever, my
king and my God.
  or:
R℣. Alleluia.

Let all your works give you thanks, O
    Lord,
  and let your faithful ones bless you.
Let them discourse of the glory of your
    kingdom
  and speak of your might.

R℣. I will praise your name forever, my
king and my God.
  or:
R℣. Alleluia.

Let them make known your might to the
    children of Adam,
  and the glorious splendor of your
    kingdom.
Your kingdom is a kingdom for all ages,
  and your dominion endures through all
    generations.

R℣. I will praise your name forever, my
king and my God.
  or:
R℣. Alleluia.

SECOND READING
Rev 21:1-5a

Then I, John, saw a new heaven and a new
    earth.
The former heaven and the former earth
    had passed away,
  and the sea was no more.
I also saw the holy city, a new Jerusalem,
  coming down out of heaven from God,
    prepared as a bride adorned for her
    husband.
I heard a loud voice from the throne
    saying,
  "Behold, God's dwelling is with the
    human race.
He will dwell with them and they will be
    his people
  and God himself will always be with
    them as their God.
He will wipe every tear from their eyes,
  and there shall be no more death or
    mourning, wailing or pain,
  for the old order has passed away."

The One who sat on the throne said,
  "Behold, I make all things new."

✝ CATECHESIS

About Liturgy

Eucharistic praying and love: Since the *new* commandment to love one another as Jesus has loved us is so essential in the life of his disciples, we would naturally expect that our eucharistic prayers reflect this same commandment of love. And, indeed, they do in at least two ways.

First, excluding the prefaces, the word "love" appears in almost all of our eucharistic prayers. The Eucharistic Prayer for Reconciliation II continues after the institution narrative with these words: "Celebrating, therefore, the memorial of the Death and Resurrection of your Son, who left us this pledge of his love, we offer you what you have bestowed on us, the Sacrifice of perfect reconciliation." What is the antecedent of "this"? What is the "pledge of his love"? It would seem to be not only the institution narrative itself and the command to "Do this in memory of me," but also the eucharistic acclamation in which we proclaim our faith in terms of Jesus' dying and rising. Jesus' pledge of love is his continual giving of Self to us. This leads to the second way the eucharistic prayers reflect the commandment of love.

All the eucharistic prayers clearly narrate for us Jesus' self-giving—both in terms of his sacrifice on the cross as well as his sacrifice on this altar which becomes his Body and Blood given as our heavenly Food. Thus the eucharistic prayers not only *narrate* Jesus' love, but they model again and again within the whole eucharistic action the *meaning* and *demands* of this love—giving oneself over for the good of others.

About Liturgical Music

Music suggestions: An excellent hymn speaking of the new creation ushered in by Christ's resurrection would be "We Know That Christ Is Raised and Dies No More." The text speaks of sharing by water in Jesus' death and new life. Especially apropos is verse 4: "A new creation comes to life and grows As Christ's new body takes on flesh and blood. The universe restored and whole will sing." This hymn would be appropriate for the entrance procession or for the sprinkling rite. Another hymn relating to the new creation is Brian Wren's "Christ Is Risen! Shout Hosanna!" The catchy, upbeat tune would make the hymn work well either for the entrance procession or as a song of praise after Communion.

The gospel reveals that a central part of the new creation in Christ is his command that we love one another as he has loved us. A setting of *Ubi Caritas* would be most appropriate for Communion, as would James Chepponis's "Love One Another." Two contemporary texts that could be sung during the preparation of the gifts are Herman Stuempfle's "Lord, Help Us Walk Your Servant Way" (in *Hymns for the Gospels*, GIA) and Ruth Duck's "The Call Is Clear and Simple" (in *Dancing in the Universe*, GIA).

SPIRITUALITY

GOSPEL ACCLAMATION
John 14:23

R⁊. Alleluia, alleluia.
Whoever loves me will keep my word, says the
     Lord,
and my Father will love him and we will come
     to him.
R⁊. Alleluia, alleluia.

Gospel

John 14:23-29; L57C

Jesus said to his disciples:
     "Whoever loves me will
          keep my word,
     and my Father will love
          him,
     and we will come to him and
          make our dwelling with
          him.
Whoever does not love me does not
     keep my words;
     yet the word you hear is not mine
     but that of the Father who sent me.

"I have told you this while I am with
     you.
The Advocate, the Holy Spirit,
     whom the Father will send in my
          name,
     will teach you everything
     and remind you of all that I told you.
Peace I leave with you; my peace I give
     to you.
Not as the world gives do I give it to
     you.
Do not let your hearts be troubled or
     afraid.
You heard me tell you,
     'I am going away and I will come
          back to you.'
If you loved me,
     you would rejoice that I am going to
          the Father;
     for the Father is greater than I.
And now I have told you this before it
     happens,
     so that when it happens you may
          believe."

Reflecting on the Gospel

We have little problem understanding how love is an action. We can *see* love: the care parents give children, the care adult children give their elderly parents, the generosity of youth in responding to disasters, the goodness of volunteers who keep so many programs viable. These and many other expressions of love are observable every day of our lives, if we but open our eyes to see. We see love expressed by those close to us and strangers, by the successful and those who are struggling, by young and old alike. But we rarely think of believing as an action. Yet it is. Believing is as concrete and visible an action as love.

Jesus promises to send us the Holy Spirit who will "teach [us] everything." The Holy Spirit does not teach us *what* to believe, but to *believe*. To believe means to live out of the divine indwelling, live out of the peace given, live out of the mutual exchange of love between God and us and each other. Believing is living what the Spirit teaches us. Believing is an action that marries love with presence.

God's love *is* divine life, divine indwelling. The Holy Spirit given to us *is* divine life, divine indwelling. The key to understanding the many parts of this gospel—loving, keeping Jesus' word, teaching and learning, receiving peace, believing—is divine indwelling. All these parts of the gospel are really expressions of our surrender to the God who dwells within us. Jesus' ascension paves the way for the Holy Spirit to come and dwell within us. This indwelling of divine Life teaches us to live with all the compassion and mercy, love and obedience, care and concern that exists within the Trinity itself. What the Holy Spirit teaches us is surrender of our very selves to God's Life within us, a surrender which prompts obedience to what God asks and opens us to receive the peace only God can give.

The peace we receive is not absence of strife or contention, but the fruit of the Holy Spirit dwelling in us. Such love God gives us! We need not "be troubled or afraid." We only need to love in return. Here is what is wholly new: God dwells within us! This intimate union between God and humanity is made possible by Jesus' farewell gift, the Holy Spirit. Indeed, in the Spirit all things are new!

Living the Paschal Mystery

The new creation and new life effected by Christ's resurrection resulted in an entirely new self-understanding by the first Christian communities (as reported in Acts) and a new religious order (as described in Revelation). Because we Christians today are so inundated with words and pay little attention to most of them, it is possible that any newness of the Resurrection escapes us or else the newness has become so commonplace that it has lost its power. The challenge is to shift from words and believing as an intellectual exercise to love motivating us to respond to the Spirit's presence within us. Believing is an action; it is a response to the Holy Spirit's promptings to do good, to live faithfully the divine Life that has been given to us.

Each year our Easter celebration challenges us to assess our treasure trove: God's dwelling among us, the relationship of hearing (living) God's word and loving as Jesus did, being taught by the Holy Spirit. These cannot remain simply concepts; these gifts are given to us so that we are Easter made visible.

Focusing the Gospel

Key words and phrases: Whoever loves me, Father will love, make our dwelling, Holy Spirit . . . will teach you everything, peace I give you, may believe

To the point: Jesus promises to send us the Holy Spirit who will "teach [us] everything." The Holy Spirit does not teach us *what* to believe, but to *believe*. To believe means to live out of the divine indwelling, live out of the peace given, live out of the mutual exchange of love between God and us. Believing is living what the Spirit teaches us.

Connecting the Gospel

to the second reading: The second reading describes the heavenly Jerusalem which "gleam[s] with the splendor of God . . . and the Lamb." The divine indwelling in us and our believing make us citizens of this city.

to experience: Gifts are most often tangible and the most prized ones satisfy our wants and desires. Jesus offers us a gift beyond anything we can imagine or desire—his risen presence as the Holy Spirit dwelling within us. This gift satisfies beyond all human expectations.

Connecting the Responsorial Psalm

to the readings: Psalm 67 was a hymn of thanksgiving for a fruitful harvest. The Israelites prayed that God would extend these abundant blessings to all the earth. In this way all nations would know God's saving care and offer joyful praise. In the context of this Sunday's readings, Psalm 67 invites us to make our very way of living the abundant harvest God offers the world. When we love Jesus and keep his word, we move beyond the temptation to limit God's presence and power to specific practices (first reading) and places (second reading). We become the very dwelling place of God on earth (gospel). Let us pray together that our manner of living and relating will make God's way "known upon earth" (psalm) and that through us all nations will come to know salvation.

to psalmist preparation: The harvest for which you praise God in this responsorial psalm is the salvation wrought through the death and resurrection of Christ. You pray that all nations will come to know this salvation. Who has helped you come to know and believe in it? To whom are you making it known?

**ASSEMBLY &
FAITH-SHARING GROUPS**

- The Holy Spirit has taught me that . . . I still need to learn . . .
- My believing looks like . . .
- God dwelling within me shapes the way I choose to live in that . . .

PRESIDERS
My love for my people witnesses to God's love for them when I . . .

DEACONS
I have glimpsed the "splendor of God" (second reading) while ministering to God's people when . . .

HOSPITALITY MINISTERS
I am sharing Jesus' peace with others whenever I . . .

MUSIC MINISTERS
When I have reflected on the mutual exchange of love between God and me, my music making sounds like . . .

ALTAR MINISTERS
My serving witnesses to the presence of the Spirit in that . . .

LECTORS
When I live what I believe, my proclamation sounds like . . .

**EXTRAORDINARY MINISTERS
OF HOLY COMMUNION**
When my believing in the real Presence includes the divine indwelling in others, my living looks like . . .

✝ CELEBRATION

Model Rite of Blessing and Sprinkling of Water

Presider: Water is a gift which sustains life. Let us ask God to bless this water and bring us to deeper gratitude for the divine life within us . . . [pause]

> *[continue with the third choice, "during Easter time," for the blessing of water]*

Homily Points

• All our lives, we teach and learn. Our first teachers are parents and school teachers. Maturing into adulthood, our teachers are honest friends, loving spouses, those who challenge us and our way of living. But how many of us think very often of the Holy Spirit as our teacher?

• When we hear the word "believe," we often think of what we believe, such as the tenets of the Creed. But this is only one small part of believing. The Holy Spirit is our constant teacher who guides us in our daily choices, bringing us to the kind of believing made visible in the way we live. Believing is living what the Spirit teaches us.

• The easier challenge is believing the tenets of the Creed. The difficult challenge is experiencing how the Spirit who dwells within us actually guides us. Sometimes this guidance comes through the good counsel of spouse, friends, and colleagues. At other times this guidance becomes apparent through quiet moments of reflection on our lives. Sometimes this guidance is experienced through our witnessing the good others do. Our responses to these promptings of the Spirit are expressions of believing. Believing is living what the Spirit teaches us.

Model Universal Prayer (Prayer of the Faithful)

Presider: The Spirit who dwells within us teaches us how to respond to the needs that bring us to prayer. And so we pray.

Response:

Lord, hear our prayer.

Cantor:

we pray to the Lord,

For the church, the embodiment of the Spirit's peace and love . . . [pause]

For the world, called to salvation by God's abiding presence . . . [pause]

For the troubled and afraid, in whom God dwells . . . [pause]

For ourselves here gathered, loved by the Father, raised to new life by Jesus, taught by the Holy Spirit . . . [pause]

Presider: Loving God, your Son promised the descent of the Spirit who teaches us all things: hear these our prayers that we may one day enjoy eternal life. We ask this through Christ our Lord. **Amen.**

Let us pray

Pause for silent prayer

Grant, almighty God,
that we may celebrate with heartfelt
   devotion these days of joy,
which we keep in honor of the risen Lord,
and that what we relive in remembrance
we may always hold to in what we do.
Through our Lord Jesus Christ, your Son,
who lives and reigns with you in the unity
   of the Holy Spirit,
one God, for ever and ever.
Amen.

FIRST READING
Acts 15:1-2, 22-29

Some who had come down from Judea were
   instructing the brothers,
   "Unless you are circumcised according
      to the Mosaic practice,
   you cannot be saved."
Because there arose no little dissension
   and debate
   by Paul and Barnabas with them,
   it was decided that Paul, Barnabas, and
      some of the others
   should go up to Jerusalem to the
      apostles and elders
   about this question.

The apostles and elders, in agreement
   with the whole church,
   decided to choose representatives
   and to send them to Antioch with Paul
      and Barnabas.
The ones chosen were Judas, who was
   called Barsabbas,
   and Silas, leaders among the brothers.
This is the letter delivered by them:

"The apostles and the elders, your brothers,
   to the brothers in Antioch, Syria, and
      Cilicia
   of Gentile origin: greetings.
Since we have heard that some of our
   number
   who went out without any mandate
      from us
   have upset you with their teachings
   and disturbed your peace of mind,
   we have with one accord decided to
      choose representatives
   and to send them to you along with our
      beloved Barnabas and Paul,
   who have dedicated their lives to the
      name of our Lord Jesus Christ.

So we are sending Judas and Silas
   who will also convey this same message
      by word of mouth:
   'It is the decision of the Holy Spirit and
      of us
   not to place on you any burden beyond
      these necessities,
   namely, to abstain from meat sacrificed
      to idols,
   from blood, from meats of strangled
      animals,
   and from unlawful marriage.
If you keep free of these,
   you will be doing what is right. Farewell.'"

RESPONSORIAL PSALM

Ps 67:2-3, 5, 6, 8

R̷. (4) O God, let all the nations praise you!
   or:
R̷. Alleluia.

May God have pity on us and bless us;
   may he let his face shine upon us.
So may your way be known upon earth;
   among all nations, your salvation.

R̷. O God, let all the nations praise you!
   or:
R̷. Alleluia.

May the nations be glad and exult
   because you rule the peoples in equity;
   the nations on the earth you guide.

R̷. O God, let all the nations praise you!
   or:
R̷. Alleluia.

May the peoples praise you, O God;
   may all the peoples praise you!
May God bless us,
   and may all the ends of the earth fear
      him!

R̷. O God, let all the nations praise you!
   or:
R̷. Alleluia.

SECOND READING

Rev 21:10-14, 22-23

See Appendix A, p. 300.

Or, where the Ascension is celebrated on
Sunday, the second reading and gospel for
the Seventh Sunday of Easter may be used
on this Sunday.

Rev 22:12-14, 16-17, 20, p. 133.

John 17:20-26, p. 130.

✠ CATECHESIS

About Liturgy

Lectors, God's word, and the Holy Spirit as teacher: More than readers, lectors are those who *proclaim* God's word. One difference between reading and proclaiming lies in lectors' "owning" the word before they approach the ambo. This means that, first, they must prayerfully read over their selection (this has traditionally been called "divine reading" or *lectio divina*) and learn to love God's word. Only after prayerful reading will lectors be able to live the word during the week preceding their ministry. Only after living the word—the word in action—will lectors truly *proclaim* the word. Proclamation, then, involves prayer, making the word one's own, living it, and loving it. This is no small task, but lectors must always remember that Jesus sends his Spirit to be with them.

The Spirit within teaches the lectors and moves them from reading to proclamation. This teaching does not happen in a classroom but in the school of daily living. With the Scriptures written in our hearts, we respond to life's situations and challenges from a divine perspective.

About Liturgical Music

Music suggestions: "For Your Gift of God the Spirit" (in *Hymns for the Gospels*, GIA) combines thanksgiving for the gift of the Spirit with proclamation about what this Spirit does within us—stirs life, interprets Scripture, gives strength to conquer evil, etc. Verse 3 is particularly relevant to this Sunday's gospel: "He, himself the living Author, Wakes to life the sacred Word, Reads with us its holy pages And reveals our risen Lord. . . ." The final verse is a petition that God give this Spirit full sway in our hearts. Sung to a strong tune such as HYMN TO JOY or ABBOT'S LEIGH, this would make a stirring entrance song. Sung to a more lilting tune such as HOLY MANNA or PLEADING SAVIOR, this would work well at the preparation of the gifts provided this ritual element be long enough to accommodate all the verses.

Two Easter hymns from Africa which fit this Sunday's readings are "Christ Has Risen" and "Jesus Has Conquered Death" (both in *Lead Me, Guide Me*, GIA). The first uses a verse-refrain format with a soloist singing the verses and would be wonderful during the Communion procession. The second uses call-response style, and would work well either for the entrance procession or the preparation of the gifts. Both songs sound best with simple percussion accompaniment (see *Leading the Church's Song*, Augsburg Fortress #3-402, for input on African rhythmic patterns).

SPIRITUALITY

GOSPEL ACCLAMATION
Matt 28:19a, 20b

R⁷. Alleluia, alleluia.
Go and teach all nations, says the Lord;
I am with you always, until the end of the world.
R⁷. Alleluia, alleluia.

Gospel

Luke 24:46-53; L58C

Jesus said to his disciples:
  "Thus it is written that
    the Christ would
    suffer
  and rise from the dead on
    the third day
  and that repentance, for
    the forgiveness of
    sins,
  would be preached in his
    name
  to all the nations, beginning from
    Jerusalem.
You are witnesses of these things.
And behold I am sending the promise
    of my Father upon you;
  but stay in the city
  until you are clothed with power
    from on high."

Then he led them out as far as
    Bethany,
  raised his hands, and blessed them.
As he blessed them he parted from
    them
  and was taken up to heaven.
They did him homage
  and then returned to Jerusalem with
    great joy,
  and they were continually in the
    temple praising God.

Reflecting on the Gospel

The English word "homage" comes from the Latin *homo* meaning "man." In Medieval times it was the ceremony by which a vassal pledged his allegiance to his lord. Homage, then, predicates relationship, obedience, service, respect, fidelity. Jesus' last earthly gesture toward the disciples was to *bless* them. In response, the disciples "did him homage" and experienced "great joy." This response was not to Jesus' departure from them, but was an expression of a new relationship to him, the risen One. Now instead of *accompanying* him in his ministry, they were "clothed with power from on high" to *be* his presence and *do* his ministry. In essence, Jesus' last gesture toward the disciples was to *empower* them to be "witnesses of these things." His blessing empowered them to live a wholly new relationship with him, one that would be expressed in their obedience to his word, in their serving his saving mission, in their respecting his continued presence, and in their continued fidelity to everything Jesus had taught them.

Although Jesus "was taken up to heaven," the ascension does not end Jesus' work but inaugurates a new way of carrying it out: Jesus passes the mission on to his disciples ("you are witnesses of these things") and promises them the power to fulfill it ("clothed with power from on high"). The mission and the power are now theirs. With Jesus' ascension, the necessity of discipleship is clear. The ascension of Jesus prepares the way for the powerful and enduring presence of the Holy Spirit in the disciples who continue his ministry.

True, the one in whom the disciples had placed their hope had ascended to the right hand of God. Interestingly enough, rather than leaving the disciples alone, Jesus' ascension leads them to grasp what being a community of disciples really means. They witness, pay homage, and are "continually in the temple praising God." With Jesus' ascension and blessing, the disciples live a whole new relationship with him. Rather than simply as vassals to a lord, their relationship is a response to the Lord of Life who now dwells within them through his Holy Spirit. Now we are his disciples, we are the ones in whom the Holy Spirit dwells. We are the living presence of the risen Christ in our world today!

Living the Paschal Mystery

The "two men dressed in white garments" told the disciples that Jesus would "return in the same way as you have seen him going into heaven." The ascension challenges us to look beyond this time to the Christ of glory. Resurrection is fulfilled only on the last day. Thus, absence and presence refer to even more than Jesus' ascension and sending of the Spirit to dwell within us. They also remind us that our suffering and rising, repenting and forgiving, preaching, witnessing, and blessing all carry us forward to that final day of hope when we, too, share in Jesus' glory. Hope itself is an act of discipleship! Our joy is great when our hope is firm.

The challenge which remains is to make all this practical in our daily living. Perhaps we could begin the habit of thinking about those we are with every day in terms of "Body of Christ." Perhaps we could make it a point to say an encouraging word to someone each week. Perhaps we could encourage others who have been absent to come to church to worship on Sunday. In all these ways we are disciples, making Jesus' risen life present to others. In all these ways we are making visible our own relationship with the risen Christ, witness to how we have grafted our life onto his, how our discipleship continues his own ministry.

Focusing the Gospel

Key words and phrases: witnesses of these things, clothed with power from on high, blessed them, did him homage, great joy

To the point: Jesus' last earthly gesture toward the disciples was to *bless* them. In response, the disciples "did him homage" and experienced "great joy." This response was not to Jesus' departure from them, but was an expression of a new relationship to him, the risen One. Now instead of *accompanying* him in his ministry, they were "clothed with power from on high" to *be* his presence and *do* his ministry. In essence, Jesus' last gesture toward the disciples was to *empower* them to be "witnesses of these things."

Connecting the Gospel

to the first reading: The "power from on high" with which Jesus promised his disciples would be clothed before his ascension (gospel) is made explicit in the first reading. It is the Holy Spirit whom they receive and who empowers them to be faithful witnesses "to the ends of the earth."

to experience: When a strong cultic leader is present, a cult thrives and grows. In the absence of such a leader, a cult most often diminishes. This is not so with Christianity. The ascension of Jesus prepares the way for the powerful and enduring presence of the Holy Spirit in the disciples who continue his ministry and witness to his risen presence.

Connecting the Responsorial Psalm

to the readings: Psalm 47 was an enthronement psalm used when the Ark of the Covenant was carried in procession into the Temple. It celebrated God's sovereignty over all heaven and earth. The song contains verses (omitted from this responsorial psalm) which express Israel's belief that God chose them to play a special role in establishing God's kingship over all nations.

Knowing the full text of this psalm brings its use on this solemnity into fuller perspective. The psalm is not just about the historical ascension of Jesus to the throne of God, but includes our participation in his ascendancy. We, too, "have confidence of entrance into the sanctuary" (second reading). Though we do not know the time of the kingdom's coming, we do witness to its presence (first reading). We have been blessed by Christ to tell of it (gospel). By Jesus' ascension all humanity is raised to the glory of God. When we sing Psalm 47 on this solemnity, this is what we witness to, celebrate, and proclaim.

to psalmist preparation: On the surface you can interpret this psalm as a celebration of the historical event of Jesus' ascension. But it is about far more than that. The psalm is about the complete victory of the whole Body of Christ over the forces of sin and death. Who sits on the "holy throne"? You do. The assembly does. The church does. As you prepare to sing this psalm, you need to reflect on this fuller understanding so that you can move the assembly, and yourself, from historicizing about Jesus' life and mission to personally participating in it.

ASSEMBLY & FAITH-SHARING GROUPS

- Jesus blesses me today when . . .
- When it comes to continuing Jesus' ministry, I am a witness in my daily living to . . .
- Where I have learned to depend on being "clothed with power from on high" is . . .

PRESIDERS

At the end of Mass, when I bless the assembly, I empower them to . . .

DEACONS

My serving others brings them great joy when . . .

HOSPITALITY MINISTERS

The very gathering of the assembly moves me to praise God and offer God homage because . . .

MUSIC MINISTERS

I feel Jesus blessing me in my music ministry when . . . I feel myself blessing the church through my music making when . . .

ALTAR MINISTERS

Serving others is an act of homage to the risen Lord because . . .

LECTORS

My proclamation announces to the assembly the presence of the risen Lord when I . . .

EXTRAORDINARY MINISTERS OF HOLY COMMUNION

I shall consider how my *Amen* at Eucharist announces my promise to witness to Christ in my daily living . . .

Model Rite of Blessing and Sprinkling of Water

Presider: Today we celebrate the risen Christ's return to glory at the right hand of God. With the disciples we await the coming of the Spirit to clothe us with power from on high. Let us ask God to bless this water over which the Spirit moves . . . [pause]

[continue with the third choice, "during Easter time," for the blessing of water]

Homily Points

• When someone we love must leave us—a parent in the armed services is deployed, grandparents return to their home in another state, parents sending their little ones off to school—we are saddened. The physical absence of loved ones imparts an emptiness and longing in a relationship. Jesus' blessing of the disciples at the moment of his ascension erased emptiness and longing and instilled in them joy and firmness of purpose.

• Everything about Jesus' life—preaching and forgiveness of sins, dying and rising—is passed on to the disciples at Jesus' ascension. Filled with "power from on high," the disciples returned to Jerusalem from where their ministry would begin. Though they would not escape the plight of Jesus ("the Christ would suffer"), his blessing empowered them to be "witnesses of these things" as sharers in his risen life. Jesus' ascension is a promise of their own ascension to fulfillment. They saw the end before they even began their ministry.

• When we experience an emptiness and longing in our relationship with God, it is sometimes a sign that we have strayed from fidelity to Jesus' ministry and are not living the blessing we have been given. This emptiness and longing call us to renew our relationship with the risen Lord, our firmness of purpose in continuing the ministry of Jesus, and our keeping before us the promise of our own ascension to fulfillment. Throughout our daily living we must always remember Jesus' blessing and the empowerment of the indwelling Spirit.

Model Universal Prayer (Prayer of the Faithful)

Presider: Just as Jesus blessed his disciples before ascending into heaven, so will God bless us with whatever we need. So we pray with confidence.

Response:

Lord, hear our prayer.

Cantor:

we pray to the Lord,

That the church may continue Jesus' reconciling and forgiving ministry with joy . . . [pause]

That all people of the world may be blessed with peace and joy . . . [pause]

That those seeking repentance and forgiveness may be embraced by the mercy of God . . . [pause]

That we disciples gathered here faithfully take up Jesus' ministry and continually praise God by our lives . . . [pause]

Presider: O God, you are faithful to your promises: hear these our prayers and lead us to share in glory with you and the Son, in the unity of the Holy Spirit, for ever and ever. **Amen.**

COLLECT

Let us pray

Pause for silent prayer

Gladden us with holy joys, almighty God,
and make us rejoice with devout
    thanksgiving,
for the Ascension of Christ your Son
is our exaltation,
and, where the Head has gone before in
    glory,
the Body is called to follow in hope.
Through our Lord Jesus Christ, your Son,
who lives and reigns with you in the unity
    of the Holy Spirit,
one God, for ever and ever. **Amen.**

or:

Grant, we pray, almighty God,
that we, who believe that your Only
    Begotten Son, our Redeemer,
ascended this day to the heavens,
may in spirit dwell already in heavenly
    realms.
Who lives and reigns with you in the unity
    of the Holy Spirit,
one God, for ever and ever. **Amen.**

FIRST READING

Acts 1:1-11

In the first book, Theophilus,
    I dealt with all that Jesus did and taught
    until the day he was taken up,
    after giving instructions through the
        Holy Spirit
    to the apostles whom he had chosen.
He presented himself alive to them
    by many proofs after he had suffered,
    appearing to them during forty days
    and speaking about the kingdom of
        God.
While meeting with them,
    he enjoined them not to depart from
        Jerusalem,
    but to wait for "the promise of the
        Father
    about which you have heard me speak;
    for John baptized with water,
    but in a few days you will be baptized
        with the Holy Spirit."

When they had gathered together they
    asked him,
    "Lord, are you at this time going to
        restore the kingdom to Israel?"
He answered them, "It is not for you to
    know the times or seasons
    that the Father has established by his
        own authority.
But you will receive power when the Holy
    Spirit comes upon you,

and you will be my witnesses in
Jerusalem,
throughout Judea and Samaria,
and to the ends of the earth."
When he had said this, as they were
looking on,
he was lifted up, and a cloud took him
from their sight.
While they were looking intently at the
sky as he was going,
suddenly two men dressed in white
garments stood beside them.
They said, "Men of Galilee,
why are you standing there looking at
the sky?
This Jesus who has been taken up from
you into heaven
will return in the same way as you have
seen him going into heaven."

RESPONSORIAL PSALM

Ps 47:2-3, 6-7, 8-9

R7. (6) God mounts his throne to shouts of
joy: a blare of trumpets for the Lord.
or:
R7. Alleluia.

All you peoples, clap your hands,
shout to God with cries of gladness,
for the LORD, the Most High, the awesome,
is the great king over all the earth.

R7. God mounts his throne to shouts of joy:
a blare of trumpets for the Lord.
or:
R7. Alleluia.

God mounts his throne amid shouts of joy;
the LORD, amid trumpet blasts.
Sing praise to God, sing praise;
sing praise to our king, sing praise.

R7. God mounts his throne to shouts of joy:
a blare of trumpets for the Lord.
or:
R7. Alleluia.

For king of all the earth is God;
sing hymns of praise.
God reigns over the nations,
God sits upon his holy throne.

R7. God mounts his throne to shouts of joy:
a blare of trumpets for the Lord.
or:
R7. Alleluia.

SECOND READING

Eph 1:17-23

or

Heb 9:24-28; 10:19-23

See Appendix A, p. 301.

About Liturgy

Ascension and forty days: Luke's time frame for these events is different from that recorded in John's gospel. In John, Jesus ascends to the Father and sends the Spirit on resurrection day itself. In Luke, Jesus ascends to the Father forty days after the resurrection and sends the Spirit after fifty days, on Pentecost. While we have two different gospel traditions concerning Ascension and Pentecost, we must always be careful not to "historicize" these events. The timing does not matter; what does matter is that Jesus ascended into heaven to take his place of glory at the right hand of his Father and sent the Spirit to dwell within us.

There are a number of uses of the number "forty" in Scripture, but perhaps the one most important for this solemnity is Jesus' forty-day sojourn in the desert prior to the inauguration of his public ministry. We might interpret, intimated by Luke, that during the forty days after his resurrection, Jesus was preparing the disciples for their ministry of witnessing to all nations. The number is symbolic: their preparation was adequate or complete, surely brought to a climax on Pentecost with the sending of the Spirit.

In our language about the Ascension, we need to monitor our "literal" expressions and be leery about spatial images (up, up and away!) which convey only absence or any disruption in the unity and integrity of our fifty-day celebration of Easter.

About Liturgical Music

Music suggestions: Hymns celebrating the ascension of Jesus into heaven are readily marked in every hymn resource. Particularly appropriate are texts which connect Jesus' ascension with the elevation of all humanity to glory. One Easter hymn which does this is "Up from the Earth." Its style and energy make it suitable either for the entrance procession or for a song of praise after Communion.

Other good choices this day are hymns for Christ the King, such as "To Jesus Christ Our Sovereign King" and "Rejoice, the Lord Is King." A very good contemporary text for the recessional would be Sylvia Dunstan's Ascension hymn "Lift Up Your Hearts, Believers" (in *Hymns for the Gospels*, GIA).

MAY 9, 2013 (Thursday) or MAY 12, 2013
THE ASCENSION OF THE LORD

✝ SPIRITUALITY

GOSPEL ACCLAMATION
cf. John 14:18

R̸. Alleluia, alleluia.
I will not leave you orphans, says the Lord.
I will come back to you, and your hearts will
      rejoice.
R̸. Alleluia, alleluia.

Gospel

John 17:20-26; L61C

Lifting up his eyes to
      heaven, Jesus prayed,
      saying:
   "Holy Father, I pray not
      only for them,
   but also for those who will believe
      in me through their word,
   so that they may all be one,
   as you, Father, are in me and I in you,
   that they also may be in us,
   that the world may believe that you
      sent me.
And I have given them the glory you
      gave me,
   so that they may be one, as we are
      one,
   I in them and you in me,
   that they may be brought to
      perfection as one,
   that the world may know that you
      sent me,
   and that you loved them even as you
      loved me.
Father, they are your gift to me.
I wish that where I am they also may be
      with me,
   that they may see my glory that you
      gave me,
   because you loved me before the
      foundation of the world.
Righteous Father, the world also does
      not know you,
   but I know you, and they know that
      you sent me.
I made known to them your name and I
      will make it known,
   that the love with which you loved me
   may be in them and I in them."

Reflecting on the Gospel

One of the best compliments children can pay their parents is to mimic them. Small children seem to do it naturally. We've all seen the little guy take large steps and put a swagger in his walk, imitating his father. Or we've seen the little gal wait for the right moment to get at her mother's makeup and apply it—usually with rather garish results! When the relationship between children and parents is healthy and strong, the children grow up to imitate their parents in much more consequential ways; for example, in continuing family values, upright living, or rearing their own children through loving relationships. Jesus' prayer in this Sunday's gospel is essentially a prayer that we imitate Jesus.

This Sunday's gospel—just a week before Pentecost—situates us with Jesus at the Supper with his disciples the night before he died. Jesus, always the loving one, naturally turns to prayer for his disciples: Jesus prays that the intimate love and union he shares with his Father may take root in his disciples. Experiencing such divine love and intimate union enables and sustains the disciples who are to take up Jesus' mission to the world. In fact, love and unity among believers is their primary mission, their first witness to the glory of the risen presence of Christ. Our love for each other is God's love in us spilling over. Our unity as the Body of Christ is God's life abounding in us in word and truth. This love and unity is a sign to the world about who Jesus is: the risen One united perfectly with his Father and with us.

The first reading illustrates for us a disciple's love and intimate union with Jesus. Stephen's vision of the "glory of God" was possible because the love of God had taken such deep root in him. This love sustained him and kept him focused on God even at the moment of his martyrdom. In his very moment of martyrdom Stephen repeats the words of Jesus from the cross: "receive my spirit" and "do not hold this sin against them." He witnesses union with Jesus, the Father, and the human community, the very things for which Jesus prays in the gospel. He witnesses how faithful disciples imitate the risen One. He witnesses where faithful and deep love take us: to eternal glory.

This is the greatest compliment we can pay to Jesus: imitate him. Ultimately, this is what discipleship means: imitate him. This is how we are to live as disciples: imitate him. This is the call of the new life of resurrection: imitate him. This is the challenge of Pentecost: imitate him.

Living the Paschal Mystery

Paschal transformation is allowing ourselves to be made into a gift—wrapped in love, tied by unity, and delivered by the word. The first reading is a concrete example of a disciple who is a gift to Jesus. Stephen puts the paschal mystery into action, where the gospel always takes us. He preaches the Good News, accepts the fatal consequences, and forgives those who love not. Stephen willingly embraces his death because he knows this is the way to eternal glory and life.

We have been given the glory (presence) of Jesus so that others may see the glory. How do others see the glory? Through our love, unity, and forgiveness which reflect the glory of God. Thus paschal mystery living is more than a "not yet" ideal for which we strive and one day at the end of our human lives will be brought to perfection. It is at the same time the "already" of the glory of God revealed first through Jesus and now through us, his disciples.

Focusing the Gospel

Key words and phrases: given them the glory, brought to perfection as one, that the world may know that you sent me, love . . . may be in them

To the point: Jesus prays that the intimate love and union he shares with his Father may take root in his disciples. Experiencing such divine love and intimate union enables and sustains the disciples who are to take up Jesus' mission to the world. In fact, love and unity among believers is their primary mission, their first witness to the glory of the risen presence of Christ.

Connecting the Gospel

to the second reading: John's vision is of the fulfillment of time when Jesus returns to gather the faithful to share his eternal glory. When we disciples embrace the love and unity for which Jesus prays in the gospel, we are responding to Jesus' invitation to "Come."

to experience: Too often, the notion of love portrayed in our society does not bring unity but disharmony because the love is selfish. Unselfish love is about care for the other and this care strengthens relationships and is tangible in the unity of minds and hearts.

Connecting the Responsorial Psalm

to the readings: Psalm 97 is a hymn celebrating God's sovereignty over all that exists. The verses used here retell the vision which strengthens Stephen to remain steadfast in discipleship to the point of death (first reading). Stephen sees the glory of God in heaven and Jesus standing at God's right hand and proclaims what he sees to the people surrounding him. Even more, he dies as Jesus did, giving himself over to God and forgiving those who have murdered him. In return he is raised to the glory of eternal life (second reading). We sing these psalm verses because we have been granted the same vision as Stephen and we have been called to the same discipleship. In singing this psalm we acclaim that we, too, have seen the glory of Jesus and that we, too, will stake our lives on it.

to psalmist preparation: Because Psalm 97 is a generic text about the glory of God, it would be easy to sing it in a perfunctory way. But the context of Stephen's martyrdom (first reading) and Jesus' prayer that his disciples be one with him and the Father (gospel) invite a much deeper interpretation. To see the glory of God means to discover the mystery of your own glory. To become one with Christ means to accept that such glorification can come only through death. To sing these verses means to lay down your life in surrender and belief as did Stephen. This, then, is no simple song. Are you willing to sing it?

ASSEMBLY & FAITH-SHARING GROUPS

- I experience God's love for me when . . . I am able to love others with God's love when . . .
- Some ways I am a living answer to Jesus' prayer for unity are . . .
- I witness to the glory of the risen presence of Christ when I . . .

PRESIDERS

Ways I assist the community's diversity and differences to be united in Christ are . . .

DEACONS

My serving others brings them the hope of a share in eternal glory when I . . .

HOSPITALITY MINISTERS

My hospitality promotes unity among the assembly whenever I . . .

MUSIC MINISTERS

The primary mission of my music making is . . .

ALTAR MINISTERS

The humility of serving others prepares me to "enter the city" of God (second reading) in that . . .

LECTORS

Jesus' prayer for unity challenges me to work on forgiveness and reconciliation with . . . This affects my proclamation in these ways . . .

EXTRAORDINARY MINISTERS OF HOLY COMMUNION

Communion entails unity with the Lord *and* with each other. I foster communion with each other in our parish by . . .

Model Rite of Blessing and Sprinkling of Water

Presider: Jesus prays that we be one as he and the Father are one. We ask God to bless this water from which our baptismal unity as the Body of Christ flows . . . [pause]
[continue with the third choice, "during Easter time," for the blessing of water]

Homily Points

• Tree and plant roots are invisible but so vital: they spread sometimes to unimaginable length, they nourish, they anchor, they harbor life when what is above ground is dead. Invisible roots make possible the beauty and joy of the visible leaves, fruit, or flowers.

• This is one of the few times when a gospel records actual words of Jesus' prayer. And this prayer is for us. His prayer is for our life. His prayer is for the love and unity among us that makes visible the glory of the risen presence of Christ.

• When Jesus prays that his and the Father's love and unity take root in his disciples, he is praying that we may go to great lengths to continue his mission, may nourish others, may be support for others during difficult times, may bring new life and hope when life seems dead. The glory of new life comes from faithful discipleship and witness.

Model Universal Prayer (Prayer of the Faithful)

Presider: We are united with Jesus and the Father through love. Let us express this love by praying for our own needs and those of the church and world.

Response:

Lord, hear our prayer.

Cantor:

we pray to the Lord,

That all members of the church may grow in love and unity and bear fruit for God's people . . . [pause]

That all peoples of the world, divided by war and violence, may be united in peace and justice . . . [pause]

That fractured relationships may be healed in love . . . [pause]

That we here gathered may faithfully witness to the presence of the risen Lord and the glory he promises . . . [pause]

Presider: Loving God, you call us to unity with you through Christ in the Spirit: hear these our prayers that we may grow in our love for you and one another and come to share in your eternal glory. We ask this through Christ our Lord. **Amen.**

COLLECT

Let us pray

Pause for silent prayer

Graciously hear our supplications, O Lord,
 so that we, who believe that the Savior of
  the human race
is with you in your glory,
may experience, as he promised,
until the end of the world,
his abiding presence among us.
Who lives and reigns with you in the unity
  of the Holy Spirit,
one God, for ever and ever.
Amen.

FIRST READING

Acts 7:55-60

Stephen, filled with the Holy Spirit,
 looked up intently to heaven and saw
  the glory of God
 and Jesus standing at the right hand of
  God,
 and Stephen said, "Behold, I see the
  heavens opened
 and the Son of Man standing at the
  right hand of God."
But they cried out in a loud voice,
 covered their ears, and rushed upon him
  together.
They threw him out of the city, and began
 to stone him.
The witnesses laid down their cloaks
 at the feet of a young man named Saul.
As they were stoning Stephen, he called
 out,
 "Lord Jesus, receive my spirit."
Then he fell to his knees and cried out in a
 loud voice,
 "Lord, do not hold this sin against
  them";
 and when he said this, he fell asleep.

RESPONSORIAL PSALM
Ps 97:1-2, 6-7, 9

R. (1a and 9a) The Lord is king, the most high over all the earth.
or:
R. Alleluia.

The LORD is king; let the earth rejoice;
   let the many islands be glad.
Justice and judgment are the foundation of
   his throne.

R. The Lord is king, the most high over all the earth.
or:
R. Alleluia.

The heavens proclaim his justice,
   and all peoples see his glory.
All gods are prostrate before him.

R. The Lord is king, the most high over all the earth.
or:
R. Alleluia.

You, O LORD, are the Most High over all
   the earth,
   exalted far above all gods.

R. The Lord is king, the most high over all the earth.
or:
R. Alleluia.

SECOND READING
Rev 22:12-14, 16-17, 20

I, John, heard a voice saying to me:
   "Behold, I am coming soon.
I bring with me the recompense I will give
   to each
   according to his deeds.
I am the Alpha and the Omega, the first
   and the last,
   the beginning and the end."

Blessed are they who wash their robes
   so as to have the right to the tree of life
   and enter the city through its gates.

"I, Jesus, sent my angel to give you this
   testimony for the churches.
I am the root and offspring of David,
   the bright morning star."

The Spirit and the bride say, "Come."
Let the hearer say, "Come."
Let the one who thirsts come forward,
   and the one who wants it receive the gift
   of life-giving water.

The one who gives this testimony says,
   "Yes, I am coming soon."
Amen! Come, Lord Jesus!

About Liturgy

Seventh Sunday of Easter readings: In all of Canada and most U.S. dioceses, Ascension Thursday is transferred to the following Sunday, so this Sunday's proper readings (for the Seventh Sunday of Easter) are not proclaimed. This is unfortunate since these readings are so important: they clearly bring home the mission to bring others to believe in Jesus the Messiah and the inevitable consequences disciples of Jesus must bear because of their commitment. This Sunday—surely preparing for the celebration of the coming of the Spirit on Pentecost—reminds us that the paschal mystery is not only Jesus' way of living, dying, and rising but also our own.

Supporting the importance of the readings for the Seventh Sunday of Easter, the Lectionary note before the Sixth Sunday of Easter says that "[w]hen the Ascension of the Lord is celebrated the following Sunday, the second reading and Gospel from the Seventh Sunday of Easter [see nos. 59–61] may be read on the Sixth Sunday of Easter."

Mother's Day and Mary: This Sunday is Mother's Day; it is also the month of May. There may be a tendency here to focus on mothers and Mary, but that runs the risk of overshadowing the Easter season. Perhaps the hospitality ministers could wish the mothers well on their special day, but it is best to let the liturgy reflect the Easter season.

It is always appropriate, however, to include another intention at the general intercessions on days like this. Here is a model: For all mothers, models of self-giving and love . . . [pause]

The *Book of Blessings* includes an Order for the Blessing of Mothers on Mother's Day (Chapter 55) and gives sample intercessions which may be added to those of the day as well as a Prayer over the People used at the end of Mass in the place of the usual blessing before dismissal.

About Liturgical Music

Music suggestions: A very appropriate hymn for Communion this Sunday would be "At That First Eucharist" with its refrain, "Thus may we all one Bread, one Body be, Through this blessed Sacrament of Unity." A good choice for the preparation of the gifts would be "Eternal Christ, Who, Kneeling" (in *Hymns for the Gospels*, GIA). Its opening verse reads, "Eternal Christ, who, kneeling When earthly tasks were done, Turned unto God appealing, 'That they may all be one,' We thank you for your vision of unity un-torn, Of faith without division With which your church was born."

A good choice for choral prelude would be Owen Alstott's "We Have No Glory" (OCP 8971). The refrain reads, "We have no glory, we have no name. We are as grains of sand upon the shore. Our only glory, our only name, is Jesus Christ." The verses speak of Christ as the source of all our life and being, and of our mission to "become the name of Christ upon the earth."

✛ SPIRITUALITY

GOSPEL ACCLAMATION

R̓. Alleluia, alleluia.
Come, Holy Spirit, fill the hearts of your faithful
and kindle in them the fire of your love.
R̓. Alleluia, alleluia.

Gospel   John 14:15-16, 23b-26; L63C

Jesus said to his disciples:
  "If you love me, you will keep my
    commandments.
And I will ask the Father,
  and he will give you another Advocate
    to be with you always.

"Whoever loves me will keep my word,
  and my Father will love him,
  and we will come to him and make
    our dwelling with him.
Those who do not love me do not keep
    my words;
  yet the word you hear is not mine
  but that of the Father who sent me.

"I have told you this while I am with you.
The Advocate, the Holy Spirit whom the
    Father will send in my name,
  will teach you everything
  and remind you of all that I told you."

or John 20:19-23

On the evening of that first day of the
    week,
  when the doors were locked, where the
    disciples were,
  for fear of the Jews,
  Jesus came and stood in their midst
  and said to them, "Peace be with you."
When he had said this, he showed them
    his hands and his side.
The disciples rejoiced when they saw the
    Lord.
Jesus said to them again, "Peace be with
    you.
As the Father has sent me, so I send you."
And when he had said this, he breathed
    on them and said to them,
  "Receive the Holy Spirit.
Whose sins you forgive are forgiven them,
  and whose sins you retain are retained."

Reflecting on the Gospel

"*If* you love me." "*Whoever* loves me." (emphases added) Our love is always a free choice and, as human beings, we are never quite sure of our choices. God's love, on the other hand, is sure and steady. God continually sends the Spirit to dwell within us. This indwelling Spirit empowers us to love with God's steadfastness. Transformed by the Spirit, our love moves from "if" to "I can, I choose, I will." On this festival of Pentecost which concludes our celebration of the resurrection, we are given a Gift of Life so that we can faithfully take up Jesus' saving mission. Pentecost is an invitation to choose to love, to choose to do, to choose to be risen Presence. This is the power of Pentecost and why we can continue Jesus' ministry: the Spirit imbues us with God's love.

In this gospel the emphasis is not so much on God's power as on our receptivity to God's indwelling presence which enables us to be faithful disciples. Both power and gentle relationship characterize the disciple who has received the Spirit. God's power in the Spirit gives birth to a new relationship of love and divine indwelling. The Spirit's dwelling within us *is* the Father's and Jesus' love and the precondition for why we can continue Jesus' mission. The Spirit is our "soul's most welcome guest," our "strength" (sequence). The Spirit is the source of the disciple's life and mission. Filled with this Spirit, the disciples are able to love as Jesus loves.

We can be sure of God's steadfast Love dwelling within us because God's very nature is to be love and God cannot act against the divine nature. God *is* love. For God to act is to love. The Father's love for disciples and Jesus' abiding presence with and in them *is* the Holy Spirit. Here is the import of Pentecost: divine indwelling ("make our dwelling"), outfitting for mission ("teach you everything and remind you of all that I told you"), and way of life ("love me . . . keep my commandments . . . keep my word"). Easter culminates in Pentecost when Jesus' risen life is shared with us in a most profound way through the coming of the Spirit. We ourselves now go forth to carry on Jesus' mission, equipped with divine indwelling. We are never alone in our demanding discipleship; the Spirit is always with us.

Living the Paschal Mystery

The Spirit is not a Gift like other gifts we might receive—open them, appreciate and use them, wear them out or discard them. The Spirit is received in baptism and the Spirit's presence is strengthened in confirmation so that we might carry on Jesus' saving mission. The more we respond to the Spirit's indwelling, the more we are immersed in God's very love. The choice to love becomes more clear, more focused. The Spirit brings us to a single-mindedness about our love and about our choice to take up Jesus' saving mission.

Sometimes in our lives we might witness to a *powerful* presence of the Spirit. Perhaps we must confront another who has done wrong and refuses to change, stand up to injustice, or challenge another to more ethical and generous living. Sometimes in our lives we might witness to a gentler, *relational* Spirit. Perhaps we spend extra quality time with the children, or visit elderly relatives and bring them some cheer, or help someone pick up the pile of oranges which has come tumbling down in the grocery. In these great and simple acts the Spirit works through us and moves us from "if" to "I can, I choose, I will."

Focusing the Gospel *(John 14:15-16, 23b-26)*

Key words and phrases: If, Whoever, Father will love, the Holy Spirit whom the Father will send

To the point: "If you love me." *"Whoever* loves me." (emphases added) Our love is always a free choice and, as human beings, we are never quite sure of our choices. God's love, on the other hand, is sure and steady. God continually sends the Spirit to dwell within us. This indwelling Spirit empowers us to love with God's steadfastness. Transformed by the Spirit, our love moves from "if" to "I can, I choose, I will."

Connecting the Gospel

to the second reading: Saint Paul enumerates the effects of the Spirit's dwelling within us: we belong to Christ, are made righteous, are given new life, become adopted children and heirs of God. Here is God's gift of Love to us: an unprecedented relationship made possible by the indwelling of the Holy Spirit.

to experience: It is so much easier to act with love when we know we are loved. We can act with love in all times and places, all situations and circumstances, because we know we are filled with the Spirit who is God's love.

Connecting the Responsorial Psalm

to the readings: Psalm 104 is a masterful hymn praising God for the creation of the cosmos. It unfolds in a seven-part structure paralleling the creation account in Genesis 1. The Hebrews believed the cause of creation to be God's breath or spirit *(ruach).* Take breath away and creatures would die; give them breath/spirit and they would live (vv. 29-30).

In the first reading this breath of God comes like a "strong driving wind" which enables the disciples to witness to "the mighty acts of God." In the second reading this breath comes as a "spirit of adoption" making us sons and daughters of God. In the gospel this breath comes as Advocate sent in Jesus' name to teach us all things. This is the Spirit we ask God to send us in the responsorial psalm: the power pushing us forward in mission, the love which is God's very life within us, and the spokesperson reminding us of all that Jesus has taught—truly a Breath that will re-create the universe!

to psalmist preparation: You pray in this responsorial psalm for the renewal of the church—the renewal of her knowledge of Christ (gospel), the renewal of her sense of identity as one Body (second reading), and the renewal of her commitment to mission (first reading). How have these weeks of Easter celebration renewed you as a member of the church?

**ASSEMBLY &
FAITH-SHARING GROUPS**

- I experience the Spirit empowering me to . . . when . . .
- Because of the Spirit's indwelling, I have come to love . . . I express this love by . . .
- My love of others is a sure "I can, I choose, I will" when . . .

PRESIDERS
Some ways that I affirm and nurture the presence and power of the Spirit within the community are . . .

DEACONS
My serving makes visible the Spirit's love when I . . .

HOSPITALITY MINISTERS
My manner of my greeting those who are gathering encourages them to make a choice to participate more fully in liturgy when I . . .

MUSIC MINISTERS
My music making is a choice to love whenever I . . .

ALTAR MINISTERS
My serving witnesses to the presence of the loving Spirit within me when I . . .

LECTORS
When I intentionally open myself to the Spirit's power, my proclamation of the word is like . . .

**EXTRAORDINARY MINISTERS
OF HOLY COMMUNION**
My distributing the Sacrament of Love enables communicants to know they are loved when . . .

Model Rite of Blessing and Sprinkling of Water

Presider: The Spirit of Love given at Pentecost is the Spirit given to us through the waters of baptism. We ask God to bless this water and to renew us in this Spirit . . . [pause]

[continue with the third choice, "during Easter time," for the blessing of water]

Homily Points

• What energizes us? Rousing music. Inspiring words. Touching gestures. Successful ventures. Listening ears. Hearty laughter. Loving encounters. Loving actions. Loving responses. In all of this, something new happens within us. The energy generates new life. The most profound and all-embracing new life is generated by Love.

• Jesus makes a simple condition for the Father's love: we are to keep his word, his commandments. More than conformity to law, Jesus is inviting us to the kind of choices that make love the center of our lives and source of our energy. This love is made possible by the indwelling of the Holy Spirit.

• The Spirit dwells within us, empowering us to love with more energy, more enthusiasm, more confidence and courage. The Spirit enables us to see beyond present limitations to new possibilities. The Spirit is God's transforming Life, God's creating Energy, God's abiding Love. Our choice? To trust that the Spirit moves our tentative discipleship from "if" to "I can, I choose, I will." Something new is happening.

Model Universal Prayer (Prayer of the Faithful)

Presider: Let us ask our loving God to strengthen us in the Spirit, so that we love others with God's love.

Response:

Lord, hear our prayer.

Cantor:

we pray to the Lord,

That Christian churches throughout the world be renewed in their love by the power and presence of the Holy Spirit . . . [pause]

That all people of the world make choices for their daily living that bring new life and love . . . [pause]

That all those who yearn for a fuller and more loving life might be renewed in the Spirit . . . [pause]

That all of us here be faithful to our choice for discipleship by loving and caring for others as Jesus did . . . [pause]

Presider: O God, you send the Spirit and fill us with your life: hear our prayers that we may grow in love and one day be united with you forever. We ask this through Christ our Lord. **Amen.**

COLLECT

Let us pray

Pause for silent prayer

O God, who by the mystery of today's
  great feast
sanctify your whole Church in every people
  and nation,
pour out, we pray, the gifts of the Holy Spirit
across the face of the earth
and, with the divine grace that was at work
when the Gospel was first proclaimed,
fill now once more the hearts of believers.
Through our Lord Jesus Christ, your Son,
who lives and reigns with you in the unity
  of the Holy Spirit,
one God, for ever and ever.
Amen.

FIRST READING
Acts 2:1-11

When the time for Pentecost was fulfilled,
  they were all in one place together.
And suddenly there came from the sky
  a noise like a strong driving wind,
  and it filled the entire house in which
    they were.
Then there appeared to them tongues as
    of fire,
  which parted and came to rest on each
    one of them.
And they were all filled with the Holy Spirit
  and began to speak in different tongues,
  as the Spirit enabled them to proclaim.

Now there were devout Jews from every
    nation under heaven
      staying in Jerusalem.
At this sound, they gathered in a large
    crowd,
  but they were confused
  because each one heard them speaking
    in his own language.
They were astounded, and in amazement
    they asked,
  "Are not all these people who are
      speaking Galileans?
Then how does each of us hear them in his
    native language?
We are Parthians, Medes, and Elamites,
  inhabitants of Mesopotamia, Judea and
      Cappadocia,
  Pontus and Asia, Phrygia and Pamphylia,
  Egypt and the districts of Libya near
      Cyrene,
  as well as travelers from Rome,
  both Jews and converts to Judaism,
      Cretans and Arabs,
  yet we hear them speaking in our own
      tongues
  of the mighty acts of God."

RESPONSORIAL PSALM

Ps 104:1, 24, 29-30, 31, 34

R⁷. (cf. 30) Lord, send out your Spirit, and renew the face of the earth.
or: R⁷. Alleluia.

Bless the LORD, O my soul!
   O LORD, my God, you are great indeed!
How manifold are your works, O LORD!
   The earth is full of your creatures.

R⁷. Lord, send out your Spirit, and renew the face of the earth.
or: R⁷. Alleluia.

If you take away their breath, they perish
   and return to their dust.
When you send forth your spirit, they are created,
   and you renew the face of the earth.

R⁷. Lord, send out your Spirit, and renew the face of the earth.
or: R⁷. Alleluia.

May the glory of the LORD endure forever;
   may the LORD be glad in his works!
Pleasing to him be my theme;
   I will be glad in the LORD.

R⁷. Lord, send out your Spirit, and renew the face of the earth.
or: R⁷. Alleluia.

SECOND READING

Rom 8:8-17

or

1 Cor 12:3b-7, 12-13

See Appendix A, p. 301.

SEQUENCE

See Appendix A, p. 302.

About Liturgy

Pentecost sequence: This is one of only two Sundays of the year (Easter is the other one) when a sequence is obligatory. Sung as an extension of the gospel acclamation, a sequence can be an occasion for a more lengthy gospel procession which clearly draws attention to the gospel as central to the Liturgy of the Word and central in Christians' lives. On this day, Pentecost, when the church celebrates the coming of the Spirit and the sending of the disciples to continue Jesus' saving mission, it is especially fitting to draw attention to the gospel as we sing our request for the Spirit to come and dwell within us. If the worship space permits it, the gospel proclaimer might process throughout the church and hold the gospel book so people can reach out and reverence it.

Neither the Lectionary (no. 63) nor the GIRM (no. 64) mentions a rubric for posture during the sequence, but since it is really a hymn it would seem that the assembly ought at least to be standing. This is a festive hymn to the Holy Spirit and the music setting needs to reflect this joyous occasion.

About Liturgical Music

Music suggestions: Hymns to the Holy Spirit abound, so the task is to be judicious about what we sing, when we sing it, and how. For example, "O Holy Spirit, Come to Bless" would be suitable for the preparation of the gifts but not for the entrance procession because the tune to which it is commonly set (ST. COLUMBA) is too gentle. Sung to the stronger tune MORNING HYMN, however, it would make a very fitting entrance hymn. For another example, even though the refrain of David Haas's "Send Us Your Spirit" is almost identical to the refrain of the responsorial psalm, it would not make a good substitution for the psalm because its verses are not the psalm text. This piece would be better used as a prayerful prelude with assembly joining in on the canonic refrain. For a third example, singing texts that are tried and true such as "Come, Holy Ghost" reminds us that we are part of a community of faithful disciples that spans generations. On the other hand, singing a contemporary text refreshes our sense of what Pentecost means. One such text is Herman Stuempfle's "Wind of the Spirit" (in *Redeeming the Time*, GIA). Over three verses the hymn develops three progressive images of the Spirit: "Wind of the spirit . . . make us new!" (v. 1); "Flame of the spirit . . . make us bold!" (v. 2); "Dove of the Spirit . . . make us one!" (v. 3).

Finally, it is important not to overuse Holy Spirit hymns on this day. Singing one for the entrance procession and another for the preparation of the gifts is sufficient. Excellent examples of hymns appropriate for Pentecost though not directed to the Holy Spirit include "We Know That Christ Is Raised"; "The Church of Christ in Every Age"; and "Go to the World!"

Ordinary Time II

✚ SPIRITUALITY

℟. Alleluia, alleluia.
Glory to the Father, the Son, and the Holy Spirit;
to God who is, who was, and who is to come.
℟. Alleluia, alleluia.

Gospel

John 16:12-15; L166C

Jesus said to his disciples:
"I have much more to tell you, but
you cannot bear it now.
But when he comes, the Spirit
of truth,
he will guide you to all truth.
He will not speak on his own,
but he will speak what he hears,
and will declare to you the things
that are coming.
He will glorify me,
because he will take from what is
mine and declare it to you.
Everything that the Father has is mine;
for this reason I told you that he will
take from what is mine
and declare it to you."

Reflecting on the Gospel

When advertising makes a bold statement, we tend to be skeptical. And a downright preposterously bold statement—such as a laundry soap that removes virtually every stain, even when dried on for ten years; or a diet pill that guarantees loss of weight while one doesn't have to exercise or watch what one eats; or a beauty cream keeps wrinkles away no matter what the age—doesn't leave us skeptical, but outright unbelievers. The gospel for this solemnity makes some downright preposterously bold statements. In fact, the mystery itself we celebrate is pretty bold!

The Spirit guides us to *all* truth. Such a bold statement! That truth is the Holy Spirit, is the Life given by the Spirit. *Everything* the Father has is given us. An even bolder statement! What the Father gives us is divine Life. And it is for Jesus' glory that his disciples are empowered by the Spirit to bear what belongs to Jesus and the Father: divine Life. Our triune God holds back nothing from us. And here we have a double bold statement: our God is triune—three divine Persons in One God—and this God gives us everything we need to grow in the Life given us.

The indwelling of the Spirit—divine Life—assures us of the *triune* God's working within and through us: the Father's love, the Son's mission, the Spirit's truth. We need not fear to take up the Son's mission; the gospel assures us we are not alone. Thus, the gospel illuminates two aspects of the Trinity. First, that everything the Father has belongs also to the Son and Spirit. Second, all that God has is given to us through Jesus who sends us the Spirit. Here is the great mystery and grace of Trinity: the riches of God's own life are given to us, empowering us to take up the divine saving mission.

This life "poured . . . into our hearts" empowers us to "boast . . . in the glory of God" and even to "boast of our afflictions" (second reading). Because of the Trinity's divine life within us, even our afflictions become gift, strengthening us for the mission entrusted to us. Because of the Trinity's divine life within us, we weak human beings can be disciples who fruitfully carry on the very work of God.

The Trinity is, indeed, a lofty mystery. In one sense, though, the Trinity's dwelling within us and entrusting us with continuing Jesus' mission of saving the world is an even loftier mystery! We have been raised to the dignity of sharing in triune Life and continuing the divine saving mission! We spend our entire lives growing into this mystery of divine indwelling, of more faithfully carrying forth Jesus' saving mission, of witnessing to the truth of God's presence.

Living the Paschal Mystery

The Trinity is, indeed, a lofty mystery which comes down from the "heights" when we ourselves make God's presence known by the way we live. The triune mystery is revealed in our own loving others, in our doing good for others, in our being persons of integrity and truth. The mystery of the Trinity is concrete when we act out of the dignity which has been bestowed upon us—those who carry divine Life within them.

The Spirit not only guides us to all truth, but bears what we cannot bear on our own. Jesus' mission, then, is not entirely on our shoulders. Jesus, through his Spirit, is still present to us; it is always Jesus' mission. We are disciples doing what he commanded—teaching others what he declares to us by the Holy Spirit.

Focusing the Gospel

Key words and phrases: Spirit of truth, all truth, glorify me, Everything that the Father has, declare it to you

To the point: The Spirit guides us to *all* truth. Such a bold statement! That truth is the Holy Spirit, is the Life given by the Spirit. *Everything* the Father has is given us. An even bolder statement! What the Father gives us is divine Life. And it is for Jesus' glory that his disciples are empowered by the Spirit to bear what belongs to Jesus and the Father: divine Life. Our triune God holds back nothing from us.

Connecting the Gospel

to the second reading: Since we have received everything that is of God, the Trinity's divine life is within us (see gospel). This life "poured . . . into our hearts" empowers us to be justified and even to "boast of our afflictions" (second reading).

to experience: Our age has an inherent optimism about unraveling the mysteries of life, whether it be the origins of the universe or the genetic makeup of a person. If there's a mystery, "we'll solve it." This solemnity presents the Trinity as a mystery not to be "solved" or "explained," but as a Trinity of Persons who share their very Life with us.

Connecting the Responsorial Psalm

to the readings: The responsorial psalm for this solemnity of The Most Holy Trinity asks who we are in the eyes of God. The readings for this Sunday reveal the high value God places on us human beings. In the first reading the wisdom of God "[plays] on the surface of the earth" and "[finds] delight in the human race." In the second reading God pours God's own love into our hearts through the gift of the Holy Spirit. In the gospel Jesus promises that the Spirit will give to us everything that belongs to him and the Father. Truly God has made us "little less than the angels" and has "crowned [us] with glory and honor" (psalm). In singing this psalm we acknowledge the greatness of the Trinity who gives all so that we might become more.

to psalmist preparation: This responsorial psalm is not so much about your greatness as a human being as about the beneficence of God who treats you with unimaginable dignity and grace. How this week might you treat those whom you meet with this same dignity and grace—at home? at work? on the street?

ASSEMBLY & FAITH-SHARING GROUPS

- The Father has given me . . . Jesus has given me . . . The Spirit has given me . . .
- I believe that the "Spirit of truth" is guiding me to . . .
- Believing that I bear God's divine life within me influences my daily living in that . . .

PRESIDERS

My preaching witnesses to all truth as God's Life within me and the assembly when I . . .

DEACONS

My diaconal service communicates the mystery and majesty of God by . . .

HOSPITALITY MINISTERS

My care and concern for others manifests the "love of God" being "poured" into their hearts (see second reading) whenever I . . .

MUSIC MINISTERS

The truth of my music making is . . . What the Father gives me through my music making is . . .

ALTAR MINISTERS

My ministry is a bold statement about God's Life given to me when I . . .

LECTORS

Contemplating the mystery and majesty of the triune God impacts how I proclaim the word in that . . .

EXTRAORDINARY MINISTERS OF HOLY COMMUNION

Some ways I acknowledge, affirm, and build up the divine indwelling in members of the Body of Christ are . . .

Model Penitential Act

Presider: On this Trinity Sunday, we profess that our God is three divine Persons in One. This Trinity dwells within us. As we prepare to celebrate these mysteries, let us reflect on whether we have been faithful to this divine indwelling . . . [pause]

> Lord Jesus, you are glorified by your Father and by us: Lord . . .
>
> Christ Jesus, you are one with your Father and Spirit: Christ . . .
>
> Lord Jesus, you send the Spirit of truth to dwell within us: Lord . . .

Homily Points

• When do we hold back? When we don't quite trust the other or ourselves. When we are hesitant about outcomes. When another has hurt us. When we don't have all the facts. When we are too selfish to care about others. We human beings all know that at times each of us holds back. Our triune God, however, holds back nothing from us.

• The dynamism of divine Life within the Trinity cannot be held back. God desires to guide each of us to all truth which is the fullness of Life. This Life empowers us to hold nothing back and aptly describes discipleship.

• The first task of a faithful disciple is to become aware of God's Life within and live accordingly. So gifted, a faithful disciple begins to trust more freely, becomes bold in living the Gospel, lives out of the certainty that the outcome of faithful discipleship is eternal life, moves beyond hurt to forgiveness, has the freedom to act even without all the facts because the truth has been given, responds in love to the needs of others. Because we have been given so much—God's very life—faithful disciples need hold nothing back.

Model Universal Prayer (Prayer of the Faithful)

Presider: Our triune God gives us all we need to live the fullness of truth and Life. And so we pray.

Response:

Lord, hear our prayer.

Cantor:

we pray to the Lord,

That the church, guided by the Spirit of truth, may glorify God by living faithfully all that Christ has taught . . . [pause]

That the people of the world, guided by the Spirit of truth, may live in the peace and love of God . . . [pause]

That families torn by strife, guided by the Spirit of truth, may be reconciled with one another . . . [pause]

That all of us here, guided by the Spirit of truth, may hold nothing back as we live the Gospel . . . [pause]

Presider: O God, you will that all people share in your triune Life: hear these our prayers that we might one day enjoy everlasting life with you. We ask this through Jesus Christ our Lord in the Holy Spirit, one God. **Amen.**

COLLECT

Let us pray

Pause for silent prayer

God our Father, who by sending into the world
the Word of truth and the Spirit of sanctification
made known to the human race your wondrous mystery,
grant us, we pray, that in professing the true faith,
we may acknowledge the Trinity of eternal glory
and adore your Unity, powerful in majesty.
Through our Lord Jesus Christ, your Son,
who lives and reigns with you in the unity of the Holy Spirit,
one God, for ever and ever.
Amen.

FIRST READING

Prov 8:22-31

Thus says the wisdom of God:
"The LORD possessed me, the beginning of his ways,
  the forerunner of his prodigies of long ago;
from of old I was poured forth,
  at the first, before the earth.
When there were no depths I was brought forth,
  when there were no fountains or springs of water;
before the mountains were settled into place,
  before the hills, I was brought forth;
while as yet the earth and fields were not made,
  nor the first clods of the world.

"When the Lord established the heavens I was there,
  when he marked out the vault over the face of the deep;
when he made firm the skies above,
  when he fixed fast the foundations of the earth;
when he set for the sea its limit,
  so that the waters should not transgress his command;
then was I beside him as his craftsman,
  and I was his delight day by day,
playing before him all the while,
  playing on the surface of his earth;
  and I found delight in the human race."

RESPONSORIAL PSALM
Ps 8:4-5, 6-7, 8-9

℟. (2a) O Lord, our God, how wonderful your name in all the earth!

When I behold your heavens, the work of your fingers,
the moon and the stars which you set in place—
what is man that you should be mindful of him,
or the son of man that you should care for him?

℟. O Lord, our God, how wonderful your name in all the earth!

You have made him little less than the angels,
and crowned him with glory and honor.
You have given him rule over the works of your hands,
putting all things under his feet.

℟. O Lord, our God, how wonderful your name in all the earth!

All sheep and oxen,
yes, and the beasts of the field,
the birds of the air, the fishes of the sea,
and whatever swims the paths of the seas.

℟. O Lord, our God, how wonderful your name in all the earth!

SECOND READING
Rom 5:1-5

Brothers and sisters:
Therefore, since we have been justified by faith,
we have peace with God through our Lord Jesus Christ,
through whom we have gained access by faith
to this grace in which we stand,
and we boast in hope of the glory of God.
Not only that, but we even boast of our afflictions,
knowing that affliction produces endurance,
and endurance, proven character,
and proven character, hope,
and hope does not disappoint,
because the love of God has been poured out into our hearts
through the Holy Spirit that has been given to us.

About Liturgy

Grace as God's indwelling: Many Catholics have grown up thinking about grace as a *quantity*, something they can "get." Liturgy is where we "get more graces." While there is some truth to this understanding, we have come to a deeper appreciation for understanding grace in terms of God's indwelling life. Rather than a quantity to be had, grace is God's life within us which brings us to a unique relationship with God—as beloved daughters and sons (see CCC no. 1997). Basic to any notion of grace is that it is a gracious gift of God, a bestowal of God's favor on us.

It is not insignificant that the Latin word for grace, *gratia*, has as one of its meanings "thanksgiving." This is, of course, the same word which is the meaning of the Greek *eucharistia*. Grace, then, is God's life within us which first and foremost evokes in us an attitude and relationship of thanksgiving. We might speak of the "grace" of the Mass in terms of our making visible our thankful posture toward God and in that very posture our relationship with God is deepened and strengthened. In this vein, it is clear that any good we do is because of God's grace—because of God's indwelling life, strength, and power.

Any consideration of our continuing Jesus' mission as his faithful disciples must be made within the context of this grace which has been given us. It is not primarily our doing (although we surely do cooperate with God and make a conscious choice to live the Gospel and continue as Jesus did), but God's grace which enables us to be disciples.

About Liturgical Music

Hymn suggestions: Many hymns to the Trinity exist, but most fitting would be ones which connect to this year's readings. An example is Brian Wren's text, "How Wonderful the Three-in-One." The first two verses capture especially well the content of the first reading, "How wonderful the Three-in-One, Whose energies of dancing light Are undivided, pure and good, Communing love in shared delight. Before the flow of dawn and dark, Creation's lover dreamed of earth, And with a caring deep and wise, All things conceived and brought to birth." Since the tune may be unfamiliar to many, the choir could sing the hymn as a prelude or during the preparation of the gifts with the assembly joining in on the last verse.

Another example is Mary Louise Bringle's "Play of the Godhead," which begins with the phrase, "The play of the Godhead, the Trinity's dance, Embraces the earth in a sacred romance. . . ." This hymn would work well during preparation of the gifts. A third example is Bernadette Farrell's "God beyond All Names," which proclaims that the God beyond "our dreams . . . all names . . . all words . . . all time . . ." is also the "God of tender care" who has "cradled us in goodness" and "mothered us in wholeness" and "loved us into birth." This hymn would fit either the preparation of the gifts or the Communion procession.

✝ SPIRITUALITY

GOSPEL ACCLAMATION
John 6:51

℟. Alleluia, alleluia.
I am the living bread that came down from heaven, says the Lord; / whoever eats this bread will live forever.
℟. Alleluia, alleluia.

Gospel Luke 9:11b-17; L169C

Jesus spoke to the
    crowds about the
        kingdom of God,
    and he healed those
        who needed to be
        cured.
As the day was drawing
    to a close,
    the Twelve approached him
        and said,
    "Dismiss the crowd
    so that they can go to the
        surrounding villages and farms
    and find lodging and provisions;
    for we are in a deserted place here."
He said to them, "Give them some food
    yourselves."
They replied, "Five loaves and two fish
    are all we have,
    unless we ourselves go and buy food
        for all these people."
Now the men there numbered about
    five thousand.
Then he said to his disciples,
    "Have them sit down in groups of
        about fifty."
They did so and made them all sit down.
Then taking the five loaves and the two
    fish,
    and looking up to heaven,
    he said the blessing over them, broke
        them,
    and gave them to the disciples to set
        before the crowd.
They all ate and were satisfied.
And when the leftover fragments were
    picked up,
    they filled twelve wicker baskets.

Reflecting on the Gospel

Healing, nourishment, satisfaction, and abundance are all signs of the presence of the kingdom of God. Jesus' actions in this gospel, however, reveal an even more telling sign. By taking, blessing, breaking, and giving the bread and fish, he foreshadows the total gift of his very self—on the Cross, in the Eucharist. The fullest presence of the kingdom of God is revealed by the total gift of self. When we receive Jesus' gift of self in the Eucharist and choose to be transformed into being that same gift for others, we are the visible presence of the kingdom of God. The kingdom of God comes to fulfillment in every act of total self-giving.

Jesus is the one who gave himself totally and continues to give himself to us in the Eucharist. In this Sunday's gospel Jesus not only fills the hungry with good things, he fills them to overflowing. This solemnity reminds us that Jesus' generous extravagance is not measured only by the amount of food but by the kind of Food he offers—his very self in his Body and Blood. The presence of the kingdom of God is an extravagant presence revealed in the signs of nourishment and abundance, in the signs of total gift of self.

The food the Twelve offered in response to Jesus' command "Give them some food yourselves" was a few loaves and a couple fish, insufficient for so large a crowd. The food Jesus offered was abundant—foreshadowing his own ultimate and abundant self-giving. Human food leaves us hungry and desiring more. Jesus' food leaves us satisfied. But the satisfaction comes not simply from eating and drinking the Food Jesus offers. The real satisfaction comes from what the eating and drinking lead us to do: give ourselves over to others in self-surrender as Jesus did. The focus of this solemnity, therefore, is not limited to the eucharistic elements, but leads to our eating and drinking as a proclamation of living the paschal mystery: "For as often as you eat this bread and drink the cup, you proclaim the death of the Lord until he comes" (second reading). Our eating and drinking is our own pledge of self-giving.

Living the Paschal Mystery

Our sharing in the Body and Blood of Christ isn't just for ourselves; St. Paul in his First Letter to the Corinthians makes it clear that we eat and drink ourselves into the paschal mystery. That is, when our eating and drinking truly "proclaim the death of the Lord until he comes," we ourselves "hand over" our bodies—our lives—for the salvation of others. What the Twelve were not able to do for the crowd—provide food for so many—we can do if we do as Jesus did: hand ourselves over.

Discipleship is both accepting the abundance of what God gives us and living out the responsibility having that abundance implies. When we eat and drink the Body and Blood of Christ, we ourselves are transformed more perfectly into the presence of that risen Christ for others. This transformation is both gift and challenge. It is the gift and pledge that what we have now—Jesus' Body and Blood—we will also have even more fully at the messianic banquet. It is the challenge to spend ourselves for others, to give of ourselves. Herein is the mystery!

The deepest mystery this solemnity celebrates is not only that Jesus gives us his own Body and Blood as nourishment which satisfies us fully. It is also that we, too, must give our very own body and blood to others so that they might be satisfied. And when the "leftover fragments" of ourselves are gathered up, we will find ourselves sharing in the everlasting abundance of the messianic banquet. Such a mystery!

Key words and phrases: kingdom of God, healed, gave, all ate, satisfied, fragments . . . filled

To the point: Healing, nourishment, satisfaction, and abundance are all signs of the presence of the kingdom of God. Jesus' actions in this gospel, however, reveal an even more telling sign. By taking, blessing, breaking, and giving the bread and fish, he foreshadows the total gift of his very self—on the Cross, in the Eucharist. The fullest presence of the kingdom of God is revealed by the total gift of self. When we receive Jesus' gift of self in the Eucharist and choose to be transformed into being that same gift for others, we are the visible presence of the kingdom of God. The kingdom of God comes to fulfillment in every act of total self-giving.

Connecting the Gospel

to the second reading: The focus of this solemnity is not limited to our eating and drinking the eucharistic elements, but leads to our living the total self-giving of Christ: "For as often as you eat this bread and drink the cup, you proclaim the death of the Lord until he comes."

to experience: Total self-giving seems beyond human capability. Only little by little do we grow in our capacity to give ourselves as Jesus did. The Eucharist nourishes and encourages us as we more and more in our daily lives choose self-giving.

Connecting the Responsorial Psalm

to the readings: Psalm 110 was a royal psalm used at the coronation ceremony of a king descended from the line of David. The text promised the king a place of honor next to God, victory over enemies, and a priestly role before the people. In the first reading Melchizedek, "a priest of God Most High," gives food, drink, and blessing to Abram. In the gospel Jesus heals those in need and feeds the starving crowd, creating an amazing abundance out of a meager supply. In the second reading Paul reminds us that the food and drink Jesus gives us is his very Body and Blood. In singing this psalm we recognize what Jesus does and who Jesus is. He is the one victorious over all that impedes fullness of life. He is the one who feeds us with his very self. He is the completion of the Davidic line and a "Priest forever, in the line of Melchizedek."

to psalmist preparation: The psalm you sing this Sunday acclaims the power and priesthood of Christ, both most evident to us in the gift of his Body and Blood for food. What might you do this week to affirm your personal faith in Jesus and express your gratitude for what he does in giving us the Eucharist?

ASSEMBLY & FAITH-SHARING GROUPS

- Signs of the kingdom of God I see in my daily living are . . .
- I hunger to be nourished by the Body and Blood of Christ when . . . I feel satisfied when . . .
- I grow in self-giving when . . . I feel satisfied when . . .

PRESIDERS

"This is my body that is for you" (second reading). I not only pray these words but live them when I . . .

DEACONS

My serving ministry makes visible the kingdom of God when I . . .

HOSPITALITY MINISTERS

My hospitality is marked by self-giving when . . . and the signs of this are . . .

MUSIC MINISTERS

My participation in music ministry is a gift of self when . . . Eucharist nourishes my ability to give self in this music ministry by . . .

ALTAR MINISTERS

Serving others is an occasion to grow in self-giving in that . . .

LECTORS

My time with God's word helps me live the eucharistic mystery—giving self for others—because . . .

EXTRAORDINARY MINISTERS OF HOLY COMMUNION

My ministry goes beyond formality to genuine self-giving—imitating Christ's own self-giving in the Eucharist—when I . . .

Model Penitential Act

Presider: The Body and Blood of Christ sustains our Gospel call to self-giving. As we prepare to celebrate this liturgy, let us reflect on how we have faithfully given self for others . . . [pause]

Lord Jesus, you give us the Gift of yourself in the Eucharist: Lord . . .

Christ Jesus, you are the fulfillment of the kingdom of God: Christ . . .

Lord Jesus, your Body and Blood are the pledge of eternal life: Lord . . .

Homily Points

• Generosity abounds. Habitat for Humanity, Peace Corps, Doctors without Borders do not want for volunteers. Parents' self-giving seems heroic. A good friend's availability is constant. These and many other simple acts of daily self-giving are signs of the presence of the kingdom of God among us.

• The gospel describes two kinds of Jesus' self-giving: he heals the sick and feeds the hungry crowd, he foreshadows his total self-giving on the Cross and in the Eucharist. In this self-giving does Jesus make clear that the kingdom of God is present. The kingdom of God comes to fulfillment in every act of total self-giving.

• Everyday simple acts of sharing are a sign of the presence of the kingdom of God. The gospel challenges us to see our daily generosity and self-giving as "eucharistic actions" that make present God's kingdom. Eucharist cannot be limited to receiving the total Gift of Christ's Body and Blood. Eucharist is also a way of life expressed in the total gift of self for the sake of others. This eucharistic living is the visible sign of the kingdom of God.

Model Universal Prayer (Prayer of the Faithful)

Presider: The God who nourishes us abundantly surely hears our prayers. And so we lift them to God with confidence.

Response:

Lord, hear our prayer.

Cantor:

we pray to the Lord,

May all members of the Body of Christ imitate Jesus in self-giving for the sake of others . . . [pause]

May all people of the world share in the abundant gifts of God's unending generosity . . . [pause]

May all those who hunger and thirst for food, justice, mercy, forgiveness, and peace be satisfied . . . [pause]

May all of us here grow into being more perfectly the Body of Christ living eucharistic lives . . . [pause]

Presider: Generous God, you give us the Body and Blood of your Son as food for our journey: hear our prayers that one day we may come to the eternal banquet you have prepared for us. We ask this through Christ our Lord. **Amen.**

COLLECT

Let us pray

Pause for silent prayer

O God, who in this wonderful Sacrament
have left us a memorial of your Passion,
grant us, we pray,
so to revere the sacred mysteries of your
    Body and Blood
that we may always experience in
    ourselves
the fruits of your redemption.
Who live and reign with God the Father
in the unity of the Holy Spirit,
one God, for ever and ever.
Amen.

FIRST READING
Gen 14:18-20

In those days, Melchizedek, king of Salem,
    brought out bread and wine,
    and being a priest of God Most High,
    he blessed Abram with these words:
"Blessed be Abram by God Most High,
    the creator of heaven and earth;
    and blessed be God Most High,
    who delivered your foes into your
        hand."
Then Abram gave him a tenth of
    everything.

RESPONSORIAL PSALM

Ps 110:1, 2, 3, 4

R⁄. (4b) You are a priest forever, in the line of Melchizedek.

The LORD said to my Lord: "Sit at my right hand
till I make your enemies your footstool."

R⁄. You are a priest forever, in the line of Melchizedek.

The scepter of your power the LORD will stretch forth from Zion:
"Rule in the midst of your enemies."

R⁄. You are a priest forever, in the line of Melchizedek.

"Yours is princely power in the day of your birth, in holy splendor;
before the daystar, like the dew, I have begotten you."

R⁄. You are a priest forever, in the line of Melchizedek.

The LORD has sworn, and he will not repent:
"You are a priest forever, according to the order of Melchizedek."

R⁄. You are a priest forever, in the line of Melchizedek.

SECOND READING

1 Cor 11:23-26

Brothers and sisters:
I received from the Lord what I also handed on to you,
that the Lord Jesus, on the night he was handed over,
took bread, and, after he had given thanks,
broke it and said, "This is my body that is for you.
Do this in remembrance of me."
In the same way also the cup, after supper, saying,
"This cup is the new covenant in my blood.
Do this, as often as you drink it, in remembrance of me."
For as often as you eat this bread and drink the cup,
you proclaim the death of the Lord until he comes.

OPTIONAL SEQUENCE

See Appendix A, p. 302.

About Liturgy

This solemnity and Ordinary Time: At first look, it may be tempting to see this solemnity simply as a "devotional" feast. In fact, it developed at a time in the church's eucharistic spirituality when people rarely actually received the Eucharist, but gazed on the exposed Host and adored it. Many in the church today can still recall the lavish *Corpus Christi* processions from their youth; some parishes or other liturgical communities are reviving this popular devotion. On Holy Thursday the church celebrates Jesus' giving his Body and Blood, in the context of service. Since so much during the Triduum directs our attention elsewhere, this solemnity allows further reflection on that great mystery inaugurated at the Lord's Supper.

Now, however, the context is Ordinary Time. This is the time when we might reflect on Jesus' gift of his very own Body and Blood in the context of our developing notion of discipleship. This solemnity challenges us to move our eucharistic piety beyond prayer and liturgy to a lived, everyday expression of the love that Eucharist embodies.

Optional sequence: The sequence for this day is optional, but it ought not be dismissed too lightly. There is a profound theology contained therein, especially with the last five verses (the shorter form). If a parish liturgy preparation team does not use the sequence as part of an extended gospel procession, it might at least be used at a liturgy committee meeting for deeper reflection on the mystery of Eucharist. It would be time well spent!

About Liturgical Music

Music suggestions: Steven Janco's "Draw Near" is a lovely verse-refrain setting of the seventh century hymn *Sancti, venite, Christi corpus sumite.* The song invites us to draw near and receive Christ's gift of himself to us in the Eucharist. Also appropriate for Communion on this solemnity would be songs which express our participation in Christ's feeding of the hungry. David Haas's "Now We Remain" comes to mind not only because of its refrain but also because of its final verse, "We are the presence of God; this is our call. Now to become bread and wine: food for the hungry, life for the weary, for to live with the Lord, we must die with the Lord." Tom Porter's "Let Us Be Bread" offers this refrain: "Let us be bread, blessed by the Lord, broken and shared, life for the world. Let us be wine, love freely poured. Let us be one in the Lord." Marty Haugen's litanic "Bread to Share" is uplifting with its repetition of "You have plenty to share, you have plenty of bread to share." Rory Cooney's "Bread of Life/*Pan de Vida*" uses the refrain, "I myself am the bread of life. You and I are the bread of life, taken and blessed, broken and shared by Christ that the world might live." Delores Dufner's "We Come with Joy" (in *Hymns for the Gospels*, GIA) combines narration of the story of Jesus' feeding the crowd with the call that we do likewise, "For Christ will bless our bit of bread, The loaves our hands provide, Till empty baskets overflow And all are satisfied." This hymn could be sung during the preparation of the gifts, during the Communion procession, or after Communion as a song of praise.

✝ SPIRITUALITY

GOSPEL ACCLAMATION
Matt 11:29ab

℟. Alleluia, alleluia.
Take my yoke upon you, says the Lord;
and learn from me, for I am meek and humble
     of heart.
℟. Alleluia, alleluia.

or

1 John 4:10b

℟. Alleluia, alleluia.
God first loved us
and sent his Son as expiation for
     our sins.
℟. Alleluia, alleluia.

Gospel

Luke 15:3-7; L172C

Jesus addressed this
     parable to the Pharisees and
     scribes:
"What man among you having a
     hundred sheep and losing one of
     them
     would not leave the ninety-nine in the
          desert
     and go after the lost one until
          he finds it?
And when he does find it,
     he sets it on his shoulders with great
          joy
     and, upon his arrival home,
     he calls together his friends and
          neighbors and says to them,
     'Rejoice with me because I have
          found my lost sheep.'
I tell you, in just the same way
     there will be more joy in heaven over
          one sinner who repents
     than over ninety-nine righteous
          people
     who have no need of repentance."

See Appendix A, p. 303, for other readings.

Reflecting on the Gospel
The human heart is a symbol for love and life. This gospel depicts both: the shepherd's love for the lost sheep (sinner); the life celebrated in the joy of the lost being found. The Sacred Heart is a divine heart that loves totally, rejoices fully, and gives life freely. How blessed are we to be sheep of his flock, recipients of his care, sharers in his life! This solemnity in honor of the Sacred Heart of Jesus is a day on which we not only rejoice in Jesus' intimate relationship with us, but also in his incredible sacrificial love.

The gospel, first reading, and responsorial psalm use the image of the good shepherd to define the mystery of the Sacred Heart. Such is the love which seeks the lost, heals the wounded, protects from death, and gives its own life. In this, "God proves his love for us" (second reading). Jesus' sacrificial love is to be the way we love. He gave his life for us sinners (second reading). We are to give our lives for others.

The second reading gives us a hint as to why so many people can take up the sacrificial and life-giving love of Christ: "The love of God has been poured out into [their] hearts through the Holy Spirit that has been given to [them]." This is why this solemnity is cause for rejoicing and not cringing: sacrifice is nothing to shrink from, but something to embrace. Because that is where Life is. That is where Love is. That is where Heart is.

The gospel uses the word "joy" twice and "rejoice" once. Although we know that the Sacred Heart is a symbol of self-giving sacrificial love, the Sacred Heart is also a symbol of great happiness. Jesus rejoices in his work of redemption, when the lost are found (saved). We rejoice because we have such a Good Shepherd to care for us.

Living the Paschal Mystery
This solemnity might hold challenges for two different groups of people. First, those who have yet to develop a life patterned after Jesus' sacrificial love must take it up, since "we are now justified by [Christ's] blood" (second reading). This solemnity, coming early in our resumption of Ordinary Time, encourages us to travel the paschal journey with Christ in which we take up our own cross for the sake of sinners. This solemnity urges us to have the heart of Christ: one which gives all for even one out of love and compassion. This solemnity calls us to embrace the one precept of the Sacred Heart/Good Shepherd: love that even searches for the lost, embraces those who are different, cares for the unacceptable, is tolerant of the irresponsible, rejoices over the repentant sinner.

Second, many among us already live sacrificial—indeed, even heroic—lives characterized by great generosity. Our nation virtually saves billions of dollars each year because of the millions of volunteers who do everything from taking meals to homebound people, to calling the sick and elderly and making sure they are okay, to serving meals to the homeless. How many people give of their holiday time so that the hungry can be fed? For these already very generous people, the challenge of this solemnity is to couch their generosity and self-sacrificing love within the context of the redeeming love of Christ. The challenge is to see those they serve as Christ himself and to realize that their sacrificial love is Christ's Sacred Heart in them. And it is Christ's Sacred Heart being made present to others. It is the Good Shepherd made visible today.

Focusing the Gospel

Key words and phrases: go after the lost one, great joy, rejoice with me, found, joy in heaven

To the point: The human heart is a symbol for love and life. This gospel depicts both: the shepherd's love for the lost sheep (sinner); the life celebrated in the joy of the lost being found. The Sacred Heart is a divine heart that loves totally, rejoices fully, and gives life freely. How blessed are we to be sheep of his flock, recipients of his care, sharers in his life!

Model Penitential Act

Presider: On this Friday we celebrate the solemnity of the Most Sacred Heart of Jesus. Let us open ourselves to the Good Shepherd's tender love and ask to be truly faithful in following him . . . [pause]

Lord Jesus, you seek out the lost: Lord . . .

Christ Jesus, you love us and bring us joy: Christ . . .

Lord Jesus, you shepherd us on the path to life: Lord . . .

Model Universal Prayer (Prayer of the Faithful)

Presider: The God whose own Son is our Good Shepherd hears our prayers and answers our needs. And so we pray.

Response:

Cantor:

That the church may always faithfully follow the Good Shepherd . . . [pause]

That world leaders always shepherd their people with care and justice . . . [pause]

That the lost be found, the unloved be loved, sinners be reconciled . . . [pause]

That the love of the Sacred Heart be poured forth into our hearts in good measure . . . [pause]

Presider: O God of boundless love, you faithfully hear the prayers of those who cry out to you: may we imitate the Sacred Heart of Jesus by growing in our love for others. We ask this through Christ our Lord. **Amen.**

COLLECT

Let us pray

Pause for silent prayer

Grant, we pray, almighty God,
that we, who glory in the Heart of your
    beloved Son
and recall the wonders of his love for us,
may be made worthy to receive
an overflowing measure of grace
from that fount of heavenly gifts.
Through our Lord Jesus Christ, your Son,
who lives and reigns with you in the unity
    of the Holy Spirit,
one God, for ever and ever. **Amen.**

FOR REFLECTION

- I experience Jesus' love and life when . . .
- I am lost when . . . Jesus finds me through . . . I experience joy in that . . .
- I imitate the Sacred Heart of Jesus in my care for others when I . . .

Homily Points

• This parable of the Good Shepherd in search of the lost sheep contrasts the tenderness of Jesus' Heart with the hardness of the hearts of the Pharisees and scribes. These Jewish leaders of his time shun those whom they judge are lost—those who stray from any precept of their law. The Pharisees and scribes hardly love with tenderness and compassion; instead, they place burdens on the shoulders of the very people they ought to shepherd.

• Often we make others earn our love by demanding they follow our precepts. This festival reminds us of the free, abundant, tender love of the Sacred Heart who is much more concerned about inviting others to grow in new life than chastising them for straying from his fold. This festival calls us to move beyond our limited embrace to the all-encompassing embrace of the Sacred Heart/Good Shepherd. We are to follow his precept of love, acceptance, forgiveness.

✠ SPIRITUALITY

GOSPEL ACCLAMATION
Luke 7:16

R⁊. Alleluia, alleluia.
A great prophet has risen in our midst,
God has visited his people.
R⁊. Alleluia, alleluia.

Gospel

Luke 7:11-17; L90C

Jesus journeyed to a city called
   Nain,
   and his disciples and a large
      crowd accompanied him.
As he drew near to the gate of the
      city,
   a man who had died was being
      carried out,
   the only son of his mother, and
      she was a widow.
A large crowd from the city was with
      her.
When the Lord saw her,
   he was moved with pity for her and
      said to her,
   "Do not weep."
He stepped forward and touched the
      coffin;
   at this the bearers halted,
   and he said, "Young man, I tell you,
      arise!"
The dead man sat up and began to
      speak,
   and Jesus gave him to his mother.
Fear seized them all, and they glorified
      God, exclaiming,
   "A great prophet has arisen in our
      midst,"
   and "God has visited his people."
This report about him spread through
      the whole of Judea
   and in all the surrounding region.

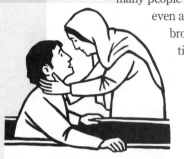

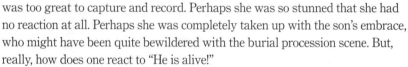

Reflecting on the Gospel

Loving children prepare emotionally and spiritually (and often financially) their whole lives for the death and burial of their parents. This is the way it should be. No parents can prepare to bury their child. This isn't the way it should be. The parents are the older generation; they pass away first. While there is always grief at the death of parents, there is also no small measure of comfort in reminiscing about a life well spent, hopefully a long life that has influenced many people and achieved much good. When a child dies, however— even an adult child—we have a sense that the life the parents have brought into this world has been cheated by the brevity of its time on this earth. Not everything has been accomplished. The younger generation just doesn't die first. That's not the way things are supposed to be.

In this Sunday's gospel a burial procession is taking place. A son has died. The dead man was the widow's only son. Naturally, she was weeping. Nothing could have prepared her for the grief she felt at her only son's death. Nothing could assuage the grief. So she thought. Jesus, out of pity, raised the dead son to life again, who "sat up and began to speak." He is alive! The gospel does not record the widow's response to this unexpected turn of events. It only tells us that "Jesus gave him to his mother." Perhaps her joy was too great to capture and record. Perhaps she was so stunned that she had no reaction at all. Perhaps she was completely taken up with the son's embrace, who might have been quite bewildered with the burial procession scene. But, really, how does one react to "He is alive!"

The crowd was in awe and "glorified God" for the miracle. Little did they know how in an even fuller and more life-giving way "God has visited his people." This God-man is an only Son, too. He, too, will die. He, too, will be raised up to new life. He, too, speaks. Then. And now, to us. He, too, gives life. Then. And now, to us. When Jesus speaks to us the word of life—Arise!—he is offering us more than human life. He is offering us a share in his risen life.

There is a connection between the gospel and first reading beyond the obvious parallels of a widow, son, death, new life, giving son back to a mother, acknowledgment of God's presence and power. Elijah "stretched himself out upon the child" and called out to God to "let the life breath return." These actions point to Jesus stretched out on the cross and the Spirit coming to breathe new life into us. Bringing new life from death is a paschal event. We share now in the risen life Jesus gives us through the Spirit.

Living the Paschal Mystery

We have only recently completed our annual celebration of the season of Easter. Yet our return to Ordinary Time begins with a story of Jesus raising a dead man to life. God brings us new life out of death every day of our Christian journey. Every day Jesus encounters us on the way and has pity on us. His love and compassion are so great and so enduring that Jesus is always loving us into ever deeper risen life. Every day he is saying to us "Arise!" when we think we are going to break from too much tension, are discouraged with always playing catch-up, are doubting our ability to make a difference in our world. What is our response to his ever-present gift of Life?

Focusing the Gospel

Key words and phrases: man had died, only son, arise, began to speak, God has visited his people

To the point: The dead man was the widow's only son. Naturally, she was weeping. Jesus, out of pity, raised the man to life again, who "sat up and began to speak." He is alive! The crowd "glorified God" for the miracle. Little did they know how in an even fuller and more life-giving way "God has visited his people." This God-man is an only Son, too. He, too, will die. He, too, will be raised up to new life. He, too, speaks. Then. And now, to us. He, too, gives life. Then. And now, to us.

Connecting the Gospel

to the first reading: The widow recognizes Elijah as truly a "man of God" when he restores life to her dead son. Jesus reveals the presence and power of God when he raises another widow's son from the dead. The sign that God is acting in our midst is that God overcomes death to bring new life.

to experience: We think of death as final. We weep. Jesus establishes that death is not final, but is the beginning of fuller and everlasting life. For this we rejoice and glorify God.

Connecting the Responsorial Psalm

to the readings: The Sunday Lectionary uses Psalm 30 four times (Easter Vigil 4, Third Sunday of Easter C, Tenth Sunday in Ordinary Time C, and Thirteenth Sunday in Ordinary Time B) and each time the readings deal with our need to be delivered from death. Even though God has made all things for life, we nonetheless experience death coming toward us over and over, bringing pain, grief, and even guilt (first reading). The stories of these two grieving widows, however, show us a God acting to change our weeping into rejoicing, our mourning into dancing (psalm). God restores life through the prayer of a faithful prophet. God restores life through the words and actions of Christ who holds power over death. These verses from Psalm 30 acknowledge what oftentimes only our faith can see: that death with its contingent weeping and mourning is not the end of the story—life is.

to psalmist preparation: When you sing this psalm, you embody the confidence of the entire Body of Christ that God saves from death, even when the whole world groans under its threat. Pray this week for those who are facing death in any form—physical, mental, emotional. Pray that your singing may be a song of hope for them.

ASSEMBLY & FAITH-SHARING GROUPS

- God visits me when . . . I glorify God by . . .

- I hear Jesus speaking to me these words . . . I hear Jesus say to me "arise!" when . . .

- The fuller life I experience when I encounter Jesus is . . .

PRESIDERS

My preaching brings new life to my people when I say . . .

DEACONS

My serving brings new life to those who feel "dead" when I . . .

HOSPITALITY MINISTERS

My greeting is a word of life when I . . .

MUSIC MINISTERS

When I am aware of Jesus' life-giving presence and power, my music making sounds like . . .

ALTAR MINISTERS

My serving at the altar witnesses to the life I have been given by God when I . . .

LECTORS

When I am aware of God visiting me during my preparation of the readings, my proclamation sounds like . . .

EXTRAORDINARY MINISTERS OF HOLY COMMUNION

I see the glory of God on the faces of communicants when I . . .

Model Penitential Act

Presider: Just as Jesus gave life back to the only son of the widow of Nain, so does God offer us new life during this celebration. Let us open ourselves to God's presence and new life . . . [pause]

Lord Jesus, you are the only Son of God: Lord . . .

Christ Jesus, you are the resurrection and the life: Christ . . .

Lord Jesus, you speak to us words of life: Lord . . .

Homily Points

• Death is harsh. Death is final. We have no response but to weep over the loss of life. We readily identify with the grief of the widow in this Sunday's gospel. Her life was effectively over. Her only son's death was death for her.

• With the death of her son, the widow had lost her future as well as her present. By raising her son back to life Jesus restored her present possibilities and revealed God's promise concerning our future: death is not the end, but the beginning of the fullness of life God intends for us.

• Our Christian journey is a constant opening of ourselves to new life that comes from God. We most often experience receiving this new life through others. Parents constantly encourage their little ones to try new things and grow in new directions. Teachers constantly seek to bring students in touch with the God-given gifts within them, stretching them beyond limits they tend to set for themselves. Friends constantly support and bring new understanding to one another. In such encounters Jesus himself comes to us with the words, "arise!" be alive! These encounters point to the end of our journey: the fullness of life God intends for us.

Model Universal Prayer (Prayer of the Faithful)

Presider: God desires that we have new life. And so we are confident to make our life needs known.

Response:

Lord, hear our prayer.

Cantor:

we pray to the Lord,

That all members of the church may speak Jesus' words of new life to all whom they meet . . . [pause]

That leaders of nations may always lead their people to fuller life . . . [pause]

That those who grieve may be comforted by Jesus' promise of fullness of life . . . [pause]

That each of us here reach out with support and encouragement to those who seem discouraged with life . . . [pause]

Presider: God of life, your only Son died so that we might have new life: hear these our prayers and bring us to eternal life. We ask this through Christ our Lord. **Amen.**

COLLECT

Let us pray

Pause for silent prayer

O God, from whom all good things come,
grant that we, who call on you in our need,
may at your prompting discern what is
right,
and by your guidance do it.
Through our Lord Jesus Christ, your Son,
who lives and reigns with you in the unity
of the Holy Spirit,
one God, for ever and ever.
Amen.

FIRST READING

1 Kgs 17:17-24

Elijah went to Zarephath of Sidon to the
house of a widow.
The son of the mistress of the house fell
sick,
and his sickness grew more severe until
he stopped breathing.
So she said to Elijah,
"Why have you done this to me, O man
of God?
Have you come to me to call attention to
my guilt
and to kill my son?"
Elijah said to her, "Give me your son."
Taking him from her lap, he carried the
son to the upper room
where he was staying, and put him on
his bed.
Elijah called out to the LORD:
"O LORD, my God,
will you afflict even the widow with
whom I am staying
by killing her son?"
Then he stretched himself out upon the
child three times
and called out to the LORD:
"O LORD, my God,
let the life breath return to the body of
this child."
The LORD heard the prayer of Elijah;
the life breath returned to the child's
body and he revived.
Taking the child, Elijah brought him down
into the house
from the upper room and gave him to
his mother.
Elijah said to her, "See! Your son is alive."
The woman replied to Elijah,
"Now indeed I know that you are a man
of God.
The word of the LORD comes truly from
your mouth."

RESPONSORIAL PSALM

Ps 30:2, 4, 5-6, 11, 12, 13

R⁊. (2a) I will praise you, Lord, for you have rescued me.

I will extol you, O LORD, for you drew me clear
    and did not let my enemies rejoice over me.
O LORD, you brought me up from the nether world;
    you preserved me from among those going down into the pit.

R⁊. I will praise you, Lord, for you have rescued me.

Sing praise to the LORD, you his faithful ones,
    and give thanks to his holy name.
For his anger lasts but a moment;
    a lifetime, his good will.
At nightfall, weeping enters in,
    but with the dawn, rejoicing.

R⁊. I will praise you, Lord, for you have rescued me.

Hear, O LORD, and have pity on me;
    O LORD, be my helper.
You changed my mourning into dancing;
    O LORD, my God, forever will I give you thanks.

R⁊. I will praise you, Lord, for you have rescued me.

SECOND READING

Gal 1:11-19

I want you to know, brothers and sisters,
    that the gospel preached by me is not of human origin.
For I did not receive it from a human being, nor was I taught it,
    but it came through a revelation of Jesus Christ.

For you heard of my former way of life in Judaism,
    how I persecuted the church of God beyond measure
    and tried to destroy it, and progressed in Judaism
    beyond many of my contemporaries among my race,
    since I was even more a zealot for my ancestral traditions.

Continued in Appendix A, p. 303.

About Liturgy

Rite of Christian Burial: When we Catholics think of funerals, we usually focus on the funeral Mass. In reality, the Rite of Christian Burial is a full and rich celebration consisting of three liturgies and two processions. Each has a distinctive purpose.

The first liturgy most often occurs at funeral homes, although more and more families are opting to have visitation in the church. The Vigil for the Deceased takes place before the funeral Mass. It is a celebration of the Word or it may be part of the Liturgy of the Hours, usually Evening Prayer. Through song and proclamation, intercession and blessing we pray for the deceased person and all those who mourn this loss. There is great latitude in how this prayer might unfold. This is a good time for eulogies, for recalling stories about the deceased person that eases the pain of loss for the loved ones. The vigil can be a time to express grief and be comforted by the gathered community.

This liturgy is followed by the first procession (there may be some time lapse here), to the church where the funeral Mass will be celebrated. Processions always symbolize a movement from here (a place, an attitude, a need) to there (a different place, a refreshed attitude, a different need). Moving to church might symbolize a movement from focusing on loss and grief to the focus of the funeral Mass which is a celebration of new and eternal life.

Finally, the second procession is from the church to the place of burial. Here the movement is toward surrender and final committal to the earth, whence human flesh first comes. This is the final act of reverence for the deceased person's body.

When the funeral rites are celebrated in all their fullness, they are a clear and visible sign of the dying and rising mystery of Christ into which we were immersed at baptism. Death is both a time for grieving over loss and a celebration of new and eternal life gained.

About Liturgical Music

Music suggestions: A good opening song for this Sunday would be "Your Hands, O Lord, in Days of Old." In this hymn we ask Christ whose hands "triumphed over pain and death, Fought darkness and the grave" (v. 1) to "be our mighty healer still" (v. 3). A fitting choice for the preparation of the gifts would be Herman Stuempfle's "The Ranks of Death with Trophy Grim" (in *Hymns for the Gospels*, GIA). Written with this Sunday's gospel in mind, this hymn tells how "The ranks of death and Lord of Life Stood face to face that hour," and Christ "With words of awesome power" left death defeated on the road (v. 2). The "embrace" of death which "bears us toward the tomb" has been broken by the power of Christ (v. 3). Examples of appropriate choices for Communion include "I Am the Bread of Life" and "Shepherd Me, O God." Finally, an apt recessional song would be "We Know That Christ Is Raised." This hymn with its sweeping melody sings of our union through baptism in both Christ's death and his resurrection. The rising alleluia which concludes each verse would make a fitting conclusion to this day's celebration of the paschal mystery.

SPIRITUALITY

GOSPEL ACCLAMATION
1 John 4:10b

Ry. Alleluia, alleluia.
God loved us and sent his Son
as expiation for our sins.
Ry. Alleluia, alleluia.

Gospel

Luke 7:36–8:3; L93C

A Pharisee invited Jesus to dine
with him,
and he entered the Pharisee's
house and reclined at table.
Now there was a sinful woman in
the city
who learned that he was at
table in the house of the
Pharisee.
Bringing an alabaster flask of
ointment,
she stood behind him at his feet
weeping
and began to bathe his feet with her
tears.
Then she wiped them with her hair,
kissed them, and anointed them with
the ointment.
When the Pharisee who had invited
him saw this he said to
himself,
"If this man were a prophet,
he would know who and what sort of
woman this is who is touching
him,
that she is a sinner."
Jesus said to him in reply,
"Simon, I have something to say to
you."
"Tell me, teacher," he said.
"Two people were in debt to a certain
creditor;
one owed five hundred days' wages
and the other owed fifty.
Since they were unable to repay the
debt, he forgave it for both.
Which of them will love him more?"

Continued in Appendix A, p. 304.

Reflecting on the Gospel

The familiar and comfortable context of dining at table becomes an occasion charged with tension. The tensions are many: a sinful woman intimately touches Jesus in public, a host does not extend simple gestures of hospitality, others at table are indignant at Jesus assuming the power and authority to forgive sins. Simon and his guests not only judge the sinful woman, but they also judge Jesus. They fail to see who Jesus is: the One who came to bring the "good news of the kingdom of God." In this kingdom sinners touch God, receive forgiveness, and are granted peace. In this kingdom it is not tension and judgment that triumph, but love.

The woman's encounter with Jesus not only brought her forgiveness, but also was an occasion for her to show her "great love." Forgiveness is a sign of mutual acceptance. Forgiveness is a sign of peace sought. Forgiveness is a sign of love exchanged. Of such is the "good news of the kingdom of God."

The gospel and first reading manifest one of the most significant aspects of the relationship between God and human beings: God is the one who forgives sins; human beings are those who sin. The issue is not whether we sin (we do and will!), but whether we will open ourselves to the judgment and mercy of God. This woman does; David does (first reading); Simon, however, resists. Simon himself sits in judgment; the woman kneels in repentance. The gospel concludes with Simon being rebuked and the woman being forgiven.

Simon thought that Jesus was unaware of the "sort of woman" who was lovingly "touching him." In response to Simon's judgment about the woman, Jesus constructed his parable to open Simon's eyes to see the great love within the heart of this sinful woman. The woman, who knows only too well how great is her sin, throws herself on Jesus' mercy and receives forgiveness. We do not know Simon's response. We do know the woman's response: loving action. Do we know what *we* need to do? how *we* need to respond?

Living the Paschal Mystery

Most of us are more like Simon than like the woman. It's far easier to see what is wrong in another than it is to see what is wrong in ourselves. Nathan's work as a prophet was to help David see his sinfulness. Because David acknowledges his sin, he is met with forgiveness. Like David, sometimes we need a "prophet" to help us look deeply into our own hearts and see what needs healing and forgiving.

One way that we might more easily come to acknowledge our own sinfulness is, as Nathan reminded David, to recall all the good God has done for us. David had been anointed king, rescued from Saul, given possessions and family, and even more. In forgetting all this good, he lusted after what he did not have and sinned grievously. If we keep our eyes turned toward all the good God has given us, we ourselves might more easily overcome whatever temptations to sin come our way.

Perhaps one way to live this gospel would be to sit down and make a list of all the good God has given us. This is something we probably have never done. We are good at enumerating our sinfulness; perhaps the challenge of these readings is to enumerate all the good in our lives. And then take some time to utter a prayer of loving thanks to this God who is so merciful and gracious to us. This God who loves us even when we sin.

Focusing the Gospel

Key words and phrases: bathe his feet with her tears, Your sins are forgiven, Who is this, go in peace, good news of the kingdom of God

To the point: The familiar and comfortable context of dining at table becomes an occasion charged with tension. The tensions are many: a sinful woman intimately touches Jesus in public, a host does not extend simple gestures of hospitality, others at table are indignant at Jesus assuming the power and authority to forgive sins. Simon and his guests not only judge the sinful woman, but they also judge Jesus. They fail to see who Jesus is: the One who came to bring the "good news of the kingdom of God." In this kingdom sinners touch God, receive forgiveness, and are granted peace. In this kingdom it is not tension and judgment that triumph, but love.

Connecting the Gospel

to the first reading: Despite all God has done for David, David knowingly and grievously sins against God. Confronted by Nathan the prophet for what he has done, David acknowledges his sin and is assured of God's forgiveness. David does what the sinful woman in the gospel does. Simon and his guests do not.

to experience: Seeking forgiveness from another whom we have grievously wronged is difficult. What often gives us the courage to go to the other to seek reconciliation is the desire to ease the tension and restore the relationship.

Connecting the Responsorial Psalm

to the readings: In this responsorial psalm the psalmist calls those who have experienced God's forgiveness "blessed" and relates a personal experience of having confessed sin and received divine mercy. The Lectionary omits the verses of Psalm 32 where the psalmist admits to having initially refused to name his or her guilt (vv. 3-4). For some time the psalmist resists self-examination and honest confession. When the psalmist finally relents and confesses, the forgiveness God grants is overwhelming. God replaces guilt (v. 5) with freedom (v. 7). The Lectionary did not need to include these verses because their story is dramatically told in both the first reading and the gospel. Moreover, how often it is told dramatically in our own lives. This Sunday's first reading, psalm, and gospel urge us to confess our sinfulness so that we might receive the forgiveness of God. Like the psalmist, we will find that the latter far surpasses the former.

to psalmist preparation: Spend some time this week reflecting on the overwhelming mercy of God who longs to forgive no matter what the sin. What moves you to ask for this forgiveness? What moves you to resist it?

ASSEMBLY & FAITH-SHARING GROUPS

- Like Simon, I am quick to judge another when . . .
- What I need to learn from the sinful woman is . . .
- I see love triumphing when . . . I recognize this as God's kingdom when . . .

PRESIDERS

When I am like Simon my priesthood looks like . . . When I am like the woman my priesthood looks like . . .

DEACONS

I touch others with the healing and peace of God when . . .

HOSPITALITY MINISTERS

The way I extend hospitality eases the inevitable tensions in community when I . . .

MUSIC MINISTERS

My music making creates a context for peace and forgiveness in the community when I . . .

ALTAR MINISTERS

My serving witnesses to God's abiding love when I . . .

LECTORS

When I allow myself to be touched by God's presence as I prepare to lector, my proclamation touches the community because . . .

EXTRAORDINARY MINISTERS OF HOLY COMMUNION

My ministry witnesses to God's love abounding among the members of the Body of Christ when . . .

Model Penitential Act

Presider: In this gospel a sinful woman touches Jesus as she washes his feet with her tears. Let us open ourselves to this Jesus who will touch us during our celebration . . . [pause]

> Lord Jesus, you forgive the repentant sinner: Lord . . .
> Christ Jesus, you are the Good News of God's love: Christ . . .
> Lord Jesus, you bring salvation and peace: Lord . . .

Homily Points

• Sometimes everything and everyone must fit into our perception of things. The child might determine who and how someone else might play with her or his toys. The parent might insist that the house look a certain way. The friend might demand that choices always go his or her way. All of these behaviors create tensions that harm relationships. When these behaviors are left unchecked, love cannot grow.

• Jesus looked beyond the sinfulness of the woman to see her great capacity for love, tenderness, and faith. In contrast, Simon and his guests clung to their self-righteous perception of things and their narrow judgment about the sinful woman. They fail to see who the woman is or even who Jesus is. They cannot accept Jesus' power to forgive because they cannot accept the woman as one who chooses to repent and seek forgiveness. Ultimately, they cannot embrace the love essential to enter the kingdom of God.

• In the gospel Jesus confronts Simon's self-righteousness and judgment about the woman. Jesus also confronts us, when, for example, someone challenges our prejudicial behavior, a friend shows how the outcome of a situation reveals we made some unloving choices, a spouse points out a tendency to be unforgiving toward others. In all these interactions Jesus is inviting us to embrace the love which establishes the kingdom of God among us.

Model Universal Prayer (Prayer of the Faithful)

Presider: Our God is merciful and forgiving; we make our needs known to such a loving God.

Response:

Cantor:

That the church may always be a sign of that love revealing the presence of the kingdom of God among us . . . [pause]

That leaders of nations may always judge rightly . . . [pause]

That those wronged or misjudged by others may find peace . . . [pause]

That each of us reach out to others with loving mercy and forgiveness . . . [pause]

Presider: Gracious God, you call us to your kingdom of love and forgiveness: hear our prayers that we may embrace this kingdom and one day enjoy everlasting life with you. We ask this through Christ our Lord. **Amen.**

COLLECT
Let us pray

Pause for silent prayer

O God, strength of those who hope in you,
graciously hear our pleas,
and, since without you mortal frailty can
  do nothing,
grant us always the help of your grace,
that in following your commands
we may please you by our resolve and our
  deeds.
Through our Lord Jesus Christ, your Son,
who lives and reigns with you in the unity
  of the Holy Spirit,
one God, for ever and ever.
Amen.

FIRST READING
2 Sam 12:7-10, 13

Nathan said to David:
"Thus says the LORD God of Israel:
  'I anointed you king of Israel.
I rescued you from the hand of Saul.
I gave you your lord's house and your
  lord's wives for your own.
I gave you the house of Israel and of
  Judah.
And if this were not enough, I could count
  up for you still more.
Why have you spurned the LORD and done
  evil in his sight?
You have cut down Uriah the Hittite with
  the sword;
  you took his wife as your own,
  and him you killed with the sword of
    the Ammonites.
Now, therefore, the sword shall never
  depart from your house,
  because you have despised me
  and have taken the wife of Uriah to be
    your wife.'"
Then David said to Nathan,
  "I have sinned against the LORD."
Nathan answered David:
  "The LORD on his part has forgiven your
    sin:
  you shall not die."

RESPONSORIAL PSALM

Ps 32:1-2, 5, 7, 11

R℣. (cf. 5c) Lord, forgive the wrong I have done.

Blessed is the one whose fault is taken away,
   whose sin is covered.
Blessed the man to whom the LORD imputes not guilt,
   in whose spirit there is no guile.

R℣. Lord, forgive the wrong I have done.

I acknowledged my sin to you,
   my guilt I covered not.
I said, "I confess my faults to the LORD,"
   and you took away the guilt of my sin.

R℣. Lord, forgive the wrong I have done.

You are my shelter; from distress you will preserve me;
   with glad cries of freedom you will ring me round.

R℣. Lord, forgive the wrong I have done.

Be glad in the LORD and rejoice, you just;
   exult, all you upright of heart.

R℣. Lord, forgive the wrong I have done.

SECOND READING

Gal 2:16, 19-21

Brothers and sisters:
We who know that a person is not
      justified by works of the law
   but through faith in Jesus Christ,
   even we have believed in Christ Jesus
   that we may be justified by faith in
      Christ
   and not by works of the law,
   because by works of the law no one will
      be justified.
For through the law I died to the law,
   that I might live for God.
I have been crucified with Christ;
   yet I live, no longer I, but Christ lives
      in me;
   insofar as I now live in the flesh,
   I live by faith in the Son of God
   who has loved me and given himself up
      for me.
I do not nullify the grace of God;
   for if justification comes through the
      law,
   then Christ died for nothing.

About Liturgy

Sacrament of penance: The church has given us a wonderful way to seek forgiveness by an outward sign: the sacrament of penance. There is much talk about how little Catholics avail themselves of this sacrament of forgiveness and peace. Perhaps some of the reason is a misunderstanding of sin and forgiveness.

The sacrament of penance is not about lists of sins and numbers. It is about acknowledging our sinfulness, our culpability in weakened and broken relationships, our need to seek reconciliation with others and God. Rather than a negative experience, the sacrament of penance is intended to be a positive experience of God's loving mercy and forgiveness.

Father's Day: A model fifth general intercession for this Sunday might be "That all fathers may be models of self-giving love, generous forgiveness, and merciful compassion in their families . . ." (BofB no. 1730 allows for an extra intention to be added to the general intercessions on Father's Day and allows for adaptions; no. 1732 provides other models). Chapter 56 of the *Book of Blessings* provides a special Prayer over the People for the blessing at the end of Mass on this day.

About Liturgical Music

Music suggestions: Appropriate this Sunday would be songs celebrating God's life-giving mercy and our need to admit sinfulness and seek forgiveness. Examples include "Amazing Grace"; "Grant to Us, O Lord"; "There's a Wideness in God's Mercy"; "With the Lord"; "Hosea"; "Softly and Tenderly Jesus Is Calling"; "Come, You Sinners, Poor and Needy." Also appropriate would be songs which call us to offer the same forgiving mercy to one another, such as "The Master Came to Bring Good News" and "Forgive Our Sins [as We Forgive]."

Mary Louise Bringle's "In Boldness, Look to God" (in *Joy and Wonder, Love and Longing*, GIA) speaks of many women in Scripture who dared address God with boldness. Verse 1 uses the story of the Canaanite woman who begged Jesus to cure her ailing child. Verse 2 draws on the courage of the woman who sought healing by reaching out to touch Jesus' hem. Verse 3 tells of Mary who risked censure to sit at Jesus' feet and listen to his teaching. Verse 4 honors the sinful woman who, despite "the world's harsh stare," washed Jesus' feet and wiped them with her hair. Sung during the preparation of the gifts, this hymn would make an excellent reflection on the gospel.

SPIRITUALITY

GOSPEL ACCLAMATION
John 10:27

R⁊. Alleluia, alleluia.
My sheep hear my voice, says the Lord;
I know them, and they follow me.
R⁊. Alleluia, alleluia.

Gospel

Luke 9:18-24; L96C

Once when Jesus was
     praying in solitude,
   and the disciples were
        with him,
   he asked them, "Who
        do the crowds say
        that I am?"
They said in reply, "John
     the Baptist;
   others, Elijah;
   still others, 'One of the ancient
        prophets has arisen.'"
Then he said to them, "But who do you
     say that I am?"
Peter said in reply, "The Christ of
     God."
He rebuked them
   and directed them not to tell this to
        anyone.

He said, "The Son of Man must suffer
     greatly
   and be rejected by the elders, the
        chief priests, and the scribes,
   and be killed and on the third day be
        raised."
Then he said to all,
   "If anyone wishes to come after me,
        he must deny himself
   and take up his cross daily and follow
        me.
For whoever wishes to save his life will
     lose it,
   but whoever loses his life for my sake
        will save it."

Reflecting on the Gospel

None of us likes to be rebuked. Corrections, we can tolerate—especially when we know we're wrong. But rebuke—that sharp, harsh word that leaves us beaten down and not feeling good about ourselves—is hard to take. After Peter's truthful answer of Jesus' question, "But who do you say that I am?" he is reproved by Jesus rather than congratulated. This is hardly what we would expect to a correct answer! We can well imagine (and feel in ourselves) Peter's chagrin. This opens up an opportunity for Jesus to teach perhaps his most difficult lesson. Discipleship is not easy. Discipleship is costly. Discipleship means identifying with the Master. In everything.

In the Greek text Jesus' rebuke of Peter and the language about cruel treatment of the Messiah are one single sentence. The latter disclosure about what is in store for the Christ gives the reason for rebuking Peter and admonishing the disciples not to announce his identity abroad. Jesus is warning the disciples that this Christ is not the Messiah they and the people of his time expect. It would seem that they are not ready to have their expectations about the Messiah changed, are not ready to hear about the harsh reality of the Savior.

What the disciples answer as the general perception about who Jesus is—John, Elijah, a prophet—is in sharp contrast to Peter's confession of Jesus as "The Christ of God." What Peter doesn't know at this point, however, is that the Messiah is One who must suffer, be rejected, be killed, and be raised up. What Peter also doesn't know is that Jesus' revelation about his identity is a direct challenge to the identity of the disciples: to follow Jesus is to deny oneself and take up the cross daily. The dare of the gospel is that to answer who Jesus is, is to answer who his followers are.

When we bring suffering, rejection, death, and being raised to new life into the realm of self-identity, we imply that these cannot be avoided. We would like to have the new life, but want to fend off any cost. To identify with who Jesus is means we accept *all* that happens to Jesus as being part of who we are and how we are to be. It is much easier to construct a self-identity in terms of power, glory, and majesty and to follow anyone who promises them. It is an unheard of challenge to construct a self-identity in terms of denying oneself, taking up suffering and rejection that accompany faithfulness to the saving mission, and giving up one's life for the good of another and then to follow the One who promises these. But here is the point: to save our life, we must lose it.

Asking who Jesus is can be a very costly question. How do *we* answer who Jesus is?

Living the Paschal Mystery

Children learn early on that bad tasting medicine is good—it will make them feel better and well again. Suffering and rejection and dying are not merely "bad tasting medicine" that we must take so we can have the new life Jesus promises. Rather, fidelity as disciples to the Good News of salvation sometimes involves taking the "bad tasting medicine," but our focus is not on suffering or giving up. That is not the end. The end is being faithful to our identity as followers of Jesus, continuing Jesus' saving ministry, receiving new life. This is who Jesus is; this is who we are. The way to new life is through dying to self. When we keep the gift of new life our focus, then the burden of being faithful to Jesus is lessened.

Focusing the Gospel

Key words and phrases: Who do the crowds say that I am, Who do you say that I am, The Christ of God, must suffer . . . be rejected . . . be killed . . . be raised, If anyone wishes to come after me

To the point: What the disciples answer as the general perception about who Jesus is—John, Elijah, a prophet—is in sharp contrast to Peter's confession of Jesus as "The Christ of God." What Peter doesn't know at this point, however, is that the Messiah is One who must suffer, be rejected, be killed, and be raised up. What Peter also doesn't know is that Jesus' revelation about his identity is a direct challenge to the identity of the disciples: to follow Jesus is to deny oneself and take up the cross daily. The dare of the gospel is that to answer who Jesus is, is to answer who his followers are. How do *we* answer who Jesus is?

Connecting the Gospel

to the first reading: Zechariah prophesied that the "house of David" would look upon one whom "they have pierced" and would "mourn for him as one mourns for an only son." Prophets of old made clear that the Messiah would be one who would suffer and die. The people did not listen. Do we?

to experience: How many of us seeking to make our mark in life would expect that we find our place in the world only by giving up our life? Yet this is the only way disciples of Jesus become who they are and make a difference.

Connecting the Responsorial Psalm

to the readings: The responsorial psalm reminds us that prayer—thirsting for God—is the doorway to redemption. On the one hand, prayer is a gift from God (first reading). On the other, we learn from the example of Jesus that it is a choice on our part (gospel). Always it is a relationship that reveals both who God is and who we are. Prayer teaches us that we are souls in need of divine nourishment (psalm), sinners in need of repentance and purification (first reading), and disciples called to acknowledge Christ and carry the cross (gospel). Prayer also teaches us that God is our greatest good and ultimate satisfaction, that God acts to bring us to repentance, and that God in Christ takes up the cross ahead of us. May we know for whom we thirst, and may we drink deeply and be transformed.

to psalmist preparation: In the context of this Sunday's readings, this responsorial psalm is a courageous, and confident, prayer to make. Jesus pours out his thirst for God as he seeks the reassurance he needs to bear the suffering and death incumbent upon him (gospel). You lead the assembly in joining Jesus in this prayer and the commitment it implies. Do you accept where thirsting for God will ultimately lead you? Do you believe that only carrying the cross will bring ultimate satisfaction?

ASSEMBLY & FAITH-SHARING GROUPS

- What I know about suffering and rejection is . . . This affects how I understand myself because . . .
- My daily cross looks like . . .
- For me, Jesus is . . .

PRESIDERS

My preaching reveals to others who Jesus is to me in these ways . . .

DEACONS

My serving others helps them relate their suffering to the suffering of Jesus when I . . .

HOSPITALITY MINISTERS

My greeting leads those gathering for liturgy to ask who Jesus is for them when I . . .

MUSIC MINISTERS

My liturgical music making challenges my sense of who I am when . . . It helps me follow Jesus more faithfully by . . .

ALTAR MINISTERS

My manner of serving reveals to others how I have answered who Jesus is for me when I . . .

LECTORS

I learn more about who Jesus is and who I am as his follower when I prepare to proclaim the word in this way . . .

EXTRAORDINARY MINISTERS OF HOLY COMMUNION

I help communicants grasp that they have already been given risen life when I . . .

Model Penitential Act

Presider: Jesus in this gospel asks the disciples about who he is. As we prepare to celebrate this liturgy, let us open ourselves to encounter who Jesus is and choose to become more like him . . . [pause]

Lord Jesus, you are the Christ of God: Lord . . .

Christ Jesus, you were raised on the third day: Christ . . .

Lord Jesus, you call us to take up our cross daily and follow you: Lord . . .

Homily Points

• Our self-worth is often measured by external successes such as more money and possessions, higher position and prestige, popularity and adulation. Who would ever measure personal identity and success by rejection, suffering, death? Yet this is what Jesus teaches his disciples.

• In this gospel Jesus asks the question about his identity in order to lead the disciples to a deeper understanding of who he is and his mission. The Messiah does not come in triumph to restore Israel to earthly glory, but to show that the way to lasting glory is to let go of our life, to be true to who Jesus calls us to be, to pour out ourselves for others. He challenges us disciples to take up our own cross daily if we are to follow him faithfully. The way to glory is through suffering. The way to risen life is through death.

• Those of us who follow Jesus today are called to carry our cross and to lay down our lives for others. We lay down our lives, for example, when we put aside our own convenience to meet someone else's need, when we embrace the stranger in our midst and help him or her feel at home, when we are patient with someone who regularly "pushes our buttons." In these and many other ways we are shaping our identity to be more in conformity with who Jesus is. This is our way through death to new life. This is our greatest success story.

Model Universal Prayer (Prayer of the Faithful)

Presider: God sent the only Son to show us the way to fullness of life. Let us pray that we might be faithful along our journey.

Response:

Lord, hear our prayer.

Cantor:

we pray to the Lord,

That all members of the church may willingly take up their cross daily and follow Jesus to fullness of life . . . [pause]

That leaders of nations may always respond to the needs of those who are suffering and dying . . . [pause]

That the needs of the poor be addressed by the willingness of this community to pour out their lives for others . . . [pause]

That each of us here comes to know more fully who Jesus is and live more completely who we are as his faithful disciples . . . [pause]

Presider: God of life, your Son showed us how to pour out our lives for others: hear these our prayers and strengthen us to be his faithful disciples. We ask this through Christ our Lord. **Amen.**

OPENING PRAYER

Let us pray
   [to God whose fatherly love keeps us safe]

Pause for silent prayer

Father,
guide and protector of your people,
grant us an unfailing respect for your
   name,
and keep us always in your love.

Grant this through our Lord Jesus Christ,
   your Son,
who lives and reigns with you and the
   Holy Spirit,
one God, for ever and ever. **Amen.**

FIRST READING

Zech 12:10-11; 13:1

Thus says the LORD:
   I will pour out on the house of David
   and on the inhabitants of Jerusalem
   a spirit of grace and petition;
   and they shall look on him whom they
      have pierced,
   and they shall mourn for him as one
      mourns for an only son,
   and they shall grieve over him as one
      grieves over a firstborn.

On that day the mourning in Jerusalem
      shall be as great
   as the mourning of Hadadrimmon in
      the plain of Megiddo.

On that day there shall be open to the
      house of David
   and to the inhabitants of Jerusalem,
   a fountain to purify from sin and
      uncleanness.

RESPONSORIAL PSALM

Ps 63:2, 3-4, 5-6, 8-9

R̸. My soul is thirsting for you, O Lord my God.

O God, you are my God whom I seek;
   for you my flesh pines and my soul
      thirsts
   like the earth, parched, lifeless and
      without water.

R̸. My soul is thirsting for you, O Lord my God.

Thus have I gazed toward you in the
      sanctuary
   to see your power and your glory,
for your kindness is a greater good than
      life;
   my lips shall glorify you.

R̸. My soul is thirsting for you, O Lord my God.

Thus will I bless you while I live;
    lifting up my hands, I will call upon
        your name.
As with the riches of a banquet shall my
      soul be satisfied,
    and with exultant lips my mouth shall
        praise you.

R̸. My soul is thirsting for you, O Lord my
God.

You are my help,
    and in the shadow of your wings I
        shout for joy.
My soul clings fast to you;
    your right hand upholds me.

R̸. My soul is thirsting for you, O Lord my
God.

SECOND READING
Gal 3:26-29

Brothers and sisters:
Through faith you are all children of God
    in Christ Jesus.
For all of you who were baptized into
    Christ
    have clothed yourselves with Christ.
There is neither Jew nor Greek,
    there is neither slave nor free person,
    there is not male and female;
    for you are all one in Christ Jesus.
And if you belong to Christ,
    then you are Abraham's descendant,
    heirs according to the promise.

CATECHESIS

About Liturgy

Who are we? Just as it's easy to focus more on suffering and losing one's life than on the gift of new Life that Jesus gives to those who are faithful, so is it easier to focus more on our sinful selves rather than on our identity as the redeemed, beloved daughters and sons of God, brothers and sisters in Christ. While always acknowledging that we are sinful, this gospel challenges us to keep our eyes on the real goal of discipleship: fidelity to our identity as followers of Christ.

Two questions loom: How do we *first* think of ourselves—as sinners or as beloved of Christ? How do we *first* regard our life—as filled with suffering and rejection or as basking in the Life that we have been given? Neither of these questions, of course, is an either/or one. We are both sinners and redeemed; dying is the only way to new Life.

This is the paschal mystery: Life is in dying. When we announce the Gospel by the way we live, we are choosing others ahead of ourselves. There is dying. But in this choice to be faithful, we are a visible sign of the presence of the Christ. We are growing in our fidelity to him, growing in our self-identity as members of the Body of Christ. The choice to identify more closely with him is a choice for Life.

About Liturgical Music

Music suggestions: In this Sunday's gospel the disciples grow in their awareness of who Jesus is and are confronted with the challenge of the cross. Songs about Jesus' identity as Messiah and the necessity of his suffering and death would fit the liturgy well. For example, "Jesus Christ, by Faith Revealed" would work well for the entrance procession. "Let Kings and Prophets Yield Their Name" (in *Hymns for the Gospels*, GIA) was composed specifically for this gospel reading and would make an excellent text to sing during the preparation of the gifts. "Lord of the Dance/I Danced in the Morning" would be most suitable during Communion.

Songs calling us to take up the cross as Jesus' disciples include "Only This I Want" for the preparation of the gifts or Communion; "Take Up Your Cross" for the preparation of the gifts; Bernadette Farrell's "Unless a Grain of Wheat" for Communion. Owen Alstott's "We Have No Glory" reminds us that our identity, "our only glory," and "our only name" are found in Jesus Christ; this hymn would work well either during the preparation of the gifts or Communion.

SPIRITUALITY

GOSPEL ACCLAMATION
cf. Luke 1:76

R/. Alleluia, alleluia.
You, child, will be called prophet of the Most High,
for you will go before the Lord to prepare his way.
R/. Alleluia, alleluia.

Gospel   Luke 1:57-66, 80; L587

When the time arrived for Elizabeth
     to have her child
     she gave birth to a son.
Her neighbors and relatives heard
     that the Lord had shown his
          great mercy toward her,
     and they rejoiced with her.
When they came on the eighth
     day to circumcise the
     child,
they were going to call him
     Zechariah after his father,
but his mother said in reply,
     "No. He will be called John."
But they answered her,
     "There is no one among your relatives
          who has this name."
So they made signs, asking his father what
     he wished him to be called.
He asked for a tablet and wrote, "John is his
     name,"
     and all were amazed.
Immediately his mouth was opened, his
     tongue freed,
     and he spoke blessing God.
Then fear came upon all their neighbors,
     and all these matters were discussed
     throughout the hill country of Judea.
All who heard these things took them to
     heart, saying,
     "What, then, will this child be?"
For surely the hand of the Lord was with him.

The child grew and became strong in spirit,
     and he was in the desert until the day
     of his manifestation to Israel.

*See Appendix A, pp. 304–305, for the other
readings.*

Reflecting on the Gospel

Many remarkable circumstances surrounded the conception and birth of John the Baptist! An angel announces his conception to Zechariah while he is performing his priestly duties. Zechariah and his wife Elizabeth are beyond child-bearing years. But the centerpiece of the gospel for this solemnity is not about the remarkable circumstances of John's conception; rather, the naming of John, the name given to Zechariah by Gabriel, is central because it points to being gifted and the ensuing mission.

The people in the gospel ask, "What, then, will this child be?" In a number of ways the gospel reveals who John is. He is God's gift of mercy to his parents, he is God's gracious gift to all of us ("John" means "the Lord is gracious"), he is recipient of God's gift of a strong spirit, he is the manifestation of God's coming Gift of salvation. The Good News of the gospel—and our living of it—also reveals how we are gifted by God. And so who are we to be?

The Lord is gracious, certainly, in granting Zechariah and Elizabeth a son; gracious, certainly, in sending John to herald the coming of Jesus (see second reading); but most gracious in sending the Son to bring "salvation . . . to the ends of the earth" (first reading). In celebrating the birth of John the Baptist we are, indeed, celebrating the manifold graciousness of God in granting us salvation. We are celebrating the wondrous gifts God has given each of us. We are challenged to discern our gifts, use them to cooperate with God in the divine work of salvation, and to grow through our gifts into the persons God desires us to be.

John was chosen, conceived, born, named, missioned, preached, died—all pointing to Christ. "What, then, will this child be?" John was the precursor. He pointed the way to Jesus and to salvation. He witnesses to us that being God's gracious gift for others is the way salvation is continued. God's manifold graciousness continues into our own graced and gifted lives. With us, however, God's interventions might not be so dramatic as with John. But God still acts on behalf of each of us. If we are as faithful as John, we, too, will share in God's abundant graciousness and blessing. We, too, will share in the glory of the One whom we serve.

Living the Paschal Mystery

John was the precursor who preceded Jesus; we are the disciples who follow Jesus. Our own bold announcing of the Messiah's presence and Good News does not flow from miraculous conception and naming. This, however, hardly makes us any less precious in God's graciousness. We, too, are "precursors" of the Lord's coming. By our own faithfulness to who we are we witness to the presence of the risen Christ among us.

We must be as faithful to our identity and mission as was John. We often think of God's graciousness in terms of receiving graces, getting what we pray for, good things in life which come our way, etc. Each of these is a manifestation of God's ultimate graciousness in bringing us to salvation. Less often, probably, do we think of ourselves as manifestations of God's graciousness, but we are!

We do not need to look to big things to witness to Jesus' presence and God's graciousness; we must do the simple, everyday things well, in Jesus' name. Thus our smiling at someone who is obviously weary, taking a few extra minutes to put someone at ease, eating a bit less and less well to give some money or food to a soup kitchen are all gracious behaviors which model to those around us the presence of Jesus. We truly are precursors, too!

Focusing the Gospel

Key words and phrases: the Lord has shown his great mercy; John is his name; What, then, will this child be?; strong in spirit; manifestation to Israel

To the point: "What, then, will this child be?" In a number of ways the gospel reveals who John is. He is God's gift of mercy to his parents, he is God's gracious gift to all of us ("John" means "the Lord is gracious"), he is recipient of God's gift of a strong spirit, he is the manifestation of God's coming Gift of salvation. The Good News of the gospel—and our living of it—also reveals how we are gifted by God. And so who are we to be?

Model Penitential Act

Presider: This solemnity honoring the birth of John the Baptist celebrates God's ongoing graciousness to us. Let us reflect on how we have responded to that graciousness . . . [pause]

Lord Jesus, you are God's gracious Gift of salvation to us: Lord . . .

Christ Jesus, you are a Light to the nations: Christ . . .

Lord Jesus, you are the Messiah to whom John pointed: Lord . . .

Model Universal Prayer (Prayer of the Faithful)

Presider: God is gracious and gives us all the gifts we need to come to salvation. Let us offer our prayers to such a good God.

Response:

Cantor:

That all members of the church may faithfully herald the Good News of salvation . . . [pause]

That the hand of the Lord be upon leaders of the world, strengthening them to bring peace and justice to all . . . [pause]

That God's graciousness deliver the poor and needy . . . [pause]

That all of us here continually discover who we are in God's sight and how we are called to share ourselves with others . . . [pause]

Presider: Gracious God, you graciously give us all we need to come to salvation: hear these our prayers that one day we might join John the Baptist in eternal glory and praise you forever and ever. **Amen.**

COLLECT

Let us pray

Pause for silent prayer

O God, who raised up Saint John the Baptist
to make ready a nation fit for Christ the
    Lord,
give your people, we pray,
the grace of spiritual joys
and direct the hearts of all the faithful
into the way of salvation and peace.
Through our Lord Jesus Christ, your Son,
who lives and reigns with you in the unity
    of the Holy Spirit,
one God, for ever and ever.
Amen.

FOR REFLECTION

- God has been gracious to me in these ways . . .
- I feel the movement of God's strong spirit within me when . . .
- I manifest God's gracious Gift of salvation when I . . .

Homily Points

- We easily point to other persons we consider "gifted," but we hesitate to acknowledge ourselves as being gifted. In the plan of God, however, each one of us has, like John, been uniquely and powerfully gifted to play a role in the fulfillment of God's work of salvation.

- Like John who spent time alone in the desert, we, too, need solitude and discernment to discover God's graciousness to us and how we are to share our gifts with others. Our role in the work of salvation is continually to discover God's gifts to us given for the sake of others. And so we will continually discover anew who we are. Receiving and sharing God's gifts is who we are to be. God gifts us throughout our lifetime and so learning who we are and how we are to be is a lifelong journey.

SPIRITUALITY

R∕. Alleluia, alleluia.
You are Peter and upon this rock I will build my
    church,
and the gates of the netherworld shall not
    prevail against it.
R∕. Alleluia, alleluia.

Gospel   Matt 16:13-19; L591

When Jesus went into the re-
    gion of Caesarea Philippi
    he asked his disciples,
    "Who do people say
        that the Son of
        Man is?"
They replied, "Some
    say John the Bap-
    tist, others Elijah,
    still others Jeremiah
        or one of the
        prophets."
He said to them, "But who do you say
    that I am?"
Simon Peter said in reply,
    "You are the Christ, the Son of the liv-
        ing God."
Jesus said to him in reply, "Blessed are
    you, Simon son of Jonah.
For flesh and blood has not revealed this
    to you, but my heavenly Father.
And so I say to you, you are Peter,
    and upon this rock I will build my
        Church,
        and the gates of the netherworld shall
            not prevail against it.
I will give you the keys to the Kingdom of
    heaven.
Whatever you bind on earth shall be
    bound in heaven;
    and whatever you loose on earth shall
        be loosed in heaven."

*See Appendix A, pp. 305–306, for the other
readings.*

Reflecting on the Gospel

This solemnity of Peter (Apostle to the Jews) and Paul (Apostle to the Gentiles) celebrates both the historical figures and their symbolic roles as representatives of the church. These two great apostles represent for us a church in communion with Christ continuing his saving work.

In response to Jesus' question about who he is (the gospel), Peter names him as "the Christ, the Son of the living God." In turn, Jesus names Peter as the "rock" upon which the church will be built. Like Peter, we must come to know who Jesus is and who we are in relation to him if, like Paul, we are to finish the race, keep the faith, and receive the crown of life (see second reading). Thus, we can only carry forth Jesus' saving mission if we know who Jesus is. Also, only by knowing who Jesus is can we come to salvation. Peter and Paul both model for us followers of Jesus who knew intimately their Lord and Master.

Neither Peter nor Paul lived for themselves once they encountered Jesus and knew who he was: the Savior of the world. The grace to identify Christ always circles back and creates our own identity in relation to Christ. Now we spend our lives learning about who Christ is and how to find Christ in all the circumstances of our lives. We come to know Christ and realize that we are his presence in our world. This is what it means to be church! Church is neither building nor empty space; church is Christ's Body carrying on his saving work.

Peter and Paul were unshakeable in their belief that Jesus was the Christ. Both lived and preached the Good News that Jesus revealed; both were rocks upon whom the church is built; both were faithful to Jesus, even to the point of giving their own lives. Like them, we must come to know who Jesus is and spend our own lives making Jesus known to others. Because it is Jesus working through Peter and Paul and now working through us, nothing will prevail against the church remaining unshakeable in her mission to announce the Good News to all.

Living the Paschal Mystery

Paul's words in the second reading spell out concretely how baptism plunges us into living the paschal mystery. This mystery means dying: "poured out like a libation," "compet[ing] well," "finish[ing] the race," "[keeping] the faith," completing the proclamation, finding ourselves in "the lion's mouth," having "evil threat[s]." It also means rising: "crown of righteousness await[ing]," "award . . . me . . . his appearance," "gave me strength," "rescued," "bring me safe to his heavenly kingdom." The challenge of this solemnity is to take this dying and rising message of Paul (and Peter) and translate it into our everyday lives.

Our dying may be staying up all night with a sick child, being willing to go the extra step for someone, being satisfied with less, having God as a priority in our lives, not putting material gains ahead of spiritual gains. Our rising may be in recognizing the risen Jesus in the grateful smile of another, the satisfaction of a job well done even if no one else recognizes it, the inner peace that comes from knowing our life is on course. Peter and Paul were called upon to be leaders in the early church and they responded with heroic actions. Our heroic actions are the simple, everyday things we do to make Christ no less present in our own day. This way of living is how and who we are to be. This is how and who church is. Peter and Paul have shown us the way.

Focusing the Gospel

Key words and phrases: You are the Christ, rock, build my church, shall not prevail against it

To the point: Peter and Paul were unshakeable in their belief that Jesus was the Christ. Both lived and preached the Good News that Jesus revealed; both were rocks upon whom the church is built; both were faithful to Jesus, even to the point of giving their own lives. Like them, we must come to know who Jesus is and spend our own lives making Jesus known to others. Because it is Jesus working through Peter and Paul and now working through us, nothing will prevail against the church remaining unshakeable in her mission to announce the Good News to all.

Model Penitential Act

Presider: Today we honor Ss. Peter and Paul who were chosen by Christ to be leaders of the church and who remained faithful to their Savior even unto death. Let us reflect on our own dedication to Christ and our faithfulness to announcing his Good News . . . [pause]

Lord Jesus, you are the Christ, the Son of the living God: Lord . . .

Christ Jesus, you are the Good News of our salvation: Christ . . .

Lord Jesus, you are our strength and courage: Lord . . .

Model Universal Prayer (Prayer of the Faithful)

Presider: Through the saving work of Jesus God established the church. Let us make our needs known so the church can grow in strength and grace.

Response:

Lord, hear our prayer.

Cantor:

we pray to the Lord,

That each member of the church always remain steadfast in announcing the Good News of salvation . . . [pause]

That all peoples of the world may come to salvation . . . [pause]

That those struggling with uncertainty and seemingly insurmountable challenges in their life be strengthened by Jesus' unfailing presence . . . [pause]

That each of us may build our lives on unshakeable faith in Jesus . . . [pause]

Presider: O God, you build up your church through your faithful people: hear these our prayers that we may one day join with Peter and Paul in proclaiming forever your praises. We ask this through Jesus Christ our Lord. **Amen.**

COLLECT

Let us pray

Pause for silent prayer

O God, who on the Solemnity of the Apostles
    Peter and Paul
give us the noble and holy joy of this day,
grant, we pray, that your Church
may in all things follow the teaching
of those through whom she received
the beginnings of right religion.
Through our Lord Jesus Christ, your Son,
who lives and reigns with you in the unity of
    the Holy Spirit,
one God, for ever and ever. **Amen.**

FOR REFLECTION

• My response to Jesus' question "Who do you say that I am?" would be . . . I live that answer by . . .

• For me, the church is . . . What I think is trying to prevail against it is . . .

• I announce Jesus' Good News by . . . when . . . for . . .

Homily Points

• What are people today unshakeable about? Probably not much, if anything, since our world always seems to be in such a state of flux. This feast day calls us to reflect on that which must be unshakeable for us: our faith in Jesus, who he is, and what he asks of us.

• Fruitfully discerning who Jesus is and who we are to be in relation to him requires faithfully following Jesus down the road of discipleship, intimate conversation with him along the way, and openness to hearing and announcing to others his Good News. What is absolutely unshakeable is that Jesus is always with us as we, like Peter and Paul, give our lives for the sake of the salvation Jesus came to bring.

✚ SPIRITUALITY

GOSPEL ACCLAMATION
1 Sam 3:9; John 6:68c

R℟. Alleluia, alleluia.
Speak, Lord, your servant is listening;
you have he words of everlasting life.
R℟. Alleluia, alleluia.

Gospel   Luke 9:51-62; L99C

When the days for Jesus' being
    taken up were fulfilled,
he resolutely determined to
    journey to Jerusalem,
and he sent messengers ahead
    of him.
On the way they entered a
    Samaritan village
to prepare for his reception there,
but they would not welcome him
because the destination of his journey
    was Jerusalem.
When the disciples James and John saw this
    they asked,
"Lord, do you want us to call down fire
    from heaven
to consume them?"
Jesus turned and rebuked them, and they
    journeyed to another village.

As they were proceeding on their journey
    someone said to him,
"I will follow you wherever you go."
Jesus answered him,
    "Foxes have dens and birds of the sky
      have nests,
    but the Son of Man has nowhere to rest
      his head."

And to another he said, "Follow me."
But he replied, "Lord, let me go first and
    bury my father."
But he answered him, "Let the dead bury
    their dead.
But you, go and proclaim the kingdom of
    God."
And another said, "I will follow you, Lord,
    but first let me say farewell to my family
      at home."
To him Jesus said, "No one who sets a hand
    to the plow
    and looks to what was left behind is fit for
      the kingdom of God."

Reflecting on the Gospel

Few journeys we undertake require of us absolute single-mindedness and deter-mination. And the journeys we undertake that cause us to set aside any detour tend to be journeys of great importance. We might journey, for example, to a new city to take up a new job. Nothing along the way can deter us from getting to our destination and work on time so that we can provide for our family. This is certainly an important journey to take! The journey Jesus undertakes in this Sunday's gospel is more than important. It is a journey of death and life. It is a journey of salvation. It is a journey that invites us into the very mystery of Jesus himself. The challenge of the gospel, then, is whether we are willing, single-minded, and resolute in our own journey of following Jesus.

This Lectionary gospel begins with "When the days for Jesus' being taken up were fulfilled . . ." This indicates to us a radical shift in Luke's gospel account: the Galilean portion of Jesus' ministry is completed; now, Jesus is off to Jerusalem. The rest of Luke's gospel unfolds as Jesus' journey to Jerusalem, symbolic of his accepting his des-tiny to be nailed to a cross and coming closer to fulfilling it. Moreover, this gospel reminds us that Jesus' journey to Jerusalem is not only his journey—faithful followers also journey to Jerusalem, to dying and rising.

As Jesus "resolutely determine[s] to journey to Jerusalem," he encounters a number of conflicts. Jesus is not welcome in a Samaritan village, he rebukes dis-ciples who want to take revenge, he predicts the lack of comfort and security for his followers, he chides those who have excuses for not immediately following him. These conflicts arise because the journey to Jerusalem entails death: dying to self in facing this journey's conflicts; death at this journey's end. Nevertheless, the journey must be made—by Jesus, by his disciples, by us—because this is the only journey that leads to life. This is the only journey that leads to salvation.

Single-mindedly following Jesus would seem like an ideal; yet that is exactly what Jesus asks. We must put Jesus and his mission ahead of everything— even more than the Law, even to the point of putting into a different perspec-tive our relationship to family. We must put our hand to the plow and not look back. Is this possible? Not alone. But if we remember that as we follow Jesus to Jerusalem he is ahead of us leading the way, then it is possible—not easy, but possible. We only need to say, "I will follow you wherever you go." And be abso-lutely determined to be faithful.

Living the Paschal Mystery

Jesus' invitation to "Follow me" is addressed to everyone. Our baptism begins our paschal journey with Jesus and initiates our response to follow Jesus "to Jerusalem." We spend our whole lives working out what began at baptism: fol-lowing Jesus through death into life. We spend our whole lives learning how to be resolutely determined and faithful on our journey.

Jesus invites us to follow him in the ordinary circumstances of our lives. This is where the going gets tough: not in the extraordinary, but in the ordinary things do we witness to our faithful following. Sometimes when we read the Scriptures we might be discouraged by the leadership of the prophets or early disciples. We always need extraordinary leaders to help us know where we are going in following Jesus. But the church is mostly made up of ordinary people whose very faithfulness to the gospel is an extraordinary way to follow Jesus.

Focusing the Gospel

Key words and phrases: resolutely determined to journey to Jerusalem, rebuked them, Follow me

To the point: As Jesus "resolutely determine[s] to journey to Jerusalem," he encounters a number of conflicts. Jesus is not welcome in a Samaritan village, he rebukes disciples who want to take revenge, he predicts the lack of comfort and security for his followers, he chides those who have excuses for not immediately following him. These conflicts arise because the journey to Jerusalem entails death: dying to self in facing this journey's conflicts; death at this journey's end. Nevertheless, the journey must be made—by Jesus, by his disciples, by us—because this is the only journey that leads to life.

Connecting the Gospel

to the first reading: Just as the continuation of Elijah's prophetic mission was assured by the call of Elisha, so is the continuation of Jesus' saving mission assured by the call of disciples who follow him on his journey through death to life.

to experience: Often opposition and conflict enable us to clarify our goals, strengthen our conviction, and increase our courage in pursuit of a vision. So it is with the inevitable conflicts that arise when we follow Jesus on the journey through dying to new life.

Connecting the Responsorial Psalm

to the readings: Both the first reading and the gospel this Sunday remind us that discipleship demands giving up everything. The first reading sets an example of instant and complete response. The gospel advises caution about the radical cost. The responsorial psalm invites us to look beyond the price of discipleship to the relationship with God which is its reward. The inheritance of those who give up all for God is the gift of the very presence of God. The inheritance of those who choose discipleship is fullness of life and the guidance of God along its path. While the readings ask us if we are aware of the costs of discipleship, the psalm asks if we are cognizant of the rewards. Full of divine promise and presence, the psalm gives us the courage to answer the call.

To psalmist preparation: This Sunday's psalm tells of all that you have been given because you have chosen discipleship: counsel, joy, life, refuge. Above all you have been given God's very self as your "portion" and "lot." Your singing this psalm testifies that you know the reward of discipleship is far greater than its cost. How have you come to know this? Who has taught you this? To whom are you teaching it?

**ASSEMBLY &
FAITH-SHARING GROUPS**

- In following Jesus, my "Jerusalem" looks like . . . The conflicts I encounter along the way are . . .
- Where and how I struggle most with dying to self along my life's journey is . . .
- The new life I seek is . . . The new life Jesus offers me is . . .

PRESIDERS

Ways I support others to follow Jesus "resolutely" and without excuses are . . .

DEACONS

Part of my ministry is to help those I serve embrace the dying entailed to be a faithful disciple of Jesus, and so I . . .

HOSPITALITY MINISTERS

My hospitality fortifies others on their paschal journey to Jerusalem whenever I . . .

MUSIC MINISTERS

The dying to self that music ministry requires of me is . . . I feel overwhelmed when . . . What helps me stay faithful whenever I am feeling this way is . . .

ALTAR MINISTERS

The dying to self that my serving requires of me is . . . The conflict I face because of this is . . .

LECTORS

What gives me strength to proclaim the radical demands of God's word is . . .

**EXTRAORDINARY MINISTERS
OF HOLY COMMUNION**

The manner of my distributing Holy Communion reminds others of the Life promised to those who faithfully embrace the journey of discipleship when I . . .

167

Model Penitential Act

Presider: Being Jesus' disciples means journeying with him to Jerusalem and the cross. Let us reflect on how faithful we have been in following him . . . [pause]

Lord Jesus, your journey led through death to life: Lord . . .

Christ Jesus, you call us to follow you on your journey: Christ . . .

Lord Jesus, you show us the path to life: Lord . . .

Homily Points

• We've all had an experience of having a goal so clearly in mind that no matter what challenges, obstacles, or conflicts arise on our way to the goal, we still plod ahead. It's the goal itself that keeps us going no matter what. Jesus clearly had such a goal: Jerusalem. He kept going no matter what.

• Resolutely on his way to Jerusalem, Jesus doesn't waste any time on those like the Samaritan villagers who are closed to his presence. He doesn't candy coat the demands of discipleship. He doesn't waste words with those who do not make following him their first priority. He is intent on his mission of salvation and relentless in calling us to this same level of intensity.

• What enables us to accept the demands of discipleship is Jesus' resolute dedication to and care for us. We are never alone on our journey as his followers. He wants us in his service. He wants us with him on the road to Jerusalem. His choice of us to be his disciples is a yes that has no "but . . ." May our response likewise be a yes that has no "but."

Model Universal Prayer (Prayer of the Faithful)

Presider: God faithfully strengthens those who follow Jesus, the divine Son. Let us confidently lift our prayers to God.

Response:

Lord, hear our prayer.

Cantor:

we pray to the Lord,

That all members of the church may courageously respond to Jesus' invitation to follow him to Jerusalem . . . [pause]

That all peoples find the path to life and fullness of joy in God's presence . . . [pause]

That those who struggle to make good decisions, to face conflicts, to have the courage of their convictions find strength in Jesus' presence . . . [pause]

That all of us here grow in choosing to die to self that we may receive the fullness of life . . . [pause]

Presider: O God, you call us to follow your Son without counting the cost: hear these our prayers that we might journey with your Son through death to eternal life with you in your kingdom. We ask this through Christ our Lord. **Amen.**

COLLECT

Let us pray

Pause for silent prayer

O God, who through the grace of adoption chose us to be children of light, grant, we pray, that we may not be wrapped in the darkness of error but always be seen to stand in the bright light of truth. Through our Lord Jesus Christ, your Son, who lives and reigns with you in the unity of the Holy Spirit, one God, for ever and ever. **Amen.**

FIRST READING

1 Kgs 19:16b, 19-21

The LORD said to Elijah:
"You shall anoint Elisha, son of Shaphat of Abel-meholah, as prophet to succeed you."

Elijah set out and came upon Elisha, son of Shaphat, as he was plowing with twelve yoke of oxen; he was following the twelfth. Elijah went over to him and threw his cloak over him. Elisha left the oxen, ran after Elijah, and said, "Please, let me kiss my father and mother goodbye, and I will follow you." Elijah answered, "Go back! Have I done anything to you?" Elisha left him and, taking the yoke of oxen, slaughtered them; he used the plowing equipment for fuel to boil their flesh, and gave it to his people to eat. Then Elisha left and followed Elijah as his attendant.

RESPONSORIAL PSALM

Ps 16:1-2, 5, 7-8, 9-10, 11

R̸. (cf. 5a) You are my inheritance, O Lord.

Keep me, O God, for in you I take refuge;
    I say to the LORD, "My Lord are you.
O LORD, my allotted portion and my cup,
    you it is who hold fast my lot."

R̸. You are my inheritance, O Lord.

I bless the LORD who counsels me;
    even in the night my heart exhorts me.
I set the LORD ever before me;
    with him at my right hand I shall not be
        disturbed.

R̸. You are my inheritance, O Lord.

Therefore my heart is glad and my soul
        rejoices,
    my body, too, abides in confidence
because you will not abandon my soul to
        the netherworld,
    nor will you suffer your faithful one to
        undergo corruption.

R̸. You are my inheritance, O Lord.

You will show me the path to life,
    fullness of joys in your presence,
    the delights at your right hand forever.

R̸. You are my inheritance, O Lord.

SECOND READING

Gal 5:1, 13-18

Brothers and sisters:
For freedom Christ set us free;
    so stand firm and do not submit again
        to the yoke of slavery.

For you were called for freedom, brothers
        and sisters.
But do not use this freedom
    as an opportunity for the flesh;
    rather, serve one another through love.
For the whole law is fulfilled in one
        statement,
    namely, *You shall love your neighbor as
        yourself.*
But if you go on biting and devouring one
        another,
    beware that you are not consumed by
        one another.

I say, then: live by the Spirit
    and you will certainly not gratify the
        desire of the flesh.
For the flesh has desires against the Spirit,
    and the Spirit against the flesh;
    these are opposed to each other,
    so that you may not do what you want.
But if you are guided by the Spirit, you are
    not under the law.

About Liturgy

Ordinary Time journey: This Sunday's gospel readily captures the intent of Ordinary Time: to walk with Jesus on his paschal journey. The color for Ordinary Time is green, the same as that of nature during a period of life and growth. As we journey deeper into the paschal mystery during these months until Advent, it is good for us to keep the life-giving aspect of this time of the year in mind. What Ordinary Time is about is our walking with Jesus to Jerusalem and salvation. It is by embracing the dying and rising mystery of Jesus that we receive the life of God within us and renew it each time we celebrate liturgy. Although much of Ordinary Time unfolds during the summer months when many are on vacations, when the heat brings us to slow down our pace of life, when there is a change of pace in our lives if for no other reason than that for most children school is out, we must be careful that Ordinary Time doesn't become a temptation to "vacation" from the demands of faithfully following Jesus.

July 4: July 4 occurs this week, and it would be pastorally good to celebrate liturgy on that day (there is a votive Mass for celebrating Independence Day in the US edition of *The Roman Missal*). But it would do an injustice to the incredible paschal message of this Sunday if the homily and music were to anticipate July 4. Let Sunday be Sunday!

About Liturgical Music

Music suggestions: In the song "Come and Journey with a Savior" we call one another to follow Jesus wherever he leads and whatever the cost, knowing he will always be present with us, leading the way. The song would be an appropriate entrance hymn for this Sunday. Tracing salvation history from Abraham and Sarah, to Joseph and Mary, to Matthew and Martha, John Bell's "God It Was" describes the practical consequences of God's call with tangible and picturesque imagery. Sung during the preparation of the gifts, the song would be an effective reflection on the gospel. More meditative in tone, "Jesus, Lead the Way" asks Jesus to be our light in darkness, our strength in grief, our source of "redeeming graces," even when leading us "through rough places." This, also, would be an effective reflection on the gospel during the preparation of the gifts. A good choice for Communion would be "The Love of the Lord" in which we declare that sharing in Jesus' suffering and death matters more to us than all the riches of the earth. Another good choice for Communion would be "Jerusalem, My Destiny" in which we sing that we have set our hearts, like Jesus, on the journey to Jerusalem.

Finally, the gospel hymn "A Follower of Christ" would make an excellent recessional song with its repetitions of "What do I have to do? What do I have to say? How do I have to walk each and ev'ry day? Tell me what does it cost if I carry the cross? Just let me be a follower of Christ."

JUNE 30, 2013
THIRTEENTH SUNDAY
IN ORDINARY TIME

SPIRITUALITY

GOSPEL ACCLAMATION
Col 3:15a, 16a

R℣. Alleluia, alleluia.
Let the peace of Christ control your hearts;
let the word of Christ dwell in you richly.
R℣. Alleluia, alleluia.

Gospel   Luke 10:1-12, 17-20; L102C

At that time the Lord appointed
    seventy-two others
  whom he sent ahead of him in pairs
  to every town and place he intended
      to visit.
He said to them,
  "The harvest is abundant but the
      laborers are few;
  so ask the master of the harvest
  to send out laborers for his harvest.
Go on your way;
  behold, I am sending you like lambs
      among wolves.
Carry no money bag, no sack, no
      sandals;
  and greet no one along the way.
Into whatever house you enter, first say,
  'Peace to this household.'
If a peaceful person lives there,
  your peace will rest on him;
  but if not, it will return to you.
Stay in the same house and eat and
      drink what is offered to you,
  for the laborer deserves his payment.
Do not move about from one house to
      another.
Whatever town you enter and they
      welcome you,
  eat what is set before you,
  cure the sick in it and say to them,
  'The kingdom of God is at hand for
      you.'
Whatever town you enter and they do
      not receive you,
  go out into the streets and say,
  'The dust of your town that clings to
      our feet,
  even that we shake off against you.'

Continued in Appendix A, p. 306.

Reflecting on the Gospel

Some of us, when we have many tasks to do on a day, make out a list and cross off each task as it is completed. Ah, how good it feels to see our list of ten tasks now with just seven, now three, then almost complete. To give ourselves a boost we might prioritize our list and begin with the easiest jobs that are most quickly accomplished. Thus in the first hour of work we might cross off four items and this gives us a boost of energy for tackling the rest of our more difficult challenges. This gospel talks about labors—but there is no list. There is no prioritizing to begin with easy tasks. Jesus sends us out on a challenging, difficult task. This task cannot be accomplished in a single day, but requires a lifetime of faithful labor.

Jesus sends the disciples out to plant the seed of the Good News and harvest its fruit of peace and the in-breaking of the kingdom of God. The "kingdom of God is at hand" because wherever disciples are present and received, God is present and received. Despite the disciples facing "wolves" and sometimes being rejected, their labor will bear fruit for it is God's power that works through them. It is God's work.

Isaiah's vision uses different images to describe the same reality presented in the gospel. The fruit of the disciples' labors (peace, healing, and God's kingdom at hand) are described in Isaiah as comfort, abundance, and prosperity. Both readings envision God's power and presence now and a future when our "heart[s] shall rejoice." In Isaiah, however, the future is not yet a reality for Israel; but it is a reality for the disciples. Isaiah's wonderful future is being fulfilled in Christ. In us.

Jesus admonishes them not to keep their sights on the things they've accomplished, but on a future glory which still awaits them. The harvest is not what they did in accomplishing healing and casting out demons. The harvest Jesus sends his disciples out to bring in is the larger, even more abundant harvest of heaven. This labor is never our own alone. Without the Power given us by Jesus—the indwelling of the Holy Spirit—we would not labor fruitfully. For this divine power and presence the disciples—and we—rejoice.

Living the Paschal Mystery

The disciple's journey to Jerusalem includes both dying and rising. When we describe paschal mystery journey and Gospel living as dying and rising, we are using a metaphor which has any number of interpretations and applications. In this Sunday's context of discipleship, we are saying that ministry brings us to a kind of dying (the pain of the disciple when others don't accept the Gospel) as well as rising (the rejoicing that is ours because we are doing the work of God). The end of the journey in Jerusalem brings both dying and rising, too: cross and resurrection. If the journey is undertaken alone, we will fail. We are successful, however, when the journey is faithful to Jesus' ministry and we are open to the Power—the Holy Spirit dwelling within us—given us.

Any faithful discipleship and Gospel living calls for an openness to God's presence to us. Part of our very ministry, then, and of living the dying and rising mystery is to spend time every day in prayer being attentive to God's presence, the gifts God gives us to be successful, and the power of the Spirit which washes over us. This kind of prayer helps us remember that the ministry is not ours, but Christ's.

Focusing the Gospel

Key words and phrases: Go on your way, peace will rest, the kingdom of God is at hand, I have given you the power, rejoice

To the point: Jesus sends the disciples out to plant the seed of the Good News and harvest its fruit of peace and the in-breaking of the kingdom of God. The "kingdom of God is at hand" because wherever disciples are present and received, God is present and received. Despite the disciples facing "wolves" and sometimes being rejected, their labor will bear fruit for it is God's power that works through them. For this divine power and presence the disciples—and we—rejoice.

Connecting the Gospel

to the first reading: Isaiah's vision uses different images to describe the same reality presented in the gospel. The fruit of the disciples' labors (peace, healing, and God's kingdom at hand) are described in Isaiah as comfort, abundance, and prosperity. Both readings envision God's power and presence now and a future when our "heart[s] shall rejoice."

to experience: Many people live in fear of a future marked by destruction and chaos; they have abandoned hope. These readings invite us to hope in the future God has in store for us, one of blessing and joy. At the same time, because God's kingdom is already at hand, we live in this blessing and joy now.

Connecting the Responsorial Psalm

to the readings: In these verses from Psalm 66 the psalmist calls the entire earth to come and see the marvelous works of the Lord and to shout praises for God who has wrought such "tremendous . . . deeds!" In the first reading it is the Lord who calls the people to rejoice over marvelous deeds done on behalf of Jerusalem. In her arms the people will be fed and comforted and will discover how God has acted to save and restore. In the gospel Jesus sends his disciples out to proclaim the same message: God is acting to save, the kingdom is at hand. Some will welcome this message, others will reject it. But regardless the response, the coming of the kingdom of God will not be thwarted: evil will be destroyed, healing will come, and peace will prevail. In this psalm we "cry out . . . with joy" over the abundant works of God for the salvation of the world.

to psalmist preparation: In this Sunday's gospel Jesus sends the disciples on mission to announce his coming. Your singing of the responsorial psalm is part of that mission for it is a hymn of praise telling of God's saving deeds. Where have you experienced these deeds in your own life? in the lives of others? How have you announced them to the world?

**ASSEMBLY &
FAITH-SHARING GROUPS**

- I bring the kingdom of God to . . . when . . . Its fruit is . . .
- I sense the power of God working through me when . . . for . . .
- I rejoice that God has . . .

PRESIDERS
My labor to make God's kingdom present bears fruit when I . . . The "wolves" and rejection I sometimes face are . . .

DEACONS
God's motherly comfort shapes my service (see first reading) in that . . .

HOSPITALITY MINISTERS
My greeting and assistance is a prayer of peace for those gathering whenever I . . .

MUSIC MINISTERS
Through my music ministry I plant the seed of the Good News by . . . I experience its harvest of peace when . . .

ALTAR MINISTERS
The payment which inspires me to labor for God's harvest is . . .

LECTORS
My prayerful time with the word challenges me to be God's presence when . . . This makes a difference in my proclamation in that . . .

**EXTRAORDINARY MINISTERS
OF HOLY COMMUNION**
I am drawn to rejoice in God's presence when I distribute Holy Communion when . . .

Model Penitential Act

Presider: Christ sends us out as laborers for his harvest. Let us reflect on how well we have labored and ask that we may rejoice now in the gifts God gives us . . . [pause]

Lord Jesus, you send laborers to reap the harvest of God's kingdom: Lord . . .

Christ Jesus, you announce that the kingdom of God is at hand: Christ . . .

Lord Jesus, you bring faithful disciples into the joy of your kingdom: Lord . . .

Homily Points

• Every gardener knows that when planting a seed, the harvest is iffy. It takes much outside help for the seed to come to fruition: food, water, weeding, sun, protection from high winds and harsh weather. As the seed sprouts and grows, every gardener is delighted at the life and beauty that comes forth. So do disciples rejoice when the seed of the Good News they sow during their labors bears the kingdom of God.

• The gospel describes aptly the life and challenges of discipleship: much work for too few laborers, and difficulties and rejection, on the one hand; God's divine power working through them, and presence within them, on the other hand. Jesus promises that they will succeed in their mission and rejoice in the abundant harvest.

• Those who are accompanied by the Spirit of Jesus and labor with that Power within them will plant the seed of Good News with a greater sense of peace and less apprehension about forces opposed to the in-breaking of God's presence. The assurance of God's presence and power doesn't diminish the demands of the labor, but it does give strength and courage to the laborers. Their work will bear the fruit of the presence of the kingdom of God. They will be God's presence. For this they rejoice.

Model Universal Prayer (Prayer of the Faithful)

Presider: The God who sends us as laborers to gather the harvest is present to us and helps us. So we are encouraged to make our needs known.

Response:

Lord, hear our prayer.

Cantor:

we pray to the Lord,

That all members of the church might plant the seeds of Good News and see the fruit of God's presence . . . [pause]

That all peoples of the world share in the abundant harvest of God's salvation . . . [pause]

That the sick be healed, the sorrowful be comforted, and the distressed find peace . . . [pause]

That all here may rejoice at being chosen to labor in God's kingdom . . . [pause]

Presider: Bountiful God, you send us as laborers to gather your harvest: be with us, help us to rejoice, and make our labors fruitful. We ask this through Christ our Lord. **Amen.**

COLLECT

Let us pray

Pause for silent prayer

O God, who in the abasement of your Son have raised up a fallen world, fill your faithful with holy joy, for on those you have rescued from slavery to sin you bestow eternal gladness. Through our Lord Jesus Christ, your Son, who lives and reigns with you in the unity of the Holy Spirit, one God, for ever and ever. **Amen.**

FIRST READING

Isa 66:10-14c

Thus says the LORD:
Rejoice with Jerusalem and be glad
    because of her,
  all you who love her;
exult, exult with her,
  all you who were mourning over her!
Oh, that you may suck fully
  of the milk of her comfort,
that you may nurse with delight
  at her abundant breasts!
  For thus says the LORD:
Lo, I will spread prosperity over Jerusalem
    like a river,
  and the wealth of the nations like an
    overflowing torrent.
As nurslings, you shall be carried in her
    arms,
  and fondled in her lap;
as a mother comforts her child,
  so will I comfort you;
in Jerusalem you shall find your
    comfort.

When you see this, your heart shall rejoice
  and your bodies flourish like the grass;
the LORD's power shall be known to his
    servants.

CATECHESIS

RESPONSORIAL PSALM

Ps 66:1-3, 4-5, 6-7, 16, 20

R̦. (1) Let all the earth cry out to God with joy.

Shout joyfully to God, all the earth,
    sing praise to the glory of his name;
    proclaim his glorious praise.
Say to God, "How tremendous are your
        deeds!"

R̦. Let all the earth cry out to God with joy.

"Let all on earth worship and sing praise
        to you,
    sing praise to your name!"
Come and see the works of God,
    his tremendous deeds among the
        children of Adam.

R̦. Let all the earth cry out to God with joy.

He has changed the sea into dry land;
    through the river they passed on foot;
    therefore let us rejoice in him.
He rules by his might forever.

R̦. Let all the earth cry out to God with joy.

Hear now, all you who fear God,
    while I declare what he has done for me.
Blessed be God who refused me not
    my prayer or his kindness!

R̦. Let all the earth cry out to God with joy.

SECOND READING

Gal 6:14-18

Brothers and sisters:
May I never boast except in the cross of
    our Lord Jesus Christ,
    through which the world has been
        crucified to me,
    and I to the world.
For neither does circumcision mean
        anything, nor does uncircumcision,
    but only a new creation.
Peace and mercy be to all who follow this
        rule
    and to the Israel of God.

From now on, let no one make troubles
    for me;
    for I bear the marks of Jesus on my
        body.

The grace of our Lord Jesus Christ be
    with your spirit,
    brothers and sisters. Amen.

About Liturgy

Liturgy of the Word and paschal mystery: Both Isaiah (for example, see Isa 63:1-6) and Luke (for example, the woes recorded in the skipped verses from this Sunday's gospel, vv. 13-16) speak harshly of those who do not hear and accept God's word. The Lectionary selections for this Sunday are for the most part only encouraging words (especially the selection from Isaiah). Although the Liturgy of the Word is always a challenging time, we must be careful not to lose sight of the consolation and encouragement that God's word also brings. This is another play of the dying/rising rhythm of the paschal mystery.

A good pastoral practice is to accustom ourselves to hearing both the challenge to die to self as well as the consolation in the Liturgy of the Word and the new life God promises. Both may not be present each Sunday, so this is a good way to begin to connect the Sundays so that we recognize the rhythm of dying and rising, challenge and consolation, death and new life. Connecting the Sundays is also a good way for us to enter more surely into the rhythm of the paschal mystery which is unfolded each liturgical year.

About Liturgical Music

Music suggestions: Verse 1 of Carl Daw's "Not Alone, but Two by Two" (in *Hymns for the Gospels*, GIA) tells the story of this Sunday's gospel. Verse 2 applies the story to us: "Have we still such daring hearts? Can we claim their faith and nerve? Do we truly love the world Jesus calls for us to serve? Can we plant again the seed Sown in mutual ministry, Patterned on a life of faith Rooted in community?" Verse 3 is a prayer to the Holy Spirit to bind us in the unity we need to carry out the mission given to us. This hymn would make an excellent reflection on the gospel reading during the preparation of the gifts or an excellent recessional song. Suitable for either the entrance procession or the preparation of the gifts would be "God Is Working His Purpose Out." Other good choices for the recessional would be "City of God"; "Go to the World"; and "God's Blessing Sends Us Forth."

✠ SPIRITUALITY

GOSPEL ACCLAMATION
cf. John 6:63c, 68c

R7. Alleluia, alleluia.
Your words, Lord, are Spirit and life;
you have the words of everlasting life.
R7. Alleluia, alleluia.

Gospel
Luke 10:25-37; L105C

**There was a scholar of
the law who stood up
to test Jesus and said,
"Teacher, what must I
do to inherit eternal
life?"
Jesus said to him, "What is written in
the law?
How do you read it?"
He said in reply,
*"You shall love the Lord, your God,
with all your heart,
with all your being,
with all your strength,
and with all your mind,
and your neighbor as
yourself."*
He replied to him, "You have
answered correctly;
do this and you will live."**

**But because he wished to justify
himself, he said to Jesus,
"And who is my neighbor?"
Jesus replied,
"A man fell victim to robbers
as he went down from Jerusalem to
Jericho.
They stripped and beat him and went
off leaving him half-dead.
A priest happened to be going down
that road,
but when he saw him, he passed by
on the opposite side.
Likewise a Levite came to the place,
and when he saw him, he passed by
on the opposite side.**

Continued in Appendix A, p. 306.

Reflecting on the Gospel

Only a few people never organize themselves. Most of us get up in the morning and think through our day. Sometimes we prioritize what we need to do. If the day promises to be filled with important tasks and deadlines, we may make a list to make sure we don't forget anything. Organizing ourselves helps us accomplish things; it keeps us moving forward; it minimizes the time we need to spend thinking about "What's next?" But those of us who are organizers know that writing lists or having clear goals is not the *end* of what we are trying to accomplish. We look beyond the organizing to what needs to get finished. We look beyond getting finished to success and reward. Keeping laws is a kind of way to organize ourselves in community, whether that be family, workplace, or even social milieu. The end of laws is the *relationships* that are strengthened by being together.

"What is written in the law?" Jesus asks the "scholar of the law" in this Sunday's gospel. Many would tend to answer by citing the Ten Commandments or civil law. But the lawyer in the gospel answered correctly when he named love as *the* law. Law is not about keeping rules, or even organizing ourselves, but about loving others. And, above all, love is about relationships. Eternal life is not inherited by keeping laws, but by caring for others and treating them with mercy. The law of love teaches us to "love . . . with all . . . with all . . . with all . . ." Love is nothing less than the unconditional gift of self.

The parable about the Good Samaritan is a perfect example of unconditional gift of self. The Samaritan traveler "was moved with compassion" when he saw the half-dead man along the side of the road. But this kind man went beyond the minimum acts of bandaging the victim's wounds and taking him to an inn to heal. The Samaritan traveler left money for his continued care. The Good Samaritan promised the innkeeper he would pay any more expenses upon his return.

Perhaps the Samaritan traveler hadn't planned on returning this way. But he had built a relationship of compassion and love with the victim traveler. His returning by way of the inn was probably less a matter of paying any further expenses of the victim, but more of checking on how he is recovering. Every detail about the Good Samaritan's actions models for us love as nothing less than the unconditional gift of self to another.

Living the Paschal Mystery

This is what the First Letter of John reminds us: "for whoever does not love a brother whom he has seen cannot love God whom he has not seen" (1 John 4:20b). Each of us must go beyond minimum requirements of good relationships to extending the kind of love that is the fullest gift of self. As followers of Jesus, we are to love, care for, and have mercy on others as he did: giving ourselves entirely.

The "dying" part of Gospel living can get awfully burdensome if we always think of it in negative terms. Our reflection on this gospel invites us to place our self-sacrificing to meet the needs of others in the larger context of love. Love is made concrete in our care for others. This is more than just preaching a "social gospel." It is saying that there is an indissoluble link between caring for others and loving, between loving others and loving God. Thus doing for others is more than a nice act; it is a way we make God's kingdom come.

Focusing the Gospel

Key words and phrases: What is written in the law?, love . . . with all . . . with all . . . with all . . .

To the point: "What is written in the law?" Jesus asks the "scholar of the law." Many would tend to answer by citing the Ten Commandments or civil law. But the lawyer in the gospel answered correctly when he named love as *the* law. Law is not about keeping rules, but about loving others. Eternal life is not inherited by keeping laws, but by caring for others and treating them with mercy. The law of love teaches us to "love . . . with all . . . with all . . . with all . . ." Love is nothing less than the unconditional gift of self.

Connecting the Gospel

to the first reading: The Law is not "mysterious and remote," but is "already in [our] mouths and in [our] hearts." We "have only to carry it out" and, as the gospel reminds us, it bears the human face of our neighbor in need.

to experience: As a framework to guide human behavior, law is good and necessary. Even when rearing children, we teach them to go beyond mere observance of laws' external demands to grasping the laws' deeper intent: building a community of care, respect, mercy—love.

Connecting the Responsorial Psalm

to the readings: At first glance these verses of Psalm 69 seem unrelated to either the first reading or the gospel. But further reflection reveals a rich and rewarding connection.

In the first reading Moses counsels the people that the commandments are not beyond them, but within them. In the gospel Jesus teaches that the commandments to love God and neighbor are not hazy, but clear and applicable: to love God means to love the immediate neighbor in need. Psalm 69 reminds us that whenever we have been in need God has responded without hesitation. We know God's law of love because we have experienced God loving us—directly and personally. And we know who is the neighbor in need because we have been that neighbor. It is this knowledge which fills our hearts and inspires us to act compassionately toward others. Psalm 69 grounds our ability to love in the One who has first loved us.

to psalmist preparation: To love one's neighbor as oneself is a tall order, and even more so when that neighbor is a stranger or an enemy. But you have only to turn to God for the strength you need to love in this way (see psalm refrain). When has the grace of God helped you love a neighbor in need?

**ASSEMBLY &
FAITH-SHARING GROUPS**

- Keeping laws means to me . . . Keeping laws leads to . . .
- What makes it hard for me to "love . . . with all" is . . . What makes it easier is . . .
- I was the neighbor in need when . . . and . . . loved me "with all" by . . .

PRESIDERS
As an ordained priest among the people, I model the law of love when I . . .

DEACONS
My service ministry makes visible God's law of love in that . . . It makes visible my gift of self in that . . .

HOSPITALITY MINISTERS
My care and concern for those gathering models the law of love in that . . .

MUSIC MINISTERS
For me as a music minister, my neighbor is . . . One way I love my neighbor as myself is . . .

ALTAR MINISTERS
My serving at the altar makes visible the law of love when I . . .

LECTORS
I have come to realize that God's word "is something very near" (first reading), already in my mouth and heart, by . . . This makes a difference in my proclamation in that . . .

**EXTRAORDINARY MINISTERS
OF HOLY COMMUNION**
I see those coming for Holy Communion as neighbors to whom I must reach out with care and love by . . .

Model Penitential Act

Presider: In today's gospel Jesus tells the parable of the Good Samaritan, instructing us to treat our neighbor with love and mercy. Let us open ourselves to the love and mercy Jesus offers us during this celebration . . . [pause]

Lord Jesus, you are the Teacher who calls us to love God and neighbor: Lord . . .

Christ Jesus, you are the Law of love written in our hearts: Christ . . .

Lord Jesus, you are the fullness of kindness and mercy: Lord . . .

Homily Points

• All communities, clubs, organizations, families have "bylaws." These bylaws are not ends in themselves, however, but means for helping the group achieve its purpose. The same is true for God's laws.

• Jesus makes explicit what is the purpose of the law and it seems so simple: to love God and neighbor. Yet the kind of love Jesus describes through the parable of the Good Samaritan is anything but simple. It requires of us the unconditional gift of self.

• What Jesus does make simple is that love of neighbor is practical, concrete, readily identifiable. Jesus challenges us to see and respond to the hurt and bleeding persons lying beside the road of our own daily life. We walk past people in need sometimes because we are too busy, sometimes because we are too intent on where we are going, or sometimes because we are too afraid to get involved. The law of love challenges us constantly to reevaluate our priorities and discern where we need to grow in the unconditional gift of self. We need to see . . . Then we need to . . .

Model Universal Prayer (Prayer of the Faithful)

Presider: Jesus gives us a concrete example of love and care for our neighbor. We are confident that God hears our prayers with the same loving care.

Response:

Lord, hear our prayer.

Cantor:

we pray to the Lord,

That all members of the church may recognize those in need and respond with love and compassion . . . [pause]

That all leaders of nations may promote laws that express love and care for their people . . . [pause]

That all those harmed by abuse, violence, or neglect may receive care and compassion . . . [pause]

That all of us here may love others with an unconditional gift of self . . . [pause]

Presider: Merciful God, you hear our prayers: help us grow in your love, reach out to others in need, and show your mercy to all. We ask this through Christ our Lord. **Amen.**

COLLECT
Let us pray
Pause for silent prayer

O God, who show the light of your truth
to those who go astray,
so that they may return to the right path,
give all who for the faith they profess
are accounted Christians
the grace to reject whatever is contrary to
    the name of Christ
and to strive after all that does it honor.
Through our Lord Jesus Christ, your Son,
who lives and reigns with you in the unity
    of the Holy Spirit,
one God, for ever and ever.
Amen.

FIRST READING
Deut 30:10-14

Moses said to the people:
    "If only you would heed the voice of the
        LORD, your God,
  and keep his commandments and statutes
    that are written in this book of the law,
  when you return to the LORD, your God,
    with all your heart and all your soul.

"For this command that I enjoin on you
    today
  is not too mysterious and remote for you.
It is not up in the sky, that you should say,
  'Who will go up in the sky to get it for us
    and tell us of it, that we may carry it out?'
Nor is it across the sea, that you should
    say,
  'Who will cross the sea to get it for us
    and tell us of it, that we may carry it out?'
No, it is something very near to you,
  already in your mouths and in your
    hearts;
  you have only to carry it out."

RESPONSORIAL PSALM
Ps 69:14, 17, 30-31, 33-34, 36, 37

R♭. (cf. 33) Turn to the Lord in your need, and you will live.

I pray to you, O LORD,
  for the time of your favor, O God!
In your great kindness answer me
  with your constant help.
Answer me, O LORD, for bounteous is your
    kindness:
  in your great mercy turn toward me.

R♭. Turn to the Lord in your need, and you will live.

I am afflicted and in pain;
    let your saving help, O God, protect me.
I will praise the name of God in song,
    and I will glorify him with
        thanksgiving.

R⃫. Turn to the Lord in your need, and you
will live.

"See, you lowly ones, and be glad;
    you who seek God, may your hearts
        revive!
For the LORD hears the poor,
    and his own who are in bonds he spurns
        not."

R⃫. Turn to the Lord in your need, and you
will live.

For God will save Zion
    and rebuild the cities of Judah.
The descendants of his servants shall
        inherit it,
    and those who love his name shall
        inhabit it.

R⃫. Turn to the Lord in your need, and you
will live.

OR

RESPONSORIAL PSALM
Ps 19:8, 9, 10, 11

See Appendix A, p. 306.

SECOND READING
Col 1:15-20

Christ Jesus is the image of the invisible
    God,
    the firstborn of all creation.
For in him were created all things in
        heaven and on earth,
    the visible and the invisible,
    whether thrones or dominions or
        principalities or powers;
all things were created through him and
        for him.
He is before all things,
    and in him all things hold together.
He is the head of the body, the church.
He is the beginning, the firstborn from the
        dead,
    that in all things he himself might be
        preeminent.
For in him all the fullness was pleased to
        dwell,
    and through him to reconcile all things
        for him,
    making peace by the blood of his cross
    through him, whether those on earth or
        those in heaven.

About Liturgy

Liturgy and liturgical law: The readings for this Sunday provide an opportunity for a practical reflection on our attitude toward and application of liturgical law. It is too easy to get caught up in the intricacies of "getting liturgy right" (as important as that might be), and lose sight of the larger picture: the Body of Christ at prayer and worship. Liturgical law is for the sake of prayerful worship for all. That is the goal, not keeping the law in itself. At a time when it seems like liturgical rules reign supreme, it is good always to remind ourselves about what we really do when we gather for liturgy: surrender ourselves to God and raise our hearts and voices in thanksgiving and praise. Worship is an act of unconditional love, of unconditional gift of self. Christ shows us the way; we only need to follow.

It is equally easy to disregard the law and do in worship what we like and what makes us feel good. It is helpful when worship is pleasing and affects us personally in positive ways, but this can also run the risk of our worship becoming self-centered. Worship is not ultimately about us (although we are surely central players, in that we are transformed as the gifts of bread and wine are transformed), but about our giving God praise and thanks and love.

About Liturgical Music

Music suggestions: In Herman Stuempfle's "We Sing Your Praise, O Christ" (in *Hymns for the Gospels*, GIA) we ask the Lord's forgiveness for the times "when we fail to hear Our neighbor's anguished cry" (v. 1) and we pray that our "love of you be manifest In serving other's needs" (v. 3). This hymn would make an appropriate entrance song on this Sunday when the gospel of the Good Samaritan is proclaimed. Also in keeping with the gospel proclamation, songs about the command to love God and one another wholeheartedly would be appropriate. "Where Charity and Love Prevail" would fit either during the preparation of the gifts or during Communion. James Chepponis's "Love One Another" and Michael Joncas's "No Greater Love" would be suitable during Communion. A good choice for the recessional would be "What Does the Lord Require" with its repeated phrase, "Do justly; Love mercy; Walk humbly with your God."

JULY 14, 2013
FIFTEENTH SUNDAY
IN ORDINARY TIME

SPIRITUALITY

R⫾. Alleluia, alleluia.
Blessed are they who have kept the word with a
    generous heart
and yield a harvest through perseverance.
R⫾. Alleluia, alleluia.

Gospel

Luke 10:38-42; L108C

Jesus entered a village
    where a woman whose name was
        Martha welcomed him.
She had a sister named Mary
    who sat beside the Lord at his feet
        listening to him speak.
Martha, burdened with much serving,
    came to him and said,
"Lord, do you not care
    that my sister has left me by myself
        to do the serving?
Tell her to help me."
The Lord said to her in reply,
    "Martha, Martha, you are anxious
        and worried about many things.
There is need of only one thing.
Mary has chosen the better part
    and it will not be taken from her."

Reflecting on the Gospel

When someone lives alone, it is challenging to have guests in for dinner. The host needs to be busy about getting the drinks and hors d'oeuvres, finishing up dinner, etc. At the same time, the host wants to be with his or her guests. This raises an important question: how can one serve and be hospitable at the same time one is attentive to guests? This can sometimes be a tricky balancing act. But every good host knows that the guests are far more important than anything else.

The gospel demonstrates many expressions of hospitality: welcoming, listening, serving. While each expression is valuable, none is complete in itself nor an end in itself. There is no one way to be hospitable. Hospitality in its deepest meaning makes possible a personal encounter of the kind that Mary is having with Jesus. This is the "better part" to which Jesus refers. Martha's generous hospitality is marred by her upbraiding Jesus and complaining to him about Mary. Rather than being truly hospitable, she is "anxious and worried" only about accomplishing a task. Her welcome shifts away from Jesus to herself. Busy about herself, she misses the "better part": centering on Jesus. The "better part" is to be undividedly present to the person of Jesus. Even when serving.

Hospitality—genuine welcome of the other and surrender to the other—facilitates encounter; one critical aspect of discipleship is being attentive to Jesus' presence. Abraham (in the first reading) is totally attentive to the three strangers: he greets them and bows down in respect; he extends an invitation to remain a while, and then does what he needs to do to make his guests comfortable. Abraham's hospitality was an attentiveness to his guests. In contrast, Martha is "anxious and worried." She loses sight of her Guest and gets wrapped up in her task, as well-meaning as that may be.

The gospel teaches us about encountering the Lord. Martha surrendered to anxiety and worry rather than to the presence of her Guest. What is the "better part"? As important as certain aspects of hospitality are, the "better part" is to surrender to the presence of the Lord. Faithful discipleship depends upon keeping the Lord at the center of all we are and do. Faithful discipleship depends upon encountering the Lord.

Living the Paschal Mystery

How do we keep Jesus at the center of our lives when we are always so busy? One way is to practice seeing Jesus in every person we meet. Another way is to remember that all the good we have and do ultimately comes from God who is the source of all good. Yet another way is to stop and think about why we are doing things: simply to accomplish a task, or to build a stronger relationship with others?

In the "busy-ness" of the average person's everyday life, we must take time to be present to others so that we truly *encounter* them. This is primary if we disciples are not to lose sight of the One who teaches us—and often teaches us through those to whom we are truly hospitable. Discipleship relativizes our noble and pious instincts to be busy about others and calls us to become present and take the other into our heart. It necessarily requires our surrender to the One who speaks, and that surrender looks like self-giving. The encounter with Jesus is essential for Christian hospitality. Let us hear that well!

Focusing the Gospel

Key words and phrases: Martha welcomed him, burdened with much serving, do you not care, anxious and worried, better part

To the point: Martha's generous hospitality is marred by her upbraiding Jesus and complaining to him about Mary. Rather than being truly hospitable, she is "anxious and worried" only about accomplishing a task. Her welcome shifts away from Jesus to herself. Busy about herself, she misses the "better part": centering on Jesus. The "better part" is to be undividedly present to the person of Jesus. Even when serving.

Connecting the Gospel

to the first reading: Abraham exhibited true hospitality. All of his efforts and busyness were directed toward the presence of his guests and their comfort and needs. This is what Martha in the gospel failed to do: keep persons at the heart of hospitality.

to experience: How uncomfortable we feel when our presence takes second place in the attention of a host who is busy about the details of our being there! On the other hand, how welcome we feel when we are the host's center of concern and attention.

Connecting the Responsorial Psalm

to the readings: Psalm 15 was part of a ritual followed whenever a person wished to gain admittance to the Temple. Because the Temple was God's dwelling, one could not enter without permission. Instead the person was questioned at the gate by a priest who would ask, "Lord, who may abide in your tent?" (v. 1 of the psalm, omitted in the Lectionary). The person then answered by reciting the subsequent verses of Psalm 15: one who does justice, thinks truth, slanders not, etc. This ritual expressed Israel's understanding that entrance into God's dwelling place required right living.

In the first reading Abraham stands as type of the right living which grants entrance into the divine presence. He receives strangers with hospitality and is blessed for it. That he responds so immediately to their needs, however, indicates he was already living "in the presence of the Lord" (psalm refrain). Such was the consistent orientation of his life. This is the orientation to which the psalm calls us and to which Jesus calls us when he praises Mary's choice of the "better part" in the gospel. May our central desire be to live in the presence of God and may that Presence be the source of our manner of living.

to psalmist preparation: In preparing to sing this responsorial psalm, spend some time reflecting on how you choose to live in the presence of God and how that choice shapes your manner of living. When and how do you take time to be with God? How, in concrete ways, do you let God's presence challenge your manner of living?

**ASSEMBLY &
FAITH-SHARING GROUPS**

- To be less "anxious and worried" and become more attentive to the needs of those around me, I need to . . .

- What helps me be undividedly present to the person of Jesus is . . . What interferes with this is . . .

- I understand the "better part" chosen by Mary to mean . . .

PRESIDERS

In the midst of busy ministry, what helps me remain genuinely present and attentive to others is . . .

DEACONS

In order to safeguard the "one thing" necessary, what I need to revise is . . .

HOSPITALITY MINISTERS

When I recall that welcoming members of the assembly is welcoming Jesus, then my hospitality is like . . .

MUSIC MINISTERS

My music ministry helps me be more attentive to the presence of Jesus when . . .

ALTAR MINISTERS

As I attend to the "many things" needed for liturgy, I keep focused on the centrality of encountering Jesus by . . .

LECTORS

When I prepare to minister by being attentive to Jesus' presence (like Mary) throughout the week, my proclamation is like . . .

**EXTRAORDINARY MINISTERS
OF HOLY COMMUNION**

The sort of hospitality necessary in my heart in order to hear the Word and distribute the Body of Christ is . . .

Model Penitential Act

Presider: In the gospel story of Martha and Mary, Martha is more concerned about serving than about being present to Jesus. Let us open ourselves to Jesus' presence during this celebration . . . [pause]

Lord Jesus, you are divine Presence within and among us: Lord . . .

Christ Jesus, you speak Words of life: Christ . . .

Lord Jesus, you have shown us the better part: Lord . . .

Homily Points

• In our daily living, we would choose the "better part" as often as we could: seats on the fifty yard line, first class seats on an airplane, the biggest slice of cake or piece of candy, sitting next to Grandma or Grandpa at table. This last example is truly a "better part" to be chosen. The children want to be near a special guest who loves them and whom they love.

• The gospel names the "special guest" whom we choose to be near: Jesus. While all of us most days need to go about many tasks as did Martha, this gospel calls us to choose the "better part" by not forgetting to keep Jesus at the center of our lives. Always. Even when serving.

• When we have family and friends in for dinner, a big part of the gathering is the exchange of happenings in each other's lives. The children are asked about how school is going, the person looking for work is asked about job prospects, the hosts are asked how dinner is coming along. In all these cases, paying attention to persons with their concerns and needs, their joys and successes is the "better part." It is the "better part" because to be present to others is to be undividedly present to the Jesus who is within them.

Model Universal Prayer (Prayer of the Faithful)

Presider: God is attentive to those who make their needs known. And so we pray.

Response:

Lord, hear our prayer.

Cantor:

we pray to the Lord,

That each member of the church become more attentive to the presence of Jesus in others . . . [pause]

That world leaders listen to their people with receptive hearts . . . [pause]

That those who are in any need be graciously shown love and hospitality by others . . . [pause]

That each of us here never lose sight of Jesus as the center of our lives . . . [pause]

Presider: Merciful God, you hear the prayers of those who cry to you: help us to listen to your Son with hospitable and attentive hearts, that we may always be faithful disciples. We ask this through that same Son Jesus Christ our Lord. **Amen.**

COLLECT

Let us pray

Pause for silent prayer

Show favor, O Lord, to your servants
and mercifully increase the gifts of your grace,
that, made fervent in hope, faith and charity,
they may be ever watchful in keeping your commands.
Through our Lord Jesus Christ, your Son,
who lives and reigns with you in the unity of the Holy Spirit,
one God, for ever and ever.
Amen.

FIRST READING
Gen 18:1-10a

The Lord appeared to Abraham by the terebinth of Mamre,
as he sat in the entrance of his tent,
while the day was growing hot.
Looking up, Abraham saw three men standing nearby.
When he saw them, he ran from the entrance of the tent to greet them;
and bowing to the ground, he said:
"Sir, if I may ask you this favor,
please do not go on past your servant.
Let some water be brought, that you may bathe your feet,
and then rest yourselves under the tree.
Now that you have come this close to your servant,
let me bring you a little food, that you may refresh yourselves;
and afterward you may go on your way."
The men replied, "Very well, do as you have said."

Abraham hastened into the tent and told Sarah,
"Quick, three measures of fine flour! Knead it and make rolls."
He ran to the herd, picked out a tender, choice steer,
and gave it to a servant, who quickly prepared it.
Then Abraham got some curds and milk,
as well as the steer that had been prepared,
and set these before the three men;
and he waited on them under the tree while they ate.

They asked Abraham, "Where is your wife Sarah?"
He replied, "There in the tent."
One of them said, "I will surely return to you about this time next year,

and Sarah will then have a son."

RESPONSORIAL PSALM

Ps 15:2-3, 3-4, 5

R̸. (1a) He who does justice will live in the presence of the Lord.

One who walks blamelessly and does justice;
    who thinks the truth in his heart
    and slanders not with his tongue.

R̸. He who does justice will live in the presence of the Lord.

Who harms not his fellow man,
    nor takes up a reproach against his neighbor;
by whom the reprobate is despised,
    while he honors those who fear the LORD.

R̸. He who does justice will live in the presence of the Lord.

Who lends not his money at usury
    and accepts no bribe against the innocent.
One who does these things
    shall never be disturbed.

R̸. He who does justice will live in the presence of the Lord.

SECOND READING

Col 1:24-28

Brothers and sisters:
Now I rejoice in my sufferings for your sake,
    and in my flesh I am filling up
what is lacking in the afflictions of Christ
    on behalf of his body, which is the church,
    of which I am a minister
in accordance with God's stewardship given to me
to bring to completion for you the word of God,
    the mystery hidden from ages and from generations past.
But now it has been manifested to his holy ones,
to whom God chose to make known the riches of the glory
of this mystery among the Gentiles;
    it is Christ in you, the hope for glory.
It is he whom we proclaim,
    admonishing everyone and teaching everyone with all wisdom,
that we may present everyone perfect in Christ.

About Liturgy

Hospitality ministers and encountering Christ: Each gospel proclaimed every Sunday always challenges the assembly in some way. This Sunday's gospel has a number of challenges for hospitality ministers in particular.

First, hospitality ministers must make sure their welcome of the members of the gathering assembly is a welcome of Jesus himself. Members of the assembly are members of the Body of Christ. The focus of the hospitality ministers is, therefore, on Christ himself.

Second, hospitality ministers, in their very greeting of those who are gathering, already play an important part in helping the assembly members have a listening attitude toward the God whom they will encounter in the celebration of liturgy. All the warmth and friendliness of the hospitality minister, then, is directed to opening those they greet to encounter God during liturgy.

Third, the hospitality members themselves must practice being present to others in their daily living if they are to help assembly members encounter God. Their ministry is essentially a ministry modeling how to encounter others.

Fourth, this gospel challenges hospitality ministers to focus on their actions as ministry, always serving the greater good of gathering those who come to liturgy as the one Body of Christ.

About Liturgical Music

Music suggestions: Herman Stuempfle's "Lord, Grant Us Grace to Know the Time" recognizes the value of both Martha's concern about serving Jesus and Mary's choice to sit at his feet and listen: "We seek your Word, as Mary sought; We wait in quietness, And yet we ask for strength to serve With Martha's faithfulness" (v. 2). We need help to discern which ought to be our priority when "Lord, grant us grace to know the time Of action or of prayer, Which hour to crowd with waiting work and which with you to share" (v. 1). Sung during the preparation of the gifts, this hymn would make an excellent reflection on the gospel reading.

John Bell, on the other hand, takes Martha to task in "God It Was" and does so with delightful, down-home imagery: "Christ it was who said to Martha, 'Listen first, then make the tea!'" (v. 4). This hymn is a lengthy one that needs to be sung in its entirety. It would work well during the preparation of the gifts if sufficient time is available. Otherwise, the choir could have some fun singing this as a prelude, trading around voices and parts to highlight when God/Christ is speaking and when a narrator is telling the story.

Mary Louise Bringle's "In Boldness, Look to God" (in *Joy and Wonder, Love and Longing*, GIA), with its verse about Mary risking censure to sit and listen to Jesus' teaching, would be worth repeating this week during the preparation of the gifts.

✢ SPIRITUALITY

GOSPEL ACCLAMATION
Rom 8:15bc

℞. Alleluia, alleluia.
You have received a Spirit of adoption,
through which we cry, Abba, Father.
℞. Alleluia, alleluia.

Gospel
Luke 11:1-13; L111C

Jesus was praying in
      a certain place,
      and when he had
      finished,
   one of his disciples
      said to him,
   "Lord, teach us to pray
      just as John taught his disciples."
He said to them, "When you pray, say:
   Father, hallowed be your name,
      your kingdom come.
   Give us each day our daily bread
   and forgive us our sins
   for we ourselves forgive everyone
      in debt to us,
   and do not subject us to the final
      test."

And he said to them, "Suppose one of
      you has a friend
   to whom he goes at midnight and says,
   'Friend, lend me three loaves of bread,
   for a friend of mine has arrived at
      my house from a journey
   and I have nothing to offer him,'
   and he says in reply from within,
   'Do not bother me; the door has
      already been locked
   and my children and I are already in
      bed.
I cannot get up to give you anything.'
I tell you,
   if he does not get up to give the
      visitor the loaves
   because of their friendship,
   he will get up to give him whatever
      he needs
   because of his persistence.

Continued in Appendix A, p. 307.

Reflecting on the Gospel

Prayer is not magic; we cannot expect to receive whatever we want from God just because we ask. If this were so, many of us would be praying to win the lottery with great fervor! No, praying to win the lottery won't make us rich. But praying for what we need and what is good for us opens us to God's presence, helps us gain God's perspective on our lives, challenges us to think broader than our immediate needs. Prayer always includes a discernment of *what God wants for us*, not simply what we want for ourselves.

Jesus did not just teach the disciples simply to say words in prayer. Oh, yes, he gave them the words to what we now know as the "Lord's Prayer." Beyond the words, though, he taught his disciples what prayer truly is: seeking God's presence and what *God wants for us*. And perhaps this is the most difficult thing about prayer. Instead of always praying for and fulfilling our own shortsighted needs (although sometimes this is perfectly legitimate, necessary, and good prayer!), authentic prayer leads us to know God's will for us, to receive the Holy Spirit, to open us in new ways to God's goodness. Authentic prayer draws us out of ourselves toward the God who wishes all good for us and gives us all we need to grow in our relationship with God and each other.

In this gospel Jesus instills confidence in his disciples that they will receive from God that for which they pray. He teaches them (and us) to pray for daily needs: the food we need to live, the forgiveness we need to grow in our relationships, the protection we need to remain faithful. Because of what we have already received (our daily needs), we are certain that God will give even more to those who ask: the Holy Spirit, a share in the plenitude of God's very Life. Such a Gift! Why would we not ask?

Living the Paschal Mystery

Most of us first learned to pray by saying prayers—meal prayers, bedtime prayer, the Guardian Angel prayer, the Our Father and Hail Mary. This is a good beginning, because it gives us an anchor. It gives us the words to get started. As we grow older and we come to know God better, however, there is always the risk that these "memorized prayers," prayers known by heart and so familiar to us, might become rote. We could end up just "saying prayers." Some people are proud of the fact that they say three rosaries or more a day. That may be good. Or it may not be so good, if all they are doing is rattling through words.

The kind of prayer Jesus taught is prayer from the heart, a prayer of communion, a prayer of attentiveness to divine Presence, a prayer seeking God's will. We cannot ask or seek or find if we are not sure of the presence of the Other. Praying—even saying familiar and much-loved memorized prayers—must bring us to divine encounter and to listen to God's will for us. Prayer is the communion of Person with person. It is the utterance of spirit to Spirit. Of life to Life.

Prayer cannot be limited to set times, although that is necessary, too. The gospel says Jesus was "praying in a certain place." We know that the Mount of Olives was one of his favorite places for prayer. Jesus had set times for prayer: before undertaking a mission, during ministry, early in the morning. Jesus also was constantly in communion with his Father; this is the "always" of prayer. This is what we really wish to emulate: communion with God as abiding presence. Lord, teach us to pray!

Focusing the Gospel

Key words and phrases: When you pray, say; Give us; give good gifts; give the Holy Spirit to those who ask

To the point: In this gospel Jesus instills confidence in his disciples that they will receive from God that for which they pray. He teaches them (and us) to pray for daily needs: the food we need to live, the forgiveness we need to grow in our relationships, the protection we need to remain faithful. Because of what we have already received (our daily needs), we are certain that God will give even more to those who ask: the Holy Spirit, a share in the plenitude of God's very Life. Such a Gift! Why would we not ask?

Connecting the Gospel

to the first reading: Abraham directly, confidently, persistently, and courageously petitions God to spare the people of Sodom and Gomorrah. In the gospel Jesus teaches us to pray with the same directness, confidence, persistence, and courage.

to experience: Nothing breeds confidence like success. This is also true when we turn to God in prayer. Although not always in the way we expect, God always answers our prayer.

Connecting the Responsorial Psalm

to the readings: In the gospel Jesus responds on several levels to the disciples' request that he show them how to pray: he teaches them the Our Father, he encourages them to be persistent, he subtly suggests what it is they are to pray for (the gift of the Holy Spirit), and he calls them to ground their prayer in the goodness of God who is their Father. The first reading gives us a dramatic example of such prayer. Abraham persists in his petition. He remains humble yet audacious, speaking to God directly and forcefully. Finally, what he prays for is righteous judgment and protection of the innocent. On the divine side the story reveals that God waits for such prayer. God stands directly in front of Abraham and invites the conversation. God listens each time Abraham speaks and grants his request. Clearly this is a God who desires salvation and who seeks human collaboration in bringing it about.

The responsorial psalm confirms that what grounds confidence in prayer is the nature of God who is great in kindness and true to every promise. God will answer when we call; God will complete the work of salvation begun in us. We need have no hesitation to petition such a God. We have only to carefully discern for what it is we ask.

to psalmist preparation: When you sing the responsorial psalm, what the assembly hears more than the beauty of your voice is the sound of your praying. Ask Christ this week to teach you *how to pray* the psalm.

**ASSEMBLY &
FAITH-SHARING GROUPS**

- The daily need I must pray for most diligently is . . .
- I ask the Father for the gift of the Holy Spirit when . . . because . . .
- The prayers God has most surely answered for me are . . . In these "answers," I have experienced the plenitude of God's Life in that . . .

PRESIDERS
I assist others to desire what the Father wants for them, namely, the Holy Spirit, by . . .

DEACONS
I assist others to remain persistent in prayer by . . .

HOSPITALITY MINISTERS
When my hospitality unfolds from prayer, my care and concern is like . . .

MUSIC MINISTERS
My ministry is that of leading the assembly in sung prayer. What helps me pray through my music-making is . . . What sometimes gets in the way of my praying is . . .

ALTAR MINISTERS
What helps me keep the liturgy as an encounter with divine Presence is . . .

LECTORS
The difference in my proclamation when it comes out of Spirit-filled prayer is . . .

**EXTRAORDINARY MINISTERS
OF HOLY COMMUNION**
I am most aware that in my ministry I distribute the plenitude of God's Life when I . . .

Model Penitential Act

Presider: In today's gospel Jesus teaches the disciples the Lord's Prayer. Let us prepare ourselves to pray as Jesus has taught us . . . [pause]

Lord Jesus, teach us to pray as you did: Lord . . .

Christ Jesus, give us this day our daily bread: Christ . . .

Lord Jesus, forgive our sins as we forgive one another: Lord . . .

Homily Points

• How can we say that God answers our prayer to provide for our daily needs when sick people don't get well, the jobless are still searching after months of unemployment, family members are still estranged, people are still hungry, disasters still happen? Praying for daily needs is, however, more a matter of opening ourselves to God's sure presence than receiving that for which we specifically pray. It is God's presence that gives us confidence our prayers have been heard.

• In the mystery of God's love for us, the answer to every prayer is God's presence in the power of the Holy Spirit, the plenitude of God's very Life. Divine presence is the underlying Gift for which we need to ask in every prayer.

• No matter what we pray for, authentic prayer is not solely about getting what we ask for. Prayer is ultimately less about receiving and more about opening ourselves to perceive new possibilities with a broader vision of what God is doing for us and offering us in terms of fullness of Life. All prayer, then, seeks the Gift of the Holy Spirit. Such a Gift! Why would we not ask?

Model Universal Prayer (Prayer of the Faithful)

Presider: God is generous beyond measure to those who make their needs known. And so we pray.

Response:

Lord, hear our prayer.

Cantor:

we pray to the Lord,

That all members of the church remain diligent in prayer, always seeking God's presence in the Spirit . . . [pause]

That all peoples of the world come to the plenitude of the Life God offers . . . [pause]

That those who feel their prayer is fruitless find hope in God's abiding presence . . . [pause]

That our prayer opens us to new possibilities and a broader vision for what God wants for us . . . [pause]

Presider: Generous God, you hear the prayers of those who ask, seek, and knock: open the door of your mercy and grant these our prayers which we ask through Christ our Lord. **Amen**.

COLLECT

Let us pray

Pause for silent prayer

O God, protector of those who hope in you,
without whom nothing has firm
        foundation, nothing is holy,
bestow in abundance your mercy upon us
and grant that, with you as our ruler and
        guide,
we may use the good things that pass
in such a way as to hold fast even now
to those that ever endure.
Through our Lord Jesus Christ, your Son,
who lives and reigns with you in the unity
        of the Holy Spirit,
one God, for ever and ever. **Amen.**

FIRST READING

Gen 18:20-32

In those days, the LORD said: "The outcry
        against Sodom and Gomorrah is so
        great,
    and their sin so grave,
    that I must go down and see whether or
        not their actions
    fully correspond to the cry against them
        that comes to me.
I mean to find out."

While Abraham's visitors walked on
        farther toward Sodom,
    the LORD remained standing before
        Abraham.
Then Abraham drew nearer and said:
    "Will you sweep away the innocent with
        the guilty?
Suppose there were fifty innocent people in
        the city;
    would you wipe out the place, rather
        than spare it
    for the sake of the fifty innocent people
        within it?
Far be it from you to do such a thing,
    to make the innocent die with the guilty
    so that the innocent and the guilty would
        be treated alike!
Should not the judge of all the world act
        with justice?"
The LORD replied,
    "If I find fifty innocent people in the city
        of Sodom,
    I will spare the whole place for their sake."
Abraham spoke up again:
    "See how I am presuming to speak to
        my Lord,
    though I am but dust and ashes!
What if there are five less than fifty
        innocent people?
Will you destroy the whole city because of
        those five?"
He answered, "I will not destroy it, if I find
        forty-five there."
But Abraham persisted, saying, "What if
        only forty are found there?"

CATECHESIS

He replied, "I will forbear doing it for the
sake of the forty."
Then Abraham said, "Let not my Lord
grow impatient if I go on.
What if only thirty are found there?"
He replied, "I will forbear doing it if I can
find but thirty there."
Still Abraham went on,
   "Since I have thus dared to speak to my
      Lord,
   what if there are no more than twenty?"
The LORD answered, "I will not destroy it,
   for the sake of the twenty."
But he still persisted:
   "Please, let not my Lord grow angry if I
      speak up this last time.
What if there are at least ten there?"
He replied, "For the sake of those ten, I will
   not destroy it."

RESPONSORIAL PSALM
Ps 138:1-2, 2-3, 6-7, 7-8

R∕. (3a) Lord, on the day I called for help,
you answered me.

I will give thanks to you, O LORD, with all
      my heart,
   for you have heard the words of my
      mouth;
   in the presence of the angels I will sing
      your praise;
I will worship at your holy temple
   and give thanks to your name.

R∕. Lord, on the day I called for help, you
answered me.

Because of your kindness and your truth;
   for you have made great above all things
   your name and your promise.
When I called you answered me;
   you built up strength within me.

R∕. Lord, on the day I called for help, you
answered me.

The LORD is exalted, yet the lowly he sees,
   and the proud he knows from afar.
Though I walk amid distress, you preserve
      me;
   against the anger of my enemies you
      raise your hand.

R∕. Lord, on the day I called for help, you
answered me.

Your right hand saves me.
   The LORD will complete what he has
      done for me;
your kindness, O LORD, endures forever;
   forsake not the work of your hands.

R∕. Lord, on the day I called for help, you
answered me.

SECOND READING
Col 2:12-14

See Appendix A, p. 307.

About Liturgy

Praying liturgy: Just as personal prayer runs a risk of becoming rote, just saying prayers, so does liturgy. One of the important things an assembly must always keep in mind is to surrender themselves to the ritual action in such a way as to really *pray* at liturgy.

One of the big mistakes we often make in liturgy is to make choices (about music, environment, introductions, etc.) which are directed to catching people's attention. Rather, efforts by all present must constantly be put forth in order to draw each member of the assembly through prayer into the depths of the mystery being celebrated, which ultimately means encounter with the redeeming God.

We sometimes forget how much our own presence and prayer affect those around us at liturgy, and even the entire assembly. If my posture and attitude is lackadaisical, that affects how the whole Body present is praying. If I am deeply immersed in prayer, that draws those around me into deeper prayer. If I sing wholeheartedly, that adds to the swell of sung prayer of the whole assembly. If I respond well, that adds to the full voice of the prayer. Liturgy is celebrated by a *community* and each member affects the prayer of each other member. It is not good enough just to be there. We must all be persistent in surrendering to God in prayer, listening for God's will, and welcoming the Holy Spirit into our hearts.

About Liturgical Music

Music suggestions: Throughout the verses of Herman Stuempfle's "Lord, Teach Us How to Pray" (in *Hymns for the Gospels*, GIA) we ask to be taught how to pray when our "hearts are dull and dead," when our "faith . . . has fled," and when "cares distract the mind." We ask the Lord to remind us "That you wait eagerly to hear Before we think to pray." This hymn could be sung either as the entrance song or during the preparation of the gifts. Both "Seek Ye First" and Eugene Englert's "Ask and You Shall Receive" would be suitable during the preparation of the gifts. Suggestions for Communion include Anne Quigley's "There Is a Longing"; David Haas's "Increase Our Faith"; and the Taizé ostinato "O Lord, Hear My Prayer." This last will need to be lengthened (in Taizé fashion) with choral embellishments and instrumental interludes.

JULY 28, 2013
**SEVENTEENTH SUNDAY
IN ORDINARY TIME**

SPIRITUALITY

GOSPEL ACCLAMATION
Matt 5:3

R∕. Alleluia, alleluia.
Blessed are the poor in spirit,
for theirs is the kingdom of heaven.
R∕. Alleluia, alleluia.

Gospel
Luke 12:13-21; L114C

Someone in the crowd
    said to Jesus,
  "Teacher, tell my
      brother to share
      the inheritance
      with me."
He replied to him,
  "Friend, who appointed me as your
      judge and arbitrator?"
Then he said to the crowd,
  "Take care to guard against all greed,
  for though one may be rich,
  one's life does not consist of
      possessions."

Then he told them a parable.
"There was a rich man whose land
      produced a bountiful harvest.
He asked himself, 'What shall I do,
  for I do not have space to store my
      harvest?'
And he said, 'This is what I shall do:
  I shall tear down my barns and build
      larger ones.
There I shall store all my grain and
      other goods
  and I shall say to myself, "Now as for
      you,
  you have so many good things stored
      up for many years,
  rest, eat, drink, be merry!"'
But God said to him,
  'You fool, this night your life will be
      demanded of you;
  and the things you have prepared, to
      whom will they belong?'
Thus will it be for all who store up
      treasure for themselves
  but are not rich in what matters to
      God."

Reflecting on the Gospel

What small child doesn't dream of growing up to be rich so he or she can have everything he or she wants? What adult doesn't dream of having sufficient resources put aside to assure him or her of a secure retirement? Dreaming of having enough isn't so bad! Focusing all our energy, relationships, and even our whole life only on acquiring possessions is another story. The gospel is going far beyond "you can't take it with you." It pointedly reminds us that wealth isn't everything. In this gospel Jesus challenges the crowd to "guard against all greed." The rich man in the parable judges he has stored up enough possessions to guarantee a good life without worries—so he thinks. Any reliance on wealth and possessions, however, is pure folly—both worldly possessions and this life are fleeting. What truly matters is the inheritance that only God can give: the fullness of eternal life. What "matters to God" is spending our life dispossessing ourselves of anything which hinders us from growing into the fullness of life.

On God's scale of values, this man is foolish because the things of this world are fleeting (see first reading). The first reading describes in even greater detail the misfortune which befalls the rich man in the gospel parable. According to Qoheleth, laboring for wealth and possessions is not only foolish but results in sorrow, grief, and anxiety. Jesus teaches us that the only wealth worth acquiring is to become "rich in what matters to God." Clearly, in things, possessions, there is no lasting profit. There is only lasting profit in that which leads us to "seek what is above" (second reading) because we recognize that "Christ is all and in all." Thus, what really matters to God is that we learn a new set of priorities. The readings and psalm give us ample suggestions: wisdom of heart, kindness, joy, gladness, gracious care, putting to death what is "earthly," putting on a new self, living in the image of our Creator, opening ourselves to the "Christ [who] is all and in all." In these ways we are invited to shift our priorities to what matters most: growing into the fullness of life.

It is no wonder that we tend to lose ourselves in possessions—this is so much easier than pursuing only what matters to God! When we make the effort, however, to reorganize our priorities and keep our sight on God, then we gain what the man in the gospel never achieved—absolute security in our future. This is a future which is not in barns filled with grain and other earthly goods; this is a future in God! This future is eternal life!

Living the Paschal Mystery

Discipleship requires self-emptying. Dying to our own needs and wants and pleasures is what God wants (see second reading). When we so die, we come to see things as God sees them. And when that happens, our needs and desires gradually change as our practical, everyday choices begin to square up with "what matters to God."

This is not to say that discipleship means we must give up all possessions. That is neither practical nor necessary. There is nothing wrong with possessions in themselves and there is everything wrong with destitution, no matter what its cause. All of us have a right to whatever material things we need to pursue a wholesome life. The problem arises when concern for our possessions or the drive to have more and more is our highest priority. The issue is valuing things appropriately, and then making choices so that our priorities remain clear and never compromised. Possessions must take second place to "what matters to God." Emptying ourselves of whatever stands in the way of that value is much more difficult than building bigger barns—but also more lasting. For self-emptying leads us to eternal glory with God.

Focusing the Gospel

Key words and phrases: guard against all greed, what matters to God

To the point: The rich man in the parable judges he has stored up enough possessions to guarantee a good life without worries—so he thinks. Any reliance on wealth and possessions, however, is pure folly—both worldly possessions and this life are fleeting. What truly matters is the inheritance that only God can give: the fullness of eternal life. What "matters to God" is spending our life dispossessing ourselves of anything which hinders us from growing into the fullness of life.

Connecting the Gospel

to the first reading: The first reading describes in greater detail the misfortune which befalls the rich man in the gospel parable. According to Qoheleth, laboring for wealth and possessions is not only foolish but results in sorrow, grief, and anxiety.

to experience: We naturally and responsibly store up wealth to take care of our future. There is nothing wrong with this kind of planning. The issue of the gospel is that we must look beyond the wealth, guard against sheer greed, and keep our eye turned toward what "matters to God."

Connecting the Responsorial Psalm

to the readings: In this responsorial psalm we sing about things which fade away: time, human life, the grass of the fields. The readings advise us not to put our hope in material possessions or hard work for these, too, fade away. Yet in the psalm we also ask God to "prosper the work of our hands." What is the work which needs to prosper? The psalm tells us: growth in the wisdom to value things rightly; growth in the capacity to see the kindness and care God grants us every day; growth in the courage to hear what God is saying to us and to change our hearts accordingly. In the end it is not labor that determines the direction of our lives, but the object for which we labor. May the goal of all our work be that Christ become our "all in all" (see second reading) and eternal life with God our ultimate reward.

to psalmist preparation: The refrain for this responsorial psalm is challenging: often when God speaks the human heart resists. This is normal and to be expected, for conversion is never easy. When do you find yourself resisting God's voice? Who or what helps you open your heart to "what matters to God" (gospel)?

ASSEMBLY & FAITH-SHARING GROUPS

- Where greed tempts me to lose sight of God and the life God offers me is . . .
- I have learned the folly of storing up possessions because . . .
- In order to become "rich in what matters to God," I need to dispossess myself of . . .

PRESIDERS

My daily living manifests to others what "matters to God" in that . . .

DEACONS

That which helps me grow into the fullness of life and strengthens my ministry to help others grow is . . .

HOSPITALITY MINISTERS

My manner of greeting those gathering for liturgy helps them to experience that they "[matter] to God" when I . . .

MUSIC MINISTERS

As a music minister the possessions I focus on are . . . What sometimes points my heart in the wrong direction is . . . What brings me back to what "matters to God" is . . .

ALTAR MINISTERS

Serving others keeps before me how to become "rich in what matters to God" because . . .

LECTORS

I need to dispossess myself of . . . in order to proclaim the word authentically.

EXTRAORDINARY MINISTERS OF HOLY COMMUNION

In order to be "rich in what matters to God," I need to empty myself of . . . This kind of self-emptying makes me more like Christ in that . . .

Model Penitential Act

Presider: In this Sunday's gospel Jesus warns us how foolish it is to place our hopes in earthly possessions. Let us prepare to receive the riches God gives us in this celebration . . . [pause]

Lord Jesus, you teach us where true riches lie: Lord . . .

Christ Jesus, you lead us to our eternal inheritance: Christ . . .

Lord Jesus, you call us to seek what truly matters to God: Lord . . .

Homily Points

• When Jesus admonishes in the gospel that we "Take care to guard against all greed," he is not asking us to dispossess ourselves of everything we own. Greed is not defined by how many or what kind of possessions we have, but by focusing totally on those possessions, by being possessed by them, or by directing all our decisions in life to protecting what we have. Greed turns us from what really matters to us—and surely what matters to God.

• Possessions do not guarantee life; God alone does. What alone lasts, what alone merits our time, energy, and concern, is our growing toward possessing the inheritance only God can give—fullness of eternal life.

• We cannot grow into fullness of life if we are glued to the things we have and love. We cannot grow in our relationship with God if we are self-occupied with resting, eating, drinking, and being merry. We cannot grow in our care for others if we are not rich in what matters most: love, compassion, mercy, trust, kindness, forgiveness, fidelity. These are the choices that matter to God and bring us our eternal inheritance.

Model Universal Prayer (Prayer of the Faithful)

Presider: Let us ask God for those gifts which bring true and lasting wealth.

Response:

Lord, hear our prayer.

Cantor:

we pray to the Lord,

May all members of the church grow toward receiving the eternal inheritance of life that God offers . . . [pause]

May the peoples of the world guard against all greed . . . [pause]

May the greedy become generous and the dispossessed receive a wealth of blessings . . . [pause]

May all of us pattern our lives after what matters to God . . . [pause]

Presider: Good and generous God, you know what we need to have in order to possess eternal life: hear these our prayers that we may share in your glory, through Jesus Christ our Lord. **Amen.**

COLLECT

Let us pray

Pause for silent prayer

Draw near to your servants, O Lord,
and answer their prayers with unceasing
kindness,
that, for those who glory in you as their
Creator and guide,
you may restore what you have created
and keep safe what you have restored.
Through our Lord Jesus Christ, your Son,
who lives and reigns with you in the unity
of the Holy Spirit,
one God, for ever and ever.
Amen.

FIRST READING

Eccl 1:2; 2:21-23

Vanity of vanities, says Qoheleth,
vanity of vanities! All things are vanity!

Here is one who has labored with wisdom
and knowledge and skill,
and yet to another who has not labored
over it,
he must leave property.
This also is vanity and a great misfortune.
For what profit comes to man from all the
toil and anxiety of heart
with which he has labored under the
sun?
All his days sorrow and grief are his
occupation;
even at night his mind is not at rest.
This also is vanity.

RESPONSORIAL PSALM

Ps 90:3-4, 5-6, 12-13, 14 and 17

℟. (8) If today you hear his voice, harden
not your hearts.

You turn man back to dust,
saying, "Return, O children of men."
For a thousand years in your sight
are as yesterday, now that it is past,
or as a watch of the night.

℟. If today you hear his voice, harden not
your hearts.

You make an end of them in their sleep;
the next morning they are like the
changing grass,
which at dawn springs up anew,
but by evening wilts and fades.

℟. If today you hear his voice, harden not
your hearts.

Teach us to number our days aright,
that we may gain wisdom of heart.
Return, O Lord! How long?
Have pity on your servants!

R⁊. If today you hear his voice, harden not your hearts.

Fill us at daybreak with your kindness,
    that we may shout for joy and gladness
        all our days.
And may the gracious care of the LORD
    our God be ours;
    prosper the work of our hands for us!
    Prosper the work of our hands!

R⁊. If today you hear his voice, harden not your hearts.

SECOND READING
Col 3:1-5, 9-11

Brothers and sisters:
If you were raised with Christ, seek what
        is above,
    where Christ is seated at the right hand
        of God.
Think of what is above, not of what is on
        earth.
For you have died,
    and your life is hidden with Christ in
        God.
When Christ your life appears,
    then you too will appear with him in
        glory.

Put to death, then, the parts of you that
        are earthly:
    immorality, impurity, passion, evil
        desire,
    and the greed that is idolatry.
Stop lying to one another,
    since you have taken off the old self
        with its practices
    and have put on the new self,
    which is being renewed, for knowledge,
    in the image of its creator.
Here there is not Greek and Jew,
    circumcision and uncircumcision,
    barbarian, Scythian, slave, free;
    but Christ is all and in all.

About Liturgy

Second reading during Ordinary Time: Usually during Ordinary Time the second reading is not related to the gospel or first reading. Instead, the second reading is a sequential selection from one of the New Testament letters; that is, one letter is read for a number of Sundays until it is completed, then another letter is begun. Almost always it takes a great deal of "mental gymnastics" to connect the second reading to the first reading or the gospel. Consequently, the second reading is best disregarded when preparing the communal celebration of liturgy during Ordinary Time and best used for private prayer and preparation for Sunday liturgy.

This Sunday, however, the second reading from Colossians is a happy coincidence. It not only fits nicely with the first reading and gospel, it even adds perspective and depth to the gospel parable. This Sunday it would be advantageous to dwell on the second reading, especially on the phrase "Christ is all and in all" with respect to Christian priorities of discipleship.

About Liturgical Music

Music suggestions: An appropriate song for either the entrance procession or the preparation of the gifts would be "O God, Our Help in Ages Past" in which we sing of the fleetingness of human life and proclaim our confidence in God who is our ultimate hope and eternal home. In "Seek Ye First" we challenge one another to pursue first and foremost the things of God; this song would work well during the preparation of the gifts. A good choice for either the preparation of the gifts or Communion would be "The Love of the Lord" in which we profess that "faith in the promise of Christ" is worth more to us than any riches, honors, or "earthly delights." In "Only This I Want" we claim as loss everything but the cross of Christ; this song would be suitable during the preparation of the gifts or Communion. In "Be Thou My Vision" we tell God, "Riches I heed not, or man's empty praise, Thou my inheritance, now and always: Thou and Thou only, first in my heart, High King of heaven, my treasure Thou art." This ancient Irish hymn would work well during the preparation of the gifts. Finally, another possible choice for Communion would be Paul Inwood's "Center of My Life." In this song based on Psalm 16, we tell God "you are the center of my life: I will always praise you, I will always serve you, I will always keep you in my life."

SPIRITUALITY

GOSPEL ACCLAMATION
Matt 24:42a, 44

R̸. Alleluia, alleluia.
Stay awake and be ready!
For you do not know on what day the Son of
    Man will come.
R̸. Alleluia, alleluia.

Gospel
Luke 12:32-48; L117C

Jesus said to his disciples:
    "Do not be afraid any longer,
        little flock,
    for your Father is pleased to
        give you the kingdom.
Sell your belongings and give
    alms.
Provide money bags for yourselves
    that do not wear out,
    an inexhaustible treasure in heaven
    that no thief can reach nor moth
        destroy.
For where your treasure is, there also
    will your heart be.

"Gird your loins and light your lamps
    and be like servants who await their
        master's return from a wedding,
    ready to open immediately when he
        comes and knocks.
Blessed are those servants
    whom the master finds vigilant on his
        arrival.
Amen, I say to you, he will gird
    himself,
    have them recline at table, and
        proceed to wait on them.
And should he come in the second or
    third watch
    and find them prepared in this way,
    blessed are those servants.
Be sure of this:
    if the master of the house had
        known the hour
    when the thief was coming,
    he would not have let his house be
        broken into.

Continued in Appendix A, p. 307.

Reflecting on the Gospel

We all dream of finding treasures. Usually our "treasure" is money, a special heirloom, a cherished memory. Ordinarily, we don't think of "treasure" as a person. Yes, we do speak of two people deeply in love as treasuring each other. Parents treasure their children. People can be treasures. This gospel speaks of treasure, but a very special one. This treasure is Life. This treasure is Master. This treasure is Messiah. This treasure is Son.

What, really, does the Father give us? What is the treasure that is to claim our hearts? The "inexhaustible treasure in heaven" the Father gives us is the Son (the Master). Our hearts must lie with the Son, for *he* is our Treasure. Those servants who are formed by this Treasure abide by the Son's expectations and seek to carry them out. Faithful servants do as the Son would do—their actions follow their heart. When our hearts lie where our treasure is, it is not overly difficult to do what the Son would do.

Jesus admonishes his disciples to be vigilant for the "master's return," to be eager to learn and do the "master's will," and to be "faithful" though the master's coming is delayed. Though much is required of them, more will be given to them: "your Father is pleased to give you the kingdom." In the gospel, the kingdom we seek is not a place, but it is divine Presence. It is manifested when we followers of Jesus are faithful to our Master's will. God's kingdom is present when we are engaged in an activity of "doing God." That is, when our doing is God-like: when it is creating and loving, merciful and forgiving, faithful and prudent.

What helps us in our daily "doing God" is vigilant preparation. This preparation is not about busyness, but it is about keeping our lives focused on God who entrusts us with much: preparing ourselves for the coming of "the Son of Man." Receiving this inexhaustible treasure depends upon our readiness. Delay does not matter; seeking God does.

Living the Paschal Mystery

There are many treasures found in this life, for example, family, home, community, friendship, integrity. Good as these are, they are nonetheless exhaustible. What the Father offers us is an inexhaustible Treasure: the fullness of the Life of the risen Lord. Possessing this divine Life is possessing the Spirit of the risen Son who dwells within those of us who are faithful stewards.

We live according to where our treasure is. This is why the way we live as disciples is so critical. This is why being a disciple is not something we slot into our already too busy schedules: one hour a week for Mass, so much money in the collection basket, another hour a week doing some volunteer work. Being a disciple is just that—*being*. It is much more a matter of the surrender of our whole selves to the "master's will" which means, first, being true to making present the kingdom which is already within and among us. This is the "much" with which we have been entrusted: who we are and how we live makes present God's kingdom.

The way we live, therefore, witnesses to where our treasure is. Our very living challenges others to prioritize their own treasures. Clearly, God must have priority in our lives. We make this apparent when religion is not so much practices we do as a loving relationship we develop as we encounter God and then extend that life we are given to others.

Focusing the Gospel

Key words and phrases: Father is pleased to give you, inexhaustible treasure, there also will your heart be, servant . . . doing so

To the point: What, really, does the Father give us? What is the treasure that is to claim our hearts? The "inexhaustible treasure in heaven" the Father gives us is the Son (the Master). Our hearts must lie with the Son, for *he* is our Treasure. Those servants who are formed by this Treasure abide by the Son's expectations and seek to carry them out. Faithful servants do as the Son would do—their actions follow their heart.

Connecting the Gospel

to the first reading: The "holy children of the good" were putting God's plan into effect just as the "faithful and prudent steward" in the gospel was putting into effect the Master's will.

to experience: There are many treasures found in this life, for example, family, home, community, friendship, integrity. Good as these are, they are nonetheless exhaustible. What the Father offers us is an inexhaustible Treasure: the fullness of the Life of the risen Lord.

Connecting the Responsorial Psalm

to the readings: Jesus tells us in this Sunday's gospel that where our treasure is there will be our heart. Along this very line the responsorial psalm says something remarkable about God: we are God's treasure, chosen as "his own inheritance." And where God's treasure is, God's heart will be.

This is the reason why we can wait with hope and "sure knowledge" for the deliverance promised us, whether we know the hour of its arrival (first reading) or not (gospel). God has chosen us and already given us the kingdom (gospel). Our response is to keep our eyes turned toward the God whose eyes are fixed upon us (psalm) by being faithful servants who fulfill the Lord's will in season and out (gospel). We are but returning the gift.

to psalmist preparation: Jesus calls you as cantor to be a faithful and vigilant servant, ever ready for his coming. How does Jesus come to you in the Liturgy of the Word each week? How does he come to you as you prepare to sing the responsorial psalm? How does he come to the assembly as you lead them in singing the psalm?

ASSEMBLY & FAITH-SHARING GROUPS

- I treasure . . . When I remember my Treasure is the Son, I . . .
- The Son has formed me to do . . .
- My actions best follow my heart when I . . .

PRESIDERS

I help people know the Treasure given them when I . . .

DEACONS

My faithfully serving others makes visible the Treasure in my heart when I . . .

HOSPITALITY MINISTERS

Tending to the demands of hospitality forms me into a vigilant servant because . . .

MUSIC MINISTERS

Jesus tells his disciples that those who have been entrusted with much will have much required of them. As a music minister, God has entrusted me with . . . What God expects of me is . . .

ALTAR MINISTERS

My fidelity to the details of faithfully serving at the altar best expresses Who is in my heart when I . . .

LECTORS

The kind of treasure my way of living proclaims to others is . . . This comes through in my proclamation of the word when . . .

EXTRAORDINARY MINISTERS OF HOLY COMMUNION

I am most aware that I am distributing the "inexhaustible treasure in heaven" when I . . .

✠ CELEBRATION

Model Penitential Act

Presider: God promises inexhaustible treasure in heaven for servants who are vigilant and faithful. Let us prepare to celebrate the inexhaustible Treasure given to us in this Eucharist . . . [pause]

> Lord Jesus, you are the Gift of the Father's inexhaustible Treasure: Lord . . .
> Christ Jesus, you are the Son of Man who will return in glory: Christ . . .
> Lord Jesus, you show us how to have faithful hearts: Lord . . .

Homily Points

• Truly charismatic leaders inspire others to continue their vision even when they are no longer present. Martin Luther King, Jr. initiated a path of nonviolent confrontation of injustice that continues in many ways today. So did Gandhi. So did Jesus.

• The work of salvation begun by Jesus is continued by his faithful followers. The treasure given us by the Father to carry on this saving work is the very risen Life of the Son. Further, the treasure is the Son. Faithful servants can do as the Son would do because of the Life dwelling within them, their greatest Treasure. To be faithful, disciples of Jesus must simply make sure their actions follow the One who dwells in their heart.

• Lead by doing. Follow your heart. These aphorisms are true for disciples of Jesus when he abides in their heart. We follow the Treasure in our heart when we, for example, treat others with the mercy and compassion of Jesus, when we strive to build a just society (both at home and around the world), when we forgive those who have hurt us, when we help those in need, when we heal those who are hurting. Faithful servants do as the Son would do—their actions follow their heart.

Model Universal Prayer (Prayer of the Faithful)

Presider: God is the faithful One who makes good on the promise to give us abundant Treasure. Let us pray with confidence for our needs.

Response:

Cantor:

That all members of the church cherish the Treasure God has placed in their hearts . . . [pause]

That all people of the world may know God's will for them and act accordingly . . . [pause]

That those who lack their proper share in the treasures of this earth receive justice . . . [pause]

That all of us here may serve others with generosity and compassion as did Jesus . . . [pause]

Presider: Good and gracious God, you give inexhaustible treasure to those who serve you faithfully: hear these our prayers that one day we might share fully in your glory. We ask this through Christ our Lord. **Amen.**

COLLECT

Let us pray

Pause for silent prayer

Almighty ever-living God,
whom, taught by the Holy Spirit,
we dare to call our Father,
bring, we pray, to perfection in our hearts
the spirit of adoption as your sons and
    daughters,
that we may merit to enter into the
    inheritance
which you have promised.
Through our Lord Jesus Christ, your Son,
who lives and reigns with you in the unity
    of the Holy Spirit,
one God, for ever and ever.
Amen.

FIRST READING
Wis 18:6-9

The night of the passover was known
    beforehand to our fathers,
    that, with sure knowledge of the oaths
        in which they put their faith,
    they might have courage.
Your people awaited the salvation of the
    just
    and the destruction of their foes.
For when you punished our adversaries,
    in this you glorified us whom you had
        summoned.
For in secret the holy children of the good
    were offering sacrifice
    and putting into effect with one accord
        the divine institution.

RESPONSORIAL PSALM

Ps 33:1, 12, 18-19, 20-22

℟. (12b) Blessed the people the Lord has chosen to be his own.

Exult, you just, in the Lord;
  praise from the upright is fitting.
Blessed the nation whose God is the Lord,
  the people he has chosen for his own
    inheritance.

℟. Blessed the people the Lord has chosen to be his own.

See, the eyes of the Lord are upon those
    who fear him,
  upon those who hope for his kindness,
to deliver them from death
  and preserve them in spite of famine.

℟. Blessed the people the Lord has chosen to be his own.

Our soul waits for the Lord,
  who is our help and our shield.
May your kindness, O Lord, be upon us
  who have put our hope in you.

℟. Blessed the people the Lord has chosen to be his own.

SECOND READING

Heb 11:1-2, 8-19

Brothers and sisters:
Faith is the realization of what is hoped for
  and evidence of things not seen.
Because of it the ancients were well attested.

By faith Abraham obeyed when he was
    called to go out to a place
  that he was to receive as an inheritance;
  he went out, not knowing where he was
    to go.
By faith he sojourned in the promised land
    as in a foreign country,
  dwelling in tents with Isaac and Jacob,
    heirs of the same promise;
  for he was looking forward to the city
    with foundations,
  whose architect and maker is God.
By faith he received power to generate,
  even though he was past the normal age
  —and Sarah herself was sterile—
  for he thought that the one who had
    made the promise was trustworthy.

Continued in Appendix A, p. 308.

✠ CATECHESIS

About Liturgy

Sunday collection and responsibility as parish community: This Sunday invites us not only to consider where our own treasure lies, but also to consider where our treasure as a parish community lies. Each Sunday a collection is taken up. Most of the money goes to the necessary financial obligations of the parish—salaries, building upkeep, programs and services. It is good to remind ourselves regularly, in addition to these necessary costs, that some of our gifts each Sunday must be set aside so that others less fortunate than us can share more equally in the treasures of this earth. Yes, each parish community has financial obligations; but each parish community also has *people* obligations. We witness to where our treasure really lies when we make some of our resources available to those less fortunate than we.

Most parishes nowadays are pretty strapped financially. In many cases staffs are being cut, programs curtailed, services less apparent. These are the times when it is very tempting to be less resolved about sharing despite our need with those even more needy. Yet this sharing despite our need is really what constitutes our "inexhaustible treasure."

About Liturgical Music

Music suggestions: In "God Whose Giving Knows No Ending" we sing of the treasure God has entrusted to us from God's "rich and endless store" and ask to be made servants who use our "skills and time For pressing toward the goals of Christ." This hymn is set to a majestic 4/4 tune (RUSTINGTON) that gives the text power and sweep. It would work well for the entrance procession or during the preparation of the gifts. In Delores Dufner's "Of You My Heart Is Speaking" (in *The Glimmer of Glory in Song*, GIA) we pray, "Wherever is my treasure, my heart will also be. O let it be with you, God, for all eternity." This hymn would be appropriate during the preparation of the gifts. The verse-refrain form of Marty Haugen's "Where Your Treasure Is" would lend itself well for singing during the Communion procession.

AUGUST 11, 2013
NINETEENTH SUNDAY IN ORDINARY TIME

SPIRITUALITY

GOSPEL ACCLAMATION

R⁄. Alleluia, alleluia.
Mary is taken up to heaven;
a chorus of angels exults.
R⁄. Alleluia, alleluia.

Gospel   Luke 1:39-56; L622

Mary set out
   and traveled to the hill
      country in haste
   to a town of Judah,
   where she entered the house
      of Zechariah
   and greeted Elizabeth.
When Elizabeth heard Mary's
      greeting,
   the infant leaped in her womb,
   and Elizabeth, filled with the Holy Spirit,
   cried out in a loud voice and said,
   "Blessed are you among women,
   and blessed is the fruit of your womb.
And how does this happen to me,
   that the mother of my Lord should
      come to me?
For at the moment the sound of your
      greeting reached my ears,
   the infant in my womb leaped for joy.
Blessed are you who believed
   that what was spoken to you by the
      Lord
   would be fulfilled."

And Mary said:
   "My soul proclaims the greatness of
      the Lord;
      my spirit rejoices in God my Savior
      for he has looked with favor on his
         lowly servant.
   From this day all generations will call
      me blessed:
      the Almighty has done great things
         for me,
      and holy is his Name.
   He has mercy on those who fear him
      in every generation.
   He has shown the strength of his arm,
      and has scattered the proud in their
         conceit.

Continued in Appendix A, p. 308–309.

Reflecting on the Gospel

We tend not to like people who boast about themselves and their accomplishments. Often the boasts are more than a bit exaggerated. At the same time, people who constantly put themselves down—are self-deprecating—tire us out as well. Whole people know a balance between who they are and who they are not. Saying honestly who we are is healthy. In the song known as the *Magnificat* Mary is honest about who she is. Her honesty derives from her keen awareness of God's gifts to her.

In response to Elizabeth's greeting, Mary not only proclaims the greatness of God, but also acknowledges that God "has done great things" for her. Her greatness is brought to completion in her assumption when this lowly maiden of Nazareth is "clothed with the sun" (first reading). God's greatness and Mary's greatness commingle through her yes to being the mother of our Savior. God's greatness fills us when we, like Mary, say yes to God's plan of salvation and give birth to the Son through the way we live each day. The most honest we can be with and about ourselves is to acknowledge, like Mary, the great things God has done for us.

Mary responded to God's initiatives with her whole being and life, and now "all generations will call [her] blessed." On this festival we honor Mary for her fidelity and we celebrate God's faithfulness in bringing us salvation through the divine Son. Mary's assumption of body and soul into heaven is a dogma defined by the church. It is fitting that we thus honor Mary because it was her body which was the first temple for the Son of God. She conceived, nurtured, allowed to grow, and gave birth to Jesus—all because she willingly gave her body as an instrument for God to work the wonders of salvation. This holy body now enjoys full union with her divine Son in eternal glory. By her assumption into glory, God has "shown the strength of his arm" and the greatness of his love. God will do the same for us.

Living the Paschal Mystery

We have many examples from Scripture where God uses mighty things to carry forward God's plan of salvation. We have only to think of the ten plagues, manna in the desert, overcoming Israel's Canaanite enemies so they could occupy the promised land. God also uses colorful and forceful people. We have only to think of the power of Moses' staff, the wisdom of Solomon, the love of David, the moving and poetic prophecies of Isaiah, the fire of Elijah.

God also uses simple things and persons in the plan of salvation. On this solemnity we honor Mary—a simple maiden without title or means. She it was who in her very being bore the Christ. She it was who heard the word, bore the Word, and then in her very being was a herald of the Word. If this simple maiden girl can change the course of history with her fervent yes, can we not model our own lives after hers?

Just as God chose this simple maiden, so does God choose each of us. Like Mary, we only need to say yes and be faithful to that commitment. Like Mary, we must hear the word, bear the Word, and herald the Word. And to do this honestly and fruitfully, we need to remember that the Word is made flesh and dwells in us just as in Mary. We are given God's Life at baptism; we become members of the Body of Christ; we receive Holy Communion and Christ's body commingles with our body. Like Mary, we bear divine Presence. We, too, are temples of the Son of God.

Focusing the Gospel

Key words and phrases: the mother of my Lord, greatness of the Lord, the Almighty has done great things for me

To the point: In response to Elizabeth's greeting, Mary not only proclaims the greatness of God, but also acknowledges that God "has done great things" for her. Her greatness is brought to completion in her assumption when this lowly maiden of Nazareth is "clothed with the sun" (first reading). God's greatness and Mary's greatness commingle through her yes to being the mother of our Savior. God's greatness fills us when we, like Mary, say yes to God's plan of salvation and give birth to the Son through the way we live each day.

Model Penitential Act

Presider: Today we honor Mary who was taken body and soul into heaven to share the divine glory of the One to whom she gave birth. Let us prepare to encounter her Son, the source of our salvation, during this liturgy . . . [pause]

Lord Jesus, you were born of the virgin Mary: Lord . . .

Christ Jesus, you are the Son of God: Christ . . .

Lord Jesus, your Father did great things for Mary: Lord . . .

Model Universal Prayer (Prayer of the Faithful)

Presider: God did mighty things for Mary, and will do mighty things for us. And so we are encouraged to lift our needs to God.

Response:

Lord, hear our prayer.

Cantor:

we pray to the Lord,

That all members of the church may faithfully say yes to all God asks of us . . . [pause]

That all peoples of the world surrender themselves to God's plan of salvation . . . [pause]

That the poor be lifted up and the hungry be satisfied . . . [pause]

That all of us here shine forth God's greatness in all we do . . . [pause]

Presider: All powerful God, you accomplish your plan of salvation through the simple and faithful: hear these our prayers that we might one day share in the glory of your eternal life. We ask this through Jesus Christ. **Amen.**

COLLECT

Let us pray

Pause for silent prayer

Almighty ever-living God,
who assumed the Immaculate Virgin Mary,
    the Mother of your Son,
body and soul into heavenly glory,
grant, we pray,
that, always attentive to the things that are
    above,
we may merit to be sharers of her glory.
Through our Lord Jesus Christ, your Son,
who lives and reigns with you in the unity
    of the Holy Spirit,
one God, for ever and ever. **Amen.**

FOR REFLECTION

* The hope I gain by recalling the "great things" God has done for Mary is . . .

* I imitate Mary and proclaim the "greatness of the Lord" when I . . .

* I give birth to the Son in my daily life in these ways . . .

Homily Points

* One of the greatest sources of pride for many people is giving birth to a child. As the child grows, parents become more and more aware of how the child is an extension of themselves, their values, their gifts, and their lives. The child's success (greatness) redounds to the parents. So it is with we who are children of God.

* God's greatness—gifts, goodness, strength, mercy, justice—fills us when we, like Mary, say yes to God's plan of salvation and give birth to the risen Life of the Son through the way we live each day. When we are generous, it is God's gifts shining through us; when we respond to the needs of others, it is God's mercy shining through us; when we are strong in face of wrong, it is God's justice enacted through us. Our "success" as God's children is drawn from and leads others to the greatness of God. Like Mary, our faithfulness will one day bring us to the completion of God's Life within us, to the glory of the Son.

SPIRITUALITY

℟. Alleluia, alleluia.
My sheep hear my voice, says the Lord;
I know them, and they follow me.
℟. Alleluia, alleluia.

Gospel

Luke 12:49-53; L120C

Jesus said to his disciples:
"I have come to set the
earth on fire,
and how I wish it were
already blazing!
There is a baptism with which
I must be baptized,
and how great is my anguish
until it is accomplished!
Do you think that I have come
to establish peace on the
earth?
No, I tell you, but rather division.
From now on a household of five will
be divided,
three against two and two against
three;
a father will be divided against his
son
and a son against his father,
a mother against her daughter
and a daughter against her mother,
a mother-in-law against her
daughter-in-law
and a daughter-in-law against her
mother-in-law."

Reflecting on the Gospel

Most people naturally shun fighting. We want to live our lives in peace. We pray for peace in the world. But what is peace? Jesus makes clear in this gospel that it is not absence of strife. In fact, he intimates that being on fire to accomplish his mission will bring serious divisions. The issue here isn't to sow division, but to be faithful to the saving mission for which Jesus was sent. We have the deepest peace when we ourselves take up and are faithful to Jesus' saving mission. Even in the midst of strife, we can know peace.

In this gospel fire is an image referring to divine judgment. Jesus is clearly stating that he has come to judge the people. His own faithfulness to this task and to his saving mission led to his great anguish and ultimately to his passion and death. So will we, his faithful disciples, be treated. Jesus' intent here is not primarily to condemn people, but to challenge them to right living according to the covenant established with God. So must this be our intent. Integrity of mission and commitment means facing opposition. The critical question for Jesus' disciples is whether or not we are enough on fire to continue his saving mission, no matter what the cost.

The pivotal point is that neither Jesus nor we *choose* division and strife; we choose to speak God's word and preach the values consistent with God's reign. Divisions occur simply by being faithful to God's message. This is the real shock value of the gospel: being a faithful disciple of Jesus will often instigate a clash of values, of principles, of priorities. The judgment we ourselves must make each day—and many times each day—is whether or not we are faithful to the Gospel values and challenges Jesus has taught us.

Jesus' very message is divisive because it calls people to a radical way of living—self-giving for the good of others. We must make a decision to follow him or not, to share his Passion ("baptism") or not, to be self-giving as he is. This choice results in division, even within families, because all of us do not make the same choice to follow Jesus.

Jesus came to preach the Good News of radical fidelity to God. Paradoxically, being faithful to Jesus (even when this brings strife and divisions) is how we come to lasting peace. If we compromise our Gospel message in order to have peace now, we forfeit the everlasting peace which is promised the faithful disciple. The choice is ours.

Living the Paschal Mystery

Realistically, most of us do not live our discipleship this dramatically nor are we faced with such consequential choices. We are hardly called like Jeremiah in the first reading to announce to the Israelites that their beloved Jerusalem will fall into the hands of the Babylonians—nor are we thrown into a cistern to die! Nor like Jesus will we be nailed to a cross because of our preaching and teaching. Nevertheless, we are called to be faithful to God's word in the small, everyday things as well as at times when the more serious challenges come along.

We do not seek division, but we seek consistency in living Gospel values. The very way we live our lives is a way to preach the Gospel. Sometimes strife and division is a sign of our faithful commitment. Gospel living is not always easy!

Focusing the Gospel

Key words and phrases: I have come, on fire, I must be baptized, anguish until it is accomplished

To the point: In this gospel fire is an image referring to divine judgment. Jesus is clearly stating that he has come to judge the people. His own faithfulness to this task led to his great anguish and ultimately to his passion and death. So will we his faithful disciples be treated. Jesus' intent here is not primarily to condemn people, but to challenge them to right living according to the covenant established with God. So must this be our intent.

Connecting the Gospel

to the first reading: Jeremiah's preaching divided the city and incited such opposition that people sought his death. Standing in this prophetic tradition, Jesus, too, preaches a word which divides families and leads ultimately to his death.

to experience: None of us seeks or desires division and strife, especially among those whom we cherish most. Sometimes, however, the choice is so clear and the values are so important, that we accept division and strife as a consequence of our choice.

Connecting the Responsorial Psalm

to the readings: In the first reading Jeremiah is thrown into a muddy cistern because he challenged the leaders of Israel. Jesus tells us in the gospel that we, too, will face extreme opposition if we follow him. Discipleship demands a willingness to stand alone, to be cut off even from those close to us when the call of Christ requires it. But the responsorial psalm reminds us that we are not, in fact, left alone. When human persons turn away from or against us because of our fidelity to discipleship, God will stoop close. Nothing can eradicate the cost of discipleship, but neither can anything destroy God's care for and protection of us. Though we may die, as did Jesus, God will not abandon us to death but will raise us to new life. This psalm expresses our absolute trust that God will "hold not back" anything in our support.

to psalmist preparation: In this psalm you call upon God to "come to my aid." In the context of the readings, this is a cry raised in the face of persecution experienced because you are being faithful to discipleship. When have you found yourself meeting such opposition? What helped you remain faithful? How did God come to your aid?

ASSEMBLY & FAITH-SHARING GROUPS

- Where I experience "great . . . anguish" for Jesus' mission to be "accomplished" is . . .
- Commitment to my relationship with God has brought divisiveness into my life when . . .
- My intent for living the Gospel is . . .

PRESIDERS

I support and strengthen others who struggle to remain faithful to their relationship with God by . . .

DEACONS

My serving others strengthens their relationship with God in that . . .

HOSPITALITY MINISTERS

I assist the assembly to be vulnerable before God's radical call to discipleship whenever I . . .

MUSIC MINISTERS

The judgment Jesus would bring to my manner of doing music ministry would be . . .

ALTAR MINISTERS

I serve others by helping them to choose Jesus and follow him faithfully by . . .

LECTORS

The word stirs up a fire inside me to accomplish God's will when . . .

EXTRAORDINARY MINISTERS OF HOLY COMMUNION

The Eucharist brings me peace by . . . the Eucharist challenges me by . . .

Model Penitential Act

Presider: Jesus was always faithful to his mission even to the point of death. In this liturgy let us pray that we may be strengthened to be faithful to him in all things . . . [pause]

Lord Jesus, you bring peace to those who are faithful: Lord . . .

Christ Jesus, you come to set the earth on fire: Christ . . .

Lord Jesus, you strengthen us to do your will: Lord . . .

Homily Points

• The most honorable judges are experienced, wise, and impartial. Their rule for judgment is the law and the good order of society. Jesus is the just Judge whose rule for judgment is God's will (law) and the right relationships he intends for his followers.

• Jesus came to judge us wisely. His rule of judgment is God's will. His intent is that we be in right relationship with each other, an indication of our right relationship with God. When we do God's will, we need not fear Jesus' judgment nor its effects. Even when our faithfulness brings us anguish, misunderstanding, division from others, we can be at peace because of our relationship with God.

• Like Jesus, we must be judges. We are constantly challenged about how we are to live and be in right relationship with others. The danger is that sometimes we can be so obstinate about how we see things that we do not judge according to God's will for us or for the good of deepening right relationships. Another danger is that we don't take the time needed to judge with honesty and sufficient reflection. Yet another danger is that our own desires get in the way of healthy discernment. The ultimate sign of our faithfulness to Jesus is not absence of anguish, misunderstanding, or division, but the deep peace that comes from right relationship with God and others.

Model Universal Prayer (Prayer of the Faithful)

Presider: God hears the cry of the faithful. Let us confidently place our needs in God's hands.

Response:

Lord, hear our prayer.

Cantor:

we pray to the Lord,

That all members of the church may make wise judgments for being faithful to their relationships with God and others . . . [pause]

That all people of the world may strive for peace in the midst of divisions . . . [pause]

That the sick, poor, and those who are suffering receive what they need from those who are faithful in discerning God's caring intent for others . . . [pause]

That each of us here be wise in our judgments, faithful in our actions, and steadfast in face of opposition . . . [pause]

Presider: O God, you inflame our hearts with passion for the saving work of your Son: hear these our prayers that we remain faithful. We ask this through Christ our Lord. **Amen.**

COLLECT

Let us pray

Pause for silent prayer

O God, who have prepared for those who love you
good things which no eye can see,
fill our hearts, we pray, with the warmth of your love,
so that, loving you in all things and above all things,
we may attain your promises,
which surpass every human desire.
Through our Lord Jesus Christ, your Son,
who lives and reigns with you in the unity of the Holy Spirit,
one God, for ever and ever.
Amen.

FIRST READING
Jer 38:4-6, 8-10

In those days, the princes said to the king:
    "Jeremiah ought to be put to death;
    he is demoralizing the soldiers who are left in this city,
    and all the people, by speaking such things to them;
    he is not interested in the welfare of our people,
    but in their ruin."
King Zedekiah answered: "He is in your power";
    for the king could do nothing with them.
And so they took Jeremiah
    and threw him into the cistern of Prince Malchiah,
    which was in the quarters of the guard,
    letting him down with ropes.
There was no water in the cistern, only mud,
    and Jeremiah sank into the mud.

Ebed-melech, a court official,
    went there from the palace and said to him:
    "My lord king,
    these men have been at fault
    in all they have done to the prophet Jeremiah,
    casting him into the cistern.
He will die of famine on the spot,
    for there is no more food in the city."
Then the king ordered Ebed-melech the Cushite
    to take three men along with him,
    and draw the prophet Jeremiah out of the cistern before he should die.

RESPONSORIAL PSALM
Ps 40:2, 3, 4, 18

R̶⁊. (14b) Lord, come to my aid!

I have waited, waited for the LORD,
   and he stooped toward me.

R̶⁊. Lord, come to my aid!

The LORD heard my cry.
He drew me out of the pit of destruction,
   out of the mud of the swamp;
he set my feet upon a crag;
   he made firm my steps.

R̶⁊. Lord, come to my aid!

And he put a new song into my mouth,
   a hymn to our God.
Many shall look on in awe
   and trust in the LORD.

R̶⁊. Lord, come to my aid!

Though I am afflicted and poor,
   yet the LORD thinks of me.
You are my help and my deliverer;
   O my God, hold not back!

R̶⁊. Lord, come to my aid!

SECOND READING
Heb 12:1-4

Brothers and sisters:
Since we are surrounded by so great a
   cloud of witnesses,
   let us rid ourselves of every burden and
     sin that clings to us
   and persevere in running the race that
     lies before us
   while keeping our eyes fixed on Jesus,
   the leader and perfecter of faith.
For the sake of the joy that lay before him
   he endured the cross, despising its
     shame,
   and has taken his seat at the right of
     the throne of God.
Consider how he endured such opposition
   from sinners,
   in order that you may not grow weary
     and lose heart.
In your struggle against sin
   you have not yet resisted to the point of
     shedding blood.

About Liturgy

Liturgy and strife: Strife and divisiveness is not always located within family households; it can also be evidenced on liturgy committees and in parishes! There are probably few things in parish life which cause divisions the way the decisions about the celebration of liturgy can. Is it not ironic that the very celebration whereby we express our unity in the Body of Christ can be the cause for so much anger, anguish, and divisiveness?

    Sometimes a parish can be radically split about how to celebrate liturgy because "good" liturgy is judged in terms of what individuals or groups want, desire, or find satisfying. Ideally, everyone would come to Sunday Mass each Sunday and go home satisfied, filled, and spiritually and emotionally fed. In reality, this does not happen to everyone in the same way and at the same time. One way to deal with this issue is to remember that the purpose of liturgy is not primarily our own satisfaction; rather, the purpose of liturgy is to give God praise and thanksgiving by offering ourselves with Christ on the altar. Only by such self-giving, and by keeping this the focus, can we hope to overcome divisions and improve our celebration of liturgy.

About Liturgical Music

Music suggestions: In Sylvia Dunstan's "Christus Paradox" we name Christ "peace-maker and swordbringer" and call "worthy" his "defeat and vict'ry" . . . his "peace and strife." This hymn would be appropriate during the preparation of the gifts after the gospel has been proclaimed. If sung at too fast a tempo, however, the multiple paradoxes within the text fly by at too fast a pace to grasp. This one needs to be savored and mulled over. A fitting recessional song this Sunday would be "God, Whose Purpose Is to Kindle." In verse 1 we ask God to "ignite us with your fire; While the earth awaits your burning, With your passion us inspire. Overcome our sinful calmness, Stir us with your saving name; Baptize with your fiery Spirit, Crown our lives with tongues of flame." In verse 3 we ask God who delivers a sword rather than a "placid peace" to "With your sharpened word disturb us, From complacency release!"

✠ SPIRITUALITY

GOSPEL ACCLAMATION
John 14:6

R⁊. Alleluia, alleluia.
I am the way, the truth and the life, says the
Lord;
no one comes to the Father, except through me.
R⁊. Alleluia, alleluia.

Gospel
Luke 13:22-30; L123C

Jesus passed through towns and
villages,
teaching as he went and making his
way to Jerusalem.
Someone asked him,
"Lord, will only a few people be
saved?"
He answered them,
"Strive to enter through the narrow
gate,
for many, I tell you, will attempt to
enter
but will not be strong enough.
After the master of the house has arisen
and locked the door,
then will you stand outside knocking
and saying,
'Lord, open the door for us.'
He will say to you in reply,
'I do not know where you are from.'
And you will say,
'We ate and drank in your company
and you taught in our streets.'
Then he will say to you,
'I do not know where you are from.
Depart from me, all you evildoers!'
And there will be wailing and grinding of
teeth
when you see Abraham, Isaac, and Jacob
and all the prophets in the kingdom of
God
and you yourselves cast out.
And people will come from the east and
the west
and from the north and the south
and will recline at table in the kingdom
of God.
For behold, some are last who will be first,
and some are first who will be last."

Reflecting on the Gospel
This Sunday's gospel uses an image of a *narrow* gate. The image suggests stricture, difficulty, squeezing by. Entering the narrow gate to salvation is not guaranteed by privilege or tradition (those who perceive themselves to be first), but guaranteed by openness to the in-breaking of the Messiah (those who perceive themselves to be last). The gate is narrow because the way is difficult—journeying with Jesus leads to Jerusalem and the cross. The strength needed to persist on this journey comes from reclining "at [his] table in the kingdom of God." It comes from eating and drinking the messianic Food with the Messiah.

Followers of Jesus feed on the messianic Food he gives us to strengthen us and overcome any difficulties or fears. We cannot claim merely eating and drinking with Jesus as our "ticket" to heaven. We must recline at the table with him, remain in his presence, and become transformed into his presence for others. In other words, we must live what we have become: we must be messianic Food; we must be Eucharist for others. Long ago (early second century) St. Ignatius of Antioch referred to the Eucharist as the "medicine of immortality" (Letter of Ignatius to the Ephesians 20:2). The narrow gate is thrown open more widely when we are strengthened by this Eucharist which is our antidote to difficulties and fears and our strength to be steadfast on our own journey to a share in the risen Life of Jesus. We know where Jesus is going (Jerusalem) and must ask ourselves whether we are willing to go there with him. The surprise of the gospel is that being saved is not accomplished by mere association with Jesus, but by the *transformation* which comes from sharing in his life, death, and resurrection, by sharing in the "medicine of immortality."

What is required for salvation? We must walk with Jesus to Jerusalem! Like Jesus, we, too, will meet opposition; we, too, must die to ourselves in self-giving to others. Alone, this is a daunting task. But we are not alone; Jesus is with us to support us and give us strength. We need only keep close to him. We need only keep our eyes on him rather than count the cost. Then we, too, can "recline at table in the kingdom of God" with him. His table is the banquet of eternal life. This is why the demands of discipleship do not overwhelm us completely. Sure, it costs. Sure, there is dying. At the same time there is also the rising!

Living the Paschal Mystery
Usually parents barely have begun a long trip with the children when they begin the chant, "Aren't we there yet?" Sometimes this is our chant, too, on our paschal journey. We want the dying to be over. We want the risen Life which comes from knowing who Jesus is, journeying with him, and being faithful to him. In God's good time, that will come. In the meantime, we are to walk with him to Jerusalem.

Part of discipleship is to be faithful to the everyday "plodding" of our paschal journey. If we try and rush it, we will miss opportunities—graced moments which bring us closer to salvation. Discipleship requires consistent and faithful decisions so that Jesus gets to "know us" on the way. Then we are invited to be his guest at his table. Then we find ourselves numbered among the first. More is required for salvation than eating and drinking—ultimately, we must share in Jesus' passion and death by eating and drinking his Body and Blood now.

Focusing the Gospel

Key words and phrases: making his way to Jerusalem, will only a few be saved?, narrow gate, strong enough, last who will be first

To the point: Entering the narrow gate to salvation is not guaranteed by privilege or tradition (those who perceive themselves to be first), but guaranteed by openness to the in-breaking of the Messiah (those who perceive themselves to be last). The gate is narrow because the way is difficult—journeying with Jesus leads to Jerusalem and the cross. The strength needed to persist on this journey comes from reclining "at [his] table in the kingdom of God." It comes from eating and drinking the messianic Food with the Messiah.

Connecting the Gospel

to the first reading: Isaiah prophesies that salvation is offered to all peoples ("from all the nations"). The gospel makes clear a condition for salvation: those who desire salvation must journey with Jesus to Jerusalem and accept all this entails.

to experience: Our society tends to declare, "*numero uno!*" We tend to want to be first, to find things easy, to have everything handed to us on a silver platter. This gospel says exactly the opposite. We are not first—Christ is. Things will not be easy—the road to salvation is narrow, difficult, demanding. Everything will not be handed to us—rather, we are asked to hand ourselves over.

Connecting the Responsorial Psalm

to the readings: Jesus challenges us in this Sunday's gospel with the harsh reality that not everyone will be admitted to the kingdom of God. His message, however, is for those who have heard the Good News of salvation, not for those who have "never heard of [God's] fame, or seen [God's] glory" (first reading). To these God will send messengers to tell them the Good News and gather them to the holy dwelling, Jerusalem. For those who have already heard, radical demands are in place (Jesus has been spelling these out in previous Sundays' gospels). And the responsorial psalm gives yet another command: we are to be the messengers who spread the Good News of God's salvation to all the world. The psalm reminds us that we are a necessary part of God's plan of salvation for all. It also suggests that we cannot recline at God's table if we have not invited everyone else to be there with us.

to psalmist preparation: In singing this psalm you command the assembly to tell the world the Good News of salvation. Who in your life is especially in need of hearing this news? How do you tell them?

ASSEMBLY & FAITH-SHARING GROUPS

- When I hear Jesus say, "Strive to enter through the narrow gate," I . . .
- When my journey to salvation gets narrow and challenging, I tend to . . . Jesus then . . .
- What sustains me most on my journey to Jerusalem is . . .

PRESIDERS

The way I strengthen my people on their journey to Jerusalem is . . . They strengthen me when . . .

DEACONS

My serving others seems overly demanding for me when . . . What strengthens me to continue my faithful service is . . .

HOSPITALITY MINISTERS

My hospitality is shaped (and limited) by my presumptions of who is "first" and "last" in the kingdom in that . . .

MUSIC MINISTERS

My music ministry becomes very difficult for me when . . . What strengthens me to continue on this road to salvation is . . .

ALTAR MINISTERS

Serving others is a fitting way of striving to enter through the "narrow gate" because . . .

LECTORS

When I embrace the narrowness of the journey to salvation in my daily living, my proclamation opens up for the people . . .

EXTRAORDINARY MINISTERS OF HOLY COMMUNION

Like the Eucharist, I help others be "strong enough" to enter the "narrow gate" whenever I . . .

Model Penitential Act

Presider: In the gospel for today, Jesus encourages us to strive to enter the narrow gate to salvation. Let us open ourselves to receive the strength offered at God's table . . . [pause]

Lord Jesus, you open wide the narrow door to salvation: Lord . . .

Christ Jesus, you invite all to your messianic table: Christ . . .

Lord Jesus, you strengthen us on our journey: Lord . . .

Homily Points

• Stenophobia is fear of narrow places. Even those of us who do not suffer from stenophobia can find being enclosed in a medical device for an MRI or CAT scan anxiety-producing. We naturally favor open spaces that give us room and freedom. And yet in this gospel Jesus is inviting us deliberately to enter a narrow gate!

• Why would we choose a narrow entry to a difficult and long journey? Jesus gives us the answer: this is the only way to salvation. We are strengthened by the reality that Jesus himself has already trod the journey to Jerusalem and the cross, and shown us that the end of this journey opens onto the wide and free space of new Life.

• Some of the "narrow places" we might encounter along our journey toward salvation include choosing to embrace a new challenge or task that frightens us, reestablishing trust with someone who has previously broken that trust, forgiving another who repeatedly hurts us, surrendering our time and talent for the good of someone who never says thank you, caring for someone outside our "circle." We are strengthened to enter these "narrow places" by others who know us and understand our fear, by past good experiences of having been stretched beyond ourselves, by the Bread of Life given us by the One who leads us on our journey.

Model Universal Prayer (Prayer of the Faithful)

Presider: Jesus desires that all will be saved. And so we pray for our needs with confidence.

Response:

Lord, hear our prayer.

Cantor:

we pray to the Lord,

That all members of the church may courageously walk with Jesus to Jerusalem and the cross . . . [pause]

That all peoples from east and west and from north and south find a place at God's table . . . [pause]

That those who are poor and needy find a place at the table of the world's abundant resources . . . [pause]

That all of us will be strong enough to enter through the narrow gate of faithful discipleship . . . [pause]

Presider: Generous God, you invite all to come to your table: help us to meet faithfully the demands of discipleship so that one day we might be with you to share your abundant feast. We ask this through Christ our Lord. **Amen.**

COLLECT
Let us pray

Pause for silent prayer

O God, who cause the minds of the faithful
to unite in a single purpose,
grant your people to love what you
    command
and to desire what you promise,
that, amid the uncertainties of this world,
our hearts may be fixed on that place
where true gladness is found.
Through our Lord Jesus Christ, your Son,
who lives and reigns with you in the unity
    of the Holy Spirit,
one God, for ever and ever.
Amen.

FIRST READING
Isa 66:18-21

Thus says the LORD:
I know their works and their thoughts,
and I come to gather nations of every
    language;
  they shall come and see my glory.
I will set a sign among them;
  from them I will send fugitives to the
    nations:
  to Tarshish, Put and Lud, Mosoch,
    Tubal and Javan,
  to the distant coastlands
  that have never heard of my fame, or
    seen my glory;
  and they shall proclaim my glory
    among the nations.
They shall bring all your brothers and
    sisters from all the nations
  as an offering to the LORD,
  on horses and in chariots, in carts, upon
    mules and dromedaries,
  to Jerusalem, my holy mountain, says
    the LORD,
  just as the Israelites bring their offering
  to the house of the LORD in clean
    vessels.
Some of these I will take as priests and
    Levites, says the LORD.

RESPONSORIAL PSALM

Ps 117:1, 2

℟. (Mark 16:15) Go out to all the world and tell the Good News.
  or:
℟. Alleluia.

Praise the LORD, all you nations;
  glorify him, all you peoples!

℟. Go out to all the world and tell the Good News.
  or:
℟. Alleluia.

For steadfast is his kindness toward us,
  and the fidelity of the LORD endures
    forever.

℟. Go out to all the world and tell the Good News.
  or:
℟. Alleluia.

SECOND READING

Heb 12:5-7, 11-13

Brothers and sisters,
You have forgotten the exhortation
    addressed to you as children:
  "My son, do not disdain the discipline
      of the Lord
    or lose heart when reproved by him;
  for whom the Lord loves, he disciplines;
    he scourges every son he
      acknowledges."
Endure your trials as "discipline";
  God treats you as sons.
For what "son" is there whom his father
    does not discipline?
At the time,
  all discipline seems a cause not for joy
      but for pain,
  yet later it brings the peaceful fruit of
      righteousness
  to those who are trained by it.

So strengthen your drooping hands and
    your weak knees.
Make straight paths for your feet,
    that what is lame may not be disjointed
      but healed.

About Liturgy

Eucharist and salvation: Sunday Mass is as much a part of our week as eating and sleeping. This is not to say we take it for granted; most of us take our Sunday celebrations quite seriously and know they nourish and strengthen us for our weekly journey in discipleship. At the same time, few of us probably think of the direct relationship between Sunday Mass and salvation, other than that we receive grace from a worthy celebration. This is very true, but we can say so much more.

The eucharistic prayers especially talk about how "we offer you [the Father] his Body and Blood, the sacrifice acceptable to you which brings salvation to the whole world" (Eucharistic Prayer IV). The prayers also specifically mention the chalice of salvation or saving chalice. It is too easy to think of this language as only referring to Christ and his sacrifice. At Mass we place ourselves on the altar with Christ in self-sacrifice; thus our own self-giving united with Christ's is part of bringing "salvation to the whole world."

There is another way to look at Eucharist and salvation. When we come to the table and share in the Body and Blood of Christ, we are coming to the "table in the kingdom of God." In other words, our sharing in the eucharistic Body and Blood of Christ at Mass is already a sharing in the eternal banquet of everlasting salvation. Our eating and drinking at God's table already brings us to the end of our paschal journey to Jerusalem, even while we are still plodding along on the way!

About Liturgical Music

A change in service music: At this point in Luke's Gospel, Jesus is making his way intentionally toward Jerusalem where he will face his death and resurrection. When asked who will be saved, he responds that the gate is narrow and great strength will be required to pass through it. It will not be enough merely to have eaten with him and listened to him speak. To enter into risen life we must journey with him to Jerusalem, we must join him in his self-emptying on the cross. One way to indicate our willingness to walk with Jesus to Jerusalem and the cross is to make this Sunday the day we change the service music we have been singing for Mass (note the change this day, for example, in the music for the Model Universal Prayer). Changing the service music marks a change in our sense of direction, and expresses an intensified choice on our part to walk the way of discipleship to its very end.

Note to the music director: To help people understand the reason for changing service music this week you might run a short blurb in the bulletin saying why the change has been made. Explain the connection between this change and Jesus' choice in the gospel to walk deliberately toward Jerusalem. Run the blurb both this week and next to give people time to reflect on it.

AUGUST 25, 2013
TWENTY-FIRST SUNDAY IN ORDINARY TIME

SPIRITUALITY

GOSPEL ACCLAMATION
Matt 11:29ab

R⁄. Alleluia, alleluia.
Take my yoke upon you, says the Lord;
and learn from me, for I am meek and humble
   of heart.
R⁄. Alleluia, alleluia.

Gospel   Luke 14:1, 7-14; L126C

On a sabbath Jesus went to dine
   at the home of one of the
      leading Pharisees,
   and the people there
      were observing him
      carefully.

He told a parable to those
   who had been invited,
   noticing how they were
      choosing the places of honor at
      the table.
"When you are invited by someone to a
      wedding banquet,
   do not recline at table in the place of
      honor.
A more distinguished guest than you
      may have been invited by him,
   and the host who invited both of you
      may approach you and say,
   'Give your place to this man,'
   and then you would proceed with
      embarrassment
   to take the lowest place.
Rather, when you are invited,
   go and take the lowest place
   so that when the host comes to you
      he may say,
   'My friend, move up to a higher
      position.'
Then you will enjoy the esteem of your
      companions at the table.
For everyone who exalts himself will
      be humbled,
   but the one who humbles himself will
      be exalted."

Continued in Appendix A, p. 309.

Continued in Appendix A, p. 309.

Reflecting on the Gospel

At formal dinners such as wedding banquets, seats of honor are assigned and a place at the table is limited only to invited guests. How cheeky someone would be to dare breach this protocol and come to a wedding banquet uninvited or take a seat assigned to someone else! Certain occasions require certain protocols. And protocols are for the benefit of right relationships. In this gospel Jesus challenges both guests and host at a dinner. But here the issue isn't one of protocol; much more is at stake.

Jesus calls the guests to let go of seeking places of honor and to choose seats that lead to being called "to a higher position." Jesus calls the host to invite as his guests those who have only themselves to give in return, for which he will be repaid at the "resurrection of the righteous." Ultimately this gospel is about relationships. Relationships among ourselves that build upon true humility and unrequited generosity deepen our relationship with the divine Host who desires our presence at the everlasting wedding Banquet where we will be the honored guests. Jesus in this gospel brings us to a longer vision—not to be concerned with our immediate honor or satisfaction, but to put first what has eternal value.

While at table, Jesus' eye is on the "wedding banquet" in God's kingdom where human expectations are reversed: the humble are exalted and the exalted are humbled. At that same heavenly Table, service to those who cannot repay ("the poor, the crippled, the lame, the blind") is repaid by God in "the resurrection of the righteous." Acts of earthly humility and generosity are met with heavenly exaltation and God's generosity. Humility is, in part, knowing one's strengths and weaknesses (see first reading) and one's place (gospel). But it is more. Humility is the virtue by which we acknowledge our status before God: we are "the poor, the crippled, the lame, the blind" who come to God's table because of God's invitation and generosity.

Thus Jesus' remarks in this gospel remind us about our truest identity in relation to God. As deeply humble people, we come to God empty and open ourselves to God's filling us with what is lasting. This reward—everlasting life at God's messianic Banquet—is ours if we but treat others as God treats us—we ourselves must bestow dignity and generosity on others. It is God who exalts us, not our own choosing or actions. It is God who repays us with the most unimaginable gift of all—everlasting life. Humility helps us shift our limited vision and relationship to an enduring perspective which keeps our focus on God.

Living the Paschal Mystery

Jesus is calling the disciples back to the authentic Jewish tradition of caring for the "widow, orphan, and sojourner" (see, for example, Exod 22:21 and Zech 7:10). These three groups in Israelite society were symbolic of those who were in a position of needing others to look after their well-being. Israel's care for them concretized God's care for Israel. Jesus is calling us to authentic relationship with God by caring for those who cannot care for themselves. The surprise: total self-giving to the lowly and needy means reward in heaven—eternal glory with God!

The lowly are those who need food, clothing, and shelter; our cities are full of these kinds of dispossessed people. The lowly are also the children in our midst; the physically, emotionally, mentally, or spiritually challenged; the elderly. We do not need to look very far to put Jesus' teaching this week into practice!

Focusing the Gospel

Key words and phrases: choosing places of honor; move up to a higher position; do not invite your friends . . . ; invite the poor, the crippled, the lame, the blind; resurrection of the righteous

To the point: In this gospel Jesus challenges both guests and host at a dinner. Jesus calls the guests to let go of seeking places of honor and to choose seats that lead to being called "to a higher position." Jesus calls the host to invite as his guests those who have only themselves to give in return, for which the host will be repaid at the "resurrection of the righteous." Ultimately this gospel is about relationships. Relationships among ourselves that build upon true humility and unrequited generosity deepen our relationship with the divine Host who desires our presence at the everlasting wedding Banquet where we will be the honored guests.

Connecting the Gospel

to the first reading: Humility is, in part, knowing one's strengths and weaknesses (see first reading) and one's place (gospel). But it is more. Humility is the virtue by which we acknowledge our status before God: we are "the poor, the crippled, the lame, the blind" who come to God's table because of God's invitation and generosity.

to experience: Jesus in this gospel is not negating meals with family and friends! He is teaching us that our generosity must extend beyond our immediate circle to include everyone—especially those in need—whom we might meet.

Connecting the Responsorial Psalm

to the readings: In this Sunday's gospel the people were "observing [Jesus] carefully." In the responsorial psalm we observe God carefully. What we see is a God who "gives a home to the forsaken" and provides "for the needy." When Jesus in the gospel advises us to invite to our table "the poor, the crippled, the lame, the blind," he is challenging us to model what we see God doing. And when we do so we experience a remarkable reversal in our own position. Choosing to give up the first place so that room is made for the poor and needy exalts us. Our humility "find[s] favor with God" (first reading). Even more, we become like God. When we sing this psalm, then, we are praying to become like the God we praise.

to psalmist preparation: This psalm praises God for goodness to the poor and needy. Only those who recognize themselves among the poor and needy can see what God is doing to lift them up. How are you poor and needy? How does God lift you up by inviting you to the banquet of Jesus' Body and Blood? How do you invite others to join you at this banquet?

ASSEMBLY & FAITH-SHARING GROUPS

- I seek a place of honor when . . . I am offered a "higher position" when . . .
- I care for those who cannot repay me whenever I . . .
- My relationships include . . . They lead me to Jesus when . . .

PRESIDERS

I am tempted to exalt myself when . . . My ministry brings me to true humility by . . .

DEACONS

As I gather and work with God's lowly ones, I recognize in them the divine Host when . . .

HOSPITALITY MINISTERS

I make the Sunday gathering a home for the disadvantaged whenever I . . .

MUSIC MINISTERS

As a music minister, I find myself clamoring for position when . . . What helps me at these times see myself as God does is . . .

ALTAR MINISTERS

Serving has taught me that true humility is . . .

LECTORS

When my preparation for lectoring includes conscious choices to be generous to others, my proclamation sounds like . . .

EXTRAORDINARY MINISTERS OF HOLY COMMUNION

I see "the poor, the crippled, the lame, the blind" in those who come to Holy Communion and this moves me to . . .

Model Penitential Act

Presider: The divine Host invites us to his banquet of generosity and love. Let us prepare ourselves to be humble guests who rejoice that we are called to this Table . . . [pause]

Lord Jesus, you are our heavenly Food and Drink: Lord . . .

Christ Jesus, you lift up the lowly: Christ . . .

Lord Jesus, you show us the way to the resurrection of the righteous: Lord . . .

Homily Points

• Different types of relationships are often revealed at meals. When the extended family gathers for a holiday, the children are often relegated to a "children's table" and eat first so the adults can interact about their adult concerns. The conversation is free to be light or even to address more serious concerns with long-range effects such as who is seriously ill, how long a job search has been, a child who seems to be going off the deep end.

• Jesus challenges us to right relationships by using the two specific examples of not choosing for ourselves places of honor and not inviting only people into our lives who can return our favors. Like family conversations, his concern is beyond the immediate to what ultimately matters—a life of righteous living. It is only right relationships that lead to ful-filling our deepest longing: presence at the everlasting wedding Banquet.

• Grabbing places of honor for ourselves can be as ordinary as pushing ahead of others in a grocery line, expecting special treatment at work or school, feeling entitled to hav-ing everything we want. Opening ourselves to a broader circle of relationships can be as ordinary as having a conversation with a shy coworker, supporting those who are trying to make changes for the good, reaching out to those who are alone and in need. These righ-teous ways of acting not only help the other, but also give us the satisfaction of deepening relationships. Not only with others, but with the divine Host himself.

Model Universal Prayer (Prayer of the Faithful)

Presider: Let us make our needs known to the God who draws us to "the resurrection of the righteous."

Response:

Lord, hear our prayer.

Cantor:

we pray to the Lord,

That all members of the church invite others into their lives in such a way as to deepen their relationship with God . . . [pause]

That world leaders strive to build the right relationships among nations that bring peace and justice to all . . . [pause]

That "the poor, the crippled, the lame, the blind" be invited to take their rightful place in the community . . . [pause]

That all of us here embrace true humility and unreserved generosity for the good of all . . . [pause]

Presider: O God, you provide for all our needs: hear these our prayers that one day we might feast at your everlasting Banquet. We ask this through Christ our Lord. **Amen.**

COLLECT

Let us pray

Pause for silent prayer

God of might, giver of every good gift,
put into our hearts the love of your name,
so that, by deepening our sense of
    reverence,
you may nurture in us what is good
and, by your watchful care,
keep safe what you have nurtured.
Through our Lord Jesus Christ, your Son,
who lives and reigns with you in the unity
    of the Holy Spirit,
one God, for ever and ever.
Amen.

FIRST READING
Sir 3:17-18, 20, 28-29

My child, conduct your affairs with
    humility,
    and you will be loved more than a giver
      of gifts.
Humble yourself the more, the greater
    you are,
    and you will find favor with God.
What is too sublime for you, seek not,
    into things beyond your strength search
      not.
The mind of a sage appreciates proverbs,
    and an attentive ear is the joy of the
      wise.
Water quenches a flaming fire,
    and alms atone for sins.

CATECHESIS

RESPONSORIAL PSALM
Ps 68:4-5, 6-7, 10-11

R℣. (cf. 11b) God, in your goodness, you have made a home for the poor.

The just rejoice and exult before God;
    they are glad and rejoice.
Sing to God, chant praise to his name;
    whose name is the LORD.

R℣. God, in your goodness, you have made a home for the poor.

The father of orphans and the defender of
        widows
    is God in his holy dwelling.
God gives a home to the forsaken;
    he leads forth prisoners to prosperity.

R℣. God, in your goodness, you have made a home for the poor.

A bountiful rain you showered down, O
        God, upon your inheritance;
    you restored the land when it
        languished;
your flock settled in it;
    in your goodness, O God, you provided
        it for the needy.

R℣. God, in your goodness, you have made a home for the poor.

SECOND READING
Heb 12:18-19, 22-24a

Brothers and sisters:
You have not approached that which could
        be touched
    and a blazing fire and gloomy darkness
    and storm and a trumpet blast
    and a voice speaking words such that
        those who heard
    begged that no message be further
        addressed to them.
No, you have approached Mount Zion
    and the city of the living God, the
        heavenly Jerusalem,
    and countless angels in festal gathering,
    and the assembly of the firstborn
        enrolled in heaven,
    and God the judge of all,
    and the spirits of the just made perfect,
    and Jesus, the mediator of a new
        covenant,
    and the sprinkled blood that speaks
        more eloquently than that of Abel.

About Liturgy

"Liturgy"—the meaning of the word: The very word "liturgy" derives from two Greek words meaning "the work (or service) of the people." In ancient Greece "liturgists" were those who performed public works on behalf of society. In the context of Christian worship, the etymology of the word "liturgy" suggests that worship cannot be separated from doing—serving others, especially those in need. Sometimes we understand liturgy in terms of "the work of the people" to mean that we must work hard to make liturgy beautiful and meaningful. That is only partially true. The real work of liturgy actually begins at the dismissal, when we are sent off to do what we have celebrated—to serve others, to spend our lives for the good of others.

All of us must also accept the responsibility for helping our parish communities come to understand and live out the everyday, practical, social demands of true worshipers. The greatest worship we can give to God is to reach out with God's generosity toward those around us in need. Worship does not only happen within church buildings; it characterizes our relationship to God and to each other—a relationship of humility and service.

Labor Day: This is Labor Day weekend, and it would be very appropriate to add a fifth petition at the prayer of the faithful. Here is a model: That all our nation's laborers work with dignity and honor and receive just compensation for their service . . . [pause]

About Liturgical Music

Singing the acclamations: The acclamations (i.e., the gospel acclamation; the Holy, Holy; the mystery of faith; and the great amen, the latter three of which are part of the eucharistic prayer) developed as a direct result of Vatican II's recovery of the priesthood of all the baptized and the essential nature of the liturgy as the celebration of all the people. They are *actions* in the form of song. As the ancient adage states, to sing is to pray twice. When we sing, we become more present, more attentive, more participative, and more powerful. When we sing, we enfold all the other members of the assembly with our voice, and communicate our choice to participate fully in the liturgical action, and vice versa. We sing the acclamations, then, not only to address God but also to direct personal support to one another in living out our identity and mission as the Body of Christ. The singing of the acclamations is neither neutral nor inconsequential, for it expresses in an intense way the triple directedness of the liturgy toward God, toward our fellow members in Christ, and toward the world. Our singing of the acclamations amplifies their energy and intent: their sound moves out from each of us as individual source, encircles all of us in mutual support, and sends us as community on mission. The more we understand their importance and the more intentionally we sing them, the more we will both deepen our participation in liturgy and our living out of the mission of the church.

✦ SPIRITUALITY

GOSPEL ACCLAMATION
Ps 119: 135

℞. Alleluia, alleluia.
Let your face shine upon your servant;
and teach me your laws.
℞. Alleluia, alleluia.

Gospel   Luke 14:25-33; L129C

Great crowds were traveling with Jesus,
  and he turned and addressed them,
    "If anyone comes to me without
      hating his father and
      mother,
  wife and children, brothers and
      sisters,
  and even his own life,
  he cannot be my disciple.
Whoever does not carry his
    own cross and come after me
  cannot be my disciple.
Which of you wishing to construct a
    tower
  does not first sit down and calculate
    the cost
  to see if there is enough for its
    completion?
Otherwise, after laying the foundation
  and finding himself unable to finish the
    work
  the onlookers should laugh at him and
    say,
  'This one began to build but did not
    have the resources to finish.'
Or what king marching into battle would
    not first sit down
  and decide whether with ten thousand
    troops
  he can successfully oppose another
    king
  advancing upon him with twenty
    thousand troops?
But if not, while he is still far away,
  he will send a delegation to ask for
    peace terms.
In the same way,
  anyone of you who does not renounce
    all his possessions
  cannot be my disciple."

Reflecting on the Gospel

Noah was enjoying his fourth birthday. It was a grand party and time to open gifts and cards. One card had four one-dollar bills in it and he was delighted. Four was a big number. He was rich! He could buy the new Wii game he wanted. The adults were smiling—they knew that he was not old enough yet to calculate the cost of real things. They knew he would have to open lots of cards with dollar bills and probably forgo some other thing he would like to have before he would have enough money to buy the new game. As is typical with a child, however, Noah soon became lost in opening his other gifts and forgot the four dollars and what he wanted to buy with them. In this gospel, Jesus challenges those following him to "calculate the cost" of discipleship. This cost is steep.

Discipleship requires both renunciation and calculation. Those who wish to follow Jesus must renounce everyone and everything that gets in the way of a single-minded response to Jesus' invitation to be his disciple. At the same time, disciples are not naively to follow Jesus. They must calculate and consent to the cost— the price is giving their all, even their own life. What the One who calls gives disciples in return, however, is beyond calculation—fullness of new Life.

Jesus is using pretty radical language about renunciation and calculation in order to give us a chance to consider carefully what we do when we say yes to discipleship. Like so many things about life, we might enter into following Jesus with great enthusiasm and energy. But the cost of discipleship might soon dampen our spirits and lead us to lose sight of the gift of new Life Jesus offers us.

Being a disciple is not something we can undertake halfheartedly or frivolously. It is a decision to be pondered and weighed. The cost is steep; like Jesus, we give our lives over for the good of others. Are we willing to pay the price? Every day? Do we calculate carefully?

Living the Paschal Mystery

The radical cost of discipleship suggests that our yes is one that must be learned; we grow into it. As we make choices to live out our discipleship, we enter more deeply into its meaning and demands. At the same time as we are faithful disciples, we also continually receive from God the strength to follow Jesus no matter what the cost.

Our yes to being followers of Jesus and taking up his mission is first ritualized at our baptism. Whether babies or adults makes no difference: that yes is always less than perfect. There is always room in our lives to grow deeper into Christ. Our ongoing baptismal yes is our ongoing assessment of the self-emptying stance of discipleship. Jesus is constantly inviting us to listen to him. We spend our whole lives bringing our fullest attention to what he is saying. This gospel gives us no hint about what happens if we cannot follow through on these radical demands of discipleship. From the history of God's dealing with the chosen people, we know God is a God of mercy, compassion, and forgiveness. Jesus lays out the radical demands of discipleship. Our human weakness begs us to call on God's mercy and forgiveness when we cannot quite measure up. In all things, God will sustain us. God never goes back on the divine promise to give new Life to those who are faithful.

Focusing the Gospel

Key words and phrases: hating . . . even his own life, carry his own cross, come after me, calculate the cost

To the point: Discipleship requires both renunciation and calculation. Those who wish to follow Jesus must renounce everyone and everything that gets in the way of a single-minded response to Jesus' invitation to be his disciple. At the same time, disciples are not naively to follow Jesus. They must calculate and consent to the cost—the price is giving their all, even their own life. What the One who calls gives disciples in return, however, is beyond calculation— fullness of new Life.

Connecting the Gospel

to the first reading: The reading from Wisdom reminds us that "the deliberations of mortals are timid." Jesus, however, challenges us to be anything but timid. With bold calculation and conviction we are to embrace the cross. This is the way of discipleship.

to experience: We take much time and care over major decisions, for example, buying a house, marrying, having children, taking a new job. Nevertheless, each of these brings its own surprises and new challenges, not initially considered. The same is true for committed discipleship—even after we make the informed decision to follow Jesus, there are still many surprises on the road of discipleship.

Connecting the Responsorial Psalm

to the readings: The first reading reminds us of a truth with which we are already familiar: "the deliberations of mortals are timid, and unsure." But Jesus challenges us in the gospel to be neither timid nor unsure when deliberating the cost of discipleship. It is total. Relationships must be abandoned, possessions must be renounced, the cross must be carried. The responsorial psalm promises, however, that we will not be left with only our own meager strength. God will grant us "wisdom" and will "prosper the work of our hands." God will give us both the wisdom to calculate the cost and the courage to pay it (first reading). God knows the all-encompassing cost of discipleship and will be with us when we need strength, support, encouragement, and mercy. In singing this psalm we profess our confidence in God who knows even better than we do what will be exacted of us and who has promised to see us through.

to psalmist preparation: The cost of following Christ is immense, but this responsorial psalm reminds you that you have more than yourself to depend upon: your faithfulness will prosper because God has underwritten your discipleship. Sing with confidence in God and share this confidence with the assembly!

ASSEMBLY & FAITH-SHARING GROUPS

- The price I must keep paying to be a disciple of Jesus is . . .
- What I need to renounce in order to follow Jesus faithfully is . . . What I need to calculate more clearly is . . .
- The next step for me in order to move beyond halfhearted to single-minded discipleship is . . .

PRESIDERS

I find it hardest to give my all when . . . When I do, what I am given in return is . . .

DEACONS

In my service ministry the demand of Jesus I experience is . . . What I am given in return is . . .

HOSPITALITY MINISTERS

I help those gathering to be open to Jesus' challenging call to discipleship whenever I . . .

MUSIC MINISTERS

One of the costs of music ministry which has surprised me is . . . What keeps me faithful despite the cost is . . .

ALTAR MINISTERS

The costs of my serving are . . . What helps me embrace these costs is . . .

LECTORS

When I am timid about the cost of discipleship and following Jesus, my proclamation sounds like . . .

EXTRAORDINARY MINISTERS OF HOLY COMMUNION

At each Eucharist I deepen my baptismal choice to follow Jesus by . . .

Model Penitential Act

Presider: In today's gospel, Jesus challenges us to calculate the cost of discipleship. In this celebration, let us ask for the grace to be faithful disciples . . . [pause]

Lord Jesus, you challenge us to follow you wholeheartedly: Lord . . .

Christ Jesus, you give to your faithful followers an abundance of Life: Christ . . .

Lord Jesus, you bring to completion the good work you have begun in us: Lord . . .

Homily Points

• In trying economic times, most people need to calculate carefully how they spend their money. They choose to renounce having some things they would like to have because other things are more essential to life. Often the reward from this pattern of calculation and renunciation becomes valuable enough that even when better economic circumstances develop, they continue in this way of living.

• Discipleship is constantly about renunciation and calculation. Following Jesus is an ongoing choice with ongoing demands. Disciples would become discouraged if they did not keep focused on where faithful discipleship leads—to fullness of new Life. Renunciation brings abundance; calculation ensures fidelity.

• If we clearly calculated the costs and assessed our resources before beginning the journey of discipleship, none of us would ever begin! The fact is, we ourselves don't have what we need to be faithful disciples. But Jesus does and he gives us his power and grace to "finish the work." So what we are to calculate is not what we lack, but what Jesus continually gives. We can give our all because Jesus has first given his all to us.

Model Universal Prayer (Prayer of the Faithful)

Presider: God gives us the grace to meet the challenges of discipleship. We now pray for the needs of the church and world.

Response:

Lord, hear our prayer.

Cantor:

we pray to the Lord,

That all members of the church renounce anything that stands in the way of faithfully following Jesus . . . [pause]

That peoples of all nations receive what they need from the abundance of this earth . . . [pause]

That those who are sick, suffering, or in any need receive from the resources of the community of the faithful . . . [pause]

That none of us here be overcome by the costs of faithful discipleship but rejoice in the Life with which Jesus continually empowers us . . . [pause]

Presider: O God, you are with us as we shoulder the cost of following faithfully your Son: hear these our prayers that one day we share forever in the new Life he offers. We ask this through Christ our Lord. **Amen.**

COLLECT
Let us pray

Pause for silent prayer

O God, by whom we are redeemed and receive adoption,
look graciously upon your beloved sons and daughters,
that those who believe in Christ may receive true freedom
and an everlasting inheritance.
Through our Lord Jesus Christ, your Son,
who lives and reigns with you in the unity of the Holy Spirit,
one God, for ever and ever.
Amen.

FIRST READING
Wis 9:13-18b

Who can know God's counsel,
    or who can conceive what the LORD intends?
For the deliberations of mortals are timid,
    and unsure are our plans.
For the corruptible body burdens the soul
    and the earthen shelter weighs down the mind that has many concerns.
And scarce do we guess the things on earth,
    and what is within our grasp we find with difficulty;
    but when things are in heaven, who can search them out?
Or who ever knew your counsel, except you had given wisdom
    and sent your holy spirit from on high?
And thus were the paths of those on earth made straight.

RESPONSORIAL PSALM
Ps 90:3-4, 5-6, 12-13, 14, 17

R℞. (1) In every age, O Lord, you have been our refuge.

You turn man back to dust,
    saying, "Return, O children of men."
For a thousand years in your sight
    are as yesterday, now that it is past,
    or as a watch of the night.

R℞. In every age, O Lord, you have been our refuge.

You make an end of them in their sleep;
   the next morning they are like the
      changing grass,
which at dawn springs up anew,
   but by evening wilts and fades.

R⫽. In every age, O Lord, you have been
our refuge.

Teach us to number our days aright,
   that we may gain wisdom of heart.
Return, O Lord! How long?
   Have pity on your servants!

R⫽. In every age, O Lord, you have been
our refuge.

Fill us at daybreak with your kindness,
   that we may shout for joy and gladness
      all our days.
And may the gracious care of the Lord
     our God be ours;
   prosper the work of our hands for us!
   Prosper the work of our hands!

R⫽. In every age, O Lord, you have been
our refuge.

SECOND READING
Phlm 9-10, 12-17

I, Paul, an old man,
   and now also a prisoner for Christ Jesus,
   urge you on behalf of my child
      Onesimus,
   whose father I have become in my
      imprisonment;
   I am sending him, that is, my own heart,
      back to you.
I should have liked to retain him for
     myself,
   so that he might serve me on your
      behalf
   in my imprisonment for the gospel,
   but I did not want to do anything
      without your consent,
   so that the good you do might not be
      forced but voluntary.
Perhaps this is why he was away from you
     for a while,
   that you might have him back forever,
   no longer as a slave
   but more than a slave, a brother,
   beloved especially to me, but even more
      so to you,
   as a man and in the Lord.
So if you regard me as a partner, welcome
   him as you would me.

About Liturgy

The challenge of liturgy committees: The task and responsibilities of a liturgy committee may sometimes seem as overwhelming as the cost of discipleship! If committee members were dependent upon their own means to be successful in their ministry, they would surely be crushed by the weight of the cost. What carries them through—enables them to continue to say yes both to this ministry and to their following Jesus every day of their lives—is the strength that God gives to each of them. This is why prayer—both individually and together as a committee—is so important for their liturgical ministry (and, indeed, for all ministry).

It might be encouraging and helpful to committee members if the parish liturgist or liturgy committee coordinator would use the blessing over the oil of catechumens (RCIA no. 207) to begin a meeting when things seem tense and overwhelming. That prayer assures the members of wisdom and strength; through their prebaptismal anointing they are able to be brought to a "deeper understanding of the Gospel" and able to "accept the challenge of Christian living."

Using this prayer also reminds us that baptism and confirmation are hardly sacraments which happen only in ritual time. They bestow God's graces on us to help us meet whatever challenges of discipleship come our way. So it is good practice regularly to go back to the prayers of our sacraments and implement them in other situations.

About Liturgical Music

Music suggestions: A setting of "Take Up Your Cross" would be appropriate for either the entrance song or the song during the preparation of the gifts. In "Only This I Want" we express our choice to bear the cross with Christ with full awareness that all other things will seem as loss, that the choice will have its price, but that such a choice will bring gladness of heart. The song would be appropriate either as a choir prelude or during the preparation of the gifts. In the Indian folk song "I Have Decided to Follow Jesus" we proclaim, "The world behind me, the cross before me" we'll follow Jesus with "No turning back, no turning back!" This song would make a good response to the gospel during the preparation of the gifts. In Thomas Troeger's "For God Risk Everything" (in *Hymns for the Gospels*, GIA) we beg, "From hearts that hide and hoard the treasures that you send Free us, till we by faith, O Lord, Shall act as you intend, Till we risk all for you, risk ev'rything you give, And risking, learn what Jesus knew: By risking all, we live." This hymn would make a fitting recessional song.

✝ SPIRITUALITY

GOSPEL ACCLAMATION
2 Cor 5:19

℟. Alleluia, alleluia.
God was reconciling the world to himself in Christ
and entrusting to us the message of reconciliation.
℟. Alleluia, alleluia.

Gospel
Luke 15:1-32; L132C

Tax collectors and sinners were all
   drawing near to listen to Jesus,
   but the Pharisees and scribes began
      to complain, saying,
   "This man welcomes sinners and
      eats with them."
So to them he addressed this parable.
"What man among you having a
      hundred sheep and losing one of
      them
   would not leave the ninety-nine in the
      desert
   and go after the lost one until he
      finds it?
And when he does find it,
   he sets it on his shoulders with great
      joy
   and, upon his arrival home,
   he calls together his friends and
      neighbors and says to them,
   'Rejoice with me because I have
      found my lost sheep.'
I tell you, in just the same way
   there will be more joy in heaven over
      one sinner who repents
   than over ninety-nine righteous people
      who have no need of repentance.

"Or what woman having ten coins and
      losing one
   would not light a lamp and sweep the
      house,
   searching carefully until she finds it?

Continued in Appendix A, p. 310.

Reflecting on the Gospel

Prodigality is evident in all three parables. But there are two sides to the kind of excess that the characters in the parables exhibit. On the one hand, the shepherd is unbelievably caring when he leaves the ninety-nine sheep to find one and tenderly carries it back to the fold on his own shoulders. The woman unrealistically wastes oil to light a lamp and time to sweep the house to find a single lost coin. The father lavishly bestows "the finest robe," a ring and sandals, and a "fattened calf" on his irresponsible son to welcome him back home. In these three characters prodigality leads to rejoicing and celebrating new life. On the other hand, the younger son totally wastes his inheritance. The older son is abundantly angry, resentful, and jealous of his brother. But in spite of the younger son's wastefulness, his decision to return home and beg his father for forgiveness brings him life. The older son, however, refuses to celebrate life. He chooses death.

What the shepherd, the woman, and the father all have in common is having lost something dear to them. When they find what they have lost, they rejoice extravagantly. In the parable of the prodigal son, he is found because he chooses to return to his father's house: he chooses life. By contrast, the older son—in his anger, resentment, and jealousy—is truly the one who is lost because he refuses to rejoice in his father's mercy and goodness: he chooses death. The extravagant mercy and goodness of our divine Father urges us to choose life over death. The challenge of this gospel is to let go of being lost and choose to be found; it is to let go of death and choose life.

God's response to our being lost (choosing sinfulness) is always one of mercy, compassion, and forgiveness. God always seeks the lost (even when it includes an intentional turning from God). God is always faithful in giving us all we need to choose life over death.

Living the Paschal Mystery

Being a faithful disciple does not mean always doing the logical thing nor the most practical thing. Like God in the first reading—who relented punishing Israel for unfaithfulness because God "brought [them] out of the land of Egypt"—we, too, must put aside our shortsightedness and be merciful and forgiving. If we find this difficult, we only need to remember God's utter fidelity and compassion toward us.

Forgiveness is never easy, and so much more difficult when the other seems to hurt us intentionally. Perhaps one way to approach this is to consider the good in the other who needs our forgiveness. When we are angry, recite a "litany" of positive virtues. When we want to strike back, think of the dignity of the other because he or she is a baptized son or daughter of God. Maybe we also need to consider our own goodness!

If we allow anger, resentment, or jealousy to fester in us (as did the older son in the gospel), we are blocking our ability to grow. We are limiting our openness to being found when we are lost. What may help us let go of choosing death is to remember God's mercy and compassion so faithfully shown us throughout history. We don't know the next chapter in the prodigal son's family saga, but we do know the father's response: he welcomed his son back home with great rejoicing. Such is so very true for our heavenly Father.

Focusing the Gospel

Key words and phrases: go after the lost one, Rejoice with me, got up and went back, let us celebrate with a feast, refused to enter the house, has come to life again

To the point: What the shepherd, the woman, and the father all have in common is having lost something dear to them. When they find what they have lost, they rejoice extravagantly. In the parable of the prodigal son, he is found because he chooses to return to his father's house: he chooses life. By contrast, the older son—in his anger, resentment, and jealousy—is truly the one who is lost because he refuses to rejoice in his father's mercy and goodness: he chooses death. The extravagant mercy and goodness of our divine Father urges us to choose life over death.

Connecting the Gospel

to the first reading: Both readings describe the mercy God extends to sinners, whether the sin is idolatry (first reading); dissolute living (younger son); or anger, resentment, and jealousy (older son). Such divine mercy begets new life.

to experience: Many parents anguish as they watch a son or daughter go astray in life. They will do anything to help their children come to their senses and turn their life around. Parents only want life for their children, although sometimes children seem to choose death for themselves.

Connecting the Responsorial Psalm

to the readings: In the first reading Moses talks God into relenting of the punishment unfaithful Israel deserves. In the gospel the prodigal son relents of his sinfulness and is embraced by his father. The Pharisees and scribes, on the other hand, refuse to relent in their judgment against Jesus for eating with sinners. The elder son refuses to relent of his resentment at his prodigal brother and his anger at his forgiving father.

The responsorial psalm for this Sunday, taken from Psalm 51, is our song of relenting. Through it we align ourselves with the tax collectors and sinners, with the lost sheep, and with the prodigal son. Such alignment is part of the radical gift of self which discipleship demands for through it we give up any vestige of false self-image. We can be found because we admit that we are lost. We can receive God's unrestricted and limitless mercy because we confess we are in need of it.

to psalmist preparation: Your singing these verses from Psalm 51 is a public act of confession for you stand before the assembly and admit sinfulness. But even more importantly, you confess the mercy of God who never spurns a contrite and humbled heart. As you prepare to sing this psalm, what forgiveness might you ask of God? What relenting of sin and pride might you need to do?

**ASSEMBLY &
FAITH-SHARING GROUPS**
- When I consider that God searches for me when I am lost, I think . . .
- I choose life when . . . I choose death when . . .
- The lost I must seek are . . . I rejoice and celebrate when . . .

PRESIDERS
I help the lost who come to me to choose life by . . .

DEACONS
I am like the good shepherd and seek the lost in the community by . . .

HOSPITALITY MINISTERS
My welcome of those gathering for liturgy helps them choose life when I . . .

MUSIC MINISTERS
The life music making brings to me is . . . I choose this life by . . .

ALTAR MINISTERS
My serving models choosing life in that . . .

LECTORS
I proclaim God's extravagant mercy and forgiveness in my life whenever I . . .

**EXTRAORDINARY MINISTERS
OF HOLY COMMUNION**
Eucharist is a sacrament of Life in that . . .

Model Penitential Act

Presider: God cares for each one of us and seeks us when we stray. Let us reflect on God's compassion and mercy and open ourselves to choose God's gift of new Life . . . [pause]

Lord Jesus, you are the Good Shepherd who seeks the lost sheep: Lord . . .

Christ Jesus, you rejoice when even one sinner repents: Christ . . .

Lord Jesus, you give us Life in abundance: Lord . . .

Homily Points

• Expectation is a strong motivator. When we expect guests for dinner, we buy groceries, clean the house, cook dinner. When we expect a promotion at our job, we work harder and longer and even plan the celebration of our success. Expectation generates action, action leads to success, success brings rejoicing and satisfaction.

• The shepherd and the woman expect to find the lost sheep and coin, or they would never have wasted their time searching. Their diligent action brings them to rejoice and celebrate. We don't know if the father expected his younger son to return, but when he "caught sight of him" he springs into action: he runs to meet him and clothes him with dignity and honor. He rejoices and calls all to a celebration of new life.

• When our own expectations are limited because we are angry, resentful, or jealous, we close off possibilities for success, new life, restored relationships, joy, celebration. When our expectations are high because we are hopeful, diligent, and welcoming, we open up possibilities for success, restored relationships, acceptance, deep satisfaction—that is, we choose new life. The extravagant mercy and goodness of our divine Father shapes our expectations and enables us to choose life over death.

Model Universal Prayer (Prayer of the Faithful)

Presider: No one is so lost that they are not sought by our divine Father to receive his goodness and mercy. We are encouraged to pray for our needs.

Response:

Lord, hear our prayer.

Cantor:

we pray to the Lord,

That the church always seek those who are lost and bring them the new life of God's mercy and goodness . . . [pause]

That world leaders generously show compassion and mercy toward the powerless and the poor . . . [pause]

That those struggling with anger, resentment, or jealousy may choose conversion of heart . . . [pause]

That all of us rejoice that our divine Father always seeks the lost to bring them back into the divine embrace . . . [pause]

Presider: O God, we praise you for your mercy and goodness: look kindly on our needs and hear our prayers that we may one day rejoice with you in your kingdom of heaven. We ask this through Christ our Lord. **Amen.**

COLLECT

Let us pray

Pause for silent prayer

Look upon us, O God,
Creator and ruler of all things,
and, that we may feel the working of your mercy,
grant that we may serve you with all our heart.
Through our Lord Jesus Christ, your Son,
who lives and reigns with you in the unity of the Holy Spirit,
one God, for ever and ever.
Amen.

FIRST READING

Exod 32:7-11, 13-14

The LORD said to Moses,
"Go down at once to your people,
whom you brought out of the land of Egypt,
for they have become depraved.
They have soon turned aside from the way I pointed out to them,
making for themselves a molten calf and worshiping it,
sacrificing to it and crying out,
'This is your God, O Israel,
who brought you out of the land of Egypt!'
I see how stiff-necked this people is,"
continued the LORD to Moses.
"Let me alone, then,
that my wrath may blaze up against them to consume them.
Then I will make of you a great nation."

But Moses implored the LORD, his God, saying,
"Why, O LORD, should your wrath blaze up against your own people,
whom you brought out of the land of Egypt
with such great power and with so strong a hand?
Remember your servants Abraham, Isaac, and Israel,
and how you swore to them by your own self, saying,
'I will make your descendants as numerous as the stars in the sky;
and all this land that I promised,
I will give your descendants as their perpetual heritage.'"
So the LORD relented in the punishment he had threatened to inflict on his people.

RESPONSORIAL PSALM
Ps 51:3-4, 12-13, 17, 19

R̸. (Luke 15:18) I will rise and go to my father.

Have mercy on me, O God, in your
     goodness;
   in the greatness of your compassion
        wipe out my offense.
Thoroughly wash me from my guilt
   and of my sin cleanse me.

R̸. I will rise and go to my father.

A clean heart create for me, O God,
   and a steadfast spirit renew within me.
Cast me not out from your presence,
   and your Holy Spirit take not from me.

R̸. I will rise and go to my father.

O Lord, open my lips,
   and my mouth shall proclaim your
        praise.
My sacrifice, O God, is a contrite spirit;
   a heart contrite and humbled, O God,
        you will not spurn.

R̸. I will rise and go to my father.

SECOND READING
1 Tim 1:12-17

Beloved:
I am grateful to him who has strengthened
     me, Christ Jesus our Lord,
   because he considered me trustworthy
   in appointing me to the ministry.
I was once a blasphemer and a persecutor
     and arrogant,
   but I have been mercifully treated
   because I acted out of ignorance in my
        unbelief.
Indeed, the grace of our Lord has been
        abundant,
   along with the faith and love that are in
        Christ Jesus.
This saying is trustworthy and deserves
        full acceptance:
   Christ Jesus came into the world to save
        sinners.
Of these I am the foremost.
But for that reason I was mercifully
     treated,
   so that in me, as the foremost,
   Christ Jesus might display all his
        patience as an example
   for those who would come to believe in
        him for everlasting life.
To the king of ages, incorruptible,
        invisible, the only God,
   honor and glory forever and ever. Amen.

About Liturgy

Proclaiming familiar parables: Parables are short stories or sayings which use familiar situations and images to teach a truth. They are metaphorical, that is, they have a hidden meaning which is grasped only through the obvious meaning. The speaker may use a parable in order to grab and hold the hearer's attention; the story is catchy and the hearer wants to know how it ends. The parable is an indirect way for the speaker to get the hearer to apply a message to him- or herself which would otherwise be dismissed. In the classical Greek sense of "rhetoric," parables are to persuade us to a certain viewpoint.

The challenge for the gospel reader (deacon or presider) is how to proclaim the gospel when the assembly already knows the ending of these parables. The surprise, "catchy" element is gone. The reader might think in terms of "pregnant pauses" at unexpected places during the proclamation, or strong emphasis on words that the assembly might not expect. Most important, however, is that the proclaimer cannot read the parable with a tone of voice that really says, "I know this parable and let's just get through it." The reader's voice must say, "This is exciting and there is something new here. This parable can speak to us today."

Long or short form of the gospel: The long form of the gospel for this Sunday includes the parable of the Prodigal Son. If only the short form of the gospel is proclaimed (given as an alternative for this Sunday), the impact of the responsorial psalm which obviously leads to the Prodigal Son parable would be curtailed. Moreover, during this Year C of the three-year Lectionary cycle, we also heard the Prodigal Son parable on the Fourth Sunday of Lent. The Lenten context invited us to interpret this parable in terms of mercy, forgiveness, reconciliation, repentance, conversion, etc. The Ordinary Time context, along with the other two parables preceding the Prodigal Son story in this Sunday's gospel, invites us to interpret the parable along different lines. Different liturgical year contexts suggest different approaches to familiar parables.

About Liturgical Music

Music suggestions: In "All Who Hunger Gather Gladly" we call all who "once were lost and scattered" to come to the table of the Lord as "welcome guest[s]." The HOLY MANNA setting would work well for the entrance procession, while Bob Moore's verse-refrain setting would be excellent at Communion with choir or cantor singing the verses and the assembly the refrain. Lucien Deiss's classic verse-refrain piece "Yes, I Shall Arise" would also be a good choice for Communion, as would Michael Joncas's setting of Psalm 103, "With the Lord."

Herman Stuempfle's "Shepherd, Do You Tramp the Hills" (in *Hymns for the Gospels*, GIA) retells all three of this Sunday's gospel parables in question and answer format. In v. 1 we ask, "Shepherd, do you tramp the hills, Tracking down one straying sheep . . . ?" and the shepherd answers, "But that one I call by name; she will hear and know my voice . . ." In v. 2 we ask "Woman, do you scour the house Just to find one coin that's lost . . . ?" and the woman answers, "But that coin you count so small Has for me a special worth . . ." In v. 3 we ask the father, "Father, does your heart still bleed For a child who chose to roam . . . ?" and the father answers, "but that restless, reckless boy Never can my love outrun! . . ." Verse 4 wraps up the whole: "Shepherd, searcher, parent's care—By what image can we name Spendthrift love, impassioned grace, Incandescent as a flame? Christ, beyond all words you spoke, Stories that with wonder glow, You have shown us on a cross Love that will not let us go!" Sung in antiphonal fashion between the assembly and various soloists, this hymn would be a perfect response to the gospel reading during the preparation of the gifts.

SEPTEMBER 15, 2013
TWENTY-FOURTH SUNDAY IN ORDINARY TIME

✝ SPIRITUALITY

GOSPEL ACCLAMATION
2 Cor 8:9

℟. Alleluia, alleluia.
Though our Lord Jesus Christ was rich, he
became poor,
so that by his poverty you might become rich.
℟. Alleluia, alleluia.

Gospel

Luke 16:1-13; L135C

Jesus said to his disciples,
  "A rich man had a steward
  who was reported to him for
      squandering his property.
He summoned him and said,
  'What is this I hear about you?
Prepare a full account of your
      stewardship,
  because you can no longer be
      my steward.'
The steward said to himself,
  'What shall I do,
  now that my master is taking
      the position of steward away
      from me?
I am not strong enough to dig and I am
      ashamed to beg.
I know what I shall do so that,
  when I am removed from the
      stewardship,
  they may welcome me into their
      homes.'
He called in his master's debtors one
      by one.
To the first he said,
  'How much do you owe my master?'
He replied, 'One hundred measures of
      olive oil.'
He said to him, 'Here is your
      promissory note.
Sit down and quickly write one for
      fifty.'
Then to another the steward said, 'And
      you, how much do you owe?'
He replied, 'One hundred kors of wheat.'

Continued in Appendix A, p. 311.

Reflecting on the Gospel

If the unscrupulous steward in the gospel deserved to be removed from his position for squandering his master's possessions, how much more did he deserve to be dismissed for forgiving debts that were not his to forgive! But at least the steward was acting consistently: he squandered and gave away what was not his. However, the point of this gospel is not really about honesty or how to handle another's property. This gospel pivots around something much more serious: our ultimate future. This is ours to squander by the choices we make every day. But why would we want to do that when our future is concerned with "eternal dwellings"?

The wily servant has concern only for his immediate future and uses underhanded means to assure that his needs are met. In his efforts to protect his future, however, he limits it—he will only be welcomed into the homes of those whose favor he bought dishonestly with his master's wealth. By serving himself, the wily servant ultimately limits his world of possibilities. By contrast, disciples are to serve in such a way that they open their future to unending possibilities. Faithful disciples first choose not themselves nor the things of this world, but to serve God and others. This choice leads to an eternal future ("eternal dwellings"). At the end the gospel implies an important question related to the kind of future we deserve: Which God do we serve? The answer to that question determines whether or not we share in everlasting life.

The context for this gospel, then, is final judgment; the end is near and so we do anything necessary with prudence and decisiveness in order to be saved. Jesus is emphasizing what we must do in order to secure our desired future. We "make friends" with the things of this world as a means to an end: the end must shape our present behavior, our daily choices. The more we keep our eyes focused on God, the easier it is to keep the things of this world in perspective. "Mammon" is a necessary part of this world. The choice is always to use it with a longer view in sight—eternal life. The "full account" of our stewardship will not be a matter of spreadsheets and ledgers. It will be a matter of how well we have been faithful disciples; how well we have consistently kept our life focused on God as the center; how well we have made choices to serve God and others.

Living the Paschal Mystery

Just as the steward was decisive in how he used his master's possessions to gain his favorable end, so are we to be decisive in our use of possessions and which God we serve in order to gain our eternal end. Eternal life, then, is dependent upon two things: we are to be prudent and decisive in this life, and do all we can to gain eternal life; we are to constantly monitor which God it is we serve.

Most of us do not go through life thinking through each action in terms of eternal life. This would be pretty impossible and probably more than a little distracting! Keeping ourselves focused on God is as simple as doing little acts of kindness each day for the good of others. It may be as demanding as resisting temptation to do something sinful. Keeping ourselves focused on God also means that we do take time each day to pray—to pour out our hearts to God and acknowledge God as the Lord and center of our lives. In these simple, everyday ways we make choices about prudence and decisiveness, mammon or God, our "eternal dwelling."

Focusing the Gospel

Key words and phrases: What shall I do, may welcome me into their homes, eternal dwellings, cannot serve both God and mammon

To the point: The wily servant has concern only for his immediate future and uses underhanded means to assure that his needs are met. In his efforts to protect his future, however, he limits it—he will only be welcomed into the homes of those whose favor he bought dishonestly with his master's wealth. By serving himself, the wily servant ultimately limits his world of possibilities. By contrast, disciples are to serve in such a way that they open their future to unending possibilities. Faithful disciples first choose not themselves nor the things of this world, but to serve God and others. This choice leads to an eternal future ("eternal dwellings").

Connecting the Gospel

to the first reading: The first reading presents the same scenario about the future as does the gospel. God will hold accountable those who serve themselves for personal gain, and will never forget "a thing they have done."

to experience: In the everyday humdrum of life, we rarely think about the ultimate future. Life itself pressures us into shortsighted choices for living. Discipleship, on the other hand, calls us to live in such a way that our daily choices form patterns of behavior that move us toward God's promise of life eternal.

Connecting the Responsorial Psalm

to the readings: The connection of the responsorial psalm to the first reading is obvious. In the first reading God swears never to forget an injustice done to the poor. In the psalm God redresses such wrongs and raises the poor from dust to nobility. The relationship of the psalm to the gospel, however, is not so clear. Both the first reading and the gospel relate incidences of unjust and dishonest behavior pursued for the sake of personal gain. The intimation is that these stories exemplify the choice to serve mammon rather than God. Yet while Jesus condemns dishonest behavior, he commends the dishonest steward for pursuing it.

What Jesus invites, however, is not emulation of the behavior but emulation of the shrewdness which motivates it. We are to act in service of what is true and just. The role of the psalm, then, becomes clear. Our real model of behavior is God who redresses wrongs and raises up the poor. In praying this psalm we are singing the praises of the One whom we wish to be like. We are choosing our Master.

to psalmist preparation: In singing this psalm you invite the assembly to praise God for acting on behalf of the poor and oppressed. By implication you also invite them to imitate God in their own manner of acting. In what ways do you choose God as your Master and guide? In what ways do you struggle with this choice? How might Christ help you?

ASSEMBLY & FAITH-SHARING GROUPS

- Jesus uses the dishonest steward to teach me that . . .
- The choices I am making now that lead to an "eternal [dwelling]" place are . . .
- Some examples which show that I am serving God over "mammon" are . . . I am using my "mammon" to serve God whenever I . . .

PRESIDERS

I guide the community to prepare for eternal, rather than earthly, dwellings whenever I . . .

DEACONS

My serving others broadens my possibilities for both this life and the next in that . . .

HOSPITALITY MINISTERS

The manner of my hospitality points the assembly to "eternal dwellings" whenever I . . .

MUSIC MINISTERS

The manner of my music making opens up possibilities for the assembly's deeper worship when I . . .

ALTAR MINISTERS

How I transform my busy activity into an interior serving of others *for God* is . . .

LECTORS

My life announces a choosing of God over mammon whenever I . . . This affects my proclamation in that . . .

EXTRAORDINARY MINISTERS OF HOLY COMMUNION

The Eucharist keeps me focused on "eternal dwellings" in that . . .

217

Model Penitential Act

Presider: The gospel this Sunday faces us with the choice to serve God or mammon. As we prepare to celebrate this liturgy, let us open our hearts to God's presence and guidance . . . [pause]

    Lord Jesus, you show us how to serve God and others: Lord . . .

    Christ Jesus, you lead us to your eternal dwelling place: Christ . . .

    Lord Jesus, you guide us along the path of life: Lord . . .

Homily Points

• Speculators who engage in Ponzi schemes and other dishonest financial manipulations gain short term wealth spent on multiple mansions, yachts, classy cars. Yet their future is often very limited—spent in a 10 x 10 cell! The unlimited pursuit of this world's wealth always limits our future.

• Jesus challenges disciples to be as shrewd as the wily servant in the gospel but not as shortsighted. This gospel pivots around the kind of future we choose for ourselves. Choosing to serve God and others often places limits on our present way of living. But it opens us up to a limitless future—an eternal future in God's eternal dwelling place.

• Preoccupation with "mammon"—the world's values, material wealth and possessions, satisfying self—limits our future because it traps us in only the immediate things of this world. Gospel living calls us to have a longer and wider view of this world so we can be led to a fuller future. We must make choices in this life that open us to the next. For example, instead of pining for and buying the latest electronic gadget, we might give of time and "mammon" to those without the barest necessities of life. Instead of choosing to go our separate ways for entertainment, we might spend a family night together at home. The unlimited pursuit of this world's wealth always limits our future. The unlimiting choice for the wealth God gives through serving others always brings us more wealth than we can imagine—fullness of life.

Model Universal Prayer (Prayer of the Faithful)

Presider: Let us ask God for what we need to one day enter into God's eternal dwelling place.

Response:

Lord, hear our prayer.

Cantor:

we pray to the Lord,

That all members of the church may embrace without limit the things of God rather than the things of this world . . . [pause]

That all people of the world may come to the fullness of life . . . [pause]

That those in need find assistance and support . . . [pause]

That all of us here may serve God in each other all the days of our lives . . . [pause]

Presider: Ever-living God, you call us to serve you and others: hear these our prayers that we might one day enter your eternal dwelling place. We ask this through Christ our Lord. **Amen.**

COLLECT

Let us pray

Pause for silent prayer

O God, who founded all the commands of
    your sacred Law
upon love of you and of our neighbor,
grant that, by keeping your precepts,
we may merit to attain eternal life.
Through our Lord Jesus Christ, your Son,
who lives and reigns with you in the unity
    of the Holy Spirit,
one God, for ever and ever.
Amen.

FIRST READING
Amos 8:4-7

Hear this, you who trample upon the
    needy
    and destroy the poor of the land!
"When will the new moon be over," you
    ask,
    "that we may sell our grain,
    and the sabbath, that we may display
        the wheat?
We will diminish the ephah,
    add to the shekel,
    and fix our scales for cheating!
We will buy the lowly for silver,
    and the poor for a pair of sandals;
    even the refuse of the wheat we will
        sell!"
The LORD has sworn by the pride of Jacob:
    Never will I forget a thing they have
        done!

RESPONSORIAL PSALM
Ps 113:1-2, 4-6, 7-8

℟. (cf. 1a, 7b) Praise the Lord, who lifts up
the poor.
    or:
℟. Alleluia.

Praise, you servants of the LORD,
    praise the name of the LORD.
Blessed be the name of the LORD
    both now and forever.

℟. Praise the Lord, who lifts up the poor.
    or:
℟. Alleluia.

High above all nations is the Lord;
   above the heavens is his glory.
Who is like the Lord, our God, who is
   enthroned on high
   and looks upon the heavens and the
      earth below?

R̸. Praise the Lord, who lifts up the poor.
   or:
R̸. Alleluia.

He raises up the lowly from the dust;
   from the dunghill he lifts up the poor
to seat them with princes,
   with the princes of his own people.

R̸. Praise the Lord, who lifts up the poor.
   or:
R̸. Alleluia.

SECOND READING
1 Tim 2:1-8

Beloved:
First of all, I ask that supplications,
   prayers,
   petitions, and thanksgivings be offered
      for everyone,
   for kings and for all in authority,
   that we may lead a quiet and tranquil
      life
   in all devotion and dignity.
This is good and pleasing to God our
      savior,
   who wills everyone to be saved
   and to come to knowledge of the truth.
      For there is one God.
      There is also one mediator between God
         and men, the man Christ Jesus,
      who gave himself as ransom for all.
This was the testimony at the proper time.
For this I was appointed preacher and
      apostle
   —I am speaking the truth, I am not
      lying—,
   teacher of the Gentiles in faith and
      truth.

It is my wish, then, that in every place the
      men should pray,
   lifting up holy hands, without anger
      or argument.

About Liturgy
Eucharist and eschatology, part 1: Already by now, nearing the end of September, the church begins to think about the parousia (Christ's Second Coming) and eschatological fulfillment, with which the liturgical year ends. Although these motifs are evident in the Liturgy of the Word toward the end of the Lectionary year, eschatology is a motif present in every celebration of Eucharist. Two of the three eucharistic acclamations explicitly mention the Second Coming of Christ. Number 8 of SC mentions that earthly liturgy is a foretaste of heavenly liturgy, so the assembly already shares to some extent in eschatological glory. Each time we sing the Holy, Holy, Holy at the end of the preface, we explicitly join our praise and thanks to the heavenly choir giving worship to God.

Eschatology is a difficult theme. It refers to the end times when all will be brought to fulfillment in Christ. Since most of us are pretty taken up with the present and getting through the demands of each day, our thoughts about the future rarely include more than perhaps looking to the end of the month and bills to pay or perhaps planning a vacation. This time of the year when the church's liturgy turns us toward the end time is an opportunity to remind ourselves that the way we live now does make a difference in how we will spend our eternal future! A good weekly practice would be to keep our eternal future and eschatology in mind as we celebrate Eucharist each week, keying into those elements which remind us of what is to come.

About Liturgical Music
Music suggestions: Songs which express being decisive and faithful in our choice to serve God above all would connect well with this Sunday's celebration, as would songs which sing of Christ as the center and foundation of our lives. Some good examples for the entrance procession are "Rise Up, O Saints of God"; "Praise to You, O Christ Our Savior"; "Glorious in Majesty"; and "Be Light for Our Eyes." Good choices for the preparation of the gifts include "Guide My Feet"; "I Bind My Heart"; "Be Thou My Vision"; and "Seek Ye First the Kingdom of God." Appropriate songs for Communion include "The Love of the Lord" and "Center of My Life."

✠ SPIRITUALITY

GOSPEL ACCLAMATION
2 Cor 8:9

℟. Alleluia, alleluia.
Though our Lord Jesus Christ was rich, he became poor,
so that by his poverty you might become rich.
℟. Alleluia, alleluia.

Gospel
Luke 16:19-31; L138C

Jesus said to the Pharisees:
  "There was a rich man who
    dressed in purple garments
    and fine linen
  and dined sumptuously each
    day.
And lying at his door was a poor
    man named Lazarus, covered
    with sores,
  who would gladly have eaten his fill of
    the scraps
  that fell from the rich man's table.
Dogs even used to come and lick his
    sores.
When the poor man died,
  he was carried away by angels to the
    bosom of Abraham.
The rich man also died and was buried,
  and from the netherworld, where he
    was in torment,
  he raised his eyes and saw Abraham
    far off
  and Lazarus at his side.
And he cried out, 'Father Abraham, have
    pity on me.
Send Lazarus to dip the tip of his finger
    in water and cool my tongue,
  for I am suffering torment in these
    flames.'
Abraham replied,
  'My child, remember that you received
    what was good during your lifetime
  while Lazarus likewise received what
    was bad;
  but now he is comforted here, whereas
    you are tormented.

Continued in Appendix A, p. 311.

Reflecting on the Gospel

Before speaking of the "great chasm" that divides the saved from the punished after death, this gospel hints at two other chasms. There is a "great chasm" between the rich man who wears fine clothes and eats "sumptuously each day" and the poor man Lazarus whose body is covered not with rich clothes but festering sores and who longs to eat "the scraps that fell from the rich man's table." The other "great chasm" is between sinners and those who are righteous. Lazarus is a supporting character in this gospel who reveals the rich man's sinfulness.

The rich man in the gospel can neither see nor hear: he does not see Lazarus in need at his door; he does not listen to Moses and the prophets who guide him in right ways. The rich man is not in "the netherworld, where he was in torment" simply because of the good he received during his lifetime, but because his self-contained, self-satisfied lifestyle was not faithful to the teaching and practice of the Mosaic covenant. This is the rich man's sinfulness: he was so wrapped up in himself and his riches that he failed to pay attention to just relationships among those who are bound together in covenant with God.

We who live today have even a further revelation beyond Moses and the prophets: we are to hear and put into practice the truth of the Gospel affirmed by Jesus who rose from the dead. By so doing, we choose now on which side of the chasm we will be in the next life. The chasm which separated the rich man and Lazarus after death is already present while they are living. This chasm—much more than the breach between rich and poor—is a gulf of uncaring. During his earthly life the rich man could have chosen to act differently and close the chasm. This gospel is a call to us: now is the time to act; once we enter the next life, the chasm will remain forever.

The gospel uses the metaphor "great chasm" and paints a clear picture of what happens on each side: rich/poor, dined sumptuously/eat scraps, netherworld/bosom of Abraham, received good/received bad, torment/comforted, place of torment/rise from the dead. Although the wealth and comfort of this life are attractive, in the face of eternity they are too fleeting to choose. What really counts is living faithfully now so we are on the right side of the chasm in eternity!

Living the Paschal Mystery

Although the "great chasm" metaphor in the gospel leads us to compare the two possibilities of the afterlife (heaven or hell), the metaphor also applies to this life and how we are living today, for how we are living now is how we will be living for all eternity. The present moment is amplified in eternity. Ultimately, how we live both now and in eternity is our choice. God makes good (or bad) on our choice! What guides us in this choice is the Gospel. Jesus made with us a new covenant, the heart of which is love of God and each other.

The problem is not that we do not know how to live our lives. The problem is, we tend to talk about the poor and those in need of our care globally and in abstract terms. In this gospel, the poor and needy one is presented as an individual with a name lying on a nearby doorstep. Besides Moses and the prophets, we also have Jesus to teach us; we, too, only need to listen. Jesus teaches us how to see those in need around us and reach out in concern. There can be no great chasms between us.

Focusing the Gospel

Key words and phrases: a rich man, received what was good, great chasm, Moses and the prophets, listen, someone should rise from the dead

To the point: The rich man in the gospel can neither see nor hear: he does not see Lazarus in need at his door; he does not listen to Moses and the prophets who guide him in right ways. The rich man is not in "the netherworld, where he was in torment" simply because of the good he received during his lifetime, but because his self-contained, self-satisfied lifestyle was not faithful to the teaching and practice of the Mosaic covenant. We who live today have even a further revelation beyond Moses and the prophets: we are to hear and put into practice the truth of the Gospel affirmed by Jesus who rose from the dead. By so doing, we choose now on which side of the chasm we will be in the next life.

Connecting the Gospel

to the first reading: The rich man's problem is not his wealth but his complacency. Like the "complacent in Zion" who "are not made ill by the collapse of Joseph," the rich man is unconcerned for Lazarus because he has not listened well to "Moses and the prophets" nor acting according to their dictates to be concerned for one's neighbor.

to experience: We tend not to listen to those who challenge us to hear the truth about ourselves and how we should live. But we have also learned that when we take to heart the challenge to listen, we grow toward fullness of life.

Connecting the Responsorial Psalm

to the readings: Both the first reading and the gospel relate stories of indifference to human suffering. In the first reading the complacent revel in wine and music while society collapses around them. In the gospel the rich man gorges himself while the beggar dies of hunger at his gate. Had they heeded Moses and the prophets (gospel), they would have lived differently and secured a different future for themselves. The responsorial psalm relates a contrasting story. In the psalm God secures justice for the oppressed, feeds the hungry, raises up the poor, and cares for those in need.

In a sense the psalm is our message from Moses and the prophets. By praising God for never being indifferent to human suffering, the psalm challenges us to act likewise. We have been sent the message, then; it is for us to hear and heed. May our singing of this psalm be a sign that we have heard and have chosen to heed.

to the psalmist's preparation: As with last Sunday's psalm, this psalm holds God up as the model of behavior for faithful disciples. The church is called to act on behalf of the poor and suffering just as God does. In singing this psalm you invite the assembly to respond to this call. In what ways are you responding? In what ways do you need to grow in your response?

ASSEMBLY & FAITH-SHARING GROUPS

- To avoid the complacency of the rich man, I need to . . .
- I need to listen to . . . I hear . . .
- I need to see . . . Seeing leads me to . . .

PRESIDERS

I help others truly to hear the message of Moses, the prophets, and the risen Christ when I . . .

DEACONS

I challenge the community to get beyond "complacency" to compassion for the needy (see first reading) whenever I . . .

HOSPITALITY MINISTERS

The manner of my hospitality prepares those gathering for liturgy truly to hear God's word when I . . .

MUSIC MINISTERS

In my music ministry I must listen to . . .

ALTAR MINISTERS

Serving others has aligned me with the poor (and with Christ) in that . . .

LECTORS

My manner of proclamation reveals to the assembly how well I have listened to God's word and put it into practice in these ways . . .

EXTRAORDINARY MINISTERS OF HOLY COMMUNION

Holy Communion strengthens me to live God's word in these ways . . .

Model Penitential Act

Presider: Today's gospel is the parable of the rich man and Lazarus. Let us prepare ourselves for this liturgy, so that one day we might join Lazarus in everlasting life with God . . . [pause]

    Lord Jesus, you are the Word who teaches us the way of life: Lord . . .

    Christ Jesus, you are the risen One who leads us to everlasting glory: Christ . . .

    Lord Jesus, you are the Way, the Truth, and the Life: Lord . . .

Homily Points

• What makes us complacent? Sometimes, having too much of a good thing, or even enough of everything. At other times, laziness, self-absorption, self-satisfaction, frustration, too much praise, lack of challenge. All these things turn us inward and close us off from hearing or noticing what we need to get out of ourselves. Growing toward fuller life means shaking ourselves out of complacency, hearing and accepting new challenges, and seeing the good we are called to do.

• In the gospel, the rich man is complacent because he cannot see or hear beyond himself. Despite the fact that God has given him all good things—Lazarus to see the action he should take, Moses and the prophets to hear the word he should live—he chooses to remain complacent and in so doing loses for all eternity the everlasting good God bestows.

• We, too, have been given all good things by God. We cannot afford to be complacent. We cannot ignore the poor man at our door, the child who needs a listening ear, the coworker who needs words of encouragement. We cannot ignore speaking words of challenge or affirmation, offering words of forgiveness or understanding, seeking words of guidance or strength. By so doing, we choose now on which side of the chasm we will be in the next life.

Model Universal Prayer (Prayer of the Faithful)

Presider: God offers us the joy and comfort of everlasting life. Let us pray that we may live today in such a way that we grow into the fullness of life.

Response:

Lord, hear our prayer.

Cantor:

we pray to the Lord,

That all members of the church spend the good God has given them for the sake of others . . . [pause]

That all leaders of the world call forth the good in others for the betterment of society . . . [pause]

That the poor receive what they need from the fullness of the world's riches . . . [pause]

That all of us here listen to the words of the risen Christ and live as faithful disciples . . . [pause]

Presider: God of all goodness, you offer us fullness of life: hear these our prayers that one day we might share in your everlasting glory. We ask this through Christ our Lord. **Amen.**

COLLECT

Let us pray

Pause for silent prayer

O God, who manifest your almighty power above all by pardoning and showing
    mercy,
bestow, we pray, your grace abundantly
    upon us
and make those hastening to attain your
    promises
heirs to the treasures of heaven.
Through our Lord Jesus Christ, your Son,
who lives and reigns with you in the unity
    of the Holy Spirit,
one God, for ever and ever.
Amen.

FIRST READING

Amos 6:1a, 4-7

Thus says the LORD, the God of hosts:
Woe to the complacent in Zion!
Lying upon beds of ivory,
    stretched comfortably on their couches,
they eat lambs taken from the flock,
    and calves from the stall!
Improvising to the music of the harp,
    like David, they devise their own
        accompaniment.
They drink wine from bowls
    and anoint themselves with the best oils;
    yet they are not made ill by the collapse
        of Joseph!
Therefore, now they shall be the first to go
        into exile,
    and their wanton revelry shall be done
        away with.

RESPONSORIAL PSALM
Ps 146:7, 8-9, 9-10

R̆. (1b) Praise the Lord, my soul!
  or:
R̆. Alleluia.

Blessed is he who keeps faith forever,
  secures justice for the oppressed,
  gives food to the hungry.
The LORD sets captives free.

R̆. Praise the Lord, my soul!
  or:
R̆. Alleluia.

The LORD gives sight to the blind.
  The LORD raises up those who were
    bowed down.
The LORD loves the just.
  The LORD protects strangers.

R̆. Praise the Lord, my soul!
or:
R̆. Alleluia.

The fatherless and the widow he sustains,
  but the way of the wicked he thwarts.
The LORD shall reign forever;
  your God, O Zion, through all
    generations. Alleluia.

R̆. Praise the Lord, my soul!
  or:
R̆. Alleluia.

SECOND READING
1 Tim 6:11-16

But you, man of God, pursue righteousness,
  devotion, faith, love, patience, and
    gentleness.
Compete well for the faith.
Lay hold of eternal life, to which you were
  called
  when you made the noble confession in
    the presence of many witnesses.
I charge you before God, who gives life to
  all things,
  and before Christ Jesus,
  who gave testimony under Pontius
    Pilate for the noble confession,
  to keep the commandment without stain
    or reproach
  until the appearance of our Lord Jesus
    Christ
  that the blessed and only ruler
  will make manifest at the proper time,
  the King of kings and Lord of lords,
  who alone has immortality, who dwells
    in unapproachable light,
  and whom no human being has seen or
    can see.
To him be honor and eternal power. Amen.

About Liturgy

Liturgy of the Word and eternal life: Probably most of us would not readily connect our hearing the word proclaimed at Sunday Mass with eternal life. This Sunday's gospel suggests how we might make this connection.

When the rich man asks Abraham to send someone to warn his brothers about the life they are leading and what eternity will bring them, Abraham replies that they already have more than enough—they need expect no miraculous revelation because they have always had Moses and the prophets, and now Jesus, to teach them to live righteously. We, too, have such a word preached to us each Sunday. This gospel reminds us of the grave importance of attentiveness to the Liturgy of the Word. There is far more at stake than simply listening to the readings and homily. We are hearing *God's* word spoken to us, both as a warning and a challenge.

One way of "actively listening" to the readings each Sunday is to take a moment after each reading and the homily to ask, "How is this calling me to righteous living? How am I called to be sensitive and compassionate to those around me in need? How does this help me live more perfectly the baptismal covenant I made with God and community?" Hopefully, this silent time is already incorporated into the way the Liturgy of the Word is celebrated; if not, take some time after leaving church or arriving home to do this important reflecting.

About Liturgical Music

Music suggestions: The rich man who ignored the poor man dying on his doorstep finds himself condemned to eternal torment after his own death when it is too late to change the choices he made in life. There are a number of songs available which call us to act now on behalf of the poor and needy in our midst. "God of Day and God of Darkness" offers an excellent text; its length indicates it might work best during the preparation of the gifts. "Abundant Life" calls us to live in such a way "that all may have abundant life"; its gentle melody and tempo would be best suited for the preparation of the gifts. The energy of "Let Justice Roll Like a River" suggests its suitability for the entrance or recessional; its length, however, might work better during the preparation of the gifts or Communion. A superb choice for either the entrance or the recessional would be "God Whose Purpose Is to Kindle" in which we ask God to "overcome our sinful calmness" and "disturb" the "complacency" we feel in face of "our neighbor's misery." Other good choices for the recessional would be "We Are Called," "What Does the Lord Require," and "The Church of Christ in Every Age."

SPIRITUALITY

GOSPEL ACCLAMATION
1 Pet 1:25

R̸. Alleluia, alleluia.
The word of the Lord remains forever.
This is the word that has been proclaimed to you.
R̸. Alleluia, alleluia.

Gospel

Luke 17:5-10; L141C

The apostles said to the Lord,
    "Increase our faith."
The Lord replied,
  "If you have faith the size of a
      mustard seed,
  you would say to this mulberry tree,
  'Be uprooted and planted in the sea,'
      and it would obey you.

"Who among you would say to
      your servant
  who has just come in from plowing or
      tending sheep in the field,
  'Come here immediately and take
      your place at table'?
Would he not rather say to him,
  'Prepare something for me to eat.
Put on your apron and wait on me while
      I eat and drink.
You may eat and drink when I am
      finished'?
Is he grateful to that servant because
      he did what was commanded?
So should it be with you.
When you have done all you have been
      commanded,
  say, 'We are unprofitable servants;
  we have done what we were obliged
      to do.'"

Reflecting on the Gospel

When we hear (L.: *ob audire* = to hear before = obedience) something that strikes a chord within us, we are moved to respond. But the first step is *to hear*. The issue in the gospel is that the servant is to be faithful to the master and his commands. To be faithful requires that we *hear*. It is by such hearing and fidelity that faith increases.

In fact, a reflection on faith does not begin with ourselves at all, but with the Master, with God. In the Hebrew Scriptures, Israel has faith because God has unfailingly made good on God's promise to enact mighty deeds of salvation. Israel's faith, then, is a trusting response to a faithful God. Faith is relational—we put our faith not in something but in *Someone*. God is true to who God is when God carries forward the plan for our salvation. We are true to who we are when we obediently cooperate in that plan of salvation. But fulfilling our Christian obligations is more than simply an exercise of responsibility or obedience. Fidelity expresses and reinforces our relationship to Jesus. He is the Master, we are servants.

Jesus tells the disciples that even a smidgen of faith can achieve great things. How do we increase faith? Faith increases through decisive obedience to what is commanded. How do we measure this kind of faith? We measure our faith by measuring our faithfulness. The faithful disciple of Jesus is never finished serving. The faith of a disciple is never finished increasing.

Faith is a way of life. Thus, the important thing to remember here is that faith is more a verb than a noun. Faith is expressed in the way we act. Faith is faithfulness. Here is the crunch: faith is truly extraordinary, not in the stupendous acts we might do for God and others, but in terms of the consistent and enduring choices we make daily to act righteously, humbly, mercifully, and justly as well as being forgiving and reconciling—that is, to be obedient to all that Jesus has asked of us. Faith is a way of living, a way of expressing our true selves such that we act toward others like the Divine has acted toward us. What increases our faith is faithfulness.

Living the Paschal Mystery

We tend to think of everyday responsibilities as mundane, and they are! But this gospel reveals the hidden dimension of such ordinary actions—they reveal and increase our faith. We Catholics definitely have the idea that if we are good during this life our "reward" is heaven. The second part of this gospel suggests to us that we are to do simply what is obliged of us and expect nothing more. This is what the "unprofitable" in the last line means. We do not do what we are supposed to do in order to be rewarded, but we do it simply because that is what is expected of us because of the relationship we have established with our God.

Thus, one aspect of faith is recognizing that doing what disciples are supposed to do in itself does not earn God's beneficence. Heaven is not a "reward" for being faithful. Heaven is the amplification of the way we live our present life. What we are "obliged to do" is be faithful. What is being faithful? Being servant of all. Habakkuk in the first reading teaches us that faithfulness is trusting while we are waiting for fulfillment of the vision of everlasting goodness and righteousness. Faithfulness is confidence that God will fulfill God's promise to us of salvation and deliverance. Being faithful in this life is already living what heaven will be!

Focusing the Gospel

Key words and phrases: Increase our faith, did what was commanded, So should it be with you

To the point: Jesus tells the disciples that even a smidgen of faith can achieve great things. How do we increase faith? Faith increases through decisive obedience to what is commanded. How do we measure this kind of faith? We measure our faith by measuring our faithfulness. The faithful disciple of Jesus is never finished serving. The faith of a disciple is never finished increasing.

Connecting the Gospel

to the first reading: The prophet Habakkuk shows us in the first reading where our never-finished, increasing faith leads: to life.

to experience: We tend to think of everyday responsibilities as mundane, and they are! But this gospel reveals the hidden dimension of such ordinary actions—they reveal and increase our faith.

Connecting the Responsorial Psalm

to the readings: When the disciples ask Jesus to increase their faith, his answer seems unrelated to their request (gospel). The first reading, however, puts his answer in context. To have faith means to maintain hope in God's promise despite the long delay in its fulfillment (first reading). To have faith means to keep working at the task of discipleship even when we think that surely the task has been completed (gospel).

The responsorial psalm adds the dimension that having faith means to keep trudging on the journey to the promised land even when the going is rough and the goal far off. The first two strophes of the psalm have us arriving at the goal with joyful song. The final strophe, however, reminds us we are still on the journey and that the temptation to give up faith and quit the task—as did many Israelites in the desert—is real. May we not harden our hearts when God calls us to keep moving. May we remain faithful and keep working.

to psalmist preparation: The harsh shift between the beginning of this responsorial psalm and its conclusion only makes sense when you acknowledge how easy it is to give up on the task of faithful discipleship. In the refrain you call the assembly to remain faithful despite setbacks and hardships. Where in your own life do you struggle with these setbacks and hardships? What do you hear God saying to you at these times? What helps you listen and respond with faith?

ASSEMBLY & FAITH-SHARING GROUPS

- I have wished my faith to be increased when . . . My faith is increased when . . .
- Decisive obedience is asked of me in these situations . . . I respond by . . .
- The measure of my faithfulness is . . .

PRESIDERS

For me, the most difficult part about remaining faithful is . . . Such reflection helps me serve others better because . . .

DEACONS

Doing ministry increases my faith because . . .

HOSPITALITY MINISTERS

The privilege of greeting others as they assemble for liturgy increases my faith in that . . .

MUSIC MINISTERS

What God expects of me as a music minister is . . . I give all that is expected when I . . . In return, God gives me more than I expect by . . .

ALTAR MINISTERS

Serving others increases my faith because . . . Serving others increases their faith in that . . .

LECTORS

My daily living is a genuine proclamation of the vision God has planned for us (see first reading) when . . .

EXTRAORDINARY MINISTERS OF HOLY COMMUNION

When I witness the assembly receiving Communion, my faith is increased because . . .

Model Penitential Act

Presider: As we prepare for this liturgy, let us open ourselves to God's presence and surrender to God's action within us so that our faith might be increased . . . [pause]

Lord Jesus, you are the One in whom we have faith: Lord . . .

Christ Jesus, you are the One who calls us to faithfulness: Christ . . .

Lord Jesus, you are the One whom we serve: Lord . . .

Homily Points

• Sometimes we have a smidgen of an idea, and when we respond to the prompting of the idea it begins to grow and become something concrete and practical. For example, redecorating a room might begin with a choice of color and grow from there. A birthday party might begin with an idea for a theme cake and grow from there. A garden plot might begin with one seed and grow from there. What begins small might end up quite large.

• Faith and faithfulness are similar. They begin small and grow slowly as we respond to God's promptings within us calling us to be servants. Being servant is not a matter of obeying single commands, but of assuming a way of living in which we are constantly responding to needs around us.

• If we ask God for an increase of faith, we are really asking for an increase of faithfulness—an increase of obedience, an increase in responding to the needs around us. Our faithfulness is increased when we, for example, persist as parents in rearing our children in right values, persist as laborers in putting out an honest day's work, persist as friends in guiding and supporting one another. The faithful disciple of Jesus is never finished serving. The faith of a disciple is never finished increasing.

Model Universal Prayer (Prayer of the Faithful)

Presider: God is ever faithful and true. Therefore, we are confident when we make our prayers known.

Response:

Lord, hear our prayer.

Cantor:

we pray to the Lord,

That all members of the church increase their faith through lives of serving others . . . [pause]

That all peoples of the world hear and respond to whatever increases the well-being of others . . . [pause]

That those in need be lifted up by the faithful service of others . . . [pause]

That all of us here increase our faith by deepening our obedience to what God asks of us . . . [pause]

Presider: Ever-faithful God, you increase the faith of those who turn to you: hear these our prayers that we might serve you in one another and attain eternal life. We ask this through Christ our Lord. **Amen.**

COLLECT

Let us pray

Pause for silent prayer

Almighty ever-living God,
who in the abundance of your kindness
surpass the merits and the desires of those
    who entreat you,
pour out your mercy upon us
to pardon what conscience dreads
and to give what prayer does not dare to
    ask.
Through our Lord Jesus Christ, your Son,
who lives and reigns with you in the unity
    of the Holy Spirit,
one God, for ever and ever.
Amen.

FIRST READING
Hab 1:2-3; 2:2-4

How long, O Lᴏʀᴅ? I cry for help
    but you do not listen!
I cry out to you, "Violence!"
    but you do not intervene.
Why do you let me see ruin;
    why must I look at misery?
Destruction and violence are before me;
    there is strife, and clamorous discord.
Then the Lᴏʀᴅ answered me and said:
    Write down the vision clearly upon the
        tablets,
    so that one can read it readily.
For the vision still has its time,
    presses on to fulfillment, and will not
        disappoint;
if it delays, wait for it,
    it will surely come, it will not be late.
The rash one has no integrity;
    but the just one, because of his faith,
        shall live.

RESPONSORIAL PSALM

Ps 95:1-2, 6-7, 8-9

R⃰. (8) If today you hear his voice, harden not your hearts.

Come, let us sing joyfully to the LORD;
   let us acclaim the Rock of our salvation.
Let us come into his presence with
      thanksgiving;
   let us joyfully sing psalms to him.

R⃰. If today you hear his voice, harden not your hearts.

Come, let us bow down in worship;
   let us kneel before the LORD who made
      us.
For he is our God,
   and we are the people he shepherds, the
      flock he guides.

R⃰. If today you hear his voice, harden not your hearts.

Oh, that today you would hear his voice:
   "Harden not your hearts as at Meribah,
   as in the day of Massah in the desert,
where your fathers tempted me;
   they tested me though they had seen my
      works."

R⃰. If today you hear his voice, harden not your hearts.

SECOND READING

2 Tim 1:6-8, 13-14

Beloved:
I remind you to stir into flame
   the gift of God that you have through the
      imposition of my hands.
For God did not give us a spirit of
      cowardice
   but rather of power and love and
      self-control.
So do not be ashamed of your testimony
      to our Lord,
   nor of me, a prisoner for his sake;
   but bear your share of hardship for the
      gospel
   with the strength that comes from God.

Take as your norm the sound words that
      you heard from me,
   in the faith and love that are in Christ
      Jesus.
Guard this rich trust with the help of the
      Holy Spirit
   that dwells within us.

About Liturgy

The Apostles' Creed: Each Sunday and solemnity the assembly makes a profession of faith by saying the Creed. The Nicene Creed comes from the fourth century and is essentially a doctrinal statement addressing the divinity of Christ. We have been saying this Creed for centuries.

In no. 19, *The Roman Missal, Third Edition* gives much more latitude for using the Apostles' Creed than we had before the implementation of this missal. There are many advantages for choosing to use this Creed. For example, it is of ancient origin, capturing the apostolic faith; it is a much more concise statement of our faith; it connects the creed we profess during Mass with the prayer with which we begin the Rosary, thus connecting liturgical and devotional prayer; it closely resembles the baptismal profession, thus reminding us that every liturgical celebration is an exercise of our baptismal share in Christ's priesthood.

The gospel this Sunday calls us to connect our profession of faith during the Apostles' Creed with the apostles' request of Jesus that he increase their faith. Each time we say the Apostles' Creed we are doing much more than making an intellectual assent to the basic tenets of our faith. We are, in fact, reminding ourselves of the relationship we have with the three Persons of the Trinity and with each other in the communion of the church and all saints. To deepen these relationships is to increase our faith.

About Liturgical Music

Music suggestions: Fred Pratt Green's "The Church of Christ in Every Age" fits the parable in this Sunday's gospel when it calls the "servant Church" to rise and carry on the task of salvation because "We have no mission but to serve In full obedience to our Lord." The hymn would work well for the entrance procession. A song which captures the hope we maintain despite the sufferings and struggles of life (see first reading) is "Eye Has Not Seen," which would work well for the preparation of the gifts or the Communion procession. "The Love of the Lord" speaks of hope grounded in the life and love of the Lord (refrain) and of faith as our greatest possession (v. 4). This song could be used during the preparation of the gifts or the Communion procession. The refrain of David Haas's "Increase Our Faith" begs, "Lord, increase our faith. With all our heart, may we always follow you. Teach us to pray always." This simple, meditative piece would work well during the preparation of the gifts with cantor or choir singing the verses.

Frederick Faber's standard "Faith of Our Fathers" has been altered for inclusive language under the new title "A Living Faith." Verse 1 speaks of the faith of our fathers, v. 2 the faith of our mothers, and v. 3 the faith of our brothers and sisters. Verse 4 addresses our faith: "Faith born of God, O call us yet; Bind us with all who follow you, Sharing the struggle of your cross Until the world is made anew, Faith born of God, O living faith, we will be true to you till death." This hymn would be effective if sung either during the preparation of the gifts or as the recessional song.

✠ SPIRITUALITY

GOSPEL ACCLAMATION
1 Thess 5:18

℟. Alleluia, alleluia.
In all circumstances, give thanks,
for this is the will of God for you in Christ Jesus.
℟. Alleluia, alleluia.

Gospel   Luke 17:11-19; L144C

As Jesus continued his journey to
     Jerusalem,
  he traveled through Samaria and
       Galilee.
As he was entering a village, ten lepers
     met him.
They stood at a distance from him and
     raised their voices, saying,
  "Jesus, Master! Have pity on us!"
And when he saw them, he said,
  "Go show yourselves to the priests."
As they were going they were cleansed.
And one of them, realizing he had been
     healed,
  returned, glorifying God in a loud
       voice;
  and he fell at the feet of Jesus and
       thanked him.
He was a Samaritan.
Jesus said in reply,
  "Ten were cleansed, were they not?
Where are the other nine?
Has none but this foreigner returned to
     give thanks to God?"
Then he said to him, "Stand up and go;
  your faith has saved you."

Reflecting on the Gospel

Sharing is something that is learned. In some families children grow up alone or with only one sibling. The natural give-and-take coming from interacting with others is much more limiting for them. These children have their own bedroom, own TV, own video games, own cell phones. So much is given them that they never really learn sharing, never really learn the natural give-and-take so essential to grow into healthy relationships with others. In other families, less is more: the children don't have their own everything. Early on they learn to share, to give-and-take, to say thank you. Sharing is fundamental to healthy relationships.

In this gospel Jesus shares much with the ten lepers. They ask Jesus to take pity on them and he heals them. But only the Samaritan leper returns to Jesus, glorifies God, and gives thanks. This leper understands the give-and-take of healthy relationships. He reveals himself as someone who knew he needed healing, but also as someone compelled to return to his Healer, throw himself at his feet, and further the fledgling relationship begun with the healing. For this action he received even more than physical healing. He hears Jesus declare to him, "your faith has saved you." This is faith: knowing who we are before God, gratefully coming to God, and ever deepening our relationship with God. And for this we always give thanks.

The ten lepers exemplify aspects of our relationship with God: acknowledgment of need ("'Have pity on us!'"), obedience ("'Go . . .' As they were going"), and reception of divine mercy ("they were cleansed"). The Samaritan leper demonstrates another aspect of this relationship: only when he returns to glorify God and thank Jesus, does Jesus reveal that he has, in fact, been saved. For us, as for the Samaritan leper, salvation is revealed and experienced in the mutual sharing of an ever deepening relationship.

Salvation, worship, and thanksgiving cement a give-and-take relationship with God. God freely offers us salvation; worship and thanksgiving manifest within the community our acknowledgment and reception of salvation. Worship and thanksgiving are our *yes* to God's gifts to us. They are our response in faith to a God who shares so much with us that we come to share everlasting life in God's eternal glory.

Living the Paschal Mystery

This is what happens on our journey to Jerusalem: on the way we are all cleansed—saved. This is one reason why all the little things of our everyday lives—those things which happen to us along the journey—are so important. They are manifestations of God's acting on our behalf, healing us and saving us. We want to seize them and give thanks. In this divine-human give-and-take, we learn that gratitude is an expression of faith, is a deepening of our relationship with God and each other.

One challenge of this Sunday's gospel is to see God's promise of salvation unfolding in the everyday events of our lives. Faithful service of others is a response to seeing God in the ordinary events of each day. Gratitude—acknowledging God's actions on our behalf—is an all-enveloping context for living our lives. When gratitude is put on as a way of living, then faith and worship, too, become a way of living. Rather than relegated to an hour on Sunday, worship is part of all the little actions which make up each of our days. For that, let us give thanks!

Focusing the Gospel

Key words and phrases: Have pity on us, they were cleansed, one . . . returned, glorifying God, thanked him, your faith has saved you

To the point: In the gospel ten lepers ask Jesus to take pity on them and he heals them. But only the Samaritan leper returns to Jesus, glorifies God, and gives thanks. This leper reveals himself as someone who knew he needed healing, but also as someone compelled to return to his Healer, throw himself at his feet, and further the fledgling relationship begun with the healing. For this action he received even more than physical healing. He hears Jesus declare to him, "your faith has saved you." This is faith: knowing who we are before God, gratefully coming to God, and ever deepening our relationship with God. And for this we always give thanks.

Connecting the Gospel

to the first reading: The first reading and gospel both present foreigners (Naaman is a Syrian, the grateful leper is a Samaritan) who are healed of leprosy and who return to their healers to give thanks. Further, their response to being healed is in "glorifying God": the Samaritan leper when he fell at Jesus' feet, Naaman when he takes home with him "two mule-loads of earth" so that he can worship the God of Israel.

to experience: The sense of entitlement often leaves a person neglecting even such common social gestures as saying thanks. The ungrateful nine lepers were the original "entitlement crowd"! We are moved beyond taking for granted that what is given to us is owed to us when we grow in the kind of mutual sharing that deepens relationships.

Connecting the Responsorial Psalm

to the readings: Psalm 98, from which this responsorial psalm is taken, is about the completion of God's saving plan for Israel. All the forces which threaten God's chosen people—depicted in various psalms as enemy nations, roaring seas, evildoers, famine, disease, etc.—have been put to rout by God. The whole world sees what God has done for Israel and rejoices.

The healing stories in the first reading and gospel are concrete dramatizations of God's saving deeds as well as of the faith responses these deeds engender. Surprisingly, it is foreigners (Naaman, the Samaritan leper, the entire world in the psalm) who acknowledge what God has done and members of the chosen people (the other nine lepers) who do not. Together the psalm and readings challenge us, then, to examine our faith response to God. As members of the church do we offer God thanks through worship and faith-filled discipleship, or do we simply take salvation for granted? Do we lead the world in offering God praise for salvation, or do we sit back and assume others will do so? Offering God our thanks is an expression of faith and it is this faith, Jesus tells us, which leads us to salvation (gospel).

to psalmist preparation: In this responsorial psalm you proclaim God's saving deeds and invite the assembly to acknowledge and give thanks for them. As preparation for singing this psalm, look each day for an example of salvation unfolding and consciously give God thanks for it.

ASSEMBLY & FAITH-SHARING GROUPS

- Like the ten lepers, I acknowledge before God my need for . . .
- Like the Samaritan leper, the multiple gifts God has given me are . . .
- To be like the Samaritan leper and "give thanks to God" means to me . . .

PRESIDERS

How I keep a *thanksgiving* heart—in the midst of many and varied daily demands on me—is . . .

DEACONS

I guide others not only to acknowledge their needs before God, but also to return to the Lord with heartfelt gratitude by . . .

HOSPITALITY MINISTERS

The manner of my greeting fosters a climate where those gathering for liturgy can deepen their relationships with God and each other in that . . .

MUSIC MINISTERS

My music making helps assembly members grow in their faith and relationship with God when I . . .

ALTAR MINISTERS

When I reflect upon God's gifts to me, my service to others looks like . . .

LECTORS

When gratitude is part of my preparation for my ministry, my proclamation sounds like . . .

EXTRAORDINARY MINISTERS OF HOLY COMMUNION

What brings me back to "the feet of Jesus" in gratitude is . . .

Model Penitential Act

Presider: Just as the ten lepers in today's gospel ask for mercy, we begin this liturgy by acknowledging our needs and praying for mercy . . . [pause]

Lord Jesus, you hear our cries for mercy: Lord . . .

Christ Jesus, you reveal God's saving power: Christ . . .

Lord Jesus, you are worthy of all thanks and praise: Lord . . .

Homily Points

• It is delightful to watch a tiny baby discover self. At first the infant is fascinated with his or her fingers and toes. As children grow, new discoveries expand beyond self to a wider world, and many come through other people—family, playmates, teachers. Thus children gradually learn who they are, and the value of gratitude, trust, sharing, care for others, mutually satisfying relationships. The Samaritan who returned to Jesus to glorify God and give thanks exemplifies someone who has learned well the importance of deepening relationships.

• Having returned to Jesus to glorify God and express his gratitude for healing, the Samaritan leper hears Jesus acknowledge his faith and consequently receives the further gift of salvation. Faith is a response to our relationship with God. As our faith grows, so do our relationships. As our relationship with God grows, we know better who we are before God, we deepen our ability to worship, and we increase our need to give thanks. Always and everywhere.

• We build relationships with others by offering gratitude, yes, but also in many other ways: by listening attentively, by helping without being asked, by affirming the other's goodness, by being honest and trustworthy. Similarly, we build our relationship with God by giving thanks often, by listening to God in Scripture and prayer, by being open to and using fruitfully God's many gifts, by faithfulness to what God asks of us. All of these actions are essential if we are to grow in faith. All of these actions open us to hearing Jesus say to us, "your faith has saved you."

Model Universal Prayer (Prayer of the Faithful)

Presider: The God to whom we open our hearts always and everywhere in gratitude for the many gifts given us will hear our prayer and answer our needs.

Response:

Cantor:

That all members of the church acknowledge God's many gifts to them and use them in the service of others . . . [pause]

That all peoples be open to the salvation God offers . . . [pause]

That the afflicted be healed and remain steadfast in faith . . . [pause]

That we always and everywhere give God praise and thanksgiving . . . [pause]

Presider: Lord God, you continue to perform mighty deeds on our behalf: may faith and gratitude be ever evident in our world as we strive to reach out to all in need. We ask this through Christ our Lord. **Amen.**

COLLECT
Let us pray

Pause for silent prayer

May your grace, O Lord, we pray,
at all times go before us and follow after
and make us always determined
to carry out good works.
Through our Lord Jesus Christ, your Son,
who lives and reigns with you in the unity
    of the Holy Spirit,
one God, for ever and ever.
Amen.

FIRST READING
2 Kgs 5:14-17

Naaman went down and plunged into the
    Jordan seven times
    at the word of Elisha, the man of God.
His flesh became again like the flesh of a
    little child,
    and he was clean of his leprosy.

Naaman returned with his whole retinue
    to the man of God.
On his arrival he stood before Elisha and
    said,
    "Now I know that there is no God in all
    the earth,
    except in Israel.
Please accept a gift from your servant."

Elisha replied, "As the LORD lives whom
    I serve, I will not take it";
    and despite Naaman's urging, he still
    refused.
Naaman said: "If you will not accept,
    please let me, your servant, have two
    mule-loads of earth,
    for I will no longer offer holocaust or
    sacrifice
    to any other god except to the LORD."

✝ CATECHESIS

RESPONSORIAL PSALM
Ps 98:1, 2-3, 3-4

R̸. (cf. 2b) The Lord has revealed to the
nations his saving power.

Sing to the LORD a new song,
   for he has done wondrous deeds;
his right hand has won victory for him,
   his holy arm.

R̸. The Lord has revealed to the nations
his saving power.

The LORD has made his salvation known:
   in the sight of the nations he has
      revealed his justice.
He has remembered his kindness and his
      faithfulness
   toward the house of Israel.

R̸. The Lord has revealed to the nations
his saving power.

All the ends of the earth have seen
   the salvation by our God.
Sing joyfully to the LORD, all you lands:
   break into song; sing praise.

R̸. The Lord has revealed to the nations
his saving power.

SECOND READING
2 Tim 2:8-13

Beloved:
Remember Jesus Christ, raised from the
      dead, a descendant of David:
   such is my gospel, for which I am
         suffering,
   even to the point of chains, like a
         criminal.
But the word of God is not chained.
Therefore, I bear with everything for the
      sake of those who are chosen,
   so that they too may obtain the
         salvation that is in Christ Jesus,
   together with eternal glory.
This saying is trustworthy:
   If we have died with him
      we shall also live with him;
   if we persevere
      we shall also reign with him.
   But if we deny him
      he will deny us.
   If we are unfaithful
      he remains faithful,
      for he cannot deny himself.

About Liturgy

Eucharist means thanksgiving: Only one leper returned to give thanks to Jesus for having been cleansed. Each Sunday the Christian assembly gathers to celebrate "Eucharist," which in Greek means "thanksgiving." Thus each Sunday the Christian community comes to Jesus to give thanks for the gifts of the week: strength and guidance, healing and cleansing, mercy and forgiveness.

Giving thanks is another reason (to celebrate the resurrection is the primary one) why Christians gather each Sunday for worship. The very nature of what is done together on Sunday is giving thanks. There is a "built in" guarantee that, like the Samaritan leper in this Sunday's gospel, Christians celebrating Eucharist formalize their thanks at least weekly as they gather. Eucharist is our way of never forgetting to raise grateful hearts to God for all we have. As we come together to remember Jesus' self-giving sacrifice for our salvation, as we place ourselves on the altar in self-giving each week, we are returning to God thanks for all that has been given us.

It is sometimes tempting to phrase a petition at the prayer of the faithful in the form of a thanksgiving; for example, to thank God for good weather for the parish picnic, or for a successful building campaign drive, or for the restoration to health of an ill parishioner. The purpose of the intercessions is not to offer God thanksgiving, however, but to make our needs known to God. It is important to keep the intercessions *petitionary*. The thanksgiving we need to offer God is done through the very doing of the Eucharist.

About Liturgical Music

Music suggestions: "Your Hands, O Lord, in Days of Old" speaks about Christ's healing power and care. This hymn would work well for the entrance procession. "Healer of Our Every Ill" would fit the preparation of the gifts. The Taizé ostinato "In the Lord I'll Be Ever Thankful" would be an excellent choice for Communion, with cantor or choir singing the verses; additional verses, instrumental parts, and a bilingual refrain can be found in *Taizé: Songs for Prayer* (GIA). Another good choice for Communion would be Tom Tomaszek's "God's Love Is Everlasting." This Sunday would be a good week to sing a hymn of praise and thanksgiving after Communion. "Thanks Be to God" with its refrain, "*Deo gratias, Deo gratias*, Thanks be to God most high" would be particularly appropriate. Finally, examples of appropriate recessional songs include "Now Thank We All Our God" and "Praise and Thanksgiving."

SPIRITUALITY

GOSPEL ACCLAMATION
Heb 4:12

R7. Alleluia, alleluia.
The word of God is living and effective,
discerning reflections and thoughts of the heart.
R7. Alleluia, alleluia.

Gospel   Luke 18:1-8; L147C
Jesus told his disciples a parable
   about the necessity for them to pray
      always without becoming weary.
He said, "There was a judge in a certain
      town
   who neither feared God nor respected
      any human being.
And a widow in that town used to come to
      him and say,
   'Render a just decision for me against
      my adversary.'
For a long time the judge was unwilling,
   but eventually he thought,
   'While it is true that I neither fear God
      nor respect any human being,
   because this widow keeps bothering me
   I shall deliver a just decision for her
   lest she finally come and strike me.'"
The Lord said, "Pay attention to what the
      dishonest judge says.
Will not God then secure the rights of his
      chosen ones
   who call out to him day and night?
Will he be slow to answer them?
I tell you, he will see to it that justice is
      done for them speedily.
But when the Son of Man comes, will he
   find faith on earth?"

Reflecting on the Gospel

Persistence is different from stubbornness. Persistence is about ongoing attitudes and/or actions that lead to a good outcome. Stubbornness is really about ourselves and self-willfulness, often for selfish gains. Persistence is often about justice; stubbornness is often about injustice. The persistence of the widow in this gospel parable is not a matter of stubbornness. The unjust judge grows weary and is annoyed with the widow. He fails to grasp the deeper meaning of her persistence: an injustice is being done and the widow seeks to change that.

In this parable the widow's persistence in petitioning the judge is directed toward changing his mind so that he will act and render a just decision. Our own prayer is not a matter of changing God's mind, however. Persistent prayer is about faithful relationship to God that expands us and our expectations of how God is to act. God always acts justly. The challenge of the gospel is to keep on praying to a God who wills only good for us, who wills that we receive salvation and eternal life. Sometimes it is required that we must change *our* minds about that for which we pray or about our perception of how God answers our prayer.

Whether the response to our own prayer is delayed or speedily given, faith and hope uphold our efforts to "pray always." Persistence requires discipline, and it rests on the hope that the desired outcome of our efforts will be achieved. For example, we are persistent in exercise routines, athletic training, musical practice. So it is with prayer: we persist because of our hope that God will hear us, that our petition is just. This hope, nonetheless, is not merely future-oriented, concerned only with receiving what we request. This hope rests on the conviction of our steadfast relationship to the God who has always been faithful and who always listens to our prayer. If faith seeks justice and salvation, then hope spawns the confidence that our prayer will be heard and one day we will share in everlasting life.

Living the Paschal Mystery

Will God "find faith on earth?" God does find faith in those who persist in prayer. But what about those of us who feel like we are praying persistently for our needs but God does not seem to be answering us?

This raises the important issue about what we pray for. If our prayer is simply about getting what we want, then our focus may only be upon ourselves. If, instead, our focus is on "justice [being] done . . . speedily," then persistence will get us that justice and, ultimately, salvation. The key is to remember that the answer to our prayers is not getting what we want now, but justice, that is, right relationship with God that leads to eternal life. Ultimately, then, our persistence in prayer leads to receiving more than we could possibly want or imagine. It leads to favorable judgment when Christ comes and our entering into eternal glory with him.

This is not to say that we forgo praying for our own needs; for example, for the good of the family, secure employment, good health, sufficiency in retirement, etc. These needs, however immediate, are always prayed for within the larger picture: what we need in order to secure right relationship with God and salvation. In this, we are always assured that our prayer will be heard.

Focusing the Gospel

Key words and phrases: pray always, Render a just decision, judge was unwilling, I shall deliver a just decision, faith on earth

To the point: In this parable the widow's persistence in petitioning the judge is directed toward changing his mind so that he will act and render a just decision. Our prayer is not a matter of changing God's mind, however. Persistent prayer is about faithful relationship to God that expands us and our expectations of how God is to act. God always acts justly. The challenge of the gospel is to keep on praying to a God who wills only good for us. Sometimes this requires that we must change *our* minds.

Connecting the Gospel

to the first reading: The obvious connection between the first reading and gospel is that both Moses and the widow persist in their petitions. But there are other connections as well: the widow and Moses are God's "chosen ones"; the petitions are in line with God's will; prayer petitions, when just, are always answered by our just and caring God.

to experience: We tend to be most persistent about what is most important to us. For example, we are persistent in exercise routines, athletic training, musical practice. So it is with prayer: we remain faithful and persistent in prayer when God is at the center of our life and that for which we ask flows from deep faith that God always hears our prayers and answers them.

Connecting the Responsorial Psalm

to the readings: Psalm 121, used in its entirety this Sunday, is a pilgrimage song. Having journeyed to Jerusalem for festival, the Israelites must now travel home. They see the dark mountains which surround them as a threat for they are the hideout of thieves and enemies, the home of wild animals. The psalm is a prayer of confidence in God's protection, perhaps said in blessing over them by the temple priest as the pilgrims begin their journey home. What motivates the prayer is surety about God. The Israelites know that God answers the prayer of those who are faithful to the covenant. Moses had such confidence (first reading) as did Jesus (gospel), as do we when we sing this psalm. May our singing reveal the "faith on earth" (gospel) for which Christ longs.

to psalmist preparation: When you sing this responsorial psalm, you are like the temple priest blessing the people as they begin their journey homeward. The people are the Body of Christ, the journey that of faithful discipleship, the homeland God's kingdom. How in your singing can you assure the assembly members of God's presence and protection on the way? How outside of Sunday Eucharist can you persist in your prayer for them?

**ASSEMBLY &
FAITH-SHARING GROUPS**

- For me to "pray always" means . . . What helps me persist through weariness and remain faithful in prayer is . . .
- My prayer is faith-filled when . . .
- With respect to my relationships with others, I need to change my mind about . . . With respect to prayer, I need to change my mind about . . .

PRESIDERS

Like Aaron and Hur (see first reading), I assist my parishioners to persist faithfully in prayer by . . .

DEACONS

I help those I serve to expand their expectations about how God is to act toward them in that . . .

HOSPITALITY MINISTERS

Some examples of when I have comforted and encouraged others when they were weary in faith are . . .

MUSIC MINISTERS

What helps me persist in music ministry is . . . What I pray to God for through this ministry is . . .

ALTAR MINISTERS

My service to others is an expression of persistent faith in God when . . .

LECTORS

When my preparation for ministry is accompanied by persistent prayer, my proclamation sounds like . . .

**EXTRAORDINARY MINISTERS
OF HOLY COMMUNION**

Like God's heavenly food, I aid and nurture those who are weary in faith by . . .

Model Penitential Act

Presider: In today's gospel, Jesus tells his disciples about the necessity to pray always. As we prepare to enter this celebration, let us open our hearts in prayer to God's abiding presence . . . [pause]

> Lord Jesus, you show us how to pray to our Father: Lord . . .
>
> Christ Jesus, you are just and merciful: Christ . . .
>
> Lord Jesus, you give us the gift of faith: Lord . . .

Homily Points

• Sometimes to accomplish a task we need other people to encourage and strengthen us, giving us confidence and support. At other times, to be persistent we need to have our expectations expanded beyond a narrow perception of how to proceed. Our expectations are expanded by receiving challenges from other people; by remembering what we have learned from past, similar experiences; by realizing the direction we are pursuing is too limited. Prayer leads us to expand our minds and hearts beyond our own limits, entrusting ourselves to the God who always acts justly and wills only good for us.

• In the gospel parable, the widow kept returning to an unjust judge whom she could petition face-to-face, and whom she could concretely judge for his lack of just action. When we pray to God, we do so personally, but we cannot judge how God responds to our prayer. The challenge of the gospel is to keep on praying to a God who wills only good for us. Sometimes this requires that we must change our minds about that for which we pray or about our perception of how God answers our prayer.

• Jesus' admonition to "pray always without becoming weary" says something about persistence in prayer as well as how we ought to pray. We become weary and discouraged in prayer when our expectations of God are too narrow either in what we want or how soon we want it. Prayer opens up for us a deeper relationship with God that expands us and our expectations of both self and God. Prayer leads us to expand our minds and hearts beyond our own limits, entrusting ourselves to the God who always acts justly and wills only good for us.

Model Universal Prayer (Prayer of the Faithful)

Presider: We are called "to pray always without becoming weary." And so we pray.

Response:

Cantor:

That all members of the church be persistent in prayer and steadfast in faith . . . [pause]

That world leaders be persistent in securing justice for all . . . [pause]

That those without hope find support in the faith and prayer of others . . . [pause]

That all of us here deepen our prayer in such a way that we are expanded in mind and heart . . . [pause]

Presider: O God, you hear the prayers of those who cry out to you: help us to persevere in prayer, that we might one day live with you forever. We ask this through Christ our Lord. **Amen.**

COLLECT

Let us pray

Pause for silent prayer

Almighty ever-living God,
grant that we may always conform our
    will to yours
and serve your majesty in sincerity of
    heart.
Through our Lord Jesus Christ, your Son,
who lives and reigns with you in the unity
    of the Holy Spirit,
one God, for ever and ever.
Amen.

FIRST READING

Exod 17:8-13

In those days, Amalek came and waged
    war against Israel.
Moses, therefore, said to Joshua,
    "Pick out certain men,
    and tomorrow go out and engage
        Amalek in battle.
I will be standing on top of the hill
    with the staff of God in my hand."
So Joshua did as Moses told him:
    he engaged Amalek in battle
    after Moses had climbed to the top of
        the hill with Aaron and Hur.
As long as Moses kept his hands raised
    up,
    Israel had the better of the fight,
    but when he let his hands rest,
    Amalek had the better of the fight.
Moses' hands, however, grew tired;
    so they put a rock in place for him to
        sit on.
Meanwhile Aaron and Hur supported his
    hands,
    one on one side and one on the other,
    so that his hands remained steady till
        sunset.
And Joshua mowed down Amalek and his
    people
    with the edge of the sword.

RESPONSORIAL PSALM

Ps 121:1-2, 3-4, 5-6, 7-8

R⁊. (cf. 2) Our help is from the Lord, who made heaven and earth.

I lift up my eyes toward the mountains;
    whence shall help come to me?
My help is from the Lord,
    who made heaven and earth.

R⁊. Our help is from the Lord, who made heaven and earth.

May he not suffer your foot to slip;
    may he slumber not who guards you:
indeed he neither slumbers nor sleeps,
    the guardian of Israel.

R℣. Our help is from the Lord, who made
heaven and earth.

The LORD is your guardian; the LORD is
        your shade;
    he is beside you at your right hand.
The sun shall not harm you by day,
    nor the moon by night.

R℣. Our help is from the Lord, who made
heaven and earth.

The LORD will guard you from all evil;
    he will guard your life.
The LORD will guard your coming and
        your going,
    both now and forever.

R℣. Our help is from the Lord, who made
heaven and earth.

SECOND READING
2 Tim 3:14–4:2

Beloved:
Remain faithful to what you have learned
        and believed,
    because you know from whom you
        learned it,
    and that from infancy you have known
        the sacred Scriptures,
    which are capable of giving you
        wisdom for salvation
    through faith in Christ Jesus.
All Scripture is inspired by God
    and is useful for teaching, for refutation,
        for correction,
    and for training in righteousness,
    so that one who belongs to God may be
        competent,
    equipped for every good work.

I charge you in the presence of God and of
        Christ Jesus,
    who will judge the living and the dead,
    and by his appearing and his kingly
        power:
    proclaim the word;
    be persistent whether it is convenient or
        inconvenient;
    convince, reprimand, encourage through
        all patience and teaching.

CATECHESIS

About Liturgy

Persistence of the prayer of the faithful: The universal prayer or prayer of the faithful concludes the Liturgy of the Word. This is no happenstance. Having heard the challenge and encouragement of the readings, the prayer of the faithful already begins the response we must make to the whole liturgy, that is, being dismissed to *live* what we have celebrated.

The nature of the prayer of the faithful is to present our needs before God. It is entirely a petitionary prayer. At the same time, the petitions are not about our own needs, but are always directed to the needs of the whole church and world, the needs of the poor and disadvantaged, the needs of this praying community. These petitions serve as a reminder to us—supporting and strengthening what we have heard in the readings and homily—that if the world is to change, we must change. We must change our minds about how we want to act as the Body of Christ, bringing Jesus' Good News of salvation and justice to all those we encounter each day. We must change our minds about the choices we make in everyday living so that others can justly share in the goods of this world. We must change our minds about how persistent we want to be to overcome hurts and misunderstandings and strained relationships.

The prayer of the faithful persistently challenges us about how we are to live. This prayer is not about reminding God of how God should act to right things, but of alerting us to the needs around us and urging us to be persistent in addressing them. The prayer of the faithful is addressed to us as much as it is addressed to God.

About Liturgical Music

The value of familiar, repeated music: There is a great deal of repetition built into the liturgy. One of the purposes of this repetition is to help us persist in prayer. The same is true for liturgical music. It is not a matter of how many new songs or new settings of the Mass we sing, but how well we pray liturgically when we sing. For this to happen, the music needs to be familiar and repeated. Constantly changing service music and introducing new hymns keeps us on the surface of the liturgy. This may be interesting, stimulating, and entertaining, but it makes liturgy a kind of musical superhighway with so many distracting billboards we lose track of what road we are on and where we are going. The real role of music, however, is to help us stay focused on where we are going—into the heart of the paschal mystery—and help us persist in the prayer needed to go there.

SPIRITUALITY

GOSPEL ACCLAMATION
2 Cor 5:19

R̸. Alleluia, alleluia.
God was reconciling the world to himself in
    Christ
and entrusting to us the message of salvation.
R̸. Alleluia, alleluia.

Gospel   Luke 18:9-14; L150C

Jesus addressed this parable
    to those who were convinced of their
        own righteousness
    and despised everyone else.
"Two people went up to the temple area
    to pray;
    one was a Pharisee and the other was a
        tax collector.
The Pharisee took up his position and
    spoke this prayer to himself,
    'O God, I thank you that I am not like
        the rest of humanity—
    greedy, dishonest, adulterous—or even
        like this tax collector.
I fast twice a week, and I pay tithes on
    my whole income.'
But the tax collector stood off at a
    distance
    and would not even raise his eyes to
        heaven
    but beat his breast and prayed,
    'O God, be merciful to me a sinner.'
I tell you, the latter went home justified,
    not the former;
    for whoever exalts himself will be
        humbled,
    and the one who humbles himself will
        be exalted."

Reflecting on the Gospel

We've all heard the proverb "Too much of a good thing is bad," and this gospel surely points to this. The Pharisee is faithful to pious practices, even does more than he is asked. But Jesus does not praise him for his pious acts; in fact, Jesus renders the harsh judgment that he will not be justified. The Pharisee, for all his supposed goodness, misses the heart of prayer: inward turning to God that carries us outward to right relationship with others. We cannot honestly pray to God if we judge harshly and set ourselves apart from those we meet every day. The tax collector is justified because he admits that he has not been in right relationships ("me a sinner"). True humility is honesty about who we are before both God and others. True prayer leads to God exalting us ("went home justified") because we have humbled ourselves before the Most High and have exalted others through our just actions toward them. True piety is directed toward humility and prayer.

This gospel parable recounts the teaching of Sirach from the first reading: "the prayer of the lowly" is willingly and speedily heard by God. Unexpectedly, it is the sinful tax collector, and not the pious Pharisee, who goes home justified. Although the Pharisee is faithful to pious practices, he is missing the heart of prayer and the core of faith demonstrated by the tax collector: dependence upon God ("be merciful") and humble acknowledgment of one's true identity ("me a sinner"). Such humility would seem to create a greater distance between the holy God and the sinful tax collector, but the opposite is true. The tax collector's humility draws him closer to God and allows him to go home justified. For ourselves to go home justified, we need to imitate the practices of the Pharisee in being faithful to prayer and gospel living. But we must always pray and live in the humble spirit of the tax collector. This is how we are justified.

The Pharisee uses his pious practices to separate himself from "the rest of humanity." Authentic religious practices—for the Pharisee and for us today—ultimately lead us to communion with God and one another and being in right relationship. The Pharisee distances himself from the rest of humanity; the tax collector, in his acknowledgment that he is a sinner, identifies with humanity. The Pharisee focuses on himself; the tax collector focuses on God. The Pharisee is thankful for his own actions; the tax collector simply acknowledges how God acts ("be merciful"). The issue here is not whether one ought to perform pious practices; of course we should! The real issue is whether those practices witness to our true selves before God.

Living the Paschal Mystery

Prayer helps us enter into and maintain an intimate relationship with God. Our final exaltation will flow from our humility, that is, our awareness of being in right relationship with God as creature to Creator. In prayer we not only express this relationship, our prayer actually helps create it. In prayer we acknowledge who we are before our merciful God.

It is difficult to pray like the tax collector! It is difficult to be faithful to prayer! Every day a hundred and one things will tempt us to let it go. Only self-emptying and focusing on God will keep us faithful to prayer. Only fidelity to prayer will bring us the true humility which justifies us—an attitude toward God which acknowledges and begs, "O God, be merciful to me a sinner."

Focusing the Gospel

Key words and phrases: I am not like, I fast . . . pay tithes, be merciful to me a sinner, justified, humbled, exalted

To the point: The Pharisee is faithful to pious practices, but he misses the heart of prayer: inward turning to God that carries us outward to right relationship with others. We cannot honestly pray to God if we judge harshly and set ourselves apart from those we meet every day. The tax collector is justified because he admits that he has not been in right relationships ("me a sinner"). True humility is honesty about who we are before both God and others. True prayer leads to God exalting us ("went home justified") because we have humbled ourselves before the Most High and have exalted others through our just actions toward them.

Connecting the Gospel

to the first reading: Sirach states in a poetic way what Jesus in the gospel parable teaches: our just God extends justice to those who petition God, serve God, and live rightly.

to experience: The Pharisee uses his pious practices to separate himself from "the rest of humanity." Authentic religious practices—for the Pharisee and for us today—ultimately lead us to communion with God and one another.

Connecting the Responsorial Psalm

to the readings: It is not the self-righteous whom God hears in prayer (gospel) but those "crushed in spirit" (responsorial psalm). God is not closed-minded to the rich; indeed, God "knows no favorites" (first reading). Rather, it is the self-satisfied who are closed to God. The Pharisee is so full of himself that he keeps God at a distance (gospel). When the tax collector, on the other hand, begs for mercy, he allows God to draw close. In this Sunday's responsorial psalm we identify ourselves with the poor, the brokenhearted, the lowly. We align ourselves with the tax collector. We acknowledge our true relationship with God—that of dependency, of humility, of need for mercy. We allow God to come close, and we are justified (gospel).

to psalmist preparation: The words of the responsorial psalm parallel the message Jesus tells in his parable of the Pharisee and the tax collector (gospel). When you sing these words, then, you know what Jesus knew, and you tell it. What was it that Jesus knew?

ASSEMBLY & FAITH-SHARING GROUPS

- My spiritual practices lead me to humility and trust in God when . . .
- God humbles me by . . . God exalts me when . . .
- I am led to lift to God in prayer my relationships with others when . . . Prayer strengthens my relationships with others in that . . .

PRESIDERS

My personal prayer leads me to be a better minister to others when . . .

DEACONS

My diaconal service for others assists my growth in humility by . . .

HOSPITALITY MINISTERS

The manner of my hospitality both at church and in my daily life witnesses to my humble praying before God when . . .

MUSIC MINISTERS

Whenever I am apt to exalt myself because of my music ministry, Jesus calls me back to humility by . . .

ALTAR MINISTERS

Serving others sends me home "justified" and "exalted" when . . .

LECTORS

When I imitate the tax collector's reverence and humility, my proclamation is like . . .

EXTRAORDINARY MINISTERS OF HOLY COMMUNION

The privilege of distributing Christ's Body and Blood humbles me and unites me more deeply with "the rest of humanity" in that . . .

Model Penitential Act

Presider: Let us come before our God in humble prayer, acknowledge our sinfulness, and ask for God's mercy . . . [pause]

    Lord Jesus, you hear the prayer of those who cry out to you: Lord . . .

    Christ Jesus, you justify the repentant sinner: Christ . . .

    Lord Jesus, you exalt those who humble themselves: Lord . . .

Homily Points

• Why do conceited people turn us off so much? Most probably because they are so stuck on themselves that we feel they separate themselves from us and that we are inferior to them. The word "Pharisee" in Hebrew means "separated ones." They separated themselves from other Israelites by the strictness and piety of their religious practices. Ironically, for some Pharisees this kind of piety was exactly what separated them from God as well.

• The gospel challenges and reverses our perception about who is pious and who is a sinner. The Pharisees placed tremendous importance on exterior behavior, but some did not have the interior attitude of humility before God and others that made their pious practices truly an act of religion. Piety without humility and right relationships is false piety and not true prayer. The Pharisee is the real sinner. The tax collector has sinned, but the humility and honesty of his prayer justify him. He is really the pious one.

• We joke about being pious and holy in church on Sunday, but our behavior in leaving the parking lot after the service is over is anything but Christian! Pious acts and prayer deepen our relationship with God, change us, and must be expressed in the way we treat each other. Respectful relating to others brings about in us true humility (truth about who we are) which, in turn, deepens our prayer and makes it more authentic. We are justified before God and others when our prayer and daily living are consistent with each other. What we do says who we really are.

Model Universal Prayer (Prayer of the Faithful)

Presider: God hears the prayer of those who humbly present their needs. And so we now pray.

Response:

Cantor:

That all members of the church may draw near to God in humble prayerfulness . . . [pause]

That all peoples of the world be authentic in their prayer and just in their relationships . . . [pause]

That those who are brokenhearted and crushed in spirit be comforted and healed . . . [pause]

That each of us here always pray in such a way that we are honest before God and live in such a way that we are honest before each other . . . [pause]

Presider: O God, you are merciful to sinners who cry out to you: hear these our prayers that we might one day be exalted with you in heaven. We ask this through Christ our Lord. **Amen.**

COLLECT

Let us pray

Pause for silent prayer

Almighty ever-living God,
increase our faith, hope and charity,
and make us love what you command,
so that we may merit what you promise.
Through our Lord Jesus Christ, your Son,
who lives and reigns with you in the unity
    of the Holy Spirit,
one God, for ever and ever.
Amen.

FIRST READING
Sir 35:12-14, 16-18

The LORD is a God of justice,
    who knows no favorites.
Though not unduly partial toward the
    weak,
    yet he hears the cry of the oppressed.
The LORD is not deaf to the wail of the
    orphan,
    nor to the widow when she pours out
      her complaint.
The one who serves God willingly is
    heard;
    his petition reaches the heavens.
The prayer of the lowly pierces the clouds;
    it does not rest till it reaches its goal,
nor will it withdraw till the Most High
    responds,
    judges justly and affirms the right,
and the LORD will not delay.

RESPONSORIAL PSALM

Ps 34:2-3, 17-18, 19, 23

R℘. (7a) The Lord hears the cry of the poor.

I will bless the LORD at all times;
    his praise shall be ever in my mouth.
Let my soul glory in the LORD;
    the lowly will hear me and be glad.

R℘. The Lord hears the cry of the poor.

The LORD confronts the evildoers,
    to destroy remembrance of them from
        the earth.
When the just cry out, the LORD hears
        them,
    and from all their distress he rescues
        them.

R℘. The Lord hears the cry of the poor.

The LORD is close to the brokenhearted;
    and those who are crushed in spirit he
        saves.
The LORD redeems the lives of his
        servants;
    no one incurs guilt who takes refuge in
        him.

R℘. The Lord hears the cry of the poor.

SECOND READING

2 Tim 4:6-8, 16-18

Beloved:
I am already being poured out like a
        libation,
    and the time of my departure is at
        hand.
I have competed well; I have finished the
        race;
    I have kept the faith.
From now on the crown of righteousness
        awaits me,
    which the Lord, the just judge,
    will award to me on that day, and not
        only to me,
    but to all who have longed for his
        appearance.

At my first defense no one appeared on
        my behalf,
    but everyone deserted me.
May it not be held against them!
But the Lord stood by me and gave me
        strength,
    so that through me the proclamation
        might be completed
    and all the Gentiles might hear it.
And I was rescued from the lion's mouth.
The Lord will rescue me from every evil
        threat
    and will bring me safe to his heavenly
        kingdom.
To him be glory forever and ever. Amen.

About Liturgy

Liturgy, pious acts, and living the Gospel: The Pharisee in the gospel performed well his religious practices, but did not carry those practices over into right relationship with God and others. This gospel leads us to reflect on our own pious acts, and whether they are leading us to live the Gospel more fully in our daily living.

Liturgy is far more than fulfilling a duty to God by coming to church once a week for an hour or so. Liturgy makes present the paschal mystery, that mystery into which we were baptized. Christ's mystery is our mystery. Our encounter with this mystery during liturgy prompts us to live like Jesus when we leave church and go about our lives. In a real sense liturgy is a "rehearsal" for how we ought to live each moment of each day: ongoing self-giving for the good of others.

To underscore that liturgy is to be lived, that liturgy draws us to living the Gospel more fully, Pope Benedict wrote two new dismissals that are included in *The Roman Missal, Third Edition.* He wants us to hear, as we are dismissed and sent forth from the liturgy, that our life is about living as Jesus did. These two dismissals are "Go and announce the Gospel of the Lord" and "Go in peace, glorifying the Lord by your life." In both dismissals it is clear that our lives are to reflect what we have celebrated. We hear these dismissals time and again. This Sunday's gospel may well remind us to hear them well. What is at stake is right living, right relationships, our hearing Jesus announce that we ourselves, like the tax collector in the gospel, are justified.

About Liturgical Music

Music suggestions: When consecutive gospel readings are as clearly related as those for this Sunday and last Sunday, repeating a hymn helps support the connection. For example, singing quiet repetitions of the Taizé "O Lord, Hear My Prayer" as a prelude, with choir and assembly singing together, would be appropriate. Songs expressing humility before God and one another include Lucien Deiss's setting of Psalm 131, "My Soul Is Longing" as well as David Haas's setting of the same, "My Soul Is Still," either of which would make an excellent Communion song. Good choices for the preparation of the gifts include the spiritual "Give Me a Clean Heart" and the Shaker hymn "'Tis the Gift to Be Simple." Also fitting for the preparation of the gifts would be "In a Lowly Manger Born" and "Eternal Spirit of the Living Christ" (both in *Hymns for the Gospels*, GIA). The first hymn cites Christ's own humility in becoming a human being as the wellspring of his acceptance of the lowly: "Sinners gladly hear his call; Publicans before him fall, For in him new life began; This is he, Behold the man!" (v. 2). The second hymn begs, "Come, pray in me the prayer I need this day; Help me to see your purpose and your will, Where I have failed, what I have done amiss; Held in forgiving love, let me be still" (v. 2).

OCTOBER 27, 2013
THIRTIETH SUNDAY IN ORDINARY TIME

✝ SPIRITUALITY

GOSPEL ACCLAMATION
Matt 11:28

R̸. Alleluia, alleluia.
Come to me, all you who labor and are burdened
and I will give you rest, says the Lord.
R̸. Alleluia, alleluia.

Gospel

Matt 5:1-12a; L667

When Jesus saw the crowds, he
    went up the mountain,
and after he had sat
        down, his disciples
        came to him.
He began to teach them,
    saying:
    "Blessed are the poor in
        spirit,
    for theirs is the Kingdom
        of heaven.
    Blessed are they who mourn,
        for they will be comforted.
    Blessed are the meek,
        for they will inherit the land.
    Blessed are they who hunger and thirst
        for righteousness,
        for they will be satisfied.
    Blessed are the merciful,
        for they will be shown mercy.
    Blessed are the clean of heart,
        for they will see God.
    Blessed are the peacemakers,
        for they will be called children of God.
    Blessed are they who are persecuted
        for the sake of righteousness,
        for theirs is the Kingdom of heaven.
    Blessed are you when they insult you
        and persecute you
    and utter every kind of evil against
        you falsely because of me.
    Rejoice and be glad,
        for your reward will be great in
            heaven."

See Appendix A, p. 312, for the other readings.

Reflecting on the Gospel

Merchant reward cards are mushrooming by leaps and bounds. So many stores have these cards, intended to establish customer loyalty. If reward points grow, it is presumed the customer will keep coming back to buy and eventually have enough points for some tangible reward. Tangible rewards—that is what we are after. We all love to get something for free. We all like to make our dollar stretch. We all want to see good results of the stewardship of our goods. In this gospel Jesus speaks of a reward, too; however, this reward is not so tangible as points or money or free merchandise. Nor is this reward free; it costs us our faithfulness, our very life. Jesus invites us to "Rejoice and be glad, for your reward will be great in heaven." This reward in heaven is promised to those who live lives that are marked by blessedness.

What is our reward in heaven? The completion and fullness of the kind of life we have chosen to live here on earth. Those who choose the ways of God (poor in spirit, meekness, righteousness, mercy, purity of heart, peace) receive—both now and in eternity—the reward of becoming like God. The blessedness of which Jesus speaks is a quality of God—God's very holiness. The reward of the saints (those in heaven, and the faithful ones on earth) is to be holy like God. This reward is worth all the points and merchandise in the world!

The saints we honor today are receiving their reward in heaven. They are forever before the throne of God, giving God unending praise. In each liturgy, in fact, we join with all the heavenly choir in giving God thanks and praise (see, for example, SC no. 8). Each time we celebrate Mass we are united in a special way with all the praise offered God in heaven and all the saints who have been granted their great reward in heaven. Thus, our celebrations now are a foretaste of the glory—of the reward—which one day we will share with these saints in heaven. Each of the Beatitudes in the gospel promises this same thing: those who are blessed now will share in eternal inheritance, the "kingdom of heaven."

Both the first reading ("salvation comes from our God") and the second reading ("see what love the Father has bestowed on us") underscore that the source of our blessedness is God's acting in us. This is what it means to be a saint: that God's work is manifested in us. Like the saints in heaven who model for us Gospel living, we must be "poor in spirit," "meek," "hunger and thirst for righteousness," "merciful," "clean of heart," "peacemakers," accepting of persecution "for the sake of righteousness." All these actual ways of living are manifestations of the blessedness already bestowed on us, who are "called children of God."

This solemnity, then, is not only about the saints in heaven. It is also about ourselves who are blessed, holy ones, saints on this earth.

Living the Paschal Mystery

This solemnity gives us a wonderful opportunity to celebrate our relationship with God and with all the saints who have gone before us. Knowing that we are already "blessed," we are fortified to assume more perfectly the demands of following in the footsteps of the saints in being faithful disciples of Jesus.

Few of us will someday be canonized saints. Nevertheless, we can live now manifesting that blessedness already bestowed on us. May we always be faithful like the saints, giving God eternal glory and praise!

Focusing the Gospel

Key words and phrases: Blessed, reward will be great

To the point: What is our reward in heaven? The completion and fullness of the kind of life we have chosen to live here on earth. Those who choose the ways of God (poor in spirit, meekness, righteousness, mercy, purity of heart, peace) receive—both now and in eternity—the reward of becoming like God. The blessedness of which Jesus speaks is a quality of God—God's very holiness. The reward of the saints (those in heaven, and the faithful ones on earth) is to be holy like God.

Model Penitential Act

Presider: The first reading for this wonderful festival honoring all the saints describes how the saints in heaven offer continuous praise to God; let us unite with them as we offer God our praise and thanksgiving . . . [pause]

> Lord Jesus, you are the fullness of new Life: Lord . . .
> Christ Jesus, you are the Lamb worthy of blessing and glory: Christ . . .
> Lord Jesus, you bless us with risen Life: Lord . . .

Model Universal Prayer (Prayer of the Faithful)

Presider: Let us ask God to bring to completion the good work begun in us.

Response:

Lord, hear our prayer.

Cantor:

we pray to the Lord,

That all members of the church continually grow in the blessedness to which they have been called . . . [pause]

That all leaders of nations be peacemakers who govern with justice and mercy . . . [pause]

That the poor, persecuted, and sorrowing be lifted up by Jesus' promise of blessedness . . . [pause]

That all of us here choose faithfully to live the ways of God . . . [pause]

Presider: O God, you are the joy of the saints: help us to bring joy and happiness to all people so that the blessedness of your kingdom may be established on earth. We ask this through Christ our Lord. **Amen.**

COLLECT

Let us pray

Pause for silent prayer

Almighty ever-living God,
by whose gift we venerate in one celebration
the merits of all the Saints,
bestow on us, we pray,
through the prayers of so many intercessors,
an abundance of the reconciliation with you
for which we earnestly long.
Through our Lord Jesus Christ, your Son,
who lives and reigns with you in the unity of
    the Holy Spirit,
one God, for ever and ever. **Amen.**

FOR REFLECTION

- I experience the blessedness received from God when I . . .
- Where I struggle most to live the ways of God is . . .
- My favorite saint is . . . because . . .

Homily Points

- What did Jesus see when he looked at the crowds? What did he see when he looked at his disciples? He saw the blessedness they already possessed and his words encouraged them to continue to grow in their holiness. He also was drawing them to the eternal reward they would one day receive for their fidelity to living his Good News. Jesus' Sermon on the Mount gave support and hope to a community of Jesus' followers who were facing persecution and insult because of their fidelity to him. It is no less an encouragement to us.

- Choosing to live God's ways faithfully is not easy. We will need to make tough decisions about money, family issues, job choices, friendships, use of the earth's goods. We make these tough decisions because of our relationship to Jesus and the Gospel he taught, and because our world view is not limited to this life, but embraces the wider reality of one day sharing with the saints in heaven. May we "rejoice and be glad" for what we have already been given (blessedness now) and what we will receive (blessed for eternity).

SPIRITUALITY

GOSPEL ACCLAMATION
cf. John 6:40

This is the will of my Father, says the Lord,
that everyone who sees the Son and believes in
   him
may have eternal life.

Gospel

John 6:37-40; L668

**Jesus said to the crowds:
"Everything that the Father gives me
   will come to me,
   and I will not reject anyone who
      comes to me,
   because I came down from heaven
      not to do my own will
   but the will of the one who sent me.
And this is the will of the one who sent
   me,
   that I should not lose anything of
      what he gave me,
   but that I should raise it on the last
      day.
For this is the will of my Father,
   that everyone who sees the Son and
      believes in him
   may have eternal life,
   and I shall raise him on the last day."**

See Appendix A, p. 313, for the other readings.

*Other readings in L668 may be chosen or those
given in the Masses for the Dead, L1011–1016.*

Reflecting on the Gospel

An increasing number of contemporary films, books, conferences, and popular songs refer to reincarnation, the process by which after death a person's soul is reborn to live again in another body. Catholics, of course, do not believe in reincarnation. But we do share with those who believe in reincarnation this concept—widely believed especially in Eastern religions—that a part of us (we call it the "soul") lives forever. We know physical death is the end of natural life; we Catholics (and many others) believe that there is life eternal. This is why we celebrate this feast day commemorating the faithful departed—we believe they live forever. We believe that God loves us so much that God wills we be united with the divine One for all eternity.

The will of the Father is that Jesus not lose any one of his disciples nor "reject anyone who comes to" him. How comforting for us is this gospel teaching! The Father gives everyone to Jesus to form and teach and nurture into a gift Jesus can return to the Father. God promises salvation and eternal life to those who, like Jesus, do the will of the Father. The choice is ours to open ourselves to Jesus to be changed into a perfect gift for the Father.

Salvation and eternal life are God's promise and gift to us. God desires that we who "have grown into union with [Jesus] through a death like his" (second reading) will live forever. As we unite ourselves with Jesus and pattern our own living after his living and dying and rising—as we are changed by Jesus into being a more perfect gift he returns to his Father—we do grow into the mystery of everlasting life. Without fully understanding life eternal, we live with the expectation that one day we will be united with Jesus in the fullness of his risen life. We respond to the promise and expectation of eternal life by believing in Jesus. Believing, in fact, is simply *living* what Jesus taught by our embracing his dying and rising mystery, by our doing his Father's will. Believing is *doing* what Jesus did: he gave himself for the good of others. As God raised Jesus up, so does God raise up those who believe and are faithful to God's will.

We remember the faithful departed this day. Remembering here is more than "recalling" our loved ones (although that may well be part of our celebrations this day); our remembering the faithful departed is broader than that. Our remembering on this feast day enables us to enter into the very mystery the faithful departed now live: whatever happens to the faithful who have believed and died, will happen to us. Remembering, then, is a way to express our belief and hope. By uniting ourselves with the faithful departed, we embrace the mystery which we cannot understand: we embrace eternal life. We become the gift Jesus returns to his Father.

Living the Paschal Mystery

This is a day to do more than celebrate the faithfulness of those who have died. This is a day to unite ourselves with their goodness in such a way that their faithful lives are mirrored in our own Gospel living.

Perhaps one good family activity might be to recount the virtues and good deeds of the family members we remember and pray for this day. Then choose one good thing to put into practice in daily living. In this way the remembering of our loved ones is translated into our daily living and becomes a permanent, visible memorial of their faithfulness.

Focusing the Gospel

Key words and phrases: the Father gives me, will not reject anyone, the will of my Father, I shall raise him

To the point: The will of the Father is that Jesus not lose any one of his disciples nor "reject anyone who comes to" him. The Father gives everyone to Jesus to form and teach and nurture into a gift Jesus can return to the Father. God promises salvation and eternal life to those who, like Jesus, do the will of the Father. The choice is ours to open ourselves to Jesus to be changed into a perfect gift for the Father.

Model Penitential Act

Presider: We gather today to remember our faithful departed. We remember our loved ones as well as all those who have died in Christ. Let us prepare to celebrate this liturgy by asking God to help us to be faithful to the divine will in our own lives . . . [pause]

Lord Jesus, you came to do the Father's will: Lord . . .

Christ Jesus, you were raised by the Father to new life: Christ . . .

Lord Jesus, you will raise us up on the last day: Lord . . .

Model Universal Prayer (Prayer of the Faithful)

Presider: The God who promises not to reject anyone who comes will surely hear our prayers. And so we are encouraged to make our needs known.

Response:

Lord, hear our prayer.

Cantor:

we pray to the Lord,

That all members of the church may be open to being formed, taught, and nurtured by Jesus, growing toward eternal life . . . [pause]

That all peoples of the world may believe in God and come to salvation . . . [pause]

That all those in need find comfort in Jesus' promise of eternal life . . . [pause]

That all the faithful departed be granted everlasting peace . . . [pause]

That each of us here learns from the goodness of our departed loved ones how to live the Gospel more steadfastly . . . [pause]

Presider: Gracious God, you raised your Son up to new life and promise eternal life to those who believe in him: hear these our prayers that one day we may come to share in your eternal glory. We pray through that same Son, Jesus Christ our Lord. **Amen.**

COLLECT (from the first Mass)

Let us pray

Pause for silent prayer

Listen kindly to our prayers, O Lord,
and, as our faith in your Son,
raised from the dead, is deepened,
so may our hope of resurrection for your
    departed servants
also find new strength.
Through our Lord Jesus Christ, your Son,
who lives and reigns with you in the unity
    of the Holy Spirit,
one God, for ever and ever.
Amen.

FOR REFLECTION

- As I consider my departed loved ones, my prayer is about . . . because . . .
- The Father's will for me is . . . Jesus forms, teaches, and nurtures me to do this will by . . .
- I experience myself as Jesus' gift to the Father when . . .

Homily Points

- The will of God is our salvation. For this purpose God sent the Son to show us the way to salvation. All who come to him—who seek him and his way of life, who trust him and his teachings, who follow him faithfully—will find salvation. The choice to come to Jesus and be changed is ours.

- The souls in purgatory have followed the Father's will, have come to Jesus, listened to him, and been changed. But not perfectly. They still are in the process of being purified to become the gift Jesus wishes to give his Father. We, too, still are in the process of being changed as we make our choices to follow Jesus more faithfully. The souls in purgatory can show us the way. We pray for them on this final stage of their journey, knowing that salvation is theirs. May it be ours as well.

SPIRITUALITY

R̶. Alleluia, alleluia.
God so loved the world that he gave his only Son,
so that everyone who believes in him might have
    eternal life.
R̶. Alleluia, alleluia.

Gospel   Luke 19:1-10; L153C

At that time, Jesus came to Jericho
    and intended to pass through
    the town.
Now a man there named Zacchaeus,
    who was a chief tax collector and
        also a wealthy man,
    was seeking to see who Jesus
        was;
    but he could not see him because
        of the crowd,
    for he was short in stature.
So he ran ahead and climbed a
    sycamore tree in order to see
    Jesus,
    who was about to pass that way.
When he reached the place, Jesus looked
    up and said,
    "Zacchaeus, come down quickly,
    for today I must stay at your house."
And he came down quickly and received
    him with joy.
When they all saw this, they began to
    grumble, saying,
    "He has gone to stay at the house of a
        sinner."
But Zacchaeus stood there and said to the
    Lord,
    "Behold, half of my possessions, Lord,
        I shall give to the poor,
    and if I have extorted anything from
        anyone
    I shall repay it four times over."
And Jesus said to him,
    "Today salvation has come to this
        house
    because this man too is a descendant
        of Abraham.
For the Son of Man has come to seek
    and to save what was lost."

Reflecting on the Gospel

Often at parades we see parents hoist their children to sit on their shoulders in order to see better. It's tough for short folks to see over people. Perhaps Zacchaeus is the first height-challenged person to be named in the gospels! He did not let his being "short in stature," however, keep him from satisfying his curiosity about Jesus. He did what many people do: he climbed a tree. He "was seeking to see who Jesus was." Little did he know that his tree-climbing efforts would allow him to see Jesus in a whole new way. Little did he know that his encounter with Jesus would change his very life.

Jesus did not intend to stop in Jericho, but Zacchaeus stopped him short! Jesus responds to Zacchaeus' uninhibited enthusiasm by doing for him the very thing Jesus came to do: "to seek out and to save what was lost." Their dramatic encounter brings out something about each of them which has escaped the grumbling crowd: Zacchaeus is open to being changed through an encounter with Jesus; Jesus is the One who inspires the kind of change that leads to salvation. We are to be just as uninhibited and enthusiastic about encountering Jesus and just as willing to be changed by him. When we truly encounter Jesus, the one who is compassionate toward those who seem lost, our lives can never be the same. Like Zacchaeus, we are changed.

Because of his encounter with Jesus, Zacchaeus receives Jesus into his own home "with joy." Moreover, this encounter brings a changed behavior in Zacchaeus: he shares his wealth with the poor and mends his sinful ways. Because of this, Jesus says to him, "Today salvation has come to this house." The dignity of means and status (Zacchaeus was a wealthy tax collector) is nothing compared to the dignity God bestows on forgiven sinners who are saved.

Jesus "intended to pass through the town," but "must stay" after encountering Zacchaeus. Jesus is the Son of Man who has come "to seek and to save what was lost." Jesus' ministry is hindered neither by wealth nor status, but by his passionate desire to bring salvation to anyone who comes seeking. Jesus' very identity and passion for others' salvation compels him to stay among us. Perhaps it was Jesus' very passion for others' salvation which aroused in Zacchaeus the passion to forget his dignity and climb that tree. This leaves us with an interesting question: Would we go to the same heights as Zacchaeus to encounter Jesus, change, and be saved?

Living the Paschal Mystery

This story of Zacchaeus reminds us that we sinners must come *seeking* Jesus if we are to have a saving encounter with divine mercy. Sometimes it may seem to many of us that our seeking Jesus is far more difficult than climbing a tree to see him! Perhaps we are having difficulty with prayer and God seems to have abandoned us. Perhaps we are being tempted in a particular and prolonged way to do something radically against Gospel values. Perhaps so much is going wrong in our lives that we are disposed to be bitter or resentful or vindictive. These are times when we can come closest to God by acknowledging our human frailty and giving ourselves over to God's care and mercy. Sometimes just a refocus of our attention away from the difficulty toward Jesus who loves us is enough to remain faithful and encounter Jesus in a new and life-giving way. The important thing is the encounter with Jesus who changes us and saves us.

Focusing the Gospel

Key words and phrases: climbed a sycamore tree, they began to grumble, I shall give . . . I shall repay, come to seek . . . to save

To the point: Jesus did not intend to stop in Jericho, but Zacchaeus stopped him short! Jesus responds to Zacchaeus' uninhibited enthusiasm by doing for him the very thing Jesus came to do: "to seek out and to save what was lost." Their dramatic encounter brings out something about each of them which has escaped the grumbling crowd: Zacchaeus is open to being changed through an encounter with Jesus; Jesus is the One who inspires the kind of change that leads to salvation. We are to be just as uninhibited and enthusiastic about encountering Jesus and just as willing to be changed by him.

Connecting the Gospel

to the first reading: The Book of Wisdom poetically describes the same dynamic dramatically depicted in the gospel that takes place between Jesus and Zacchaeus: changed behavior is called forth, God loves and spares all things, God desires conversion and grants salvation.

to experience: Some people we meet have a lasting effect on us. For example, John Paul II's effect on the young people gathered for world youth days, a respected teacher's influence on a youngster's choice of career, a beloved grandparent's impact on a youngster's behavior. The challenge of the gospel is to allow Jesus to come close enough to us to have lasting effect.

Connecting the Responsorial Psalm

to the readings: Psalm 145 is an acrostic hymn, meaning that each verse begins with a successive letter of the Hebrew alphabet. Consequently, the psalm does not develop any theme in depth but simply offers God general praise. The verses chosen for this Sunday praise God for showing mercy and compassion rather than anger, and for lifting up those who have fallen. The reading from Wisdom confirms this attitude of God when it proclaims that the Lord "overlook[s] people's sins" and gently coaxes offenders back to right living. Clearly God prefers reconciliation to condemnation.

In his encounter with Zacchaeus Jesus is the living embodiment of this orientation of God (gospel). Jesus has come to "seek and to save what was lost." In singing this psalm we are the living embodiment of Zacchaeus' response. We recognize ourselves as sinners and shout praise to the One who comes to change and save us.

to psalmist preparation: Psalm 145 praises God for all that God does but in the context of the first reading and gospel the praise is particularly for God's mercy to sinners. For what have you been shown this mercy? How have you praised God for it?

**ASSEMBLY &
FAITH-SHARING GROUPS**

- The lengths to which I would go to encounter Jesus are . . .
- My encounters with Jesus have brought me to change these things about myself . . .
- I am the presence of Jesus calling forth change from others when I . . .

PRESIDERS
I help the community realize that "[t]oday salvation has come to this house" by . . .

DEACONS
My serving others helps them encounter Jesus when I . . .

HOSPITALITY MINISTERS
The way I welcome others brings them in touch with the saving Jesus in that . . .

MUSIC MINISTERS
My participation in music ministry helps me, like Zacchaeus, to see who Jesus is by . . . One change I have made in my life because of this is . . .

ALTAR MINISTERS
My enthusiasm to serve well at the altar and in my daily living deepens my encounters with Jesus in that . . .

LECTORS
Like Zacchaeus, I enthusiastically seek Jesus in the word whenever I . . .

**EXTRAORDINARY MINISTERS
OF HOLY COMMUNION**
As I distribute Communion, I delight in the Son of Man coming "to seek and to save what was lost" when I . . .

Model Penitential Act

Presider: With great love God seeks us to save us. Let us prepare to encounter our gracious God in this liturgy . . . [pause]

Lord Jesus, you are the One we seek: Lord . . .

Christ Jesus, you are God's gift of salvation to us: Christ . . .

Lord Jesus, you came to save the lost: Lord . . .

Homily Points

• What is the catalyst that leads us to change our behaviors? Sometimes it is dissatisfaction with the way things are, sometimes it is a crisis that demands a decision, sometimes it is a person who shows us a better way. In the gospel Zacchaeus, a tax collector, sinner, and wealthy man, goes out of his way (probably out of curiosity) to encounter this Jesus about whom he has heard. Little does he know where this encounter will lead!

• The exchange between Zacchaeus and Jesus leads beyond Zacchaeus's curiosity and Jesus' staying at his house. Zacchaeus "received [Jesus] with joy," set his unjust actions aright, and obtained from Jesus the promise of salvation. Jesus excludes no one—especially not the lost—from his presence and favor.

• Jesus offers the gift of salvation; the work of change needed to receive the gift is ours. Like Zacchaeus, we must examine our own unjust actions and change our behavior. For example, we must examine our wasteful use of goods, and be more conserving. We must monitor the words we say to and about others, and be more kind in our conversations. We must proctor our use of time, and bring work, leisure, and care for others into better balance. To receive the salvation Jesus offers, we must be as uninhibited and enthusiastic about encountering Jesus as was Zacchaeus, and just as willing to be changed by Jesus.

Model Universal Prayer (Prayer of the Faithful)

Presider: The God who promises the gift of salvation to all, will give to us what we need.

 Response:

Lord, hear our prayer.

Cantor:

we pray to the Lord,

That all members of the church may enthusiastically seek Jesus and receive the gifts he offers . . . [pause]

That all peoples of the world may encounter the love of God and come to salvation . . . [pause]

That sinners may repent and the lost may be saved . . . [pause]

That each one of us here may be changed by encounters with the presence of Jesus . . . [pause]

Presider: Eternal God, you care for each one of us so that no one may be lost: hear these our prayers that we might be saved and enjoy everlasting life with you. We ask this through Christ our Lord. **Amen.**

COLLECT

Let us pray

Pause for silent prayer

Almighty and merciful God,
by whose gift your faithful offer you
right and praiseworthy service,
grant, we pray,
that we may hasten without stumbling
to receive the things you have promised.
Through our Lord Jesus Christ, your Son,
who lives and reigns with you in the unity
        of the Holy Spirit,
one God, for ever and ever.
Amen.

FIRST READING

Wis 11:22–12:2

Before the Lord the whole universe is as a
        grain from a balance
    or a drop of morning dew come down
        upon the earth.
But you have mercy on all, because you
        can do all things;
    and you overlook people's sins that they
        may repent.
For you love all things that are
    and loathe nothing that you have made;
    for what you hated, you would not have
        fashioned.
And how could a thing remain, unless you
        willed it;
    or be preserved, had it not been called
        forth by you?
But you spare all things, because they are
        yours,
    O Lord and lover of souls,
    for your imperishable spirit is in all
        things!
Therefore you rebuke offenders little by
        little,
    warn them and remind them of the sins
        they are committing,
    that they may abandon their wickedness
        and believe in you, O Lord!

RESPONSORIAL PSALM

Ps 145:1-2, 8-9, 10-11, 13, 14

℟. (cf. 1) I will praise your name forever,
my king and my God.

I will extol you, O my God and King,
   and I will bless your name forever and
      ever.
Every day will I bless you,
   and I will praise your name forever and
      ever.

R⁊. I will praise your name forever, my
king and my God.

The LORD is gracious and merciful,
   slow to anger and of great kindness.
The LORD is good to all
   and compassionate toward all his
      works.

R⁊. I will praise your name forever, my
king and my God.

Let all your works give you thanks, O
   LORD,
   and let your faithful ones bless you.
Let them discourse of the glory of your
      kingdom
   and speak of your might.

R⁊. I will praise your name forever, my
king and my God.

The LORD is faithful in all his words
   and holy in all his works.
The LORD lifts up all who are falling
   and raises up all who are bowed down.

R⁊. I will praise your name forever, my
king and my God.

SECOND READING
2 Thess 1:11–2:2

Brothers and sisters:
We always pray for you,
   that our God may make you worthy of
      his calling
   and powerfully bring to fulfillment
      every good purpose
   and every effort of faith,
   that the name of our Lord Jesus may be
      glorified in you,
   and you in him,
   in accord with the grace of our God and
      Lord Jesus Christ.

We ask you, brothers and sisters,
   with regard to the coming of our Lord
      Jesus Christ
   and our assembling with him,
   not to be shaken out of your minds
      suddenly, or to be alarmed
   either by a "spirit," or by an oral
      statement,
   or by a letter allegedly from us
   to the effect that the day of the Lord is
      at hand.

About Liturgy

Planning Advent reconciliation service: As we near the end of the church year and the beginning of Advent, many of us have already planned for this year's Advent Rite of Reconciliation celebrated in common (form B of the Sacrament of Penance). Advent and Lent seem to be the favored times for these celebrations in parishes, and rightly so. The two seasons have a different character, however, and the celebration of this sacrament has a different context according to the respective season. Jesus' Second Coming with the attendant final judgment suggests the context for such a celebration during Advent. Acknowledging our sinfulness and asking God's sacramental forgiveness is one way we prepare for the Second Coming.

The gospel for this Sunday reminds us that God is merciful and always forgives; we need only seek God. Celebrating communally the Sacrament of Penance is another concrete way to demonstrate that we seek God and have God as a priority in our lives. Taking time out during these busy holiday-preparation weeks to acknowledge our sinfulness and need for God is a way we can help ourselves stay other-centered.

About Liturgical Music

Music suggestion: Herman Stuempfle's "When Jesus Passed through Jericho" (in *Hymns for the Gospels*, GIA) turns the story of Zacchaeus into our story: "The friend of sinners Jesus was And is the same today. He never sees a lonely face And looks the other way, And looks the other way. Instead, when bowed by guilt or grief We seek the Lord to see, He sets before us bread and wine And says, 'Come, eat with me.' And says, 'Come, eat with me.'" The text needs to be sung in a light, story-telling fashion. The tune, the American folk melody DOVE OF PEACE, will probably be unfamiliar to most members of the assembly. Let alternating cantors sing verses 1-4, telling the story of Zacchaeus, then have the assembly join in for verses 5-6 when the story becomes theirs. The hymn would be very suitable either as a prelude or during the preparation of the gifts.

SPIRITUALITY

GOSPEL ACCLAMATION
Rev 1:5a, 6b

R℘. Alleluia, alleluia.
Jesus Christ is the firstborn of the dead;
to him be glory and power, forever and ever.
R℘. Alleluia, alleluia.

Gospel
Luke 20:27-38; L156C

Some Sadducees, those who
   deny that there is a
   resurrection,
came forward and put this
   question to Jesus, saying,
"Teacher, Moses wrote for us,
*If someone's brother dies
   leaving a wife but no child,
his brother must take the wife
and raise up descendants for his brother.*
Now there were seven brothers;
   the first married a woman but
   died childless.
Then the second and the third married
   her,
   and likewise all the seven died childless.
Finally the woman also died.
Now at the resurrection whose wife will
   that woman be?
For all seven had been married to her."
Jesus said to them,
   "The children of this age marry and
     remarry;
   but those who are deemed worthy to
     attain to the coming age
   and to the resurrection of the dead
   neither marry nor are given in marriage.
They can no longer die,
   for they are like angels;
   and they are the children of God
because they are the ones who will rise.
That the dead will rise
   even Moses made known in the passage
     about the bush,
   when he called out 'Lord,'
the God of Abraham, the God of Isaac,
     and the God of Jacob;
and he is not God of the dead, but of the
     living,
for to him all are alive."

or Luke 20:27, 34-38 in Appendix A, p. 314.

Reflecting on the Gospel

Belief in the afterlife is as much a struggle for some today as it was for the Sadducees and others in Jesus' time. For example, New Age concepts of cosmic unity and Eastern beliefs in reincarnation witness to our desire for continued life in some form and our struggle with what that might be like. As baptized Christians, we align ourselves with Jesus who teaches resurrection and eternal life shared with him in glory. Nonetheless, our belief in Jesus and the resurrection makes eternal life no less a mystery. We believe, however, because Jesus has died and risen. He has gone before us. He has shown us the way. His victory is our sure hope. Our choices today about whether we follow Jesus faithfully and live Gospel values by dying to ourselves for the good of others reveal the extent of our own hope in sharing in Jesus' risen life.

In the gospel, the Sadducees are putting a question to Jesus in accord with their belief that this life is all there is. In no uncertain terms, Jesus affirms resurrection and eternal life. This "hope God gives of being raised up by him" (first reading) fortifies us to remain faithful to God even when the price in this life is ultimate (an extreme example of which is given in the first reading). We can give our life because God gives us life.

The Sadducees are fixated on dying; Jesus is focused on living. The Sadducees deny there is resurrection; Jesus proves there is by rising from the dead. The Sadducees are trapped by affairs of this life; Jesus abides with the angels and "the children of God . . . who will rise." The Sadducees' idea of this life ends with death: there is nothing more. Jesus knows that this life continues in newness of life. And there is even more: we already participate in what the Sadducees deny. To God "all are alive" *now*.

Living the Paschal Mystery

These readings which lead us to reflect on Jesus' Second Coming are not included in the Lectionary and proclaimed at Sunday Mass to scare us, but to prepare us. Yes, Jesus will come to judge the living and the dead. That judgment determines whether we have everlasting glory or everlasting torment. The grace is that we are warned, so we can be prepared. We know that the choices we make now determine the judgment we receive at the Second Coming. What a positive grace—to know what is coming so that we can prepare for it! This is why the Second Coming will not take us by surprise. So let us prepare well!

Few of us will be faced with the extreme choice the brothers in the first reading must make. Nevertheless, we, like the seven brothers, live in a world beset by evil and filled with life-threatening situations (war, poverty, hunger, natural disasters). It is hope in a future that God will provide which upholds and sustains us and guides us in the choices to be faithful to the Gospel, no matter what we face.

We do face "death" every day: dying to self. Gospel living, then, is more than a matter of religious practices. Gospel living means that we align ourselves with Jesus' living and dying. He modeled for us the self-sacrificing giving which leads to eternal life. When we ourselves face conflicts (as in both the gospel and first reading), we can be assured that "the Lord is faithful; he will strengthen [us] and guard [us] from the evil one" (second reading). May we pray with Paul: "May the Lord direct [our] hearts to the love of God and to the endurance of Christ."

Focusing the Gospel
Key words and phrases: deny that there is a resurrection, the dead will rise

To the point: The Sadducees are fixated on dying; Jesus is focused on living. The Sadducees deny there is resurrection; Jesus proves there is by rising from the dead. The Sadducees are trapped by affairs of this life; Jesus abides with the angels and "the children of God . . . who will rise." The Sadducees' idea of this life ends with death: there is nothing more. Jesus knows that this life continues in newness of life. And there is even more: we already participate in what the Sadducees deny. To God "all are alive" *now*.

Connecting the Gospel
to the first reading: In no uncertain terms, Jesus affirms resurrection and eternal life. This "hope God gives of being raised up by him" (first reading) fortifies us to remain faithful to God even when the price in this life is ultimate (an extreme example of which is the death of the seven brothers). We can give our life because God gives us new life.

to experience: In the ordinariness and busyness of our everyday living, we rarely think about either the end times or eternal life. Nearing the conclusion of the liturgical year, the Lectionary readings invite us to reflect on the reality of the end of the world and God's promise and gift of fullness of life.

Connecting the Responsorial Psalm
to the readings: On this Sunday when the church begins to focus on the end times and the Second Coming of Christ, both the first reading and the gospel speak directly of God's promise to raise the just to new life after death. The martyred brothers in the first reading remain faithful to the covenant even to death, for they believe that the Giver of life and limb will never take back what has been bestowed. Jesus in the gospel asserts "the dead will rise," for God is "God . . . of the living."

Like the brothers, Jesus will be put to death for remaining faithful to the call of God. In the responsorial psalm we align ourselves with Jesus. We state our hope that on "waking" from death we shall find ourselves in the presence of God. And we make a commitment that we will remain "steadfast in [the] paths" of discipleship. As we celebrate this Eucharist and sing this psalm, we look to the glory of Christ to come and know that we shall share in that glory just as we have shared in its price.

to psalmist preparation: In this responsorial you proclaim your faith in God's promise of eternal life and your choice to remain faithful to discipleship no matter what its costs. This is no small thing considering the cost will be your life. What conversation might you have with Christ this week to give you courage and strengthen your hope?

ASSEMBLY & FAITH-SHARING GROUPS
- I am drawn to reflect on rising from the dead and eternal life when . . .
- My belief in the resurrection impacts my daily living by . . .
- I experience even now the fullness of life God offers me when . . .

PRESIDERS
I build up others' hope in the resurrection by . . .

DEACONS
My ministry embodies the God of the living for those struggling with hardships whenever I . . .

HOSPITALITY MINISTERS
My attentiveness to others is a way of helping them grow into newness of life when I . . .

MUSIC MINISTERS
One way music ministry leads me to die to myself is . . . I already experience new life through this dying in that . . .

ALTAR MINISTERS
I model a dying to self in the hope of being raised up whenever I . . .

LECTORS
My daily living the word proclaims a hope in the gift of new life in that . . .

EXTRAORDINARY MINISTERS OF HOLY COMMUNION
My receiving Christ's Life empowers me to share my life with others in that . . .

Model Penitential Act

Presider: In the Creed we profess our belief in the resurrection from the dead and the gift of everlasting life. In this hope, let us prepare ourselves to celebrate this liturgy . . . [pause]

Lord Jesus, you are the resurrection and the life: Lord . . .

Christ Jesus, you are Lord of the living and the dead: Christ . . .

Lord Jesus, you raise us to the fullness of life: Lord . . .

Homily Points

• Our entire life is filled with invitations to embrace the unknown in order to move forward: a family moves to another state or even a foreign country to follow a job opportunity, a high school graduate moves into a college dorm knowing no one but seeking further opportunities of learning and friendship, a youngster asks the parent to let go so he or she can ride the two-wheeler alone. All of these kinds of experiences unshackle us from our present moorings and free us to embark on the utterly new.

• Contemporary cosmology leaves us gasping at the seeming endlessness of space. This pales, however, in the face of the eternity of life God offers us in the gift of resurrection. We cannot experience now the full meaning of this gift, but—just as we do see and marvel at aspects of the unlimited universe—we do already receive of the new life God offers us.

• We receive God's gift of new life whenever estranged family members reconcile, when a new baby is born, when we've tried successfully a new endeavor, when the death of a loved one becomes a moment of grace, when our spirits are lifted up by someone's kind remark. All these experiences of new life are a taste now of the fullness God has in store for us. While we are bound by this life's limitations, we are at the same time unbounded by God's promise: a share now in—and after death the fullness of—risen life forever.

Model Universal Prayer (Prayer of the Faithful)

Presider: We turn to God who promises everlasting life and pray with hope.

Response:

Lord, hear our prayer.

Cantor:

we pray to the Lord,

That all members of the church may live in the hope of everlasting life . . . [pause]

That all people of the world may come to share in the fullness of life God offers those who believe . . . [pause]

That those who live in the shadow of death may find hope in the resurrection . . . [pause]

That each of us gathered here may know God's newness of life now and grow into sharing God's boundless life in eternity . . . [pause]

Presider: O God, you are the Lord of the living and the dead: guide us to live responsibly each day so that we might dwell in your glory for ever and ever. **Amen.**

COLLECT

Let us pray

Pause for silent prayer

Almighty and merciful God,
graciously keep from us all adversity,
so that, unhindered in mind and body
   alike,
we may pursue in freedom of heart
the things that are yours.
Through our Lord Jesus Christ, your Son,
who lives and reigns with you in the unity
   of the Holy Spirit,
one God, for ever and ever.
Amen.

FIRST READING 2 Macc 7:1-2, 9-14

It happened that seven brothers with their
      mother were arrested
   and tortured with whips and scourges
      by the king,
   to force them to eat pork in violation of
      God's law.
One of the brothers, speaking for the
      others, said:
   "What do you expect to achieve by
      questioning us?
We are ready to die rather than transgress
      the laws of our ancestors."

At the point of death he said:
   "You accursed fiend, you are depriving
      us of this present life,
   but the King of the world will raise us
      up to live again forever.
It is for his laws that we are dying."

After him the third suffered their cruel sport.
He put out his tongue at once when told
      to do so,
   and bravely held out his hands, as he
      spoke these noble words:
   "It was from Heaven that I received these;
   for the sake of his laws I disdain them;
   from him I hope to receive them again."
Even the king and his attendants marveled
      at the young man's courage,
   because he regarded his sufferings as
      nothing.

After he had died,
   they tortured and maltreated the fourth
      brother in the same way.
When he was near death, he said,
   "It is my choice to die at the hands of
      men
   with the hope God gives of being raised
      up by him;
   but for you, there will be no resurrection
      to life."

RESPONSORIAL PSALM
Ps 17:1, 5-6, 8, 15

R⁄. (15b) Lord, when your glory appears,
my joy will be full.

Hear, O LORD, a just suit;
    attend to my outcry;
    hearken to my prayer from lips without
        deceit.

R⁄. Lord, when your glory appears, my joy
will be full.

My steps have been steadfast in your
        paths,
    my feet have not faltered.
I call upon you, for you will answer me,
        O God;
    incline your ear to me; hear my word.

R⁄. Lord, when your glory appears, my joy
will be full.

Keep me as the apple of your eye,
    hide me in the shadow of your wings.
But I in justice shall behold your face;
    on waking I shall be content in your
        presence.

R⁄. Lord, when your glory appears, my joy
will be full.

SECOND READING
2 Thess 2:16–3:5

Brothers and sisters:
May our Lord Jesus Christ himself and
        God our Father,
    who has loved us and given us
        everlasting encouragement
    and good hope through his grace,
    encourage your hearts and strengthen
        them in every good deed and word.

Finally, brothers and sisters, pray for us,
    so that the word of the Lord may speed
        forward and be glorified,
    as it did among you,
    and that we may be delivered from
        perverse and wicked people,
    for not all have faith.
But the Lord is faithful;
    he will strengthen you and guard you
        from the evil one.
We are confident of you in the Lord that
        what we instruct you,
    you are doing and will continue to do.
May the Lord direct your hearts to the love
        of God
    and to the endurance of Christ.

About Liturgy

Early communities' expectation of the end times: Note that the second reading for both last Sunday and this one has been from the Second Letter to the Thessalonians. The first and second letters to this Christian community are considered the earliest of Paul's writings (and the earliest in the Christian Scriptures). At this time the Christian community was still expecting Jesus' imminent return and no doubt this directly shaped their attitudes and behavior as Christians—novel and daring behavior, indeed; for example, their radical, shared community life and willingness to die rather than denounce their belief in Jesus. They were to be prepared, because the end was near.

During Ordinary Time the second reading does not usually accord with the first reading and gospel. But on these last Sundays of the liturgical year there is a consistent *parousia* (a technical term referring to Christ's Second Coming) motif. Therefore, the second reading can be a lens through which the gospel and first reading are interpreted.

About Liturgical Music

Music suggestions: The readings and psalm this Sunday speak of hope in the resurrection but also of the challenge to be faithful to the demands of discipleship. "A Multitude Comes from the East and the West" speaks of many who will join Abraham, Isaac, and Jacob (gospel) at the "feast of salvation" and receive the crown of victory. The text with its lovely e-minor tune would work well during the preparation of the gifts. M. D. Ridge's "In the Day of the Lord" is an energetic song anticipating the Second Coming and the final resurrection. Since the text follows a verse-refrain rather than a hymn structure, verses can be omitted to fit ritual needs without doing damage to the meaning of the song as a whole. The style and tempo would fit the entrance procession, the preparation of the gifts, or the recessional.

Both Jeremy Young's "We Shall Rise Again" and David Haas's "We Will Rise Again" speak of the weariness and dangers which accompany discipleship and the certainty we hold in God's promise of resurrection. These verse-refrain songs would work well during the Communion procession. Another excellent choice for Communion would be Steven Warner's "Come, All You Blessed Ones," which combines a refrain about the promise of eternal joy for those "blest of a loving God" with verses based on Psalm 23 and Psalm 34. Andraé Crouch's well-known "Soon and Very Soon" would make a fitting recessional song.

SPIRITUALITY

GOSPEL ACCLAMATION
Luke 21:28

℞. Alleluia, alleluia.
Stand erect and raise your heads
because your redemption is at hand.
℞. Alleluia, alleluia.

Gospel
Luke 21:5-19; L159C

While some people were
    speaking about
    how the temple was adorned
        with costly stones and
            votive offerings,
    Jesus said, "All that you see
        here—
    the days will come when
        there will not be left
    a stone upon another stone that will
        not be thrown down."

Then they asked him,
    "Teacher, when will this happen?
And what sign will there be when all
    these things are about to happen?"
He answered,
    "See that you not be deceived,
    for many will come in my name,
        saying,
    'I am he,' and 'The time has come.'
Do not follow them!
When you hear of wars and
    insurrections,
    do not be terrified; for such things
        must happen first,
    but it will not immediately be the
        end."
Then he said to them,
    "Nation will rise against nation, and
        kingdom against kingdom.
There will be powerful earthquakes,
    famines, and plagues
    from place to place;
    and awesome sights and mighty signs
        will come from the sky.

Continued in Appendix A, p. 314.

Reflecting on the Gospel

"[D]o not be terrified." Such comforting and encouraging words of Jesus! For a number of weeks now we have been reading gospels which lead us to reflect on and prepare for the Second Coming. With the gospel of this Sunday we finally get a picture of the parousia events from every perspective: *cosmic* ("earthquakes," "awesome sights and mighty signs will come from the sky"); *social* ("wars and insurrections," "famines, and plagues"); *religious* ("temple . . . there will not be left another stone that will not be thrown down"); and *personal* ("seize you and persecute you"). In the midst of catastrophic events, Jesus instructs his disciples, "do not be terrified."

How in the world can we not be terrified of all these natural and human-made catastrophes? There is so much destruction told in this gospel. Our own experience of our world constantly tells of similar catastrophes from hurricanes and floods and wars and collapsed economies and killings and bloodshed on our streets. We lock and double lock our doors to try and keep danger out. And still we live in fear. Truly, we need to hear Jesus' words of comfort: "do not be terrified." Jesus assures us that "not a hair on [our] head will be destroyed" and by our faithfulness we will "secure [our] lives."

The readings for this Sunday are really filled with hope, not doom or fear. Along with all these terrifying things, good things happen: these things do not signal an immediate end so we have time to prepare; these things give all of us an opportunity to testify to Jesus' name and his reign; Jesus himself will give each of us the wisdom we need to speak boldly; and, most importantly, Jesus assures us that he will be the victor ("all your adversaries will be powerless to resist or refute").

Catastrophes, disasters, wars, insurrections, etc. are not signs of the end of the world, but of how far we actually are from the end. We hasten the end not by being fearful of these events, but by being faithful to Jesus' work of establishing God's kingdom. Preaching, teaching, and living in Jesus' name is the one sure way of discipleship that hastens Jesus' Second Coming and secures for us eternal life. We will know the end is near not by increased terror and hardship, rampant evil and lack of care for each other, constant upset and loss. The end is near when goodness and love are abundant, when caring and sharing mark our daily living, when all people are brothers and sisters. The end is marked by goodness, not by evil. When God's reign of peace and justice is established throughout our world, the end will be here. There will be no more work of salvation to do.

Living the Paschal Mystery

Times of adversity, whether now or in the future, are opportunities in which the wisdom of Jesus and his teachings embolden his followers to testify to him and strengthen them to persevere. The trials and tribulations we face now in our lives are preparation for the end times. Our faithfulness hastens the end times. As we grow in our readiness to be faithful to the Gospel in this life, we are already choosing our final destiny.

Before new life, there must be dying to the old self. We know that Christ is the victor, and those who persevere in their faithfulness will share in the glory of that victory. But the full victory is not yet revealed. We await. We hope.

Focusing the Gospel

Key words and phrases: what sign will there be, not immediately be the end, giving testimony, wisdom in speaking, because of my name, secure your lives

To the point: Catastrophes, disasters, wars, insurrections, etc. are not signs of the end of the world, but of how far we actually are from the end. We hasten the end not by being fearful of these events, but by being faithful to Jesus' work of establishing God's kingdom. Preaching, teaching, and living in Jesus' name is the one sure way of discipleship that hastens Jesus' Second Coming and secures for us eternal life.

Connecting the Gospel

to the first reading: The first reading describes the day when evil will be destroyed and those who fear God will walk in the light of God's justice. On this day the end will come because God's purpose will have been accomplished.

to experience: There are billboards and doomsday criers who point to catastrophes and evil as signs of the end times. What happens when we change our perspective and realize that the end times will be upon us only when goodness and justice reign?

Connecting the Responsorial Psalm

to the readings: In the context of this Sunday's first reading and gospel, Psalm 98 is a statement of absolute certainty that the power of Christ will prevail over the forces of evil. We need not lose heart when wars, insurrections, earthquakes, famines arise. We need not be surprised when fidelity to discipleship brings persecution. Even amidst the direst evil, the vision we maintain is of Christ's final coming and victory. And so we sing, blow trumpets, clap hands, and shout for joy, for we know the Lord is coming to rule with justice.

to psalmist preparation: When you sing this responsorial psalm, you stand before the assembly testifying to a vision of the future in which God reigns with justice. Do you believe in this future? Are you looking for it? Will you stake your life on it?

**ASSEMBLY &
FAITH-SHARING GROUPS**

- To prepare for Christ's Second Coming means to me . . .
- What enables me to persevere in my witness of Jesus is . . .
- I experience the presence of God's kingdom and the hastening of the end times when . . .

PRESIDERS

I help the assembly remain fixed on Christ rather than on false signs of the end by . . .

DEACONS

My ministry to the needs of others brings them hope and hastens Christ's Second Coming when I . . .

HOSPITALITY MINISTERS

The manner of my hospitality encourages others to take up the saving work of Christ when I . . .

MUSIC MINISTERS

Because the coming of Christ's kingdom instigates confrontation between good and evil, I experience this struggle in my music ministry when . . . I experience the confrontation in myself when . . .

ALTAR MINISTERS

My service models the real task of discipleship—perseverance in preaching, teaching, and living in Jesus' name—whenever I . . .

LECTORS

I struggle with these end of the liturgical year readings about the end times because . . . This struggle strengthens my proclamation by . . .

**EXTRAORDINARY MINISTERS
OF HOLY COMMUNION**

At Eucharist I celebrate my life secure in Christ because . . . I share this security with others by . . .

Model Penitential Act

Presider: In the day of Christ's coming, wrong will be righted, suffering will end, death will yield to eternal life. Let us prepare to meet Christ who comes to us in this Eucharist . . . [pause]

Lord Jesus, you come to bring salvation: Lord . . .

Christ Jesus, you promise life everlasting to those faithful to your name: Christ . . .

Lord Jesus, you strengthen and encourage those who follow you: Lord . . .

Homily Points

• People often lay their lives on the line so that good can triumph over evil. For example, the Freedom Riders risked their lives during the civil rights movement, rescue workers risk their lives to free victims of various disasters, someone speaks out for another who is falsely accused. These heroes put out of mind the danger they may undergo for the sake of the good that they hope to accomplish. Jesus put himself on the line throughout his life of preaching and teaching so that good would triumph over evil.

• The people in the gospel ask Jesus about the signs of the end times. He cautions them not to be misled by catastrophes and disasters. Before the end times happen, Jesus and his followers must work to establish God's kingdom—work to ensure that good triumphs over evil. Disciples' perseverance in ministering in Jesus' name will lead to being persecuted, and even to some losing their lives. But fidelity to Jesus' name and saving mission secures for them what no earthly being can: eternal life.

• The signs of the end times we usually name are not actually the right ones. The end will come not when evil is heightened, but when goodness overcomes evil. We bring about God's kingdom by the good we do. For example, good parents take care of the children before they look to their own needs, an older sibling might run to pull a younger child out of the street, a friend might simply be present and listen to another. The amazing thing is that these simple, everyday acts of goodness hasten the end times and eternal life.

Model Universal Prayer (Prayer of the Faithful)

Presider: Let us pray for the grace to persevere as Jesus' disciples, hastening the coming of the kingdom by the good we do.

Response:

Lord, hear our prayer.

Cantor:

we pray to the Lord,

That all members of the church may seize simple everyday opportunities to do good and hasten the coming of God's kingdom . . . [pause]

That all peoples of the world may work diligently to overcome war, famine, and disease . . . [pause]

That those suffering from fear, despair, or hopelessness may receive courage and strength . . . [pause]

That each of us may live faithfully every day, secure in the promise of eternal life . . . [pause]

Presider: O God, you are always faithful to your word: may your promise of eternal life inspire us to a life of faithful service, truthful testimony, and patient endurance. We ask this through Christ our Lord. **Amen.**

COLLECT

Let us pray

Pause for silent prayer

Grant us, we pray, O Lord our God,
the constant gladness of being devoted
    to you,
for it is full and lasting happiness
to serve with constancy
the author of all that is good.
Through our Lord Jesus Christ, your Son,
who lives and reigns with you in the unity
    of the Holy Spirit,
one God, for ever and ever.
Amen.

FIRST READING

Mal 3:19-20a

Lo, the day is coming, blazing like an oven,
    when all the proud and all evildoers will
        be stubble,
and the day that is coming will set them
    on fire,
    leaving them neither root nor branch,
    says the Lord of hosts.
But for you who fear my name, there will
    arise
    the sun of justice with its healing rays.

RESPONSORIAL PSALM

Ps 98:5-6, 7-8, 9

R℣. (cf. 9) The Lord comes to rule the earth with justice.

Sing praise to the LORD with the harp,
    with the harp and melodious song.
With trumpets and the sound of the horn
    sing joyfully before the King, the LORD.

R℣. The Lord comes to rule the earth with justice.

Let the sea and what fills it resound,
    the world and those who dwell in it;
let the rivers clap their hands,
    the mountains shout with them for joy.

R℣. The Lord comes to rule the earth with justice.

Before the LORD, for he comes,
    for he comes to rule the earth;
he will rule the world with justice
    and the peoples with equity.

R℣. The Lord comes to rule the earth with justice.

SECOND READING

2 Thess 3:7-12

Brothers and sisters:
You know how one must imitate us.
For we did not act in a disorderly way
        among you,
    nor did we eat food received free from
        anyone.
On the contrary, in toil and drudgery,
        night and day
    we worked, so as not to burden any of
        you.
Not that we do not have the right.
Rather, we wanted to present ourselves as
        a model for you,
    so that you might imitate us.
In fact, when we were with you,
    we instructed you that if anyone was
        unwilling to work,
        neither should that one eat.
We hear that some are conducting
        themselves among you in a disorderly
        way,
    by not keeping busy but minding the
        business of others.
Such people we instruct and urge in the
        Lord Jesus Christ to work quietly
    and to eat their own food.

About Liturgy

Eucharist and eschatology, part 2: The Catechesis about Liturgy for the Twenty-fifth Sunday in Ordinary Time addressed the eschatological thrust of liturgy, specifically mentioning the eucharistic acclamations and the connection of the earthly liturgy with the heavenly liturgy. It would be a good exercise for the parish liturgy committee and liturgical ministers to take *The Roman Missal* and go through the eucharistic rite to detect other areas where there is an eschatological thrust.

This motif is particularly prominent during this time of the liturgical year, but in fact every liturgy has an eschatological thread running through it. Moreover, the eucharistic liturgy itself is already a share in the messianic banquet. It is for this reason that the lines for the Communion procession need to process toward the altar, the symbol in our midst of the eschatological banquet. This helps make the connection between our receiving Holy Communion now and our share in the eschatological banquet in the future.

About Liturgical Music

Music suggestions: Timothy Dudley-Smith's "When the Lord in Glory Comes" assures us that when the end times come it will not be the thunder, the pomp, the lightning, "not the child of humble birth, not the carpenter on earth, not the man by all denied, not the victim crucified, but the God who died to save, but the victor of the grave" whose face we shall see and whose glory we shall share. Bob Moore's energetic setting, written to be led by the choir with the assembly responding on the refrain, would be an excellent prelude or hymn of praise after Communion. Another suitable choice for Communion would be "Lord of the Dance/I Danced in the Morning" with its promise that the One who danced at the beginning of time dances for all eternity and we dance with him. Good choices for the preparation of the gifts include "How Can I Keep from Singing" and "Be Not Afraid." Finally, songs worth repeating this Sunday include M. D. Ridge's "In the Day of the Lord" and Andraé Crouch's "Soon and Very Soon."

SPIRITUALITY

GOSPEL ACCLAMATION
Mark 11:9, 10

℞. Alleluia, alleluia.
Blessed is he who comes in the name of the Lord!
Blessed is the kingdom of our father David that
    is to come!
℞. Alleluia, alleluia.

Gospel

Luke 23:35-43; L162C

The rulers sneered at
    Jesus and said,
  "He saved others, let
    him save himself
  if he is the chosen
    one, the Christ of
    God."

Even the soldiers jeered at him.
As they approached to offer him wine
    they called out,
  "If you are King of the Jews, save
    yourself."
Above him there was an inscription
    that read,
  "This is the King of the Jews."

Now one of the criminals hanging there
    reviled Jesus, saying,
  "Are you not the Christ?
Save yourself and us."
The other, however, rebuking him, said
    in reply,
  "Have you no fear of God,
  for you are subject to the same
    condemnation?
And indeed, we have been condemned
    justly,
  for the sentence we received
    corresponds to our crimes,
  but this man has done nothing
    criminal."
Then he said,
  "Jesus, remember me when you come
    into your kingdom."
He replied to him,
  "Amen, I say to you,
  today you will be with me in
    Paradise."

Reflecting on the Gospel

Goals can motivate us mightily. If we want to have a nice vacation, we might give up eating out so often to save money. If we want to lose weight, we give up free time to exercise faithfully. If we want to get promoted, we struggle through night school to get the additional training we need. The more important the goal, the stronger the motivation. This Sunday we celebrate the end of the liturgical year and acknowledge Christ as our King. Ideally, this festival has been a strong motivation for us to follow our King faithfully during this year, journeying with him toward Jerusalem and the Cross, toward those paschal events that changed everything about who we are and what motivates us.

"If you are King . . . save yourself" the soldiers jeered at Jesus on the cross. So did the rulers and one criminal crucified with Jesus taunt him about saving himself. But they misunderstood what "save yourself" means and what motivated Jesus to live the way he did. The rulers, soldiers, and one criminal thought being saved meant that Jesus should come down from the cross, avoid any more suffering, certainly avoid death. But Jesus shows us through his words to the other criminal what being saved really means: "you will be with me in Paradise." Salvation is less a matter of being saved *from*, than a matter of being saved *for*. Here is our strongest motivation to live a Gospel life: Jesus invites us to share in his eternal glory.

Like Jesus, we cannot save ourselves from the daily demands of faithful discipleship. He did not come down from the cross to save himself; neither can we avoid accepting our daily cross in living as he did, giving ourselves for the sake of others. Jesus' kingdom is not located in some geographical locale. There is no country named "JCKingdom." Rather, the kingdom of God is among us, in us, and through us to the extent that we open ourselves to his risen Presence among us, in us, and through us. Being saved is a matter of embracing this Presence, living it, and allowing it to shape who we are, the decisions we make for daily living, and why we choose to follow our King through the cross to fullness of life. Our motivation for fidelity to Christ's way is the Life we receive.

Living the Paschal Mystery

How is Christ a king? Not by sitting on a throne; he hangs on a cross. Not by amassing territory; he establishes a kingdom of mercy and forgiveness. Not by wielding power; he does not save himself. What makes Christ our King is that he gave himself for the salvation of others. Here is what it means for Christ to be King: he gave his life for others. Here is what it means for us to live under his reign: to give our lives for others, too, and hear Jesus say to us, "you will be with me in Paradise." Christ our King, our Savior, offers us what no one else can: fullness of life.

With the Good Thief we, too, ask, "Jesus, remember me when you come into your kingdom." Our faith teaches us that we seek life, journey toward fullness of life. Jesus' response to us, as to the Good Thief, is "you will be with me in Paradise." Jesus promises. He always makes good on his promises. This is why we are faithful along the way. This is why we persevere in following Jesus. This is why we are willing to empty ourselves for the sake of others . . . because by giving of ourselves we enter with Jesus into Paradise. By giving of ourselves we grasp that which we are saved *for*: eternal happiness in Christ's eternal kingdom.

Focusing the Gospel

Key words and phrases: let him save himself, save yourself, Save yourself and us, you will be with me in Paradise

To the point: "If you are King . . . save yourself" the soldiers jeered at Jesus on the cross. So did the rulers and one criminal crucified with Jesus taunt him about saving himself. But they misunderstood what "save yourself" means. The rulers, soldiers, and one criminal thought being saved meant that Jesus should come down from the cross, avoid any more suffering, certainly avoid death. But Jesus shows us through his words to the other criminal what being saved really means: "you will be with me in Paradise." Salvation is less a matter of being saved *from*, than a matter of being saved *for*.

Connecting the Gospel

to the second reading: Paul expresses in the second reading what we have been saved *for*: the inheritance of holiness, membership in the kingdom of the beloved Son, a share in Christ's fullness, reconciliation with all things, and peace.

to experience: What we are celebrating with this solemnity is not a style of government (earthly kings and kingdoms), but the victory of Christ over all things—even death. Christ the King makes possible among us a reign of goodness, mercy, forgiveness, justice, reconciliation, peace.

Connecting the Responsorial Psalm

to the readings: Israelites arriving at the gates of Jerusalem for annual worship sang Psalm 122. It was a song of great joy, for entering Jerusalem meant encountering God. It meant celebrating membership in God's people. It meant reaffirming who they were and who God was for them. On this solemnity of Christ the King we, too, celebrate who we are and who God is for us. We are the people forgiven by God through Christ's redeeming death (second reading). We are the very "bone and [ ] flesh" (first reading) of Christ, members of the Body of which he is the Head (second reading). We are the ones remembered by Christ and called to his kingdom (gospel). Let us enter with rejoicing!

to psalmist preparation: In singing this responsorial psalm you invite the assembly to enter the kingdom of God. They have journeyed through all of Ordinary Time. They have struggled, they have been faithful. Bring them in with joy.

ASSEMBLY & FAITH-SHARING GROUPS

- Jesus has saved me for . . . Because of this, I . . .
- Knowing Jesus has saved me, I am opened to . . . I am free to . . .
- I am tempted to save myself when . . . From Jesus I learn . . .

PRESIDERS

In the midst of sneers and jeers, Jesus forgives and saves; where I need to embody this kind of shepherding is . . .

DEACONS

During this liturgical year, I have furthered the reign of Christ in my service ministry by . . .

HOSPITALITY MINISTERS

My care and concern helps the assembly realize they are already "in Paradise" whenever I . . .

MUSIC MINISTERS

What I hope Jesus remembers about me and my manner of doing music ministry during this liturgical year is . . .

ALTAR MINISTERS

My serving signifies to others that they "share in the inheritance of the holy ones" (second reading) when I . . .

LECTORS

My pondering and proclaiming of the word during this liturgical year has made me an "image of the invisible God" (second reading) in that . . .

EXTRAORDINARY MINISTERS OF HOLY COMMUNION

I distribute Christ the King at Eucharist; I "distribute" Christ's reign whenever . . .

Model Penitential Act

Presider: We come together to honor Christ our King. As we prepare for this liturgy, let us open ourselves to his call to share fullness of life with him in Paradise . . . [pause]

Lord Jesus, you are Christ, our King: Lord . . .

Christ Jesus, you are our Life and salvation: Christ . . .

Lord Jesus, you say to faithful followers, "you will be with me in Paradise": Lord . . .

Homily Points

• When people belittle or ridicule us, our natural reaction is to become defensive, lash out, and put them in their place. On the cross, Jesus is sneered at, jeered, and reviled. Yet he does not respond in like manner, either to the criminals hanging next to him or to the soldiers executing him. Jesus has shown us another way.

• Even on the cross, suffering and dying, Jesus does not act to save himself, but does act to save the Good Thief and declares that he will "come into his kingdom." In the kingdom of Christ we are lovingly embraced by the beloved Son who wills for us salvation—fullness of life. In this very embrace is the kingdom of God present.

• Christ is King not over a geographical realm. He reigns over the hearts of all those who open themselves to his invitation to be with him always. We are with him now—and are cooperating with him in furthering his kingdom—when we forgive those who have hurt us, reach out to those who are trying to change and grow, expand our hearts to welcome those who are marginalized. This is the way Jesus has shown us; this is what Jesus has saved us for; this is the way we live into Paradise.

Model Universal Prayer (Prayer of the Faithful)

Presider: Let us pray that we might one day share with Christ our King in the glory of Paradise.

Response:

Lord, hear our prayer.

Cantor:

we pray to the Lord,

That all members of the church, faithful to Christ's reign, embrace others with openness and forgiveness . . . [pause]

That leaders of the world reign over their people with compassion, truth, and integrity . . . [pause]

That those who have been harmed receive healing; that those who harm others change their ways . . . [pause]

That all of us here one day receive the fullness of life Christ promises to his faithful followers . . . [pause]

Presider: O God, you make us worthy members of your kingdom: hear these our prayers that one day we may be with you forever in Paradise. We ask this through Christ our Lord and King. **Amen.**

COLLECT

Let us pray

Pause for silent prayer

Almighty ever-living God,
whose will is to restore all things
in your beloved Son, the King of the universe,
grant, we pray,
that the whole creation, set free from slavery,
may render your majesty service
and ceaselessly proclaim your praise.
Through our Lord Jesus Christ, your Son,
who lives and reigns with you in the unity of the Holy Spirit,
one God, for ever and ever.
Amen.

FIRST READING

2 Sam 5:1-3

In those days, all the tribes of Israel came to David in Hebron and said:
"Here we are, your bone and your flesh.
In days past, when Saul was our king,
it was you who led the Israelites out and brought them back.
And the LORD said to you,
'You shall shepherd my people Israel
and shall be commander of Israel.'"
When all the elders of Israel came to David in Hebron,
King David made an agreement with them there before the LORD,
and they anointed him king of Israel.

RESPONSORIAL PSALM

Ps 122:1-2, 3-4, 4-5

R̰. (cf. 1) Let us go rejoicing to the house of the Lord.

I rejoiced because they said to me,
"We will go up to the house of the LORD."
And now we have set foot
within your gates, O Jerusalem.

R̰. Let us go rejoicing to the house of the Lord.

Jerusalem, built as a city
    with compact unity.
To it the tribes go up,
    the tribes of the LORD.

R7. Let us go rejoicing to the house of the Lord.

According to the decree for Israel,
    to give thanks to the name of the LORD.
In it are set up judgment seats,
    seats for the house of David.

R7. Let us go rejoicing to the house of the Lord.

SECOND READING

Col 1:12-20

Brothers and sisters:
Let us give thanks to the Father,
    who has made you fit to share
        in the inheritance of the holy ones in
            light.
He delivered us from the power of
    darkness
    and transferred us to the kingdom of
        his beloved Son,
    in whom we have redemption, the
        forgiveness of sins.

    He is the image of the invisible God,
        the firstborn of all creation.
    For in him were created all things in
            heaven and on earth,
        the visible and the invisible,
        whether thrones or dominions or
            principalities or powers;
        all things were created through
            him and for him.
    He is before all things,
        and in him all things hold together.
    He is the head of the body, the
        church.
    He is the beginning, the firstborn
        from the dead,
        that in all things he himself might
            be preeminent.
    For in him all the fullness was
            pleased to dwell,
        and through him to reconcile all
            things for him,
        making peace by the blood of his
            cross
    through him, whether those on
        earth or those in heaven.

CATECHESIS

About Liturgy

End/beginning of the liturgical year: The liturgical year concludes at the end of this Thirty-fourth Week in Ordinary Time. The motif of Christ's Second Coming which we have been focusing on especially these last weeks of the liturgical year comes to a climax as we celebrate Christ's victory and coming to glory on this solemnity of Our Lord Jesus Christ the King. But celebrating the victorious Christ does not end with this liturgical year nor with this solemnity. An eschatological motif continues into the first part of Advent which begins, not with looking to Christ's first coming, but with looking to Christ's Second Coming. In this way the liturgical year presents to us a seamless rhythm of passion and victory, death and new life. The liturgical year constantly presents to us the most positive motivation to remain faithful to the demands of discipleship throughout the year: we participate in a never-ending rhythm of dying to self and rising to new life. To fullness of life. To eternal life.

About Liturgical Music

Liturgical music and growth in discipleship: The solemnity of Christ the King is a good time to assess how we have grown this past year in and through liturgical music. How through our music have we more clearly become the Body of Christ given for the redemption of the world?

For assembly members: How have we grown in singing well together, meaning with willing heart and full voice? How have we grown in listening to each other as we sang, in becoming one Body rather than individuals singing "our own thing"?

For cantors and choir: How have we grown in focusing on Christ rather than making ourselves the "star" of the liturgy? How have we grown in treating each other as members of the one Body of Christ? How have we grown in unselfishness because of the disciplines required for our ministry?

For music directors: How have we grown in our understanding of the role of music in liturgy? How have we stayed faithful to keeping liturgy central and music secondary and supporting? How have we grown through this ministry in our relationship with Christ and in our ability to see the assembly as Body of Christ? How have we helped the cantors and the choir grow in these ways?

SPIRITUALITY

GOSPEL ACCLAMATION
1 Thess 5:18

R⁊. Alleluia, alleluia.
In all circumstances, give thanks,
for this is the will of God for you in Christ Jesus.
R⁊. Alleluia, alleluia.

Gospel

Luke 17:11-19; L947.6

As Jesus continued his journey
      to Jerusalem,
   he traveled through Samaria
      and Galilee.
As he was entering a village,
      ten lepers met him.
They stood at a distance from
      him and raised their
      voices, saying,
   "Jesus, Master! Have pity on
      us!"
And when he saw them, he said,
   "Go show yourselves to the priests."
As they were going they were cleansed.
And one of them, realizing he had been
      healed,
   returned, glorifying God in a loud voice;
   and he fell at the feet of Jesus and
      thanked him.
He was a Samaritan.
Jesus said in reply,
   "Ten were cleansed, were they not?
Where are the other nine?
Has none but this foreigner returned to
      give thanks to God?"
Then he said to him, "Stand up and go;
   your faith has saved you."

See Appendix A, p. 314, for the other readings.

Reflecting on the Gospel

On days like this one, Thanksgiving Day, we take time to say thanks to God for gifts which might not be on our minds all the time. As a country we are grateful for the abundant resources we have, for the democracy which enables us to live free lives, for the food on our tables. Thanksgiving Day is our country's collective thank you for all the good we share as a nation.

But real gratitude is not simply a matter of saying thank you, or even remembering all for which we are grateful. Real gratitude is an attitude and orientation toward another. It is an acknowledgment that we are social beings, live in relation with each other, are dependent on each other, make exchanges with one other. These exchanges need to be far more than material things. They must include the important interchanges of values, ideals, aspirations, hopes and desires. Real gratitude enlarges us to go beyond ourselves and our own little world to embrace others as equals, as critical to our own well-being, as extensions of ourselves. Real gratitude is an action of communion with all others.

It is not insignificant that Thanksgiving Day usually finds a special Mass being celebrated in our parish communities. We come to give God thanks not only for the blessings of our country, but also for all the spiritual blessings God has given us. The gospel for this day about the ten lepers reminds us to take time to give God thanks for our communion with the risen Jesus, and that this communion means we continue his saving mission. We are empowered to take up the very saving work of God. When the grateful leper fell at Jesus' feet to thank him, Jesus commanded him, "Stand up and go." Our expression of thanksgiving to God for all the blessings given us is only the beginning. Real gratitude invites us to express who we are—the Body of Christ—by living the way Jesus did. Jesus sends us forth from our giving thanks (from Eucharist, which means thanksgiving) on the mission of sharing with others what we have received. We are on Jesus' saving mission. By living faithfully, by accepting Jesus' command to "Stand up and go," do grateful hearts become a habit for us, a way to remember that all we have and all we are comes from God and is to be used for God's purposes.

Our gratitude must be more than occasional words of thanks. Real gratitude is a *daily* habit, a matter of orienting ourselves to Jesus and his saving mission. Like all giving thanks, taking up Jesus' saving mission becomes an ingrained habit by the very doing. The more of a habit we develop of giving thanks to God, the deeper and more familiar is our relationship with God. Taking up Jesus' saving mission is nothing less than allowing ourselves to become one with him, to receive from God the blessings we need to be faithful, and to open ourselves to the continued blessings God showers upon us.

Living the Paschal Mystery

It is something of a scandal that we live in a country with so much abundance, and yet so many people lack even the necessities of life. Our own thanksgiving must spill over into practical acts to alleviate the sufferings of so many who have so little. Indeed, giving to others less fortunate than we are is in itself an acknowledgment of our own giftedness and gratitude for our abundance. Gratitude includes sharing our gifts with others. Gratitude is an expression of our cooperating with Jesus' saving work.

Focusing the Gospel

Key words and phrases: fell at the feet of Jesus and thanked him, Stand up and go

To the point: When the grateful leper fell at Jesus' feet to thank him, Jesus commanded him, "Stand up and go." Our expression of thanksgiving to God for all the blessings given us is only the beginning. Jesus sends us forth from our giving thanks (from Eucharist, which means thanksgiving) on the mission of sharing with others what we have received.

Model Penitential Act

Presider: We gather today to give thanks to the God who fills us with good things. Let us prepare to celebrate this liturgy well . . .

Lord Jesus, you bring healing and salvation: Lord . . .

Christ Jesus, you do wondrous things for your people: Christ . . .

Lord Jesus, you are worthy of all glory and thanks: Lord . . .

Model Universal Prayer (Prayer of the Faithful)

Presider: Our generous God gives us all good things. And so we bring our prayers in grateful confidence.

Response:

Lord, hear our prayer.

Cantor:

we pray to the Lord,

That all members of the church express their gratitude for many blessings by sharing those blessings generously with others . . . [pause]

That our nation may cherish and safeguard the natural resources God has bestowed on us . . . [pause]

That the poor and hungry may share in the earth's abundance . . . [pause]

That each of us here generously share our love, values, and well-being with others for the good of our families and community . . . [pause]

Presider: O God, you give us all good things: hear these our prayers that one day we might share in the fullness of your goodness at the heavenly Banquet. We ask this through Christ our Lord and King. **Amen.**

COLLECT

Let us pray

Pause for silent prayer

Father all-powerful,
your gifts of love are countless
and your goodness infinite;
as we come before you on Thanksgiving Day
with gratitude for your kindness,
open our hearts to have concern
for every man, woman, and child,
so that we may share your gifts in loving service.
Through our Lord Jesus Christ, your Son,
who lives and reigns with you in the unity of
    the Holy Spirit,
one God, for ever and ever. **Amen.**

FOR REFLECTION

• The gifts for which I am thankful are . . . For this year, the most significant reason I need to return to Jesus (like the Samaritan leper) and give thanks is . . .

• Some ways I could lead my family to giving thanks to God during this holiday season are . . .

• Celebrating Eucharist leads me to be grateful when I . . . Eucharist sends me to share with others the blessings I've been given by . . .

Homily Points

• Thanksgiving Day—and our celebration of Eucharist—reminds us that it is not enough to give thanks for the gifts we have received. We are also to share what we have received with others. These gifts we share are not limited to physical possessions. Yes, we rightly give money, food, and clothing to those in need. But we also generously give others the love we have received, the values handed down to us by family, the well-being of a caring family, friends, community.

• How does the act of giving thanks move us to give of our blessings to others? In giving thanks we acknowledge, first of all, our own reality as recipients—we have needs that others can and do fill. Secondly, acknowledging our own needfulness verifies our solidarity with all others—we all have needs. Thirdly, in light of this solidarity, we give of our own goods, values and time to others, and thus strengthen our communion with all of humanity. For this we always and everywhere want to give thanks.

Readings *(continued)*

The Immaculate Conception of the Blessed Virgin Mary, *December 8, 2012*

Gospel (cont.)
Luke 1:26-38; L689

But Mary said to the angel,
   "How can this be,
   since I have no relations with a man?"
And the angel said to her in reply,
   "The Holy Spirit will come upon you,
   and the power of the Most High will overshadow you.
Therefore the child to be born
   will be called holy, the Son of God.
And behold, Elizabeth, your relative,
   has also conceived a son in her old age,
   and this is the sixth month for her who was called barren;
   for nothing will be impossible for God."
Mary said, "Behold, I am the handmaid of the Lord.
May it be done to me according to your word."
Then the angel departed from her.

FIRST READING
Gen 3:9-15, 20

After the man, Adam, had eaten of the tree,
   the LORD God called to the man and asked
      him, "Where are you?"
He answered, "I heard you in the garden;
   but I was afraid, because I was naked,
   so I hid myself."
Then he asked, "Who told you that you were
   naked?
You have eaten, then,
   from the tree of which I had forbidden you
      to eat!"
The man replied, "The woman whom you put
      here with me—
   she gave me fruit from the tree, and so I
      ate it."
The LORD God then asked the woman,
   "Why did you do such a thing?"
The woman answered, "The serpent tricked
   me into it, so I ate it."

Then the LORD God said to the serpent:
   "Because you have done this, you shall be
      banned
      from all the animals
      and from all the wild creatures;
   on your belly shall you crawl,
      and dirt shall you eat
      all the days of your life.
   I will put enmity between you and the
      woman,
      and between your offspring and hers;
   he will strike at your head,
      while you strike at his heel."

The man called his wife Eve,
   because she became the mother of all the
      living.

RESPONSORIAL PSALM
Ps 98:1, 2-3, 3-4

R̸. (1a) Sing to the Lord a new song, for he has
done marvelous deeds.

Sing to the LORD a new song,
   for he has done wondrous deeds;
His right hand has won victory for him,
   his holy arm.

R̸. Sing to the Lord a new song, for he has
done marvelous deeds.

The LORD has made his salvation known:
   in the sight of the nations he has revealed
      his justice.
He has remembered his kindness and his
   faithfulness
   toward the house of Israel.

R̸. Sing to the Lord a new song, for he has
done marvelous deeds.

All the ends of the earth have seen
   the salvation by our God.
Sing joyfully to the LORD, all you lands;
   break into song; sing praise.

R̸. Sing to the Lord a new song, for he has
done marvelous deeds.

SECOND READING
Eph 1:3-6, 11-12

Brothers and sisters:
Blessed be the God and Father of our Lord
      Jesus Christ,
   who has blessed us in Christ
   with every spiritual blessing in the
      heavens,
   as he chose us in him, before the foundation
      of the world,
   to be holy and without blemish before him.
In love he destined us for adoption to himself
      through Jesus Christ,
   in accord with the favor of his will,
   for the praise of the glory of his grace
   that he granted us in the beloved.

In him we were also chosen,
   destined in accord with the purpose of the
      One
   who accomplishes all things according to
      the intention of his will,
   so that we might exist for the praise of his
      glory,
   we who first hoped in Christ.

Gospel (cont.)
Matt 1:1-25; L13ABC

David became the father of Solomon,
  whose mother had been the wife of Uriah.
Solomon became the father of Rehoboam,
  Rehoboam the father of Abijah,
  Abijah the father of Asaph.
Asaph became the father of Jehoshaphat,
  Jehoshaphat the father of Joram,
  Joram the father of Uzziah.
Uzziah became the father of Jotham,
  Jotham the father of Ahaz,
  Ahaz the father of Hezekiah.
Hezekiah became the father of Manasseh,
  Manasseh the father of Amos,
  Amos the father of Josiah.
Josiah became the father of Jechoniah and his brothers
  at the time of the Babylonian exile.

After the Babylonian exile,
  Jechoniah became the father of Shealtiel,
  Shealtiel the father of Zerubbabel,
  Zerubbabel the father of Abiud.
Abiud became the father of Eliakim,
  Eliakim the father of Azor,
  Azor the father of Zadok.
Zadok became the father of Achim,
  Achim the father of Eliud,
  Eliud the father of Eleazar.
Eleazar became the father of Matthan,
  Matthan the father of Jacob,
  Jacob the father of Joseph, the husband of Mary.
Of her was born Jesus who is called the Christ.

Thus the total number of generations
  from Abraham to David
  is fourteen generations;
  from David to the Babylonian exile,
  fourteen generations;
  from the Babylonian exile to the Christ,
  fourteen generations.

Now this is how the birth of Jesus Christ came about.
When his mother Mary was betrothed to Joseph,
  but before they lived together,
  she was found with child through the Holy Spirit.
Joseph her husband, since he was a righteous man,
  yet unwilling to expose her to shame,
  decided to divorce her quietly.

Such was his intention when, behold,
  the angel of the Lord appeared to him in a dream and said,
  "Joseph, son of David,
  do not be afraid to take Mary your wife into your home.
For it is through the Holy Spirit
  that this child has been conceived in her.
She will bear a son and you are to name him Jesus,
  because he will save his people from their sins."
All this took place to fulfill
  what the Lord had said through the prophet:
    Behold, the virgin shall conceive and bear a son,
      and they shall name him Emmanuel,
  which means "God is with us."
When Joseph awoke,
  he did as the angel of the Lord had commanded him
  and took his wife into his home.
He had no relations with her until she bore a son,
  and he named him Jesus.

or Matt 1:18-25

This is how the birth of Jesus Christ came about.
When his mother Mary was betrothed to Joseph,
  but before they lived together,
  she was found with child through the Holy Spirit.
Joseph her husband, since he was a righteous man,
  yet unwilling to expose her to shame,
  decided to divorce her quietly.
Such was his intention when, behold,
  the angel of the Lord appeared to him in a dream and said,
  "Joseph, son of David,
  do not be afraid to take Mary your wife into your home.
For it is through the Holy Spirit
  that this child has been conceived in her.
She will bear a son and you are to name him Jesus,
  because he will save his people from their sins."
All this took place to fulfill
  what the Lord had said through the prophet:
    Behold, the virgin shall conceive and bear a son,
      and they shall name him Emmanuel,
  which means "God is with us."
When Joseph awoke,
  he did as the angel of the Lord had commanded him
  and took his wife into his home.
He had no relations with her until she bore a son,
  and he named him Jesus.

The Nativity of the Lord, *December 25, 2012 (At the Vigil Mass)*

FIRST READING
Isa 62:1-5

For Zion's sake I will not be silent,
   for Jerusalem's sake I will not be quiet,
until her vindication shines forth like the dawn
   and her victory like a burning torch.

Nations shall behold your vindication,
   and all the kings your glory;
you shall be called by a new name
   pronounced by the mouth of the LORD.
You shall be a glorious crown in the hand of
      the LORD,
   a royal diadem held by your God.
No more shall people call you "Forsaken,"
   or your land "Desolate,"
but you shall be called "My Delight,"
   and your land "Espoused."
For the LORD delights in you
   and makes your land his spouse.
As a young man marries a virgin,
   your Builder shall marry you;
and as a bridegroom rejoices in his bride
   so shall your God rejoice in you.

RESPONSORIAL PSALM
Ps 89:4-5, 16-17, 27, 29

R̸. (2a) For ever I will sing the goodness of
the Lord.

I have made a covenant with my chosen one,
   I have sworn to David my servant:
forever will I confirm your posterity
   and establish your throne for all
      generations.

R̸. For ever I will sing the goodness of the
Lord.

Blessed the people who know the joyful shout;
   in the light of your countenance, O LORD,
      they walk.
At your name they rejoice all the day,
   and through your justice they are exalted.

R̸. For ever I will sing the goodness of the
Lord.

He shall say of me, "You are my father,
   my God, the Rock, my savior."
Forever I will maintain my kindness toward
      him,
   and my covenant with him stands firm.

R̸. For ever I will sing the goodness of the
Lord.

SECOND READING
Acts 13:16-17, 22-25

When Paul reached Antioch in Pisidia and
      entered the synagogue,
   he stood up, motioned with his hand, and
      said,
   "Fellow Israelites and you others who are
      God-fearing, listen.
The God of this people Israel chose our
      ancestors
   and exalted the people during their sojourn
      in the land of Egypt.
With uplifted arm he led them out of it.
Then he removed Saul and raised up David
      as king;
   of him he testified,
   'I have found David, son of Jesse, a man
      after my own heart;
   he will carry out my every wish.'
From this man's descendants God, according
      to his promise,
   has brought to Israel a savior, Jesus.
John heralded his coming by proclaiming a
      baptism of repentance
   to all the people of Israel;
   and as John was completing his course, he
      would say,
   'What do you suppose that I am? I am not he.
Behold, one is coming after me;
   I am not worthy to unfasten the sandals of
      his feet.'"

The Nativity of the Lord, *December 25, 2012 (At the Mass during the Night)*

Gospel (cont.)
Luke 2:1-14; L14ABC

Now there were shepherds in that region living in the fields
   and keeping the night watch over their flock.
The angel of the Lord appeared to them
   and the glory of the Lord shone around them,
   and they were struck with great fear.
The angel said to them,
   "Do not be afraid;
   for behold, I proclaim to you good news of great joy
   that will be for all the people.
For today in the city of David
   a savior has been born for you who is Christ and Lord.
And this will be a sign for you:
   you will find an infant wrapped in swaddling clothes
   and lying in a manger."
And suddenly there was a multitude of the heavenly host with the
      angel,
   praising God and saying:
      "Glory to God in the highest
            and on earth peace to those on whom his favor rests."

The Nativity of the Lord, December 25, 2012 (At the Mass during the Night)

FIRST READING
Isa 9:1-6

The people who walked in darkness
    have seen a great light;
upon those who dwelt in the land of gloom
    a light has shone.
You have brought them abundant joy
    and great rejoicing,
as they rejoice before you as at the harvest,
    as people make merry when dividing
        spoils.
For the yoke that burdened them,
    the pole on their shoulder,
and the rod of their taskmaster
    you have smashed, as on the day of Midian.
For every boot that tramped in battle,
    every cloak rolled in blood,
    will be burned as fuel for flames.
For a child is born to us, a son is given us;
    upon his shoulder dominion rests.
They name him Wonder-Counselor, God-Hero,
    Father-Forever, Prince of Peace.
His dominion is vast
    and forever peaceful,
from David's throne, and over his kingdom,
    which he confirms and sustains
by judgment and justice,
    both now and forever.
The zeal of the LORD of hosts will do this!

RESPONSORIAL PSALM
Ps 96:1-2, 2-3, 11-12, 13

R℣. (Luke 2:11) Today is born our Savior,
Christ the Lord.

Sing to the LORD a new song;
    sing to the LORD, all you lands.
Sing to the LORD; bless his name.

R℣. Today is born our Savior, Christ the Lord.

Announce his salvation, day after day.
    Tell his glory among the nations;
    among all peoples, his wondrous deeds.

R℣. Today is born our Savior, Christ the Lord.

Let the heavens be glad and the earth rejoice;
    let the sea and what fills it resound;
    let the plains be joyful and all that is in
        them!
Then shall all the trees of the forest exult.

R℣. Today is born our Savior, Christ the Lord.

They shall exult before the LORD, for he
    comes;
    for he comes to rule the earth.
He shall rule the world with justice
    and the peoples with his constancy.

R℣. Today is born our Savior, Christ the Lord.

SECOND READING
Titus 2:11-14

Beloved:
The grace of God has appeared, saving all
    and training us to reject godless ways and
        worldly desires
    and to live temperately, justly, and devoutly
        in this age,
as we await the blessed hope,
    the appearance of the glory of our great
        God
    and savior Jesus Christ,
who gave himself for us to deliver us from
    all lawlessness
    and to cleanse for himself a people as his
        own,
eager to do what is good.

The Nativity of the Lord, December 25, 2012 (At the Mass at Dawn)

FIRST READING
Isa 62:11-12

See, the LORD proclaims
    to the ends of the earth:
say to daughter Zion,
    your savior comes!
Here is his reward with him,
    his recompense before him.
They shall be called the holy people,
    the redeemed of the LORD,
and you shall be called "Frequented,"
    a city that is not forsaken.

RESPONSORIAL PSALM
Ps 97:1, 6, 11-12

R℣. A light will shine on us this day: the Lord
is born for us.

The LORD is king; let the earth rejoice;
    let the many isles be glad.
The heavens proclaim his justice,
    and all peoples see his glory.

R℣. A light will shine on us this day: the Lord
is born for us.

Light dawns for the just;
    and gladness, for the upright of heart.
Be glad in the LORD, you just,
    and give thanks to his holy name.

R℣. A light will shine on us this day: the Lord
is born for us.

SECOND READING
Titus 3:4-7

Beloved:
When the kindness and generous love
    of God our savior appeared,
not because of any righteous deeds we had
        done
    but because of his mercy,
he saved us through the bath of rebirth
    and renewal by the Holy Spirit,
whom he richly poured out on us
    through Jesus Christ our savior,
so that we might be justified by his grace
    and become heirs in hope of eternal life.

Gospel (cont.)

John 1:1-18; L16ABC

The true light, which enlightens everyone,
    was coming into the world.
  He was in the world,
    and the world came to be through him,
    but the world did not know him.
  He came to what was his own,
    but his own people did not accept him.

But to those who did accept him
    he gave power to become children of God,
    to those who believe in his name,
  who were born not by natural generation
  nor by human choice nor by a man's decision
  but of God.

And the Word became flesh
    and made his dwelling among us,
    and we saw his glory,
    the glory as of the Father's only Son,
    full of grace and truth.
John testified to him and cried out, saying,
    "This was he of whom I said,
    'The one who is coming after me ranks ahead of me
    because he existed before me.'"
From his fullness we have all received,
    grace in place of grace,
  because while the law was given through Moses,
  grace and truth came through Jesus Christ.
No one has ever seen God.
The only Son, God, who is at the Father's side,
    has revealed him.

or John 1:1-5, 9-14

In the beginning was the Word,
    and the Word was with God,
    and the Word was God.
He was in the beginning with God.
All things came to be through him,
    and without him nothing came to be.
What came to be through him was life,
    and this life was the light of the human race;
  the light shines in the darkness,
    and the darkness has not overcome it.
The true light, which enlightens everyone,
    was coming into the world.
  He was in the world,
    and the world came to be through him,
    but the world did not know him.
  He came to what was his own,
    but his own people did not accept him.

But to those who did accept him
    he gave power to become children of God,
    to those who believe in his name,
  who were born not by natural generation
  nor by human choice nor by a man's decision
  but of God.
  And the Word became flesh
    and made his dwelling among us,
    and we saw his glory,
    the glory as of the Father's only Son,
    full of grace and truth.

FIRST READING

Isa 52:7-10

How beautiful upon the mountains
    are the feet of him who brings glad tidings,
announcing peace, bearing good news,
    announcing salvation, and saying to Zion,
    "Your God is King!"

Hark! Your sentinels raise a cry,
    together they shout for joy,
for they see directly, before their eyes,
    the LORD restoring Zion.
Break out together in song,
    O ruins of Jerusalem!
For the LORD comforts his people,
    he redeems Jerusalem.
The LORD has bared his holy arm
    in the sight of all the nations;
all the ends of the earth will behold
    the salvation of our God.

RESPONSORIAL PSALM

Ps 98:1, 2-3, 3-4, 5-6

R︎. (3c) All the ends of the earth have seen the saving power of God.

Sing to the LORD a new song,
    for he has done wondrous deeds;
his right hand has won victory for him,
    his holy arm.

R︎. All the ends of the earth have seen the saving power of God.

The LORD has made his salvation known:
    in the sight of the nations he has revealed
    his justice.
He has remembered his kindness and his
    faithfulness
    toward the house of Israel.

R︎. All the ends of the earth have seen the saving power of God.

All the ends of the earth have seen
    the salvation by our God.
Sing joyfully to the LORD, all you lands;
    break into song; sing praise.

R︎. All the ends of the earth have seen the saving power of God.

Sing praise to the LORD with the harp,
    with the harp and melodious song.
With trumpets and the sound of the horn
    sing joyfully before the King, the LORD.

R︎. All the ends of the earth have seen the saving power of God.

The Nativity of the Lord, December 25, 2012 (At the Mass during the Day)

SECOND READING
Heb 1:1-6

Brothers and sisters:
In times past, God spoke in partial and
    various ways
    to our ancestors through the prophets;
    in these last days, he has spoken to us
        through the Son,
    whom he made heir of all things
    and through whom he created the universe,
    who is the refulgence of his glory, the very
        imprint of his being,
    and who sustains all things by his
        mighty word.
When he had accomplished purification
    from sins,
he took his seat at the right hand of the
    Majesty on high,
as far superior to the angels
    as the name he has inherited is more
        excellent than theirs.

For to which of the angels did God ever say:
    You are my son; this day I have begotten
        you?
Or again:
    I will be a father to him, and he shall be a
        son to me?
And again, when he leads the firstborn into
    the world, he says:
    Let all the angels of God worship him.

The Holy Family of Jesus, Mary, and Joseph, December 30, 2012

Gospel (cont.)
Luke 2:41-52; L17C

When his parents saw him,
    they were astonished,
    and his mother said to him,
    "Son, why have you done this to us?
Your father and I have been looking for you
    with great anxiety."
And he said to them,
    "Why were you looking for me?
Did you not know that I must be in my
    Father's house?"
But they did not understand what he said to
    them.
He went down with them and came to
    Nazareth,
    and was obedient to them;
    and his mother kept all these things in her
       heart.
And Jesus advanced in wisdom and age and
    favor
    before God and man.

FIRST READING
Sir 3:2-6, 12-14

God sets a father in honor over his children;
    a mother's authority he confirms over her
       sons.
Whoever honors his father atones for sins,
    and preserves himself from them.
When he prays, he is heard;
    he stores up riches who reveres his mother.
Whoever honors his father is gladdened by
    children,
    and, when he prays, is heard.
Whoever reveres his father will live a long life;
    he who obeys his father brings comfort to
       his mother.

My son, take care of your father when he is old;
    grieve him not as long as he lives.
Even if his mind fail, be considerate of him;
    revile him not all the days of his life;
kindness to a father will not be forgotten,
    firmly planted against the debt of your sins
    —a house raised in justice to you.

RESPONSORIAL PSALM
Ps 128:1-2, 3, 4-5

R̸. (cf. 1) Blessed are those who fear the Lord
and walk in his ways.

Blessed is everyone who fears the LORD,
    who walks in his ways!
For you shall eat the fruit of your handiwork;
    blessed shall you be, and favored.

R̸. Blessed are those who fear the Lord and
walk in his ways.

Your wife shall be like a fruitful vine
    in the recesses of your home;
your children like olive plants
    around your table.

R̸. Blessed are those who fear the Lord and
walk in his ways.

Behold, thus is the man blessed
    who fears the LORD.
The LORD bless you from Zion:
    may you see the prosperity of Jerusalem
    all the days of your life.

R̸. Blessed are those who fear the Lord and
walk in his ways.

The Holy Family of Jesus, Mary, and Joseph, December 30, 2012

SECOND READING
Col 3:12-21

Brothers and sisters:
Put on, as God's chosen ones, holy and beloved,
    heartfelt compassion, kindness, humility,
        gentleness, and patience,
    bearing with one another and forgiving one
        another,
    if one has a grievance against another;
    as the Lord has forgiven you, so must you
        also do.
And over all these put on love,
    that is, the bond of perfection.
And let the peace of Christ control your hearts,
    the peace into which you were also called in
        one body.
And be thankful.
Let the word of Christ dwell in you richly,
    as in all wisdom you teach and admonish
        one another,

singing psalms, hymns, and spiritual songs
    with gratitude in your hearts to God.
And whatever you do, in word or in deed,
    do everything in the name of the Lord Jesus,
    giving thanks to God the Father through him.

Wives, be subordinate to your husbands,
    as is proper in the Lord.
Husbands, love your wives,
    and avoid any bitterness toward them.
Children, obey your parents in everything,
    for this is pleasing to the Lord.
Fathers, do not provoke your children,
    so they may not become discouraged.

or

Col 3:12-17

Brothers and sisters:
Put on, as God's chosen ones, holy and beloved,
    heartfelt compassion, kindness, humility,

gentleness, and patience,
    bearing with one another and forgiving one
        another,
    if one has a grievance against another;
    as the Lord has forgiven you, so must you
        also do.
And over all these put on love,
    that is, the bond of perfection.
And let the peace of Christ control your hearts,
    the peace into which you were also called in
        one body.
And be thankful.
Let the word of Christ dwell in you richly,
    as in all wisdom you teach and admonish
        one another,
    singing psalms, hymns, and spiritual songs
    with gratitude in your hearts to God.
And whatever you do, in word or in deed,
    do everything in the name of the Lord Jesus,
    giving thanks to God the Father through him.

Solemnity of the Blessed Virgin Mary, Mother of God, January 1, 2013

FIRST READING
Num 6:22-27

The LORD said to Moses:
    "Speak to Aaron and his sons and tell them:
    This is how you shall bless the Israelites.
Say to them:
    The LORD bless you and keep you!
    The LORD let his face shine upon
        you, and be gracious to you!
    The LORD look upon you kindly and
        give you peace!
So shall they invoke my name upon the
    Israelites,
    and I will bless them."

RESPONSORIAL PSALM
Ps 67:2-3, 5, 6, 8

℞. (2a) May God bless us in his mercy.

May God have pity on us and bless us;
    may he let his face shine upon us.
So may your way be known upon earth;
    among all nations, your salvation.

℞. May God bless us in his mercy.

May the nations be glad and exult
    because you rule the peoples in equity;
    the nations on the earth you guide.

℞. May God bless us in his mercy.

May the peoples praise you, O God;
    may all the peoples praise you!
May God bless us,
    and may all the ends of the earth fear him!

℞. May God bless us in his mercy.

SECOND READING
Gal 4:4-7

Brothers and sisters:
When the fullness of time had come, God sent
        his Son,
    born of a woman, born under the law,
    to ransom those under the law,
    so that we might receive adoption as sons.
As proof that you are sons,
    God sent the Spirit of his Son into our
        hearts,
    crying out, "Abba, Father!"
So you are no longer a slave but a son,
    and if a son then also an heir, through God.

The Epiphany of the Lord, January 6, 2013

Gospel (cont.)
Matt 2:1-12; L20ABC

And behold, the star that they had seen at its rising preceded them,
    until it came and stopped over the place where the child was.
They were overjoyed at seeing the star,
    and on entering the house
    they saw the child with Mary his mother.

They prostrated themselves and did him homage.
Then they opened their treasures
    and offered him gifts of gold, frankincense, and myrrh.
And having been warned in a dream not to return to Herod,
    they departed for their country by another way.

SECOND READING (cont.)
Titus 2:11-14; 3:4-7

When the kindness and generous love
  of God our savior appeared,
not because of any righteous deeds we had
    done
  but because of his mercy,
he saved us through the bath of rebirth
  and renewal by the Holy Spirit,
whom he richly poured out on us
  through Jesus Christ our savior,
so that we might be justified by his grace
  and become heirs in hope of eternal life.

or

FIRST READING
Isa 42:1-4, 6-7

Thus says the LORD:
Here is my servant whom I uphold,
  my chosen one with whom I am pleased,
upon whom I have put my spirit;
  he shall bring forth justice to the nations,
not crying out, not shouting,
  not making his voice heard in the street.
A bruised reed he shall not break,
  and a smoldering wick he shall not quench,
until he establishes justice on the earth;
  the coastlands will wait for his teaching.

I, the LORD, have called you for the victory of
    justice,
  I have grasped you by the hand;

I formed you, and set you
  as a covenant of the people,
  a light for the nations,
to open the eyes of the blind,
  to bring out prisoners from confinement,
  and from the dungeon, those who live in
    darkness.

RESPONSORIAL PSALM
Ps 29:1-2, 3-4, 3, 9-10

R̰. (11b) The Lord will bless his people with
peace.

Give to the LORD, you sons of God,
  give to the LORD glory and praise,
give to the LORD the glory due his name;
  adore the LORD in holy attire.

R̰. The Lord will bless his people with peace.

The voice of the LORD is over the waters,
  the LORD, over vast waters.
The voice of the LORD is mighty;
  the voice of the LORD is majestic.

R̰. The Lord will bless his people with peace.

The God of glory thunders,
  and in his temple all say, "Glory!"
The LORD is enthroned above the flood;
  the LORD is enthroned as king forever.

R̰. The Lord will bless his people with peace.

SECOND READING
Acts 10:34-38

Peter proceeded to speak to those gathered
  in the house of Cornelius, saying:
  "In truth, I see that God shows no
    partiality.
Rather, in every nation whoever fears him and
    acts uprightly
  is acceptable to him.
You know the word that he sent to the
    Israelites
  as he proclaimed peace through Jesus
    Christ, who is Lord of all,
what has happened all over Judea,
  beginning in Galilee after the baptism
  that John preached,
  how God anointed Jesus of Nazareth
  with the Holy Spirit and power.
He went about doing good
  and healing all those oppressed by the
    devil,
  for God was with him."

Third Sunday in Ordinary Time, January 27, 2013

Gospel (cont.)
Luke 1:1-4; 4:14-21; L69C

He has sent me to proclaim liberty to captives
  and recovery of sight to the blind,
  to let the oppressed go free,
  and to proclaim a year acceptable to the Lord.
Rolling up the scroll, he handed it back to the attendant and sat down,
  and the eyes of all in the synagogue looked intently at him.
He said to them,
  "Today this Scripture passage is fulfilled in your hearing."

Third Sunday in Ordinary Time, *January 27, 2013*

SECOND READING
1 Cor 12:12-30

Brothers and sisters:
As a body is one though it has many parts,
  and all the parts of the body, though many,
      are one body,
  so also Christ.
For in one Spirit we were all baptized into one
      body,
  whether Jews or Greeks, slaves or free
      persons,
  and we were all given to drink of one
      Spirit.

Now the body is not a single part, but many.
If a foot should say,
  "Because I am not a hand I do not belong to
      the body,"
  it does not for this reason belong any less
      to the body.
Or if an ear should say,
  "Because I am not an eye I do not belong to
      the body,"
  it does not for this reason belong any less
      to the body.
If the whole body were an eye, where would
the hearing be?
If the whole body were hearing, where would
      the sense of smell be?
But as it is, God placed the parts,
  each one of them, in the body as he
      intended.
If they were all one part, where would the
      body be?
But as it is, there are many parts, yet one
      body.
The eye cannot say to the hand, "I do not need
      you,"
  nor again the head to the feet, "I do not
      need you."
Indeed, the parts of the body that seem to be
      weaker
  are all the more necessary,
  and those parts of the body that we
      consider less honorable
  we surround with greater honor,
  and our less presentable parts are treated
      with greater propriety,
  whereas our more presentable parts do not
      need this.
But God has so constructed the body
  as to give greater honor to a part that is
without it,
  so that there may be no division in the
      body,
  but that the parts may have the same
      concern for one another.
If one part suffers, all the parts suffer with it;
  if one part is honored, all the parts share
      its joy.

Now you are Christ's body, and individually
      parts of it.
Some people God has designated in the
      church
  to be, first, apostles; second, prophets;
      third, teachers;
  then, mighty deeds;
  then gifts of healing, assistance,
      administration,
  and varieties of tongues.
Are all apostles? Are all prophets? Are all
      teachers?
Do all work mighty deeds? Do all have gifts
      of healing?
Do all speak in tongues? Do all interpret?

Fourth Sunday in Ordinary Time, *February 3, 2013*

SECOND READING
1 Cor 12:31–13:13

Brothers and sisters:
Strive eagerly for the greatest spiritual gifts.
But I shall show you a still more excellent way.

If I speak in human and angelic tongues,
  but do not have love,
  I am a resounding gong or a clashing cymbal.
And if I have the gift of prophecy,
  and comprehend all mysteries and all
      knowledge;
  if I have all faith so as to move mountains,
  but do not have love, I am nothing.
If I give away everything I own,
  and if I hand my body over so that I may
      boast,
  but do not have love, I gain nothing.

Love is patient, love is kind.
It is not jealous, it is not pompous,
  it is not inflated, it is not rude,
  it does not seek its own interests,
  it is not quick-tempered, it does not brood
      over injury,
  it does not rejoice over wrongdoing
  but rejoices with the truth.
It bears all things, believes all things,
  hopes all things, endures all things.

Love never fails.
If there are prophecies, they will be brought
      to nothing;
  if tongues, they will cease;
  if knowledge, it will be brought to
      nothing.
For we know partially and we prophesy
      partially,
but when the perfect comes, the partial will
      pass away.
When I was a child, I used to talk as a child,
  think as a child, reason as a child;
  when I became a man, I put aside childish
      things.
At present we see indistinctly, as in a mirror,
  but then face to face.
At present I know partially;
  then I shall know fully, as I am fully known.
So faith, hope, love remain, these three;
  but the greatest of these is love.

Gospel (cont.)
Luke 5:1-11; L75C

When Simon Peter saw this, he fell at the knees of Jesus and said,
    "Depart from me, Lord, for I am a sinful man."
For astonishment at the catch of fish they had made seized him
    and all those with him,
        and likewise James and John, the sons of Zebedee,
        who were partners of Simon.
Jesus said to Simon, "Do not be afraid;
    from now on you will be catching men."
When they brought their boats to the shore,
    they left everything and followed him.

SECOND READING
1 Cor 15:1-11

I am reminding you, brothers and sisters,
    of the gospel I preached to you,
        which you indeed received and in which
            you also stand.
Through it you are also being saved,
    if you hold fast to the word I preached to
        you,
    unless you believed in vain.
For I handed on to you as of first importance
        what I also received:
    that Christ died for our sins
        in accordance with the Scriptures;
    that he was buried;
    that he was raised on the third day
        in accordance with the Scriptures;
    that he appeared to Cephas, then to the
        Twelve.

After that, he appeared to more
        than five hundred brothers at once,
    most of whom are still living,
        though some have fallen asleep.
After that he appeared to James,
    then to all the apostles.
Last of all, as to one born abnormally,
    he appeared to me.
For I am the least of the apostles,
    not fit to be called an apostle,
        because I persecuted the church of God.
But by the grace of God I am what I am,
    and his grace to me has not been
        ineffective.
Indeed, I have toiled harder than all of them;
    not I, however, but the grace of God that is
        with me.
Therefore, whether it be I or they,
    so we preach and so you believed.

Ash Wednesday, *February 13, 2013*

FIRST READING
Joel 2:12-18

Even now, says the LORD,
  return to me with your whole heart,
  with fasting, and weeping, and mourning;
Rend your hearts, not your garments,
  and return to the LORD, your God.
For gracious and merciful is he,
  slow to anger, rich in kindness,
  and relenting in punishment.
Perhaps he will again relent
  and leave behind him a blessing,
Offerings and libations
  for the LORD, your God.

Blow the trumpet in Zion!
  proclaim a fast,
  call an assembly;
Gather the people,
  notify the congregation;
Assemble the elders,
  gather the children
  and the infants at the breast;
Let the bridegroom quit his room
  and the bride her chamber.
Between the porch and the altar
  let the priests, the ministers of the LORD,
    weep,
And say, "Spare, O LORD, your people,
  and make not your heritage a reproach,
  with the nations ruling over them!
Why should they say among the peoples,
  'Where is their God?'"

Then the LORD was stirred to concern for his
    land
  and took pity on his people.

RESPONSORIAL PSALM
Ps 51:3-4, 5-6ab, 12-13, 14, and 17

R̸. (see 3a) Be merciful, O Lord, for we have
sinned.

Have mercy on me, O God, in your goodness;
  in the greatness of your compassion wipe
    out my offense.
Thoroughly wash me from my guilt
  and of my sin cleanse me.

R̸. Be merciful, O Lord, for we have sinned.

For I acknowledge my offense,
  and my sin is before me always:
"Against you only have I sinned,
  and done what is evil in your sight."

R̸. Be merciful, O Lord, for we have sinned.

A clean heart create for me, O God,
  and a steadfast spirit renew within me.
Cast me not out from your presence,
  and your Holy Spirit take not from me.

R̸. Be merciful, O Lord, for we have sinned.

Give me back the joy of your salvation,
  and a willing spirit sustain in me.
O LORD, open my lips,
  and my mouth shall proclaim your praise.

R̸. Be merciful, O Lord, for we have sinned.

SECOND READING
2 Cor 5:20–6:2

Brothers and sisters:
We are ambassadors for Christ,
  as if God were appealing through us.
We implore you on behalf of Christ,
  be reconciled to God.
For our sake he made him to be sin who did
    not know sin,
  so that we might become the righteousness
    of God in him.

Working together, then,
  we appeal to you not to receive the grace of
    God in vain.
For he says:

  In an acceptable time I heard you,
    and on the day of salvation I helped you.

Behold, now is a very acceptable time;
  behold, now is the day of salvation.

First Sunday of Lent, *February 17, 2013*

SECOND READING
Rom 10:8-13

Brothers and sisters:
What does Scripture say?
  The word is near you,
    in your mouth and in your heart
  —that is, the word of faith that we preach—,
  for, if you confess with your mouth that Jesus is Lord
  and believe in your heart that God raised him from the dead,
  you will be saved.
For one believes with the heart and so is justified,
  and one confesses with the mouth and so is saved.
For the Scripture says,
  No one who believes in him will be put to shame.
For there is no distinction between Jew and Greek;
  the same Lord is Lord of all,
  enriching all who call upon him.
For "everyone who calls on the name of the Lord will be saved."

Second Sunday of Lent, *February 24, 2013*

SECOND READING
Phil 3:20–4:1

Brothers and sisters:
Our citizenship is in heaven,
  and from it we also await a savior, the Lord Jesus Christ.
He will change our lowly body
  to conform with his glorified body
  by the power that enables him also
  to bring all things into subjection to himself.

Therefore, my brothers and sisters,
  whom I love and long for, my joy and crown,
  in this way stand firm in the Lord, beloved.

SECOND READING

1 Cor 10:1-6, 10-12

I do not want you to be unaware, brothers and
    sisters,
    that our ancestors were all under the cloud
    and all passed through the sea,
    and all of them were baptized into Moses
    in the cloud and in the sea.
All ate the same spiritual food,
    and all drank the same spiritual drink,
    for they drank from a spiritual rock that
        followed them,
    and the rock was the Christ.
Yet God was not pleased with most of them,
    for they were struck down in the desert.

These things happened as examples for us,
    so that we might not desire evil things, as
        they did.
Do not grumble as some of them did,
    and suffered death by the destroyer.
These things happened to them as an
        example,
    and they have been written down as a
        warning to us,
    upon whom the end of the ages has come.
Therefore, whoever thinks he is standing
      secure
    should take care not to fall.

Gospel

John 4:5-15, 19b-26, 39a, 40-42; L28A

Jesus came to a town of Samaria called Sychar,
    near the plot of land that Jacob had given to his son Joseph.
Jacob's well was there.
Jesus, tired from his journey, sat down there at the well.
It was about noon.

A woman of Samaria came to draw water.
Jesus said to her,
    "Give me a drink."
His disciples had gone into the town to buy food.
The Samaritan woman said to him,
    "How can you, a Jew, ask me, a Samaritan woman, for a drink?"
—For Jews use nothing in common with Samaritans.—
Jesus answered and said to her,
    "If you knew the gift of God
    and who is saying to you, 'Give me a drink,'
    you would have asked him
    and he would have given you living water."
The woman said to him,
    "Sir, you do not even have a bucket and the cistern is deep;
    where then can you get this living water?
Are you greater than our father Jacob,
    who gave us this cistern and drank from it himself
    with his children and his flocks?"
Jesus answered and said to her,
    "Everyone who drinks this water will be thirsty again;
    but whoever drinks the water I shall give will never thirst;
    the water I shall give will become in him
    a spring of water welling up to eternal life."
The woman said to him,
    "Sir, give me this water, so that I may not be thirsty
    or have to keep coming here to draw water.

"I can see that you are a prophet.
Our ancestors worshiped on this mountain;
    but you people say that the place to worship is in Jerusalem."
Jesus said to her,
    "Believe me, woman, the hour is coming
    when you will worship the Father
    neither on this mountain nor in Jerusalem.
You people worship what you do not understand;
    we worship what we understand,
    because salvation is from the Jews.
But the hour is coming, and is now here,
    when true worshipers will worship the Father in Spirit and truth;
    and indeed the Father seeks such people to worship him.
God is Spirit, and those who worship him
    must worship in Spirit and truth."
The woman said to him,
    "I know that the Messiah is coming, the one called the Christ;
    when he comes, he will tell us everything."
Jesus said to her,
    "I am he, the one who is speaking with you."

Many of the Samaritans of that town began to believe in him.
When the Samaritans came to him,
    they invited him to stay with them;
    and he stayed there two days.
Many more began to believe in him because of his word,
    and they said to the woman,
    "We no longer believe because of your word;
    for we have heard for ourselves,
    and we know that this is truly the savior of the world."

Gospel
John 4:5-42; L28A

Jesus came to a town of Samaria called Sychar,
  near the plot of land that Jacob had given to his son Joseph.
Jacob's well was there.
Jesus, tired from his journey, sat down there at the well.
It was about noon.

A woman of Samaria came to draw water.
Jesus said to her,
  "Give me a drink."
His disciples had gone into the town to buy food.
The Samaritan woman said to him,
  "How can you, a Jew, ask me, a Samaritan woman, for a drink?"
—For Jews use nothing in common with Samaritans.—
Jesus answered and said to her,
  "If you knew the gift of God
  and who is saying to you, 'Give me a drink,'
  you would have asked him
  and he would have given you living water."
The woman said to him,
  "Sir, you do not even have a bucket and the cistern is deep;
  where then can you get this living water?
Are you greater than our father Jacob,
  who gave us this cistern and drank from it himself
  with his children and his flocks?"
Jesus answered and said to her,
  "Everyone who drinks this water will be thirsty again;
  but whoever drinks the water I shall give will never thirst;
  the water I shall give will become in him
  a spring of water welling up to eternal life."
The woman said to him,
  "Sir, give me this water, so that I may not be thirsty
  or have to keep coming here to draw water."

Jesus said to her,
  "Go call your husband and come back."
The woman answered and said to him,
  "I do not have a husband."
Jesus answered her,
  "You are right in saying, 'I do not have a husband.'
For you have had five husbands,
  and the one you have now is not your husband.
What you have said is true."
The woman said to him,
  "Sir, I can see that you are a prophet.
Our ancestors worshiped on this mountain;
  but you people say that the place to worship is in Jerusalem."
Jesus said to her,
  "Believe me, woman, the hour is coming
  when you will worship the Father
  neither on this mountain nor in Jerusalem.
You people worship what you do not understand;
  we worship what we understand,
  because salvation is from the Jews.

But the hour is coming, and is now here,
  when true worshipers will worship the Father in Spirit and truth;
  and indeed the Father seeks such people to worship him.
God is Spirit, and those who worship him
  must worship in Spirit and truth."
The woman said to him,
  "I know that the Messiah is coming, the one called the Christ;
  when he comes, he will tell us everything."
Jesus said to her,
  "I am he, the one who is speaking with you."

At that moment his disciples returned,
  and were amazed that he was talking with a woman,
  but still no one said, "What are you looking for?"
  or "Why are you talking with her?"
The woman left her water jar
  and went into the town and said to the people,
  "Come see a man who told me everything I have done.
Could he possibly be the Christ?"
They went out of the town and came to him.
Meanwhile, the disciples urged him, "Rabbi, eat."
But he said to them,
  "I have food to eat of which you do not know."
So the disciples said to one another,
  "Could someone have brought him something to eat?"
Jesus said to them,
  "My food is to do the will of the one who sent me
  and to finish his work.
Do you not say, 'In four months the harvest will be here'?
I tell you, look up and see the fields ripe for the harvest.
The reaper is already receiving payment
  and gathering crops for eternal life,
  so that the sower and reaper can rejoice together.
For here the saying is verified that 'One sows and another reaps.'
I sent you to reap what you have not worked for;
  others have done the work,
  and you are sharing the fruits of their work."

Many of the Samaritans of that town began to believe in him
  because of the word of the woman who testified,
  "He told me everything I have done."
When the Samaritans came to him,
  they invited him to stay with them;
  and he stayed there two days.
Many more began to believe in him because of his word,
  and they said to the woman,
  "We no longer believe because of your word;
  for we have heard for ourselves,
  and we know that this is truly the savior of the world."

Third Sunday of Lent, *March 3, 2013*

FIRST READING
Exod 17:3-7

In those days, in their thirst for water,
    the people grumbled against Moses,
    saying, "Why did you ever make us leave
        Egypt?
Was it just to have us die here of thirst
    with our children and our livestock?"
So Moses cried out to the LORD,
    "What shall I do with this people?
A little more and they will stone me!"
The LORD answered Moses,
    "Go over there in front of the people,
    along with some of the elders of Israel,
    holding in your hand, as you go,
    the staff with which you struck the river.
I will be standing there in front of you on the
        rock in Horeb.
Strike the rock, and the water will flow from it
    for the people to drink."
This Moses did, in the presence of the elders
    of Israel.
The place was called Massah and Meribah,
    because the Israelites quarreled there
    and tested the LORD, saying,
    "Is the LORD in our midst or not?"

RESPONSORIAL PSALM
Ps 95:1-2, 6-7, 8-9

R̸. (8) If today you hear his voice, harden not
your hearts.

Come, let us sing joyfully to the LORD;
    let us acclaim the Rock of our salvation.
Let us come into his presence with
        thanksgiving;
    let us joyfully sing psalms to him.

R̸. If today you hear his voice, harden not
your hearts.

Come, let us bow down in worship;
    let us kneel before the LORD who made us.
For he is our God,
    and we are the people he shepherds, the
        flock he guides.

R̸. If today you hear his voice, harden not
your hearts.

Oh, that today you would hear his voice:
    "Harden not your hearts as at Meribah,
    as in the day of Massah in the desert,
where your fathers tempted me;
    they tested me though they had seen my
        works."

R̸. If today you hear his voice, harden not
your hearts.

SECOND READING
Rom 5:1-2, 5-8

Brothers and sisters:
Since we have been justified by faith,
    we have peace with God through our Lord
        Jesus Christ,
    through whom we have gained access by
        faith
    to this grace in which we stand,
    and we boast in hope of the glory of God.

And hope does not disappoint,
    because the love of God has been poured
        out into our hearts
    through the Holy Spirit who has been given
        to us.
For Christ, while we were still helpless,
    died at the appointed time for the ungodly.
Indeed, only with difficulty does one die for a
        just person,
    though perhaps for a good person one
        might even find courage to die.
But God proves his love for us
    in that while we were still sinners Christ
        died for us.

Fourth Sunday of Lent, *March 10, 2013*

Gospel (cont.)
Luke 15:1-3, 11-32; L33C

I no longer deserve to be called your son;
    treat me as you would treat one of your hired workers.'"
So he got up and went back to his father.
While he was still a long way off,
    his father caught sight of him, and was filled with compassion.
He ran to his son, embraced him and kissed him.
His son said to him,
    'Father, I have sinned against heaven and against you;
    I no longer deserve to be called your son.'
But his father ordered his servants,
    'Quickly bring the finest robe and put it on him;
    put a ring on his finger and sandals on his feet.
Take the fattened calf and slaughter it.
Then let us celebrate with a feast,
    because this son of mine was dead, and has come to life again;
    he was lost, and has been found.'
Then the celebration began.
Now the older son had been out in the field
    and, on his way back, as he neared the house,
    he heard the sound of music and dancing.
He called one of the servants and asked what this might mean.

The servant said to him,
    'Your brother has returned
    and your father has slaughtered the fattened calf
    because he has him back safe and sound.'
He became angry,
    and when he refused to enter the house,
    his father came out and pleaded with him.
He said to his father in reply,
    'Look, all these years I served you
    and not once did I disobey your orders;
    yet you never gave me even a young goat to feast on with
        my friends.
But when your son returns
    who swallowed up your property with prostitutes,
    for him you slaughter the fattened calf.'
He said to him,
    'My son, you are here with me always;
    everything I have is yours.
But now we must celebrate and rejoice,
    because your brother was dead and has come to life again;
    he was lost and has been found.'"

Gospel
John 9:1-41; L31A

As Jesus passed by he saw a man blind from birth.
His disciples asked him,
 "Rabbi, who sinned, this man or his parents,
 that he was born blind?"
Jesus answered,
 "Neither he nor his parents sinned;
 it is so that the works of God might be made visible through him.
We have to do the works of the one who sent me while it is day.
Night is coming when no one can work.
While I am in the world, I am the light of the world."
When he had said this, he spat on the ground
 and made clay with the saliva,
 and smeared the clay on his eyes, and said to him,
 "Go wash in the Pool of Siloam"—which means Sent—.
So he went and washed, and came back able to see.

His neighbors and those who had seen him earlier as a beggar said,
 "Isn't this the one who used to sit and beg?"
Some said, "It is,"
 but others said, "No, he just looks like him."
He said, "I am."
So they said to him, "How were your eyes opened?"
He replied,
 "The man called Jesus made clay and anointed my eyes
 and told me, 'Go to Siloam and wash.'
So I went there and washed and was able to see."
And they said to him, "Where is he?"
He said, "I don't know."

They brought the one who was once blind to the Pharisees.
Now Jesus had made clay and opened his eyes on a sabbath.
So then the Pharisees also asked him how he was able to see.
He said to them,
 "He put clay on my eyes, and I washed, and now I can see."
So some of the Pharisees said,
 "This man is not from God,
 because he does not keep the sabbath."
But others said,
 "How can a sinful man do such signs?"
And there was a division among them.
So they said to the blind man again,
 "What do you have to say about him,
 since he opened your eyes?"
He said, "He is a prophet."

Now the Jews did not believe
 that he had been blind and gained his sight
 until they summoned the parents of the one who had gained his
 sight.
They asked them,
 "Is this your son, who you say was born blind?
How does he now see?"
His parents answered and said,
 "We know that this is our son and that he was born blind.
We do not know how he sees now,
 nor do we know who opened his eyes.
Ask him, he is of age;
 he can speak for himself."

His parents said this because they were afraid of the Jews,
 for the Jews had already agreed
 that if anyone acknowledged him as the Christ,
 he would be expelled from the synagogue.
For this reason his parents said,
 "He is of age; question him."

So a second time they called the man who had been blind
 and said to him, "Give God the praise!
We know that this man is a sinner."
He replied,
 "If he is a sinner, I do not know.
One thing I do know is that I was blind and now I see."
So they said to him,
 "What did he do to you?
How did he open your eyes?"
He answered them,
 "I told you already and you did not listen.
Why do you want to hear it again?
Do you want to become his disciples, too?"
They ridiculed him and said,
 "You are that man's disciple;
 we are disciples of Moses!
We know that God spoke to Moses,
 but we do not know where this one is from."
The man answered and said to them,
 "This is what is so amazing,
 that you do not know where he is from, yet he opened my eyes.
We know that God does not listen to sinners,
 but if one is devout and does his will, he listens to him.
It is unheard of that anyone ever opened the eyes of a person born
 blind.
If this man were not from God,
 he would not be able to do anything."
They answered and said to him,
 "You were born totally in sin,
 and are you trying to teach us?"
Then they threw him out.

When Jesus heard that they had thrown him out,
 he found him and said, "Do you believe in the Son of Man?"
He answered and said,
 "Who is he, sir, that I may believe in him?"
Jesus said to him,
 "You have seen him,
 and the one speaking with you is he."
He said,
 "I do believe, Lord," and he worshiped him.
Then Jesus said,
 "I came into this world for judgment,
 so that those who do not see might see,
 and those who do see might become blind."

Some of the Pharisees who were with him heard this
 and said to him, "Surely we are not also blind, are we?"
Jesus said to them,
 "If you were blind, you would have no sin;
 but now you are saying, 'We see,' so your sin remains."

Gospel

John 9:1, 6-9, 13-17, 34-38; L31A

As Jesus passed by he saw a man blind from birth.
He spat on the ground and made clay with the saliva,
  and smeared the clay on his eyes, and said to him,
  "Go wash in the Pool of Siloam"—which means Sent—.
So he went and washed, and came back able to see.

His neighbors and those who had seen him earlier as a beggar said,
  "Isn't this the one who used to sit and beg?"
Some said, "It is,"
  but others said, "No, he just looks like him."
He said, "I am."

They brought the one who was once blind to the Pharisees.
Now Jesus had made clay and opened his eyes on a sabbath.
So then the Pharisees also asked him how he was able to see.
He said to them,
  "He put clay on my eyes, and I washed, and now I can see."
So some of the Pharisees said,
  "This man is not from God,
  because he does not keep the sabbath."
But others said,
  "How can a sinful man do such signs?"

And there was a division among them.
So they said to the blind man again,
  "What do you have to say about him,
  since he opened your eyes?"
He said, "He is a prophet."

They answered and said to him,
  "You were born totally in sin,
  and are you trying to teach us?"
Then they threw him out.

When Jesus heard that they had thrown him out,
  he found him and said, "Do you believe in the Son of Man?"
He answered and said,
  "Who is he, sir, that I may believe in him?"
Jesus said to him,
  "You have seen him,
  and the one speaking with you is he."
He said,
  "I do believe, Lord," and he worshiped him.

FIRST READING   1 Sam 16:1b, 6-7, 10-13a

The LORD said to Samuel:
  "Fill your horn with oil, and be on your way.
I am sending you to Jesse of Bethlehem,
  for I have chosen my king from among his
    sons."

As Jesse and his sons came to the sacrifice,
  Samuel looked at Eliab and thought,
  "Surely the LORD's anointed is here before
    him."
But the LORD said to Samuel:
  "Do not judge from his appearance or from
    his lofty stature,
  because I have rejected him.
Not as man sees does God see,
  because man sees the appearance
  but the LORD looks into the heart."
In the same way Jesse presented seven sons
    before Samuel,
  but Samuel said to Jesse,
  "The LORD has not chosen any one of these."
Then Samuel asked Jesse,
  "Are these all the sons you have?"
Jesse replied,
  "There is still the youngest, who is tending
    the sheep."
Samuel said to Jesse,
  "Send for him;
  we will not begin the sacrificial banquet
    until he arrives here."
Jesse sent and had the young man brought to
    them.
He was ruddy, a youth handsome to behold
  and making a splendid appearance.

The LORD said,
  "There—anoint him, for this is the one!"
Then Samuel, with the horn of oil in hand,
  anointed David in the presence of his
    brothers;
  and from that day on, the spirit of the LORD
    rushed upon David.

RESPONSORIAL PSALM   Ps 23:1-3a, 3b-4, 5, 6

R͡. (1) The Lord is my shepherd; there is nothing I shall want.

The LORD is my shepherd; I shall not want.
  In verdant pastures he gives me repose;
beside restful waters he leads me;
  he refreshes my soul.

R͡. The Lord is my shepherd; there is nothing
I shall want.

He guides me in right paths
  for his name's sake.
Even though I walk in the dark valley
  I fear no evil; for you are at my side
with your rod and your staff
  that give me courage.

R͡. The Lord is my shepherd; there is nothing
I shall want.

You spread the table before me
  in the sight of my foes;
you anoint my head with oil;
  my cup overflows.

R͡. The Lord is my shepherd; there is nothing
I shall want.

Only goodness and kindness follow me
  all the days of my life;
and I shall dwell in the house of the LORD
  for years to come.

R͡. The Lord is my shepherd; there is nothing
I shall want.

SECOND READING
Eph 5:8-14

Brothers and sisters:
You were once darkness,
  but now you are light in the Lord.
Live as children of light,
  for light produces every kind of goodness
  and righteousness and truth.
Try to learn what is pleasing to the Lord.
Take no part in the fruitless works of
    darkness;
  rather expose them, for it is shameful even
    to mention
  the things done by them in secret;
  but everything exposed by the light
    becomes visible,
  for everything that becomes visible is light.
Therefore, it says:
  "Awake, O sleeper,
  and arise from the dead,
  and Christ will give you light."

Fifth Sunday of Lent, *March 17, 2013*

Gospel

John 11:1-45; L34A

Now a man was ill, Lazarus from Bethany,
  the village of Mary and her sister Martha.
Mary was the one who had anointed the Lord with perfumed oil
  and dried his feet with her hair;
  it was her brother Lazarus who was ill.
So the sisters sent word to Jesus saying,
  "Master, the one you love is ill."
When Jesus heard this he said,
  "This illness is not to end in death,
  but is for the glory of God,
  that the Son of God may be glorified through it."
Now Jesus loved Martha and her sister and Lazarus.
So when he heard that he was ill,
  he remained for two days in the place where he was.
Then after this he said to his disciples,
  "Let us go back to Judea."
The disciples said to him,
  "Rabbi, the Jews were just trying to stone you,
  and you want to go back there?"
Jesus answered,
  "Are there not twelve hours in a day?
If one walks during the day, he does not stumble,
  because he sees the light of this world.
But if one walks at night, he stumbles,
  because the light is not in him."
He said this, and then told them,
  "Our friend Lazarus is asleep,
  but I am going to awaken him."
So the disciples said to him,
  "Master, if he is asleep, he will be saved."
But Jesus was talking about his death,
  while they thought that he meant ordinary sleep.
So then Jesus said to them clearly,
  "Lazarus has died.
And I am glad for you that I was not there,
  that you may believe.
Let us go to him."
So Thomas, called Didymus, said to his fellow disciples,
  "Let us also go to die with him."

When Jesus arrived, he found that Lazarus
  had already been in the tomb for four days.
Now Bethany was near Jerusalem, only about two miles away.
And many of the Jews had come to Martha and Mary
  to comfort them about their brother.
When Martha heard that Jesus was coming,
  she went to meet him;
  but Mary sat at home.
Martha said to Jesus,
  "Lord, if you had been here,
  my brother would not have died.
But even now I know that whatever you ask of God,
  God will give you."
Jesus said to her,
  "Your brother will rise."
Martha said to him,
  "I know he will rise,
  in the resurrection on the last day."
Jesus told her,

"I am the resurrection and the life;
  whoever believes in me, even if he dies, will live,
  and everyone who lives and believes in me will never die.
Do you believe this?"
She said to him, "Yes, Lord.
I have come to believe that you are the Christ, the Son of God,
  the one who is coming into the world."

When she had said this,
  she went and called her sister Mary secretly, saying,
  "The teacher is here and is asking for you."
As soon as she heard this,
  she rose quickly and went to him.
For Jesus had not yet come into the village,
  but was still where Martha had met him.
So when the Jews who were with her in the house comforting her
  saw Mary get up quickly and go out,
  they followed her,
  presuming that she was going to the tomb to weep there.
When Mary came to where Jesus was and saw him,
  she fell at his feet and said to him,
  "Lord, if you had been here,
  my brother would not have died."
When Jesus saw her weeping and the Jews who had come with her
    weeping,
  he became perturbed and deeply troubled, and said,
  "Where have you laid him?"
They said to him, "Sir, come and see."
And Jesus wept.
So the Jews said, "See how he loved him."
But some of them said,
  "Could not the one who opened the eyes of the blind man
  have done something so that this man would not have died?"

So Jesus, perturbed again, came to the tomb.
It was a cave, and a stone lay across it.
Jesus said, "Take away the stone."
Martha, the dead man's sister, said to him,
  "Lord, by now there will be a stench;
  he has been dead for four days."
Jesus said to her,
  "Did I not tell you that if you believe
  you will see the glory of God?"
So they took away the stone.
And Jesus raised his eyes and said,
  "Father, I thank you for hearing me.
I know that you always hear me;
  but because of the crowd here I have said this,
  that they may believe that you sent me."
And when he had said this,
  he cried out in a loud voice,
  "Lazarus, come out!"
The dead man came out,
  tied hand and foot with burial bands,
  and his face was wrapped in a cloth.
So Jesus said to them,
  "Untie him and let him go."

Now many of the Jews who had come to Mary
  and seen what he had done began to believe in him.

Gospel

John 11:3-7, 17, 20-27, 33b-45; L34A

The sisters of Lazarus sent word to Jesus, saying,
   "Master, the one you love is ill."
When Jesus heard this he said,
   "This illness is not to end in death,
   but is for the glory of God,
   that the Son of God may be glorified through it."
Now Jesus loved Martha and her sister and Lazarus.
So when he heard that he was ill,
   he remained for two days in the place where he was.
Then after this he said to his disciples,
   "Let us go back to Judea."

When Jesus arrived, he found that Lazarus
   had already been in the tomb for four days.
When Martha heard that Jesus was coming,
   she went to meet him;
   but Mary sat at home.
Martha said to Jesus,
   "Lord, if you had been here,
   my brother would not have died.
But even now I know that whatever you ask of God,
   God will give you."
Jesus said to her,
   "Your brother will rise."
Martha said,
   "I know he will rise,
   in the resurrection on the last day."
Jesus told her,
   "I am the resurrection and the life;
   whoever believes in me, even if he dies, will live,
   and everyone who lives and believes in me will never die.
Do you believe this?"
She said to him, "Yes, Lord.
I have come to believe that you are the Christ, the Son of God,
   the one who is coming into the world."

He became perturbed and deeply troubled, and said,
   "Where have you laid him?"
They said to him, "Sir, come and see."
And Jesus wept.
So the Jews said, "See how he loved him."
But some of them said,
   "Could not the one who opened the eyes of the blind man
   have done something so that this man would not have died?"

So Jesus, perturbed again, came to the tomb.
It was a cave, and a stone lay across it.
Jesus said, "Take away the stone."
Martha, the dead man's sister, said to him,
   "Lord, by now there will be a stench;
   he has been dead for four days."
Jesus said to her,
   "Did I not tell you that if you believe
   you will see the glory of God?"
So they took away the stone.
And Jesus raised his eyes and said,
   "Father, I thank you for hearing me.
I know that you always hear me;
   but because of the crowd here I have said this,
   that they may believe that you sent me."
And when he had said this,
   he cried out in a loud voice,
   "Lazarus, come out!"
The dead man came out,
   tied hand and foot with burial bands,
   and his face was wrapped in a cloth.
So Jesus said to them,
   "Untie him and let him go."

Now many of the Jews who had come to Mary
   and seen what he had done began to believe in him.

FIRST READING
Ezek 37:12-14

Thus says the Lord GOD:
 O my people, I will open your graves
 and have you rise from them,
 and bring you back to the land of Israel.
Then you shall know that I am the LORD,
 when I open your graves and have you rise
 from them,
 O my people!
I will put my spirit in you that you may live,
 and I will settle you upon your land;
 thus you shall know that I am the LORD.
I have promised, and I will do it, says the
 LORD.

RESPONSORIAL PSALM
Ps 130:1-2, 3-4, 5-6, 7-8

R̠. (7) With the Lord there is mercy and fullness of redemption.

Out of the depths I cry to you, O LORD;
 LORD, hear my voice!
Let your ears be attentive
 to my voice in supplication.

R̠. With the Lord there is mercy and fullness
of redemption.

If you, O LORD, mark iniquities,
 LORD, who can stand?
But with you is forgiveness,
 that you may be revered.

R̠. With the Lord there is mercy and fullness
of redemption.

I trust in the LORD;
 my soul trusts in his word.
More than sentinels wait for the dawn,
 let Israel wait for the LORD.

R̠. With the Lord there is mercy and fullness
of redemption.

For with the LORD is kindness
 and with him is plenteous redemption;
and he will redeem Israel
 from all their iniquities.

R̠. With the Lord there is mercy and fullness
of redemption.

SECOND READING
Rom 8:8-11

Brothers and sisters:
Those who are in the flesh cannot please God.
But you are not in the flesh;
 on the contrary, you are in the spirit,
 if only the Spirit of God dwells in you.
Whoever does not have the Spirit of Christ
 does not belong to him.
But if Christ is in you,
 although the body is dead because of sin,
 the spirit is alive because of righteousness.
If the Spirit of the One who raised Jesus from
 the dead dwells in you,
 the One who raised Christ from the dead
 will give life to your mortal bodies also,
 through his Spirit dwelling in you.

Gospel
Matt 1:16, 18-21, 24a; L543

Jacob was the father of Joseph, the husband of Mary.
Of her was born Jesus who is called the Christ.

Now this is how the birth of Jesus Christ came about.
When his mother Mary was betrothed to Joseph,
   but before they lived together,
   she was found with child through the Holy Spirit.
Joseph her husband, since he was a righteous man,
   yet unwilling to expose her to shame,
   decided to divorce her quietly.
Such was his intention when, behold,
   the angel of the Lord appeared to him in a dream and said,
   "Joseph, son of David,
   do not be afraid to take Mary your wife into your home.
For it is through the Holy Spirit
   that this child has been conceived in her.
She will bear a son and you are to name him Jesus,
   because he will save his people from their sins."
When Joseph awoke,
   he did as the angel of the Lord had commanded him
   and took his wife into his home.

FIRST READING
2 Sam 7:4-5a, 12-14a, 16

The LORD spoke to Nathan and said:
"Go, tell my servant David,
   'When your time comes and you rest with
      your ancestors,
   I will raise up your heir after you, sprung
      from your loins,
   and I will make his kingdom firm.
It is he who shall build a house for my name.
And I will make his royal throne firm forever.
I will be a father to him,
   and he shall be a son to me.
Your house and your kingdom shall endure
     forever before me;
   your throne shall stand firm forever.'"

RESPONSORIAL PSALM
Ps 89:2-3, 4-5, 27, and 29

R℣. (37) The son of David will live forever.

The promises of the LORD I will sing forever,
   through all generations my mouth will
      proclaim your faithfulness,
For you have said, "My kindness is
     established forever";
   in heaven you have confirmed your
     faithfulness.

R℣. The son of David will live forever.

"I have made a covenant with my chosen one;
   I have sworn to David my servant:
Forever will I confirm your posterity
   and establish your throne for all
     generations."

R℣. The son of David will live forever.

"He shall say of me, 'You are my father,
   my God, the Rock, my savior!'
Forever I will maintain my kindness toward
     him,
   my covenant with him stands firm."

R℣. The son of David will live forever.

SECOND READING
Rom 4:13, 16-18, 22

Brothers and sisters:
It was not through the law
   that the promise was made to Abraham
     and his descendants
   that he would inherit the world,
   but through the righteousness that comes
     from faith.
For this reason, it depends on faith,
   so that it may be a gift,
   and the promise may be guaranteed to all
     his descendants,
   not to those who only adhere to the law
   but to those who follow the faith of Abraham,
   who is the father of all of us, as it is written,
I have made you father of many nations.
He is our father in the sight of God,
   in whom he believed, who gives life to the
     dead
   and calls into being what does not exist.
He believed, hoping against hope,
   that he would become *the father of many*
     nations,
   according to what was said, *Thus shall*
     your descendants be.
That is why *it was credited to him as*
   righteousness.

Gospel at the Procession with Palms (cont.)
Luke 19:28-40; L37C

They proclaimed:
  "Blessed is the king who comes
    in the name of the Lord.
  Peace in heaven
    and glory in the highest."
Some of the Pharisees in the crowd said to him,
  "Teacher, rebuke your disciples."
He said in reply,
  "I tell you, if they keep silent,
  the stones will cry out!"

Gospel at Mass
Luke 22:14–23:56; L38ABC

When the hour came,
  Jesus took his place at table with the apostles.
He said to them,
  "I have eagerly desired to eat this Passover with you before I suffer,
  for, I tell you, I shall not eat it again
  until there is fulfillment in the kingdom of God."
Then he took a cup, gave thanks, and said,
  "Take this and share it among yourselves;
  for I tell you that from this time on
  I shall not drink of the fruit of the vine
  until the kingdom of God comes."
Then he took the bread, said the blessing,
  broke it, and gave it to them, saying,
  "This is my body, which will be given for you;
  do this in memory of me."
And likewise the cup after they had eaten, saying,
  "This cup is the new covenant in my blood,
  which will be shed for you.

"And yet behold, the hand of the one who is to betray me
  is with me on the table;
  for the Son of Man indeed goes as it has been determined;
  but woe to that man by whom he is betrayed."
And they began to debate among themselves
  who among them would do such a deed.

Then an argument broke out among them
  about which of them should be regarded as the greatest.
He said to them,
  "The kings of the Gentiles lord it over them
  and those in authority over them are addressed as 'Benefactors';
  but among you it shall not be so.
Rather, let the greatest among you be as the youngest,
  and the leader as the servant.
For who is greater:
  the one seated at table or the one who serves?
Is it not the one seated at table?
I am among you as the one who serves.
It is you who have stood by me in my trials;
  and I confer a kingdom on you,
  just as my Father has conferred one on me,
  that you may eat and drink at my table in my kingdom;
  and you will sit on thrones
  judging the twelve tribes of Israel.

"Simon, Simon, behold Satan has demanded
  to sift all of you like wheat,

but I have prayed that your own faith may not fail;
  and once you have turned back,
  you must strengthen your brothers."
He said to him,
  "Lord, I am prepared to go to prison and to die with you."
But he replied,
  "I tell you, Peter, before the cock crows this day,
  you will deny three times that you know me."

He said to them,
  "When I sent you forth without a money bag or a sack or sandals,
  were you in need of anything?"
"No, nothing," they replied.
He said to them,
  "But now one who has a money bag should take it,
  and likewise a sack,
  and one who does not have a sword
  should sell his cloak and buy one.
For I tell you that this Scripture must be fulfilled in me,
  namely, *He was counted among the wicked;*
  and indeed what is written about me is coming to fulfillment."
Then they said,
  "Lord, look, there are two swords here."
But he replied, "It is enough!"

Then going out, he went, as was his custom, to the Mount of Olives,
  and the disciples followed him.
When he arrived at the place he said to them,
  "Pray that you may not undergo the test."
After withdrawing about a stone's throw from them and kneeling,
  he prayed, saying, "Father, if you are willing,
  take this cup away from me;
  still, not my will but yours be done."
And to strengthen him an angel from heaven appeared to him.
He was in such agony and he prayed so fervently
  that his sweat became like drops of blood
  falling on the ground.
When he rose from prayer and returned to his disciples,
  he found them sleeping from grief.
He said to them, "Why are you sleeping?
Get up and pray that you may not undergo the test."

While he was still speaking, a crowd approached
  and in front was one of the Twelve, a man named Judas.
He went up to Jesus to kiss him.
Jesus said to him,
  "Judas, are you betraying the Son of Man with a kiss?"
His disciples realized what was about to happen, and they asked,
  "Lord, shall we strike with a sword?"
And one of them struck the high priest's servant
  and cut off his right ear.
But Jesus said in reply,
  "Stop, no more of this!"
Then he touched the servant's ear and healed him.
And Jesus said to the chief priests and temple guards
  and elders who had come for him,
  "Have you come out as against a robber, with swords and clubs?
Day after day I was with you in the temple area,
  and you did not seize me;
  but this is your hour, the time for the power of darkness."

After arresting him they led him away
  and took him into the house of the high priest;
  Peter was following at a distance.

They lit a fire in the middle of the courtyard and sat around it,
  and Peter sat down with them.
When a maid saw him seated in the light,
  she looked intently at him and said,
  "This man too was with him."
But he denied it saying,
  "Woman, I do not know him."
A short while later someone else saw him and said,
  "You too are one of them";
  but Peter answered, "My friend, I am not."
About an hour later, still another insisted,
  "Assuredly, this man too was with him,
  for he also is a Galilean."
But Peter said,
  "My friend, I do not know what you are talking about."
Just as he was saying this, the cock crowed,
  and the Lord turned and looked at Peter;
  and Peter remembered the word of the Lord,
  how he had said to him,
  "Before the cock crows today, you will deny me three times."
He went out and began to weep bitterly.
The men who held Jesus in custody were ridiculing and beating him.
They blindfolded him and questioned him, saying,
  "Prophesy! Who is it that struck you?"
And they reviled him in saying many other things against him.

When day came the council of elders of the people met,
  both chief priests and scribes,
  and they brought him before their Sanhedrin.
They said, "If you are the Christ, tell us,"
  but he replied to them, "If I tell you, you will not believe,
  and if I question, you will not respond.
But from this time on the Son of Man will be seated
  at the right hand of the power of God."
They all asked, "Are you then the Son of God?"
He replied to them, "You say that I am."
Then they said, "What further need have we for testimony?
We have heard it from his own mouth."

Then the whole assembly of them arose and brought him before Pilate.
They brought charges against him, saying,
  "We found this man misleading our people;
  he opposes the payment of taxes to Caesar
  and maintains that he is the Christ, a king."
Pilate asked him, "Are you the king of the Jews?"
He said to him in reply, "You say so."
Pilate then addressed the chief priests and the crowds,
  "I find this man not guilty."
But they were adamant and said,
  "He is inciting the people with his teaching
    throughout all Judea,
  from Galilee where he began even to here."

On hearing this Pilate asked if the man was a Galilean;
  and upon learning that he was under Herod's jurisdiction,
  he sent him to Herod who was in Jerusalem at that time.
Herod was very glad to see Jesus;
  he had been wanting to see him for a long time,
  for he had heard about him
  and had been hoping to see him perform some sign.
He questioned him at length,
  but he gave him no answer.

The chief priests and scribes, meanwhile,
  stood by accusing him harshly.
Herod and his soldiers treated him contemptuously and mocked him,
  and after clothing him in resplendent garb,
  he sent him back to Pilate.
Herod and Pilate became friends that very day,
  even though they had been enemies formerly.
Pilate then summoned the chief priests, the rulers, and the people
  and said to them, "You brought this man to me
  and accused him of inciting the people to revolt.
I have conducted my investigation in your presence
  and have not found this man guilty
  of the charges you have brought against him,
  nor did Herod, for he sent him back to us.
So no capital crime has been committed by him.
Therefore I shall have him flogged and then release him."

But all together they shouted out,
  "Away with this man!
  Release Barabbas to us."
—Now Barabbas had been imprisoned for a rebellion
  that had taken place in the city and for murder.—
Again Pilate addressed them, still wishing to release Jesus,
  but they continued their shouting,
  "Crucify him! Crucify him!"
Pilate addressed them a third time,
  "What evil has this man done?
  I found him guilty of no capital crime.
Therefore I shall have him flogged and then release him."
With loud shouts, however,
  they persisted in calling for his crucifixion,
  and their voices prevailed.
The verdict of Pilate was that their demand should be granted.
So he released the man who had been imprisoned
  for rebellion and murder, for whom they asked,
  and he handed Jesus over to them to deal with as they wished.

As they led him away
  they took hold of a certain Simon, a Cyrenian,
  who was coming in from the country;
  and after laying the cross on him,
  they made him carry it behind Jesus.
A large crowd of people followed Jesus,
  including many women who mourned and lamented him.
Jesus turned to them and said,
  "Daughters of Jerusalem, do not weep for me;
  weep instead for yourselves and for your children
  for indeed, the days are coming when people will say,
  'Blessed are the barren,
  the wombs that never bore
  and the breasts that never nursed.'
At that time people will say to the mountains,
  'Fall upon us!'
  and to the hills, 'Cover us!'
  for if these things are done when the wood is green
  what will happen when it is dry?"
Now two others, both criminals,
  were led away with him to be executed.

When they came to the place called the Skull,
  they crucified him and the criminals there,
  one on his right, the other on his left.

Then Jesus said,
"Father, forgive them, they know not what they do."
They divided his garments by casting lots.
The people stood by and watched;
the rulers, meanwhile, sneered at him and said,
"He saved others, let him save himself
if he is the chosen one, the Christ of God."
Even the soldiers jeered at him.
As they approached to offer him wine they called out,
"If you are King of the Jews, save yourself."
Above him there was an inscription that read,
"This is the King of the Jews."

Now one of the criminals hanging there reviled Jesus, saying,
"Are you not the Christ?
Save yourself and us."
The other, however, rebuking him, said in reply,
"Have you no fear of God,
for you are subject to the same condemnation?
And indeed, we have been condemned justly,
for the sentence we received corresponds to our crimes,
but this man has done nothing criminal."
Then he said,
"Jesus, remember me when you come into your kingdom."
He replied to him,
"Amen, I say to you,
today you will be with me in Paradise."

It was now about noon and darkness came over the whole land
until three in the afternoon
because of an eclipse of the sun.
Then the veil of the temple was torn down the middle.
Jesus cried out in a loud voice,
"Father, into your hands I commend my spirit";
and when he had said this he breathed his last.

Here all kneel and pause for a short time.

The centurion who witnessed what had happened glorified God and said,
"This man was innocent beyond doubt."
When all the people who had gathered for this spectacle
saw what had happened,
they returned home beating their breasts;
but all his acquaintances stood at a distance,
including the women who had followed him from Galilee
and saw these events.

Now there was a virtuous and righteous man named Joseph who,
though he was a member of the council,
had not consented to their plan of action.
He came from the Jewish town of Arimathea
and was awaiting the kingdom of God.
He went to Pilate and asked for the body of Jesus.
After he had taken the body down,
he wrapped it in a linen cloth
and laid him in a rock-hewn tomb
in which no one had yet been buried.
It was the day of preparation,
and the sabbath was about to begin.
The women who had come from Galilee with him followed behind,
and when they had seen the tomb
and the way in which his body was laid in it,
they returned and prepared spices and perfumed oils.
Then they rested on the sabbath according to the commandment.

or Luke 23:1-49

The elders of the people, chief priests and scribes,
arose and brought Jesus before Pilate.
They brought charges against him, saying,
"We found this man misleading our people;
he opposes the payment of taxes to Caesar
and maintains that he is the Christ, a king."
Pilate asked him, "Are you the king of the Jews?"
He said to him in reply, "You say so."
Pilate then addressed the chief priests and the crowds,
"I find this man not guilty."
But they were adamant and said,
"He is inciting the people with his teaching
throughout all Judea,
from Galilee where he began even to here."

On hearing this Pilate asked if the man was a Galilean;
and upon learning that he was under Herod's jurisdiction,
he sent him to Herod who was in Jerusalem at that time.
Herod was very glad to see Jesus;
he had been wanting to see him for a long time,
for he had heard about him
and had been hoping to see him perform some sign.
He questioned him at length,
but he gave him no answer.
The chief priests and scribes, meanwhile,
stood by accusing him harshly.
Herod and his soldiers treated him contemptuously and mocked him,
and after clothing him in resplendent garb,
he sent him back to Pilate.
Herod and Pilate became friends that very day,
even though they had been enemies formerly.
Pilate then summoned the chief priests, the rulers, and the people
and said to them, "You brought this man to me
and accused him of inciting the people to revolt.
I have conducted my investigation in your presence
and have not found this man guilty
of the charges you have brought against him,
nor did Herod, for he sent him back to us.
So no capital crime has been committed by him.
Therefore I shall have him flogged and then release him."

But all together they shouted out,
"Away with this man!
Release Barabbas to us."
—Now Barabbas had been imprisoned for a rebellion
that had taken place in the city and for murder.—
Again Pilate addressed them, still wishing to release Jesus,
but they continued their shouting,
"Crucify him! Crucify him!"
Pilate addressed them a third time,
"What evil has this man done?
I found him guilty of no capital crime.
Therefore I shall have him flogged and then release him."
With loud shouts, however,
they persisted in calling for his crucifixion,
and their voices prevailed.
The verdict of Pilate was that their demand should be granted.
So he released the man who had been imprisoned
for rebellion and murder, for whom they asked,
and he handed Jesus over to them to deal with as they wished.

Gospel (cont.)
Luke 23:1-49

As they led him away
   they took hold of a certain Simon, a Cyrenian,
   who was coming in from the country;
   and after laying the cross on him,
   they made him carry it behind Jesus.
A large crowd of people followed Jesus,
   including many women who mourned and lamented him.
Jesus turned to them and said,
   "Daughters of Jerusalem, do not weep for me;
   weep instead for yourselves and for your children
   for indeed, the days are coming when people will say,
   'Blessed are the barren,
   the wombs that never bore
   and the breasts that never nursed.'
At that time people will say to the mountains,
   'Fall upon us!'
   and to the hills, 'Cover us!'
   for if these things are done when the wood is green
   what will happen when it is dry?"
Now two others, both criminals,
   were led away with him to be executed.

When they came to the place called the Skull,
   they crucified him and the criminals there,
   one on his right, the other on his left.
Then Jesus said,
   "Father, forgive them, they know not what they do."
They divided his garments by casting lots.
The people stood by and watched;
   the rulers, meanwhile, sneered at him and said,
   "He saved others, let him save himself
   if he is the chosen one, the Christ of God."
Even the soldiers jeered at him.

As they approached to offer him wine they called out,
   "If you are King of the Jews, save yourself."
Above him there was an inscription that read,
   "This is the King of the Jews."

Now one of the criminals hanging there reviled Jesus, saying,
   "Are you not the Christ?
   Save yourself and us."
The other, however, rebuking him, said in reply,
   "Have you no fear of God,
   for you are subject to the same condemnation?
And indeed, we have been condemned justly,
   for the sentence we received corresponds to our crimes,
   but this man has done nothing criminal."
Then he said,
   "Jesus, remember me when you come into your kingdom."
He replied to him,
   "Amen, I say to you,
   today you will be with me in Paradise."

It was now about noon and darkness came over the whole land
   until three in the afternoon
   because of an eclipse of the sun.
Then the veil of the temple was torn down the middle.
Jesus cried out in a loud voice,
   "Father, into your hands I commend my spirit";
   and when he had said this he breathed his last.

Here all kneel and pause for a short time.

The centurion who witnessed what had happened glorified God and said,
   "This man was innocent beyond doubt."
When all the people who had gathered for this spectacle
   saw what had happened,
   they returned home beating their breasts;
   but all his acquaintances stood at a distance,
   including the women who had followed him from Galilee
   and saw these events.

Gospel (cont.)
John 13:1-15; L39ABC

Simon Peter said to him,
"Master, then not only my feet, but my hands and head as well."
Jesus said to him,
"Whoever has bathed has no need except to have his feet washed,
for he is clean all over;
so you are clean, but not all."
For he knew who would betray him;
for this reason, he said, "Not all of you are clean."

So when he had washed their feet
and put his garments back on and reclined at table again,
he said to them, "Do you realize what I have done for you?
You call me 'teacher' and 'master,' and rightly so, for indeed I am.
If I, therefore, the master and teacher, have washed your feet,
you ought to wash one another's feet.
I have given you a model to follow,
so that as I have done for you, you should also do."

FIRST READING
Exod 12:1-8, 11-14

The LORD said to Moses and Aaron in the
land of Egypt,
"This month shall stand at the head of
your calendar;
you shall reckon it the first month of the
year.
Tell the whole community of Israel:
On the tenth of this month every one of
your families
must procure for itself a lamb, one apiece
for each household.
If a family is too small for a whole lamb,
it shall join the nearest household in
procuring one
and shall share in the lamb
in proportion to the number of persons
who partake of it.
The lamb must be a year-old male and
without blemish.
You may take it from either the sheep or the
goats.
You shall keep it until the fourteenth day of
this month,
and then, with the whole assembly of Israel
present,
it shall be slaughtered during the evening
twilight.
They shall take some of its blood
and apply it to the two doorposts and the
lintel
of every house in which they partake of
the lamb.
That same night they shall eat its roasted
flesh
with unleavened bread and bitter herbs.

"This is how you are to eat it:
with your loins girt, sandals on your feet
and your staff in hand,
you shall eat like those who are in flight.

It is the Passover of the LORD.
For on this same night I will go through Egypt,
striking down every firstborn of the land,
both man and beast,
and executing judgment on all the gods of
Egypt—I, the LORD!
But the blood will mark the houses where you
are.
Seeing the blood, I will pass over you;
thus, when I strike the land of Egypt,
no destructive blow will come upon you.

"This day shall be a memorial feast for you,
which all your generations shall celebrate
with pilgrimage to the LORD, as a perpetual
institution."

RESPONSORIAL PSALM
Ps 116:12-13, 15-16bc, 17-18

R̞. (cf. 1 Cor 10:16) Our blessing-cup is a communion with the Blood of Christ.

How shall I make a return to the LORD
for all the good he has done for me?
The cup of salvation I will take up,
and I will call upon the name of the LORD.

R̞. Our blessing-cup is a communion with the Blood of Christ.

Precious in the eyes of the LORD
is the death of his faithful ones.
I am your servant, the son of your handmaid;
you have loosed my bonds.

R̞. Our blessing-cup is a communion with the Blood of Christ.

To you will I offer sacrifice of thanksgiving,
and I will call upon the name of the LORD.
My vows to the LORD I will pay
in the presence of all his people.

R̞. Our blessing-cup is a communion with the Blood of Christ.

SECOND READING
1 Cor 11:23-26

Brothers and sisters:
I received from the Lord what I also handed
on to you,
that the Lord Jesus, on the night he was
handed over,
took bread, and, after he had given thanks,
broke it and said, "This is my body that is
for you.
Do this in remembrance of me."
In the same way also the cup, after supper,
saying,
"This cup is the new covenant in my blood.
Do this, as often as you drink it, in
remembrance of me."
For as often as you eat this bread and drink
the cup,
you proclaim the death of the Lord until he
comes.

Gospel (cont.)

John 18:1–19:42; L40ABC

So the band of soldiers, the tribune, and the Jewish guards seized Jesus,
  bound him, and brought him to Annas first.
He was the father-in-law of Caiaphas,
  who was high priest that year.
It was Caiaphas who had counseled the Jews
  that it was better that one man should die rather than the people.

Simon Peter and another disciple followed Jesus.
Now the other disciple was known to the high priest,
  and he entered the courtyard of the high priest with Jesus.
But Peter stood at the gate outside.
So the other disciple, the acquaintance of the high priest,
  went out and spoke to the gatekeeper and brought Peter in.
Then the maid who was the gatekeeper said to Peter,
  "You are not one of this man's disciples, are you?"
He said, "I am not."
Now the slaves and the guards were standing around a charcoal fire
  that they had made, because it was cold,
  and were warming themselves.
Peter was also standing there keeping warm.

The high priest questioned Jesus
  about his disciples and about his doctrine.
Jesus answered him,
  "I have spoken publicly to the world.
I have always taught in a synagogue
  or in the temple area where all the Jews gather,
  and in secret I have said nothing. Why ask me?
Ask those who heard me what I said to them.
They know what I said."
When he had said this,
  one of the temple guards standing there struck Jesus and said,
  "Is this the way you answer the high priest?"
Jesus answered him,
  "If I have spoken wrongly, testify to the wrong;
  but if I have spoken rightly, why do you strike me?"
Then Annas sent him bound to Caiaphas the high priest.

Now Simon Peter was standing there keeping warm.
And they said to him,
  "You are not one of his disciples, are you?"
He denied it and said,
  "I am not."
One of the slaves of the high priest,
  a relative of the one whose ear Peter had cut off, said,
  "Didn't I see you in the garden with him?"
Again Peter denied it.
And immediately the cock crowed.

Then they brought Jesus from Caiaphas to the praetorium.
It was morning.
And they themselves did not enter the praetorium,
  in order not to be defiled so that they could eat the Passover.
So Pilate came out to them and said,
  "What charge do you bring against this man?"
They answered and said to him,
  "If he were not a criminal,
  we would not have handed him over to you."
At this, Pilate said to them,
  "Take him yourselves, and judge him according to your law."

The Jews answered him,
  "We do not have the right to execute anyone,"
  in order that the word of Jesus might be fulfilled
  that he said indicating the kind of death he would die.
So Pilate went back into the praetorium
  and summoned Jesus and said to him,
  "Are you the King of the Jews?"
Jesus answered,
  "Do you say this on your own
  or have others told you about me?"
Pilate answered,
  "I am not a Jew, am I?
Your own nation and the chief priests handed you over to me.
What have you done?"
Jesus answered,
  "My kingdom does not belong to this world.
If my kingdom did belong to this world,
  my attendants would be fighting
  to keep me from being handed over to the Jews.
But as it is, my kingdom is not here."
So Pilate said to him,
  "Then you are a king?"
Jesus answered,
  "You say I am a king.
For this I was born and for this I came into the world,
  to testify to the truth.
Everyone who belongs to the truth listens to my voice."
Pilate said to him, "What is truth?"

When he had said this,
  he again went out to the Jews and said to them,
  "I find no guilt in him.
But you have a custom that I release one prisoner to you at Passover.
Do you want me to release to you the King of the Jews?"
They cried out again,
  "Not this one but Barabbas!"
Now Barabbas was a revolutionary.

Then Pilate took Jesus and had him scourged.
And the soldiers wove a crown out of thorns and placed it on his head,
  and clothed him in a purple cloak,
  and they came to him and said,
  "Hail, King of the Jews!"
And they struck him repeatedly.
Once more Pilate went out and said to them,
  "Look, I am bringing him out to you,
  so that you may know that I find no guilt in him."
So Jesus came out,
  wearing the crown of thorns and the purple cloak.
And he said to them, "Behold, the man!"
When the chief priests and the guards saw him they cried out,
  "Crucify him, crucify him!"
Pilate said to them,
  "Take him yourselves and crucify him.
I find no guilt in him."
The Jews answered,
  "We have a law, and according to that law he ought to die,
  because he made himself the Son of God."

Now when Pilate heard this statement,
he became even more afraid,
and went back into the praetorium and said to Jesus,
"Where are you from?"
Jesus did not answer him.
So Pilate said to him,
"Do you not speak to me?
Do you not know that I have power to release you
and I have power to crucify you?"
Jesus answered him,
"You would have no power over me
if it had not been given to you from above.
For this reason the one who handed me over to you
has the greater sin."
Consequently, Pilate tried to release him; but the Jews cried out,
"If you release him, you are not a Friend of Caesar.
Everyone who makes himself a king opposes Caesar."

When Pilate heard these words he brought Jesus out
and seated him on the judge's bench
in the place called Stone Pavement, in Hebrew, Gabbatha.
It was preparation day for Passover, and it was about noon.
And he said to the Jews,
"Behold, your king!"
They cried out,
"Take him away, take him away! Crucify him!"
Pilate said to them,
"Shall I crucify your king?"
The chief priests answered,
"We have no king but Caesar."
Then he handed him over to them to be crucified.

So they took Jesus, and, carrying the cross himself,
he went out to what is called the Place of the Skull,
in Hebrew, Golgotha.
There they crucified him, and with him two others,
one on either side, with Jesus in the middle.
Pilate also had an inscription written and put on the cross.
It read,
"Jesus the Nazorean, the King of the Jews."
Now many of the Jews read this inscription,
because the place where Jesus was crucified was near the city;
and it was written in Hebrew, Latin, and Greek.
So the chief priests of the Jews said to Pilate,
"Do not write 'The King of the Jews,'
but that he said, 'I am the King of the Jews.'"
Pilate answered,
"What I have written, I have written."

When the soldiers had crucified Jesus,
they took his clothes and divided them into four shares,
a share for each soldier.
They also took his tunic, but the tunic was seamless,
woven in one piece from the top down.
So they said to one another,
"Let's not tear it, but cast lots for it to see whose it will be,"
in order that the passage of Scripture might be fulfilled that says:
They divided my garments among them,
and for my vesture they cast lots.

This is what the soldiers did.
Standing by the cross of Jesus were his mother
and his mother's sister, Mary the wife of Clopas,
and Mary of Magdala.
When Jesus saw his mother and the disciple there whom he loved
he said to his mother, "Woman, behold, your son."
Then he said to the disciple,
"Behold, your mother."
And from that hour the disciple took her into his home.

After this, aware that everything was now finished,
in order that the Scripture might be fulfilled,
Jesus said, "I thirst."
There was a vessel filled with common wine.
So they put a sponge soaked in wine on a sprig of hyssop
and put it up to his mouth.
When Jesus had taken the wine, he said,
"It is finished."
And bowing his head, he handed over the spirit.

Here all kneel and pause for a short time.

Now since it was preparation day,
in order that the bodies might not remain
on the cross on the sabbath,
for the sabbath day of that week was a solemn one,
the Jews asked Pilate that their legs be broken
and that they be taken down.
So the soldiers came and broke the legs of the first
and then of the other one who was crucified with Jesus.
But when they came to Jesus and saw that he was already dead,
they did not break his legs,
but one soldier thrust his lance into his side,
and immediately blood and water flowed out.
An eyewitness has testified, and his testimony is true;
he knows that he is speaking the truth,
so that you also may come to believe.
For this happened so that the Scripture passage might be fulfilled:
Not a bone of it will be broken.
And again another passage says:
They will look upon him whom they have pierced.

After this, Joseph of Arimathea,
secretly a disciple of Jesus for fear of the Jews,
asked Pilate if he could remove the body of Jesus.
And Pilate permitted it.
So he came and took his body.
Nicodemus, the one who had first come to him at night,
also came bringing a mixture of myrrh and aloes
weighing about one hundred pounds.
They took the body of Jesus
and bound it with burial cloths along with the spices,
according to the Jewish burial custom.
Now in the place where he had been crucified there was a garden,
and in the garden a new tomb, in which no one had yet been
buried.
So they laid Jesus there because of the Jewish preparation day;
for the tomb was close by.

FIRST READING
Isa 52:13–53:12

See, my servant shall prosper,
  he shall be raised high and greatly exalted.
Even as many were amazed at him—
  so marred was his look beyond human
    semblance
  and his appearance beyond that of the sons
    of man—
so shall he startle many nations,
  because of him kings shall stand speechless;
for those who have not been told shall see,
  those who have not heard shall ponder it.

Who would believe what we have heard?
  To whom has the arm of the LORD been
    revealed?
He grew up like a sapling before him,
  like a shoot from the parched earth;
there was in him no stately bearing to make
    us look at him,
  nor appearance that would attract us to him.
He was spurned and avoided by people,
  a man of suffering, accustomed to infirmity,
one of those from whom people hide their faces,
  spurned, and we held him in no esteem.

Yet it was our infirmities that he bore,
  our sufferings that he endured,
while we thought of him as stricken,
  as one smitten by God and afflicted.
But he was pierced for our offenses,
  crushed for our sins;
upon him was the chastisement that makes
    us whole,
  by his stripes we were healed.
We had all gone astray like sheep,
  each following his own way;
but the LORD laid upon him
  the guilt of us all.

Though he was harshly treated, he submitted
  and opened not his mouth;
like a lamb led to the slaughter
  or a sheep before the shearers,
    he was silent and opened not his mouth.
Oppressed and condemned, he was taken away,
  and who would have thought any more of
    his destiny?
When he was cut off from the land of the living,
  and smitten for the sin of his people,
a grave was assigned him among the wicked
  and a burial place with evildoers,
though he had done no wrong
  nor spoken any falsehood.
But the LORD was pleased
  to crush him in infirmity.

If he gives his life as an offering for sin,
  he shall see his descendants in a long life,
  and the will of the LORD shall be
    accomplished through him.

Because of his affliction
  he shall see the light
  in fullness of days;
through his suffering, my servant shall justify
    many,
  and their guilt he shall bear.
Therefore I will give him his portion among
    the great,
  and he shall divide the spoils with the
    mighty,
because he surrendered himself to death
  and was counted among the wicked;
and he shall take away the sins of many,
  and win pardon for their offenses.

RESPONSORIAL PSALM
Ps 31:2, 6, 12-13, 15-16, 17, 25

℞. (Luke 23:46) Father, into your hands I
commend my spirit.

In you, O LORD, I take refuge;
  let me never be put to shame.
In your justice rescue me.
Into your hands I commend my spirit;
  you will redeem me, O LORD, O faithful God.

℞. Father, into your hands I commend my
spirit.

For all my foes I am an object of reproach,
  a laughingstock to my neighbors, and a
    dread to my friends;
  they who see me abroad flee from me.
I am forgotten like the unremembered dead;
  I am like a dish that is broken.

℞. Father, into your hands I commend my
spirit.

But my trust is in you, O LORD;
  I say, "You are my God."
In your hands is my destiny; rescue me
  from the clutches of my enemies and my
    persecutors."

℞. Father, into your hands I commend my
spirit.

Let your face shine upon your servant;
  save me in your kindness.
Take courage and be stouthearted,
  all you who hope in the LORD.

℞. Father, into your hands I commend my
spirit.

SECOND READING
Heb 4:14-16; 5:7-9

Brothers and sisters:
Since we have a great high priest who has
  passed through the heavens,
  Jesus, the Son of God,
  let us hold fast to our confession.
For we do not have a high priest
  who is unable to sympathize with our
    weaknesses,
  but one who has similarly been tested in
    every way,
  yet without sin.
So let us confidently approach the throne of
    grace
  to receive mercy and to find grace for
    timely help.

In the days when Christ was in the flesh,
  he offered prayers and supplications with
    loud cries and tears
  to the one who was able to save him from
    death,
  and he was heard because of his reverence.
Son though he was, he learned obedience
  from what he suffered;
  and when he was made perfect,
  he became the source of eternal salvation
    for all who obey him.

FIRST READING
Gen 1:1–2:2

In the beginning, when God created the
heavens and the earth,
the earth was a formless wasteland, and
darkness covered the abyss,
while a mighty wind swept over the waters.

Then God said,
"Let there be light," and there was light.
God saw how good the light was.
God then separated the light from the darkness.
God called the light "day," and the darkness
he called "night."
Thus evening came, and morning followed—
the first day.

Then God said,
"Let there be a dome in the middle of the
waters,
to separate one body of water from the
other."
And so it happened:
God made the dome,
and it separated the water above the dome
from the water below it.
God called the dome "the sky."
Evening came, and morning followed—the
second day.

Then God said,
"Let the water under the sky be gathered
into a single basin,
so that the dry land may appear."
And so it happened:
the water under the sky was gathered into
its basin,
and the dry land appeared.
God called the dry land "the earth,"
and the basin of the water he called "the
sea."
God saw how good it was.
Then God said,
"Let the earth bring forth vegetation:
every kind of plant that bears seed
and every kind of fruit tree on earth
that bears fruit with its seed in it."
And so it happened:
the earth brought forth every kind of plant
that bears seed
and every kind of fruit tree on earth
that bears fruit with its seed in it.
God saw how good it was.
Evening came, and morning followed—the
third day.

Then God said:
"Let there be lights in the dome of the sky,
to separate day from night.
Let them mark the fixed times, the days and
the years,
and serve as luminaries in the dome of the
sky,
to shed light upon the earth."
And so it happened:
God made the two great lights,
the greater one to govern the day,
and the lesser one to govern the night;
and he made the stars.
God set them in the dome of the sky,
to shed light upon the earth,
to govern the day and the night,
and to separate the light from the darkness.
God saw how good it was.
Evening came, and morning followed—the
fourth day.

Then God said,
"Let the water teem with an abundance of
living creatures,
and on the earth let birds fly beneath the
dome of the sky."
And so it happened:
God created the great sea monsters
and all kinds of swimming creatures with
which the water teems,
and all kinds of winged birds.
God saw how good it was, and God blessed
them, saying,
"Be fertile, multiply, and fill the water of
the seas;
and let the birds multiply on the earth."
Evening came, and morning followed—the
fifth day.

Then God said,
"Let the earth bring forth all kinds of
living creatures:
cattle, creeping things, and wild animals of
all kinds."
And so it happened:
God made all kinds of wild animals, all
kinds of cattle,
and all kinds of creeping things of the earth.
God saw how good it was.
Then God said:
"Let us make man in our image, after our
likeness.
Let them have dominion over the fish of the sea,
the birds of the air, and the cattle,
and over all the wild animals
and all the creatures that crawl on the
ground."
God created man in his image;
in the image of God he created him;
male and female he created them.
God blessed them, saying:
"Be fertile and multiply;
fill the earth and subdue it.
Have dominion over the fish of the sea, the
birds of the air,
and all the living things that move on the
earth."
God also said:
"See, I give you every seed-bearing plant all
over the earth
and every tree that has seed-bearing fruit
on it to be your food;
and to all the animals of the land, all the
birds of the air,
and all the living creatures that crawl on
the ground,
I give all the green plants for food."
And so it happened.
God looked at everything he had made, and
he found it very good.
Evening came, and morning followed—the
sixth day.

Thus the heavens and the earth and all their
array were completed.
Since on the seventh day God was finished
with the work he had been doing,
he rested on the seventh day from all the
work he had undertaken.

or

Gen 1:1, 26-31a

In the beginning, when God created the
heavens and the earth,
God said: "Let us make man in our image,
after our likeness.
Let them have dominion over the fish of the sea,
the birds of the air, and the cattle,
and over all the wild animals
and all the creatures that crawl on the
ground."
God created man in his image;
in the image of God he created him;
male and female he created them.
God blessed them, saying:
"Be fertile and multiply;
fill the earth and subdue it.
Have dominion over the fish of the sea, the
birds of the air,
and all the living things that move on the
earth."
God also said:
"See, I give you every seed-bearing plant all
over the earth
and every tree that has seed-bearing fruit
on it to be your food;
and to all the animals of the land, all the
birds of the air,
and all the living creatures that crawl on
the ground,
I give all the green plants for food."
And so it happened.
God looked at everything he had made, and
found it very good.

RESPONSORIAL PSALM

Ps 104:1-2, 5-6, 10, 12, 13-14, 24, 35

℟. (30) Lord, send out your Spirit, and renew the face of the earth.

Bless the LORD, O my soul!
    O LORD, my God, you are great indeed!
You are clothed with majesty and glory,
    robed in light as with a cloak.

℟. Lord, send out your Spirit, and renew the face of the earth.

You fixed the earth upon its foundation,
    not to be moved forever;
with the ocean, as with a garment, you
      covered it;
    above the mountains the waters stood.

℟. Lord, send out your Spirit, and renew the face of the earth.

You send forth springs into the watercourses
    that wind among the mountains.
Beside them the birds of heaven dwell;
    from among the branches they send forth
      their song.

℟. Lord, send out your Spirit, and renew the face of the earth.

You water the mountains from your palace;
    the earth is replete with the fruit of your
      works.
You raise grass for the cattle,
    and vegetation for man's use,
producing bread from the earth.

℟. Lord, send out your Spirit, and renew the face of the earth.

How manifold are your works, O LORD!
    In wisdom you have wrought them all—
the earth is full of your creatures.
    Bless the LORD, O my soul!

℟. Lord, send out your Spirit, and renew the face of the earth.

or

Ps 33:4-5, 6-7, 12-13, 20 and 22

℟. (5b) The earth is full of the goodness of the Lord.

Upright is the word of the LORD,
    and all his works are trustworthy.
He loves justice and right;
    of the kindness of the LORD the earth is full.

℟. The earth is full of the goodness of the Lord.

By the word of the LORD the heavens were
    made;
    by the breath of his mouth all their host.
He gathers the waters of the sea as in a
    flask;
    in cellars he confines the deep.

℟. The earth is full of the goodness of the Lord.

Blessed the nation whose God is the LORD,
    the people he has chosen for his own
      inheritance.
From heaven the LORD looks down;
    he sees all mankind.

℟. The earth is full of the goodness of the Lord.

Our soul waits for the LORD,
    who is our help and our shield.
May your kindness, O LORD, be upon us
    who have put our hope in you.

℟. The earth is full of the goodness of the Lord.

SECOND READING

Gen 22:1-18

God put Abraham to the test.
He called to him, "Abraham!"
"Here I am," he replied.
Then God said:
    "Take your son Isaac, your only one, whom
      you love,
    and go to the land of Moriah.
There you shall offer him up as a holocaust
    on a height that I will point out to you."
Early the next morning Abraham saddled his
    donkey,
    took with him his son Isaac and two of his
      servants as well,
    and with the wood that he had cut for the
      holocaust,
    set out for the place of which God had told
      him.

On the third day Abraham got sight of the
    place from afar.
Then he said to his servants:
    "Both of you stay here with the donkey,
    while the boy and I go on over yonder.
We will worship and then come back to you."
Thereupon Abraham took the wood for the
    holocaust
    and laid it on his son Isaac's shoulders,
    while he himself carried the fire and the
      knife.
As the two walked on together, Isaac spoke to
    his father Abraham:
    "Father!" Isaac said.
"Yes, son," he replied.
Isaac continued, "Here are the fire and the
    wood,
    but where is the sheep for the holocaust?"
"Son," Abraham answered,
    "God himself will provide the sheep for the
      holocaust."
Then the two continued going forward.

When they came to the place of which God
    had told him,
    Abraham built an altar there and arranged
      the wood on it.
Next he tied up his son Isaac,
    and put him on top of the wood on the altar.
Then he reached out and took the knife to
      slaughter his son.
But the LORD's messenger called to him from
    heaven,
    "Abraham, Abraham!"
"Here I am," he answered.
"Do not lay your hand on the boy," said the
      messenger.
"Do not do the least thing to him.
I know now how devoted you are to God,
    since you did not withhold from me your
      own beloved son."
As Abraham looked about,
    he spied a ram caught by its horns in the
      thicket.
So he went and took the ram
    and offered it up as a holocaust in place of
      his son.
Abraham named the site Yahweh-yireh;
    hence people now say, "On the mountain
      the LORD will see."

Again the LORD's messenger called to
    Abraham from heaven and said:
    "I swear by myself, declares the LORD,
    that because you acted as you did
    in not withholding from me your beloved
      son,
    I will bless you abundantly
    and make your descendants as countless
    as the stars of the sky and the sands of the
      seashore;
    your descendants shall take possession
    of the gates of their enemies,
    and in your descendants all the nations of
      the earth
      shall find blessing—
    all this because you obeyed my
      command."

or

Gen 22:1-2, 9a, 10-13, 15-18

God put Abraham to the test.
He called to him, "Abraham!"
"Here I am," he replied.
Then God said:
    "Take your son Isaac, your only one, whom
      you love,
    and go to the land of Moriah.
There you shall offer him up as a holocaust
    on a height that I will point out to you."

When they came to the place of which God
    had told him,
    Abraham built an altar there and arranged
      the wood on it.

Then he reached out and took the knife to
slaughter his son.
But the LORD's messenger called to him from
heaven,
"Abraham, Abraham!"
"Here I am," he answered.
"Do not lay your hand on the boy," said the
messenger.
"Do not do the least thing to him.
I know now how devoted you are to God,
since you did not withhold from me your
own beloved son."
As Abraham looked about,
he spied a ram caught by its horns in the
thicket.
So he went and took the ram
and offered it up as a holocaust in place of
his son.

Again the LORD's messenger called to
Abraham from heaven and said:
"I swear by myself, declares the LORD,
that because you acted as you did
in not withholding from me your beloved son,
I will bless you abundantly
and make your descendants as countless
as the stars of the sky and the sands of the
seashore;
your descendants shall take possession
of the gates of their enemies,
and in your descendants all the nations of
the earth
shall find blessing—
all this because you obeyed my command."

RESPONSORIAL PSALM
Ps 16:5, 8, 9-10, 11

R℟. (1) You are my inheritance, O Lord.

O LORD, my allotted portion and my cup,
you it is who hold fast my lot.
I set the LORD ever before me;
with him at my right hand I shall not be
disturbed.

R℟. You are my inheritance, O Lord.

Therefore my heart is glad and my soul rejoices,
my body, too, abides in confidence;
because you will not abandon my soul to the
netherworld,
nor will you suffer your faithful one to
undergo corruption.

R℟. You are my inheritance, O Lord.

You will show me the path to life,
fullness of joys in your presence,
the delights at your right hand forever.

R℟. You are my inheritance, O Lord.

THIRD READING
Exod 14:15–15:1

The LORD said to Moses, "Why are you crying
out to me?
Tell the Israelites to go forward.
And you, lift up your staff and, with hand
outstretched over the sea,
split the sea in two,
that the Israelites may pass through it on
dry land.
But I will make the Egyptians so obstinate
that they will go in after them.
Then I will receive glory through Pharaoh
and all his army,
his chariots and charioteers.
The Egyptians shall know that I am the LORD,
when I receive glory through Pharaoh
and his chariots and charioteers."

The angel of God, who had been leading
Israel's camp,
now moved and went around behind them.
The column of cloud also, leaving the front,
took up its place behind them,
so that it came between the camp of the
Egyptians
and that of Israel.
But the cloud now became dark, and thus the
night passed
without the rival camps coming any closer
together all night long.
Then Moses stretched out his hand over the
sea,
and the LORD swept the sea
with a strong east wind throughout the night
and so turned it into dry land.
When the water was thus divided,
the Israelites marched into the midst of the
sea on dry land,
with the water like a wall to their right and
to their left.

The Egyptians followed in pursuit;
all Pharaoh's horses and chariots and
charioteers went after them
right into the midst of the sea.
In the night watch just before dawn
the LORD cast through the column of the
fiery cloud
upon the Egyptian force a glance that
threw it into a panic;
and he so clogged their chariot wheels
that they could hardly drive.
With that the Egyptians sounded the retreat
before Israel,
because the LORD was fighting for them
against the Egyptians.

Then the LORD told Moses, "Stretch out your
hand over the sea,
that the water may flow back upon the
Egyptians,
upon their chariots and their charioteers."
So Moses stretched out his hand over the sea,
and at dawn the sea flowed back to its
normal depth.
The Egyptians were fleeing head on toward
the sea,
when the LORD hurled them into its midst.
As the water flowed back,
it covered the chariots and the charioteers
of Pharaoh's whole army
which had followed the Israelites into the sea.
Not a single one of them escaped.
But the Israelites had marched on dry land
through the midst of the sea,
with the water like a wall to their right and
to their left.
Thus the LORD saved Israel on that day
from the power of the Egyptians.
When Israel saw the Egyptians lying dead on
the seashore
and beheld the great power that the LORD
had shown against the Egyptians,
they feared the LORD and believed in him
and in his servant Moses.

Then Moses and the Israelites sang this song
to the LORD:
I will sing to the LORD, for he is gloriously
triumphant;
horse and chariot he has cast into the sea.

RESPONSORIAL PSALM
Exod 15:1-2, 3-4, 5-6, 17-18

R℟. (1b) Let us sing to the Lord; he has covered
himself in glory.

I will sing to the LORD, for he is gloriously
triumphant;
horse and chariot he has cast into the sea.
My strength and my courage is the LORD,
and he has been my savior.
He is my God, I praise him;
the God of my father, I extol him.

R℟. Let us sing to the Lord; he has covered
himself in glory.

The LORD is a warrior,
LORD is his name!
Pharaoh's chariots and army he hurled into
the sea;
the elite of his officers were submerged in
the Red Sea.

R℟. Let us sing to the Lord; he has covered
himself in glory.

The flood waters covered them,
   they sank into the depths like a stone.
Your right hand, O LORD, magnificent in
     power,
   your right hand, O LORD, has shattered the
     enemy.

R̸. Let us sing to the Lord; he has covered
himself in glory.

You brought in the people you redeemed
   and planted them on the mountain of your
     inheritance—
the place where you made your seat, O LORD,
   the sanctuary, LORD, which your hands
     established.
The LORD shall reign forever and ever.

R̸. Let us sing to the Lord; he has covered
himself in glory.

FOURTH READING
Isa 54:5-14

The One who has become your husband is
     your Maker;
   his name is the LORD of hosts;
your redeemer is the Holy One of Israel,
   called God of all the earth.
The LORD calls you back,
   like a wife forsaken and grieved in spirit,
   a wife married in youth and then cast off,
   says your God.
For a brief moment I abandoned you,
   but with great tenderness I will take you
     back.
In an outburst of wrath, for a moment
   I hid my face from you;
but with enduring love I take pity on you,
   says the LORD, your redeemer.
This is for me like the days of Noah,
   when I swore that the waters of Noah
   should never again deluge the earth;
so I have sworn not to be angry with you,
   or to rebuke you.
Though the mountains leave their place
   and the hills be shaken,
my love shall never leave you
   nor my covenant of peace be shaken,
   says the LORD, who has mercy on you.
O afflicted one, storm-battered and unconsoled,
   I lay your pavements in carnelians,
   and your foundations in sapphires;
I will make your battlements of rubies,
   your gates of carbuncles,
   and all your walls of precious stones.
All your children shall be taught by the LORD,
   and great shall be the peace of your children.
In justice shall you be established,

far from the fear of oppression,
   where destruction cannot come near you.

RESPONSORIAL PSALM
Ps 30:2, 4, 5-6, 11-12, 13

R̸. (2a) I will praise you, Lord, for you have
rescued me.

I will extol you, O LORD, for you drew me clear
   and did not let my enemies rejoice over me.
O LORD, you brought me up from the
     netherworld;
   you preserved me from among those going
     down into the pit.

R̸. I will praise you, Lord, for you have
rescued me.

Sing praise to the LORD, you his faithful ones,
   and give thanks to his holy name.
For his anger lasts but a moment;
   a lifetime, his good will.
At nightfall, weeping enters in,
   but with the dawn, rejoicing.

R̸. I will praise you, Lord, for you have
rescued me.

Hear, O LORD, and have pity on me;
   O LORD, be my helper.
You changed my mourning into dancing;
   O LORD, my God, forever will I give you
     thanks.

R̸. I will praise you, Lord, for you have
rescued me.

FIFTH READING
Isa 55:1-11

Thus says the LORD:
All you who are thirsty,
   come to the water!
You who have no money,
   come, receive grain and eat;
come, without paying and without cost,
   drink wine and milk!
Why spend your money for what is not bread,
   your wages for what fails to satisfy?
Heed me, and you shall eat well,
   you shall delight in rich fare.
Come to me heedfully,
   listen, that you may have life.
I will renew with you the everlasting
     covenant,
   the benefits assured to David.
As I made him a witness to the peoples,
   a leader and commander of nations,
so shall you summon a nation you knew not,
   and nations that knew you not shall run
     to you,

because of the LORD, your God,
   the Holy One of Israel, who has glorified you.

Seek the LORD while he may be found,
   call him while he is near.
Let the scoundrel forsake his way,
   and the wicked man his thoughts;
let him turn to the LORD for mercy;
   to our God, who is generous in forgiving.
For my thoughts are not your thoughts,
   nor are your ways my ways, says the LORD.
As high as the heavens are above the earth,
   so high are my ways above your ways
   and my thoughts above your thoughts.

For just as from the heavens
   the rain and snow come down
and do not return there
   till they have watered the earth,
   making it fertile and fruitful,
giving seed to the one who sows
   and bread to the one who eats,
so shall my word be
   that goes forth from my mouth;
my word shall not return to me void,
   but shall do my will,
   achieving the end for which I sent it.

RESPONSORIAL PSALM
Isa 12:2-3, 4, 5-6

R̸. (3) You will draw water joyfully from the
springs of salvation.

God indeed is my savior;
   I am confident and unafraid.
My strength and my courage is the LORD,
   and he has been my savior.
With joy you will draw water
   at the fountain of salvation.

R̸. You will draw water joyfully from the
springs of salvation.

Give thanks to the LORD, acclaim his name;
   among the nations make known his deeds,
   proclaim how exalted is his name.

R̸. You will draw water joyfully from the
springs of salvation.

Sing praise to the LORD for his glorious
     achievement;
   let this be known throughout all the earth.
Shout with exultation, O city of Zion,
   for great in your midst
   is the Holy One of Israel!

R̸. You will draw water joyfully from the
springs of salvation.

SIXTH READING
Bar 3:9-15, 32–4:4

Hear, O Israel, the commandments of life:
    listen, and know prudence!
How is it, Israel,
    that you are in the land of your foes,
    grown old in a foreign land,
defiled with the dead,
    accounted with those destined for the
        netherworld?
You have forsaken the fountain of wisdom!
    Had you walked in the way of God,
    you would have dwelt in enduring peace.
Learn where prudence is,
    where strength, where understanding;
that you may know also
    where are length of days, and life,
    where light of the eyes, and peace.
Who has found the place of wisdom,
    who has entered into her treasuries?

The One who knows all things knows her;
    he has probed her by his knowledge—
the One who established the earth for all
        time,
    and filled it with four-footed beasts;
he who dismisses the light, and it departs,
    calls it, and it obeys him trembling;
before whom the stars at their posts
    shine and rejoice;
when he calls them, they answer, "Here we
    are!"
    shining with joy for their Maker.
Such is our God;
    no other is to be compared to him:
he has traced out the whole way of
        understanding,
    and has given her to Jacob, his servant,
    to Israel, his beloved son.

Since then she has appeared on earth,
    and moved among people.
She is the book of the precepts of God,
    the law that endures forever;
all who cling to her will live,
    but those will die who forsake her.
Turn, O Jacob, and receive her:
    walk by her light toward splendor.
Give not your glory to another,
    your privileges to an alien race.
Blessed are we, O Israel;
    for what pleases God is known to us!

RESPONSORIAL PSALM
Ps 19:8, 9, 10, 11

℟. (John 6:68c) Lord, you have the words of
everlasting life.

The law of the LORD is perfect,
    refreshing the soul;
the decree of the LORD is trustworthy,
    giving wisdom to the simple.

℟. Lord, you have the words of everlasting life.

The precepts of the LORD are right,
    rejoicing the heart;
the command of the LORD is clear,
    enlightening the eye.

℟. Lord, you have the words of everlasting life.

The fear of the LORD is pure,
    enduring forever;
the ordinances of the LORD are true,
    all of them just.

℟. Lord, you have the words of everlasting life.

They are more precious than gold,
    than a heap of purest gold;
sweeter also than syrup
    or honey from the comb.

℟. Lord, you have the words of everlasting life.

SEVENTH READING
Ezek 36:16-17a, 18-28

The word of the LORD came to me, saying:
    Son of man, when the house of Israel lived
        in their land,
    they defiled it by their conduct and deeds.
Therefore I poured out my fury upon them
    because of the blood that they poured out
        on the ground,
    and because they defiled it with idols.
I scattered them among the nations,
    dispersing them over foreign lands;
    according to their conduct and deeds I
        judged them.
But when they came among the nations
        wherever they came,
    they served to profane my holy name,
    because it was said of them: "These are the
        people of the LORD,
    yet they had to leave their land."
So I have relented because of my holy name
    which the house of Israel profaned
    among the nations where they came.
Therefore say to the house of Israel: Thus
    says the Lord GOD:
    Not for your sakes do I act, house of Israel,
    but for the sake of my holy name,
    which you profaned among the nations to
        which you came.
I will prove the holiness of my great name,
    profaned among the nations,
    in whose midst you have profaned it.
Thus the nations shall know that I am the
    LORD, says the Lord GOD,
    when in their sight I prove my holiness
        through you.
For I will take you away from among the
    nations,
gather you from all the foreign lands,
    and bring you back to your own land.
I will sprinkle clean water upon you
    to cleanse you from all your impurities,
    and from all your idols I will cleanse you.
I will give you a new heart and place a new
        spirit within you,
    taking from your bodies your stony hearts
    and giving you natural hearts.
I will put my spirit within you and make you
    live by my statutes,
    careful to observe my decrees.
You shall live in the land I gave your fathers;
    you shall be my people, and I will be your
        God.

RESPONSORIAL PSALM
Ps 42:3, 5; 43:3, 4

℟. (42:2) Like a deer that longs for running
streams, my soul longs for you, my God.

Athirst is my soul for God, the living God.
    When shall I go and behold the face of God?

℟. Like a deer that longs for running streams,
my soul longs for you, my God.

I went with the throng
    and led them in procession to the house of
        God,
amid loud cries of joy and thanksgiving,
    with the multitude keeping festival.

℟. Like a deer that longs for running streams,
my soul longs for you, my God.

Send forth your light and your fidelity;
    they shall lead me on
and bring me to your holy mountain,
    to your dwelling-place.

℟. Like a deer that longs for running streams,
my soul longs for you, my God.

Then will I go in to the altar of God,
    the God of my gladness and joy;
then will I give you thanks upon the harp,
    O God, my God!

℟. Like a deer that longs for running streams,
my soul longs for you, my God.

or

Isa 12:2-3, 4bcd, 5-6

℟. (3) You will draw water joyfully from the
springs of salvation.

God indeed is my savior;
    I am confident and unafraid.
My strength and my courage is the LORD,
    and he has been my savior.
With joy you will draw water
    at the fountain of salvation.

℟. You will draw water joyfully from the
springs of salvation.

Give thanks to the LORD, acclaim his name;
  among the nations make known his deeds,
  proclaim how exalted is his name.

℟. You will draw water joyfully from the springs of salvation.

Sing praise to the LORD for his glorious achievement;
  let this be known throughout all the earth.
Shout with exultation, O city of Zion,
  for great in your midst
  is the Holy One of Israel!

℟. You will draw water joyfully from the springs of salvation.

or

Ps 51:12-13, 14-15, 18-19

℟. (12a) Create a clean heart in me, O God.

A clean heart create for me, O God,
  and a steadfast spirit renew within me.
Cast me not out from your presence,
  and your Holy Spirit take not from me.

℟. Create a clean heart in me, O God.

Give me back the joy of your salvation,
  and a willing spirit sustain in me.
I will teach transgressors your ways,
  and sinners shall return to you.

℟. Create a clean heart in me, O God.

For you are not pleased with sacrifices;
  should I offer a holocaust, you would not accept it.
My sacrifice, O God, is a contrite spirit;
  a heart contrite and humbled, O God, you will not spurn.

℟. Create a clean heart in me, O God.

EPISTLE
Rom 6:3-11

Brothers and sisters:
Are you unaware that we who were baptized into Christ Jesus
  were baptized into his death?
We were indeed buried with him through baptism into death,
  so that, just as Christ was raised from the dead
  by the glory of the Father,
  we too might live in newness of life.

For if we have grown into union with him through a death like his,
  we shall also be united with him in the resurrection.
We know that our old self was crucified with him,
  so that our sinful body might be done away with,
  that we might no longer be in slavery to sin.
For a dead person has been absolved from sin.
If, then, we have died with Christ,
  we believe that we shall also live with him.
We know that Christ, raised from the dead, dies no more;
  death no longer has power over him.
As to his death, he died to sin once and for all;
  as to his life, he lives for God.
Consequently, you too must think of yourselves as being dead to sin
  and living for God in Christ Jesus.

RESPONSORIAL PSALM
Ps 118:1-2, 16-17, 22-23

℟. Alleluia, alleluia, alleluia.

Give thanks to the LORD, for he is good,
  for his mercy endures forever.
Let the house of Israel say,
  "His mercy endures forever."

℟. Alleluia, alleluia, alleluia.

"The right hand of the LORD has struck with power;
  the right hand of the LORD is exalted.
I shall not die, but live,
  and declare the works of the LORD."

℟. Alleluia, alleluia, alleluia.

The stone which the builders rejected
  has become the cornerstone.
By the LORD has this been done;
  it is wonderful in our eyes.

℟. Alleluia, alleluia, alleluia.

Gospel
Luke 24:1-12; L41C

At daybreak on the first day of the week
  the women who had come from Galilee with Jesus
  took the spices they had prepared
  and went to the tomb.
They found the stone rolled away from the tomb;
  but when they entered,
  they did not find the body of the Lord Jesus.
While they were puzzling over this, behold,
  two men in dazzling garments appeared to them.
They were terrified and bowed their faces to the ground.
They said to them,
  "Why do you seek the living one among the dead?
He is not here, but he has been raised.
Remember what he said to you while he was still in Galilee,
that the Son of Man must be handed over to sinners
  and be crucified, and rise on the third day."
And they remembered his words.
Then they returned from the tomb
  and announced all these things to the eleven
  and to all the others.
The women were Mary Magdalene, Joanna, and Mary the mother of
    James;
  the others who accompanied them also told this to the apostles,
  but their story seemed like nonsense
  and they did not believe them.
But Peter got up and ran to the tomb,
  bent down, and saw the burial cloths alone;
  then he went home amazed at what had happened.

or, at an afternoon or evening Mass

Gospel
Luke 24:13-35; L46

That very day, the first day of the week,
  two of Jesus' disciples were going
  to a village seven miles from Jerusalem called Emmaus,
  and they were conversing about all the things that had occurred.
And it happened that while they were conversing and debating,
  Jesus himself drew near and walked with them,
  but their eyes were prevented from recognizing him.
He asked them,
  "What are you discussing as you walk along?"
They stopped, looking downcast.
One of them, named Cleopas, said to him in reply,
  "Are you the only visitor to Jerusalem
  who does not know of the things
  that have taken place there in these days?"
And he replied to them, "What sort of things?"
They said to him,
  "The things that happened to Jesus the Nazarene,
  who was a prophet mighty in deed and word
  before God and all the people,
  how our chief priests and rulers both handed him over
  to a sentence of death and crucified him.
But we were hoping that he would be the one to redeem Israel;
  and besides all this,
  it is now the third day since this took place.
Some women from our group, however, have astounded us:
  they were at the tomb early in the morning
  and did not find his body;
  they came back and reported
  that they had indeed seen a vision of angels
  who announced that he was alive.
Then some of those with us went to the tomb
  and found things just as the women had described,
  but him they did not see."
And he said to them, "Oh, how foolish you are!
How slow of heart to believe all that the prophets spoke!
Was it not necessary that the Christ should suffer these things
  and enter into his glory?"
Then beginning with Moses and all the prophets,
  he interpreted to them what referred to him
  in all the Scriptures.
As they approached the village to which they were going,
  he gave the impression that he was going on farther.
But they urged him, "Stay with us,
  for it is nearly evening and the day is almost over."
So he went in to stay with them.
And it happened that, while he was with them at table,
  he took bread, said the blessing,
  broke it, and gave it to them.
With that their eyes were opened and they recognized him,
  but he vanished from their sight.
Then they said to each other,
  "Were not our hearts burning within us
  while he spoke to us on the way and opened the Scriptures to us?"
So they set out at once and returned to Jerusalem
  where they found gathered together
  the eleven and those with them who were saying,
  "The Lord has truly been raised and has appeared to Simon!"
Then the two recounted
  what had taken place on the way
  and how he was made known to them in the breaking of bread.

FIRST READING

Acts 10:34a, 37-43

Peter proceeded to speak and said:
    "You know what has happened all over
        Judea,
    beginning in Galilee after the baptism
        that John preached,
    how God anointed Jesus of Nazareth
        with the Holy Spirit and power.
He went about doing good
    and healing all those oppressed by the devil,
        for God was with him.
We are witnesses of all that he did
    both in the country of the Jews and in
        Jerusalem.
They put him to death by hanging him on a
    tree.
This man God raised on the third day and
        granted that he be visible,
    not to all the people, but to us,
    the witnesses chosen by God in advance,
    who ate and drank with him after he rose
        from the dead.
He commissioned us to preach to the people
    and testify that he is the one appointed by
        God
    as judge of the living and the dead.
To him all the prophets bear witness,
    that everyone who believes in him
    will receive forgiveness of sins through his
        name."

RESPONSORIAL PSALM

Ps 118:1-2, 16-17, 22-23

R̸. (24) This is the day the Lord has made; let
us rejoice and be glad.
    or:
R̸. Alleluia.

Give thanks to the LORD, for he is good,
    for his mercy endures forever.
Let the house of Israel say,
    "His mercy endures forever."

R̸. This is the day the Lord has made; let us
rejoice and be glad.
    or:
R̸. Alleluia.

"The right hand of the LORD has struck with
        power;
    the right hand of the LORD is exalted.
I shall not die, but live,
    and declare the works of the LORD."

R̸. This is the day the Lord has made; let us
rejoice and be glad.
    or:
R̸. Alleluia.

The stone which the builders rejected
    has become the cornerstone.
By the LORD has this been done;
    it is wonderful in our eyes.

R̸. This is the day the Lord has made; let us
rejoice and be glad.
    or:
R̸. Alleluia.

SECOND READING

1 Cor 5:6b-8

Brothers and sisters:
Do you not know that a little yeast leavens all
    the dough?
Clear out the old yeast,
    so that you may become a fresh batch of
        dough,
    inasmuch as you are unleavened.
For our paschal lamb, Christ, has been
    sacrificed.

Therefore, let us celebrate the feast,
    not with the old yeast, the yeast of malice
        and wickedness,
    but with the unleavened bread of sincerity
        and truth.

or Col 3:1-4

Brothers and sisters:
If then you were raised with Christ, seek what
        is above,
    where Christ is seated at the right hand of
        God.
Think of what is above, not of what is on earth.
For you have died, and your life is hidden
    with Christ in God.
When Christ your life appears,
    then you too will appear with him in glory.

SEQUENCE *Victimae paschali laudes*

Christians, to the Paschal Victim
    Offer your thankful praises!
A Lamb the sheep redeems;
    Christ, who only is sinless,
    Reconciles sinners to the Father.
Death and life have contended in that combat
        stupendous:
    The Prince of life, who died, reigns immortal.
Speak, Mary, declaring
    What you saw, wayfaring.
"The tomb of Christ, who is living,
    The glory of Jesus' resurrection;
Bright angels attesting,
    The shroud and napkin resting.
Yes, Christ my hope is arisen;
    To Galilee he goes before you."
Christ indeed from death is risen, our new life
        obtaining.
    Have mercy, victor King, ever reigning!
    Amen. Alleluia.

Second Sunday of Easter (or Divine Mercy Sunday), *April 7, 2013*

Gospel (cont.)

John 20:19-31; L45C

Then he said to Thomas, "Put your finger here and see my hands,
    and bring your hand and put it into my side,
    and do not be unbelieving, but believe."
Thomas answered and said to him, "My Lord and my God!"
Jesus said to him, "Have you come to believe because you have seen
        me?
Blessed are those who have not seen and have believed."

Now Jesus did many other signs in the presence of his disciples
    that are not written in this book.
But these are written that you may come to believe
    that Jesus is the Christ, the Son of God,
    and that through this belief you may have life in his name.

The Annunciation of the Lord, *April 8, 2013*

FIRST READING
Isa 7:10-14; 8:10

The LORD spoke to Ahaz, saying:
Ask for a sign from the LORD, your God;
    let it be deep as the netherworld, or high as
        the sky!
But Ahaz answered,
    "I will not ask! I will not tempt the LORD!"
Then Isaiah said:
    Listen, O house of David!
Is it not enough for you to weary people,
    must you also weary my God?
Therefore the Lord himself will give you this
        sign:
    the virgin shall conceive, and bear a son,
    and shall name him Emmanuel,
    which means "God is with us!"

RESPONSORIAL PSALM
Ps 40:7-8a, 8b-9, 10, 11

R̸. (8a and 9a) Here am I, Lord; I come to do
your will.

Sacrifice or offering you wished not,
    but ears open to obedience you gave me.
Holocausts and sin-offerings you sought not;
    then said I, "Behold, I come";

R̸. Here am I, Lord; I come to do your will.

"In the written scroll it is prescribed for me.
To do your will, O God, is my delight,
    and your law is within my heart!"

R̸. Here am I, Lord; I come to do your will.

I announced your justice in the vast assembly;
    I did not restrain my lips, as you, O LORD,
        know.

R̸. Here am I, Lord; I come to do your will.

Your justice I kept not hid within my heart;
    your faithfulness and your salvation I have
        spoken of;
I have made no secret of your kindness and
        your truth
        in the vast assembly.

R̸. Here am I, Lord; I come to do your will.

SECOND READING
Heb 10:4-10

Brothers and sisters:
It is impossible that the blood of bulls and
        goats
    takes away sins.
For this reason, when Christ came into the
        world, he said:
    "Sacrifice and offering you did not desire,
        but a body you prepared for me;
    in holocausts and sin offerings you took no
        delight.
    Then I said, 'As is written of me in the scroll,
    behold, I come to do your will, O God.'"

First he says, "Sacrifices and offerings,
    holocausts and sin offerings,
    you neither desired nor delighted in."
These are offered according to the law.
Then he says, "Behold, I come to do your will."
He takes away the first to establish the
        second.
By this "will," we have been consecrated
    through the offering of the Body of Jesus
        Christ once for all.

Third Sunday of Easter, *April 14, 2013*

Gospel (cont.)
John 21:1-19; L48C

When they climbed out on shore,
    they saw a charcoal fire with fish on it and bread.
Jesus said to them, "Bring some of the fish you just caught."
So Simon Peter went over and dragged the net ashore
    full of one hundred fifty-three large fish.
Even though there were so many, the net was not torn.
Jesus said to them, "Come, have breakfast."
And none of the disciples dared to ask him, "Who are you?"
    because they realized it was the Lord.
Jesus came over and took the bread and gave it to them,
    and in like manner the fish.
This was now the third time Jesus was revealed to his disciples
    after being raised from the dead.

When they had finished breakfast, Jesus said to Simon Peter,
    "Simon, son of John, do you love me more than these?"
Simon Peter answered him, "Yes, Lord, you know that I love you."
Jesus said to him, "Feed my lambs."

He then said to Simon Peter a second time,
    "Simon, son of John, do you love me?"
Simon Peter answered him, "Yes, Lord, you know that I love you."
Jesus said to him, "Tend my sheep."
Jesus said to him the third time,
    "Simon, son of John, do you love me?"
Peter was distressed that Jesus had said to him a third time,
    "Do you love me?" and he said to him,
    "Lord, you know everything; you know that I love you."
Jesus said to him, "Feed my sheep.
Amen, amen, I say to you, when you were younger,
    you used to dress yourself and go where you wanted;
    but when you grow old, you will stretch out your hands,
    and someone else will dress you
    and lead you where you do not want to go."
He said this signifying by what kind of death he would glorify God.
And when he had said this, he said to him, "Follow me."

Third Sunday of Easter, April 14, 2013

Gospel
or John 21:1-14; L48C

At that time, Jesus revealed himself again to his disciples at the Sea of
   Tiberias.
He revealed himself in this way.
Together were Simon Peter, Thomas called Didymus,
   Nathanael from Cana in Galilee,
   Zebedee's sons, and two others of his disciples.
Simon Peter said to them, "I am going fishing."
They said to him, "We also will come with you."
So they went out and got into the boat,
   but that night they caught nothing.
When it was already dawn, Jesus was standing on the shore;
   but the disciples did not realize that it was Jesus.
Jesus said to them, "Children, have you caught anything to eat?"
They answered him, "No."
So he said to them, "Cast the net over the right side of the boat
   and you will find something."
So they cast it, and were not able to pull it in
   because of the number of fish.
So the disciple whom Jesus loved said to Peter, "It is the Lord."

When Simon Peter heard that it was the Lord,
   he tucked in his garment, for he was lightly clad,
   and jumped into the sea.
The other disciples came in the boat,
   for they were not far from shore, only about a hundred yards,
   dragging the net with the fish.
When they climbed out on shore,
   they saw a charcoal fire with fish on it and bread.
Jesus said to them, "Bring some of the fish you just caught."
So Simon Peter went over and dragged the net ashore
   full of one hundred fifty-three large fish.
Even though there were so many, the net was not torn.
Jesus said to them, "Come, have breakfast."
And none of the disciples dared to ask him, "Who are you?"
   because they realized it was the Lord.
Jesus came over and took the bread and gave it to them,
   and in like manner the fish.
This was now the third time Jesus was revealed to his disciples
   after being raised from the dead.

Fourth Sunday of Easter, April 21, 2013

SECOND READING
Rev 7:9, 14b-17

I, John, had a vision of a great multitude,
   which no one could count,
   from every nation, race, people, and tongue.
They stood before the throne and before the
   Lamb,
   wearing white robes and holding palm
      branches in their hands.

Then one of the elders said to me,
   "These are the ones who have survived the
      time of great distress;

they have washed their robes
and made them white in the blood of the
   Lamb.

   "For this reason they stand before God's
      throne
      and worship him day and night in his
         temple.
   The one who sits on the throne will
      shelter them.
   They will not hunger or thirst anymore,
      nor will the sun or any heat strike
         them.

For the Lamb who is in the center of the
   throne
   will shepherd them
   and lead them to springs of life-giving
      water,
   and God will wipe away every tear
      from their eyes."

Sixth Sunday of Easter, May 5, 2013

SECOND READING
Rev 21:10-14, 22-23

The angel took me in spirit to a great, high
   mountain
   and showed me the holy city Jerusalem
   coming down out of heaven from God.
It gleamed with the splendor of God.
Its radiance was like that of a precious stone,
   like jasper, clear as crystal.
It had a massive, high wall,
   with twelve gates where twelve angels were
      stationed

and on which names were inscribed,
   the names of the twelve tribes of the
      Israelites.
There were three gates facing east,
   three north, three south, and three west.
The wall of the city had twelve courses of
      stones as its foundation,
   on which were inscribed the twelve names
   of the twelve apostles of the Lamb.

I saw no temple in the city
   for its temple is the Lord God almighty and
      the Lamb.

The city had no need of sun or moon to shine
   on it,
   for the glory of God gave it light,
   and its lamp was the Lamb.

The Ascension of the Lord, May 9, 2013 (Thursday) or May 12, 2013

SECOND READING
Eph 1:17-23

Brothers and sisters:
May the God of our Lord Jesus Christ, the
        Father of glory,
    give you a Spirit of wisdom and revelation
    resulting in knowledge of him.
May the eyes of your hearts be enlightened,
    that you may know what is the hope that
        belongs to his call,
    what are the riches of glory
    in his inheritance among the holy ones,
    and what is the surpassing greatness of
        his power
    for us who believe,
    in accord with the exercise of his great
        might,
    which he worked in Christ,
    raising him from the dead
    and seating him at his right hand in the
        heavens,
    far above every principality, authority,
        power, and dominion,
    and every name that is named
    not only in this age but also in the one to
        come.

And he put all things beneath his feet
    and gave him as head over all things to the
        church,
    which is his body,
    the fullness of the one who fills all things
        in every way.

or

Heb 9:24-28; 10:19-23

Christ did not enter into a sanctuary made by
        hands,
    a copy of the true one, but heaven itself,
    that he might now appear before God on
        our behalf.
Not that he might offer himself repeatedly,
    as the high priest enters each year into the
        sanctuary
    with blood that is not his own;
    if that were so, he would have had to suffer
        repeatedly
    from the foundation of the world.
But now once for all he has appeared at the
        end of the ages
    to take away sin by his sacrifice.
Just as it is appointed that men and women
        die once,

and after this the judgment, so also Christ,
    offered once to take away the sins of many,
    will appear a second time, not to take away
        sin
    but to bring salvation to those who eagerly
        await him.

Therefore, brothers and sisters, since through
        the blood of Jesus
    we have confidence of entrance into the
        sanctuary
    by the new and living way he opened for us
        through the veil,
    that is, his flesh,
    and since we have "a great priest over the
        house of God,"
    let us approach with a sincere heart and in
        absolute trust,
    with our hearts sprinkled clean from an
        evil conscience
    and our bodies washed in pure water.
Let us hold unwaveringly to our confession
        that gives us hope,
    for he who made the promise is
        trustworthy.

Pentecost Sunday At the Mass during the Day, May 19, 2013

SECOND READING
Rom 8:8-17

Brothers and sisters:
Those who are in the flesh cannot please
        God.
But you are not in the flesh;
    on the contrary, you are in the spirit,
    if only the Spirit of God dwells in you.
Whoever does not have the Spirit of Christ
        does not belong to him.
But if Christ is in you,
    although the body is dead because of sin,
    the spirit is alive because of righteousness.
If the Spirit of the one who raised Jesus from
        the dead dwells in you,
    the one who raised Christ from the dead
    will give life to your mortal bodies also,
    through his Spirit that dwells in you.
Consequently, brothers and sisters,
    we are not debtors to the flesh,
    to live according to the flesh.
For if you live according to the flesh, you
        will die,
    but if by the Spirit you put to death the
        deeds of the body,
    you will live.

For those who are led by the Spirit of God are
        sons of God.
For you did not receive a spirit of slavery to
        fall back into fear,
    but you received a Spirit of adoption,
    through whom we cry, "Abba, Father!"
The Spirit himself bears witness with our
        spirit
    that we are children of God,
    and if children, then heirs,
    heirs of God and joint heirs with Christ,
    if only we suffer with him
    so that we may also be glorified with him.

or

1 Cor 12:3b-7, 12-13

Brothers and sisters:
No one can say, "Jesus is Lord," except by the
        Holy Spirit.

There are different kinds of spiritual gifts but
        the same Spirit;
    there are different forms of service but the
        same Lord;
    there are different workings but the same God
    who produces all of them in everyone.

To each individual the manifestation of the
        Spirit
    is given for some benefit.

As a body is one though it has many parts,
    and all the parts of the body, though many,
        are one body,
    so also Christ.
For in one Spirit we were all baptized into one
        body,
    whether Jews or Greeks, slaves or free
        persons,
    and we were all given to drink of one Spirit.

Pentecost Sunday At the Mass during the Day, May 19, 2013

SEQUENCE

Veni, Sancte Spiritus

Come, Holy Spirit, come!
And from your celestial home
   Shed a ray of light divine!
Come, Father of the poor!
Come, source of all our store!
   Come, within our bosoms shine.
You, of comforters the best;
You, the soul's most welcome guest;
   Sweet refreshment here below;
In our labor, rest most sweet;
Grateful coolness in the heat;
   Solace in the midst of woe.
O most blessed Light divine,
Shine within these hearts of yours,
   And our inmost being fill!

Where you are not, we have naught,
Nothing good in deed or thought,
   Nothing free from taint of ill.
Heal our wounds, our strength renew;
On our dryness pour your dew;
   Wash the stains of guilt away:
Bend the stubborn heart and will;
Melt the frozen, warm the chill;
   Guide the steps that go astray.
On the faithful, who adore
And confess you, evermore
   In your sevenfold gift descend;
Give them virtue's sure reward;
Give them your salvation, Lord;
   Give them joys that never end. Amen.
   Alleluia.

The Solemnity of the Most Holy Body and Blood of Christ, June 2, 2013

OPTIONAL SEQUENCE

Lauda Sion

Laud, O Zion, your salvation,
Laud with hymns of exultation,
   Christ, your king and shepherd true:

Bring him all the praise you know,
He is more than you bestow.
   Never can you reach his due.

Special theme for glad thanksgiving
Is the quick'ning and the living
   Bread today before you set:

From his hands of old partaken,
As we know, by faith unshaken,
   Where the Twelve at supper met.

Full and clear ring out your chanting,
Joy nor sweetest grace be wanting,
   From your heart let praises burst:

For today the feast is holden,
When the institution olden
   Of that supper was rehearsed.

Here the new law's new oblation,
By the new king's revelation,
   Ends the form of ancient rite:

Now the new the old effaces,
Truth away the shadow chases,
   Light dispels the gloom of night.

What he did at supper seated,
Christ ordained to be repeated,
   His memorial ne'er to cease:

And his rule for guidance taking,
Bread and wine we hallow, making
   Thus our sacrifice of peace.

This the truth each Christian learns,
Bread into his flesh he turns,
   To his precious blood the wine:

Sight has fail'd, nor thought conceives,
But a dauntless faith believes,
   Resting on a pow'r divine.

Here beneath these signs are hidden
Priceless things to sense forbidden;
   Signs, not things are all we see:

Blood is poured and flesh is broken,
Yet in either wondrous token
   Christ entire we know to be.

Whoso of this food partakes,
Does not rend the Lord nor breaks;
   Christ is whole to all that taste:

Thousands are, as one, receivers,
One, as thousands of believers,
   Eats of him who cannot waste.

Bad and good the feast are sharing,
Of what divers dooms preparing,
   Endless death, or endless life.

Life to these, to those damnation,
See how like participation
   Is with unlike issues rife.

When the sacrament is broken,
Doubt not, but believe 'tis spoken,

That each sever'd outward token
   doth the very whole contain.

Nought the precious gift divides,
Breaking but the sign betides
Jesus still the same abides,
   still unbroken does remain.

The shorter form of the sequence begins here.

Lo! the angel's food is given
To the pilgrim who has striven;
   See the children's bread from heaven,
   which on dogs may not be spent.

Truth the ancient types fulfilling,
Isaac bound, a victim willing,
   Paschal lamb, its lifeblood spilling,
   manna to the fathers sent.

Very bread, good shepherd, tend us,
Jesu, of your love befriend us,
   You refresh us, you defend us,
   Your eternal goodness send us
In the land of life to see.

You who all things can and know,
Who on earth such food bestow,
   Grant us with your saints, though lowest,
   Where the heav'nly feast you show,
Fellow heirs and guests to be. Amen. Alleluia.

The Solemnity of the Most Sacred Heart of Jesus, June 7, 2013

FIRST READING
Ezek 34:11-16

Thus says the Lord GOD:
　I myself will look after and tend my sheep.
As a shepherd tends his flock
　　when he finds himself among his scattered
　　　sheep,
　so will I tend my sheep.
I will rescue them from every place where
　　they were scattered
　when it was cloudy and dark.
I will lead them out from among the peoples
　and gather them from the foreign lands;
　I will bring them back to their own country
　and pasture them upon the mountains of
　　Israel
　in the land's ravines and all its inhabited
　　places.
In good pastures will I pasture them,
　and on the mountain heights of Israel
　shall be their grazing ground.
There they shall lie down on good grazing
　　ground,
　and in rich pastures shall they be pastured
　on the mountains of Israel.
I myself will pasture my sheep;
　I myself will give them rest, says the Lord
　　GOD.
The lost I will seek out,
　the strayed I will bring back,
　the injured I will bind up,
　the sick I will heal,
　but the sleek and the strong I will destroy,
　shepherding them rightly.

RESPONSORIAL PSALM
Ps 23:1-3a, 3b-4, 5, 6

R̸. (1) The Lord is my shepherd; there is nothing I shall want.

The LORD is my shepherd; I shall not want.
　In verdant pastures he gives me repose;
beside restful waters he leads me;
　he refreshes my soul.

R̸. The Lord is my shepherd; there is nothing I shall want.

He guides me in right paths
　for his name's sake.
Even though I walk in the dark valley
　I fear no evil; for you are at my side
with your rod and your staff
　that give me courage.

R̸. The Lord is my shepherd; there is nothing I shall want.

You spread the table before me
　in the sight of my foes;
you anoint my head with oil;
　my cup overflows.

R̸. The Lord is my shepherd; there is nothing I shall want.

Only goodness and kindness follow me
　all the days of my life;
and I shall dwell in the house of the LORD
　for years to come.

R̸. The Lord is my shepherd; there is nothing I shall want.

SECOND READING
Rom 5:5b-11

Brothers and sisters:
The love of God has been poured out into our
　　hearts
　through the Holy Spirit that has been given
　　to us.
For Christ, while we were still helpless,
　died at the appointed time for the ungodly.
Indeed, only with difficulty does one die for a
　　just person,
　though perhaps for a good person
　one might even find courage to die.
But God proves his love for us
　in that while we were still sinners Christ
　　died for us.
How much more then, since we are now
　　justified by his blood,
　will we be saved through him from the
　　wrath.
Indeed, if, while we were enemies,
　we were reconciled to God through the
　　death of his Son,
　how much more, once reconciled,
　will we be saved by his life.
Not only that,
　but we also boast of God through our Lord
　　Jesus Christ,
　through whom we have now received
　　reconciliation.

Tenth Sunday in Ordinary Time, June 9, 2013

SECOND READING *(cont.)*
Gal 1:11-19

But when God, who from my mother's womb
　　had set me apart
　and called me through his grace,
　was pleased to reveal his Son to me,
　so that I might proclaim him to the
　　Gentiles,
　I did not immediately consult flesh and
　　blood,
　nor did I go up to Jerusalem
　to those who were apostles before me;
　rather, I went into Arabia and then
　　returned to Damascus.

Then after three years I went up to Jerusalem
　to confer with Cephas and remained with
　　him for fifteen days.
But I did not see any other of the apostles,
　only James the brother of the Lord.

Eleventh Sunday in Ordinary Time, June 16, 2013

Gospel (cont.)

Luke 7:36–8:3; L93C

Simon said in reply,
"The one, I suppose, whose larger debt was forgiven."
He said to him, "You have judged rightly."

Then he turned to the woman and said to Simon,
"Do you see this woman?
When I entered your house, you did not give me water for my feet,
but she has bathed them with her tears
and wiped them with her hair.
You did not give me a kiss,
but she has not ceased kissing my feet since the time I entered.
You did not anoint my head with oil,
but she anointed my feet with ointment.
So I tell you, her many sins have been forgiven
because she has shown great love.
But the one to whom little is forgiven, loves little."
He said to her, "Your sins are forgiven."
The others at table said to themselves,
"Who is this who even forgives sins?"
But he said to the woman,
"Your faith has saved you; go in peace."

Afterward he journeyed from one town and village to another,
preaching and proclaiming the good news of the kingdom of God.
Accompanying him were the Twelve
and some women who had been cured of evil spirits and infirmities,
Mary, called Magdalene, from whom seven demons had gone out,
Joanna, the wife of Herod's steward Chuza,
Susanna, and many others who provided for them out of their
resources.

or Luke 7:36-50

A Pharisee invited Jesus to dine with him,
and he entered the Pharisee's house and reclined at table.
Now there was a sinful woman in the city
who learned that he was at table in the house of the Pharisee.

Bringing an alabaster flask of ointment,
she stood behind him at his feet weeping
and began to bathe his feet with her tears.
Then she wiped them with her hair,
kissed them, and anointed them with the ointment.
When the Pharisee who had invited him saw this he said to himself,
"If this man were a prophet,
he would know who and what sort of woman this is who is
touching him,
that she is a sinner."
Jesus said to him in reply,
"Simon, I have something to say to you."
"Tell me, teacher," he said.
"Two people were in debt to a certain creditor;
one owed five hundred day's wages and the other owed fifty.
Since they were unable to repay the debt, he forgave it for both.
Which of them will love him more?"
Simon said in reply,
"The one, I suppose, whose larger debt was forgiven."
He said to him, "You have judged rightly."

Then he turned to the woman and said to Simon,
"Do you see this woman?
When I entered your house, you did not give me water for my feet,
but she has bathed them with her tears
and wiped them with her hair.
You did not give me a kiss,
but she has not ceased kissing my feet since the time I entered.
You did not anoint my head with oil,
but she anointed my feet with ointment.
So I tell you, her many sins have been forgiven
because she has shown great love.
But the one to whom little is forgiven, loves little."
He said to her, "Your sins are forgiven."
The others at table said to themselves,
"Who is this who even forgives sins?"
But he said to the woman,
"Your faith has saved you; go in peace."

The Nativity of St. John the Baptist, June 24, 2013

FIRST READING

Isa 49:1-6

Hear me, O coastlands,
listen, O distant peoples.
The LORD called me from birth,
from my mother's womb he gave me my
name.
He made of me a sharp-edged sword
and concealed me in the shadow of his arm.
He made me a polished arrow,
in his quiver he hid me.
You are my servant, he said to me,
Israel, through whom I show my glory.

Though I thought I had toiled in vain,
and for nothing, uselessly, spent my strength,

yet my reward is with the LORD,
my recompense is with my God.
For now the LORD has spoken
who formed me as his servant from the
womb,
that Jacob may be brought back to him
and Israel gathered to him;
and I am made glorious in the sight of the
LORD,
and my God is now my strength!
It is too little, he says, for you to be my servant,
to raise up the tribes of Jacob,
and restore the survivors of Israel;
I will make you a light to the nations,
that my salvation may reach to the ends of
the earth.

The Nativity of St. John the Baptist, *June 24, 2013*

RESPONSORIAL PSALM
Ps 139:1b-3, 13-14ab, 14c-15

℟. (14a) I praise you, for I am wonderfully made.

O Lord, you have probed me, you know me;
    you know when I sit and when I stand;
    you understand my thoughts from afar.
My journeys and my rest you scrutinize,
    with all my ways you are familiar.

℟. I praise you, for I am wonderfully made.

Truly you have formed my inmost being;
    you knit me in my mother's womb.
I give you thanks that I am fearfully,
      wonderfully made;
    wonderful are your works.

℟. I praise you, for I am wonderfully made.

My soul also you knew full well;
    nor was my frame unknown to you
When I was made in secret,
    when I was fashioned in the depths of the
      earth.

℟. I praise you, for I am wonderfully made.

SECOND READING
Acts 13:22-26

In those days, Paul said:
    "God raised up David as their king;
    of him God testified,
    'I have found David, son of Jesse, a man
      after my own heart;
    he will carry out my every wish.'
From this man's descendants God, according to
    his promise,
has brought to Israel a savior, Jesus.
John heralded his coming by proclaiming a
    baptism of repentance
    to all the people of Israel;
    and as John was completing his course, he
      would say,
    'What do you suppose that I am? I am not he.
Behold, one is coming after me;
    I am not worthy to unfasten the sandals of
      his feet.'
"My brothers, sons of the family of Abraham,
    and those others among you who are God-
      fearing,
    to us this word of salvation has been sent."

SS. Peter and Paul, Apostles, *June 29, 2013*

FIRST READING
Acts 12:1-11

In those days, King Herod laid hands upon
    some members of the church to harm
    them.
He had James, the brother of John, killed by
    the sword,
    and when he saw that this was pleasing to
      the Jews
    he proceeded to arrest Peter also.
—It was the feast of Unleavened Bread.—
He had him taken into custody and put in
    prison
    under the guard of four squads of four
      soldiers each.
He intended to bring him before the people
    after Passover.
Peter thus was being kept in prison,
    but prayer by the church was fervently
      being made
    to God on his behalf.

On the very night before Herod was to bring
    him to trial,
    Peter, secured by double chains,
    was sleeping between two soldiers,
    while outside the door guards kept watch
      on the prison.
Suddenly the angel of the Lord stood by him
    and a light shone in the cell.
He tapped Peter on the side and awakened
    him, saying,
    "Get up quickly."
The chains fell from his wrists.

The angel said to him, "Put on your belt and
    your sandals."
He did so.
Then he said to him, "Put on your cloak and
    follow me."
So he followed him out,
    not realizing that what was happening
      through the angel was real;
    he thought he was seeing a vision.
They passed the first guard, then the second,
    and came to the iron gate leading out to
      the city,
    which opened for them by itself.
They emerged and made their way down an
    alley,
    and suddenly the angel left him.
Then Peter recovered his senses and said,
    "Now I know for certain
      that the Lord sent his angel
    and rescued me from the hand of Herod
    and from all that the Jewish people had
      been expecting."

RESPONSORIAL PSALM
Ps 34:2-3, 4-5, 6-7, 8-9

℟. (8) The angel of the Lord will rescue those
who fear him.

I will bless the Lord at all times;
    his praise shall be ever in my mouth.
Let my soul glory in the Lord;
    the lowly will hear me and be glad.

℟. The angel of the Lord will rescue those
who fear him.

Glorify the Lord with me,
    let us together extol his name.
I sought the Lord, and he answered me
    and delivered me from all my fears.

℟. The angel of the Lord will rescue those
who fear him.

Look to him that you may be radiant with joy,
    and your faces may not blush with shame.
When the poor one called out, the Lord heard,
    and from all his distress he saved him.

℟. The angel of the Lord will rescue those
who fear him.

The angel of the Lord encamps
    around those who fear him, and delivers
      them.
Taste and see how good the Lord is;
    blessed the man who takes refuge in him.

℟. The angel of the Lord will rescue those
who fear him.

SS. Peter and Paul, Apostles, June 29, 2013

SECOND READING
2 Tim 4:6-8, 17-18

I, Paul, am already being poured out like a libation,
  and the time of my departure is at hand.
I have competed well; I have finished the race;
  I have kept the faith.
From now on the crown of righteousness awaits me,
  which the Lord, the just judge,
  will award to me on that day, and not only to me,
  but to all who have longed for his appearance.

The Lord stood by me and gave me strength,
  so that through me the proclamation might be completed
  and all the Gentiles might hear it.
And I was rescued from the lion's mouth.
The Lord will rescue me from every evil threat
  and will bring me safe to his heavenly kingdom.
To him be glory forever and ever. Amen.

Fourteenth Sunday in Ordinary Time, July 7, 2013

Gospel (cont.)
Luke 10:1-12, 17-20; L102C

Yet know this: the kingdom of God is at hand.
I tell you,
  it will be more tolerable for Sodom on that day than for that town."

The seventy-two returned rejoicing, and said,
  "Lord, even the demons are subject to us because of your name."
Jesus said, "I have observed Satan fall like lightning from the sky.
Behold, I have given you the power to 'tread upon serpents' and
    scorpions
  and upon the full force of the enemy and nothing will harm you.
Nevertheless, do not rejoice because the spirits are subject to you,
  but rejoice because your names are written in heaven."

or Luke 10:1-9; L102C

At that time the Lord appointed seventy-two others
  whom he sent ahead of him in pairs
  to every town and place he intended to visit.

He said to them,
  "The harvest is abundant but the laborers are few;
  so ask the master of the harvest
  to send out laborers for his harvest.
Go on your way;
  behold, I am sending you like lambs among wolves.
Carry no money bag, no sack, no sandals;
  and greet no one along the way.
Into whatever house you enter, first say,
  'Peace to this household.'
If a peaceful person lives there,
  your peace will rest on him;
  but if not, it will return to you.
Stay in the same house and eat and drink what is offered to you,
  for the laborer deserves his payment.
Do not move about from one house to another.
Whatever town you enter and they welcome you,
  eat what is set before you,
  cure the sick in it and say to them,
  'The kingdom of God is at hand for you.'"

Fifteenth Sunday in Ordinary Time, July 14, 2013

Gospel (cont.)
Luke 10:25-37; L105C

But a Samaritan traveler who came upon him
  was moved with compassion at the sight.
He approached the victim,
  poured oil and wine over his wounds and
      bandaged them.
Then he lifted him up on his own animal,
  took him to an inn, and cared for him.
The next day he took out two silver coins
  and gave them to the innkeeper with the
      instruction,
  'Take care of him.
If you spend more than what I have given you,
  I shall repay you on my way back.'
Which of these three, in your opinion,
  was neighbor to the robbers' victim?"

He answered, "The one who treated him with
    mercy."
Jesus said to him, "Go and do likewise."

RESPONSORIAL PSALM
Ps 19:8, 9, 10, 11

R℣. (9a) Your words, Lord, are Spirit and life.

The law of the LORD is perfect,
  refreshing the soul;
the decree of the LORD is trustworthy,
  giving wisdom to the simple.

R℣. Your words, Lord, are Spirit and life.

The precepts of the LORD are right,
  rejoicing the heart;
the command of the LORD is clear,
  enlightening the eye.

R℣. Your words, Lord, are Spirit and life.

The fear of the LORD is pure,
  enduring forever;
the ordinances of the LORD are true,
  all of them just.

R℣. Your words, Lord, are Spirit and life.

They are more precious than gold,
  than a heap of purest gold;
sweeter also than syrup
  or honey from the comb.

R℣. Your words, Lord, are Spirit and life.

Seventeenth Sunday in Ordinary Time, July 28, 2013

Gospel (cont.)
Luke 11:1-13; L111C

"And I tell you, ask and you will receive;
   seek and you will find;
   knock and the door will be opened to you.
For everyone who asks, receives;
   and the one who seeks, finds;
   and to the one who knocks, the door will be opened.
What father among you would hand his son a snake
   when he asks for a fish?
Or hand him a scorpion when he asks for an egg?
If you then, who are wicked,
   know how to give good gifts to your children,
   how much more will the Father in heaven
   give the Holy Spirit to those who ask him?"

SECOND READING
Col 2:12-14

Brothers and sisters:
You were buried with him in baptism,
   in which you were also raised with him
   through faith in the power of God,
   who raised him from the dead.
And even when you were dead
   in transgressions and the uncircumcision of your flesh,
   he brought you to life along with him,
   having forgiven us all our transgressions;
   obliterating the bond against us, with its legal claims,
   which was opposed to us,
   he also removed it from our midst, nailing it to the cross.

Nineteenth Sunday in Ordinary Time, August 11, 2013

Gospel (cont.)
Luke 12:32-48; L117C

You also must be prepared, for at an hour you do not expect,
   the Son of Man will come."

Then Peter said,
   "Lord, is this parable meant for us or for everyone?"
And the Lord replied,
   "Who, then, is the faithful and prudent steward
   whom the master will put in charge of his servants
   to distribute the food allowance at the proper time?
Blessed is that servant whom his master on arrival finds doing so.
Truly, I say to you, the master will put the servant
   in charge of all his property.
But if that servant says to himself,
   'My master is delayed in coming,'
   and begins to beat the menservants and the maidservants,
   to eat and drink and get drunk,
   then that servant's master will come
   on an unexpected day and at an unknown hour
   and will punish the servant severely
   and assign him a place with the unfaithful.
That servant who knew his master's will
   but did not make preparations nor act in accord with his will
   shall be beaten severely;
   and the servant who was ignorant of his master's will
   but acted in a way deserving of a severe beating
   shall be beaten only lightly.
Much will be required of the person entrusted with much,
   and still more will be demanded of the person entrusted with more."

or Luke 12:35-40

Jesus said to his disciples:
"Gird your loins and light your lamps
   and be like servants who await their master's return from a
      wedding,
   ready to open immediately when he comes and knocks.
Blessed are those servants
   whom the master finds vigilant on his arrival.
Amen, I say to you, he will gird himself,
   have them recline at table, and proceed to wait on them.
And should he come in the second or third watch
   and find them prepared in this way,
   blessed are those servants.
Be sure of this:
   if the master of the house had known the hour
   when the thief was coming,
   he would not have let his house be broken into.
You also must be prepared, for at an hour you do not expect,
   the Son of Man will come."

SECOND READING

Heb 11:1-2, 8-19 *(cont.)*

So it was that there came forth from one man,
 himself as good as dead,
  descendants as numerous as the stars in
   the sky
 and as countless as the sands on the
  seashore.

All these died in faith.
They did not receive what had been promised
 but saw it and greeted it from afar
 and acknowledged themselves to be
  strangers and aliens on earth,
 for those who speak thus show that they
  are seeking a homeland.
If they had been thinking of the land from
 which they had come,
 they would have had opportunity to return.
But now they desire a better homeland, a
 heavenly one.
Therefore, God is not ashamed to be called
 their God,
 for he has prepared a city for them.

By faith Abraham, when put to the test,
 offered up Isaac,
 and he who had received the promises was
  ready to offer his only son,
of whom it was said,
 "Through Isaac descendants shall bear
  your name."
He reasoned that God was able to raise even
 from the dead,
 and he received Isaac back as a symbol.

or Heb 11:1-2, 8-12

Brothers and sisters:
Faith is the realization of what is hoped for
 and evidence of things not seen.
Because of it the ancients were well attested.

By faith Abraham obeyed when he was called
 to go out to a place
 that he was to receive as an inheritance;
 he went out, not knowing where he was to
  go.
By faith he sojourned in the promised land as
 in a foreign country,

dwelling in tents with Isaac and Jacob,
 heirs of the same promise;
 for he was looking forward to the city with
  foundations,
 whose architect and maker is God.
By faith he received power to generate,
 even though he was past the normal age
 —and Sarah herself was sterile—
 for he thought that the one who had made
  the promise was trustworthy.
So it was that there came forth from one man,
 himself as good as dead,
  descendants as numerous as the stars in
   the sky
 and as countless as the sands on the
  seashore.

Assumption of the Blessed Virgin Mary, August 15, 2013

Gospel (cont.)
Luke 1:39-56; L622

He has cast down the mighty from their thrones,
 and has lifted up the lowly.
He has filled the hungry with good things,
 and the rich he has sent away empty.
He has come to the help of his servant Israel
 for he has remembered his promise of mercy,
 the promise he made to our fathers,
 to Abraham and his children forever."

Mary remained with her about three months
 and then returned to her home.

Assumption of the Blessed Virgin Mary, *August 15, 2013*

FIRST READING
Rev 11:19a; 12:1-6a, 10ab

God's temple in heaven was opened,
    and the ark of his covenant could be seen in
        the temple.

A great sign appeared in the sky, a woman
        clothed with the sun,
    with the moon under her feet,
    and on her head a crown of twelve stars.
She was with child and wailed aloud in pain
    as she labored to give birth.
Then another sign appeared in the sky;
    it was a huge red dragon, with seven heads
        and ten horns,
    and on its heads were seven diadems.
Its tail swept away a third of the stars in the
    sky
    and hurled them down to the earth.
Then the dragon stood before the woman
    about to give birth,
    to devour her child when she gave birth.
She gave birth to a son, a male child,
    destined to rule all the nations with an iron
        rod.
Her child was caught up to God and his
    throne.
The woman herself fled into the desert
    where she had a place prepared by God.

Then I heard a loud voice in heaven say:
    "Now have salvation and power come,
    and the Kingdom of our God
    and the authority of his Anointed One."

RESPONSORIAL PSALM
Ps 45:10, 11, 12, 16

R̈. (10bc) The queen stands at your right
hand, arrayed in gold.

The queen takes her place at your right hand
    in gold of Ophir.

R̈. The queen stands at your right hand,
arrayed in gold.

Hear, O daughter, and see; turn your ear,
    forget your people and your father's house.

R̈. The queen stands at your right hand,
arrayed in gold.

So shall the king desire your beauty;
    for he is your lord.

R̈. The queen stands at your right hand,
arrayed in gold.

They are borne in with gladness and joy;
    they enter the palace of the king.

R̈. The queen stands at your right hand,
arrayed in gold.

SECOND READING
1 Cor 15:20-27

Brothers and sisters:
Christ has been raised from the dead,
    the firstfruits of those who have fallen
        asleep.
For since death came through man,
    the resurrection of the dead came also
        through man.
For just as in Adam all die,
    so too in Christ shall all be brought to life,
    but each one in proper order:
    Christ the firstfruits;
    then, at his coming, those who belong to
        Christ;
    then comes the end,
    when he hands over the Kingdom to his
        God and Father,
    when he has destroyed every sovereignty
    and every authority and power.
For he must reign until he has put all his
    enemies under his feet.
The last enemy to be destroyed is death,
    for "he subjected everything under his feet."

Twenty-second Sunday in Ordinary Time, *September 1, 2013*

Gospel (cont.)
Luke 14:1, 7-14; L126C

Then he said to the host who invited him,
    "When you hold a lunch or a dinner,
    do not invite your friends or your brothers
    or your relatives or your wealthy neighbors,
    in case they may invite you back and you have repayment.
Rather, when you hold a banquet,
    invite the poor, the crippled, the lame, the blind;
    blessed indeed will you be because of their inability to repay you.
For you will be repaid at the resurrection of the righteous."

Gospel (cont.)
Luke 15:1-32; L132C

And when she does find it,
    she calls together her friends and neighbors
    and says to them,
    'Rejoice with me because I have found the coin that I lost.'
In just the same way, I tell you,
    there will be rejoicing among the angels of God
    over one sinner who repents."

Then he said,
    "A man had two sons, and the younger son said to his father,
    'Father give me the share of your estate that should come to me.'
So the father divided the property between them.
After a few days, the younger son collected all his belongings
    and set off to a distant country
    where he squandered his inheritance on a life of dissipation.
When he had freely spent everything,
    a severe famine struck that country,
    and he found himself in dire need.
So he hired himself out to one of the local citizens
    who sent him to his farm to tend the swine.
And he longed to eat his fill of the pods on which the swine fed,
    but nobody gave him any.
Coming to his senses he thought,
    'How many of my father's hired workers
    have more than enough food to eat,
    but here am I, dying from hunger.
I shall get up and go to my father and I shall say to him,
    "Father, I have sinned against heaven and against you.
I no longer deserve to be called your son;
    treat me as you would treat one of your hired workers."'
So he got up and went back to his father.
While he was still a long way off,
    his father caught sight of him,
    and was filled with compassion.
He ran to his son, embraced him and kissed him.
His son said to him,
    'Father, I have sinned against heaven and against you;
    I no longer deserve to be called your son.'
But his father ordered his servants,
    'Quickly bring the finest robe and put it on him;
    put a ring on his finger and sandals on his feet.
Take the fattened calf and slaughter it.
Then let us celebrate with a feast,
    because this son of mine was dead, and has come to life again;
    he was lost, and has been found.'
Then the celebration began.
Now the older son had been out in the field
    and, on his way back, as he neared the house,
    he heard the sound of music and dancing.
He called one of the servants and asked what this might mean.

The servant said to him,
    'Your brother has returned
    and your father has slaughtered the fattened calf
    because he has him back safe and sound.'
He became angry,
    and when he refused to enter the house,
    his father came out and pleaded with him.
He said to his father in reply,
    'Look, all these years I served you
    and not once did I disobey your orders;
    yet you never gave me even a young goat to feast on with my
        friends. But when your son returns,
    who swallowed up your property with prostitutes,
    for him you slaughter the fattened calf.'
He said to him,
    'My son, you are here with me always;
    everything I have is yours.
But now we must celebrate and rejoice,
    because your brother was dead and has come to life again;
    he was lost and has been found.'"

or Luke 15:1-10

Tax collectors and sinners were all drawing near to listen to Jesus,
    but the Pharisees and scribes began to complain, saying,
    "This man welcomes sinners and eats with them."
So to them he addressed this parable.
"What man among you having a hundred sheep and losing one of them
    would not leave the ninety-nine in the desert
    and go after the lost one until he finds it?
And when he does find it,
    he sets it on his shoulders with great joy
    and, upon his arrival home,
    he calls together his friends and neighbors and says to them,
    'Rejoice with me because I have found my lost sheep.'
I tell you, in just the same way
    there will be more joy in heaven over one sinner who repents
    than over ninety-nine righteous people
    who have no need of repentance.

"Or what woman having ten coins and losing one
    would not light a lamp and sweep the house,
    searching carefully until she finds it?
And when she does find it,
    she calls together her friends and neighbors
    and says to them,
    'Rejoice with me because I have found the coin that I lost.'
In just the same way, I tell you,
    there will be rejoicing among the angels of God
    over one sinner who repents."

Twenty-Fifth Sunday in Ordinary Time, *September 22, 2013*

Gospel (cont.)
Luke 16:1-13; L135C

The steward said to him, 'Here is your promissory note;
write one for eighty.'
And the master commended that dishonest steward for acting
    prudently.

"For the children of this world
    are more prudent in dealing with their own generation
    than are the children of light.
I tell you, make friends for yourselves with dishonest wealth,
    so that when it fails, you will be welcomed into eternal dwellings.
The person who is trustworthy in very small matters
    is also trustworthy in great ones;
    and the person who is dishonest in very small matters
    is also dishonest in great ones.
If, therefore, you are not trustworthy with dishonest wealth,
    who will trust you with true wealth?
If you are not trustworthy with what belongs to another,
    who will give you what is yours?
No servant can serve two masters.
He will either hate one and love the other,
    or be devoted to one and despise the other.
You cannot serve both God and mammon."

or Luke 16:10-13

Jesus said to his disciples,
    "The person who is trustworthy in very small matters
    is also trustworthy in great ones;
    and the person who is dishonest in very small matters
    is also dishonest in great ones.
If, therefore, you are not trustworthy with dishonest wealth,
    who will trust you with true wealth?
If you are not trustworthy with what belongs to another,
    who will give you what is yours?
No servant can serve two masters.
He will either hate one and love the other,
    or be devoted to one and despise the other.
You cannot serve both God and mammon."

Twenty-Sixth Sunday in Ordinary Time, *September 29, 2013*

Gospel (cont.)
Luke 16:19-31; L138C

Moreover, between us and you a great chasm is established
    to prevent anyone from crossing who might wish to go
    from our side to yours or from your side to ours.'
He said, 'Then I beg you, father,
    send him to my father's house, for I have five brothers,
    so that he may warn them,
    lest they too come to this place of torment.'
But Abraham replied, 'They have Moses and the prophets.
Let them listen to them.'
He said, 'Oh no, father Abraham,
    but if someone from the dead goes to them, they will repent.'
Then Abraham said, 'If they will not listen to Moses and the prophets,
    neither will they be persuaded if someone should rise from the dead.'"

FIRST READING
Rev 7:2-4, 9-14

I, John, saw another angel come up from the
East,
    holding the seal of the living God.
He cried out in a loud voice to the four angels
    who were given power to damage the land
        and the sea,
    "Do not damage the land or the sea or the
        trees
    until we put the seal on the foreheads of
        the servants of our God."
I heard the number of those who had been
        marked with the seal,
    one hundred and forty-four thousand
        marked
    from every tribe of the children of Israel.

After this I had a vision of a great multitude,
    which no one could count,
    from every nation, race, people, and tongue.
They stood before the throne and before the
    Lamb,
    wearing white robes and holding palm
        branches in their hands.
They cried out in a loud voice:
    "Salvation comes from our God,
        who is seated on the throne,
    and from the Lamb."
All the angels stood around the throne
    and around the elders and the four living
        creatures.
They prostrated themselves before the throne,
    worshiped God, and exclaimed:

    "Amen. Blessing and glory, wisdom and
        thanksgiving,
        honor, power, and might
    be to our God forever and ever. Amen."
Then one of the elders spoke up and said to
        me,
    "Who are these wearing white robes, and
        where did they come from?"
I said to him, "My lord, you are the one who
        knows."
He said to me,
    "These are the ones who have survived the
        time of great distress;
    they have washed their robes
    and made them white in the Blood of the
        Lamb."

RESPONSORIAL PSALM
Ps 24:1-2, 3-4, 5-6

R̸. (cf. 6) Lord, this is the people that longs to
see your face.

The LORD's are the earth and its fullness;
    the world and those who dwell in it.
For he founded it upon the seas
    and established it upon the rivers.

R̸. Lord, this is the people that longs to see
your face.

Who can ascend the mountain of the LORD?
    or who may stand in his holy place?
One whose hands are sinless, whose heart is
    clean,
    who desires not what is vain.

R̸. Lord, this is the people that longs to see
your face.

He shall receive a blessing from the LORD,
    a reward from God his savior.
Such is the race that seeks for him,
    that seeks the face of the God of Jacob.

R̸. Lord, this is the people that longs to see
your face.

SECOND READING
1 John 3:1-3

Beloved:
See what love the Father has bestowed on us
    that we may be called the children of God.
Yet so we are.
The reason the world does not know us
    is that it did not know him.
Beloved, we are God's children now;
    what we shall be has not yet been revealed.
We do know that when it is revealed we shall
        be like him,
    for we shall see him as he is.
Everyone who has this hope based on him
        makes himself pure,
    as he is pure.

All Souls, *November 2, 2013*

(Other options can be found in the Lectionary for Mass, L668.)

FIRST READING

Wis 3:1-9

The souls of the just are in the hand of God,
  and no torment shall touch them.
They seemed, in the view of the foolish, to be
  dead;
  and their passing away was thought an
    affliction
  and their going forth from us, utter
    destruction.
But they are in peace.
For if before men, indeed they be punished,
  yet is their hope full of immortality;
chastised a little, they shall be greatly
    blessed,
  because God tried them
  and found them worthy of himself.
As gold in the furnace, he proved them,
  and as sacrificial offerings he took them to
    himself.
In the time of their visitation they shall shine,
  and shall dart about as sparks through
    stubble;
they shall judge nations and rule over
    peoples,
  and the LORD shall be their King forever.
Those who trust in him shall understand
    truth,
  and the faithful shall abide with him in
    love:
because grace and mercy are with his holy
    ones,
  and his care is with his elect.

RESPONSORIAL PSALM

Ps 23:1-3a, 3b-4, 5, 6

℟. (1) The Lord is my shepherd; there is
nothing I shall want.
  or:
℟. (4ab) Though I walk in the valley of
darkness, I fear no evil, for you are with me.

The LORD is my shepherd; I shall not want.
  In verdant pastures he gives me repose;
beside restful waters he leads me;
  he refreshes my soul.

℟. The Lord is my shepherd; there is nothing
I shall want.
  or:
℟. Though I walk in the valley of darkness, I
fear no evil, for you are with me.

He guides me in right paths
  for his name's sake.
Even though I walk in the dark valley
  I fear no evil; for you are at my side
with your rod and your staff
  that give me courage.

℟. The Lord is my shepherd; there is nothing
I shall want.
  or:
℟. Though I walk in the valley of darkness, I
fear no evil, for you are with me.

You spread the table before me
  in the sight of my foes;
you anoint my head with oil;
  my cup overflows.

℟. The Lord is my shepherd; there is nothing
I shall want.
  or:
℟. Though I walk in the valley of darkness, I
fear no evil, for you are with me.

Only goodness and kindness follow me
  all the days of my life;
and I shall dwell in the house of the LORD
  for years to come.

℟. The Lord is my shepherd; there is nothing
I shall want.
  or:
℟. Though I walk in the valley of darkness, I
fear no evil, for you are with me.

SECOND READING

Rom 6:3-9; L1014.3

Brothers and sisters:
Are you unaware that we who were baptized
    into Christ Jesus
  were baptized into his death?
We were indeed buried with him through
    baptism into death,
  so that, just as Christ was raised from the
    dead
  by the glory of the Father,
  we too might live in newness of life.

For if we have grown into union with him
    through a death like his,
  we shall also be united with him in the
    resurrection.
We know that our old self was crucified with
    him,
  so that our sinful body might be done away
    with,
  that we might no longer be in slavery to sin.
For a dead person has been absolved from sin.
If, then, we have died with Christ,
  we believe that we shall also live with him.
We know that Christ, raised from the dead,
    dies no more;
  death no longer has power over him.

Thirty-Second Sunday in Ordinary Time,
November 10, 2013

Gospel
Luke 20:27, 34-38; L156C

Some Sadducees, those who deny that there is a resurrection,
  came forward.

Jesus said to them,
  "The children of this age marry and remarry;
  but those who are deemed worthy to attain to the coming age
  and to the resurrection of the dead
  neither marry nor are given in marriage.
They can no longer die,
  for they are like angels;
  and they are the children of God
  because they are the ones who will rise.
That the dead will rise
  even Moses made known in the passage about the bush,
  when he called out 'Lord,'
  the God of Abraham, the God of Isaac, and the God of Jacob;
  and he is not God of the dead, but of the living,
  for to him all are alive."

Thirty-Third Sunday in Ordinary Time,
November 17, 2013

Gospel (cont.)
Luke 21:5-19; L159C

"Before all this happens, however,
  they will seize and persecute you,
  they will hand you over to the synagogues and to prisons,
  and they will have you led before kings and governors
  because of my name.
It will lead to your giving testimony.
Remember, you are not to prepare your defense beforehand,
  for I myself shall give you a wisdom in speaking
  that all your adversaries will be powerless to resist or refute.
You will even be handed over by parents, brothers, relatives, and
  friends,
  and they will put some of you to death.
You will be hated by all because of my name,
  but not a hair on your head will be destroyed.
By your perseverance you will secure your lives."

Thanksgiving Day, November 28, 2013
(Other options can be found in the Lectionary for Mass, L943–947.)

FIRST READING
Sir 50:22-24; L943.2

And now, bless the God of all,
  who has done wondrous things on earth;
Who fosters people's growth from their
    mother's womb,
  and fashions them according to his will!
May he grant you joy of heart
  and may peace abide among you;
May his goodness toward us endure in Israel
  to deliver us in our days.

RESPONSORIAL PSALM
Psalm 138:1-2a, 2bc-3, 4-5; L945.3

R℩. (2bc) Lord, I thank you for your
faithfulness and love.

I will give thanks to you, O LORD, with all of
    my heart,
  for you have heard the words of my mouth;
  in the presence of the angels I will sing
    your praise;
I will worship at your holy temple.

R℩. Lord, I thank you for your faithfulness and
love.

I will give thanks to your name,
Because of your kindness and your truth.
When I called, you answered me;
  you built up strength within me.

R℩. Lord, I thank you for your faithfulness and
love.

All the kings of the earth shall give thanks to
    you, O LORD,
  when they hear the words of your mouth;
And they shall sing of the ways of the LORD:
  "Great is the glory of the LORD."

R℩. Lord, I thank you for your faithfulness and
love.

SECOND READING
1 Cor 1:3-9; L944.1

Brothers and sisters:
Grace to you and peace from God our Father
  and the Lord Jesus Christ.

I give thanks to my God always on your
    account
  for the grace of God bestowed on you in
    Christ Jesus,
  that in him you were enriched in every way,
  with all discourse and all knowledge,
  as the testimony to Christ was confirmed
    among you,
  so that you are not lacking in any spiritual
    gift
  as you wait for the revelation of our Lord
    Jesus Christ.
He will keep you firm to the end,
  irreproachable on the day of our Lord Jesus
    Christ.
God is faithful,
  and by him you were called to fellowship
    with his Son, Jesus Christ our Lord.

Choral Settings for the Prayer of the Faithful

Purchasers of this volume may reproduce these choral arrangements for use in their parish or community. The music must be reproduced as given below, with composer's name and copyright line.

ADVENT

we pray to the Lord,

Lord, _____ hear our prayer.

Lord, _____ hear our prayer.

Lord, hear our prayer.

Music: Kathleen Harmon, SNDdeN, ©1999, Institute for Liturgical Ministry, 4960 Salem Avenue, Dayton OH 45416. All rights reserved.

CHRISTMAS and EASTER

we pray to the Lord,

Lord, hear our prayer.

Lord, hear our prayer.

Music: Kathleen Harmon, SNDdeN, ©1999, Institute for Liturgical Ministry, 4960 Salem Avenue, Dayton OH 45416. All rights reserved.

LENT

we pray to the Lord,

Lord, hear our prayer.

Music: Kathleen Harmon, SNDdeN, ©1999, Institute for Liturgical Ministry, 4960 Salem Avenue, Dayton OH 45416. All rights reserved.

SOLEMNITIES

we pray to the Lord,

Lord, hear our prayer.

Lord, hear our prayer.

Music: Kathleen Harmon, SNDdeN, ©1999, Institute for Liturgical Ministry, 4960 Salem Avenue, Dayton OH 45416. All rights reserved.

ORDINARY TIME, WEEKS 2-5

Music: Kathleen Harmon, SNDdeN, ©1999, Institute for Liturgical Ministry, 4960 Salem Avenue, Dayton OH 45416. All rights reserved.

ORDINARY TIME, WEEKS 10-20

Music: Kathleen Harmon, SNDdeN, ©1999, Institute for Liturgical Ministry, 4960 Salem Avenue, Dayton OH 45416. All rights reserved.

ORDINARY TIME, WEEKS 21-33

Music: Kathleen Harmon, SNDdeN, ©1999, Institute for Liturgical Ministry, 4960 Salem Avenue, Dayton OH 45416. All rights reserved.

Lectionary Pronunciation Guide

Lectionary Word	Pronunciation
Aaron	EHR-uhn
Abana	AB-uh-nuh
Abednego	uh-BEHD-nee-go
Abel-Keramin	AY-b'l-KEHR-uh-mihn
Abel-meholah	AY-b'l-mee-HO-lah
Abiathar	uh-BAI-uh-ther
Abiel	AY-bee-ehl
Abiezrite	ay-bai-EHZ-rait
Abijah	uh-BAI-dzhuh
Abilene	ab-uh-LEE-neh
Abishai	uh-BIHSH-ay-ai
Abiud	uh-BAI-uhd
Abner	AHB-ner
Abraham	AY-bruh-ham
Abram	AY-br'm
Achaia	uh-KAY-yuh
Achim	AY-kihm
Aeneas	uh-NEE-uhs
Aenon	AY-nuhn
Agrippa	uh-GRIH-puh
Ahaz	AY-haz
Ahijah	uh-HAI-dzhuh
Ai	AY-ee
Alexandria	al-ehg-ZAN-dree-uh
Alexandrian	al-ehg-ZAN-dree-uhn
Alpha	AHL-fuh
Alphaeus	AL-fee-uhs
Amalek	AM-uh-lehk
Amaziah	am-uh-ZAI-uh
Amminadab	ah-MIHN-uh-dab
Ammonites	AM-uh-naitz
Amorites	AM-uh-raits
Amos	AY-muhs
Amoz	AY-muhz
Ampliatus	am-plee-AY-tuhs
Ananias	an-uh-NAI-uhs
Andronicus	an-draw-NAI-kuhs
Annas	AN-uhs
Antioch	AN-tih-ahk
Antiochus	an-TAI-uh-kuhs
Aphiah	uh-FAI-uh
Apollos	uh-PAH-luhs
Appius	AP-ee-uhs
Aquila	uh-KWIHL-uh
Arabah	EHR-uh-buh
Aram	AY-ram
Arameans	ehr-uh-MEE-uhnz
Areopagus	ehr-ee-AH-puh-guhs
Arimathea	ehr-uh-muh-THEE-uh
Aroer	uh-RO-er

Lectionary Word	Pronunciation
Asaph	AY-saf
Asher	ASH-er
Ashpenaz	ASH-pee-naz
Assyria	a-SIHR-ee-uh
Astarte	as-TAHR-tee
Attalia	at-TAH-lee-uh
Augustus	uh-GUHS-tuhs
Azariah	az-uh-RAI-uh
Azor	AY-sawr
Azotus	uh-ZO-tus
Baal-shalishah	BAY-uhl-shuh-LAI-shuh
Baal-Zephon	BAY-uhl-ZEE-fuhn
Babel	BAY-bl
Babylon	BAB-ih-luhn
Babylonian	bab-ih-LO-nih-uhn
Balaam	BAY-lm
Barabbas	beh-REH-buhs
Barak	BEHR-ak
Barnabas	BAHR-nuh-buhs
Barsabbas	BAHR-suh-buhs
Bartholomew	bar-THAHL-uh-myoo
Bartimaeus	bar-tih-MEE-uhs
Baruch	BEHR-ook
Bashan	BAY-shan
Becorath	bee-KO-rath
Beelzebul	bee-EHL-zee-buhl
Beer-sheba	BEE-er-SHEE-buh
Belshazzar	behl-SHAZ-er
Benjamin	BEHN-dzhuh-mihn
Beor	BEE-awr
Bethany	BEHTH-uh-nee
Bethel	BETH-el
Bethesda	beh-THEHZ-duh
Bethlehem	BEHTH-leh-hehm
Bethphage	BEHTH-fuh-dzhee
Bethsaida	behth-SAY-ih-duh
Beth-zur	behth-ZER
Bildad	BIHL-dad
Bithynia	bih-THIHN-ih-uh
Boanerges	bo-uh-NER-dzheez
Boaz	BO-az
Caesar	SEE-zer
Caesarea	zeh-suh-REE-uh
Caiaphas	KAY-uh-fuhs
Cain	kayn
Cana	KAY-nuh
Canaan	KAY-nuhn
Canaanite	KAY-nuh-nait
Canaanites	KAY-nuh-naits

Lectionary Word	Pronunciation
Candace	kan-DAY-see
Capernaum	kuh-PERR-nay-uhm
Cappadocia	kap-ih-DO-shee-u
Carmel	KAHR-muhl
carnelians	kahr-NEEL-yuhnz
Cenchreae	SEHN-kree-ay
Cephas	SEE-fuhs
Chaldeans	kal-DEE-uhnz
Chemosh	KEE-mahsh
Cherubim	TSHEHR-oo-bihm
Chislev	KIHS-lehv
Chloe	KLO-ee
Chorazin	kor-AY-sihn
Cilicia	sih-LIHSH-ee-uh
Cleopas	KLEE-o-pas
Clopas	KLO-pas
Corinth	KAWR-ihnth
Corinthians	kawr-IHN-thee-uhnz
Cornelius	kawr-NEE-lee-uhs
Crete	kreet
Crispus	KRIHS-puhs
Cushite	CUHSH-ait
Cypriot	SIH-pree-at
Cyrene	sai-REE-nee
Cyreneans	sai-REE-nih-uhnz
Cyrenian	sai-REE-nih-uhn
Cyrenians	sai-REE-nih-uhnz
Cyrus	SAI-ruhs
Damaris	DAM-uh-rihs
Damascus	duh-MAS-kuhs
Danites	DAN-aits
Decapolis	duh-KAP-o-lis
Derbe	DER-bee
Deuteronomy	dyoo-ter-AH-num-mee
Didymus	DID-I-mus
Dionysius	dai-o-NIHSH-ih-uhs
Dioscuri	dai-O-sky-ri
Dorcas	DAWR-kuhs
Dothan	DO-thuhn
dromedaries	DRAH-muh-dher-eez
Ebed-melech	EE-behd-MEE-lehk
Eden	EE-dn
Edom	EE-duhm
Elamites	EE-luh-maitz
Eldad	EHL-dad
Eleazar	ehl-ee-AY-zer
Eli	EE-lai
Eli Eli Lema Sabachthani	AY-lee AY-lee luh-MAH sah-BAHK-tah-nee

Lectionary Word	Pronunciation	Lectionary Word	Pronunciation	Lectionary Word	Pronunciation
Eliab	ee-LAI-ab	Gilead	GIHL-ee-uhd	Joppa	DZHAH-puh
Eliakim	ee-LAI-uh-kihm	Gilgal	GIHL-gal	Joram	DZHO-ram
Eliezer	ehl-ih-EE-zer	Golgotha	GAHL-guh-thuh	Jordan	DZHAWR-dn
Elihu	ee-LAI-hyoo	Gomorrah	guh-MAWR-uh	Joseph	DZHO-zf
Elijah	ee-LAI-dzhuh	Goshen	GO-shuhn	Joses	DZHO-seez
Elim	EE-lihm	Habakkuk	huh-BAK-uhk	Joshua	DZHAH-shou-ah
Elimelech	ee-LIHM-eh-lehk	Hadadrimmon	hay-dad-RIHM-uhn	Josiah	dzho-SAI-uh
Elisha	ee-LAI-shuh	Hades	HAY-deez	Jotham	DZHO-thuhm
Eliud	ee-LAI-uhd	Hagar	HAH-gar	Judah	DZHOU-duh
Elizabeth	ee-LIHZ-uh-bth	Hananiah	han-uh-NAI-uh	Judas	DZHOU-duhs
Elkanah	el-KAY-nuh	Hannah	HAN-uh	Judea	dzhou-DEE-uh
Eloi Eloi Lama Sabechthani	AY-lo-ee AY-lo-ee LAH-mah sah-BAHK-tah-nee	Haran	HAY-ruhn	Judean	dzhou-DEE-uhn
		Hebron	HEE-bruhn	Junia	dzhou-nih-uh
		Hermes	HER-meez	Justus	DZHUHS-tuhs
Elymais	ehl-ih-MAY-ihs	Herod	HEHR-uhd	Kephas	KEF-uhs
Emmanuel	eh-MAN-yoo-ehl	Herodians	hehr-O-dee-uhnz	Kidron	KIHD-ruhn
Emmaus	eh-MAY-uhs	Herodias	hehr-O-dee-uhs	Kiriatharba	kihr-ee-ath-AHR-buh
Epaenetus	ee-PEE-nee-tuhs	Hezekiah	heh-zeh-KAI-uh	Kish	kihsh
Epaphras	EH-puh-fras	Hezron	HEHZ-ruhn	Laodicea	lay-o-dih-SEE-uh
ephah	EE-fuh	Hilkiah	hihl-KAI-uh	Lateran	LAT-er-uhn
Ephah	EE-fuh	Hittite	HIH-tait	Lazarus	LAZ-er-uhs
Ephesians	eh-FEE-zhuhnz	Hivites	HAI-vaitz	Leah	LEE-uh
Ephesus	EH-fuh-suhs	Hophni	HAHF-nai	Lebanon	LEH-buh-nuhn
Ephphatha	EHF-uh-thuh	Hor	HAWR	Levi	LEE-vai
Ephraim	EE-fray-ihm	Horeb	HAWR-ehb	Levite	LEE-vait
Ephrathah	EHF-ruh-thuh	Hosea	ho-ZEE-uh	Levites	LEE-vaits
Ephron	EE-frawn	Hur	her	Leviticus	leh-VIH-tih-kous
Epiphanes	eh-PIHF-uh-neez	hyssop	HIH-suhp	Lucius	LOO-shih-uhs
Erastus	ee-RAS-tuhs	Iconium	ai-KO-nih-uhm	Lud	luhd
Esau	EE-saw	Isaac	AI-zuhk	Luke	look
Esther	EHS-ter	Isaiah	ai-ZAY-uh	Luz	luhz
Ethanim	EHTH-uh-nihm	Iscariot	ihs-KEHR-ee-uht	Lycaonian	lihk-ay-O-nih-uhn
Ethiopian	ee-thee-O-pee-uhn	Ishmael	ISH-may-ehl	Lydda	LIH-duh
Euphrates	yoo-FRAY-teez	Ishmaelites	ISH-mayehl-aits	Lydia	LIH-dih-uh
Exodus	EHK-so-duhs	Israel	IHZ-ray-ehl	Lysanias	lai-SAY-nih-uhs
Ezekiel	eh-ZEE-kee-uhl	Ituraea	ih-TSHOOR-ree-uh	Lystra	LIHS-truh
Ezra	EHZ-ruh	Jaar	DZHAY-ahr	Maccabees	MAK-uh-beez
frankincense	FRANGK-ihn-sehns	Jabbok	DZHAB-uhk	Macedonia	mas-eh-DO-nih-uh
Gabbatha	GAB-uh-thuh	Jacob	DZHAY-kuhb	Macedonian	mas-eh-DO-nih-uhn
Gabriel	GAY-bree-ul	Jairus	DZH-hr-uhs	Machir	MAY-kih
Gadarenes	GAD-uh-reenz	Javan	DZHAY-van	Machpelah	mak-PEE-luh
Galatian	guh-LAY-shih-uhn	Jebusites	DZHEHB-oo-zaits	Magdala	MAG-duh-luh
Galatians	guh-LAY-shih-uhnz	Jechoniah	dzhehk-o-NAI-uh	Magdalene	MAG-duh-lehn
Galilee	GAL-ih-lee	Jehoiakim	dzhee-HOI-uh-kihm	magi	MAY-dzhai
Gallio	GAL-ih-o	Jehoshaphat	dzhee-HAHSH-uh-fat	Malachi	MAL-uh-kai
Gamaliel	guh-MAY-lih-ehl	Jephthah	DZHEHF-thuh	Malchiah	mal-KAI-uh
Gaza	GAH-zuh	Jeremiah	dzhehr-eh-MAI-uh	Malchus	MAL-kuhz
Gehazi	gee-HAY-zai	Jericho	DZHEHR-ih-ko	Mamre	MAM-ree
Gehenna	geh-HEHN-uh	Jeroham	dzhehr-RO-ham	Manaen	MAN-uh-ehn
Genesis	DZHEHN-uh-sihs	Jerusalem	dzheh-ROU-suh-lehm	Manasseh	man-AS-eh
Gennesaret	gehn-NEHS-uh-reht	Jesse	DZHEH-see	Manoah	muh-NO-uh
Gentiles	DZHEHN-tailz	Jethro	DZHEHTH-ro	Mark	mahrk
Gerasenes	DZHEHR-uh-seenz	Joakim	DZHO-uh-kihm	Mary	MEHR-ee
Gethsemane	gehth-SEHM-uh-ne	Job	DZHOB	Massah	MAH-suh
Gideon	GIHD-ee-uhn	Jonah	DZHO-nuh	Mattathias	mat-uh-THAI-uhs

Lectionary Word	Pronunciation	Lectionary Word	Pronunciation	Lectionary Word	Pronunciation
Matthan	MAT-than	Parmenas	PAHR-mee-nas	Sabbath	SAB-uhth
Matthew	MATH-yoo	Parthians	PAHR-thee-uhnz	Sadducees	SAD-dzhoo-seez
Matthias	muh-THAI-uhs	Patmos	PAT-mos	Salem	SAY-lehm
Medad	MEE-dad	Peninnah	pee-NIHN-uh	Salim	SAY-lim
Mede	meed	Pentecost	PEHN-tee-kawst	Salmon	SAL-muhn
Medes	meedz	Penuel	pee-NYOO-ehl	Salome	suh-LO-mee
Megiddo	mee-GIH-do	Perez	PEE-rehz	Salu	SAYL-yoo
Melchizedek	mehl-KIHZ-eh-dehk	Perga	PER-guh	Samaria	suh-MEHR-ih-uh
Mene	MEE-nee	Perizzites	PEHR-ih-zaits	Samaritan	suh-MEHR-ih-tuhn
Meribah	MEHR-ih-bah	Persia	PER-zhuh	Samothrace	SAM-o-thrays
Meshach	MEE-shak	Peter	PEE-ter	Samson	SAM-s'n
Mespotamia	mehs-o-po-TAY-mih-uh	Phanuel	FAN-yoo-ehl	Samuel	SAM-yoo-uhl
		Pharaoh	FEHR-o	Sanhedrin	san-HEE-drihn
Micah	MAI-kuh	Pharisees	FEHR-ih-seez	Sarah	SEHR-uh
Midian	MIH-dih-uhn	Pharpar	FAHR-pahr	Sarai	SAY-rai
Milcom	MIHL-kahm	Philemon	fih-LEE-muhn	saraph	SAY-raf
Miletus	mai-LEE-tuhs	Philippi	fil-LIH-pai	Sardis	SAHR-dihs
Minnith	MIHN-ihth	Philippians	fih-LIHP-ih-uhnz	Saul	sawl
Mishael	MIHSH-ay-ehl	Philistines	fih-LIHS-tihnz	Scythian	SIH-thee-uihn
Mizpah	MIHZ-puh	Phinehas	FEHN-ee-uhs	Seba	SEE-buh
Moreh	MO-reh	Phoenicia	fee-NIHSH-ih-uh	Seth	sehth
Moriah	maw-RAI-uh	Phrygia	FRIH-dzhih-uh	Shaalim	SHAY-uh-lihm
Mosoch	MAH-sahk	Phrygian	FRIH-dzhih-uhn	Shadrach	SHAY-drak
myrrh	mer	phylacteries	fih-LAK-ter-eez	Shalishah	shuh-LEE-shuh
Mysia	MIH-shih-uh	Pi-Hahiroth	pai-huh-HAI-rahth	Shaphat	Shay-fat
Naaman	NAY-uh-muhn	Pilate	PAI-luht	Sharon	SHEHR-uhn
Nahshon	NAY-shuhn	Pisidia	pih-SIH-dih-uh	Shealtiel	shee-AL-tih-ehl
Naomi	NAY-o-mai	Pithom	PAI-thahm	Sheba	SHEE-buh
Naphtali	NAF-tuh-lai	Pontius	PAHN-shus	Shebna	SHEB-nuh
Nathan	NAY-thuhn	Pontus	PAHN-tus	Shechem	SHEE-kehm
Nathanael	nuh-THAN-ay-ehl	Praetorium	pray-TAWR-ih-uhm	shekel	SHEHK-uhl
Nazarene	NAZ-awr-een	Priscilla	PRIHS-kill-uh	Shiloh	SHAI-lo
Nazareth	NAZ-uh-rehth	Prochorus	PRAH-kaw-ruhs	Shinar	SHAI-nahr
nazirite	NAZ-uh-rait	Psalm	Sahm	Shittim	sheh-TEEM
Nazorean	naz-aw-REE-uhn	Put	puht	Shuhite	SHOO-ait
Neapolis	nee-AP-o-lihs	Puteoli	pyoo-TEE-o-lai	Shunammite	SHOO-nam-ait
Nebuchadnezzar	neh-byoo-kuhd-NEHZ-er	Qoheleth	ko-HEHL-ehth	Shunem	SHOO-nehm
		qorban	KAWR-bahn	Sidon	SAI-duhn
Negeb	NEH-gehb	Quartus	KWAR-tuhs	Silas	SAI-luhs
Nehemiah	nee-hee-MAI-uh	Quirinius	kwai-RIHN-ih-uhs	Siloam	sih-LO-uhm
Ner	ner	Raamses	ray-AM-seez	Silvanus	sihl-VAY-nuhs
Nicanor	nai-KAY-nawr	Rabbi	RAB-ai	Simeon	SIHM-ee-uhn
Nicodemus	nih-ko-DEE-muhs	Rabbouni	ra-BO-nai	Simon	SAI-muhn
Niger	NAI-dzher	Rahab	RAY-hab	Sin (desert)	sihn
Nineveh	NIHN-eh-veh	Ram	ram	Sinai	SAI-nai
Noah	NO-uh	Ramah	RAY-muh	Sirach	SAI-rak
Nun	nuhn	Ramathaim	ray-muh-THAY-ihm	Sodom	SAH-duhm
Obed	O-behd	Raqa	RA-kuh	Solomon	SAH-lo-muhn
Olivet	AH-lih-veht	Rebekah	ree-BEHK-uh	Sosthenes	SAHS-thee-neez
Omega	o-MEE-guh	Rehoboam	ree-ho-BO-am	Stachys	STAY-kihs
Onesimus	o-NEH-sih-muhs	Rephidim	REHF-ih-dihm	Succoth	SUHK-ahth
Ophir	O-fer	Reuben	ROO-b'n	Sychar	SI-kar
Orpah	AWR-puh	Revelation	reh-veh-LAY-shuhn	Syene	sai-EE-nee
Pamphylia	pam-FIHL-ih-uh	Rhegium	REE-dzhee-uhm	Symeon	SIHM-ee-uhn
Paphos	PAY-fuhs	Rufus	ROO-fuhs	synagogues	SIHN-uh-gahgz

Lectionary Word	Pronunciation	Lectionary Word	Pronunciation	Lectionary Word	Pronunciation
Syrophoenician	SIHR-o fee-NIHSH-ih-uhn	Timon	TAI-muhn	Zebedee	ZEH-beh-dee
Tabitha	TAB-ih-thuh	Titus	TAI-tuhs	Zebulun	ZEH-byoo-luhn
Talitha koum	TAL-ih-thuh-KOOM	Tohu	TO-hyoo	Zechariah	zeh-kuh-RAI-uh
Tamar	TAY-mer	Trachonitis	trak-o-NAI-tis	Zedekiah	zeh-duh-KAI-uh
Tarshish	TAHR-shihsh	Troas	TRO-ahs	Zephaniah	zeh-fuh-NAI-uh
Tarsus	TAHR-suhs	Tubal	TYOO-b'l	Zerah	ZEE-ruh
Tekel	TEH-keel	Tyre	TAI-er	Zeror	ZEE-rawr
Terebinth	TEHR-ee-bihnth	Ur	er	Zerubbabel	zeh-RUH-buh-behl
Thaddeus	THAD-dee-uhs	Urbanus	er-BAY-nuhs	Zeus	zyoos
Theophilus	thee-AH-fih-luhs	Uriah	you-RAI-uh	Zimri	ZIHM-rai
Thessalonians	theh-suh-LO-nih-uhnz	Uzziah	yoo-ZAI-uh	Zion	ZAI-uhn
Theudas	THU-duhs	Wadi	WAH-dee	Ziph	zihf
Thyatira	thai-uh-TAI-ruh	Yahweh-yireh	YAH-weh-yer-AY	Zoar	ZO-er
Tiberias	tai-BIHR-ih-uhs	Zacchaeus	zak-KEE-uhs	Zorah	ZAWR-uh
Timaeus	tai-MEE-uhs	Zadok	ZAY-dahk	Zuphite	ZUHR-ait
		Zarephath	ZEHR-ee-fath		

INDEX OF LITURGICAL TOPICS